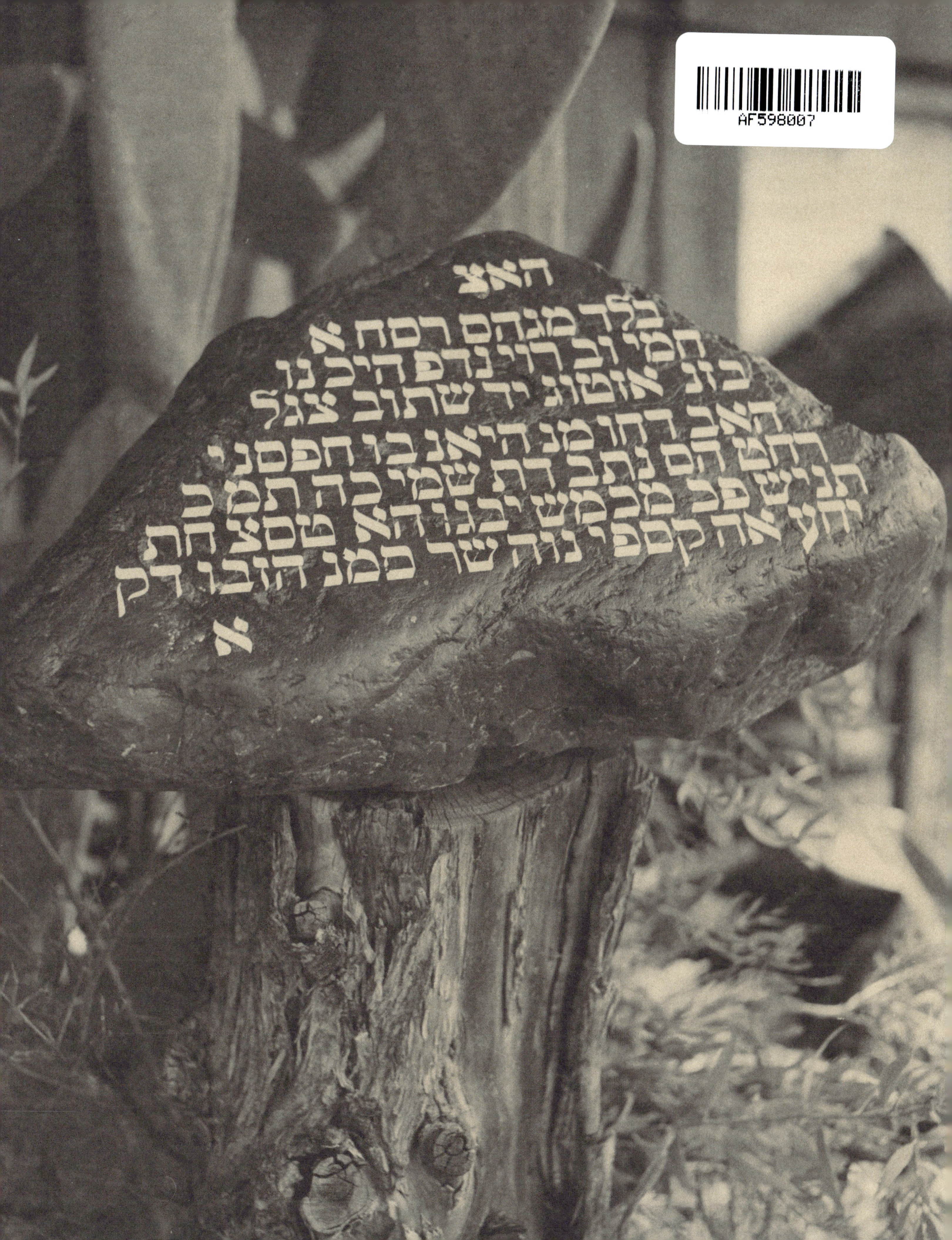

READING RECENT WORK

Sunday sept. 15 8:30

D. Meltzer
J. B. May
F. Fiedler
A. Trocchi
J. Ain
C. Larsen
J. Reed
~~C. La~~ B. Collins
Cameron
E. Teske

SEMINA
1531 Sawtelle w.l.a.

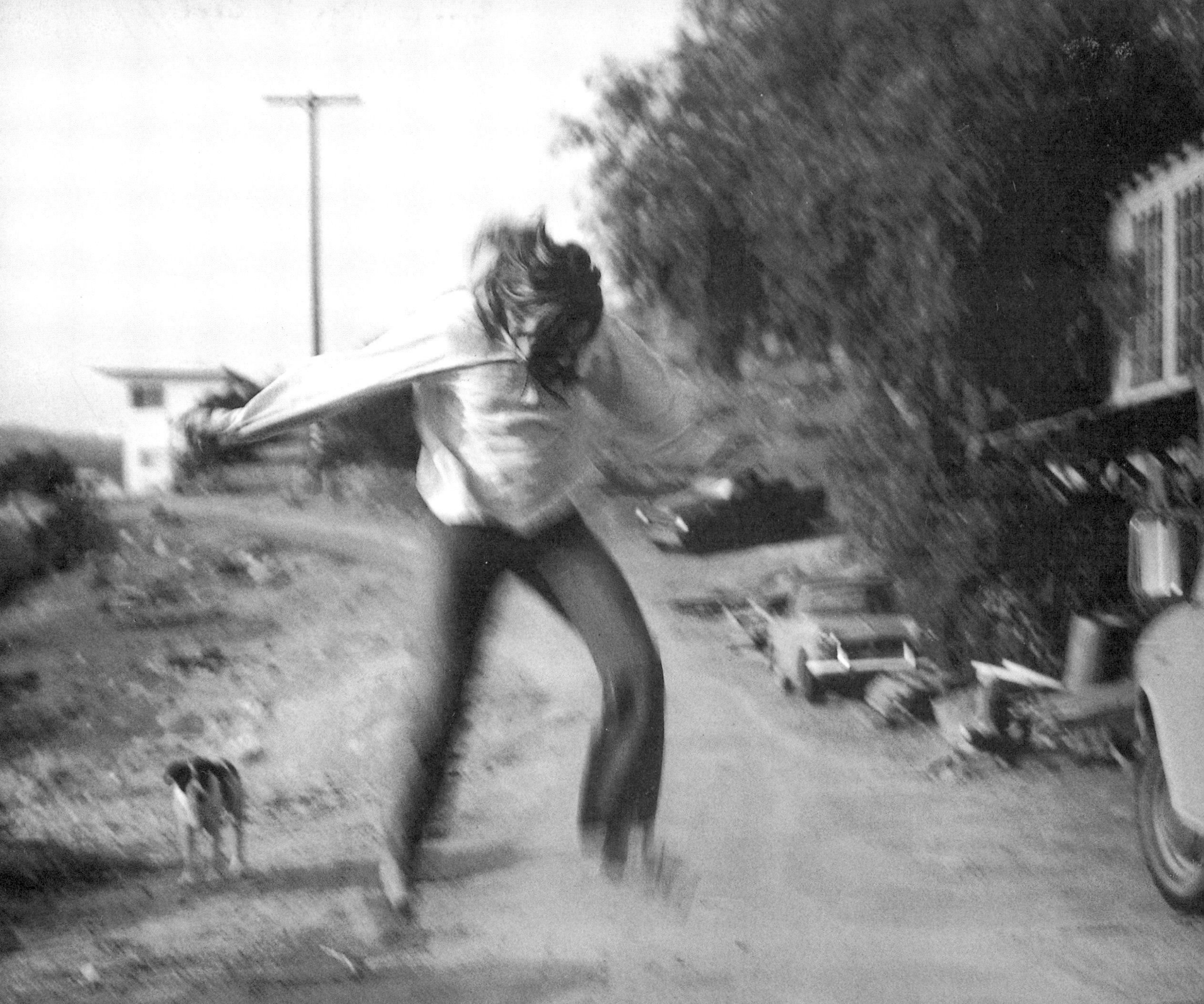

SEMINA CULTURE

Wallace Berman & His Circle

Michael Duncan and Kristine McKenna

DAP
Santa Monica Museum of Art

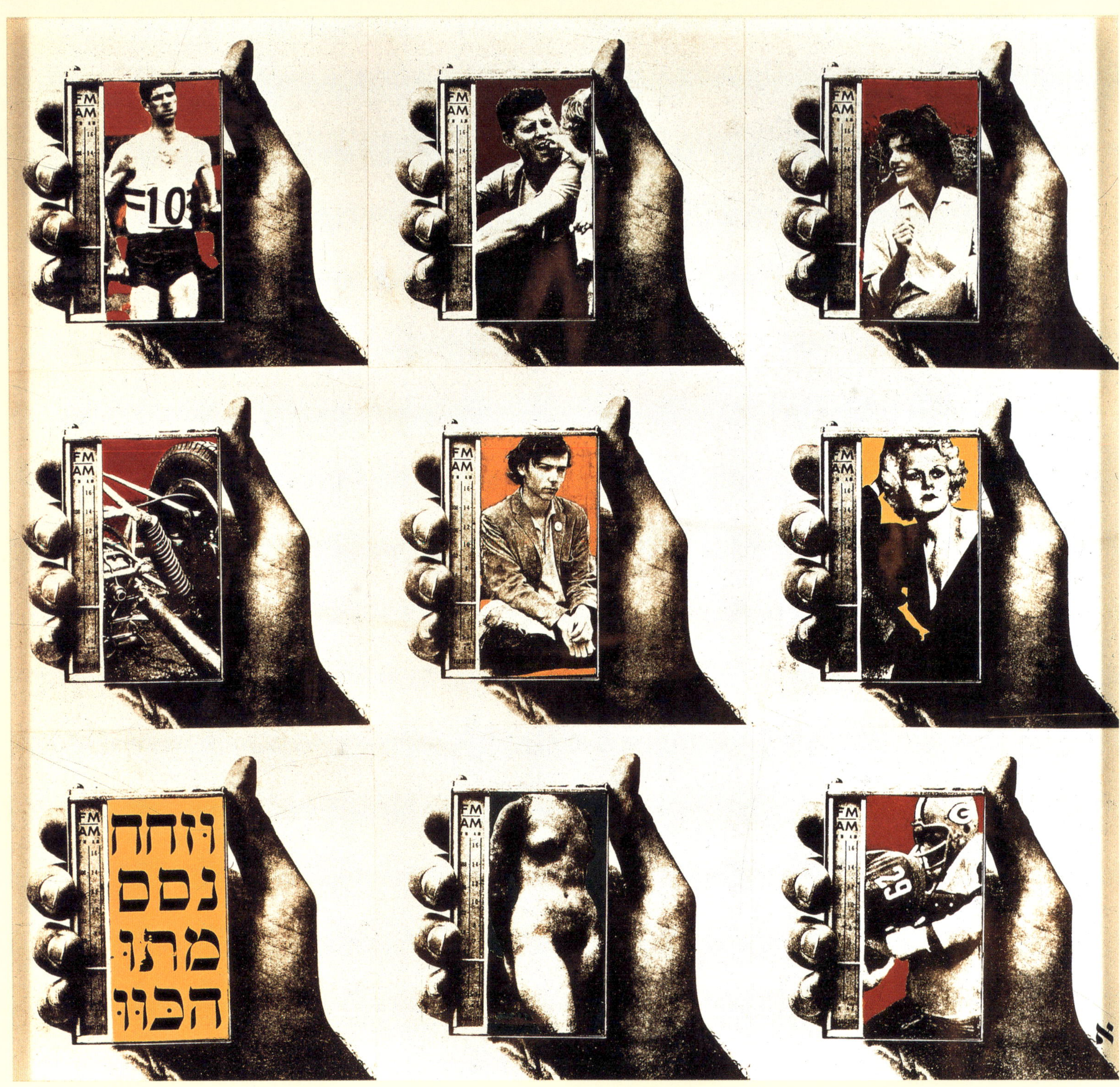

front cover Self-portrait, Crater Lane, 1955. Photograph by Wallace Berman, Courtesy Wallace Berman Estate.

back cover Self-portrait, Poet's Parade, 1959, Photograph by Wallace Berman, Collection of Philip Aarons.

p. 1 Wallace Berman, Topanga Canyon (self portrait), 1974, Photograph by Wallace Berman.

p. 2 Poster for Semina reading at Stone Brothers, 1957, Wallace Berman Archives, Archives of American Art, Smithsonian Institution.

4 Wallace Berman, Untitled, 1961–62, Verifax collage, 20 x 20 in., Courtesy of Wallace Berman Estate.

TABLE OF CONTENTS

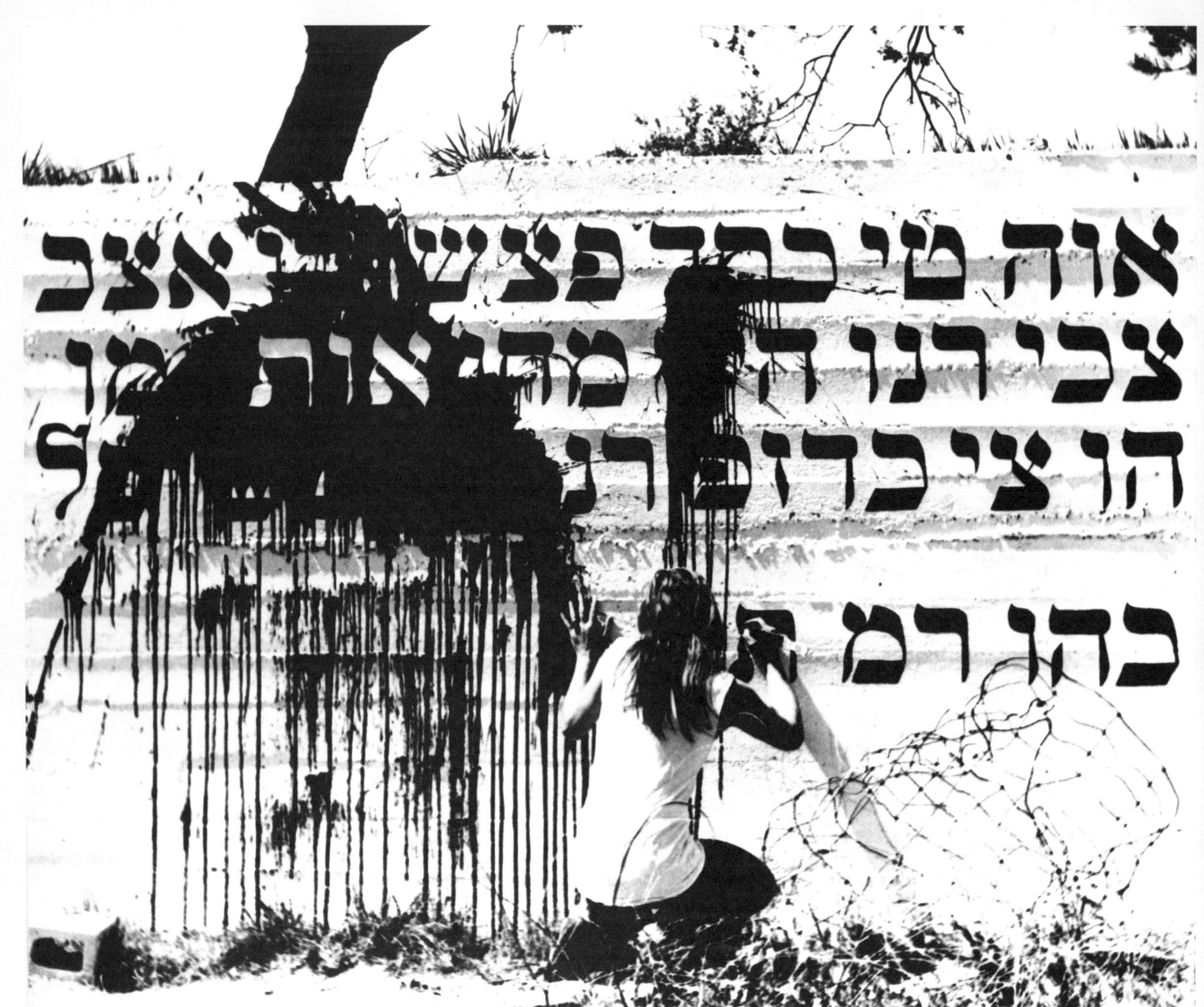

Director's Foreword

Wallace Berman is a legend in the West Coast–Beat Generation counterculture, yet the full extent of his contribution to the art, literature, and character of that era—and the resonance of his influence on future generations—is an epic story waiting to be told. Berman was both a magnet and a catalyst. Whether he lived on a houseboat in Larkspur or in a bungalow at the top of Topanga Canyon in Los Angeles, creative people gravitated to him, and stayed. Berman traveled through many worlds, carrying ideas, dreams, and images from one group of people to the next. His circle extended well beyond the borders of California to other centers of the avant-garde; Andy Warhol, Allen Ginsberg, Diane DiPrima, and Henry Miller numbered among his colleagues and friends. In addition to making revealing photographs of his family and friends and a body of compelling experimental collages, one of his greatest creations was the dynamic community of people that formed around him. That community is the true subject of "*Semina* Culture: Wallace Berman & His Circle," a traveling exhibition organized for the Santa Monica Museum of Art by co-curators Michael Duncan and Kristine McKenna.

Semina, Berman's handcrafted journal published from 1955 to 1964, provides the framework for this exhibition; original works by Berman and the more than fifty artists and poets featured in its nine issues and in his photographs comprise the subject matter. For seven years, Duncan and McKenna have conducted painstaking research into the period and the people of *Semina*; the result is a distillation of three hundred objects for this exhibition. The selection includes paintings, drawings, sculpture, writings, and artifacts as well as photographic portraits from Berman's personal archive, many printed from negatives for the first time. The curators' steadfast dedication to this project is further reflected in the enlightening texts they have written for the catalogue. Historian Stephen Fredman and curator and writer Raymond Foye have as well added informed perspectives to the story of Berman and his circle. *Elsa Longhauser*

Note to the Second Edition

Since the opening of Semina Culture in 2005, interest in Wallace Berman and his circle has burgeoned, evidenced in major retrospective exhibitions for Dennis Hopper (Museum of Contemporary Art Los Angeles, 2010), Jay DeFeo (Whitney Museum of American Art, 2012), Llyn Foulkes (Hammer Museum, 2013), Jess and Robert Duncan (Crocker Art Museum, 2013), and John Altoon (Los Angeles County Museum of Art, 2014). While Berman himself has not been the subject of a U.S. retrospective since 1978 (Otis Art Institute Gallery, Los Angeles), his works continue to resonate with contemporary audiences. Sadly, since the first edition of this book, five members of the community chronicled in Semina Culture have deceased: Philip Lamantia (2005), Bruce Conner (2008), Dennis Hopper (2010), Charles Brittin (2011), and Taylor Mead (2013). Their creative spirits added much to the tenor of the times and they are greatly missed.

Michael Duncan & Kristine McKenna

Self-portrait, Topanga Canyon, 1975, Photograph by Wallace Berman, Courtesy Wallace Berman Estate.

WALLACE BERMAN & HIS CIRCLE: Introduction

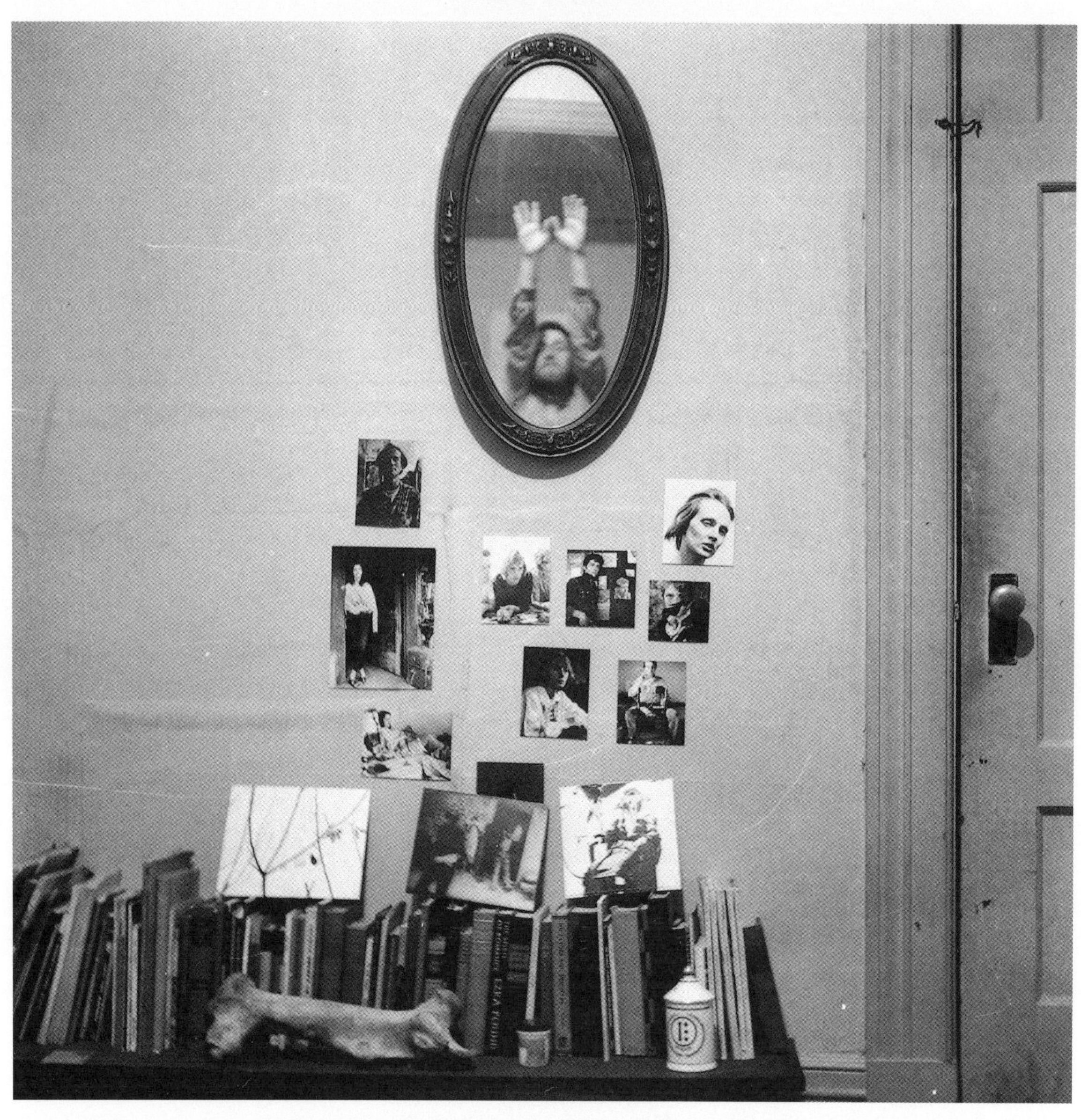

Michael Duncan

A key under-recognized artist of his generation, Wallace Berman was an enigmatic, underground figure whose collages and assemblages articulate an important strand of dark spirituality in postwar American culture. Berman's hand-printed, personally distributed literary journal, *Semina*, stands as an iconic document of its time, presaging a variety of cultural and esthetic developments and providing an outlet for some of the most innovative voices of the 1950s and 1960s. An eccentric and lyrical primer of the early counterculture, assembled against the grain of conformist Eisenhower-era America, it circumscribes a world of self-exploration, cultural alienation, esthetic indulgence, communal comforts, and spiritual transcendence.

This book and exhibition survey artworks, photographs, publications, and documents that manifest the scope and interests of "*Semina* Culture." Included in this first major examination of *Semina* are relevant works by most of the contemporary contributors to Berman's journal and by other friends and collaborators who appeared frequently in his photographs. The essays here address the impact and meaning of *Semina* as a document of its time and as a creative outlet for Wallace Berman, as well as analyze a group of artists with a new lifestyle and approach to making art.

The artists of the so-called "Beat" movement of the 1950s and 1960s pursued an alternative way of thinking about the purpose and formal nature of art. Their fervent, ephemeral, flexible, and theatrical works function in a way that is vastly different from the modernist and postmodernist art that fills our museums. Infused with nostalgia, lyricism, and feeling, these Beat collages, assemblages, photographs, paintings, and writings offer a sprawling alternative to the formal achievements of Abstract Expressionism, Minimalism, and postmodernism, one that stands outside of the traditional art-historical narrative of "progression."

Art was an integral part of Wallace Berman's everyday life. As discussed in Kristine McKenna's essay, Berman had a radical approach to the medium of photography, treating it as a kind of personal record or testing ground for art. Despite the sometimes belabored setups for the many striking portraits of artists and poets found in his existing archive of negatives, photographs were not printed in signed limited editions, but only as single prints that were on occasion cutup and pasted on mailers to friends. Berman used photography simply as a way to record the figures around him who intrigued him or were doing admirable work.

The photographic portraits from Berman's archive—many printed here for the first time—reveal the close-knit nature of this underground community of artists, performers, and poets. Berman's contacts were surprisingly broad, extending well beyond his immediate circle of friends. Based largely

Self-portrait, 707 Scott Street, San Francisco, 1960, Photograph by Wallace Berman, Courtesy Wallace Berman Estate.

in California, but with significant ties to the East Coast, the artists and poets of this exhibition were loosely connected to other important nexuses of American avant-garde production in the 1950s and 1960s: Black Mountain College (Robert Duncan, Jess, Joe Dunn, John Wieners); the New York poets and New York Poets Theatre (Allen Ginsberg, Diane DiPrima, Michael McClure, George Herms, Robert Duncan, John Wieners); avant-garde cinema (Bruce Conner, Lawrence Jordan, Paul Beattie, Toni Basil, Russel Tamblyn); and Andy Warhol's Factory (Jack Smith, Taylor Mead, Diane DiPrima).

Wallace Berman thrived on mystery and contradiction. His evocative, oracular artworks often feature hermetic symbols and images referring to jazz music, French poetry, sports, or the Kabbalah. Inside jokes, willful obfuscation, and hermetic systems abound, giving an air of insular impenetrability to the uninitiated. A conviction on charges of public obscenity for his 1957 exhibition at Ferus Gallery alienated Berman from again exhibiting his work in galleries. He preferred, as he put it, to "swing in the shadows" until the mid 1960s, when he stepped up production of what have become his best known works: enigmatic collages of newspaper and magazine images made with a Verifax machine (an early photocopying prototype).

These works are designed as grids whose unifying form is the repeated image of a hand-held transistor radio. The radio's casing is a frame for diverse images taken from the mass media. The structural device is a resonant metaphor for Berman's broader role as a transmitter of images and ideas that were metaphorically "in the air." In many ways his eclectic, esoteric tastes defined his art, clearly exemplified in the images he chose for inclusion in the Verifax works. For example, a grid of radios might include images of Charlie Parker, an Egyptian ankh, a snake, an exploding nebula, or Jean Cocteau. The serial format sets up a common space for disparate iconic images to coexist, each equally worthy of the viewer's consideration and contemplation. Collectively the images seem talismans and portents, reflecting a mystically charged, yet deeply troubled universe.

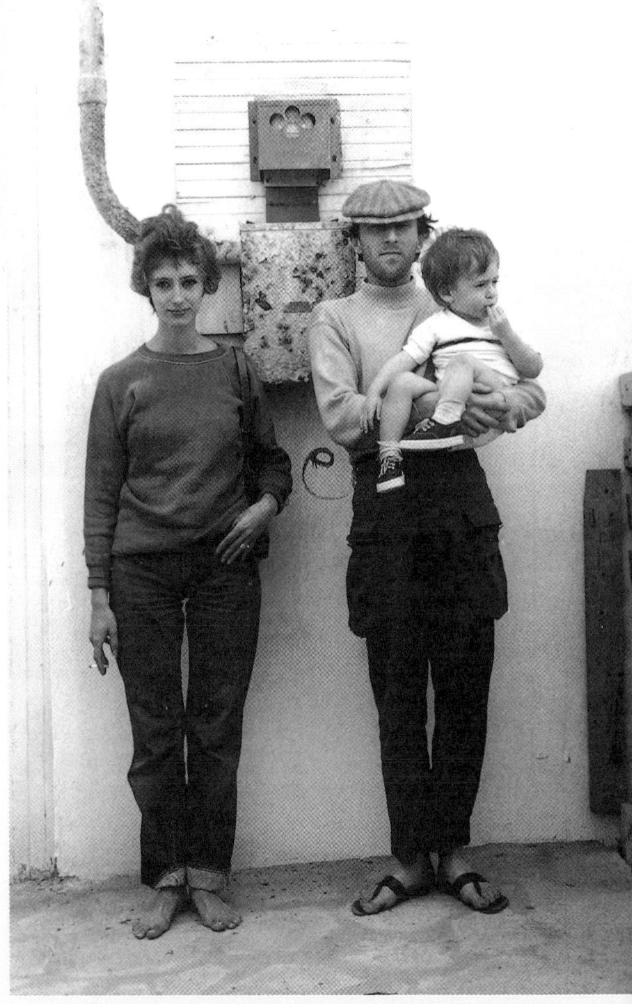

Shirley, Wallace, and Tosh Berman, 1957, Photograph by Charles Britten, Courtesy of the artist.

The mysterious nature of Berman's art was reflected in his life, which included radical shifts and surprising inconsistencies. Kristine McKenna's chronology charts Berman's interactions with his friends and collaborators as he blossomed from high-school dropout to central figure in the West Coast artistic community. The biographies of the other artists in the exhibition briefly describe the triumphs and foibles of an outsider generation caught in a time of experimentation and radical change. Berman's circle included both driven artists who created lasting bodies of work and more erratic personalities whose artworks have mostly been lost or destroyed.

Berman tended to cloak himself in mystery—especially when dealing with strangers or the press. Yet he also had a generous spirit, evident in his support for the artists in whom he believed. A man of notoriously few words, he managed to communicate his sensibility to friends through recommendations of literature, art, and music. Despite its private significance and hermetic associations, *Semina* helped nurture a sense of community spirit, defining the parameters and interests of an alternate society composed of the misfit members of a generation.

In oral histories conducted over the years with the artists and poets of this exhibition, several have emphasized their deep respect for Wallace Berman as an artistic personality and spiritual force. His support for his friends' work did not manifest itself in analysis or critique, but in tacit endorsement. Joan Brown once stated,

> *Wally was one of the most supportive people to me, without any kind of overt encouragement. It was an attitude. It was a deep kind of understanding and encouragement and bond... I was tremendously influenced by Wally Berman. But by him as a person, not by his work. He just stood, for me, for the whole idea of the individual.... He sensed that how I was and what I was doing were very right for me.*[1]

Berman folded artist friends into his supportive community, centered from 1953 through 1965 in his small house on Crater Lane. Charles Brittin described Berman's home as a kind of artistic dissemination center:

> *He wouldn't put on a show or entertain you. People came happily and sat down and left four hours later. What happened is that you'd listen to some music and you'd smoke some pot and talk and look at things. What I enjoyed was not the conversation but the things we looked at. We did a lot of that. There were books, pictures, art books, clippings from newspapers. There were evenings where there was not much talk. People would change records, walk over and say, 'Look at this. Wow!'*[2]

Through exposure to, say, issues of *View* magazine, a new recording of Bach or Charlie Parker, or a poem by Jean Cocteau, these young poets and artists were inspired to look beyond the dulling conformity of 1950s Middle America. In Berman's living room, the seeds were sown for *Semina* Culture. Significantly, Berman's tastes were cosmopolitan. An aficionado of French literature, he included poems by Charles Baudelaire and Paul Éluard in *Semina,* as well as works by the less well known surrealist poets Jules Supervielle and Pierre Jean Jouve. Stephen Fredman's essay tracing the literary sources of *Semina* discusses the importance of the Kabbalah and writings by Antonin Artaud to Berman's circle. Many in the group were fascinated by exotic and esoteric systems, as well as by drugs like peyote that radically shifted ordinary consciousness.

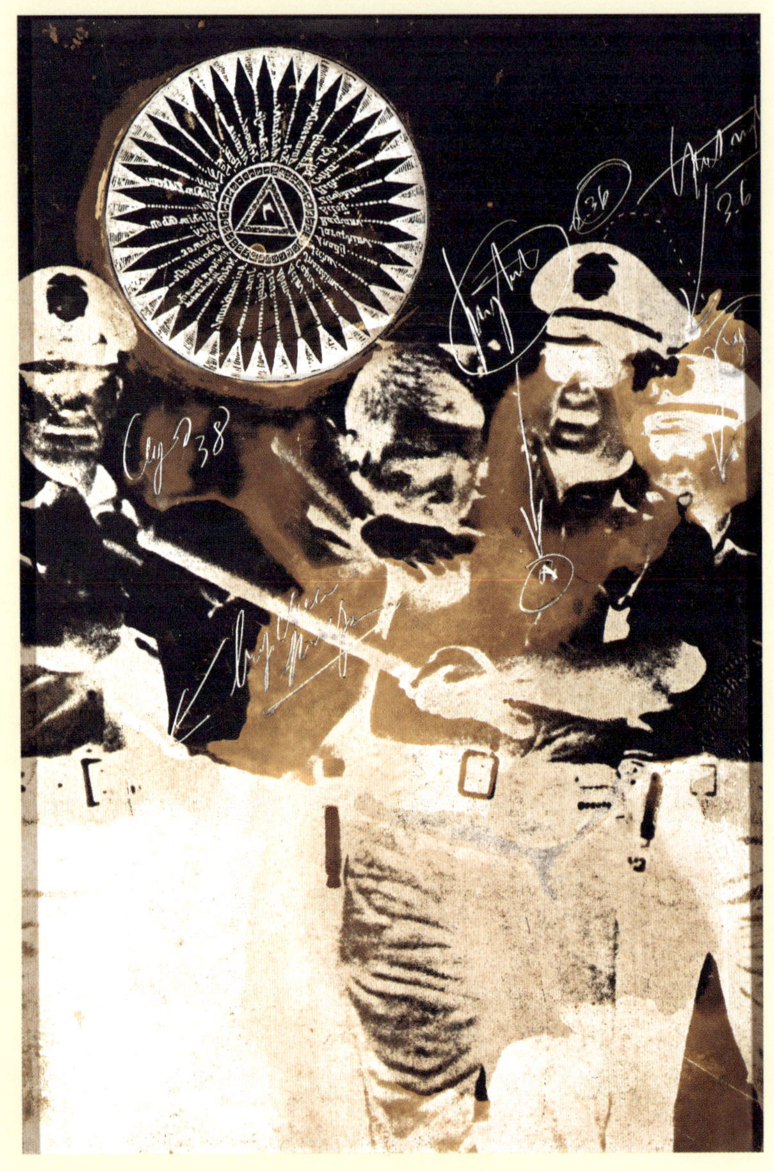

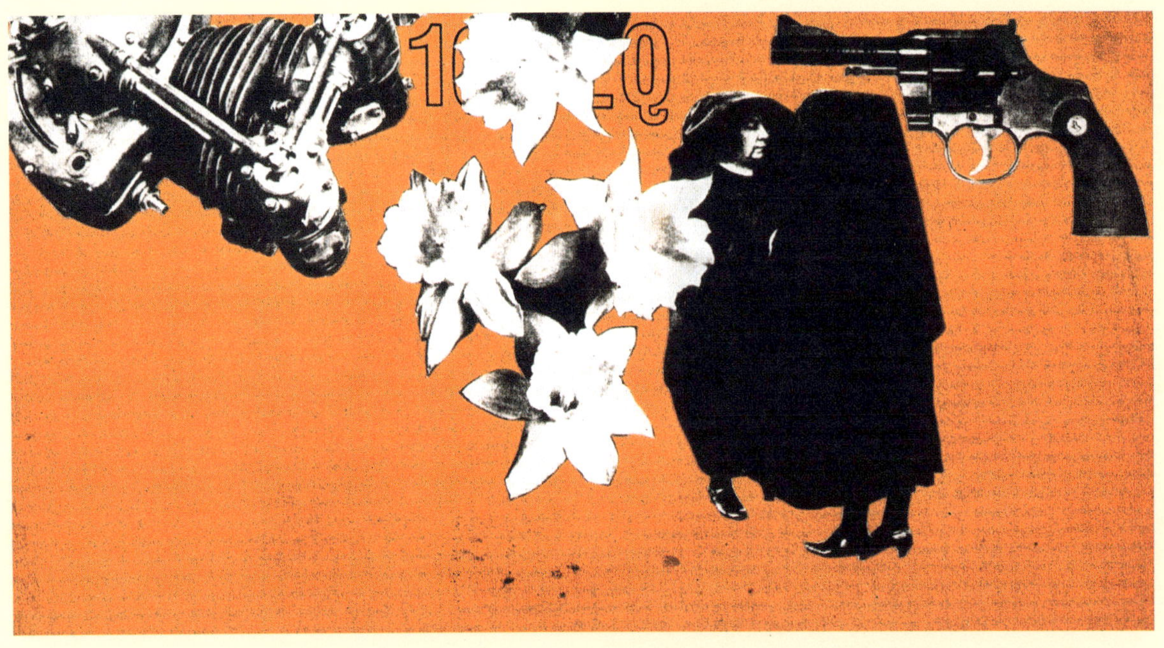

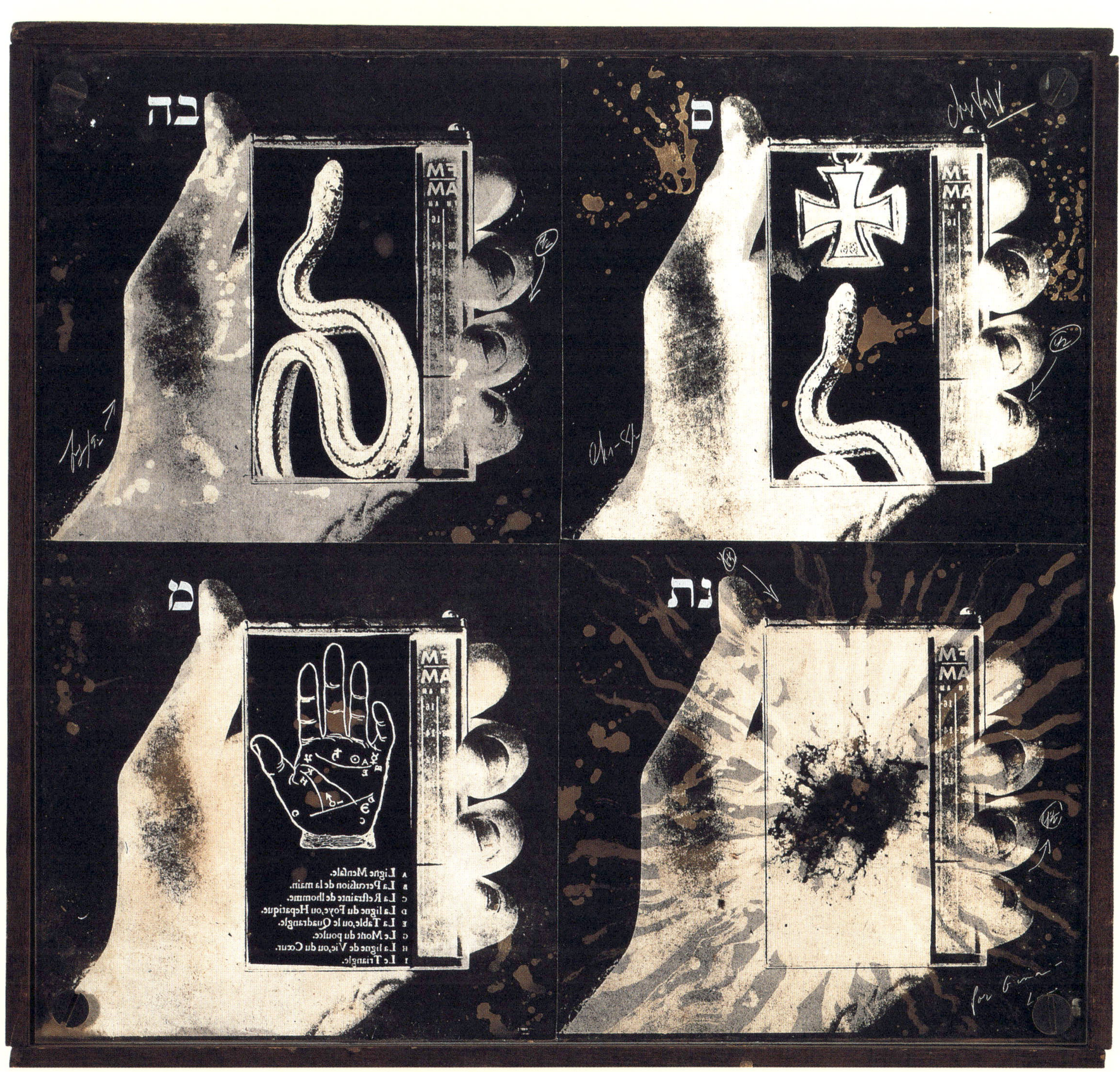

p. 12 top Wallace Berman, Untitled, 1967, Verifax collage, 9 1/2 x 6 1/2 inches, Collection of Tosh Berman.

p. 12 bottom Wallace Berman, Untitled (Engine, flowers, nuns, pistol), 1964, Verifax collage.

p. 13 Wallace Berman, Untitled, 1971–72, Verifax collage, 12 5/8 x 13 5/8 inches, Courtesy Wallace Berman Estate.

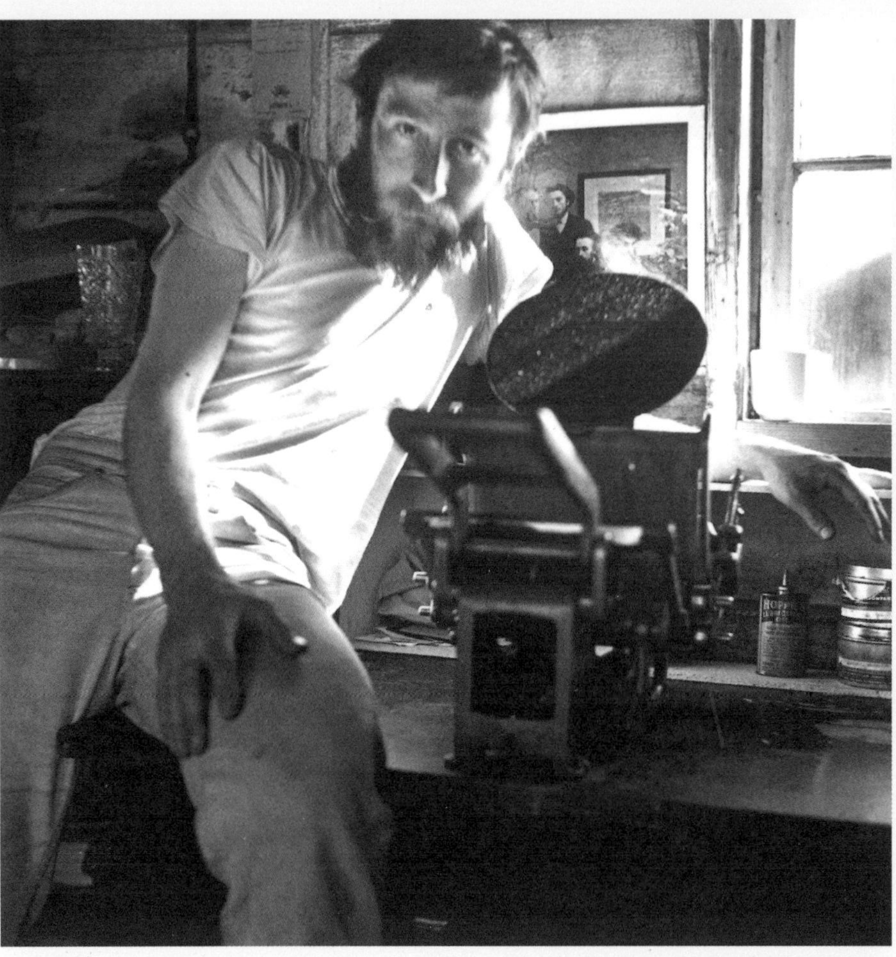

Self-portrait, Crater Lane, 1955, Photograph by Wallace Berman, Courtesy Wallace Berman Estate.

Berman was a casual connoisseur of art and personalities, as is evident in his photographs, Verifax collages, and *Semina*. As a discriminating esthete, he was, as Baudelaire was once described, "a dandy lost in Bohemia."[3] His son Tosh described him as fastidious in his dress, "It might be just jeans and a flowered shirt my mom made him, but it had to be exactly the right shirt and jeans. He wore aftershave—Royal Lime and Royal Spice—that you can't get anymore."[4] Reportedly the owner of a zootsuit in the late 1940s, Berman was one of the first men of his generation to wear long hair, and he sported an earring in the early 1970s. As can be seen in a 1964 photograph by Dennis Hopper (p. 171), his motorcycle helmet was decorated with his personal emblem, a precisely painted Hebrew aleph. His tastes in clothes, art, and pop music were always refined and ahead of the curve.

In a self-portrait photograph from around 1955, on the wall of Berman's studio can be glimpsed part of a framed reproduction of Henri Fantin-Latour's *Around the Table* (1872), a group portrait of French poets and artists, including Verlaine and Rimbaud, that was painted as homage to Baudelaire. This tribute to a cadre of poets clearly had its appeal to an artist who was busy gathering

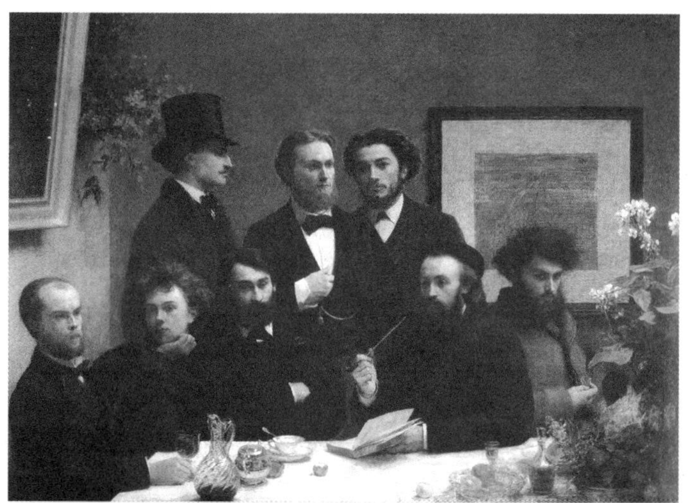

Henri Fantin-Latour, *Around the Table*, 1872,
Oil on canvas, 63 x 88 1/2 inches, Collection of Museé D'Orsay, Paris.

his own group, both in his day-to-day life and through the publication of *Semina*.

This exhibition of the works of *Semina*'s contributors, then, can be seen as a presentation of the tentacles of Berman's wideranging taste. Outlining a fuller picture of what *Semina* represents—including works of both nihilistic angst and romantic innocence, dissipated self-indulgence and spiritual transcendence—we will look at the radical West Coast generation of the 1950s and 1960s through the sensibility of one of its most charismatic and influential characters.

We have tried to select materials that show the multifarious interactions and cross-influences of members of the circle, emphasizing tributes, collaborations, and dedications. Working at cross-purposes to the 1950s American mainstream, the group gained collective strength from their individual efforts. Most were active chroniclers of what they knew were remarkable times.

With their new means of expression, these artists built an audience of fellow lost souls who were able to understand and appreciate the brutal paint smears of Jay DeFeo, John Altoon, and Arthur Richer; the dark, sardonic assemblages of Bruce Conner, George Herms, and Ben Talbert; the fanciful collages of Jean Conner, Dean Stockwell, and Russel Tamblyn; the playful mysticism of Jack Hirschman, Michael McClure, and David Meltzer; the oblique lyricism of Robert Alexander and John Reed; and the magical fantasies of Cameron and Jess. Although they made their works for each other, giving little thought to a commercial audience, today their art seems prophetic. In this decade of mass-market conformity and cultural stagnation, the art of *Semina Culture* couldn't be more refreshing and relevant.

ENDNOTES

1 "Joan Brown Interview," with Paul Karlstrom, July 1–September 9, 1975, Archives of American Art, Smithsonian Institution, Reel 3196, p. 27–28.

2 Charles Brittin, interviewed 1986 by Sandra Leonard Starr, in *Lost and Found in California: Four Decades of Assemblage Art* (Santa Monica: Corcoran, Shoshana Wayne, and Pence Galleries, 1988), p. 73. For a fuller discussion of Berman's persona and reputation, see Richard Candida Smith, *Utopia and Dissent: Art, Poetry, and Politics in California* (Berkeley: University of California Press, 1995).

3 Théophile Gautier, cited by Ellen Moers, *The Dandy* (New York: Viking Press, 1960), p. 273.

4 Tosh Berman, interview by Kristine McKenna, January 11, 1999.

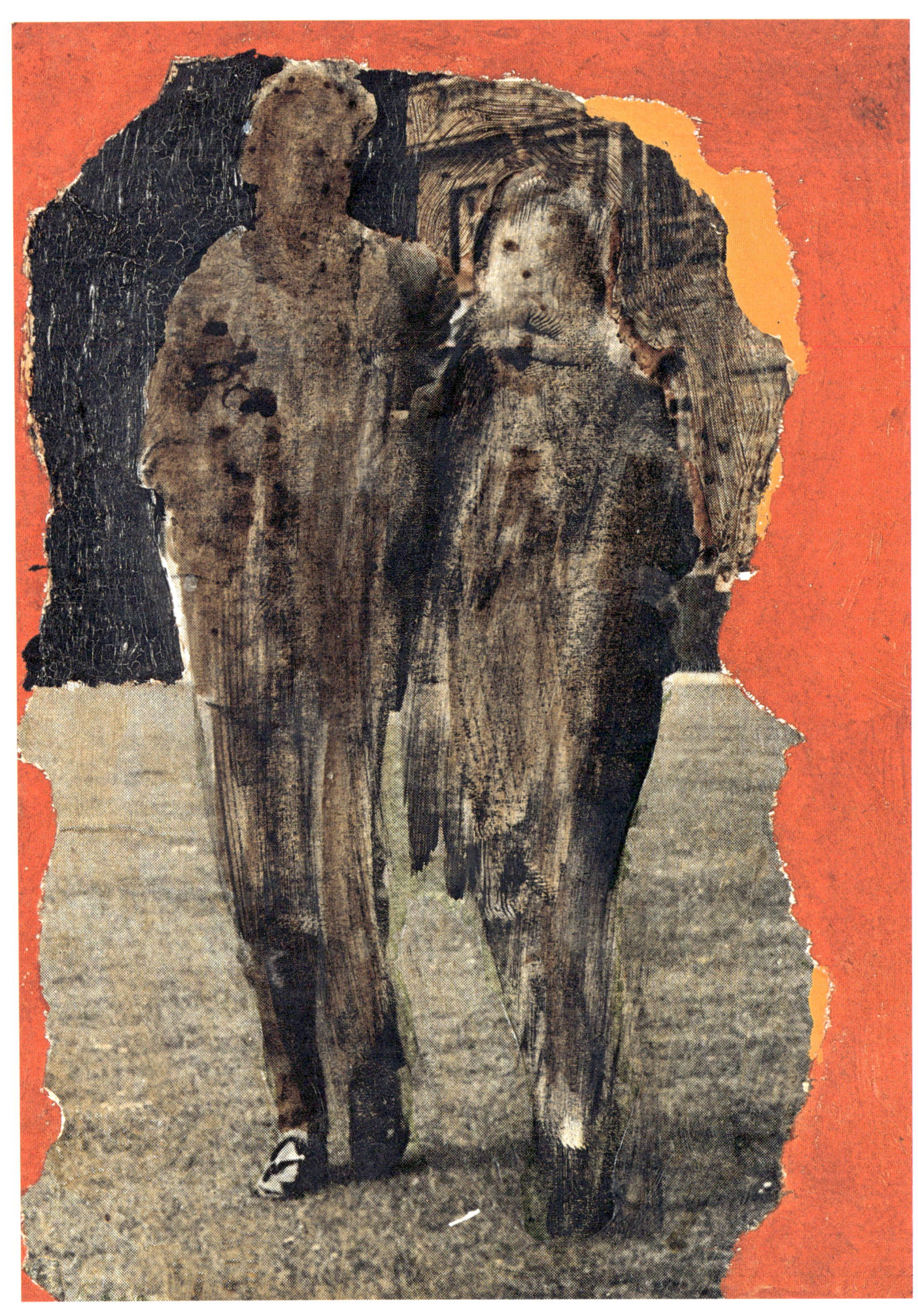

p. 16 Wallace Berman, Untitled, 1970, Verifax collage, 6 1/4 x 5 1/8 inches, Collection of Tosh Berman.

p. 17 Wallace Berman, Untitled (Lenny Bruce), 1963, Mixed media collage on paper.

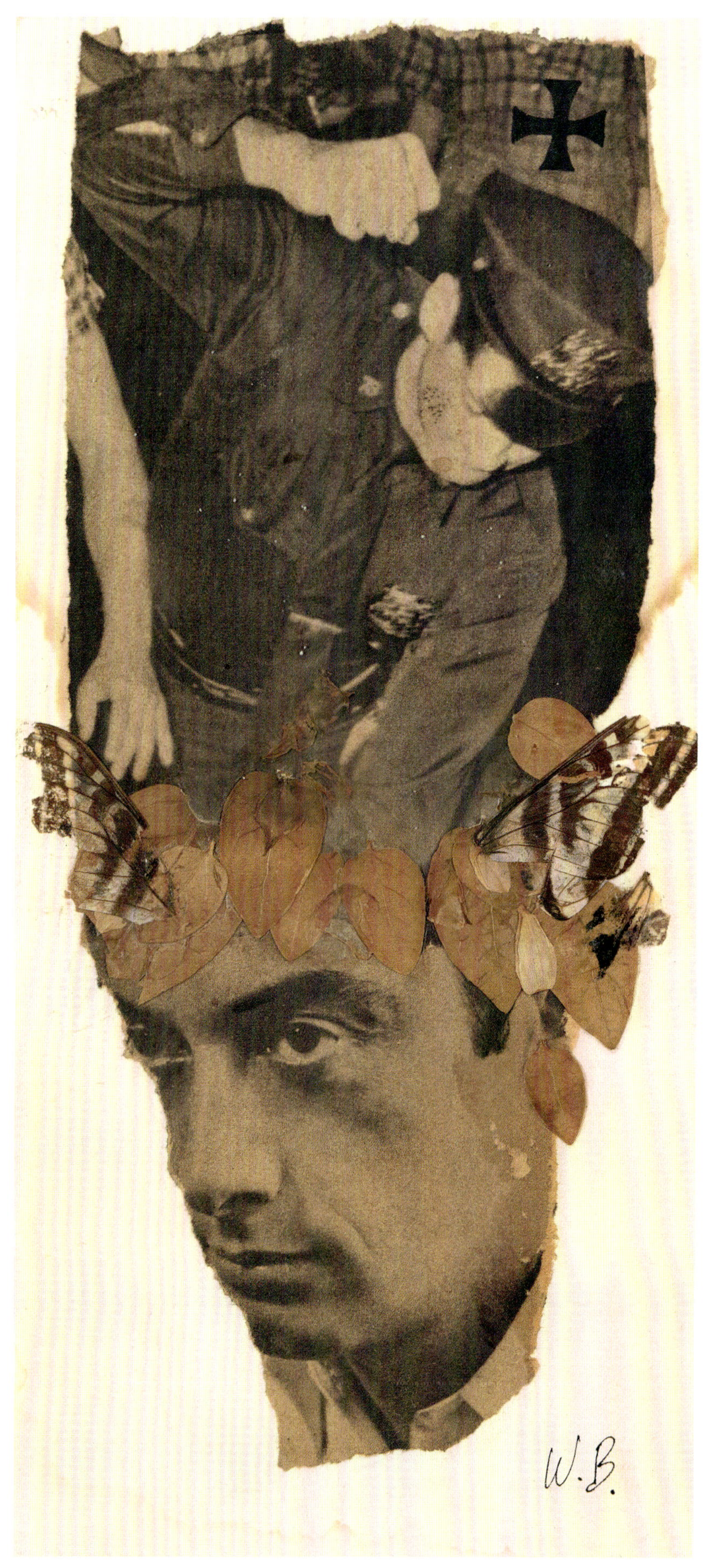
W.B.

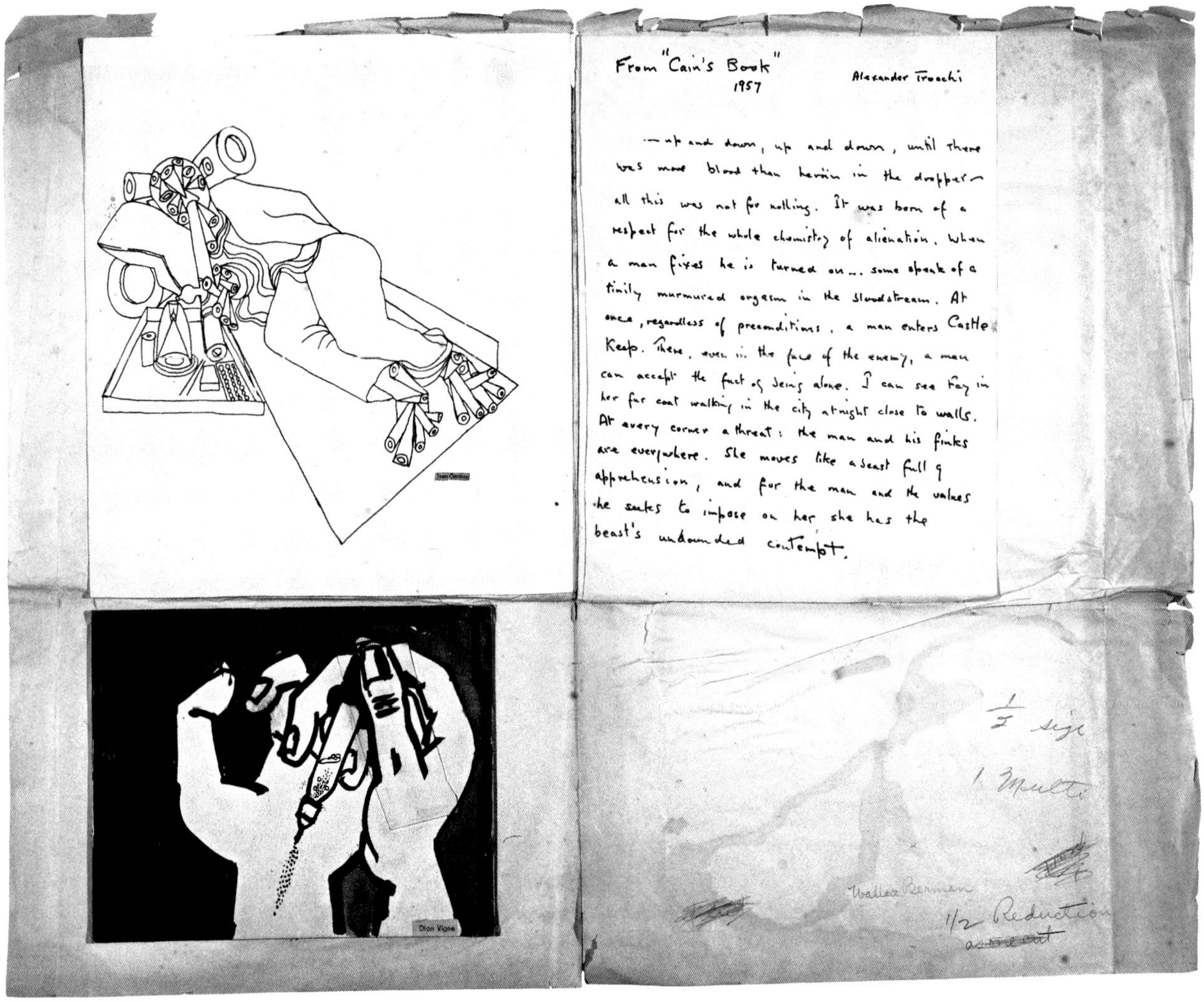

From "Cain's Book"
1957

Alexander Trocchi

—up and down, up and down, until there was more blood than heroin in the dropper— all this was not for nothing. It was born of a respect for the whole chemistry of alienation. When a man fixes he is turned on... some speak of a tinily murmured orgasm in the bloodstream. At once, regardless of preconditions, a man enters Castle Keep. There, even in the face of the enemy, a man can accept the fact of being alone. I can see Fay in her fur coat walking in the city at night close to walls. At every corner a threat: the man and his finks are everywhere. She moves like a beast full of apprehension, and for the man and the values he seeks to impose on her she has the beast's unbounded contempt.

Dion Vigné

Wallace Berman

1/2 Reduction

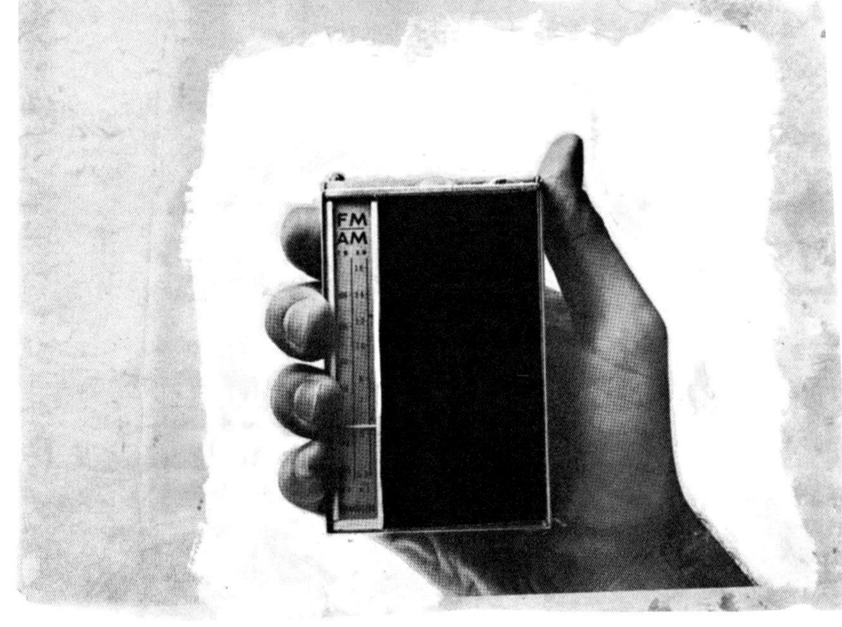

p. 18 top Pasteup for *Semina Two* (see p. 52–54) including drawing by artist/filmmaker Dion Vigné (1930–1978) that was not included in the published edition.

p. 18 bottom Wallace Berman, Prototype for Verifax collages, 1964, Collection of Dean Stockwell.

p. 19 Wallace Berman, Untitled (Wardell Dead), c. 1957, Photograph and rubber stamp letters, 10 1/2 x 9 1/2 inches, Courtesy Wallace Berman Estate.

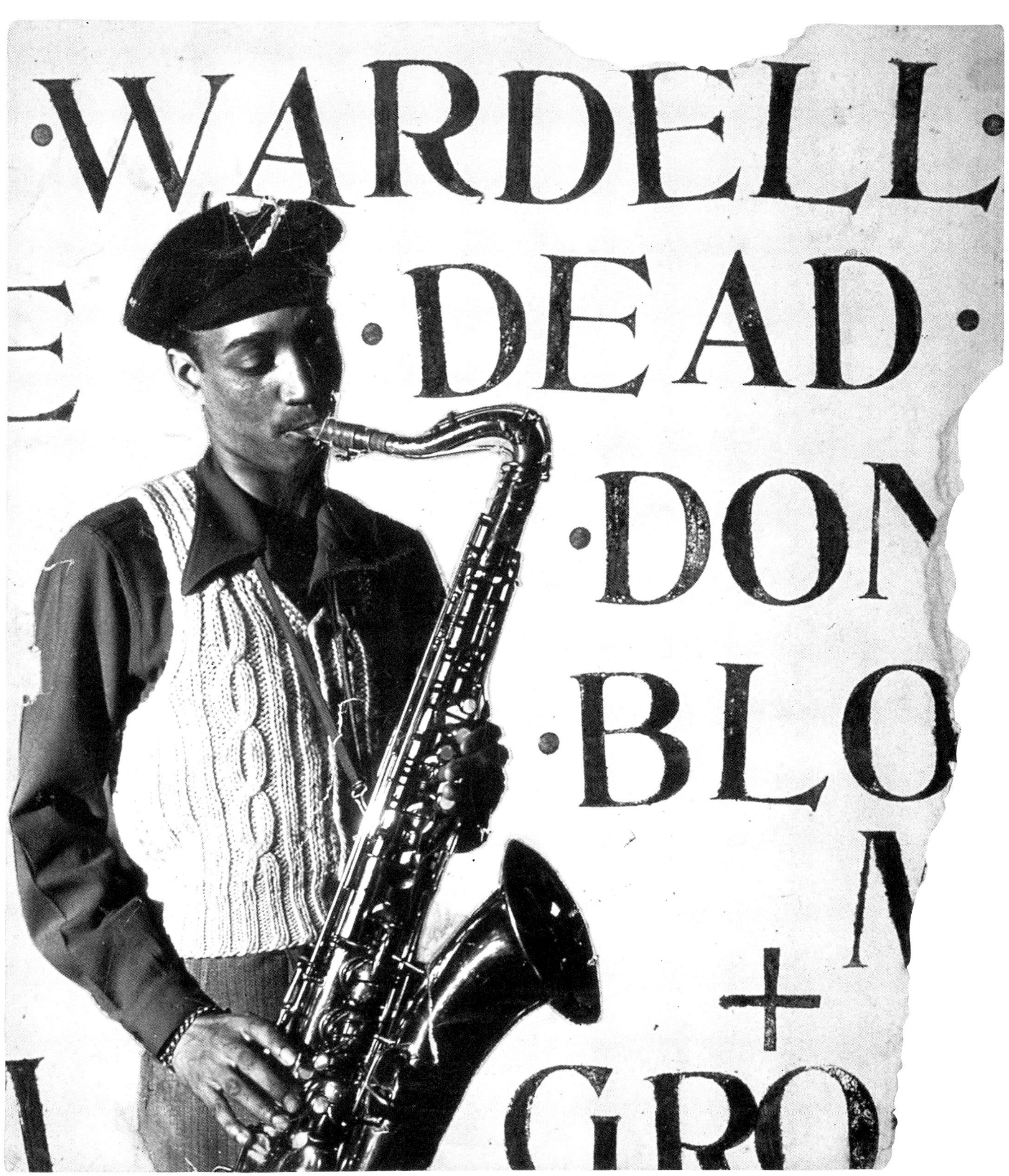
·WARDELL·
·DEAD·
·DON
·BLO
+
GRO

SEMINA as ART

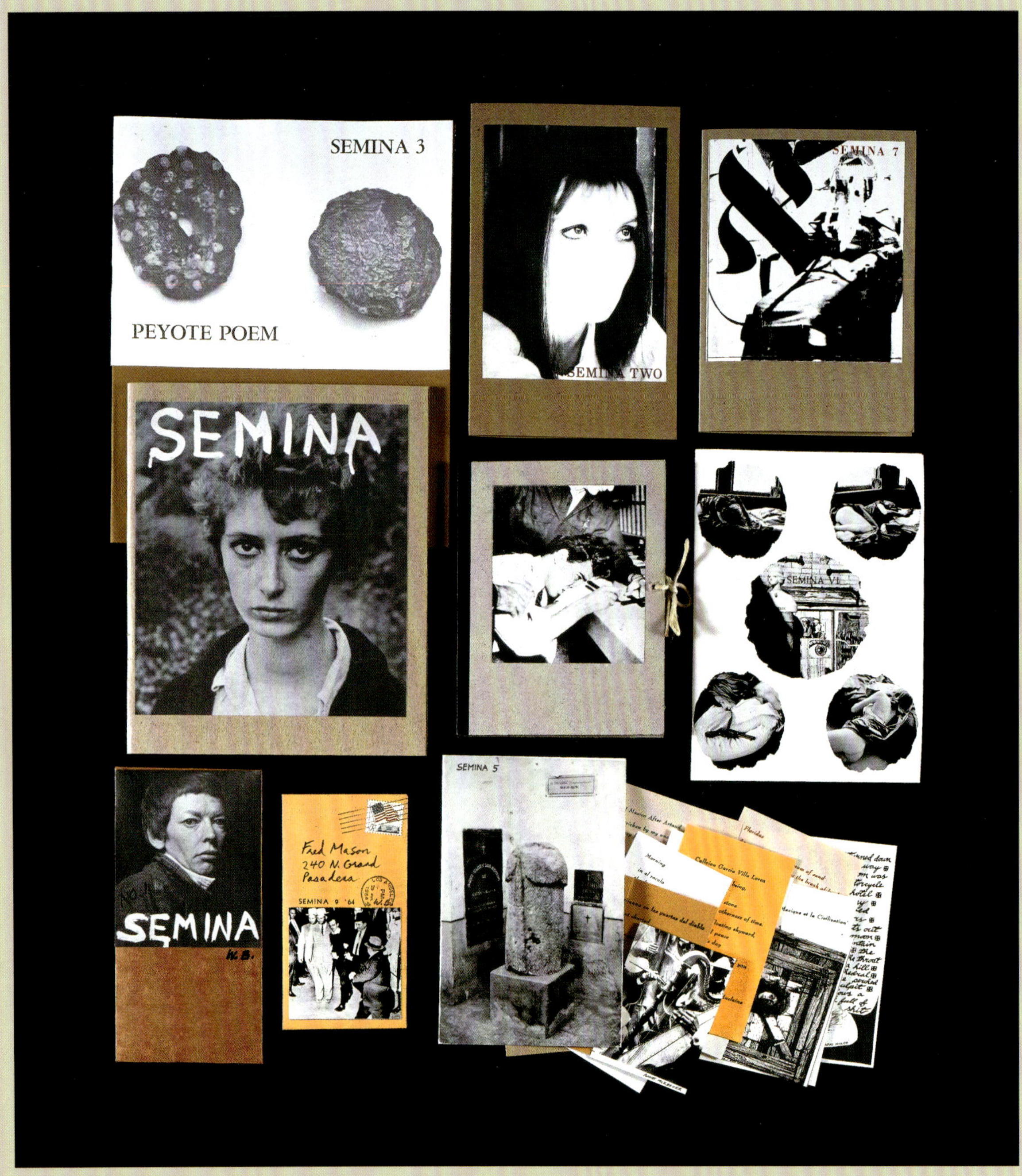

For complete listings of each issue, see "*Semina* Annotated Contents," p. 49–69.

Michael Duncan

Although printed on a handpress in editions of only a few hundred, Wallace Berman's *Semina*, a journal of poems and artworks published in nine issues from 1955 to 1964, is one of the determining works of its time, staking out a new cultural perimeter for an underground eager for change. Turning his back on the stultifying shibboleths of middle-class 1950s America, Berman presented voices of a radically different timbre. Sprinkling in works by poets from the past such as Baudelaire, Blake, Cocteau, and Artaud, *Semina* provided a context for radical new writers such as Allen Ginsberg, Cameron, William Burroughs, Michael McClure, John Wieners, Alexander Trocchi, and David Meltzer. Serving as counterpoint were unconventional artworks and photographs by Charles Brittin, Jean Cocteau, Jess, Cameron, Llyn Foulkes, Dean Stockwell, Patricia Jordan, Keith Sanzenbach, and Walter Hopps.

Berman never directly stated his intentions behind *Semina*, but an early assessment of it by James Boyer May was published in the February 1957 issue of *Trace: A Chronicle of Living Literature*. *Trace* (1952–70) was instrumental as a clearinghouse for poets and writers, directing them to little magazines and journals friendly towards experimental writing. Published at the end of his monthly roundup of new publications, May's description summed up conversations he had had with Berman about *Semina 1*:

> *This has been launched in what may be called (on the literary side) the 'pure' little-mag tradition—for Editor Wallace Berman's intentions here are comprised wholly in a serious-amateur frame. He is a graphic artist and sculptor, pretending no wide knowledge of modern literature, but with decided tastes and actuated solely by the desire to provide a medium for publication of what meets his personal aesthetic preferences. He offers no attempted theoretical rationalizations, as do so many. Neither does he publish hypotheses in relation to the photography and drawings, fields in which he qualifies as a professional. In its neat folder-format, this may become as much a collector's item as is the first* Little Man *presentation of nearly a generation ago.*[1]

May recognized the unusual integrity of Berman's project, going so far as submitting his own poems to *Semina* for publication.[2]

Despite extremely limited distribution—the publication was mostly delivered by U.S. Mail to Berman's friends—*Semina* became an underground legend.[3] Though it remains under-examined, rarely alluded to in overviews of the period, it is gaining iconic status as a stepping stone into the ethos of the mid-century counterculture, a more elliptically resonant, formally rigorous alternative to Allen Ginsberg's *Howl* (1956) and Jack Kerouac's *On the Road* (1957).

Semina (editions 1–9), Conceived and edited by Wallace Berman with various contributors, 1955–64, Mixed media limited edition artist's publication.

Although a journal comprised of contributions from a number of unique voices, *Semina* stands as an artwork in its own right, a new kind of assemblage of images and texts. Seven of its issues were printed on loose-leaf pages inserted in a sleeve; five of those issues had no prescribed order or sequence. Photographs, drawings, and collages by Berman and others were juxtaposed with texts, often on the same page. Attributions were at times enigmatic, with some texts ascribed to authors by initials and some artworks completely unattributed. Reproductions of several of Berman's mailers to friends were included, and treated as discrete works of art. Disseminated without any regular or predictable publication dates, *Semina* was sent out like a surprise communication from an erratic correspondent.

While he clearly conceived of it as a literary journal—including both contributions from friends and submissions from readers—Berman also created in *Semina* a new expressive form.[4] Its conceptually rigorous structure relates to earlier avant-garde works while presaging postmodern and contemporary artworks that step outside the norms of traditional authorship. The concept of a journal as an envelope with loose-leaf pages implies a radical notion of montage subject to chance and happenstance. Upping the ante of, say, a Max Ernst collage of engravings or an Eisenstein montage of edited film images, Berman presented a printed mélange of texts whose order was left to chance or whim. He abdicated his role as a sequencing editor, presenting an array to be experienced as a reader saw fit.

With its element of chance, *Semina* can be considered as a kind of game, offering readers playing-pieces with which they set up their own correspondences and meanings. Michael McClure has described *Semina*'s participatory structure and formal flexibility:

> Semina *is also about rules. There are so many rules in the putting together of a* Semina *and it is so precise a game of art that new freedom is created for the imagination, as in information theory: the more rules there are, the more specific something must be—then more powerful channels are created for freedom.* Semina *poises like the work of George Herms or Bruce Conner on the crack of crisis, on the lip of entropy—it's about to fall apart. Like love, a* Semina *has to be tended and displayed to exist.*[5]

An important source and analogue for Berman's interest in game systems and esoteric mysteries is Hermann Hesse's 1943 novel *Magister Ludi (The Glass Bead Game)*, a work for which Hesse received the 1946 Nobel Prize. Both *Semina 1* and *Semina Two* include poems from the novel that were purportedly written by its fictional hero, Joseph Knecht. Set in an unspecified European society of the future, Hesse's *bildungsroman* tracks Knecht's rise through the ranks of a community of philosophical scholars dedicated to a complex, mystical game whose concept is based on the idea that all knowledge can be reduced to a single, mathematically based, scientific principle.

The rules of the game are never defined in the novel, yet it is hinted that they are derived from elements of the *I Ching*, analytic geometry, astrology, classical fugue structure, Asian architecture, and the Fibonacci code of natural science. Berman's one existent sculpture from his Ferus Gallery

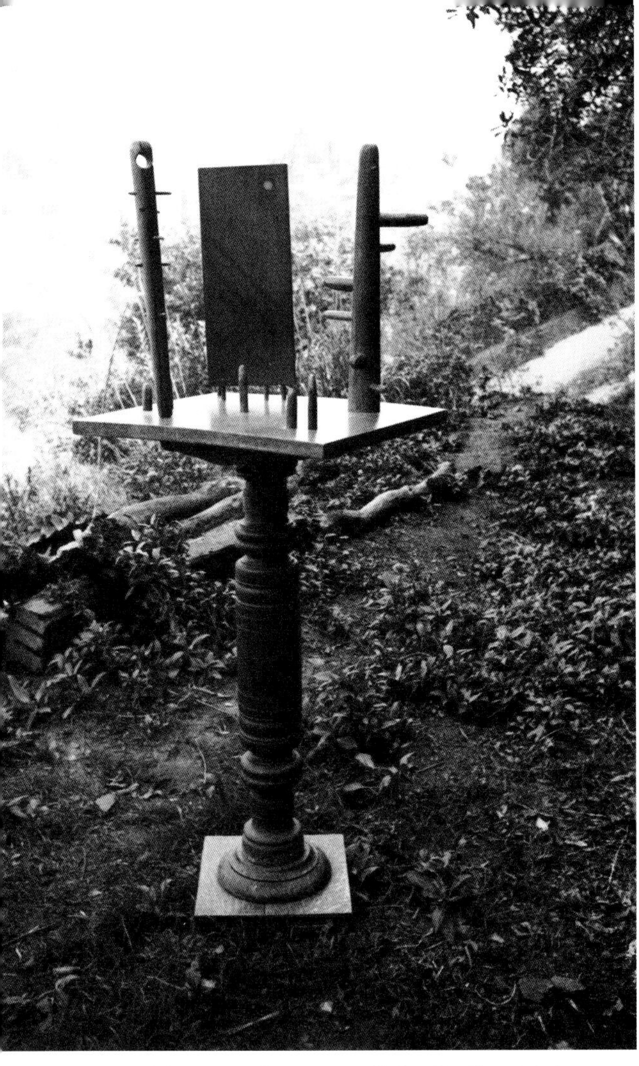

Wallace Berman, *Homage to Herman Hesse*, 1949 (modified 1954), Wood.

exhibition, *Homage to Hermann Hesse* (1949, 1954), resembles a kind of three-dimensional wooden game-board featuring geometric planes and solids. On its table-like pedestal, the clean-lined, elegant work suggests an abstract sculptural interpretation of Hesse's game.

The monastic lifestyle of the game players, aloof from the concerns of bourgeois life, would clearly have appealed to Berman. The two Hesse poems included in *Semina*, "The Bead Game" and "To a Toccata by Bach" celebrate the spiritual transcendence offered by the secret "magic formula" of the "music of the spheres." Hesse's game is treated as an alternative to art and religion, sidestepping ego, God, and the twentieth-century cult of the individual artist. The game involves a group effort dedicated to an ideal.

Yet Hesse emphasizes the inner resources necessary to generate significance from the game. Knecht's first teacher, the Music Master, preaches the integration of theory and practice: "The Godhead is in yourself, not in theories and in books. Truth must be lived, not taught."[6] Berman's trademark slogan, "Art is Love is God," included twice in *Semina*, advocates the same melding of life, religion, and esthetics. The fact that the poem, "The Bead Game," is the first entry in *Semina Two*—the one traditionally structured issue—suggests the importance of its source to Berman's enterprise. In a way, *Semina* is Berman's "glass bead game," a complex, enigmatic system of thought generated from within that touches on a universe of anxieties, truths, and feelings.

The sports and gambling-loving Berman thrived on chance and relished games such as baseball, Ping-Pong, gin rummy, snooker, and boxing. His enthusiasm for systematic rules and regulations translated into several Dada-inspired artworks that substituted enigmatic codes for the written word. For the poem "Rapist & Voicethrower" in *Semina* 7 (1961), Berman decided to replace his text with numbers in code (see p. 65).[7] The result is a nihilistic rejection of literary expression that questions the manipulative role of the author—the "rapist and voicethrower."

In *Semina* 8, the poem, "Fongmother," is printed in Chinese characters without translation; an accompanying drawing by John Reed depicts the figure of a strange trickster: a rabbit hand-puppet

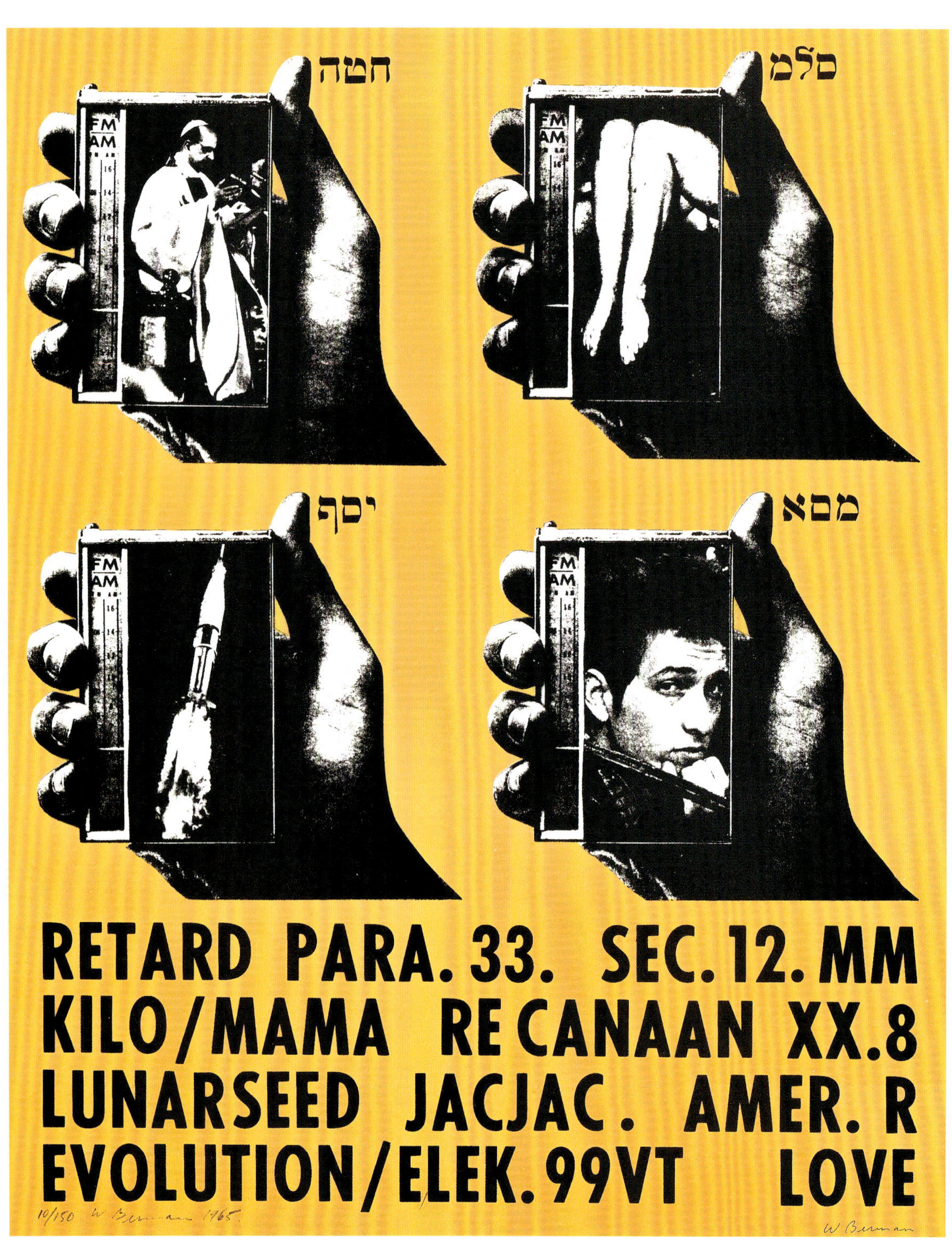

p. 24 Wallace Berman, Poster, 1965, Lithograph, ed. of 150, 21 x 17 inches, Courtesy Wallace Berman Estate.

p. 25 Wallace Berman, Untitled (Tondo), 1959, Ink and gouache on paper.

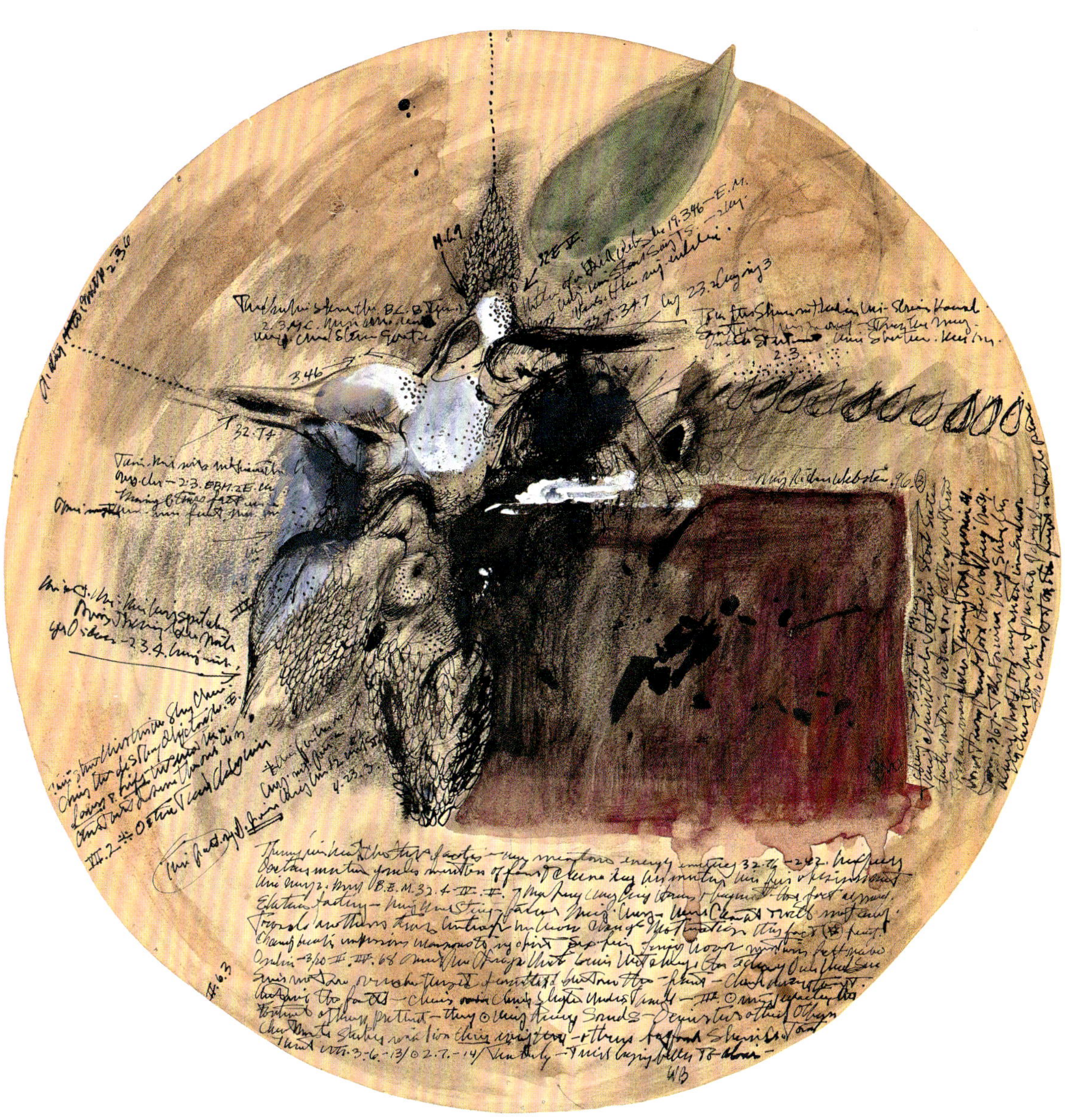

that seems to have come to life (see p. 67). Berman's personal library included a copy of Ernest Fenollosa's *The Chinese Written Character as a Medium for Poetry* (1936), edited by Ezra Pound.[8] Fenollosa's essay, written in 1904, had been instrumental in Pound's early development of the Imagist idea of a poem as a kind of ideogram emanating overtones of meaning. Pound was one of Berman's favorite poets—images of him appear in several Verifax works. Pound's interest in the poetic resonance of Chinese characters clearly influenced Berman's espousal of Hebrew letters as symbolic totems.

In a more conciliatory mode, Berman made several color lithograph posters during the mid-1960s of Verifax images with partially coded, inscrutable texts that read as abbreviated references to mysterious legal documents, Bible verses, and electronic inventory numbers.[9] These works experiment with a more austere form of non-rational language than the primal animal-talk of Michael McClure's poem cycle, *Ghost Tantras* (1964). Berman's handwritten scrawls on a mailer and drawing reproduced in *Semina VI* and *Semina 7* included indecipherable scribble mixed with legible bits of phrases or words (see p. 62 and 64). With its dense flurry of overlapping, manipulated images and symbols, Berman's film *Aleph* (1956–66) is the cinematic equivalent of an untranslated codex (see p. 57). For Berman, the message is always more than what we can comprehend; the message is more than the medium.

In his work, Berman often emulated the utterances of a seer or sibyl. As critics have pointed out, Berman's 1957 *Parchment* works—ink Hebrew characters drawn on wood-stained fragments of parchment—bear a resemblance to pages of the Dead Sea Scrolls, first uncovered and photographed in 1947 (see p. 45).[10] Like the Hebrew letters and references to the Kabbalah in his assemblages and Verifax works, the texts of the *Parchment* works were not intended to offer any precise meaning.

A free-flow bardic utterance, transcribed from an interview with Berman in 1967, best demonstrates how the Hebrew alphabet evoked for him a host of metaphorical associations:

> *The letter Beth which is the mouth as mans organ of speech.... [ellipses in text] his interior...his habitation...it denotes among many other things interior action & movement...this letter when in conjunction with the one preceding it...the Aleph...forms all ideals of progress...of graduated advance..the passage from one state into another...Locomotion..charcoal & ice..mysteries of the current event...tattooed weddings..ventriloquists with thin portfolios..musical & magical counterpoint..it's all there including the magnetic memory of volcanic rocks......impossible for me to talk about...dig the works...it's all there*[11]

What interested Berman was the mystery embodied in the fragments of letters and the elusive codes for which they stood. David Meltzer has described Berman's mystical esthetic:

> *Berman's work was both ocular and occultic...It was both revealed and concealed which gives it an interesting edge. You have to read Berman's work in that sense. You have to translate*

it in a much different way than looking at an Altoon gestural painting, where you're not reading it, you're just looking at formal ideas of space, composition, and energy.[12]

Sometimes on the cusp of the indecipherable, Berman's works demand close reading.

Another significant formal precursor for *Semina* is *The Box in a Valise* (1935–41) by the great gamesman-artist Marcel Duchamp. This carefully constructed edition consists of a briefcase filled with miniature versions of the artist's best-known works, serving as a retrospective-in-a-box. Elaborating on Duchamp's concept of an art container, Berman conceived of *Semina* as a kind of traveling group show in an envelope. Berman owned a copy of the March 1945 Duchamp issue of *View* magazine that alludes to the *Valise*. (The work had been pictured in *Time* and *Life* magazines as well.[13]) Although Berman hadn't seen the *Valise* that was part of the famed Arensberg Collection in Los Angeles, he had heard about it from his friend Walter Hopps, an avid Duchampian.[14]

Semina's unique form inspired Berman's admirers to experiment with similar variations on traditional book structures. A pirate edition of John Wieners's *Asylum Poems (for my father)* (np: Press of the Black Flag Raised, 1969; after New York: Angel Hair, 1969) was printed on eighteen sheets of colored paper and housed in an envelope with a blank mailing sticker. Punning on the etymology of *Semina's* name, Richard Brautigan's *Please Plant This Book* (San Francisco: Graham Macintosh, 1968) consisted of poems printed on actual seed packets. *A Portents Semina—Portents #6 (For Wallace Berman)* (San Francisco: Portents, 1967), edited by Samuel Charters, consisted of single-sheet broadsides and photographs housed in a pocket.

George Herms has created a number of projects in the loose-leaf style of *Semina*. His 1964 collaboration with Paul Beattie, *Game for Angels* (1963), is a set of poem-cards designed as a game and packaged in a cloth bag. The catalogue for Herms's 1992 retrospective at the Municipal Art Gallery, Los Angeles, took the form of a cardboard folio containing unbound brochure essays and postcard reproductions of works.[15]

With its playful package format designed to be sent through the mail, *Semina* clearly relates to the contemporaneous emergence of mail art as practiced by Ray Johnson and various artists associated with Fluxus. Begun in the mid-1950s and later christened the "New York Correspondence School," Johnson's massive project consisted of sending unsolicited collages and drawings to friends and art celebrities through the mail. For over forty years, he sent out thousands of goofy, absurdist missives; several from the mid-1960s appear in Wallace Berman's archive.[16]

Johnson's project was an anarchistic critique of the worlds of art and celebrity. The correspondence pranks and artwork mailers by Fluxus artists such as George Brecht, Dick Higgins, and Robert Watts also seem an ironic commentary on "high art" distribution methods.[17] Johnson used his mailings as calling cards for attention from critics, actors, curators, and artists that he admired or wished to know. Although *Semina* too is filled with inside jokes and elliptical references, its serious content and earnest intentions put it in another league. It was made for a constituency of friends and acquaintances as an esthetic and cultural expression of potent urgency.

More relevant to a consideration of *Semina* is the tradition of the "little magazines" from the 1920s such as *Transition*, *Dial*, and *Broom* that were instrumental in introducing experimental literature and art to American audiences. A specific model and precedent for *Semina*, however, is *View* magazine (1940–47), issues of which George Herms remembers excitedly perusing in Berman's living room on Crater Lane.[18] In *Semina Two*, Berman directly appropriated two proto-surrealistic photographic manipulations by Victorian writer Lewis Carroll that had appeared in the May 1942 "Tanguy/Tchelitchew" issue of the magazine. (see p. 54)

Under the editorship of Charles Henri Ford, *View* had a penchant for the unexpected and an unerring eye for quality, mixing fiction and poetry with features on Max Ernst, Pavel Tchelitchew, Hans Bellmer, Joseph Cornell, Man Ray, and Isamu Noguchi—most of whom contributed artworks for its covers.[19] Friendly to European wartime artist émigrés, *View* had a distinctly cosmopolitan bias and was the first to publish translations of works by Raymond Roussel, Jorge Luis Borges, Benjamin Peret, Albert Camus, Henri Michaux, Jean Genet, and Jean-Paul Sartre. *View* also significantly put an American spin on the Surrealist sensibility. Aztec and Native American poetry were featured, as well as Joseph Cornell's worshipful tribute to actress Hedy Lamarr.

Most importantly, *View* was a quiet yet crucial force kindling underground American culture. Nineteen fifties touchstones such as Henry Miller, Paul Bowles, Paul Goodman, and Marshall McLuhan published in the magazine. Philip Lamantia, whom Berman met in San Francisco in 1958 and published in *Semina 4* and *5*, had worked at *View* as an assistant editor after having first published in the magazine at age sixteen. In discussions about the magazine, he reportedly remembers Berman's high regard for the cohesiveness of the Surrealist movement over the years.[20] Also significant for Berman's interests were *View* associate editor Parker Tyler's critical assessments of Hollywood and avant-garde films, as well as serious articles on jazz and experimental music by critics Barry Ulanov and Roger Lyon Dodge, and composer Lou Harrison.

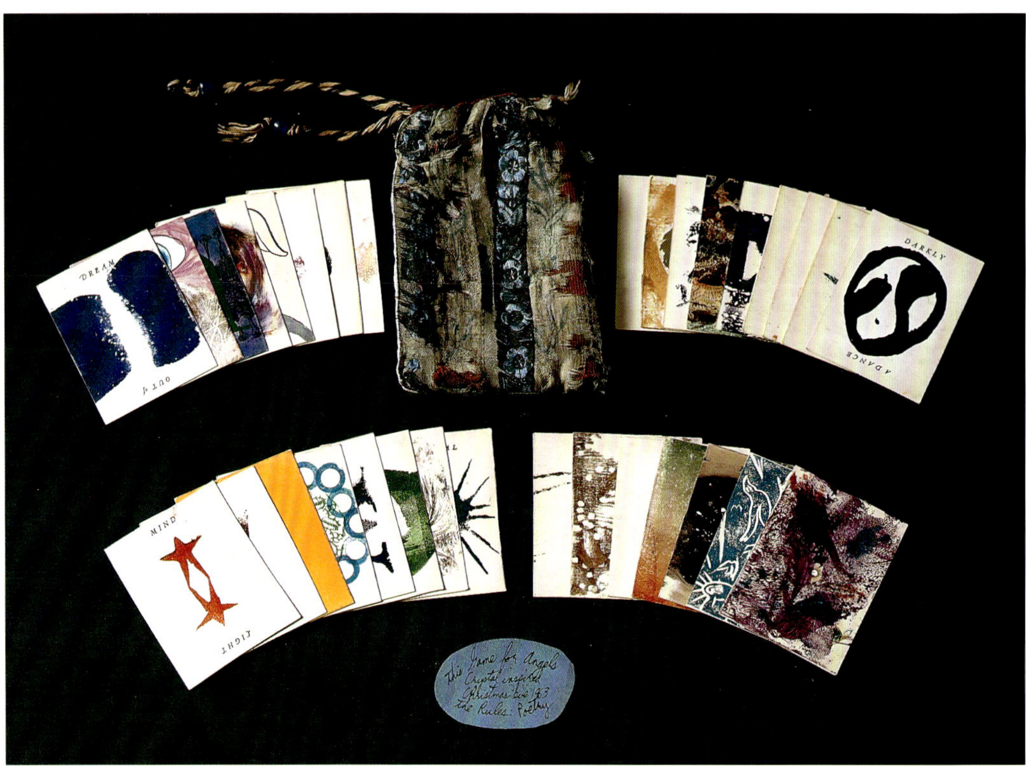

Paul Beattie (with text by George Herms), *Game for Angels*, 1963, Watercolor and text on cards in cloth bag, ed. of 50, MC Press, 1963.

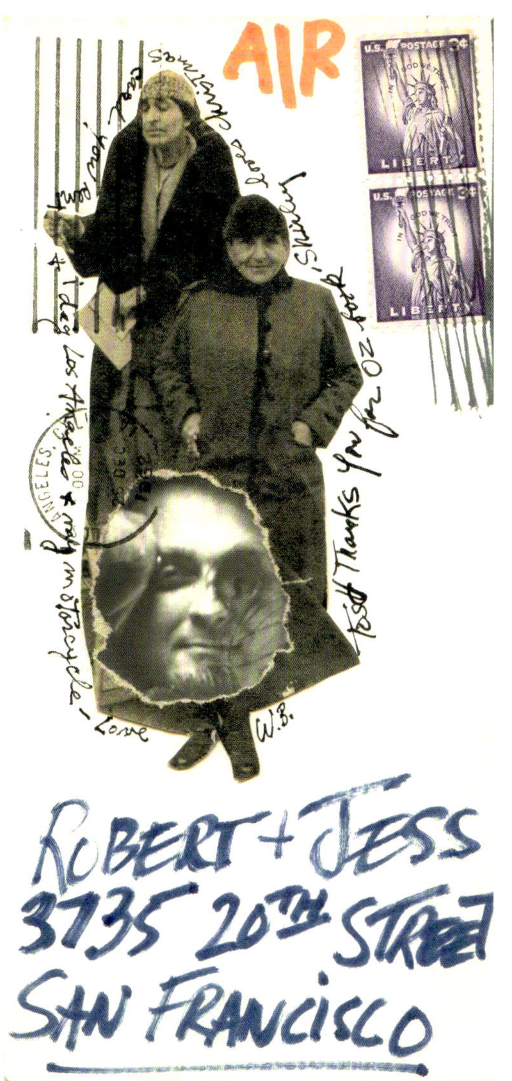

With Tyler and Ford at the helm, *View* also espoused a gay sensibility, indulgent of whimsy, sexual innuendo, eccentricity, and private jokes—qualities that prompted the disapproval of self-proclaimed surrealist kingpin and noted homophobe André Breton.[21] The homosexual subtext that offended Breton, however, was not an issue in Berman's circle. The Beats were extraordinarily sophisticated with regards to sexuality, with blanket acceptance for the tastes and proclivities of gay artists such as John Wieners, Edmund Teske, Allen Ginsberg, William Burroughs, Robert Duncan, and Jess.

The group was united more by artistic interests than sexual preference. As many of them have stated in interviews and oral histories, to look or dress like an artist in mainstream 1950s America made you an outcast. The straight, Wichita-born poet Michael McClure described how anyone in that era who was out of the ordinary was targeted:

In fact, I thought of myself as 'queer.' That's why I emphasize the word 'queer.' People would yell, "Queer!" at me when I walked down the street as easily as they would yell "Queer!" at my friend Don Love when he walked down the street. They weren't separating out young men with long hair from somebody who was apparently homosexual. I had it yelled at me as much as anyone.[22]

Wallace Berman, Mailer to Robert Duncan and Jess, n.d., Mixed media collage on paper.

Diane DiPrima's memoir *Recollections of My Life as a Woman* chronicles her complex relationships in the late 1950s with both men and women, gay and straight. As she described her group, the goal of their sexual experimentation and drug taking was *experience*:

> *Consciousness itself was a good. And anything that took us outside—that gave us the dimensions of the box we were caught in, an aerial view, as it were—showed us the exact arrangement of the maze we were walking, was a blessing. A small* satori. *Because we knew we were caught, knew beyond a doubt we were at an impasse: where to next Uncle Whitehead, Daddy Camus? But we had yet to take measure, find out all we could about what held us, kept us 'fascinated.' In the old sense of that word. Hypnotized. How to circumvent, bypass, or take on the monster.*[23]

Semina's overarching theme involved a search for how to transcend the "monster" of postwar meaninglessness. This romantic quest was pursued in the journal in several directions at once, signaled through contributors such as Antonin Artaud, who preached a revolutionary brand of primitivism and ritual; David Meltzer, whose poems tracked the role of the outsider artist in history and myth; Cameron, a practicing follower of Alastair Crowley and the occult; Alexander Trocchi, a defiant apologist for drug use; and Robert Duncan and Jess, a poet-artist couple whose works were generated out of fanciful imagination and mythological lore. In *Semina's* multivocal dialectic, all these refrains—and more—play at once.

The journal's allusions to drugs comprise a kind of paean to experimentation, evidenced in McClure's "Peyote Poem," Burroughs's "Pantapon Rose," Cocteau's sketch of an opium smoker, and many poems of *Semina 5*, the "Mexico" issue (1959). The assessment of drugs seems qualified only by Berman's pseudonymous poem in *Semina Two* credited to Pantale Xantos—also the credit for a photograph of Philip Lamantia shooting up in *Semina 5* (see p. 53). The short poem, with its reference to the "anxious needle" and the "narco myth," is placed next to Berman's two uncredited photographs of Robert Alexander shooting heroin, the first a harshly lit medium shot of the needle going into his arm, the next a shot of him from behind, slumping into himself as the drug takes effect. Over his shoulder can be seen one of Berman's *Parchment* works on the wall, ambiguously counterbalancing the act. The implication of the accompanying poem is that drugs represent a refuge for the severely alienated—those "raped by innumerable messiahs."

The spiritual quest evident in so much of *Semina* seems dedicated to keeping that alienation at bay. Berman's personal anxieties emerge most strikingly in *Semina 7* (1961), the sole issue for which he titled and claimed authorship: *ALEPH/a gesture involving photographs drawings & text by Wallace Berman* (see p. 63–65). This issue includes photographs and tributes to wife Shirley and son Tosh, as well as references to some of his closest friends: a photo of Arthur Richer, a mailer addressed to George Herms, and another addressed to David Meltzer that features a photograph of John Wieners. Other works commemorate some of Berman's favorite artists: Charlie Parker, Jean Cocteau, and Billie Holiday. Full-page photographs, including one of his wife's naked torso and one of thriving marijuana plants, are embossed with a large painted aleph, sanctified with a kind of seal of approval.

As a self-proclaimed "gesture," *ALEPH* is fraught with urgency, made at the end of the Bermans' stint living on a houseboat in Larkspur. One of the issue's autobiographical poems, "Boxed City," presents a pleasant but claustrophobic domestic scene of wife and child busying themselves while a stoned Berman continues "To separate seeds/ From the bulk." The act of discernment seems both privilege and burden. The mantra of Berman's poem, "Fairytale for Tosh"—"The wolf is dead" repeated ten times—seems less reassurance than a recurring attempt to ward off danger. A photograph of a still life presided over by photographs of Cocteau and Nijinsky is accompanied by a poem

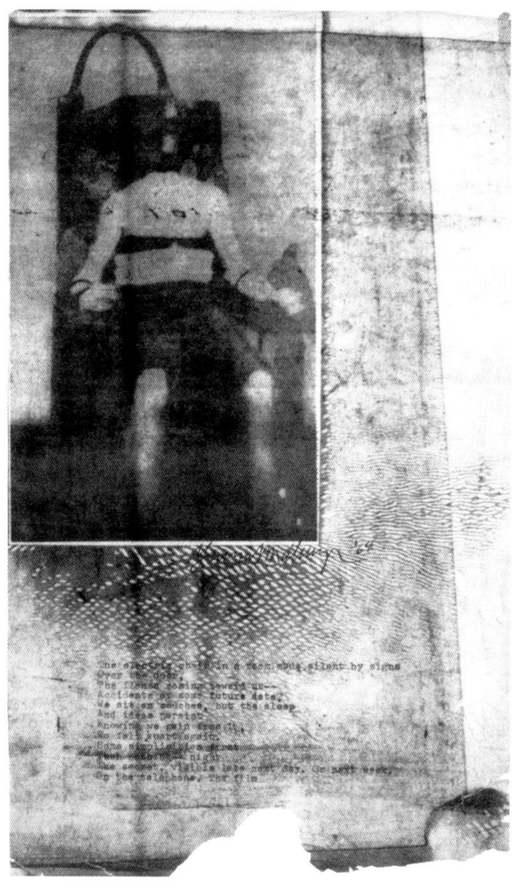

Andy Warhol and Gerard Malanga, Untitled ("The electric chair in a room made silent by signs..."), 1964, Thermofax with typewriter and ink on paper, 14 x 8 1/2 inches, Private collection, courtesy Sands + Company Fine Art, New York.

announcing the end of the Larkspur interlude and the Bermans impending return to Los Angeles:

Spurred by what reason
Do I leave this ark
For the city of degenerate
Angels 500 miles south other than to die.

This sense of doom is accented by *ALEPH*'s title page: a still from *I Want to Live* (1958, director Robert Wise) of the film's condemned killer in her electric chair, her face blotted out to become anonymous (see p. 63).

Berman's cover image preceded by two years *Lavender Disaster* (1963), Andy Warhol's acrylic and silkscreen painting of a grid of fifteen images of a photograph of an empty electric chair from Sing Sing. Accompanied by Gerard Malanga, Taylor Mead, and others, Warhol met Berman in late September 1963 while in Los Angeles for his exhibition at Ferus Gallery (see Chronology p. 347). Warhol used the backyard of Berman's Crater Lane house as one of the locations for his film, *Tarzan and Jane Regained, Sort Of...* (1963).

Impressed by the Bermans, Malanga dedicated a poem to them later that year.[24] In 1964—a year after Berman had begun making works with a Verifax machine—Warhol collaborated with Malanga on about twenty-five artworks in a style reminiscent of Berman's photo collages, juxtaposing hand-written poems by Malanga with news photos of acts of violence reproduced in sepia with a Thermofax machine. One of the works, *Untitled (The electric chair in a room made silent by signs)*, reproducing the image of a bound figure in an electric chair, directly echoed the cover of *Semina* 7.[25]

Semina 8 (1963) extended the personal angst of *Semina* 7 into a broader social context. Its contributions, credited only by initials, centered on symbolic martyrdom, epitomized by Berman's photo collages of doomed boxer Benny Peret, jazz musician Wardell Gray, and comedian Lenny Bruce. Texts by Artaud, Cameron, Kirby Doyle, and John Wieners augmented the apocalyptic tone.

The single sheet of *Semina* 9 (1964) concluded the project with the news photograph of Jack Ruby shooting Lee Harvey Oswald, altered so that the image of the government agent holding Oswald is doubled. Berman's tampered image seems inspired by the controversy surrounding the Warren Commission (1963–64) and the ambiguous evidence provided by the Abraham Zapruder home movie that documented the motorcade in Dallas. The print rights to Zapruder's 8mm film

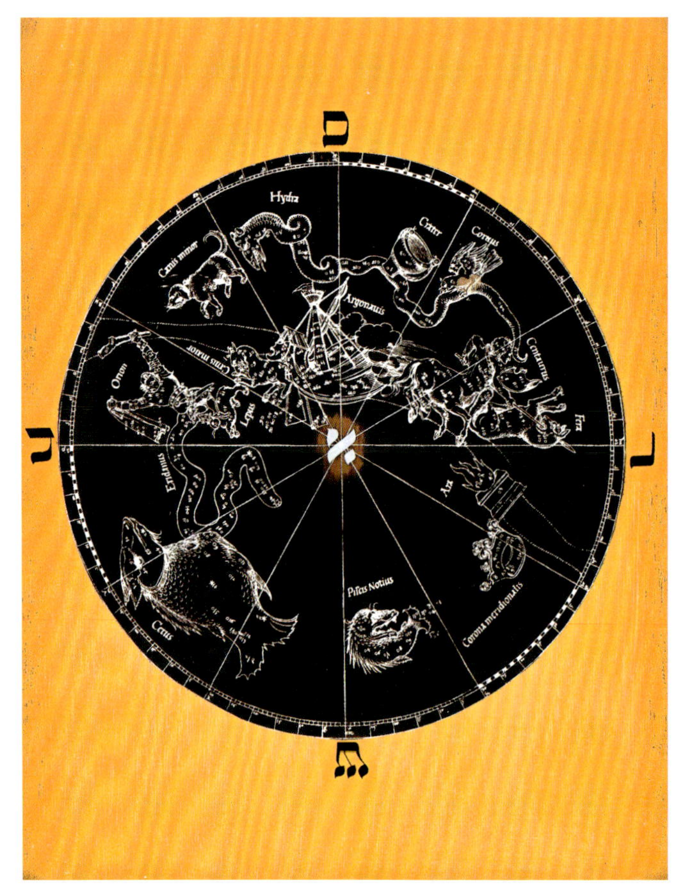

Hydra
Crater
Corvus
Argonauta
Centaurus
Fera
Orion
Lepus
Eridanus
Ara
Piscis Notius
Corona meridionalis
Cetus

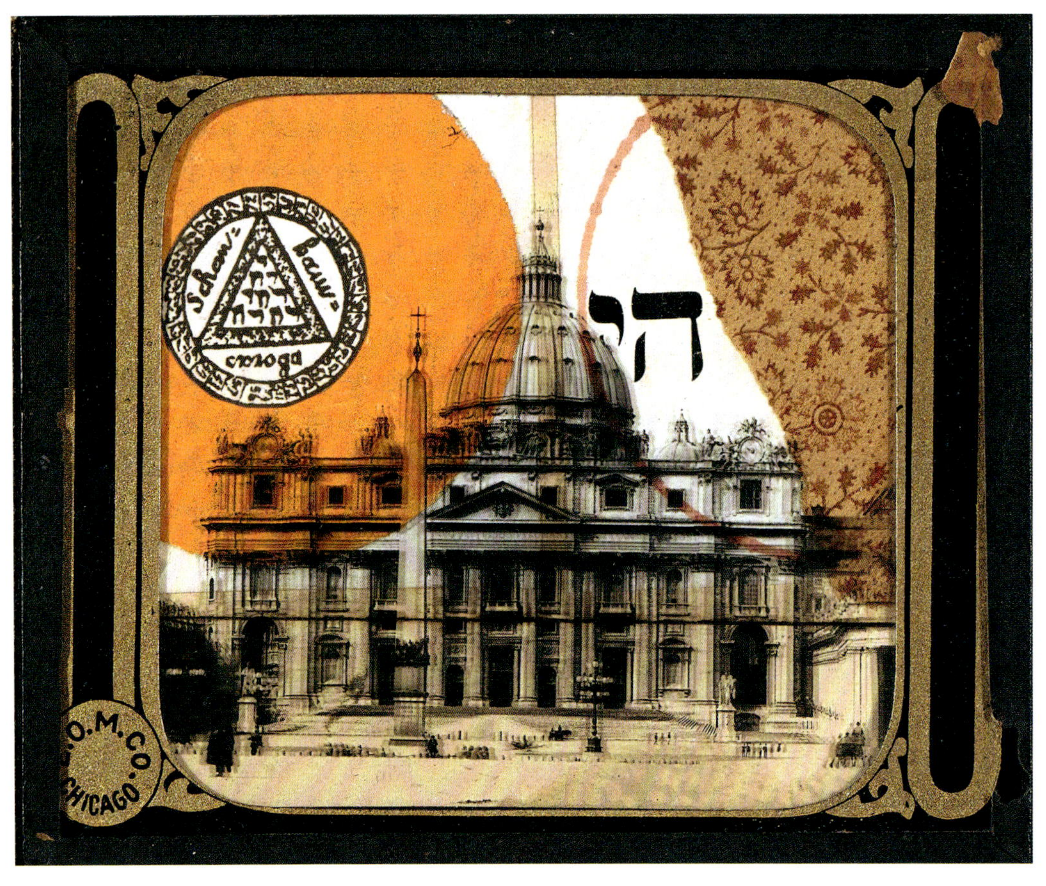

הי
O.M.CO
CHICAGO

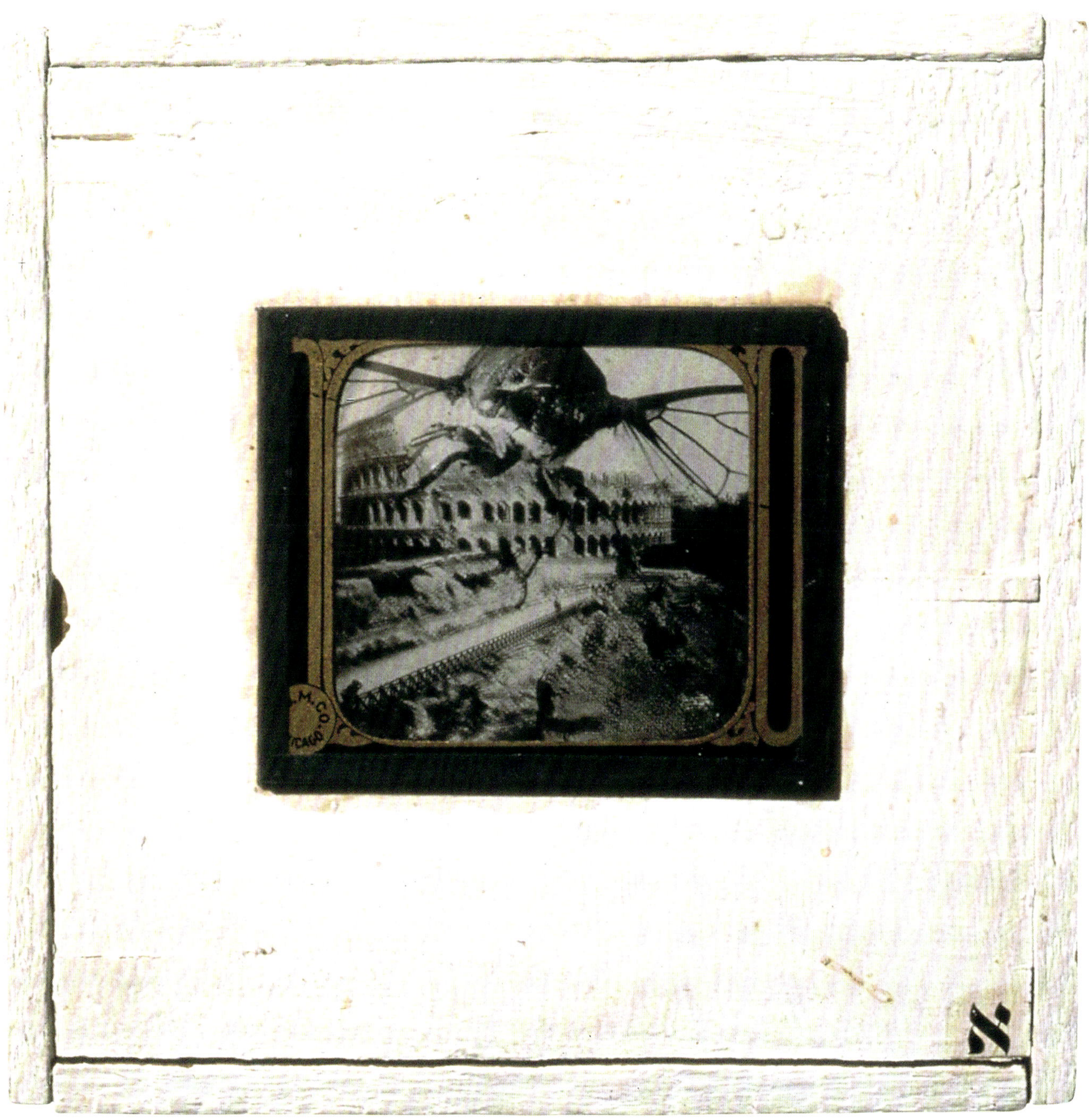

32 top Wallace Berman, Untitled, c. 1970, Verifax collage, 9 1/2 x 7 1/2 inches, Courtesy Wallace Berman Estate.

32 bottom Wallace Berman, Untitled, 1971, Glass photo collage, 8 1/2 x 9 1/4 inches, Collection of Temple of Man, Venice, Courtesy of Charles Brittin.

33 Wallace Berman, Untitled, 1971, Glass photo collage on wood, 7 5/8 x 7 3/4 inches, Collection of Nicole Klagsbrun.

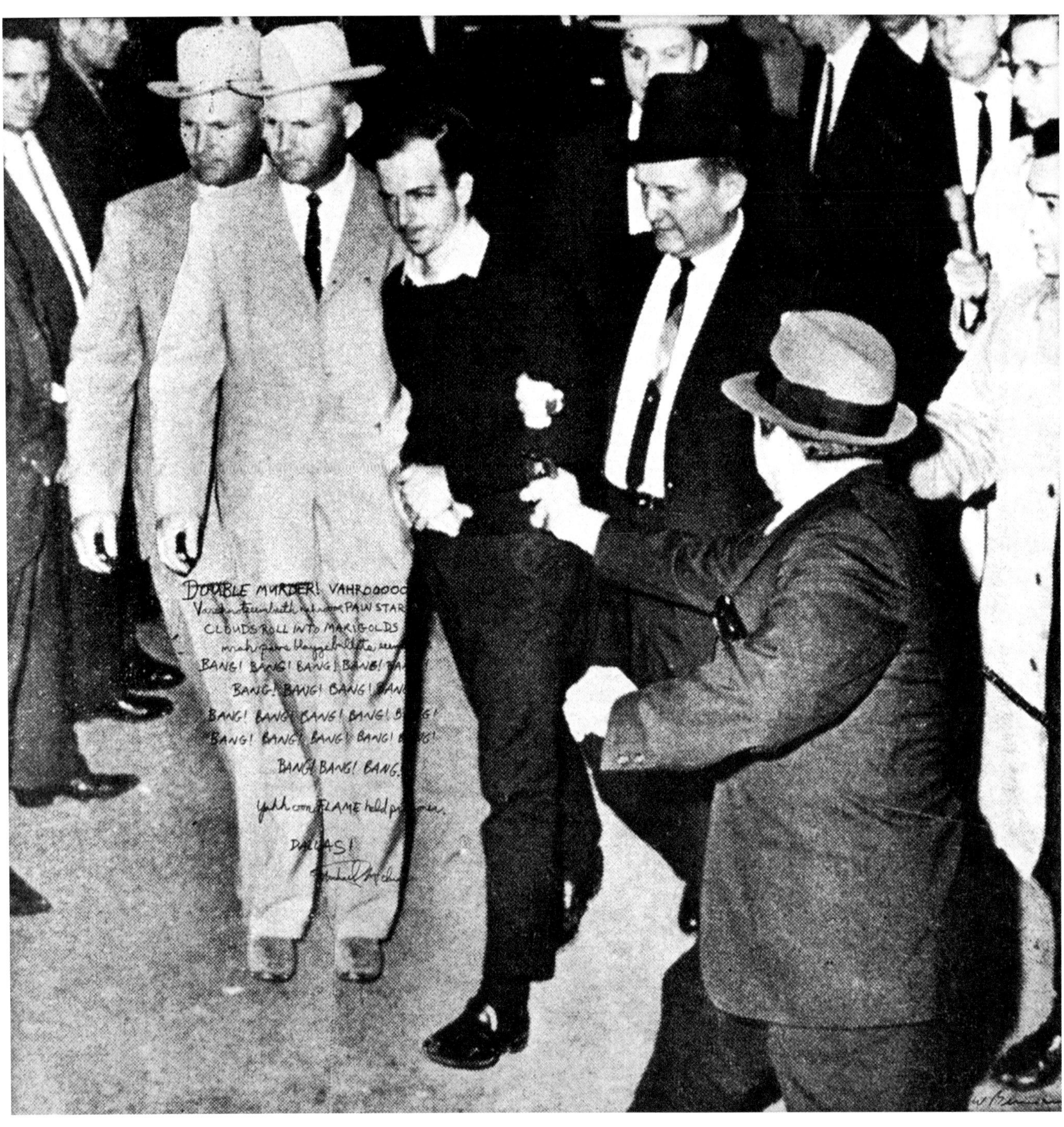
DOUBLE MURDER! VAHROOOOO
CLOUDS ROLL INTO MARIGOLDS
BANG! BANG! BANG!
BANG! BANG! BANG!
DALLAS!

were bought almost immediately by *Life* magazine and the film was confiscated by the government, not to be seen by the public until 1969. Stills from the film were printed in the November 24, 1963 issue of the magazine, sparking decades of conspiracy theories regarding the assassination.

With the simple doubling of one of the figures in this iconic photograph, Berman conjures the world of doubt that subsequent generations of disaffected Americans have felt towards officially sanctioned inquiries and mass-media images. Written after seeing the image, Michael McClure's bardic yelp—with its mantra of gunshots: "BANG! BANG! BANG! BANG! BANG!"—is a primal response to the violent acts that seemed to mark the end of the placid naïveté of the 1950s.

Friends with both Berman and McClure, Bruce Conner began working on his films *Report* (1963–67) and *Television Assassination* (1963–64, 1975) shortly after the Kennedy assassination while living in Brookline, Massachusetts, not far from the late president's birthplace. In both films, he manipulated footage taken from television reports of the events surrounding the Kennedy assassination with numerous edited repetitions, visual stutters, and reversing effects, in a sense making his own alternative, fractured Zapruder film.[26] Using additional stock footage and documentary material—including slow-motion footage and freeze-frame images of Ruby's gangland-style assassination of Oswald—the films are reveries on American myth-making and the numbing effects of mass media violence.

Similarly responding to an event that has yet to be adequately explained, Berman and Conner emphasized the unreliability and exploitative vulgarity of live-media coverage. While Andy Warhol famously looked straight ahead at the tragedy in his 1964 silkscreen paintings of Jackie Kennedy before and after the assassination, Berman and Conner seemed to step back to criticize the processes at work in the spectacles of the then new mass-media.

Pointed critique was not part of the Warhol esthetic. According to Gerard Malanga, Warhol began a film in 1966 based on the Kennedy assassination that featured two actors (Ronnie Cutrone and Malanga) in a dual role as Oswald—but the film devolved into chaos and was scrapped.[27] In the aftermath of the assassination, Warhol reportedly had been fascinated by the mystique created by the endless television replay in slow motion of the motorcade and Oswald's killing. Victor Bockris speculates that Warhol was perhaps inspired by the mesmerizing footage to project his own early films several frames more slowly than they had been shot.[28] In the projection of *Eat*, *Sleep*, and *Haircut*, Warhol employed a technique that had been used to analyze a national trauma and applied it to the most banal subject matter imaginable.

In their very different projects, Berman and Warhol both became indexers of Pop culture, surveying icons and symbols of American life. Berman's Verifax collages and Warhol's silkscreen series both cover a similarly wide range of images, including rock stars, national and religious symbols, animals, athletes, and politicians. Warhol's replicated silkscreens emphasize sameness and the machinery of mass-media culture. Although also appropriated from found images, Berman's grids of Verifax images thrive on their differences, manifested in the juxtapositions and combinations.

Wallace Berman, Untitled (Jack Ruby), 1964, Verifax with manuscript of poem by Michael McClure.

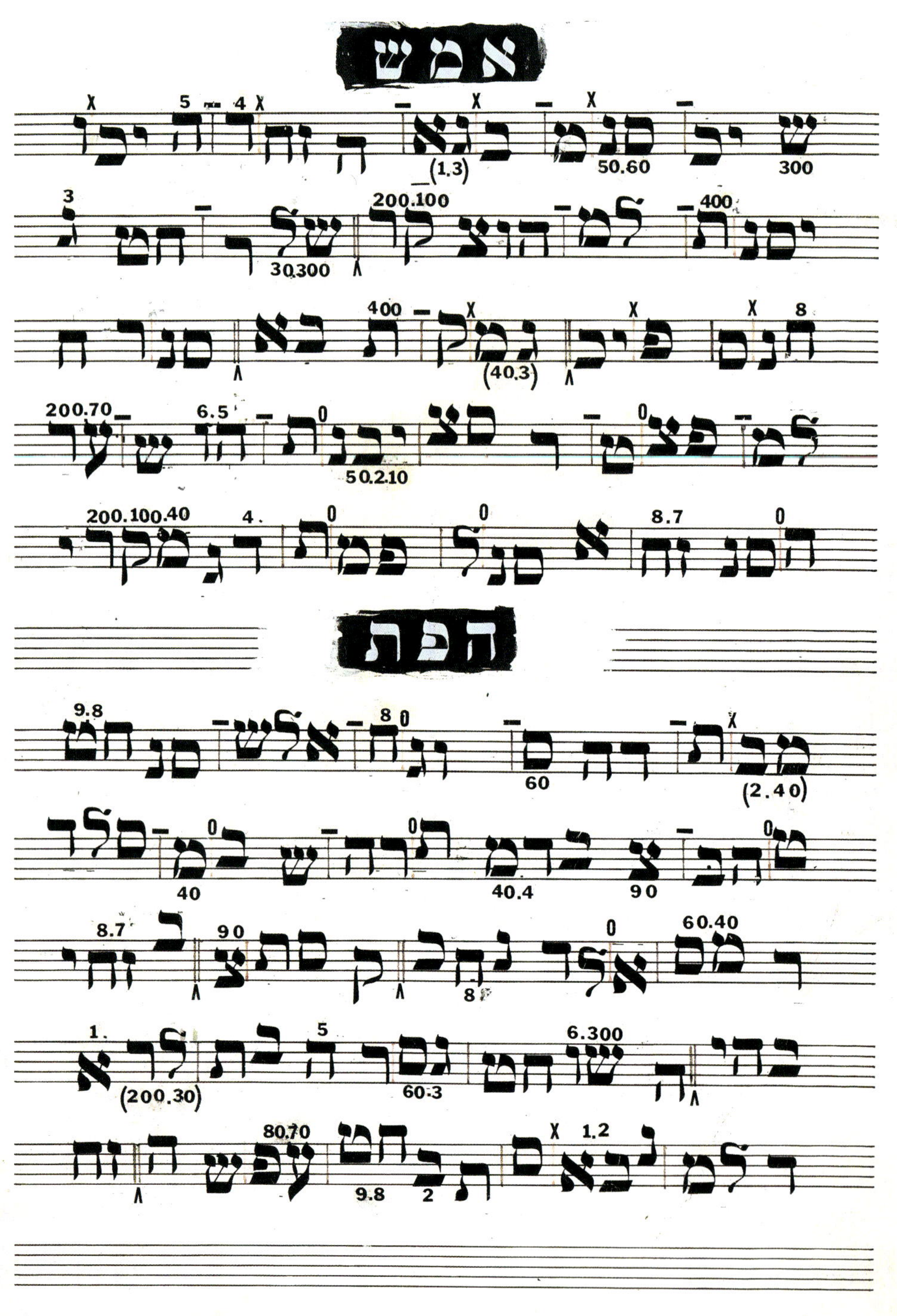

p. 36 Wallace Berman, Untitled (Music), 1974,
Ink and letraset on paper.

p. 37 Wallace Berman, Untitled, 1973, Mixed media,
9 1/2 x 9 1/2 inches, Collection of Ann Janss.

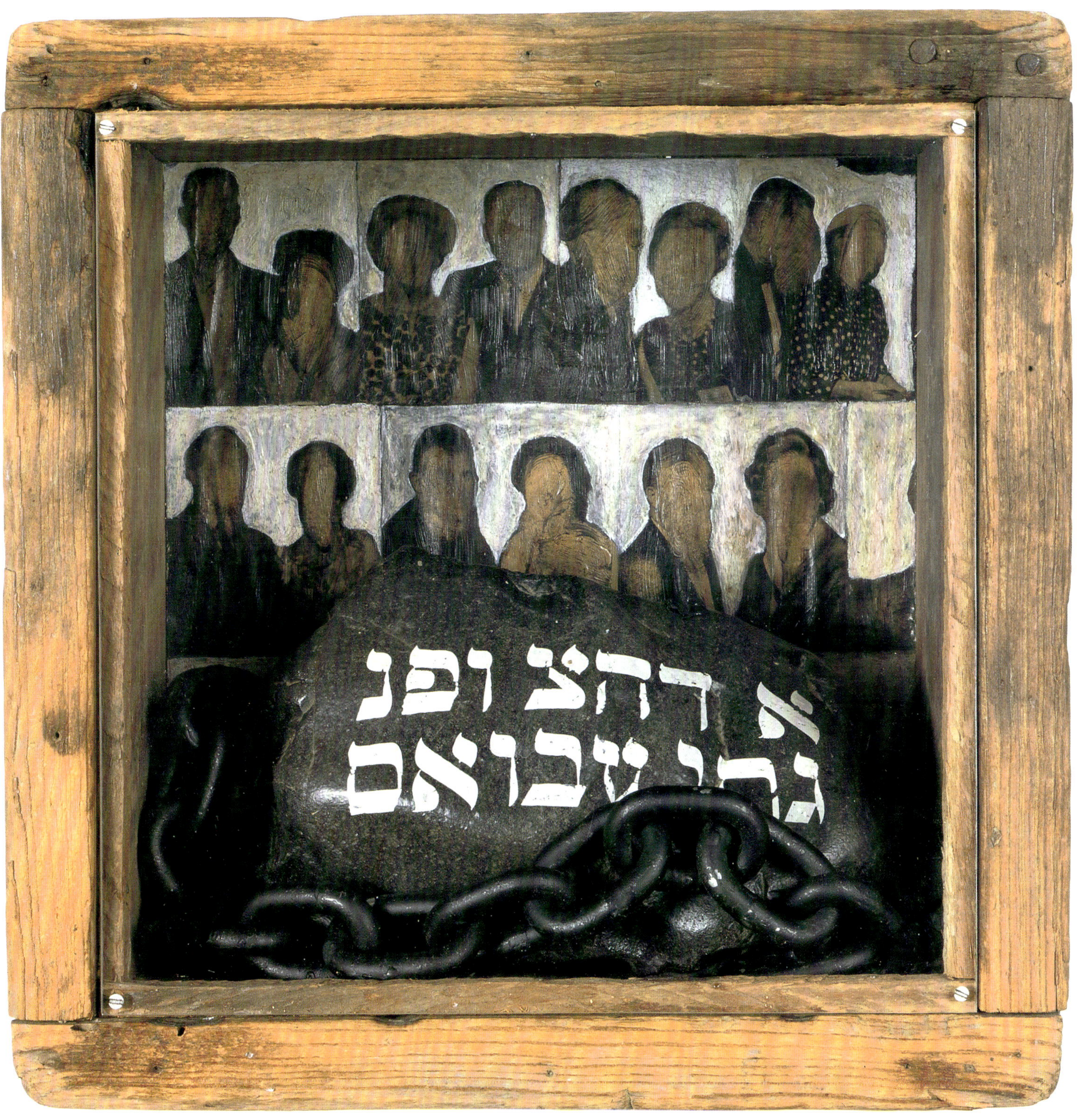
א דהצ ופנ
גחי שבואם

They reveal the shadows behind Warhol's surface glitz. In the brochure for Berman's 1970 exhibition at the Jewish Museum, James Monte noted the two artists' differences, remarking how an example of Warhol's Disaster Series "remains vague in the mind, a disaster of banality, of ennui" while a Berman collage "bombarded the viewer eliciting polymorphous esthetic responses to its varied parts."[29]

Although often included in group shows of Pop art, Berman's Verifax works are too complex and richly textured for the movement's deadpan cool. Similarly, *Semina's* poetic essence separates it from the ranks of the postmodern efforts it foreshadows. Although Berman never claimed authorship of *Semina*, his role as editor was as a kind of literary deejay, sampling texts from disparate sources and combining them to new effect. Yet his enterprise is vastly different from that of postmodern appropriators such as Sherrie Levine and Mike Bidlo, or the politically charged collectives Group Material and Gran Fury. Despite its status as a document that appropriates texts from the past and present, *Semina* is simply too earnest and mystical to fit into a proto-postmodern niche.

In his 1936 essay, "The Work of Art in the Age of Mechanical Reproduction," critic Walter Benjamin famously argued that mass-reproduction of images in the twentieth century had brought about the demystification of the "aura" surrounding traditional artworks. The decay of a work's uniqueness, according to Benjamin, provided a more social and open-ended context for art. Benjamin's ideas have helped foster postmodern art that comments on the image-glut of contemporary society, critiquing both the values and ideas of the past and present. Elevated from critique by its intrinsic mysticism, Berman's *Semina* seems to twist and defy Benjamin's theory. In each issue, the collection of replicated and re-configured poems and artworks from the past and present takes on an aggregate essence and aura beyond that of the individual components.

A triumph of the do-it-yourself esthetic, *Semina* is a fragmentary guidebook to alternative modes of thinking, living, and art-making. In the mix of texts and voices, Berman defined a new esthetic based on a romantic embrace of mysticism, individualism, and domesticity. Through *Semina*, he advocated a kind of hermetic transcendence fostered by the anxiety, comedy, darkness, and banality of the all-too-real world of 1950s America. Protected by and emanating a dark aura, Berman offered in *Semina* the seeds for a defensive counterculture capable of transcending the puritanical values of mainstream America. Now fifty years since the publication of the journal's first issue, those conservative values seem again to have a stranglehold on our culture. Yet, a resurgence of the counterculture is in the air. *Semina's* model remains potent and ready to help activate a new generation of the disaffected.

ENDNOTES

1 James Boyer May, "Addenda," *Trace: A Chronicle of Living Literature*, 21, April 1957, p. 31. A letter from May to Berman dated February 18, 1957 refers to their previous meetings and includes May's submission of several poems for publication in *Semina*, including "It's Living Now" which appears in *Semina Two*. James Boyer May Archive, University Archives and Special Collections, Pollak Library, California State University, Fullerton. *The Little Man* was published erratically in the late 1930s by Robert James Lowry in Cincinnati.

2 May also published in *Trace* 24 (October 1957) a paragraph review of I.E. (Robert) Alexander's book *Collectanea*, mentioning its cover by Wallace Berman.

3 *Semina* was listed in the "Directory" or "Chronicle" of *Trace* in issues 21 (April 1957); 25 (February 1958): "Stresses experimental art—brochure presentation of individualistic works"; 26 (April 1958); 30 (February–March 1959); 32 (June–July 1959): "Handset on 'beat' handpress but Editor Berman renounces Beat classification"; 39 (September–October 1960); 42 (Summer 1961); and 47 (Fall–Winter 1962): "*Far-out* items"). Issues were listed as being for sale for $1 and writers were instructed to make submissions to Berman's various home addresses.

4 See *Semina* Contents for some references in Berman's correspondence to *Semina* submissions. A 1959 postcard to Allen Ginsberg, for example, states: "I forgot to sound you out about poems for *Semina* Mexican issue—not more than 10 lines—also if you have anything by Burroughs that hasn't been printed yet & Kerouac—Mexican subject matter doesn't have to dominate poem—a sentence or word in poem is cool." Allen Ginsberg Archive, Box 2 Folder 31, Special Collections, Stanford University Libraries.

5 "On Semina," McClure interview with Eduardo Lipschutz-Villa, October 1992, In *Wallace Berman: Support the Revolution* (Amsterdam: Institute of Contemporary Art, 1992), p. 60–61.

6 Hermann Hesse, *Magister Ludi,* trans. by Mervyn Savill (New York: Frederick Ungar, 1949), p. 76–77.

7 Conversation with George Herms, June 4, 2004.

8 Berman's personal library is part of Wallace Berman Archive, Archives of American Art, Smithsonian Institution. For a discussion of Fenellosa and Pound, see Hugh Kenner, *The Pound Era* (Berkeley: University of California Press, 1971).

9 A 1965 poster (edition of 150) reads:

RETARD PARA.33 SEC.12.MM
KILO/MAMA RECANAAN XX.8
LUNARSEED JACJAC. AMER.R
EVOLUTION/ELEK.99VT LOVE

Another poster from 1967 reads:

OPT.82 BOOSTER BNG. ANGUINEA/Y
GOTHIC/Y FANTOM LEX.MM.44.9 STP
DEF.005.E ANGUINEA/X (BLACK) CM

10 See Christopher Knight, "Instant Artifacts," in *Wallace Berman: Support the Revolution* (Amsterdam: Institute of Contemporary Art, 1992), p. 37–38; and Sophie Dannenmuller, *Wallace Berman: California Assemblage Artist (1926–1976),* unpublished Master's Thesis, Université Paris III, Sorbonne, 2003, p. 22–24.

11 Wallace Berman, uncredited statement, undated, Wallace Berman Archive, Smithsonian Institution, Archive of American Art, Reel 5282, Frame 394. This statement is transcribed in the Archive in several different drafts, including one on a page following a 1968 letter from the Jewish Museum, New York requesting from the artist a biography and short statement about his work. This re-edit of the statement is credited as follows: "transcribed by Tanya Baum-Leh [spelled elsewhere as "Belami"], London at residence of R. Fraser, London 1967." The Bermans visited London that year and stayed in the apartment of art dealer Robert Fraser.

12 David Meltzer, interview with Kristine McKenna, November 16, 2003.

13 *Time,* September 7, 1942 issue includes an article on Duchamp with a photograph of him displaying a copy of *The Box in a Valise* in the apartment of Peggy Guggenheim; *Life*, April 1952.

14 Walter Hopps, phone conversation, February 24, 2004

15 Edward Leffingwell, *George Herms: The Secret Archives* (Los Angeles: Los Angeles Municipal Art Gallery, 1992).

16 See Wallace Berman Archive, Archives of American Art, Smithsonian Institution.

17 *Arranged Marriage*, a 1999 exhibition at New York's Roth Horowitz Gallery juxtaposed mailers of Berman and Robert Watts. Although presuming similarities, the exhibition and accompanying catalogue only made evident the artists' differences.

18 June 4, 2004 conversation with Herms.

19 For an index of articles appearing in *View*, see Judith Young Mallin, "Index to *View*: 1940–47," in Charles Henri Ford, editor, *View: Parade of the Avant-Garde: An Anthology of View Magazine (1940–47),* (New York: Thunder's Mouth Press, 1991), p. 271–282.

20 According to Rebecca Solnit, *Secret Exhibition: Six California Artists of the Cold War Era* (San Francisco: City Lights Books, 1990), p. 16.

21 See Catrina Neiman, "Introduction, *View* Magazine: Transatlantic Pact," in *View: Parade of the Avant-Garde,* p. xv.

22 Michael McClure 1992 interview with Kevin Killian, "An Empire of Signs: Jack Spicer," in *Lighting the Corners: On Art, Nature, and the Visionary* (Albuquerque: University of New Mexico, 1993), p. 116.

23 Diane DiPrima, *Recollections of My Life as a A Woman: The New York Years* (New York: Penguin Books, 2001), *p.* 202–203.

24 Gerard Malanga, "Pictures from Larkspur (for Wallace and Shirley)," December 18, 1963 correspondence, Wallace Berman Archive, Archives of American Art, Smithsonian Institution.

25 Neil Printz, *Andy Warhol: Death and Disasters,* ex.cat. (Houston: The Menil Collection, 1988), p. 26. Printz reports that in 1964–65, Factory collaborator, Billy Name made Thermofax copies of images of deaths and disasters "stockpiled by Warhol." In a September 18, 2004 email to Michael Duncan, Malanga stated, "Andy Warhol had nothing to do with the creation of the Thermofax series and was nowhere in the vicinity when they were made. The only reason for his name being attached to the series was that he owned the photocopy machine." Another of the Thermofax works, *Ghost-Written* (1964), however, bears Warhol's rubber stamp signature, *Death and Disasters,* p. 27. Over the years, many of Warhol's projects were executed or conceived by his assistants and friends. In 1963 Wallace Berman began using a Verifax machine he discovered in the studio of William Jahrmarkt; Jahrmarkt gave him the machine in 1964.

26 For a full assessment of the films, see Bruce Jenkins, "Explosion in a Film Factory: The Cinema of Bruce Conner," in *2000 BC: The Bruce Conner Story Part II* (Minneapolis: Walker Art Center, 1999), p.185–223.

27 Gerard Malanga interview with Patrick Smith, November 1, 1978; Patrick S. Smith, ed., *Andy Warhol's Art and Films* (Ann Arbor: UMI Research Press, 1986), p.394.

28 Victor Bockris, *The Life and Death of Andy Warhol* (New York: Bantam, 1989), p. 142–143.

29 James Monte, "Wallace Berman and Collage Verité," *Wallace Berman: Verifax Collages*, exhibition brochure, Jewish Museum, New York, 1968.

SURREALISM MEETS KABBALAH:

Wallace Berman and the Semina Poets

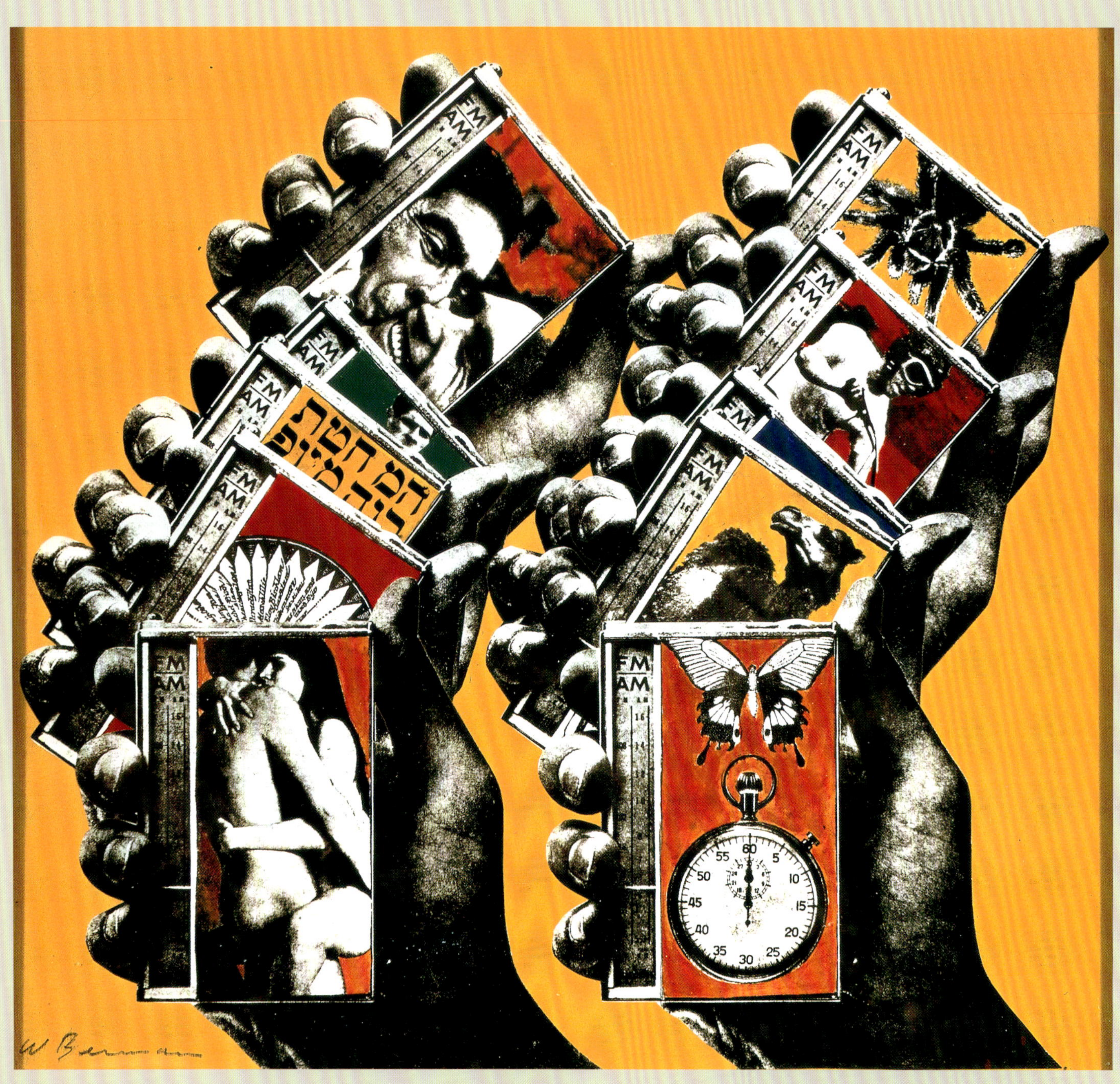

Stephen Fredman

Although Wallace Berman's *Semina* has acquired legendary status within the art world, there would be no *Semina* without the poetry that made up the majority of its contents. According to his wife, Shirley, Berman began *Semina* "because he loved poetry so much."[1] "We spent a lot of time reading poetry," she recalls, insisting that poetry was a more important source of inspiration for Berman than two other art forms he adored, music and film. Not only did Berman write poetry himself, but it formed an integral part of the discipline of his working life: "His working process was to read poetry, all the new young poets."[2] By reading seriously "new young poets" such as Robert Alexander, David Meltzer, Michael McClure, Robert Duncan, John Wieners, Philip Lamantia, Jack Hirschman, Bob Kaufman, Ray Bremser, and Kirby Doyle, Berman gained entrée into a vast range of modern and occult literary ideas and forms. His poetic explorations opened up fields of experience and experiment that took Berman far beyond what he was learning from the visual artists who gathered around him. In particular, the poets joined him in a lifelong fascination with Surrealism, especially with Jean Cocteau and Antonin Artaud. As Shirley attests, Berman "was really more involved with [Surrealist] poetry than he was with the artists—Baudelaire, Rimbaud, Mallarmé, and Cocteau."[3]

With Artaud in Mexico

Like the Surrealists, Berman and the *Semina* group consistently blurred the boundaries between life and art. In this sense, Artaud, renowned as poet, actor, theater revolutionary, and psychic pioneer, was a fertile source of inspiration for the poets and for Berman. As Shirley affirms emphatically, Berman "did love Artaud,"[4] whose texts "To Have Done with the Judgment of God" and "Concerning a Journey to the Land of the Tarahumaras" were translated early and became touchstones for the *Semina* group.[5] The ultimate psychic/artistic adventurer, Artaud had proclaimed as a young man, "Where others want to produce works of art, I aspire to no more than display my own spirit.... I cannot conceive of a work of art as distinct from life."[6] Since his death in 1948, Artaud's influence upon theater and performance art has been incalculable; he has come to be seen as the embodiment of an unswerving commitment to conducting life as a continual experimental performance. One of his experiments that greatly impressed the *Semina* group was the trek he made to Northern Mexico for

40 Wallace Berman, Untitled (Multi-color shuffle), 1967, Color Verifax collage, 13 x 14 inches, Courtesy Wallace Berman Estate.

the purpose of ingesting peyote with the Tarahumara Indians; his 1936 report contains one of the first modern depictions of psychedelic experiences. Beyond the extensive influence of his "theater of cruelty" and his dedication to personal transformation, Artaud inspired the *Semina* group directly through his description of the effects of peyote and his invocation of Mexico as a magical and forbidden realm.

In an essay entitled "Artaud: Peace Chief," Michael McClure hails Artaud as "more than a man of literature" and adds, "He has turned his body into an instrument of science and become a being of history."[7] McClure took the opportunity to turn his own body into such an instrument early in 1958, when Berman left five peyote buttons at his apartment.[8] The morning after, McClure wrote "Peyote Poem," which Berman then printed as the sole contents of *Semina 3*—graced on its cover with a photo of two peyote buttons (see p. 55). The poem portrays an ecstatic experience of expanded consciousness, in which an "I" witnesses itself intersecting with an external world in ways both fantastic and fleshly:

I am separate. I close my eyes in divinity and pain.
I blink in solemnity and unsolemn joy.
I smile at myself in my movements. Walking
I step higher in my carefulness. I fill
space with myself. I see the secret and distinct
patterns of smoke from my mouth
I am without care part of all. Distinct.
I am separate from gloom and beauty. I see all.

In certain ways, this report of McClure's echoes Ralph Waldo Emerson's famous visionary experience, in which he became a "transparent eye-ball" and reported "I am nothing; I see all; the currents of Universal Being circulate through me; I am part or particle of God."[9] The effects of their visions were different, though, because Emerson embraced his as confirming a Platonic tendency to see transcendent forms as most real, while McClure was moved by his experience to see the fleshly as inherently spiritual, an insight that set him off on the path of biological mysticism he has followed since.

The *Semina* equation of Artaud with Mexico and drugs reaches a climax in *Semina 5*, an entire issue dedicated to an Artaudian view of Mexico (see p. 59). The complementary cover images of a huge pre-Columbian stone phallus and a portrait of Sor Juana Inés de la Cruz articulate a complex union of opposites that runs throughout the issue: Both the images and the poems seek to blend antinomies such as male and female, voluptuous and

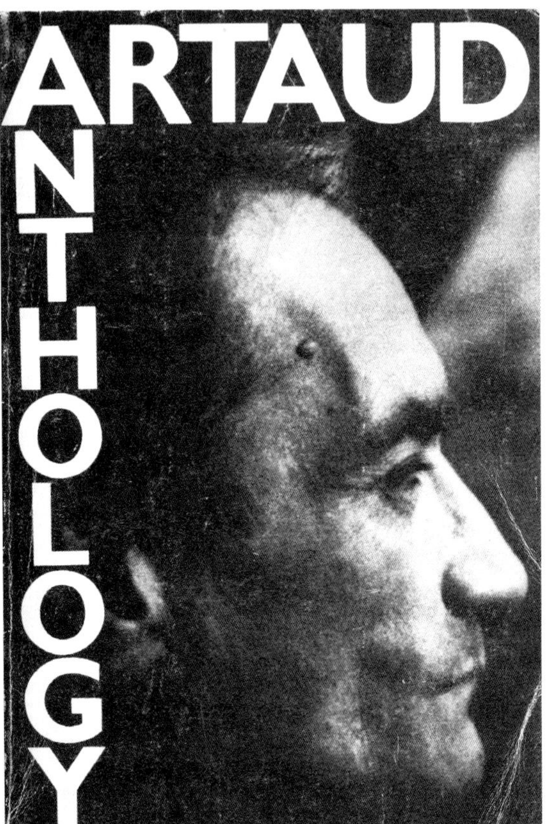

Antonin Artaud, edited by Jack Hirschman, *Artaud Anthology* (San Francisco: City Lights, 1968).

ascetic, fleshly and spiritual. Sex, drugs, and an earthy spirituality that both Artaud and the *Semina* group associate with Mexico are the catalysts that bring about a kind of alchemical conjunction of opposites. Artaud himself invokes this alchemical operation on one of the pages that contains an excerpt from a translation of his "Le Mexique et la Civilization":

and to Mercury corresponds the movement,
to Sulphur corresponds the energy,
to Salt corresponds the stable mass
even as the activity of fundamental sources
manifests the Mexican thing, an image, its
powers perpetually renewing itself.

By bringing elements fundamental to the practice of alchemy, such as mercury, sulfur, and salt, into the Mexican landscape, Artaud portrays it as a dynamic, transformative environment that is perpetually self-renewing. Possessed of remarkable alchemical abilities, Mexico seems to represent for Artaud both an image in its own right and the power to create images. He acquired this sense of the powerful, transformative quality of the landscape during peyote sessions, when the mountains and stones took on a series of biomorphic shapes: "I seemed to read everywhere a tale of childbirth amid war, a tale of genesis and chaos, with all these bodies of gods which were carved like men, and these truncated human statues."[10] In another poem from this issue of *Semina*, "I Mexico After Artaud," Kirby Doyle imitates Artaud's initiation into the dynamic powers of the Mexican landscape by throwing himself into the same crucible of madness that Artaud courted by ingesting peyote: "Stricken by my unconscious impotence, / Dizzy from intelligent spells of madness / Revealing the same thoughts, / I fall into Nature already prepared" (see p. 60).

Other works evince a similar sense of being "prepared" by Artaud. In particular, many depict states of derangement and insight achieved through the use of drugs. "Memoria" is Lamantia's paean to marijuana as a Mexican seeress, who "spoke sibyl sentences silver and cut the throats of time!" A photo by Berman of Lamantia injecting heroin on one page is matched on another by a poem by Bob Kaufman that ends with the lines, "O Mexico, give me your Easter Faced Virgin / And your Junk." Likewise, in his "Peyote Poem," John Wieners finds himself "inhabited by strange gods" and wonders, "who / are they, they walk in white trenchcoats / with pkgs. of paradise in their pockets." The filmmaker Lawrence Jordan contributes a poem, "Rockets," that seems to chronicle a peyote-enhanced trip to Mexico:

Motor oxydizing
Space-raped Breugel sand oxydizing

Blue sky oxydizing
Peyoton cloud oxydizing
Pepsi-cola oxydizing

The undeceived rearview mirror
blasting back an oxydized grey stripe.

Burnt, skin & spirit, we returned

More purified than we knew.

Through a drug-inspired vision of the world rusting away, Jordan experiences the alchemical quality of Mexico outlined by Artaud, in which breakdown and burnout are the first stages of an eventual purification and regeneration.

Just as there is a union of the opposing qualities of rust and purity in Jordan's poem, other works in this issue of *Semina* portray Mexico as either dangerous or seductive or both. John Reed invokes the Aztec-derived Mexican sense of the macabre with a drawing of a ferocious, partially skeletalized torso alongside a horrific poem presided over by vultures (see p. 60). Christopher MacLaine speaks in "Callejon García Villa Lorca" of the archetypal Mexican experience as "a stone / flung into the otherness of time." Although he invokes García Lorca in his title, MacLaine sounds more like the Mexican poet Octavio Paz when he portrays Mexico as a stone following an aberrant trajectory through history. John Chance imagines his own death, impaled on "Mexican green bull horns / Growing out of the Aztec Earth," in his poem "How I Died," while John Hoffman has a more peaceful vision of the ocean "clos[ing] the break of land / Into its time-deep crystal." David Meltzer imagines the dead Pancho Villa, whose ear "hangs like a rotted flower, / its blood nourishing the flies & / a disfigured unknown cactus." In contrast, Michael McClure's reverie about Mexico has a gentle quality, invoking "pastel / adobe houses. Pink, Salmon, and Blue / piñatas and crinoline hems." Seemingly addressed to a lover, McClure's poem opens up to the feminine side of the packet, in which Sor Juana, Mexico's first poet (translated by Lamantia), asks whether it is worse to be the seducer or the seduced, the prostitute or her client. Ruth Weiss contrasts the "calendar-poster of saints" with "the open-legged girl [who] IS the / mother of your children," in order to illustrate what she calls "the two-sided coin" of Mexico. The feminine side of Mexico is rounded out by William Margolis in a sentimental depiction of "pious-shawled women / mourning poverty in the sun / impassively with their eyes." For the *Semina* cohort, Artaud's Mexico is a place of exploration and escape, of breakdown and transformation, where the bland reality of 1950s America can be swept aside through immersion in a seductive embrace of otherness.

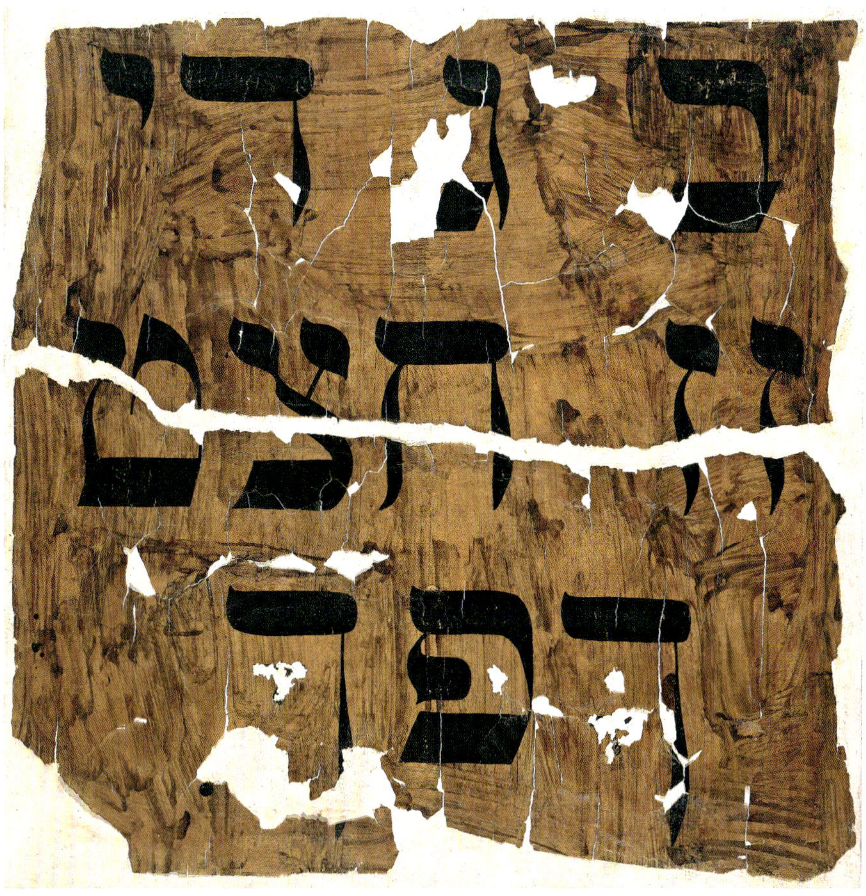

Wallace Berman, Untitled, 1956–57, Woodstain and ink on parchment, 19 1/2 x 19 1/2 inches, Collection of Hal Glicksman.

The Kabbalah and "The Artists of the Survival"

Artaud was one of a number of Surrealists, including René Daumal and Kurt Seligmann, who commandeered esoteric religious imagery for an assault on the reign of rationality. Author of an extensive *History of Magic*, Seligmann, like Artaud, made a profound impression on Philip Lamantia. As a teenager in Los Angeles and New York, Lamantia had direct access to what he calls "the Surrealist diaspora" of writers and artists who had fled Europe during World War II: "Surrealism was what brought me to what you call hermeticism.... The key for me was my weekly lunch with the painter-engraver Kurt Seligmann, who graciously allowed me to look at his many volumes of very early, amazing alchemical texts. This was an unforgettable experience."[11] Alongside alchemy, another major strand in the Western hermetic tradition, Kabbalah (literally, "tradition" or "transmission"), the mystical wing of Judaism, also held an enormous fascination for the Surrealists. Artaud, for instance, when trying to understand how patterns repeated in the Mexican landscape have a mathematical regularity—a regularity imitated in the patterns of the Tarahumara rituals and dances—turns to the Kabbalah for an explanation: "There is in the Kabbalah a music of Numbers, and this music which reduces material chaos to its prime elements explains by a kind of grandiose mathematics how Nature orders and directs the birth of forms she brings forth out of chaos. And all I beheld seemed to be governed by a Number."[12] Kabbalah has become important to modern poets not only for its numerological magic but also because of the immense, even cosmic, significance it places upon words, which are the material of poetry. As David Meltzer explains, "The Kabbalah, as much as poetry, is the study of and submission to the mysteries of the word. The language used by Kabbalists is so intricately dimensional that it is almost impossible to fully convey the simultaneous levels of meaning revealed in the simplest of words. It is said that one word is the seed of a particular universe, a system of interactions and realities as complex as the birth and death of a sun."[13] The kabbalistic conception of a word as a cosmic seed is one of the primary meanings gathered into the term "Semina"—which explains in turn why poetry, with its own insistence on the power of language, plays such a prominent part in *Semina*.

Of all the forms of magic outlined in Kurt Seligmann's *History of Magic* (astrology, numerology, divination, casting of spells, mortuary magic, alchemy, Kabbalah, Tarot, witchcraft, and black magic), Kabbalah appeals directly to poets because it is a kind of alchemy that engages with the materials of writing: the word, the letter, and the book. In Kabbalah all of the levels of occult "work"—magical practice, meditation and contemplation techniques, visionary excursions, spiritual and psychological self-transformation—can be found, as they would be in any esoteric system, but all derive from investigations of language and writing. Kabbalah made its way into the *Semina* circle primarily through the advocacy of Robert Duncan, who learned of it as a child listening in on his parents' theosophical meetings,[14] where the most important kabbalistic text, the *Zohar*, was being read as one of the keys to the mysteries of the universe. Not himself a believer in theosophy, Duncan came to view the *Zohar* as a powerful work of the imagination, calling it "the greatest mystical novel ever written."[15]

Duncan began drawing extensively upon the Kabbalah for his own poetry during the writing of the book *Letters* (1958), composed between 1953 and 1956, which was also the time period when *Semina* was born. In the preface to *Letters*, Duncan singles out Artaud as an attractive but finally destructive example of someone whose life overcomes his art: "Artaud is torn apart by actual excitations which are intolerable to his imagination and to his material."[16] Duncan sounds this cautionary note in *Letters* and continues to sound it throughout his career. In his 1978 appreciation of Berman, Duncan acknowledges the heavy reliance upon drugs in the *Semina* group and speaks parenthetically of his and his partner Jess's "avoidance of the drug culture scene so that we did not cultivate [Berman's] Larkspur house." He recognizes, though, that there was also a creative side to that dangerously self-destructive scene: "The word 'junk' that in the 1950s would have meant the trashing of the drug heroin, in the 1960s came to mean the redemption of trash in the recognition of devotional objects, emblems and signs rescued from the bottom in the art of a new context."[17] Junk art represented for Duncan an art of survival, in which the artist threatened by (self-)destruction manages to reclaim an imaginative sway over a brutal reality. In a prose poem dedicated to the Bermans from his 1964 book, *Roots and Branches* (a title that again alludes to the Kabbalah by invoking its image of the Tree of Life), Duncan speaks of "the artists of the survival" and asks, "How to shape survival! In what art to survive!"[18]

In the Kabbalah of Isaac Luria, which the *Semina* group read about in Gershom Scholem's *Major Trends in Jewish Mysticism*, the transformative art of survival is known as *tikkun*, the restoration of the broken world.[19] The sense of wholeness implied by *tikkun* is essential to Lurianic Kabbalah and is consonant with a number of other mythical kabbalistic symbols, such as the Tree of Life and the figure of Adam Kadmon, the Cosmic Human Being. Berman adopted another such symbol of wholeness, the first letter of the Hebrew alphabet, aleph, as his personal signet. Scholem points out that aleph is a silent consonant that "represents nothing more than the position taken by the larynx when a word begins with a vowel."[20] Aleph is the silent source of all articulation, the seed of the entire alphabet, "and indeed the Kabbalists always regarded it as the spiritual root of all other letters." Berman stamped the aleph everywhere, from his motorcycle helmet to *Semina 7*, entitled "ALEPH," which is an entire issue of photography, drawing, and writing by Berman dominated by the letter aleph. Speaking of Berman's collages and assemblages, Meltzer notes how the aleph functions in relation to the mundane imagery drawn from print sources: "Above the triteness and everydayness of this image continuum was Aleph—the first letter of the Hebrew alphabet, which put everything into a strange tension, because on the one hand you'd see the normative images that newspapers and magazines use to increase circulation held at bay by this letter."[21]

The aleph took on a transformative, sacralizing function, as though it were capable of conferring a blessing upon a degraded, commodified reality. In *Semina 7*, a huge aleph is stamped alongside or above a variety of photographs: a woman strapped into an electric chair, on the cover; Berman's son, Tosh, holding a rifle and wearing a Davy Crockett leather jacket; a vigorous stand of marijuana plants; a memorial collage for Charlie Parker; the torso of his wife, Shirley, with a large medallion between her exposed breasts; Patricia Jordan nude, wearing a mask and beads; a saxophone being played; and a figure seen through a window in two poses. The obsessions of Berman's life—his family, his friends, his devotion to jazz, his love of sexual display, his outrage at society as death-affirming—are all brought under the sway of the sacralizing function of aleph. Berman's use of the aleph not only introduces an "intuitive Kabbalah" that confers blessings upon the most vital facets of his life,[22] it also has an elegiac quality by virtue of its use as an iconic element so soon after World War II. Berman grew up in the Fairfax district of Los Angeles, where Hebrew lettering was prominent in the windows of shops and in the Yiddish newspapers; to invoke that world after the Holocaust is to draw attention to the death of the Hebrew letter, not only because the Yiddish-speakers of Los Angeles were dying out but also because the extermination of Jewish culture in Europe had incinerated the letters, both written and spoken, and rendered them ghostly. Like many gestures within his life and art, Berman's depiction of Hebrew letters on photographs, in assemblages, on parchment, and upon stones is fraught with opposing motives: the letters draw attention to suffering and disappearance, while at the same time invoking a promise of redemption.

Just as Berman's use of Hebrew letters runs a gamut from in-your-face protest to poignant elegy to tender utopianism, there is a unique fusion of toughness and vulnerability throughout his life and work that accounts for much of its continuing fascination. Beyond combining opposing qualities, Berman, like Artaud, achieved the most thoroughgoing fusion by intertwining his life and art so tightly that they became inseparable. In this sense, his greatest influence derives not from specific artifacts that he created but from who he was—what he thought, what he did, his attitudes toward art and life, his abilities to shine a new light on the things happening around him—as though he became a living work of art, inspiring creativity in others by his presence and example. By participating alongside the poets in the conjunction between Surrealism and Kabbalah, Berman evolved into a kind of revolutionary, shamanic figure: He refused to live his life conforming to institutional norms and social expectations; he made the conduct of life itself an ongoing artistic composition; he so conflated art and an occult spirituality that it's impossible to say which was the dominant factor in his work; he engaged in an all-consuming artistic/spiritual quest; and his personality exerted an uncanny magnetism upon other people. Fulfilling this role in a community of like-minded artists, writers, and filmmakers, Berman was able to make *Semina* the place where new experiments in art and life coalesced in a way unseen on the West Coast, helping to effect the transition from Beat culture to that of the Hippies.

ENDNOTES

1 Sandra Leonard Starr, *Lost and Found in California: Four Decades of Assemblage Art* (Santa Monica: Corcoran, Shoshana Wayne, and Pence Galleries, 1988), p. 81.
2 Ibid., p. 70.
3 Ibid.
4 Ibid.
5 Robert Duncan, *A Selected Prose*, ed. Robert J. Bertholf (New York: New Directions, 1995), p. 199.
6 Martin Esslin, *Antonin Artaud* (Harmondsworth, UK: Penguin Books, 1976), p. 5.
7 Michael McClure, *Meat Science Essays* (San Francisco: City Lights, 1963), p. 77.
8 See Richard Candida Smith, *Utopia and Dissent: Art, Poetry, and Politics in California* (Berkeley: University of California Press, 1995), p. 247; and Rebecca Solnit, *Secret Exhibition: Six California Artists of the Cold War Era* (San Francisco: City Lights Books, 1990), p. 69.
9 Ralph Waldo Emerson, *Essays and Lectures* (New York: Library of America, 1983), p. 10.
10 Antonin Artaud, *Anthology*, ed. Jack Hirschman, 2nd ed., (San Francisco: City Lights, 1965), p. 71.
11 David Meltzer, ed., *San Francisco Beat: Talking with the Poets* (San Francisco: City Lights Books, 2001), p. 137.
12 Artaud, p. 71.
13 David Meltzer, ed., *The Secret Garden: An Anthology in the Kabbalah* (Barrytown, NY: Station Hill Press, 1998), p. xiii.
14 Rodger Kamenetz, "Realms of Being: An Interview with Robert Duncan," *Southern Review* 21.1 (1985), p. 9–10.
15 Meltzer, *The Secret Garden*, p. x.
16 Robert Duncan, *Letters*, 1958, (Chicago: Flood Editions, 2003), p. x.
17 Duncan, *A Selected Prose*, p. 202.
18 Robert Duncan, *Roots and Branches* (New York: Scribner's, 1964), p. 169.
19 Gershom Scholem, *Major Trends in Jewish Mysticism*, third edition (New York: Schocken Books, 1954), p. 265–86.
20 Gershom Scholem, *On the Kabbalah and Its Symbolism*, trans. Ralph Mannheim (New York: Schocken Books, 1965), p. 30.
21 Meltzer, *San Francisco Beat,* p. 200.
22 David Meltzer, "The Door of Heaven, The Path of Letters," in Hal Glicksman, ed., *Wallace Berman Retrospective* (Los Angeles: Otis Art Institute Gallery, 1978), p. 100.

SEMINA: Annotated Contents

Michael Duncan

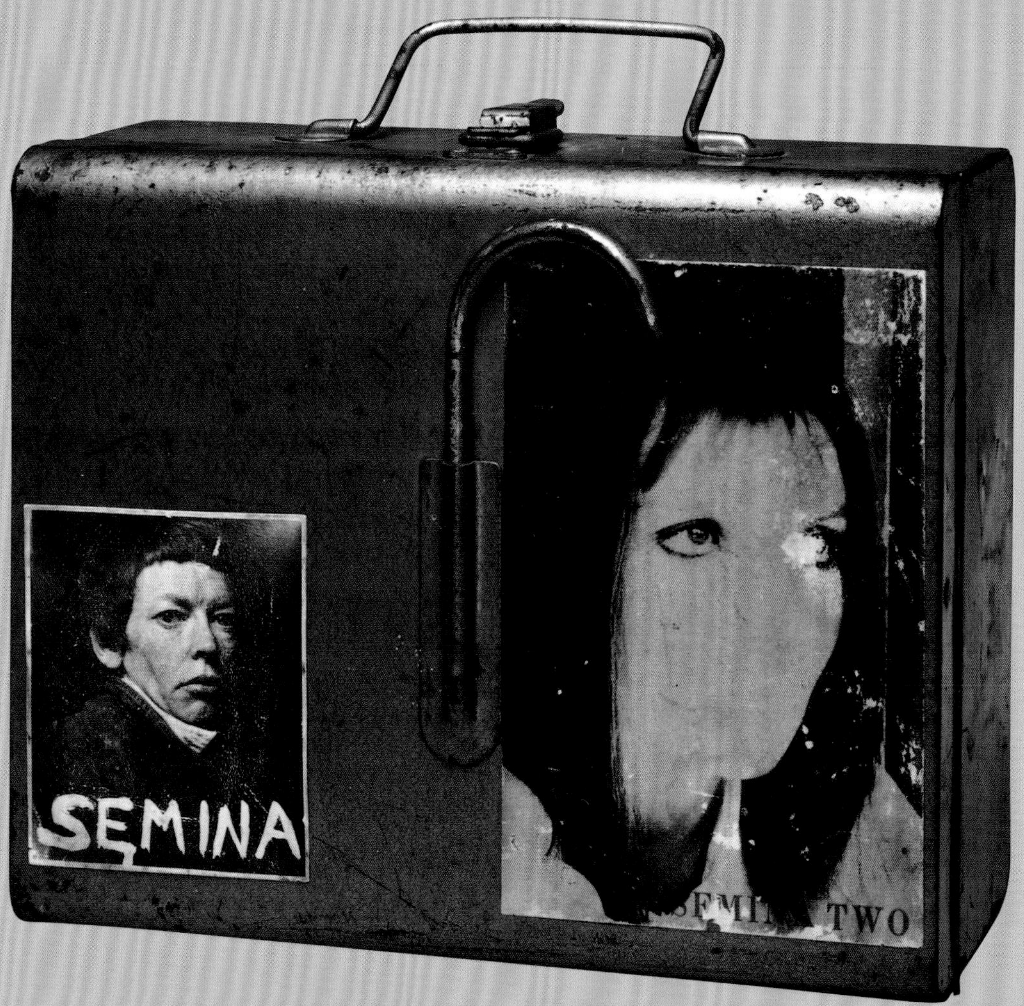

Note: The following is the first published inventory of *Semina*'s individual components, including subsequent publication history. Brief biographical information is provided for contributors not included in this exhibition. Translations for several of the poems are uncredited.

Semina 1, 4, 5, 7, and *8* include loose-leaf pages assembled in random order. Their contents are listed here in alphabetical order by author.

Wallace Berman, Carrier for *Semina*, 1957, collage on metal box, Courtesy of Shirley Berman.

a.

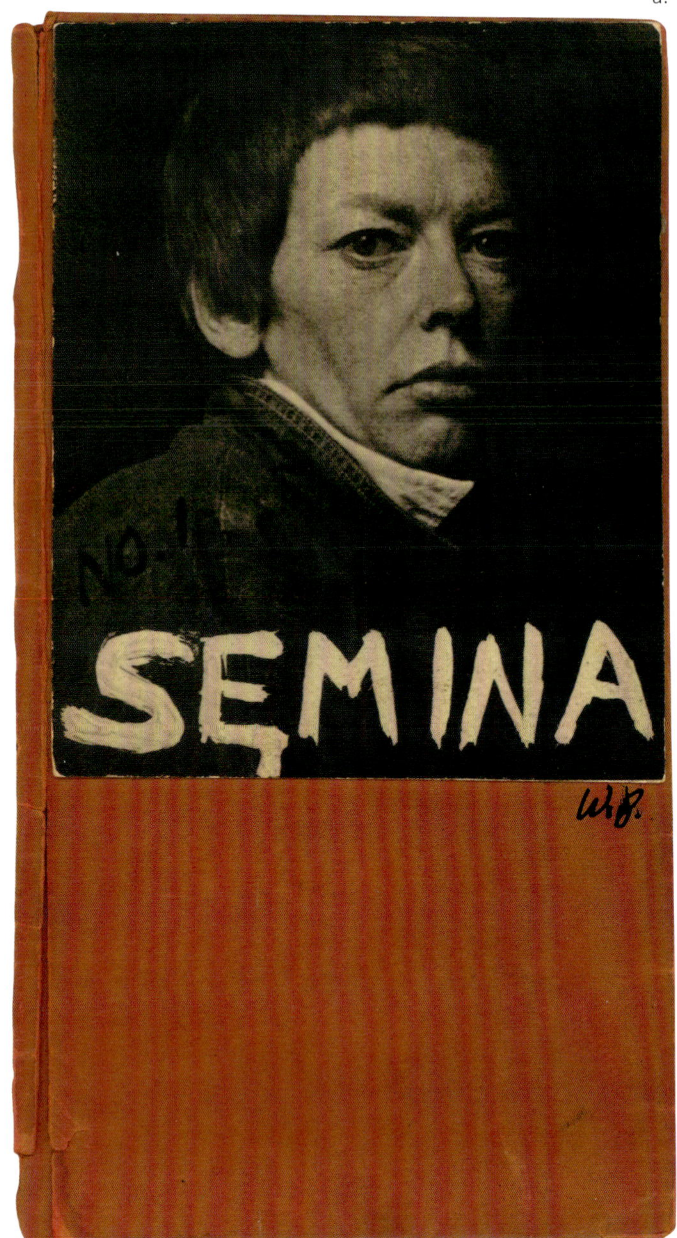

b.

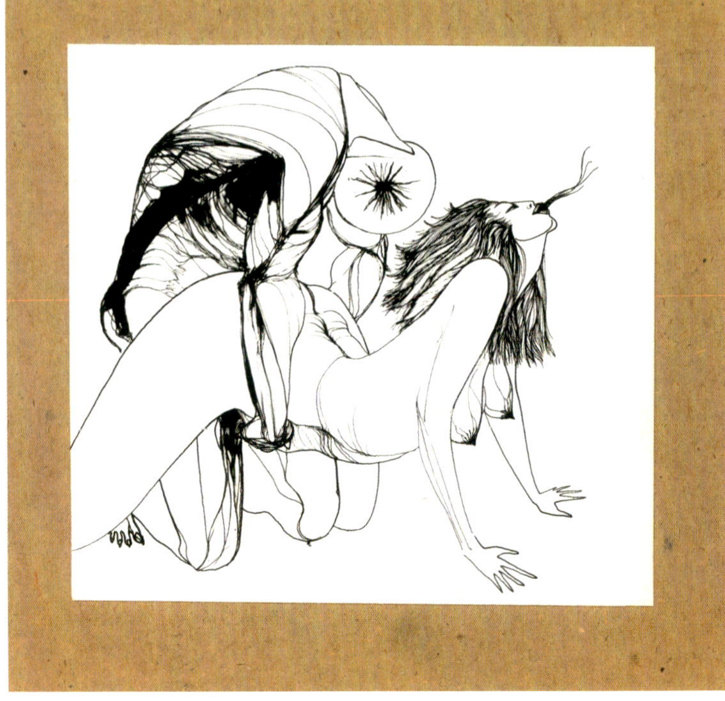

SEMINA 1

10426 Crater Lane, Los Angeles, 1955, 150 copies, 7 1/2 x 4 in.

In Wallace Berman's 1957 exhibition at Ferus Gallery, contents of *Semina 1* were scattered on the floor of his assemblage *Temple* (c. 1952–1957).

Cover: **Wallace Berman**, Photograph of Cameron. (a.)

E.I. Alexander (Robert Alexander), untitled poem ("Twelve times the door rattled and leven…"), Poem. (d.)

Charles Brittin, *Homer*, Photograph (found graffiti in Venice, California). (c.)

Cameron, *Untitled* ("peyote vision"), Ink drawing. (b.) *This* Semina *reproduction of Cameron's drawing was confiscated from Berman's Ferus exhibition by the Los Angeles Police Department and deemed obscene by Judge Kenneth Halliday in 1957 trial that convicted Berman*. (b.)

c.

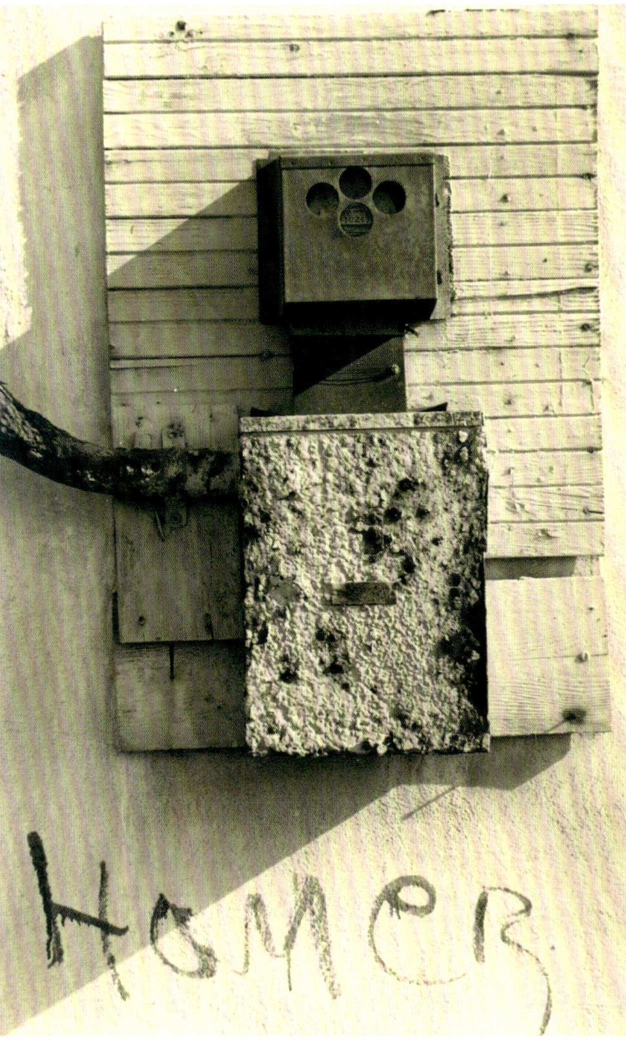

d.

e. i. alexander

twelve times the door rattled and leven
i winced in its direction. two days later
i looked out. standing there on the easel
of the opening, stood a little girl,
just nine minutes old.
-may i come in? she said.
i opened wider of the panel and walked in
back with her in front.
she flowed on the floor
and i cried, -please please! and i
gestured with my eye closed.

i remember melting and nine minutes
came into me thru my everything and i
could feel me with her and
-i shall never leave you now, she said.
-i am Your nine and you let me away.
-now you are open to me and together
We meldit xd the quantis mora.

when i opened my eye again, i was no
longer being what i was but i was being
what i am together,
me and a little girl, nine minutes old.

glory!

Jean Cocteau (1889–1963, French artist, filmmaker, poet), "The Detective," Poem (translation: Will Harriss) (originally published as "Le Détective," in *Opéra* (1925–27); republished in *Oeuvres Complètes de Jean Cocteau: Volume IV* (Paris: Marguerat, 1947), p. 140.

Marion Grogan (poet; sister-in-law of Los Angeles assemblage artist Roy Grogan), Untitled poem ("When was it warned...").

Hermann Hesse (1877–1962, Swiss novelist, poet, Nobel Prize 1946), "To a Toccata by Bach," Poem (translation: Ruth Baker Day; from "Poems of Knecht's Student Years" in *Das Glasperlenspiel (The Glass Bead Game)*, 1943, translated as *Magister Ludi*, 1949).

Walter Hopps, Untitled, Photograph (referred to by artist as *Light Drawing (tree)*, darkroom manipulation, c. 1954).

Walter Hopps, Untitled altered photograph (slow exposure of a big band jazz musician playing a tenor saxophone), c. 1949.

David Meltzer, "An Unpublished Letter to Some Lost Relatives," Poem.

a.

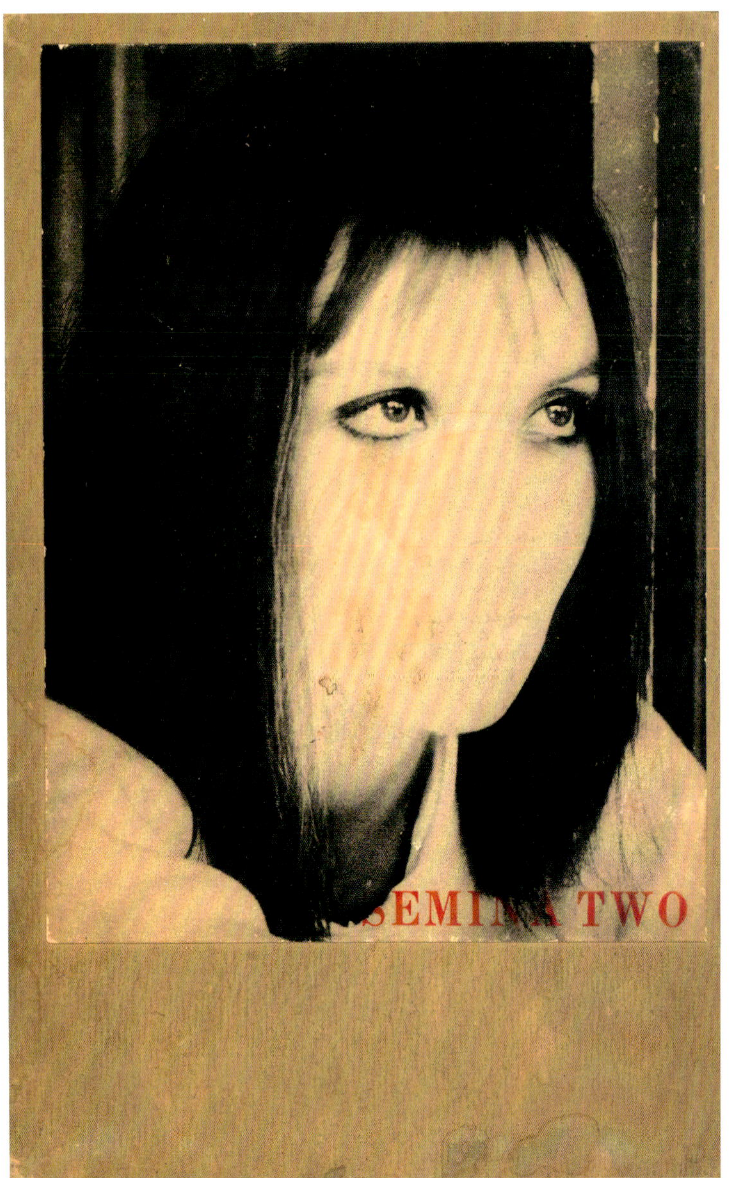

b.

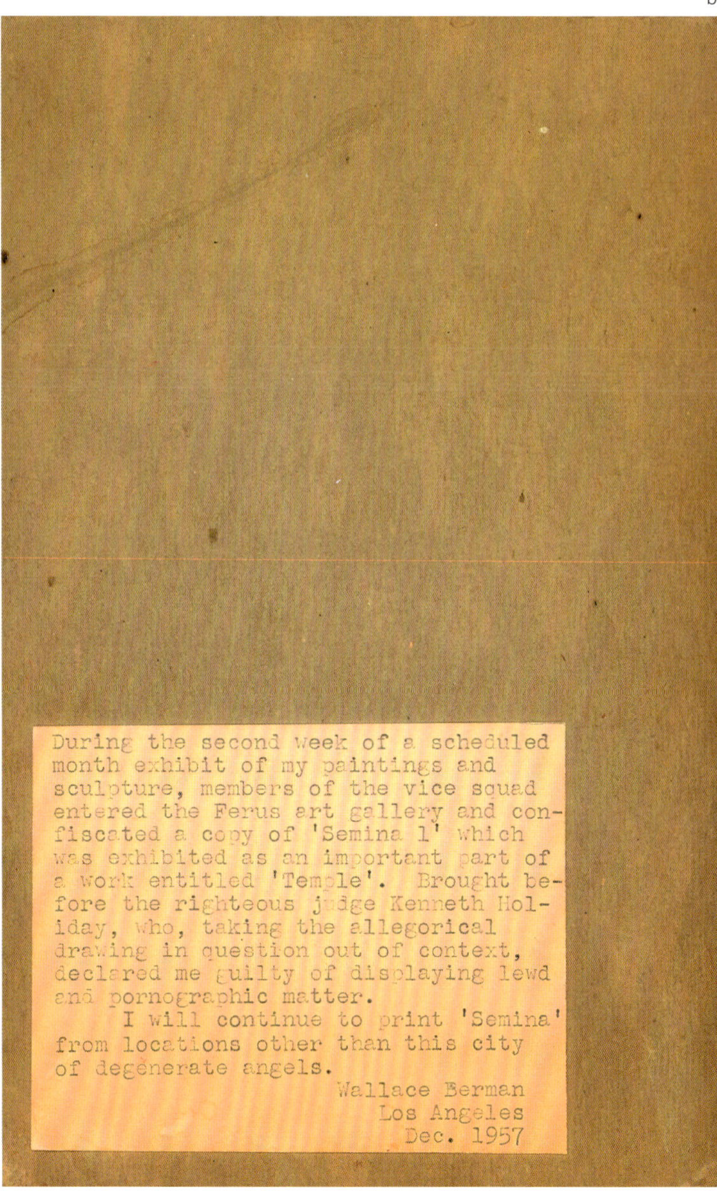

During the second week of a scheduled
month exhibit of my paintings and
sculpture, members of the vice squad
entered the Ferus art gallery and confiscated a copy of 'Semina 1' which
was exhibited as an important part of
a work entitled 'Temple'. Brought before the righteous judge Kenneth Holiday, who, taking the allegorical
drawing in question out of context,
declared me guilty of displaying lewd
and pornographic matter.
I will continue to print 'Semina'
from locations other than this city
of degenerate angels.

Wallace Berman
Los Angeles
Dec. 1957

SEMINA TWO

Stone Brothers Printing,
Sawtelle Boulevard, Los Angeles;
Jackson Street, San Francisco,
December 1957 (8 1/2 x 5 1/2 in.,
bound with individual plates,
"Handset with miscellaneous available type and papers").

Cover: **Charles Brittin**, Photograph of Suzi Hicks (niece of Loree Foxx). (a.)

Back cover: **Wallace Berman**, December 1957, Typed notice. (b.)

Hermann Hesse (see Semina 1), "The Bead Game," Poem (from "The Poetic Fragments from Knecht's Student Days" in *Magister Ludi*, translated from the German by Mervyn Savill, New York: Henry Holt and Co., 1949).

Paul Éluard (1895–1952, French surrealist poet associated with André Breton; chiefly known for love poems), "Patience," Poem (translation: Louis Renoir; originally published as "Patience," the fourth poem in a group of seven poems titled "Sur les pente inférieures," 1941, written after German occupation of France; *Oeuvres Complètes I* (Paris: Gallimard), p. 1062; set to music along with other Éluard poems in the song cycle by Francois Poulenc, *Figure Humaine*, 1946).

Jack Anderson, "Poem for Alice," Poem. *Born 1935; poet, dance historian, and dance critic for* New York Times*; submitted poem after reading about* Semina *in* Trace: A Chronicle of Living Literature *20, February 1957).*

Cameron, "Excerpt from a work in progress," Poem.

c.

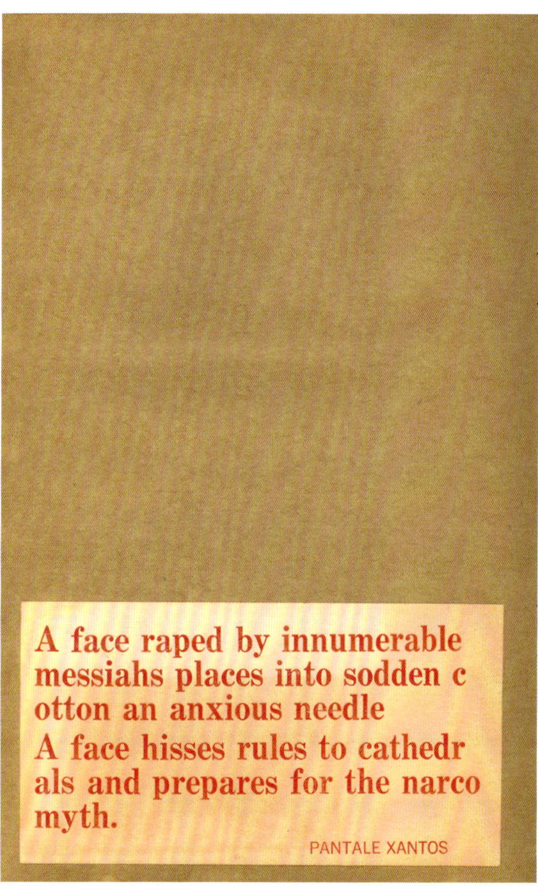

d.

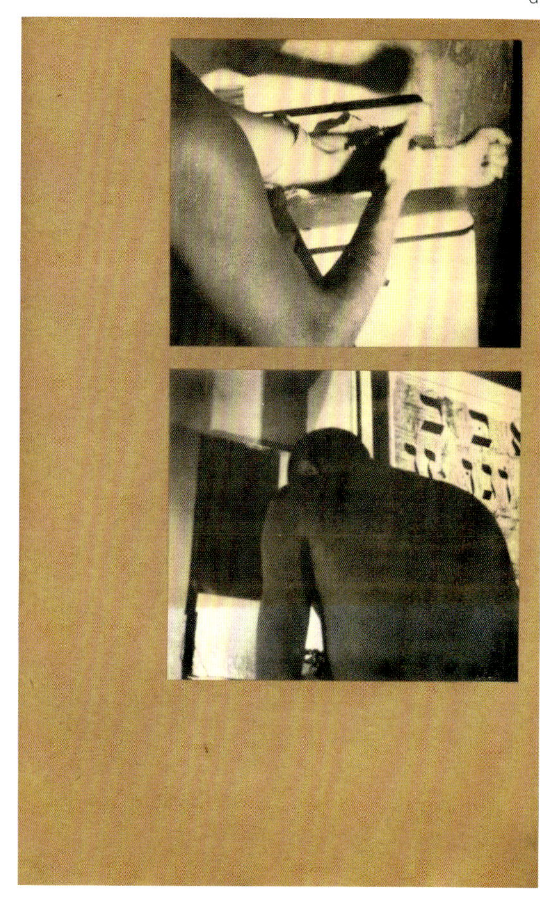

Jean Cocteau (see *Semina 1*), Untitled drawing (opium smoker), (originally published in *Journal d'une Désintoxication* (Paris: Éditions Stock. 1930), p. 191; *Opium: The Diary of a Cure*, (London: G. Allen and Unwin, 1933); republished New York: Grove Press, 1958)).

Zack Walsh, Untitled poem ("Like toys of dolls...").

Eric Cashen "Incompatible," Prose, (Canadian writer, frequent contributor to *Trace: A Chronicle of Living Literature* in late 1950s, Hollywood: Villiers Publications).

Pantale Xantos (pseudonym for Wallace Berman), Untitled poem ("A face raped by innumerable messiahs..."). (c.)

Wallace Berman, Two photographs of Robert Alexander shooting heroin from then-in-progress untitled film project by Wallace Berman (Berman's *Parchment* drawing can be seen in lower photograph). (d.)

Lynn Trocchi (Marilyn "Lyn" Rose Hicks Trocchi, 1936–1972), Untitled poem ("O God/Release my soul...). *American wife of Scottish writer Alexander Trocchi; Smith College graduate who left a New York publishing job to follow Trocchi; mother of two sons: Mark (1958–1977) and Nicolas (1966–1984); co-wrote an account of the couple's LSD experiences published in* Psychedelia Britannica: Hallucinogenic Drugs in Britain, *ed. Antonio Melechi (London: Turnaround, 1997).*

Idell T. Romero (Aya Tarlow), "Incident," Poem.

J.B. May (James Boyer May, 1904–1981), "Its Living Now,*" Poem (Southern California poet; editor of* Trace: A Chronicle of Living Literature, *1952–70, a compendium listing of little magazines; poem submitted for publication in* Semina *in February 18, 1957 correspondence to Wallace Berman, James Boyer May Archives, University Archives and Special Collections, Pollak Library, California State University, Fullerton).*

Charles Baudelaire (1821–1867, French poet), "Tomb of a Cursed Poet," Poem (originally published as "Sépulture," in *Spleen et Idéal* (Paris: Poulet-Malassis, 1857)). Translation: Hyman Lopez.

e.

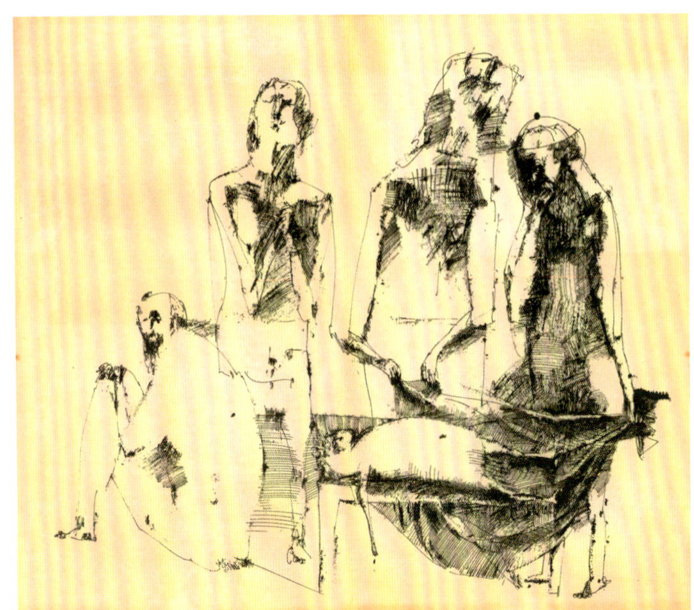

f.

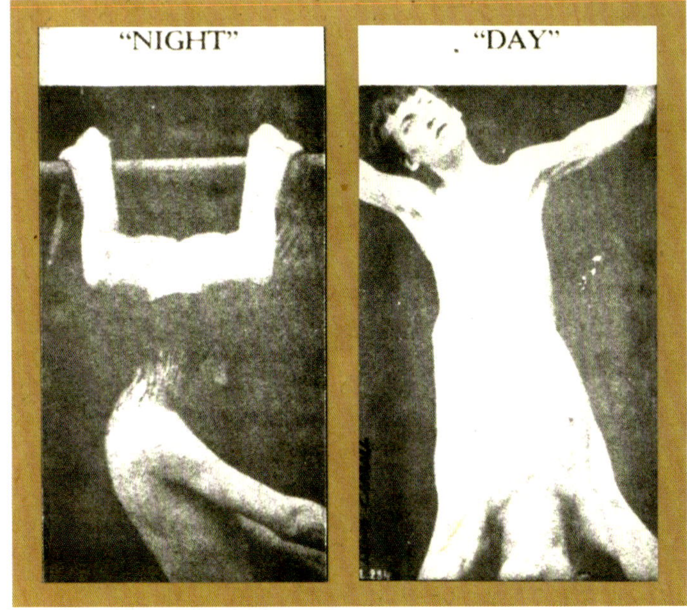

Charles Bukowski (1920–1994, Los Angeles poet), "Mine," Poem (republished in *The Days Run Away Like Wild Horses Over the Hills* (Los Angeles: Black Sparrow Press, 1969. p. 16)).

Peder Carr (poet and literature student), Untitled poem ("I shall grasp the air of the day with my sucking lungs…").

Judson Crews (1936–61, Southwest poet, printer, collage maker, and publisher; contributor to over 350 periodicals), "Does a Ghost Have Thighs," Poem.

John Reed, Untitled poem ("The Sun will touch you…)

Lewis Carroll (1832–1898, novelist, poet, photographer), *Night* and *Day,* Manipulated photographs (photographic inventory 285 & 284; published in *View*, Second Series, No. 2, May 1942, Tchelitchew/Tanguy issue). (f.).

David Meltzer, Untitled poem ("Upon a time…").

Marion Grogan (see above), Untitled poem ("When tongue forges wonder…").

Paul Valéry (1871–1945, French poet, critic), "The Sylph," poem; translation by R. Rand (originally published as *Le Sylphe* in *Charmes* (Paris: N.R.F., 1922)).

Walter Hopps, Photograph (dead shark on beach).

Alexander Trocchi, From *Cain's Book*, (later excerpted in *Paris Review* 21 (Spring-Summer 1959); published 1960, New York: Grove Press; London: John Calder).

John Altoon, Untitled ink drawing (three figures and a priest hovering over a dead child). (e.)

Marcia Jacobs (Wallace Berman pseudonym), *Circus*, poem.

Mike McClure (Michael McClure), Untitled poem ("I wanted to turn to electricity…") *Submitted in correspondence to "Walter Berman" along with two other poems on the recommendation of "Walter Hop": McClure letter, November 16, 1957, Wallace Berman Archive, Archives of American Art, Smithsonian Institution; later published in* Hymns to St. Geryon *(San Francisco: Auerhahn Press, 1959).*

Rabindranath Tagore, (1861–1941, Bengali poet, playwright, novelist, Nobel Prize 1913), "His Road." *Poem originally published in* Sheaves: Poems and Songs, *translated by Nagendranath Gupta, (Allahabad: Indian Press, 1929; New York: Philosophical Library, 1951).*

Wallace Berman, "Art is love is God," poem.

a.

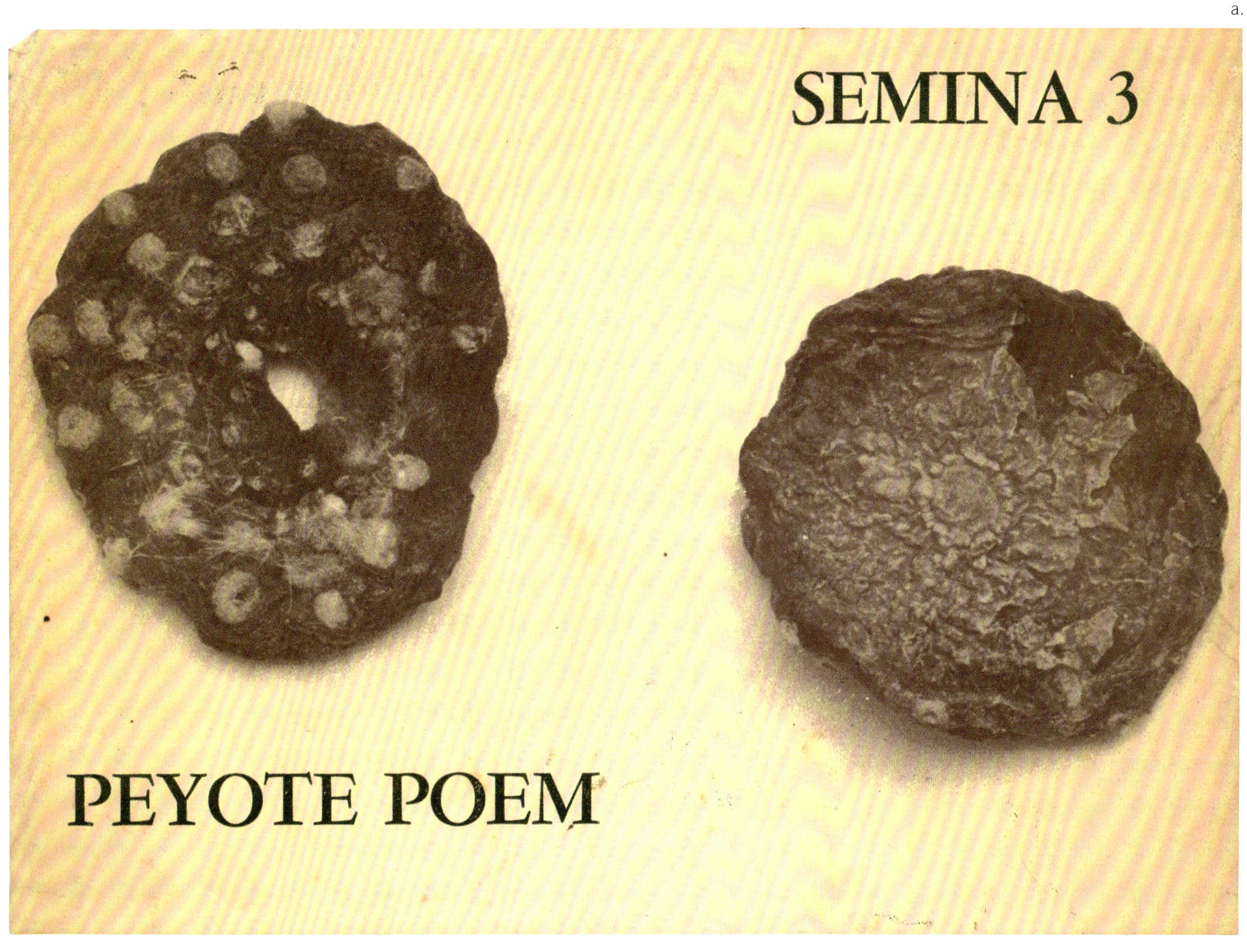

SEMINA 3

Scott Street, San Francisco, 1958,
11 x 9 in., 200 copies

Cover: **Wallace Berman**, Photograph of peyote button, front and back views. (a.)

Mike McClure (Michael McClure), "Peyote Poem" (on tipped-in, fold-out sheet, 22 x 6 3/8 in.) (later published in *Hymns to St. Geryon and Other Poems*, San Francisco: Auerhahn Press, 1959).

a.

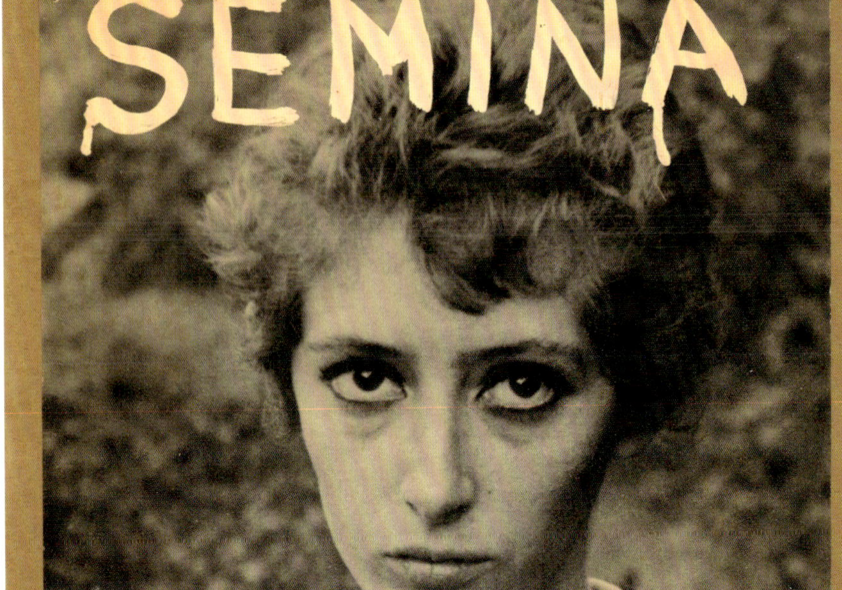

b.

boplicity

miles &
miles
for a
to hold that much cool
water water water
when I'm thirsty
plenty of ice cold
when I'm dry
when I die

Stuart Perkoff

SEMINA 4

"Type handset on Excelsior handpress," Scott Street, San Francisco, 1959, 9 1/2 x 8 in.

Cover: **Wallace Berman**, *Wife*, Photograph of Shirley Berman. (a.)

I.E. Alexander (Robert Alexander), "The Point Encased," Poem.

Wallace Berman, *Excerpts from a film now in progress entitled Semina,* (Grid of nine film stills) Stills feature (left to right) Shirley Berman, Louise Herms, a candle apparatus, a Renaissance sculpture, an image of a nun on television, Patricia and Larry Jordan, two self portraits, and Tosh Berman. (c.)

William Blake (1757–1827, English poet), "To God," Poem (originally published as "Gnomic Verses ii," From *Manuscript Notebook*, 1808–11).

Ray Bremser, "Cat Digging Walls," Poem.

William Burroughs, Excerpt from "Pantapon Rose." Slightly edited fragment republished as opening of "Have you seen Pantopon Rose" section of *Naked Lunch*, (New York: Olympia Press, 1959); other fragments from the novel had been included in *Black Mountain Review*, Autumn 1957; *Chicago Review*, Vol. 12, No. 1 (Spring 1958); *Chicago Review*, Vol. 12, No. 3 (Autumn 1958).

c.

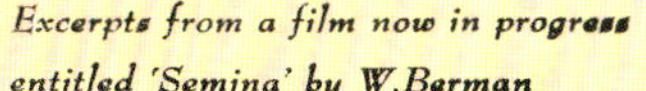

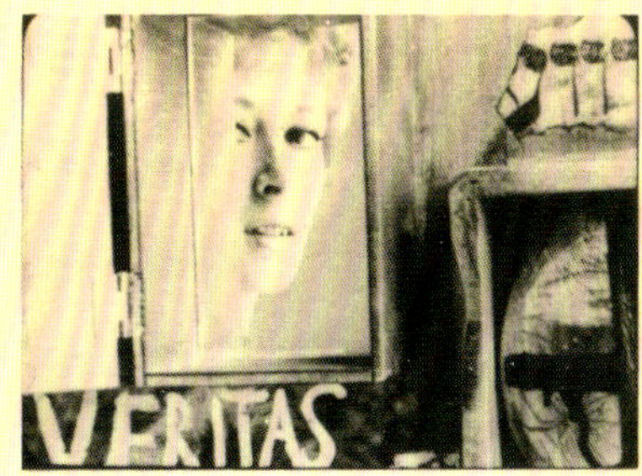

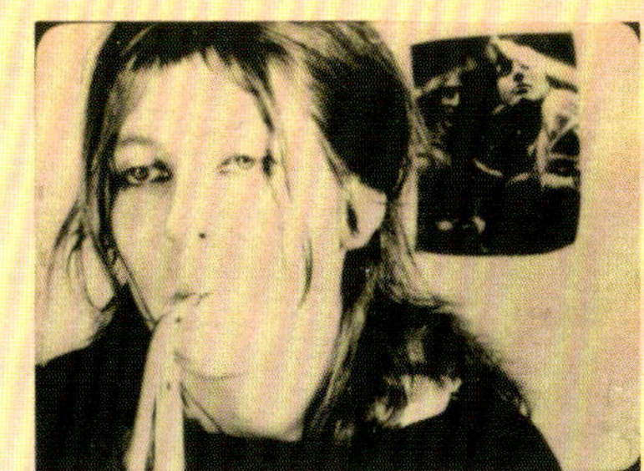

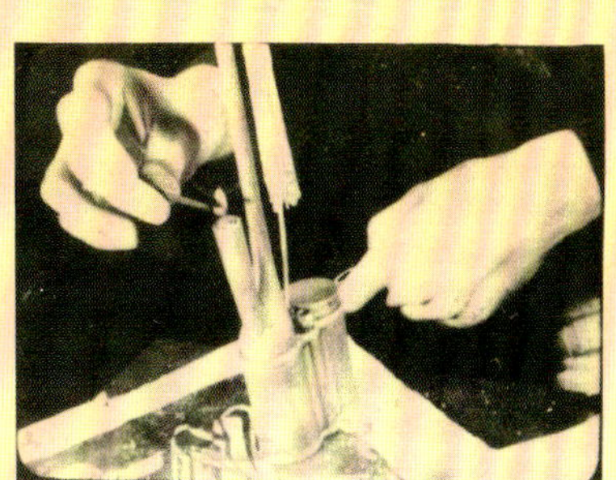

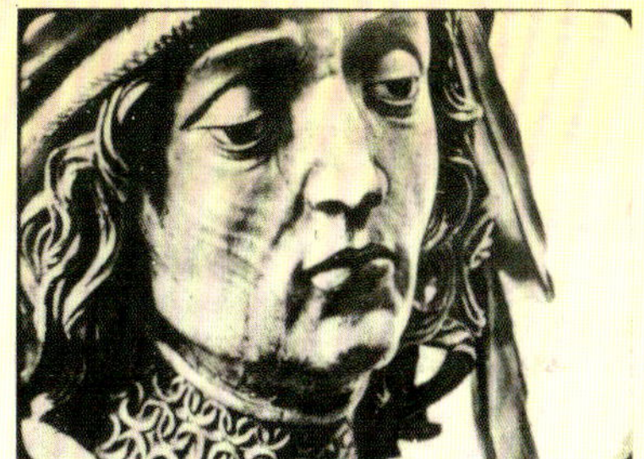

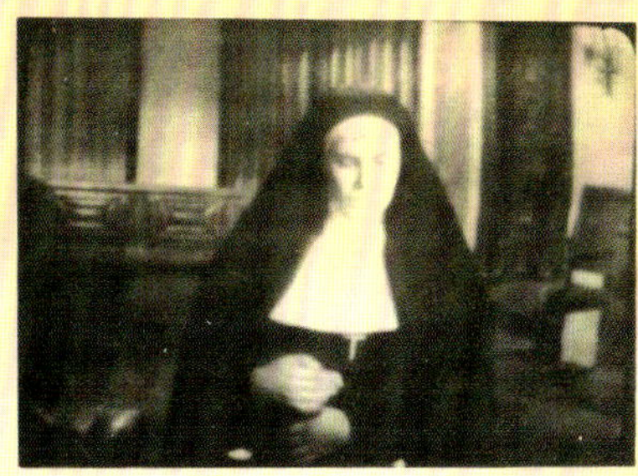

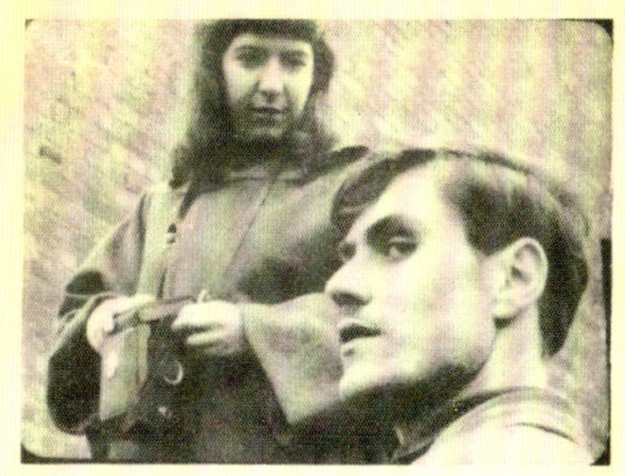

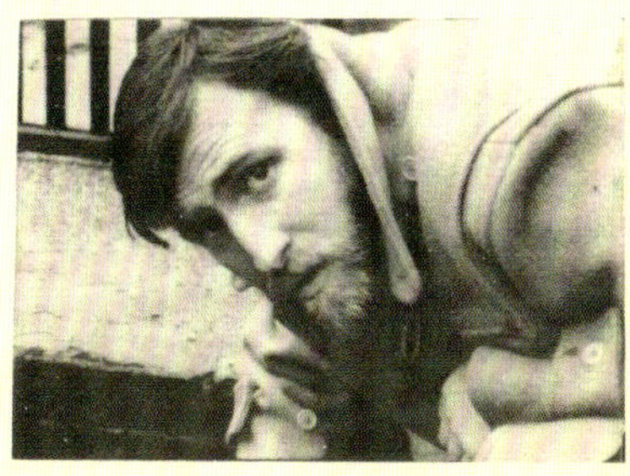

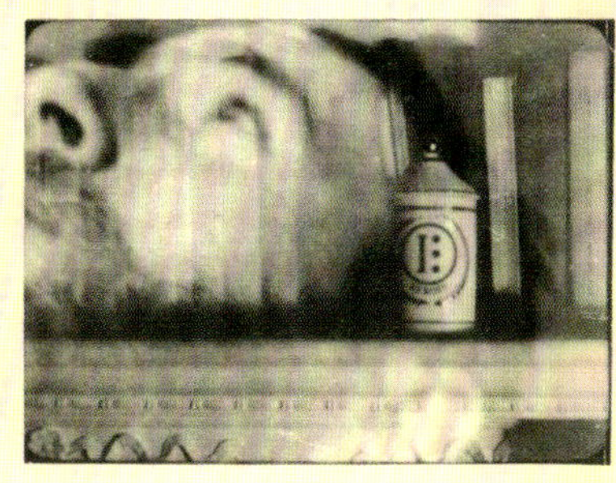

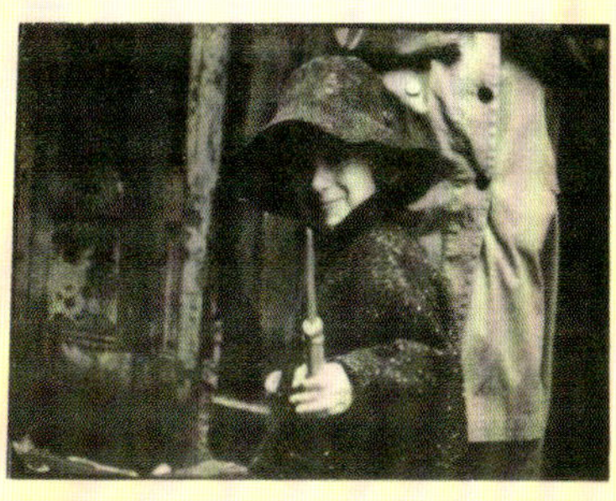

Peder Carr (see *Semina Two*), "Two Poems" ("They squeezed him into a misty little corner…" and "I smolder and smell and fume and wish for closeness…").

John Chance (San Francisco itinerant poet, published in *Beatitude*; corresponded with Ginsberg), "Talking Buddhism With My Lawyer," Poem.

Beverly Collins (poet, married to Los Angeles poet Bob Collins), Untitled poem ("Today's children…").

Judson Crews (see *Semina Two*), "Right Now I Am Not So Very Big," Poem.

Charles Foster (1922–1967, Venice poet who abandoned advertising career in 1957; published four volumes of poetry), Poem ("Paleolithic dawns…").

Allen Ginsberg, "To Lindsay," Poem (tribute to American poet Vachel Lindsay, republished in slightly edited version in *Kaddish and Other Poems* (San Francisco: City Lights Books, 1961)).

Pierre Jean Jouve (1887–1976, French poet, novelist, critic), "Sur un Mystère," Poem (published as part of "Mélodrame, Lyrique section IV—Invention sur un thème" in *Poesie X–XI,* (Paris: Mercure de France, 1957); republished in *Oeuvre I*, (Paris: Mercure de France, 1987)).Translated by Howard Shulman (Boston poet and translator living in San Francisco).

Robert Kaufman, "Dear People," Poem (republished in slighted edited version in *The Ancient Rain: Poems 1956–1978*, ed., Raymond Foye (New York: New Directions, 1981)).

Philip Lamantia, Untitled poem ("Ah Blessed Virgin Mary…") (republished in *Ekstasis*, San Francisco: Auerhahn Press, 1959).*A quotation from last verse of this poem was inscribed by Jay DeFeo in her copy of* Ekstasis*; on the page's verso DeFeo made a working sketch for* The Rose. *This quotation can also be seen painted on DeFeo's studio wall in one of Berman's 1959 photographic portraits of the artist.*

d.

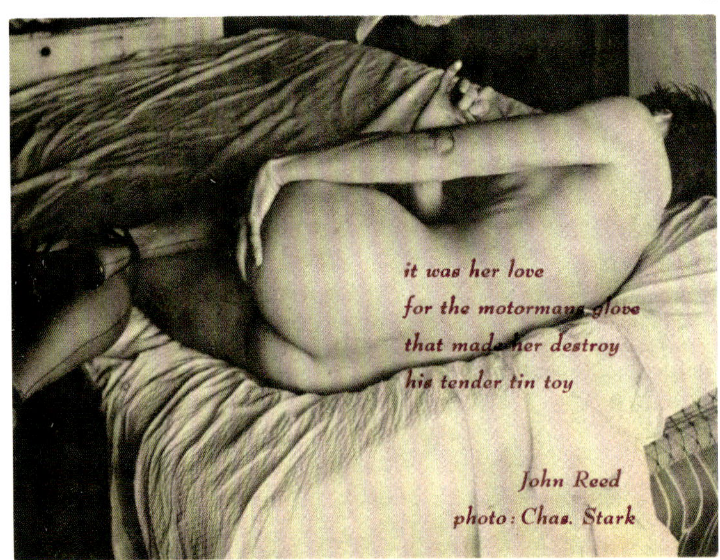

e.

Morphine mother
Heroin mother
Yage mother
Benzidrine mother
Peyote mother
Marijuana mother
Cocaine mother
Hashish mother
Mushroom mother
Opium mother
Mescalin mother

Gave my love a cherry mother
Cornbread meat and molasses mother
Chain gang mother
Alabamy bound mother
Bill Bailey mother
Midnight special mother
Stackolee mother
Rock island mother
John Henry mother
Strange fruit mother
Long John mother

Pantale Xantos

Ron Loewinsohn (Born 1937, San Francisco poet and novelist, author *Magnetic Fields* (New York: Alfred Knopf, 1983), currently Professor of English, University of California at Berkeley), Untitled poem ("The pieces of watermelon…"; republished as "Watermelons," frontispiece of *Watermelons* (New York: Totem Press, 1959)).

Michael McClure, Untitled poem ("We're in the middle of a deep cloud…").

David Meltzer, "Sampson Agonistes," Poem.

Stuart Perkoff, "Boplicity," Poem (republished in *Visions for the Tribe*, (Denver, Los Angeles: Black Ace/Temple of Man, 1976), *Voices of the Lady: Collected Poems*, (Orono, Maine: National Poetry Foundation, 1998)). (b.)

John Reed, Untitled poem ("It was her love for the motormans glove…"); **Charles Stark** (San Francisco photographer), Photograph of nude woman. (d.)

Idell T. Romero (Aya Tarlow), "A Thimble Of Goodbye," Poem.

From **Ssu-ma Ch'ien's Shih-chi** (Su Shi, 1037–1101, Chinese poet known for his satirical lyrics), Untitled poem ("Once with his young wife…"), translated by Chas. Guenther (Charles Guenther).

Jules Supervielle (1884–1960, French/Uruguayan poet, novelist, short-story writer), Untitled poem ("I felt that this ear of the soul opened…"; translated by Chas. Guenther (Charles Guenther)).

John Wieners, Untitled poem ("And what is nothingness…") (republished as "And What Is Nothingness," *Cultural Affairs in Boston: Poetry & Prose 1956–1985*, ed. by Raymond Foye (Santa Rosa: Black Sparrow Press, 1988)).

W.B. Yeats (1865–1939, Irish poet), "Oil And Blood," Poem (from *The Winding Stair and Other Poems*, 1933).

Pantale Xantos (Wallace Berman), Untitled poem ("Morphine mother…"). (e.)

a.

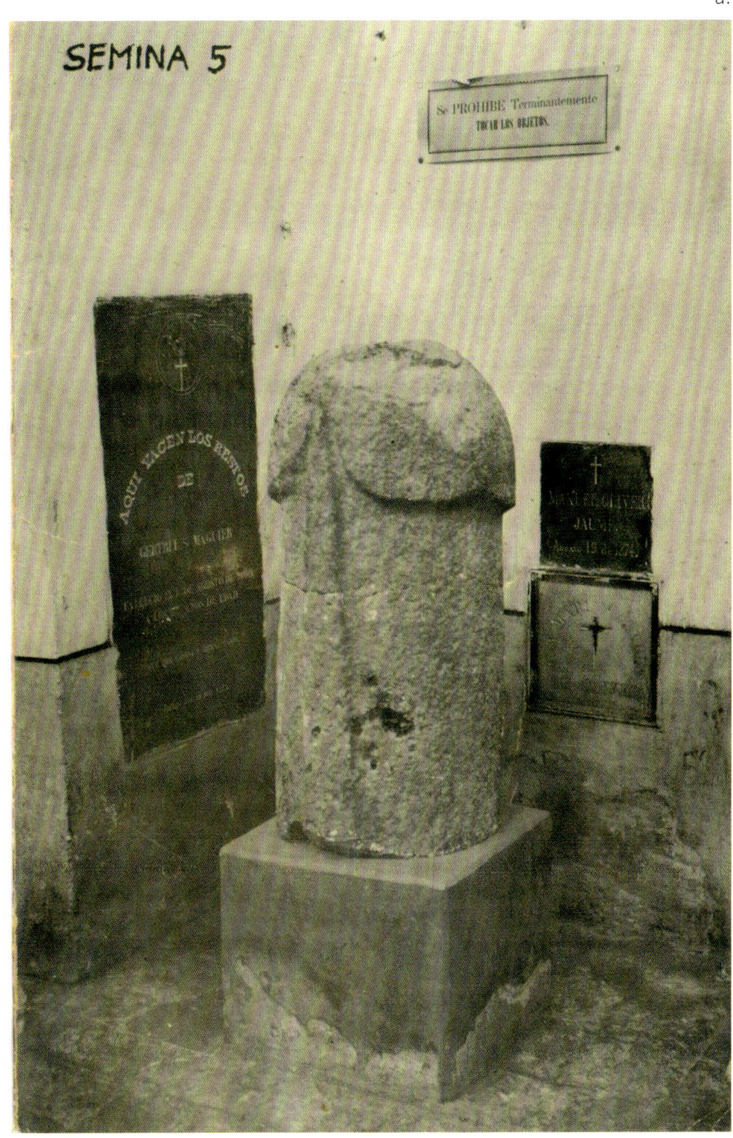

b.

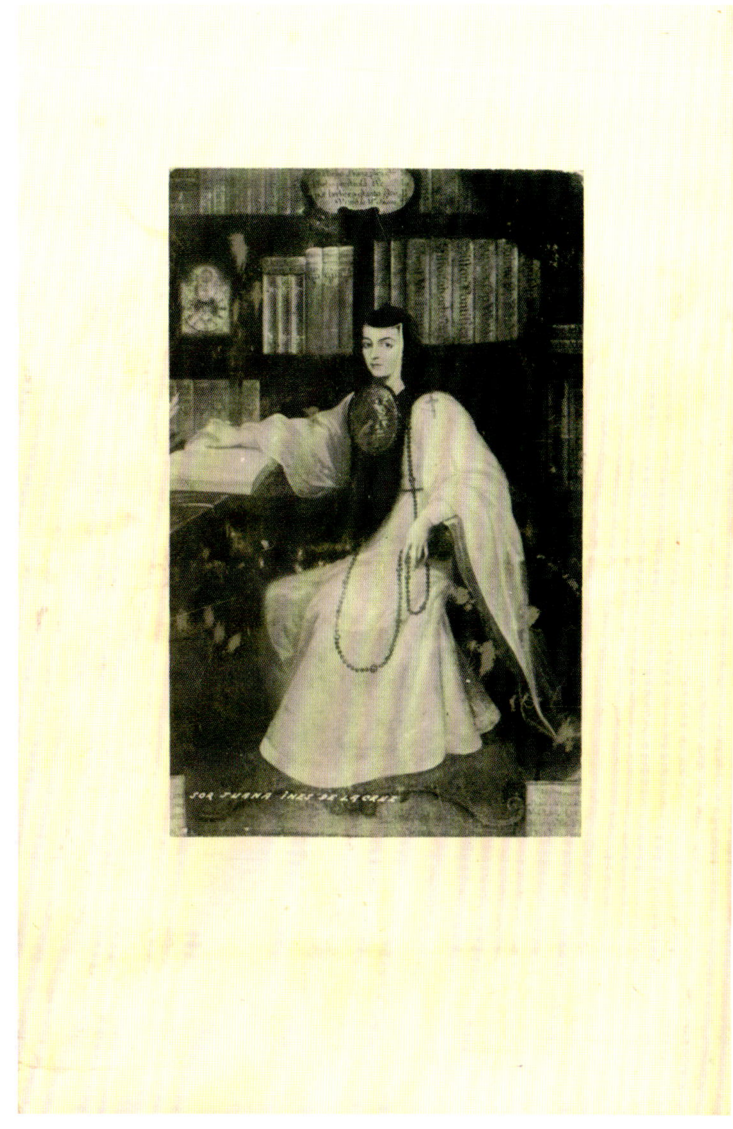

SEMINA 5

("Mexico" issue) Scott Street, San Francisco, 1959, 350 copies, 7 1/2 x 4 7/8 in.

Cover: **Charles Brittin**, Photograph of Mayan stone phallus, Stella Museum, Nuestra Señora de la Soledad, Campeche, Mexico, 1951. (a.)

Back cover: Reproduction of postcard image of Miguel Cabrera, *Retrato de la phenix Americana la madre Juana Inez de la Cruz…*, 1750, Museo Nacíonal de Historia, Mexico City. (b.)

Antonin Artaud, "Excerpt from 'Le Mexique et la Civilization,'" (translation uncredited; written 1935–36 before his trip to Mexico; originally published in *Vie et Mort de Satan-de-Feu*, Paris: Arcanes, 1953; *Oeuvres Completes VIII* (Paris: Gallimard, 1971, p. 160)).

John Chance (see above), Untitled poem ("How I Died").

d.

Callejon Garcia Villa Lorca

Beyond all this being,
crowded park:
a stone
flung into the otherness of time.

Many years, floating skyward,
did I pause
this day

and suckle at the fount of you
O Mexico
my own.

Christofer Maclaine

c.

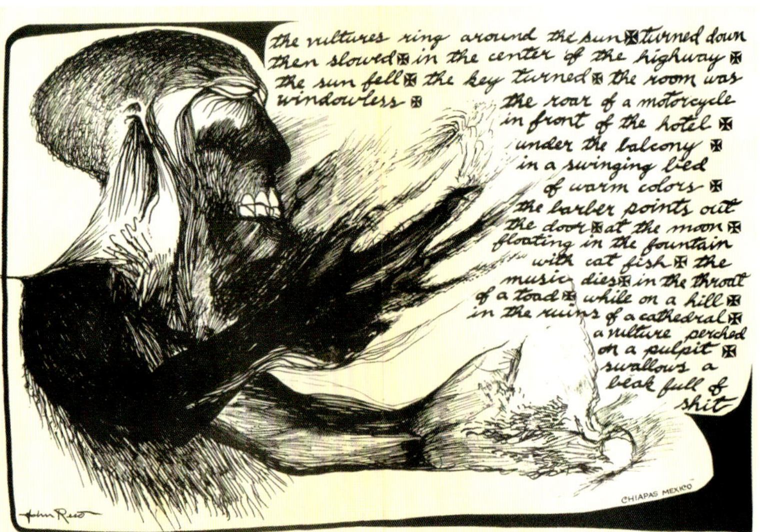

e.

I Mexico After Artaud

Stricken by my unconscious impotence,
Dizzy from intelligent spells
of madness
Revealing the same thoughts,
I fall into Nature already prepared
By the cheat of my body,
The miracle of my optical ear,
The grandiose mathematics of my love,
The numbers of my soul,
And I know there is a rage concealed
Behind my mouth, beneath my lips,
on my eyes.

KIRBY DOYLE

Kirby Doyle, "I Mexico After Artaud," Poem. (e.)

Lawrence Jordan, "Rockets," Poem.

John Hoffman (1928–1952, San Francisco poet whose works were read by Philip Lamantia at Six Gallery reading where Ginsberg's *Howl* was introduced, October 7, 1955) "Floridas," Poem, (reproduced and dated April 1950 in *Journey to the End* (San Francisco: Bern Porter, 1956) edited by Philip Lamantia and Bern Porter).

Denied economic security, holding down odd jobs for brief periods, he moved sporadically between San Francisco and New York: and, once, equipped with a copy of Lautréamont's Maldoror, *he embarked as a sailor out of New York, visiting Rio de Janeiro and Montevideo, Lautréamont's birthplace. He had the wanderlust, and after peregrinating to the central parts of Mexico (he died in Guadalajara in January 1952), he wrote me of a desire to go further south, "build a raft and make it to Ecuador": he was fated to make it to the sun.*
—Philip Lamantia, October 1954, introduction to Journey to the End.

Sor Juana Inés de la Cruz (1651–1695, Mexican saint, poet), "Sister Juana Inés of the Cross," Poem (translated by Philip Lamantia)

Robert Kaufman, Untitled poem ("O mexico your sadness is nut brown…"). (g.)

Philip Lamantia, "Memoria," Poem.

Christopher MacLaine (1923–1975, San Francisco poet and filmmaker; editor *Contour*; director of short films *The End* (1953), *Beat* (1958)), "Callejon Garcia Villa Lorca," Poem (edited version without title, substituting the word "Madness" for "Mexico," published in Section Two of *The Time Capsule* (San Francisco: 17 Adler Press, 1960). (d.)

g.

O mexico your sadness is nut brown,
Hot handed, from pushing Paracutin,
From smoky bowels, to maniac twilight,
O-Mexico, give me your Easter Faced Virgin
And your Junk.

Robt. Kaufman

f.

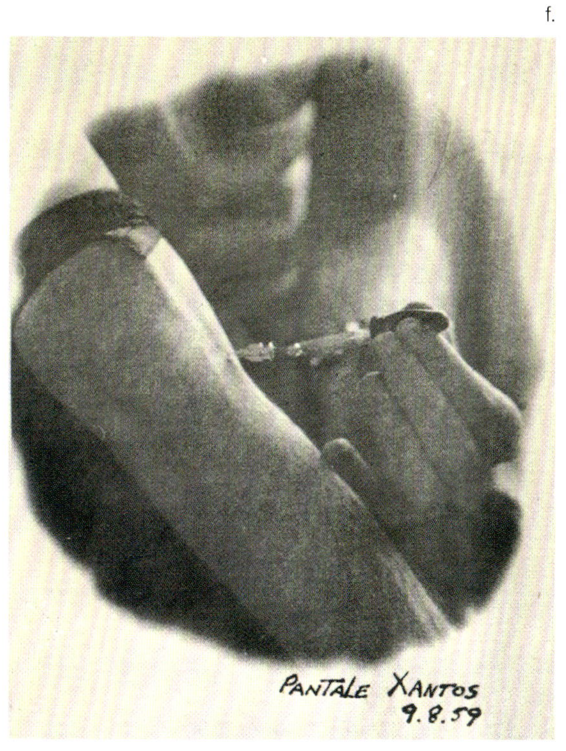

William Margolis, "Morning," Poem.

Michael McClure, Untitled poem in manuscript ("We are impervious as the skin of our dreams..." 8/2/58).

Anne McKeever (New Orleans poet, photographer; traveled in Mexico with Ruth Weiss and Philip Lamantia), Photographic collage (musicians).

David Meltzer, Untitled poem ("Todos santos...").

John Reed, Untitled ink drawing (monster) and untitled manuscript poem ("The vultures ring around the sun..."), signed "John Reed, Chiapas, Mexico". (c.)

Keith Sanzenbach (1930–1964, Bay Area artist, known for large *Mandala* paintings, several works in collection of Reidar Wennesland Collection, Kristiansand Cathedral School and Agder University College, Norway), Untitled ink drawing (Mexican lady), 1958.

Ruth Weiss (San Francisco poet and filmmaker, born Berlin, 1928; moved to San Francisco 1952; author *Gallery of Women*, 1959; director/producer *The Brink*, 1961, photographed by Paul Beattie), "From 'Compass'," Poem .

John Wieners, "Peyote Poem," Poem (reprinted in slightly edited version as "'Peyote' Poem" in Selected Poems, New York: Grossman, 1972; *Cultural Affairs in Boston: Poetry & Prose 1956–1985*, ed. Raymond Foye (Santa Rosa: Black Sparrow Press, 1988)).

Pantale Xantos (Wallace Berman), 9.5.59, Photograph of Lamantia injecting heroin (photograph incorporated in Berman's cover for Lamantia, *Narcotica*, San Francisco: Auerhahn Press, 1959). (f.)

a.

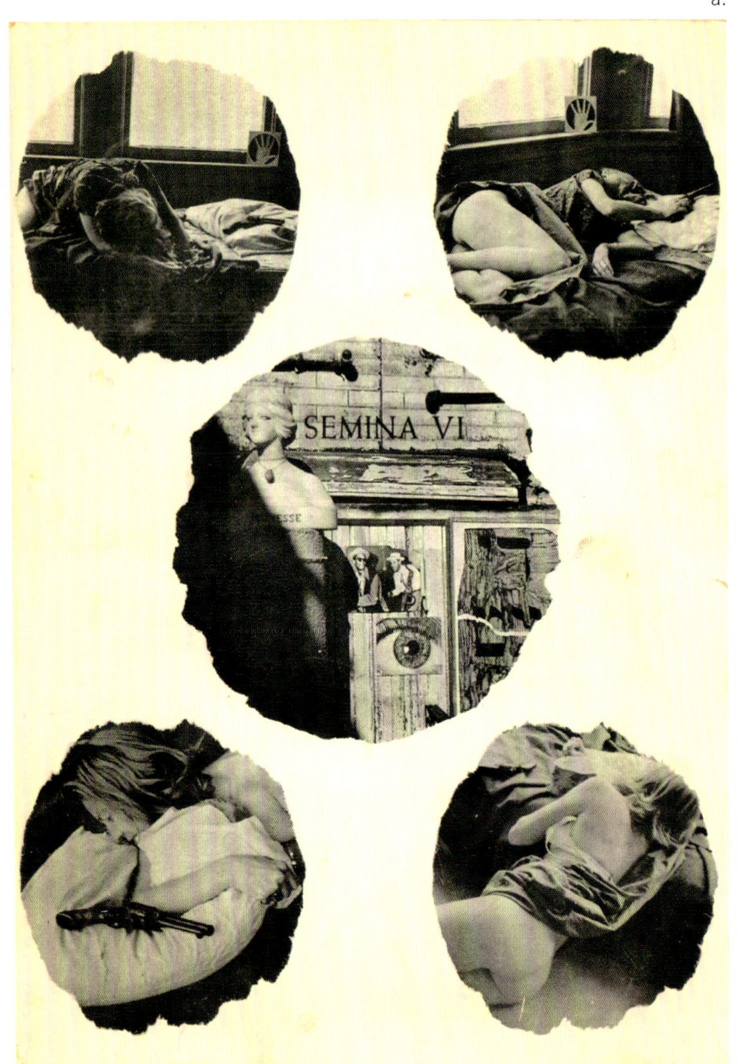

b.

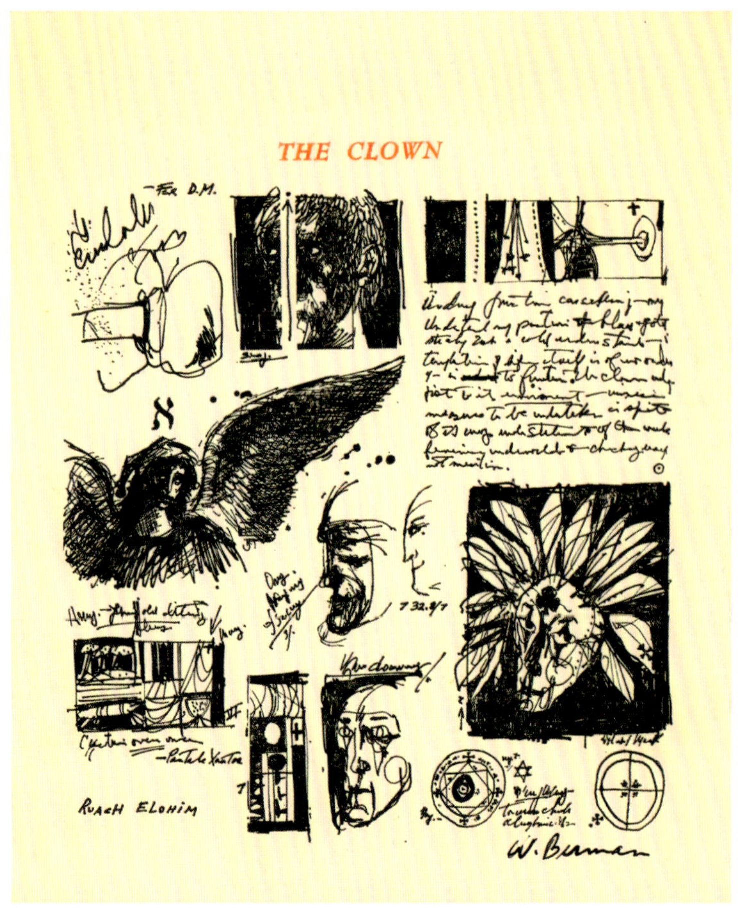

SEMINA VI

1960, Houseboat, Boardwalk #2, Larkspur, 335 copies, 8 1/2 x 6 in. ("Type handset on warped 5 x 8 inch handpress").

Cover: **Wallace Berman**, Photographic collage (four images of woman with gun (Larkspur landlady and Sausalito gallery owner Phyllis); photograph of Semina Gallery, Larkspur featuring found object, found photograph of jazz performers Wardell Grey and Dexter Gordon, and works by Berman and Charles Brittin). (a.)

Back cover: Small printed text: "Art is Love is God."

Wallace Berman, *For D.M.*, Collage of various ink drawings and texts including alchemical symbol, inscrutable inscription signed "Pantale Xantos," drawing of an angel, drawing of cowled figures, drawing of an Indian, inscrutable text. (b.)

David Meltzer, "The Clown," Thirteen-part poem.

a.

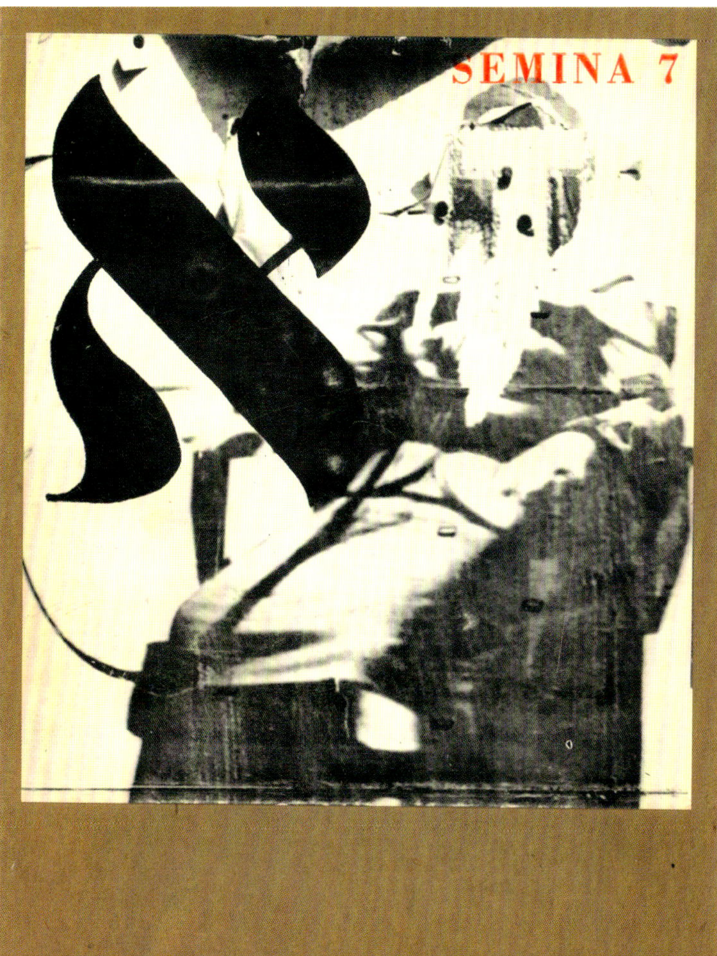

b.

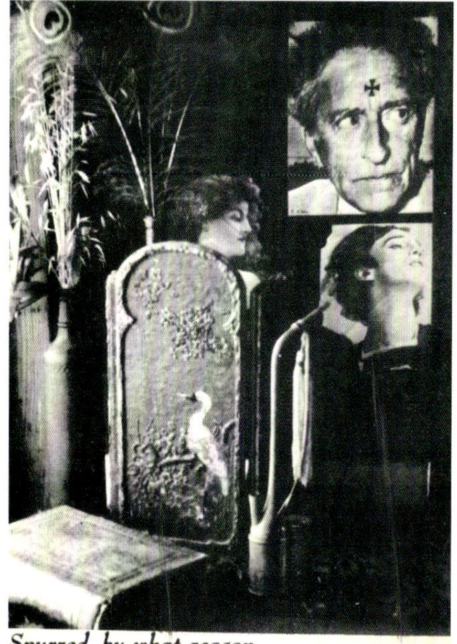

c.

ALEPH/ a gesture involving
photographs drawings & text
by Wallace Berman
200 copies Larkspur Calif 1961

for Shirley & Tosh
I love you

SEMINA 7

(with tipped-in plate reading
"ALEPH/a gesture involving photographs
drawings & text by Wallace Berman,
200 copies, Larkspur, 1961,
For Shirley and Tosh/I love you")
7 3/4 x 5 5/8 in.

Cover: Altered photographic still of actress Susan Hayward depicting Barbara Graham from *I Want to Live* (1958, directed by Robert Wise; Graham was first woman sentenced to electric chair in state of California). (a., c.)

Alternate cover: *Cannabis Sativa/ Semina VII*, printed on various found printed fragments of nineteenth-century poetry text, two copies in Wallace Berman Archive, Archives of American Art, Smithsonian Institution.

Wallace Berman, Photograph of still life featuring images of Cocteau, Nijinsky, and a Pre-Raphaelite painting; accompanied by Wallace Berman, Untitled poem ("Spurred by what reason…"). (b.)

Wallace Berman, "Art is Love is God," Poem.

Wallace Berman, "Boxed City," Poem.

f.

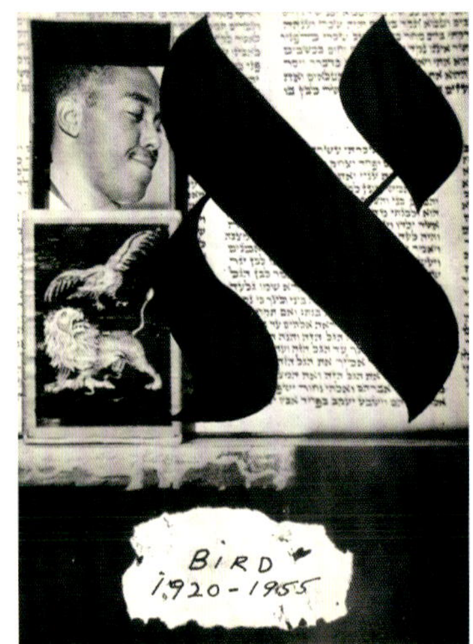

g.

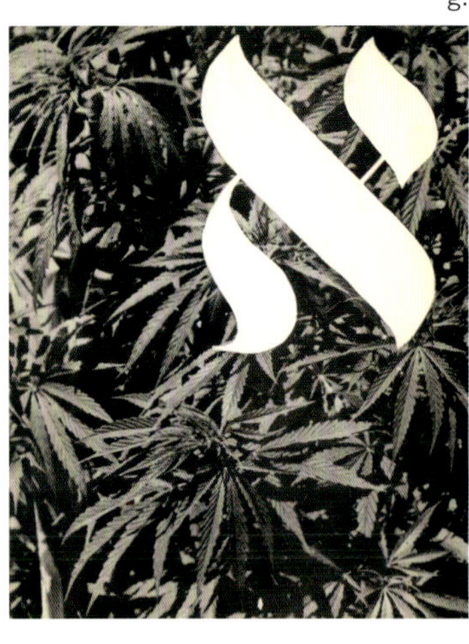

d.

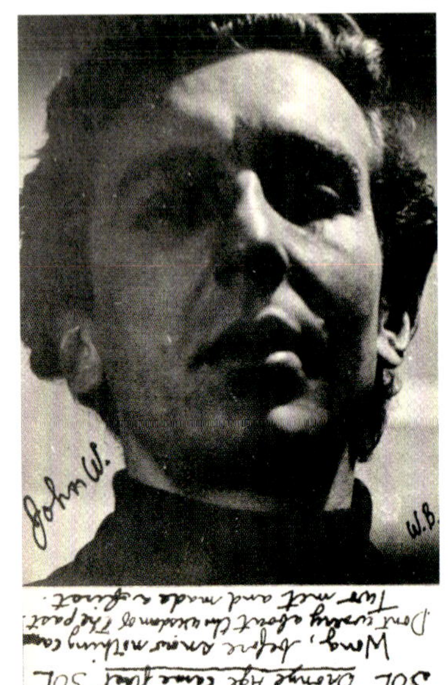

e.

Wallace Berman, "Opos," Poem.

Wallace Berman, "Fairytale for Tosh," Poem. (j.)

Wallace Berman, "First & Last Fearpoem," Poem.

Wallace Berman, Mailer to David Meltzer: Wallace Berman, Photograph of John Wieners; handwritten text: John Wieners, "The Windows of Waltham," Poem (republished as "Windows of Waltham" in *Ace of Pentacles* (New York: James F. Carr & Robert A. Wilson, 1964); *Selected Poems*, (New York: Grossman, 1972); in slightly edited version in *Selected Poems 1958–1984*, ed., Raymond Foye (Santa Barbara: Black Sparrow Books, 1986). (d.)

Wallace Berman, Mailer to George Herms (collage of various drawings and inscrutable writing, including drawing of model World War I airplane). (e.)

Wallace Berman, Photographic collage (Hebrew Aleph and Tosh and toy machine gun). (k.)

Wallace Berman, Photographic collage (Hebrew Aleph and Patricia Jordan in mask in George Herms's Larkspur studio; image of Billie Holiday added to wall). (h.)

Wallace Berman, Photographic collage (Hebrew Aleph and large pendant hanging over Shirley Berman's torso).

k.

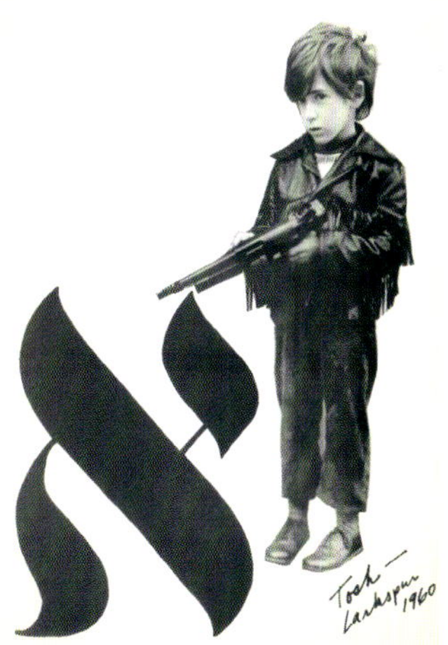

h.

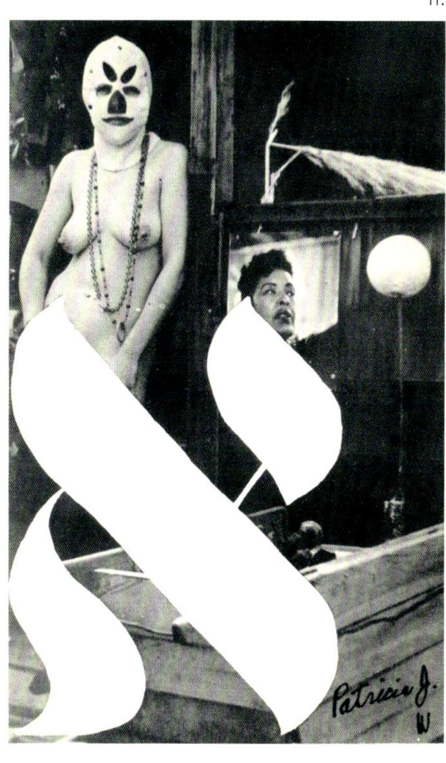

i.

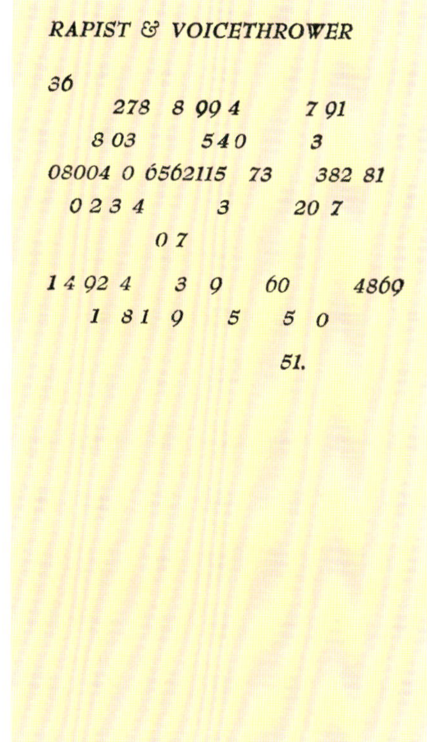
RAPIST & VOICETHROWER

36
278 8 99 4 7 91
8 03 540 3
08004 0 6562115 73 382 81
0 2 3 4 3 20 7
0 7
1 4 92 4 3 9 60 4869
1 8 1 9 5 5 0
51.

j.

FAIRYTALE FOR TOSH

The wolf is dead The wolf is dead
The wolf is dead The wolf is dead
The wolf is dead The wolf is dead
The wolf is dead The wolf is dead
The wolf is dead

The wolf is dead.

Wallace Berman, Photographic collage (Hebrew Aleph and marijuana plants). (g.)

Wallace Berman, Photographic collage (Hebrew Aleph and altered photograph of two images of Jarry Heiserman, inscribed "Jarry H. Mill Valley W.B.").

Wallace Berman, Photographic collage (Hebrew Aleph, Hebrew book, matchbook emblem of eagle and devouring lion, and Charlie Parker with inscription reading 'Bird 1920–1955'). (f.)

Wallace Berman, Photographic collage (Hebrew Aleph over photograph of Arthur Richer playing tenor saxophone).

Wallace Berman, "Rapist & Voicethrower," coded poem (numbers substituted for words). (i.)

Wallace Berman, "Some easy-rider titles by Rohmer," Poem (references to Sax Rohmer's detective novels; reference to jazz pianist Joe Albany who snitched on friends to police).

P. Xantos (Wallace Berman), Self-portrait photograph (*Embarcadero, S.F. 1959*); Wallace Berman, Untitled manuscript poem ("If someone will explain…,") with printed dedication: "For John Birch & Karl Marx".

a.

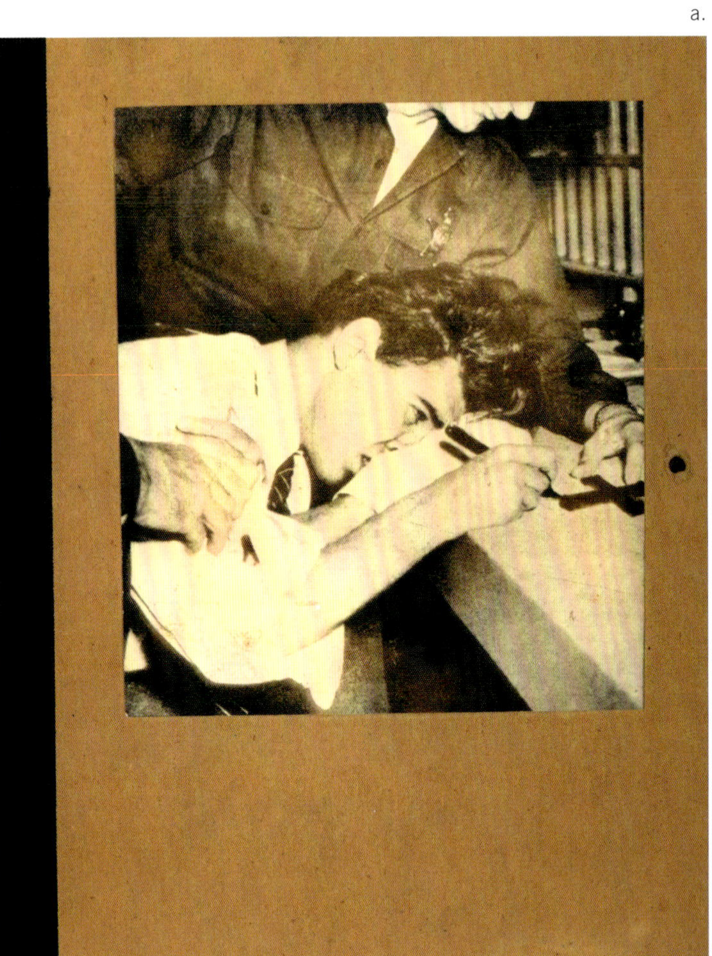

b.

It is me
Man
who will be judge
at the end of the count
it is to me
that all the elements
of substance and things
will come to refer
it is the state of my
body will carry
The Last Judgement
A. A.

SEMINA 8

Crater Lane, Los Angeles, 1963
(7 1/8 x 5 1/2 in., 149 copies in cardboard cover with string clasp).

Cover: **Dean Stockwell**, Altered press photograph of seventeen-year-old "Lipstick Killer" William George Heirens making confessions of three murders. (a.)

Back cover: Aleph in ink at lower left.

A.A. (Antonin Artaud), Untitled poetic fragment ("It is me...", provided by Jack Hirschman as explained in undated letter to Berman, Archives of American Art; published in different translation by Kenneth Rexroth in *Artaud Anthology*, edited by Jack Hirschman (San Francisco: City Lights, 1965)) Found photograph of mummy in dress. (b.)

Cameron, "June 2, 1962," Poem and drawing of sphinx-like woman. (d.)

d.

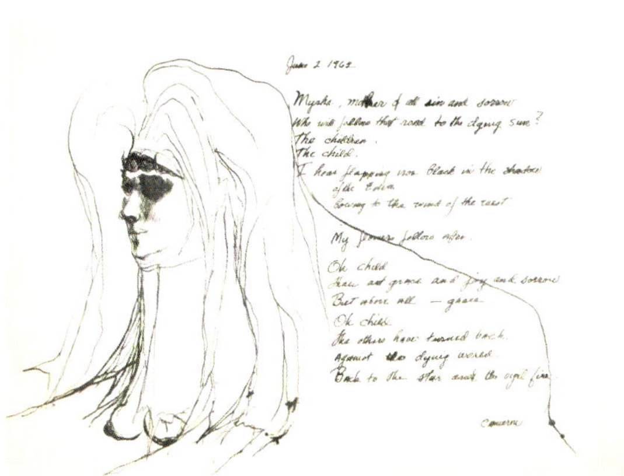

e.

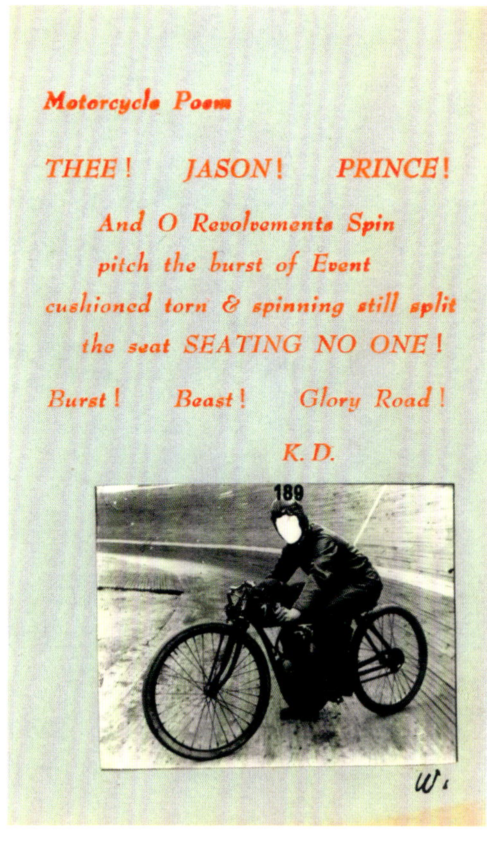

c.

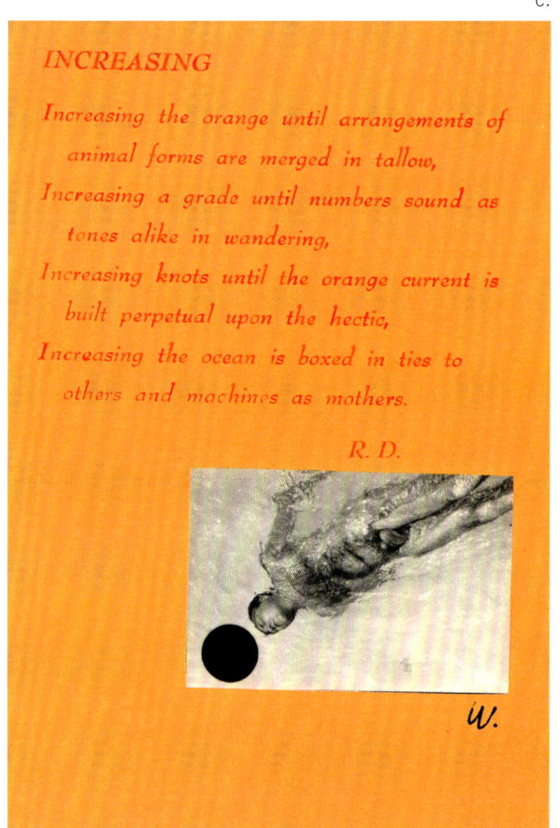

f.

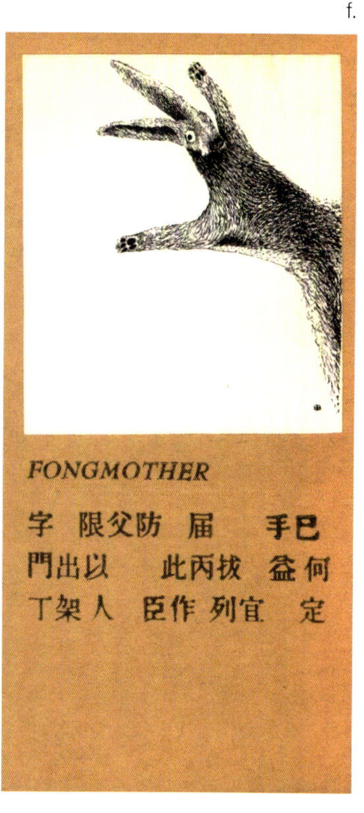

R.D. (Robert Duncan), "Increasing," Poem (published in *Writing Writing*, (Albuquerque: Sumbooks, 1964)); with **W.** (Wallace Berman), Altered photograph of nude Duncan floating in pool in Phoenix. (c.)

K.D. (Kirby Doyle), Excerpt from "Motorcycle Poem" (complete text published in *Sapphobones* (Kerhonkson, New York: The Poets Press, 1966); *The Collected Poems of Kirby Doyle* (San Francisco: Greenlight Press, 1983), p. 24; **W.** (Wallace Berman), Photographic collage (altered photograph found by George Herms of bicycle rider; Berman whitened out the face and added a number transfer). (e.)

"Fongmother," Poem in Chinese characters; **John Reed**, Untitled drawing (rabbit hand). (f.)

W.H. (William House, artist, teacher, sandal-maker, owner of Sandals Primarily, Los Angeles), Untitled drawing (abstract tree).

Jess (uncredited), Photographic collage (c. 1955, Image of cat holding briefcase leaving Turkish prison).

J.K.(Jerry Katz (b. 1934) Writer, filmmaker, and artist active in Topanga Canyon during the 1960s), Untitled poem ("I am that noise which..."); **Wallace Berman**, Photograph (raised middle finger).

h.

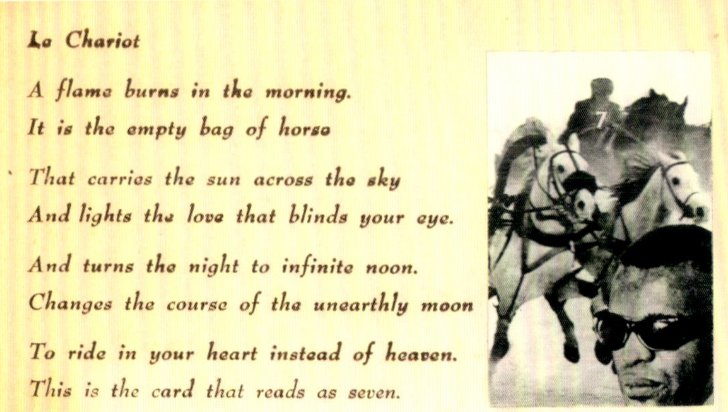

i.

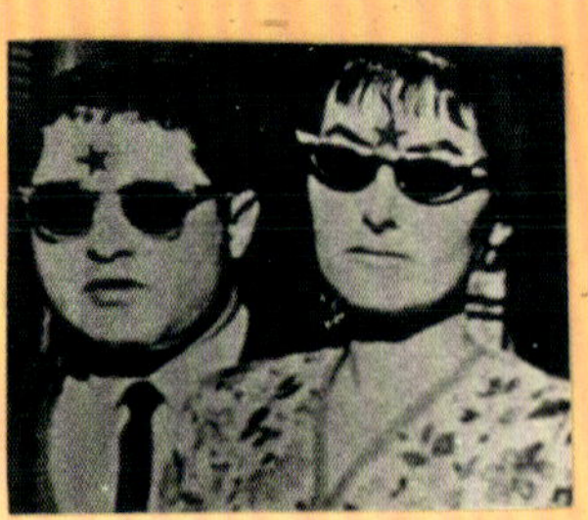

g.

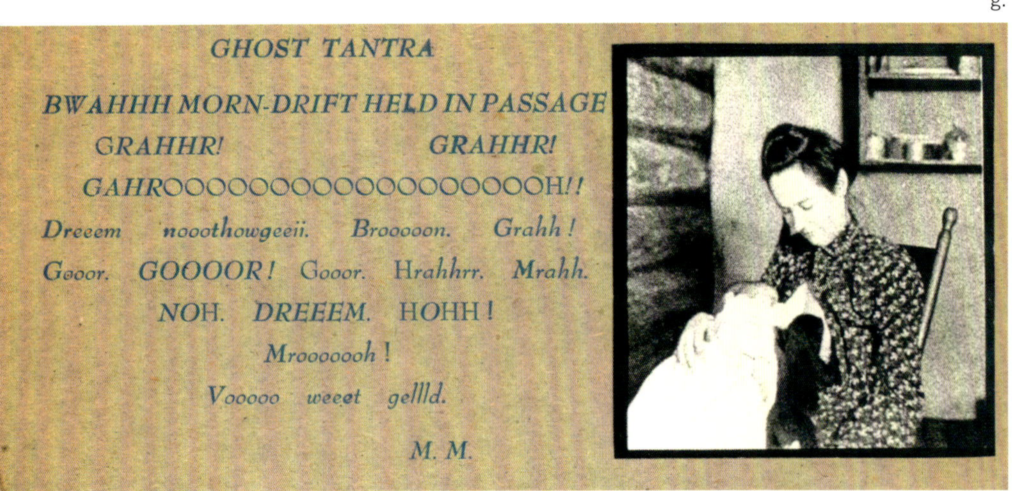

M.M. (Michael McClure), "Ghost Tantra" (later published as section 14, *Ghost Tantras* (San Francisco: Four Seasons Foundation 1969) p. 20; Found photograph of woman nursing baby and bear cub in log cabin. (g.)

I.T.R. (Aya Tarlow), Untitled poem ("my secret language"); **P.** (Patricia Jordan), Photographic collage (female servants dining juxtaposed with large human skeleton).

L.R. (Elias Romero, artist, poet; known for "Light Shows" in late 1950s), Untitled poem ("towards tall icy buttes"); **L.F.** (Llyn Foulkes), Untitled drawing (hand with cross).

W. (Wallace Berman), *Wardell Dead*, Photographic collage with text.

W. (Wallace Berman), Collage (Head of Lenny Bruce beaten by policeman with butterflies in his hair).

W. (Wallace Berman), Photographic collage (Ringside depiction of boxer Benny "the Kid" Peret on night he died in the ring in 1962 with image of flying eagle placed above his battered head).

J.W. (John Wieners), "Le Chariot," poem; W.(Wallace Berman), Photographic collage (chariot and Ray Charles) (poem submitted in correspondence, Archives of American Art, Wallace Berman Archive, February 8, 1963; republished in *Ace of Pentacles* (New York: James F. Carr & Robert A. Wilson, 1964); *Selected Poems 1958–1984*, ed., Raymond Foye (Santa Barbara: Black Sparrow Books, 1986)). (h.)

Z.W. (Zack Walsh), "Geography," Poem; **Wallace Berman**, Altered found photograph from Hollywood fan magazine. (i)

a.

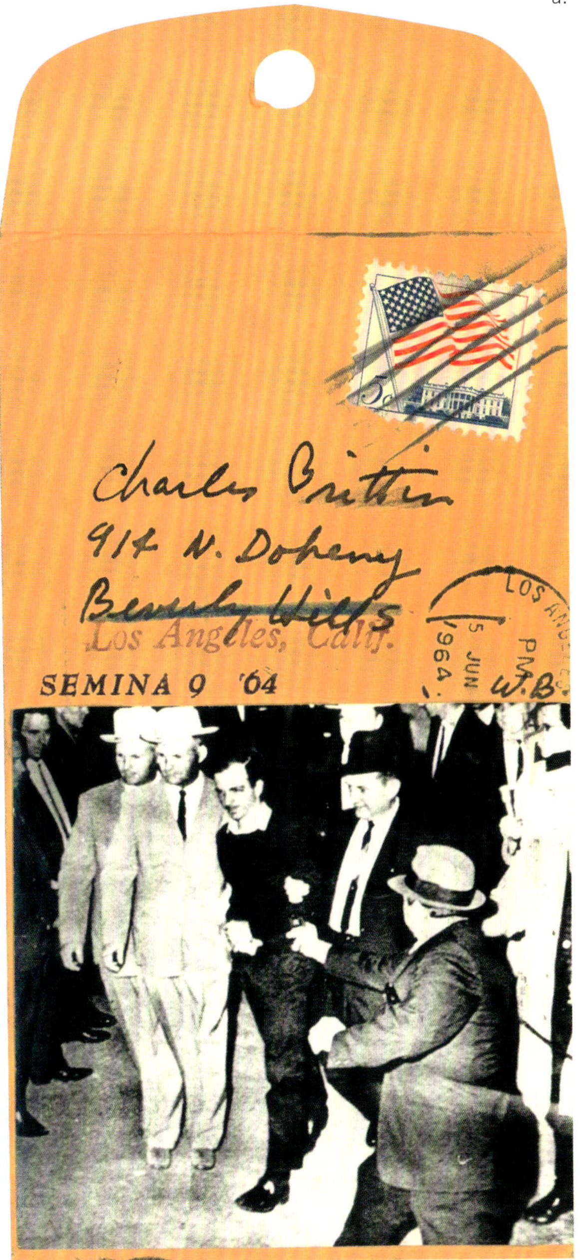

b.

DOUBLE MURDER! VAHROOOOOOOHR!
Varshnohteeembreth nahrooohr ***PAIN STAR.***
CLOUDS ROLL INTO MARIGOLDS
nrah paws blayge bullets eem air.
BANG! BANG! BANG! BANG! BANG!
BANG! BANG! BANG! BANG!
BANG! BANG! BANG! BANG! BANG!
BANG! BANG! BANG! BANG! BANG!
BANG! BANG! BANG!

Yahh oon ***FLAME held prisoner.***

DALLAS!

McClure

SEMINA 9

Crater Lane, Los Angeles, 1964,
5 1/2 x 3 1/8 in.

Cover: **Wallace Berman**, Altered photograph of Jack Ruby shooting Lee Harvey Oswald depicting a twinned image of the agent guarding Oswald. (McClure poem written in response to Berman's image.) (a.)

McClure (Michael McClure), Untitled poem, ("Double Murder! VAHROOOOOOOH R!"),(Reprinted as "November's Texas Song (for Lee Harvey Oswald and John F. Kennedy)" in *Star* (New York: Grove Press, 1970); *Huge Dreams* (New York: Penguin Poets, 1999). (b.)

Wallace, have had poem on wall for days convinced it is best recent poem. I have been reading it with "Yahh oon FLAME held prisoner," as end line as it is on mss. Page. I like DALLAS at end. Had already tried it that way mentally. This is it. Should be no more than one poem. Intensity of the shot is the knife-edge brevity. Undated correspondence from McClure to Berman accompanying submission of manuscript, Wallace Berman Archive, Archives of American Art, Smithsonian Institution

Artist Biographies

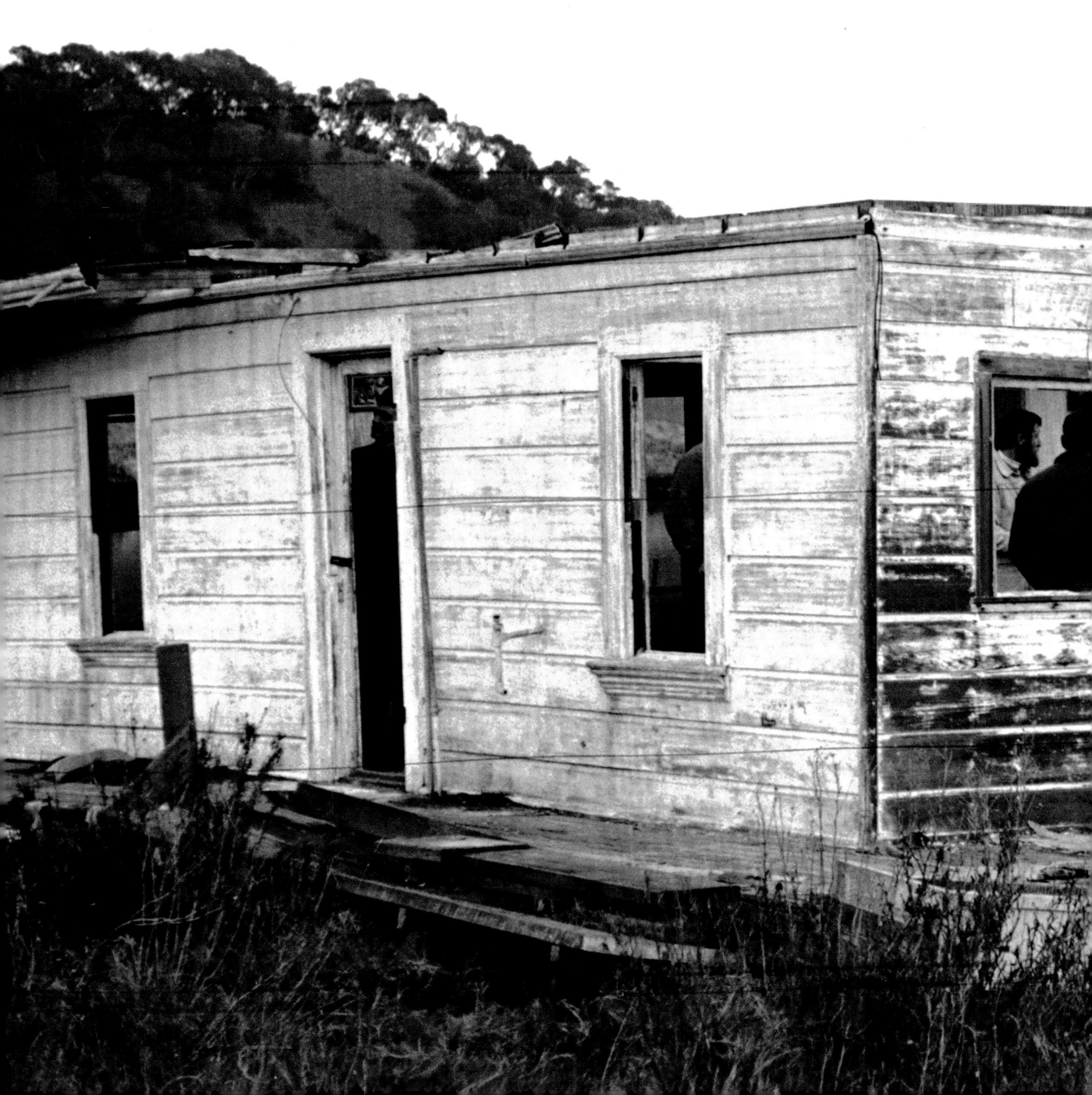

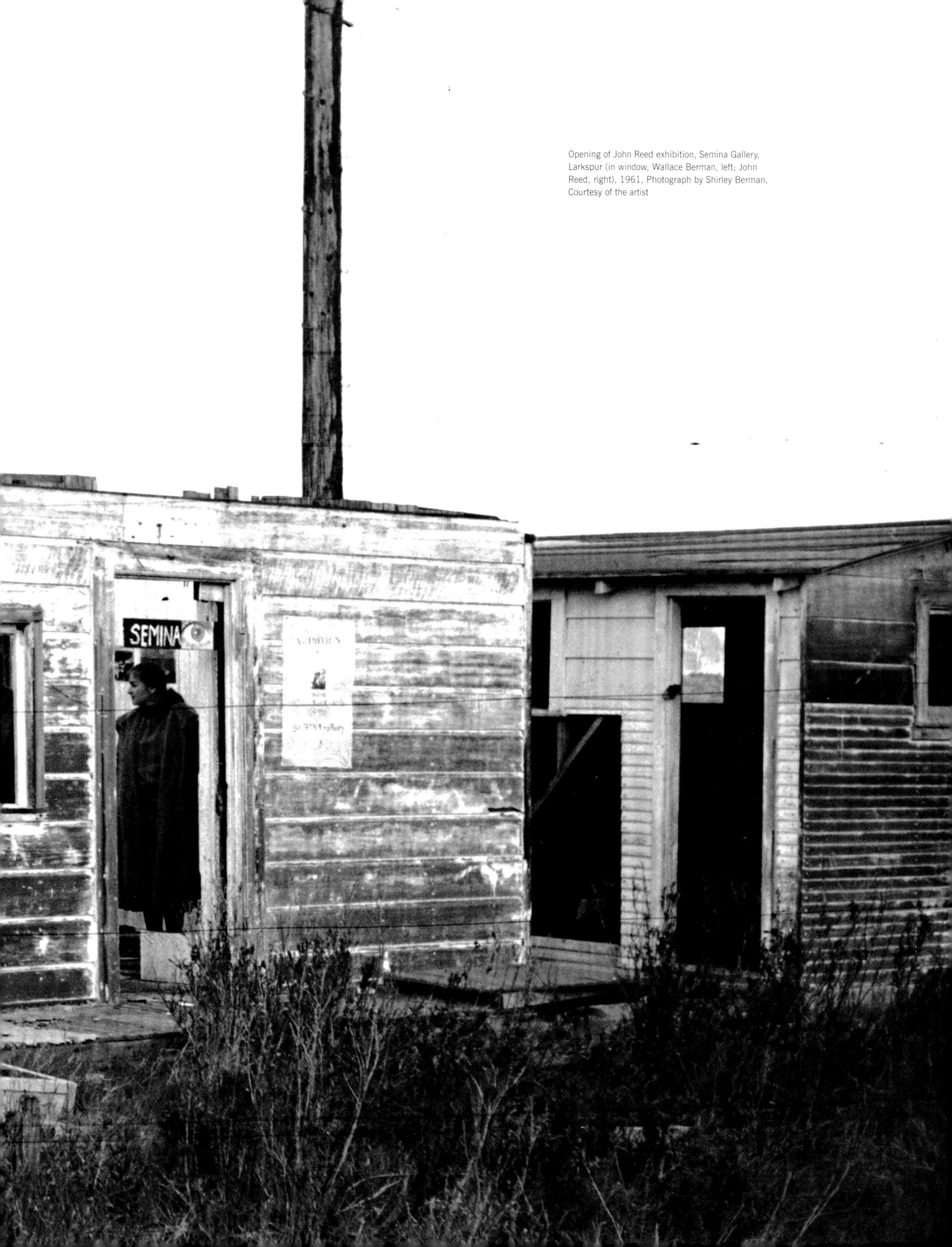

Opening of John Reed exhibition, Semina Gallery, Larkspur (in window, Wallace Berman, left; John Reed, right), 1961, Photograph by Shirley Berman, Courtesy of the artist

Robert Alexander

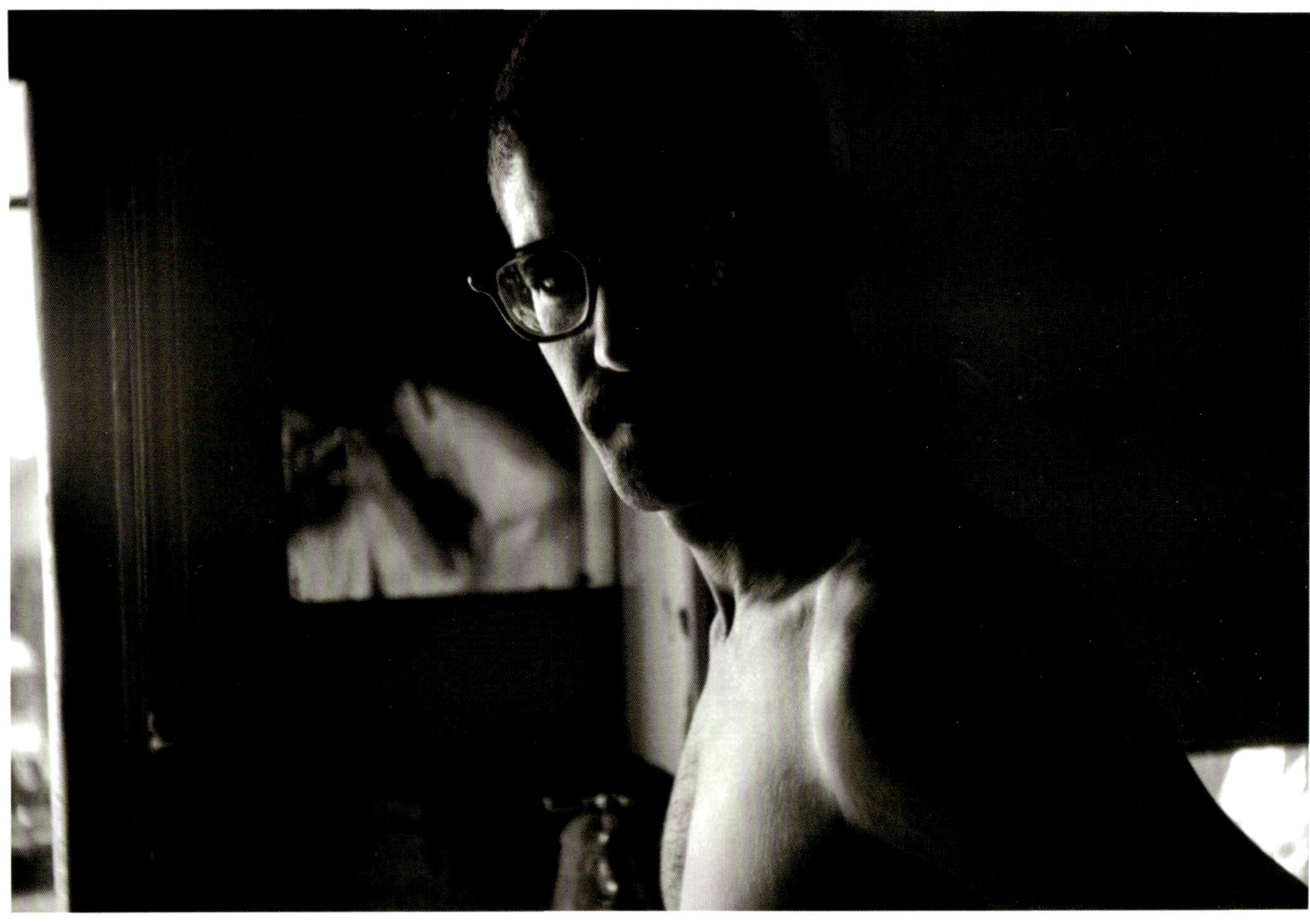

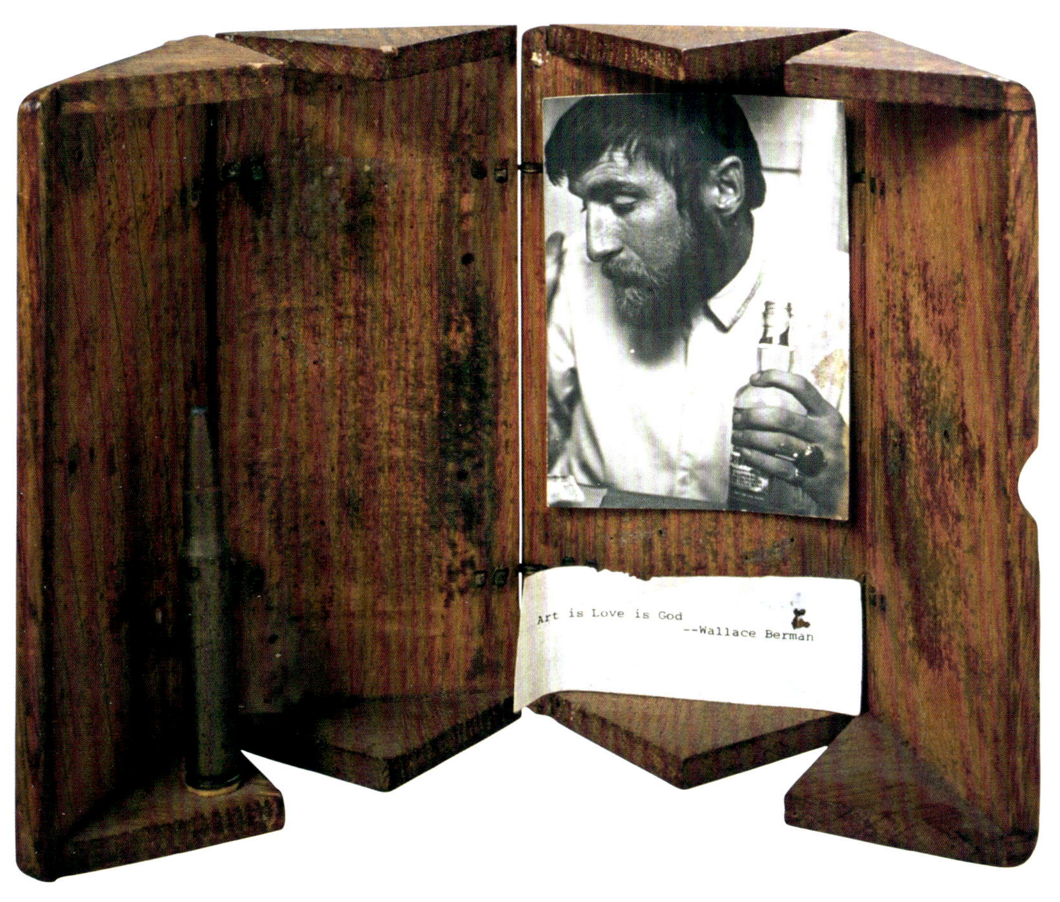
Art is Love is God
--Wallace Berman

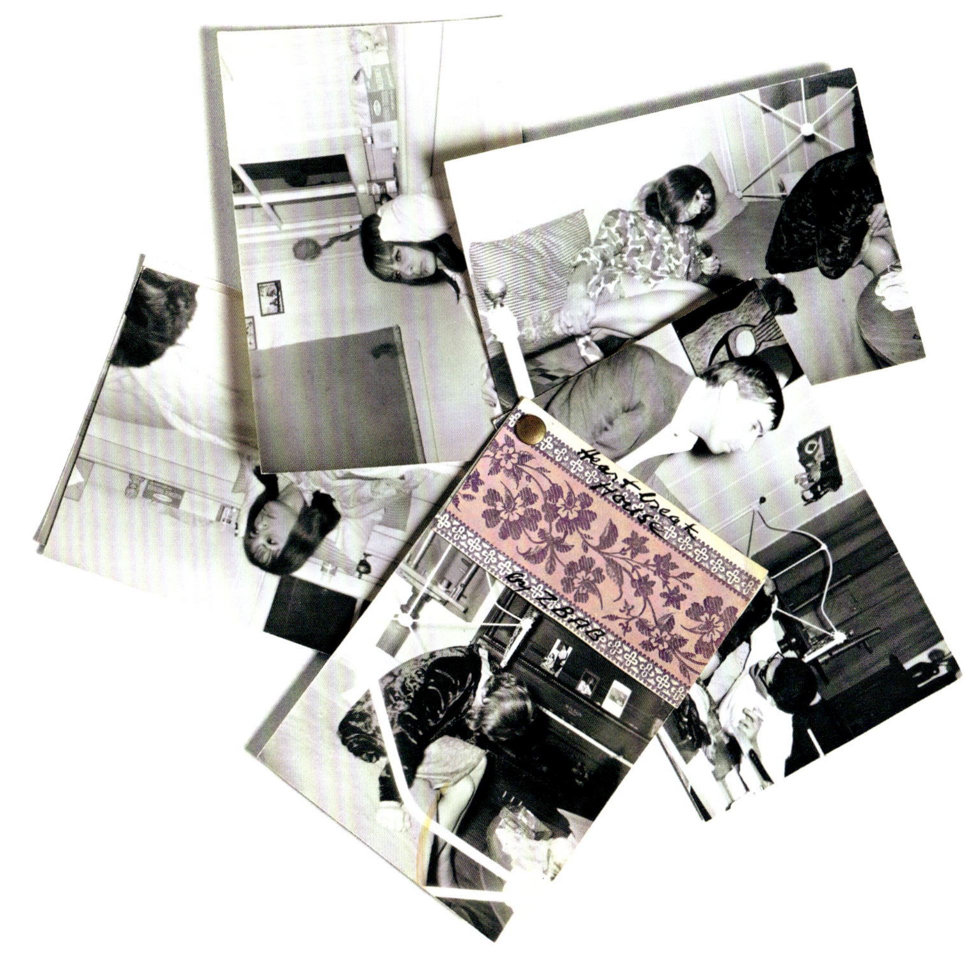

Robert Alexander was born in Chicago, Illinois in 1923. The only child of Russian immigrants, Alexander and his family relocated to Southern California shortly after he was born and settled in Boyle Heights, which then had a large community of Jewish immigrants. After Alexander finished elementary school the family moved to the West Adams district, where Alexander came of age.

Reflecting on his youth, Alexander has described himself as having had a "semi-languid messianic complex," and he marched to his own drum from the start. At age thirteen he began writing poetry, smoking marijuana, and hanging out on the Los Angeles jazz scene, which was then in its heyday. Having made himself a false I.D., he spent time in the almost exclusively black clubs of Central Avenue. During this period he also worked as a carnival barker on the boardwalks of Venice and Santa Monica, where he developed strong ties to the itinerant carny community.

p. 72
Robert Alexander, Stone Brothers Printing, Los Angeles, 1957, Photograph by Wallace Berman, Courtesy Wallace Berman Estate.

p. 73 top
Robert Alexander, Untitled ("Art is Love is God"), 1955, Mixed media assemblage.

p. 73 bottom
Robert Alexander, *Heartbreak House*, 1958, Photographic flipbook.

p. 74
Robert Alexander, *Blood of a Poet*, 1956, Mixed media with artist's blood.

p. 75
Robert Alexander, Untitled ("Mother"), 1960, Mixed media collage on paper.

In 1943 Alexander was drafted into the Army, but was given a medical discharge due to poor vision. The following year the black magazine, *Sepia*, began publishing poetry by Alexander, who also hosted a radio show on KMTR, where he produced profiles of jazz musicians. Because of a shared interest in jazz, Alexander crossed paths with Wallace Berman in 1945, and the two became fast friends. "Wally and I probably both had our lives saved by jazz music," recalled Alexander, who managed musicians Slim Gaillard and Slam Stewart during the late 1940s.[1] The downside of Alexander's immersion in the jazz world was that it exposed him to heroin, and by 1948 he'd become an addict.

As the decade wound to a close, Alexander spent four months in New York where he landed small parts in several television shows. Returning to Los Angeles in 1950, he married his first wife, Kathleen Bleiweiss, and together they opened Contemporary Bazaar, an arts and crafts store in the San Fernando Valley. The shop carried an extensive collection of smallpress publications and hosted performances by comedian Lord Buckley. Contemporary Bazaar survived until 1954, when Alexander entered a drug detoxification facility in Fort Worth, Texas following the birth of his daughter, Marika.

After completing the program in Texas, Alexander returned to Los Angeles in 1955 and separated from his wife. He moved into an abandoned real estate office on Santa Monica Boulevard that Ed Kienholz found for him, a tiny space that he rented for $25 a month and christened it the Baza Shack. During this period Kienholz opened the Now Gallery in the green room of the Coronet Louvre Theater, and at the end of 1955 Alexander had his first solo exhibition there of collaged poems. "I was taking original poems, of which I made no copies, smashing them onto a piece of something or other, and trying to make a piece out of the poem," Alexander explained.[2]

It was also in 1955 that Berman purchased a small hand-press and began publishing *Semina*. Alexander had mastered the nuts and bolts of printing in junior high school, and was of invaluable help to Berman during the early days of *Semina*. While working together on the magazine, Alexander and Berman began discussing the possibility of opening a gallery that would be "open to the outlaws," as Alexander put it.[3] Toward that end, Berman introduced Alexander to Walter Hopps, and Alexander took Hopps to meet his friend Ed Kienholz. The following

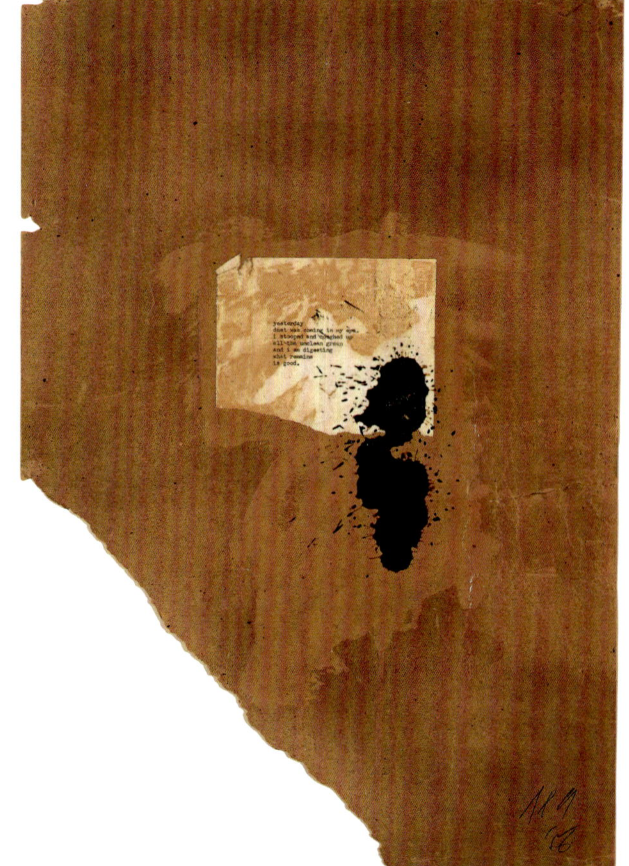

year Kienholz and Hopps collaborated on the All-City Art Festival at Barnsdall Park, where Alexander exhibited a room environment made of boxes and cigarette cork tips.

When Kienholz and Hopps opened the Ferus Gallery in 1957, Alexander did a great deal to get the gallery up and running. "The first Ferus was Baza's aesthetic," David Meltzer has recalled. "Alexander did the cleaning, hammered nails, painted walls—he played a crucial role in the early Ferus."[4] George Herms concurs that Alexander "developed some of the most well-known institutions and got zero credit for it because someone else would be the one to make it into the history books. Bob was a completely creative person...he was a poet, a collage maker, an assemblage artist and a printer."[5] Shortly after Ferus opened, Hopps rented a storefront for Alexander on Santa Monica Boulevard where he could do graphics and printing for the gallery. Dubbed "Stone Brothers Printing," it became a hangout for Alexander and Berman, who hosted poetry readings and film screenings there.

At the end of the year Alexander moved to San Francisco where he was offered a job as warehouse foreman at Paper Editions. He also worked part-time as manager of the Jazz Workshop, and collaborated with Jim Newman on the Dilexi Gallery, an exhibition space they opened above the jazz club. "Dilexi was the only gallery that had anything worth looking at at the time," Shirley Berman has recalled.[6] Nonetheless, Alexander left all his posts; after being ordained by Reverend Melvin Johnson of the Peoples' Association Church, he went back to Los Angeles at the end of the year.

On returning to Los Angeles, Alexander moved into Charles Brittin's apartment in Venice Beach and founded the Temple of Man, a nonsectarian center for poetry, jazz and art. Alexander went back to San Francisco later in the year to remodel The Cellar, a jazz club that had been destroyed by a fire, but the club went bankrupt shortly after reopening, and Alexander returned to Venice in 1961. He married again the following year, and in 1963 he and his wife, Anita, opened a print shop in Silverlake, a suburb of Los Angeles. His second marriage had a stabilizing effect on Alexander, who began working as a printer for the Los Angeles Free Press in 1968. In the early 1970s the Alexanders moved back to Venice where they remained until 1987, when Bob Alexander died of cancer.

Kristine McKenna

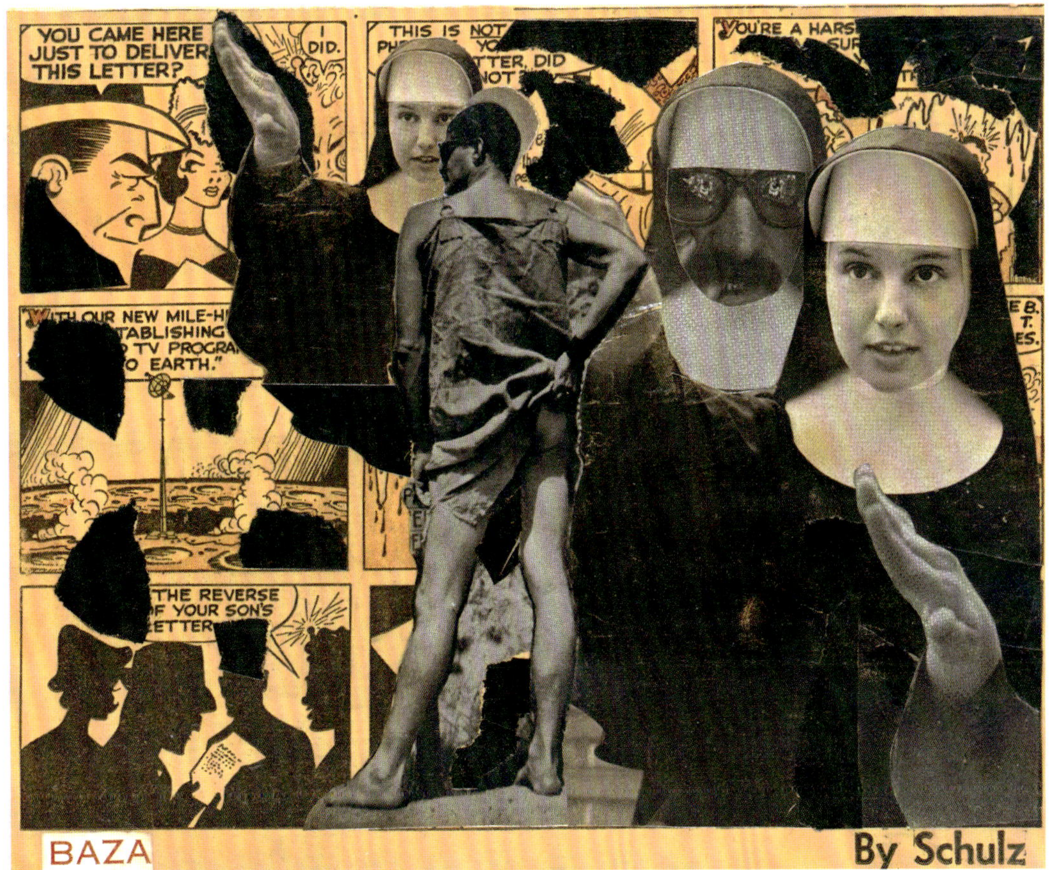

1 Sandra Leonard Starr, *Lost and Found in California: Four Decades of Assemblage Art*, (Santa Monica: James Corcoran, Shoshana Wayne, and Pence Galleries, 1988), p. 57.
2 Ibid., p. 82.
3 Ibid.
4 From a conversation with Kristine McKenna, November 18, 2003.
5 Starr, p. 88.
6 Ibid., p. 98.

John Altoon

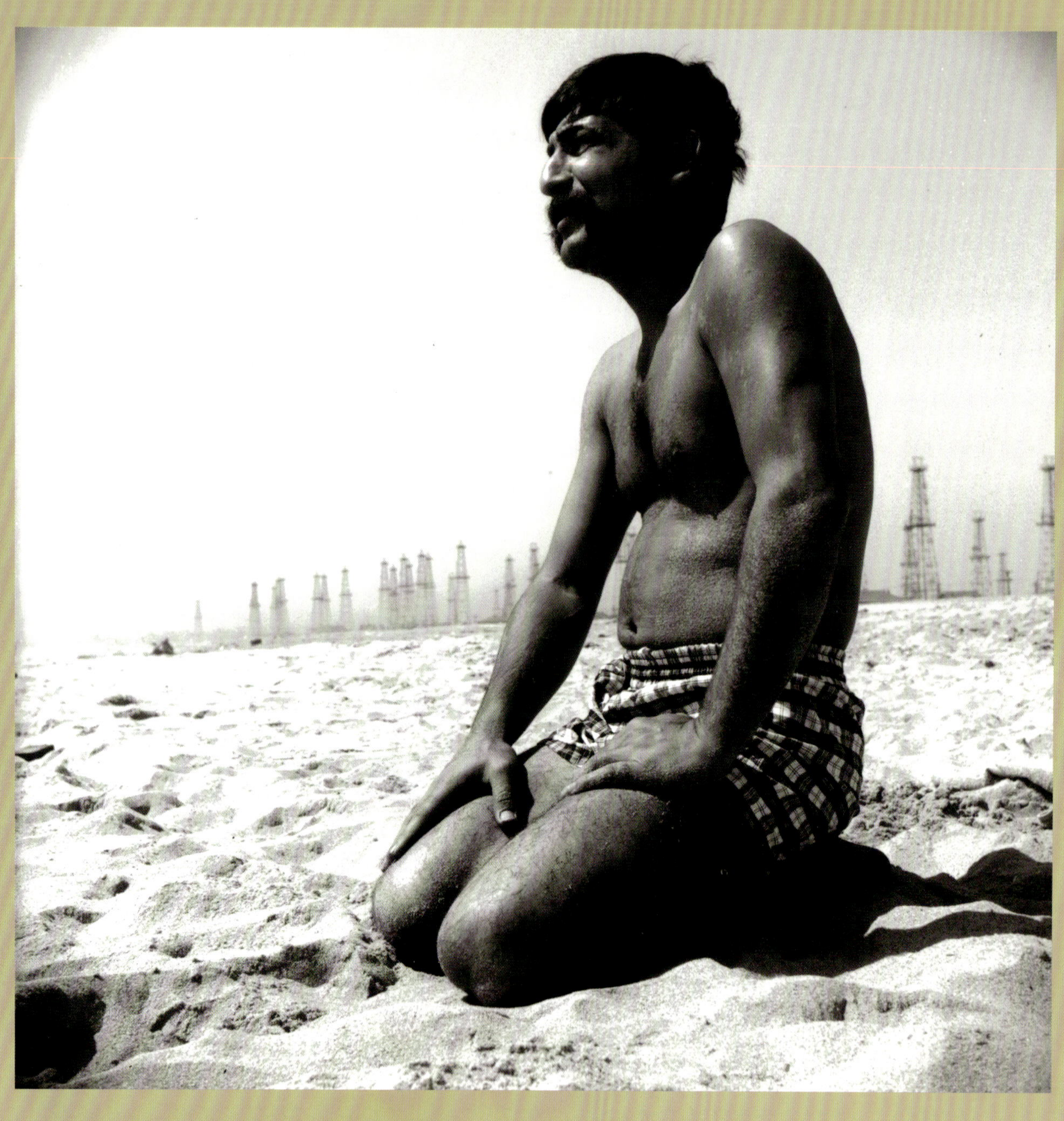

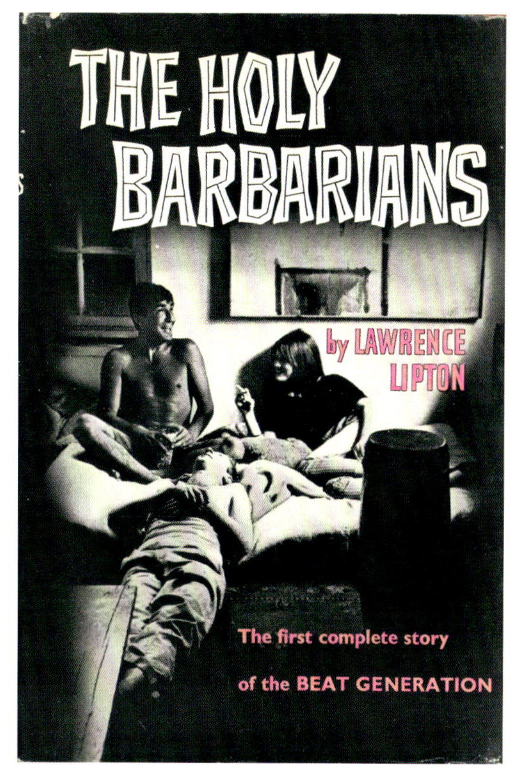

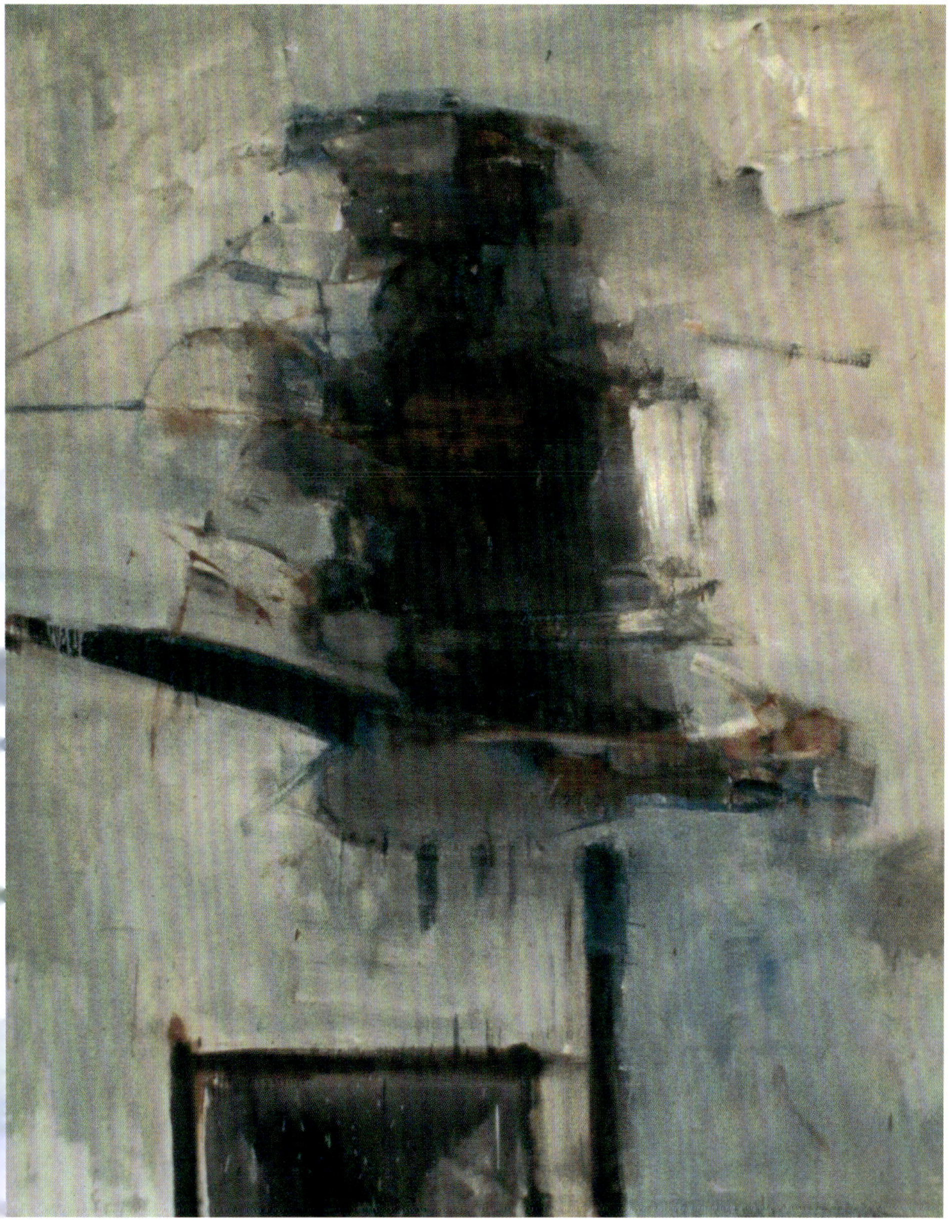

I -
in my own season
find reasons to discuss
About
a friend -
whose tires on his car
Need air -
Like
my car and tires
need air -
He -
as it is his way -
tires and gets mad
so I
in my way -
say - what is what
I can say -
like fill those mothers
and lets go -

Untitled poem from Altoon papers, undated

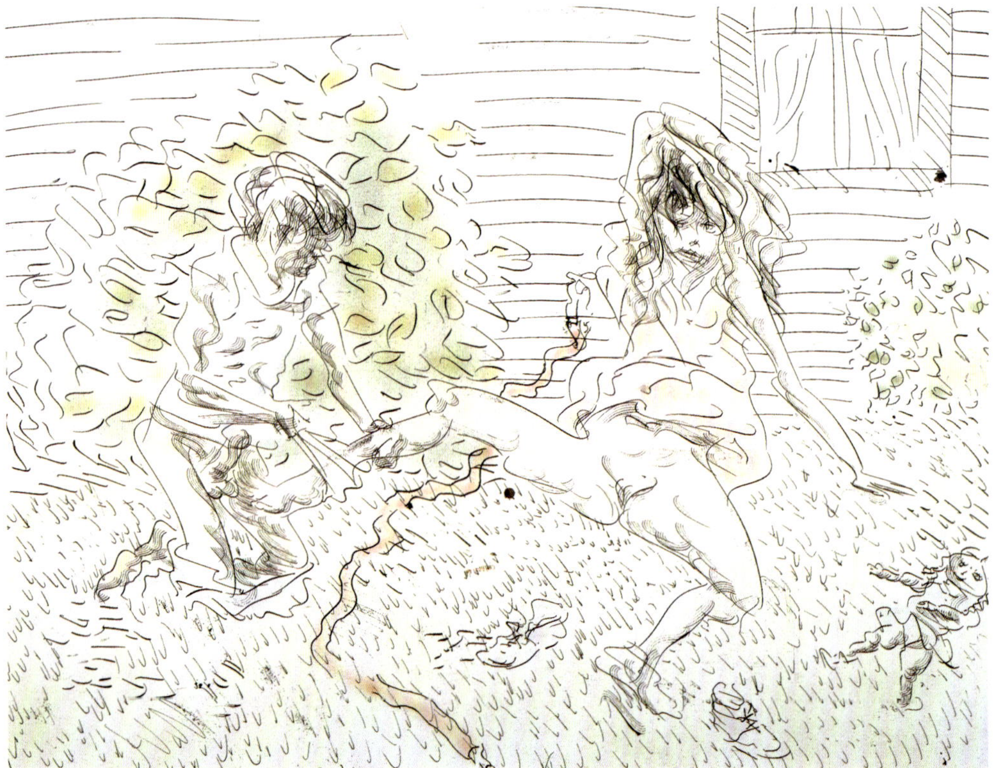

The most gifted abstract painter of the Ferus Gallery stable, Los Angeles artist John Altoon still enjoys a larger-than-life reputation for his exuberant personality and unpredictable antics. Although one of the most charismatic members of the Southern California art scene, he suffered from psychological disturbances that often led to violent outbursts and manic behavior. Despite his early death, his erotic drawings and late abstract paintings stand as two of the West Coast's most evocative bodies of work.

Born in 1925 to first generation Armenian immigrants, Altoon attended Dorsey High School in central Los Angeles. His natural abilities as a draftsman won him a scholarship to Otis Art Institute, but his studies were interrupted by wartime service in the Pacific as a Navy radar technician. After the war, he returned to Otis on the G.I. Bill, but soon transferred to Art Center School to study illustration. Objecting to the curriculum, he turned against commercial art, switching back to a program in Fine Arts at Chouinard Art Institute. Upon graduation in 1951, he enjoyed his first one-person exhibition at the Santa Barbara Museum of Art.

From 1951 to 1954 Altoon lived in New York and supported himself through commercial illustration while pursuing a career as a serious painter. An Emily Lowe Competition Grant in 1954 enabled Altoon to travel in Europe, with a sojourn in Mallorca where he met Robert Duncan, Jess, and poet Robert Creeley, with whom he later collaborated on a print portfolio (*About Women*, Gemini Ltd., 1965–66). Psychological pressures and severe depression forced him to return from Europe to live with his family in Los Angeles for several months.

Altoon began to teach drawing at Art Center School and met key members of the Los Angeles artistic community, including Walter Hopps and Ed Kienholz, who included his work in the first group exhibition at Ferus Gallery. Altoon's work won acclaim as a strong painterly response to the Abstract Expressionism of Bay Area artists such as Clyfford Still, Hassel Smith, and Richard Diebenkorn. In 1957 Wallace Berman included in *Semina Two* an ink drawing taken from one of Altoon's European sketchbooks depicting a group of mourners and a priest hovering around a child's body.

In 1960, a bout of depression led Altoon to destroy much of the work in his studio, an act that horrified members of the local art community. His Ferus solo exhibition of 1961 included, however, *Portrait of a Spanish Poet (Lorca)* (1954–59), which serves as a kind of elegy to the dead poet, with its brushy cloud of gray and blue conjuring a lyrical emanation over a rectangular, tomb-like box.

p. 76
John Altoon on Venice Beach, 1955, Photograph
by Charles Brittin.

p. 77 left
John Altoon, *Portrait of a Spanish Poet (Lorca)*, 1954–59, Oil on canvas.

p. 77 top right
Lawrence Lipton, *The Holy Barbarians* (London: W.H. Allen, 1960), Cover photograph of John Altoon and friends under John Altoon *Portrait of a Spanish Poet (Lorca)*.

p. 77 below right
John Altoon, Untitled poem, John Altoon Archive, Archives of American Art, Smithsonian Institution.

p. 78
John Altoon, *Untitled (woman, garden hose, & boy)*, 1966, Ink and gouache on paper.

Altoon's sketchbooks include poetry written in a blunt elliptical style somewhat reminiscent of Robert Creeley.[1]

In 1962 Altoon divorced his B-movie and television actress wife Fay Spain. To try to quell his manic behavior, he began regular sessions with psychiatrist Milton Wexler. The free associations of therapy seemed to open up his paintings. In 1962 Altoon moved away from the influences of Philip Guston, Willem DeKooning, and the Bay Area Abstract Expressionist painters in the *Ocean Park* series, named for Altoon's Venice studio on Marine Street that had become a local hangout for both the beach art crowd and Westside canyon dwellers. Of the group known as the "Ferus Boys," Altoon was perhaps the most socially available, allowing his studio to become a kind of crash pad. As Ed Kienholz later described it, "His habitat was the studio. The floors were covered in old canvases used as rugs. The smell was India ink and turpentine. There was always something new on the easel, and Altoon would be standing in the middle of all the mess in sandals and cut-offs petting his dog, Man."[2]

The *Ocean Park* paintings and drawings employed a brighter palette and were organized around abstracted sexual, anatomical, and botanical shapes. Although at times reminiscent of the imagery of fellow Armenian-American artist Arshile Gorky and Los Angeles artist Craig Kauffman, Altoon's biomorphic abstraction developed along brushier, more painterly lines using decidedly more playful, erotic forms. Critic Leah Ollman has stated, "Altoon's biomorphic shapes, like Gorky's align themselves within each painting or drawing according to an organic, internal logic, creating a visual current for the eye to ride, as fluid as the stream of consciousness."[3]

The abstract work seemed to distill imagery taken from the twenty to thirty freehand drawings he made each day, many of which were prompted by his teaching and occasional commercial gigs. In 1963 he began a Pop-inspired series of satires of magazine advertisements that were executed in his loose illustrational style. Altoon's outrageous sense of raunchy humor was evidenced in the narrative drawings featuring surreal animals, haplessly horny men, and sex-besotted beach bunnies. These wild, untamed works were often inspired by ideas and fantasies that surfaced during his psychoanalytic sessions.

The free spirit of the cartoon satires—some of which he referred to as *Nightmares*—seems to spring from the erotic lasciviousness of Picasso's etchings and to relate as well to the overtly sexual work of Ben Talbert. Critic Peter Selz has rightly emphasized Altoon's importance as a maker of "art of magic erotic content": "Like the work of his Surrealist precursors, the paintings of John Altoon testify to the dynamic power of the erotic to break the bourgeois web of taboos and restore the authentic human being to sensual desire."[4] In their comic portrayal of psychological fears, warped American values, bourgeois hypocrisies, and the war between the sexes, Altoon's drawings presage much contemporary work, particularly the confessional and sometimes vulgar drawings of Paul McCarthy, Raymond Pettibon, and Nicole Eisenman.

In 1964 Altoon began experimenting with air-brush effects that further loosened up his organic imagery with mists of cool color that imbued the works with a dream-like atmosphere. In 1965 he married Roberta "Babs" Lunine, a stabilizing influence on his volatile personality. To some degree the angst of his earlier years seemed to have been assuaged in the late works. His last drawings—the series *Princess and the Frog*, *Cowboy and Indian*, and an untitled series of abstracted genitalia (all 1968)—depicted more oblique narratives that were fantastical and comically absurd.

In 1969 he died suddenly of a massive heart attack after attending a party. In 1997 the San Diego Museum of Contemporary Art organized a retrospective of Altoon's work, co-curated by Andrea Hales and Hugh Davies.

Michael Duncan

1 Altoon Archive, unmicrofilmed, Archives of American Art, Smithsonian Institution.
2 Brigid S. Barton, *John Altoon*, De Saisset Museum, Santa Clara, 1980, p. 15.
3 Leah Ollman, "Altoon: Beyond the Aura," *Art in America*, Vol. 87, Issue 2, February 1999, p. 88.
4 Peter Selz, "John Altoon Reconsidered," *John Altoon* (San Diego: Museum of Contemporary Art, 1997), p. 13.

Toni Basil

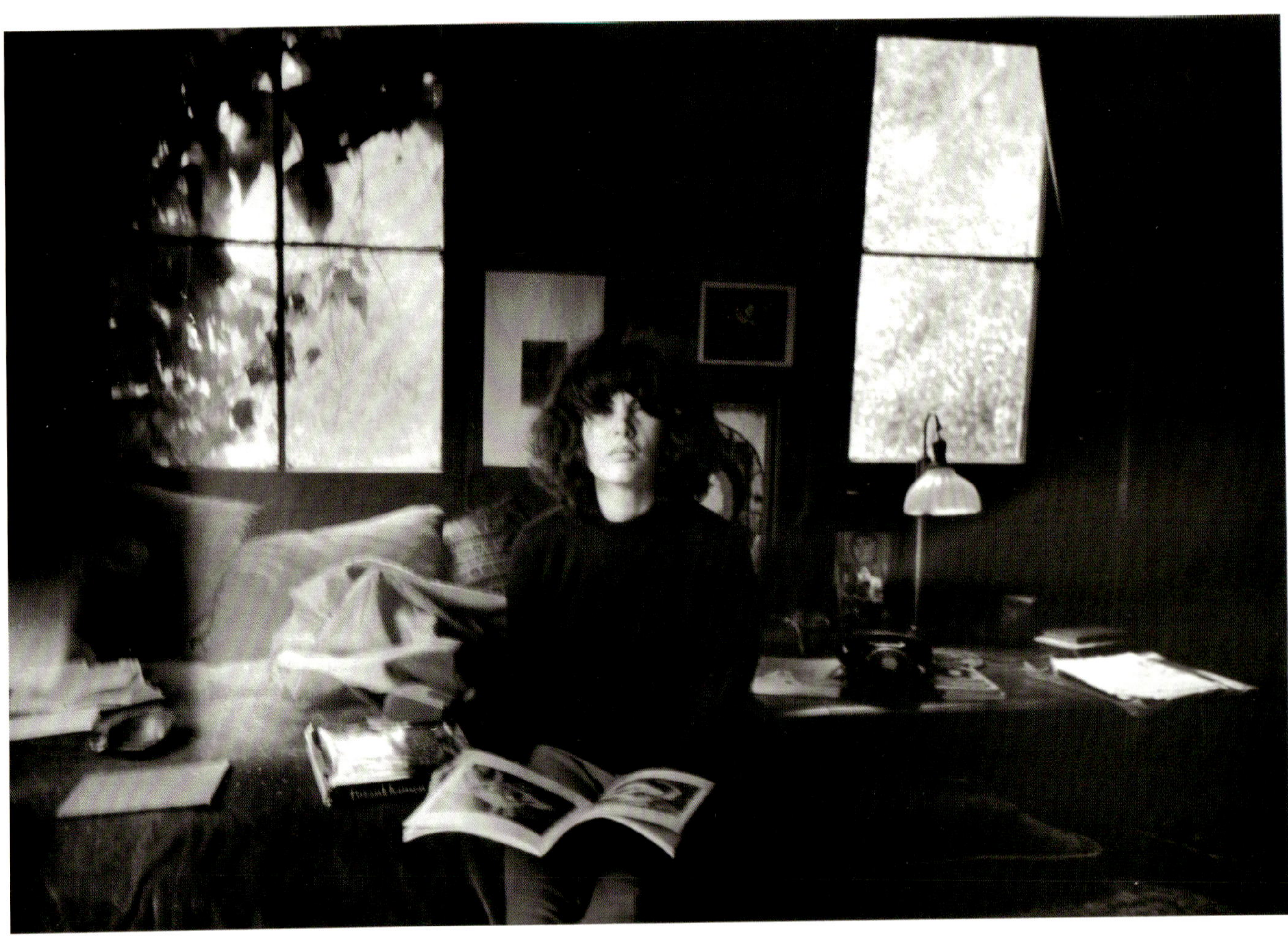

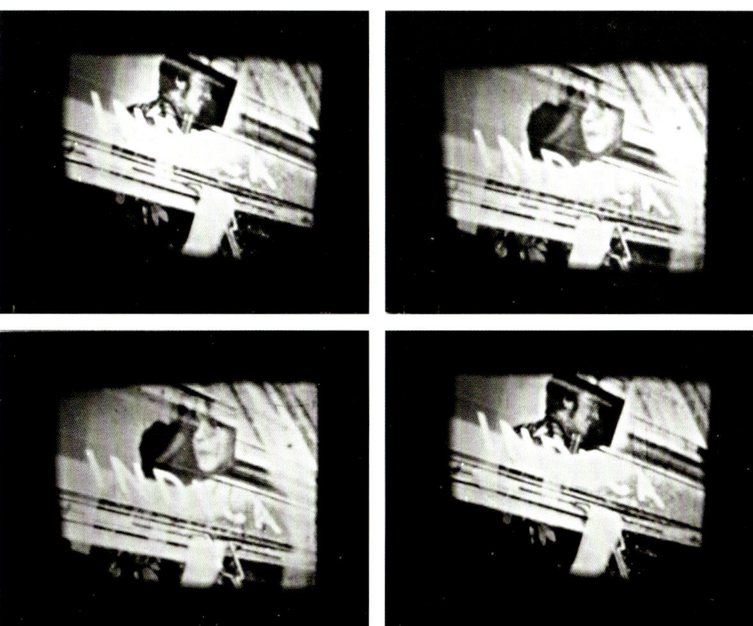

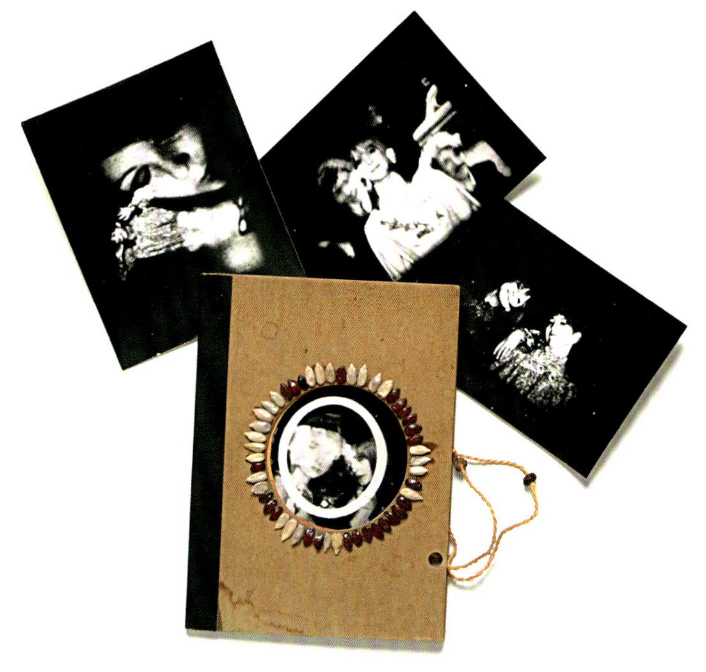

Chiefly known as a choreographer of films and videos—and as the singer of the 1982 hit single "Mickey"—Toni Basil enjoyed an underground reputation in the late 1960s Los Angeles art scene as a budding filmmaker. Born Antonia Christina Basilotta in Philadelphia in 1943 to a bandleader father and dancer mother, she spent her teenage years in Las Vegas. A cheerleader with Hollywood aspirations, she moved to Los Angeles upon graduation and soon won a few parts as a go-go dancer in teen films.

In 1963 Basil became involved in a relationship with Dean Stockwell who introduced her to the artists of Berman's circle. Basil's interest in filmmaking sprang directly on the heels of her irrepressible performance in Bruce Conner's 1966 short film *Breakaway*. The combination of Basil's choreography and Conner's quick-cut editing made the film a brilliant tour de force that presaged the MTV style of video editing. Basil's short 1967 film, *Our Trip*, recorded a rollicking European excursion made with friends Teri Garr and Ann Marshall that included shots of their encounters with The Beatles and Rolling Stones. Rhythmically edited to the songs "I Feel Free" by Cream and "Sgt. Pepper's Lonely Hearts Club Band" by The Beatles, the film is a lively portrait of young women on the loose in the 1960s.

Basil shot extended footage of Stockwell, Berman, Billy Gray, and their friends at play, including a film recording a Topanga Canyon baseball game interrupted by the arrival of a demolition bulldozer. In 1968 she made *A Dance Film Inspired by Jim Morrison*, an experimental short featuring choreography for two dancers accented by strobe-light editing effects. She appeared in small roles in *Easy Rider* (1969), *Five Easy Pieces* (1970), and *The Last Movie* (1971) for which she traveled with Stockwell to Peru.

In the late 1970s she formed the breakdancing group, The Lockers, who were seminal in the development of street-dancing and hip-hop culture. Since her flurry of activity as a performer in the 1980s, Basil has continued to choreograph and dance for films and musical productions. *Michael Duncan*

p. 80
Toni Basil at Berman home, 1964. Photograph by Wallace Berman.

p. 81 left
Toni Basil, *Our Trip (for Ann)*, 1967. Framed film stills.

p. 81 right
Toni Basil, *Our Trip (for Teri)*, 1967. Mixed media collaged book.

Paul Beattie

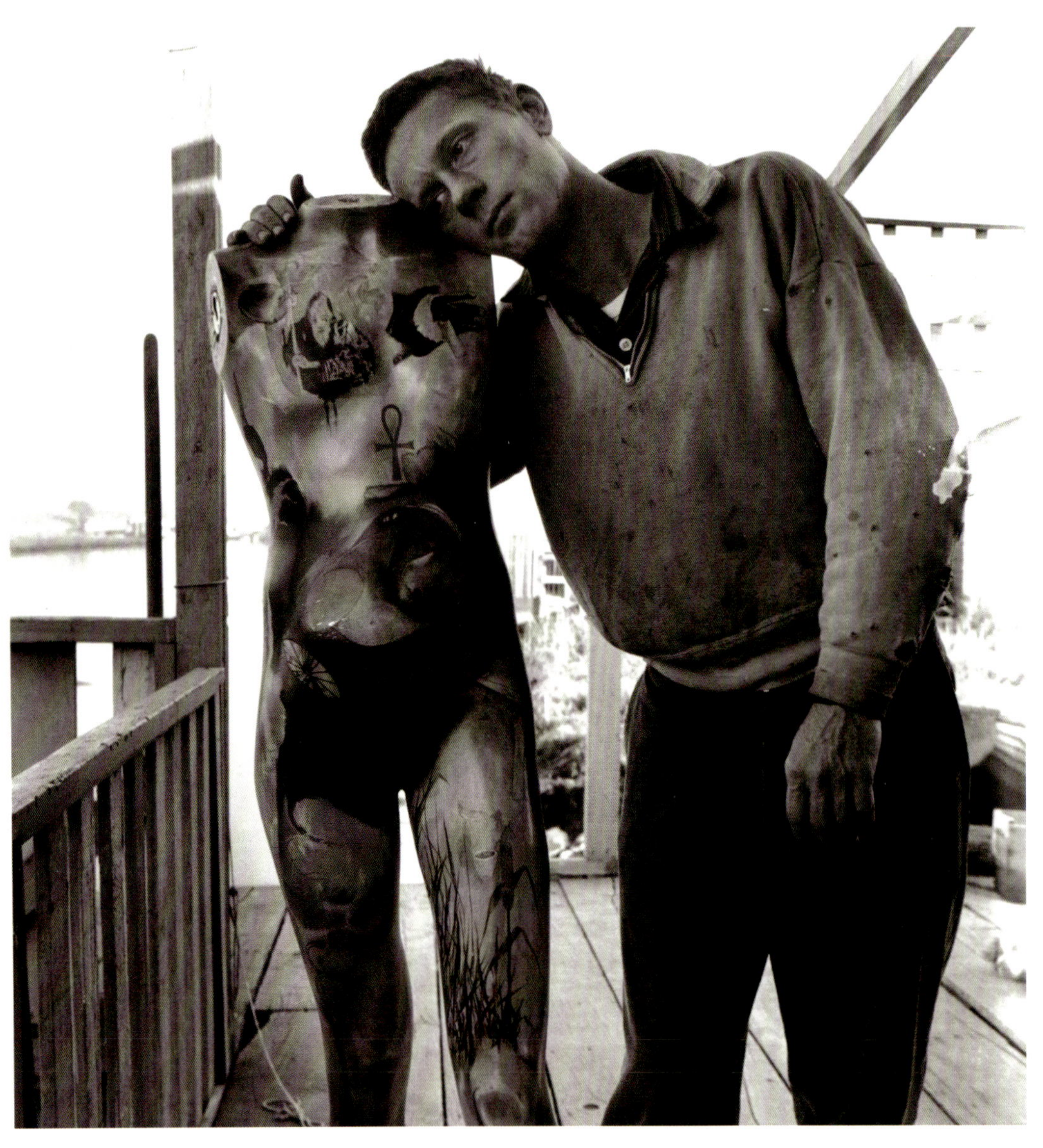

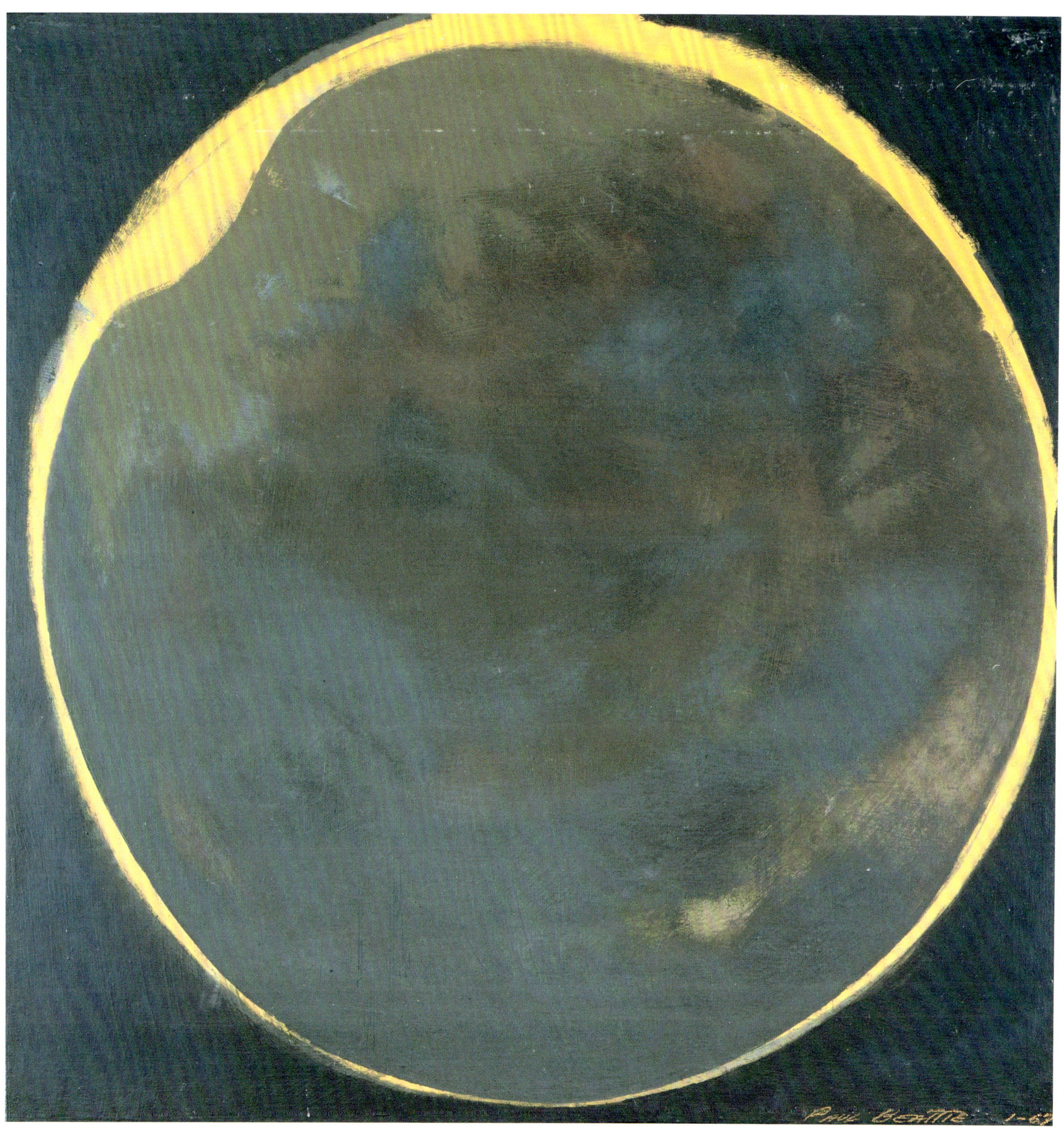
PAUL BEATTIE 1-67

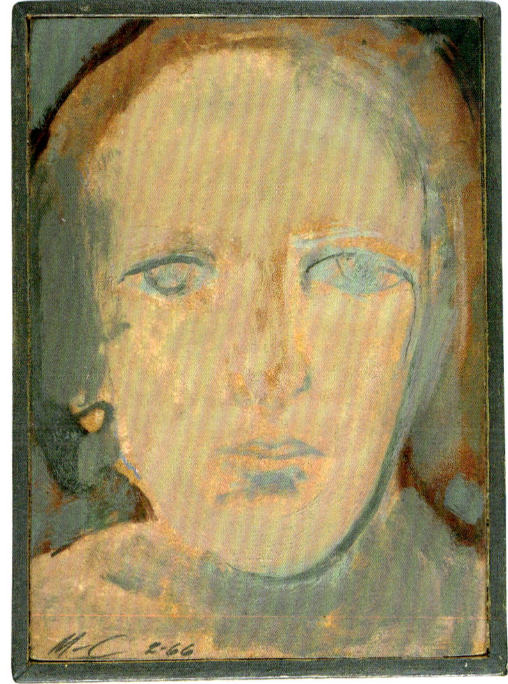

Bay Area artist and filmmaker Paul Beattie is one of the most underrated figures of the Berman circle. Born in Bay City, Michigan in 1924, Beattie attended the Detroit Society of Arts and Crafts. Moving to New York after school, he fell under the influence of the Abstract Expressionists, particularly Willem DeKooning and Jackson Pollock. In a statement written in 1975, he described his early intention "to implant more of a deep-space quality to Pollockian surface-patterned tracery."[1]

Despite a 1954 solo exhibition at the Hansa Gallery and inclusion in several group shows, Beattie became dissatisfied with the New York art scene and decided to move with his wife and young children to San Francisco. He found a niche for himself on the West Coast exploring the relationship of abstraction to natural forms. He exhibited at the best new galleries, with a solo show at The Six Gallery in 1955 and participation in group shows at Batman Gallery.

In the late 1950s, Beattie's interests turned to filmmaking, photography, and music. He became proficient in jazz saxophone and classical improvisation and completed about a dozen films in the early 1960s, including *Thimble of Goodbye* and *The T Cross* (both 1961); *Sunset* (1963); a four-part series of shorts, *L, O, V,* and *E;* and *Finger-Water-Light* (all 1963 and featuring George Herms). Beattie approached filmmaking with the eye of an abstract painter, eschewing narrative in his concentration on light and color. Beattie collaborated with Elias Romero on his light shows in 1959 and became friends with artists Warner Jepson, Ann Halprin, and Robert Morris. He shot the footage for Ruth Weiss's film, *The Brink,* in 1961.

p. 82
Paul Beattie in Larkspur, 1960, Photograph by Wallace Berman.

p. 83
Paul Beattie, *Green Disc*, 1967, Oil on board.

p. 84
Paul Beattie, *Head of Wallace Berman*, 1966, Oil on board.

p. 85 top
Paul Beattie, *Colliding Galaxies with a Plethora of Globular Clusters*, 1976, Pencil on paper.

p. 85 bottom
Paul Beattie, *George Herms (from footage of Finger-Water-Light*, 1964, gouache on board.

For many years, Beattie earned a living as a carpenter. In 1963 he moved to the forests of Sonoma County where he built a house for his family designed in a starburst shape around a central tree on Mill Creek Road near Healdsburg. He helped George Herms build a ramshackle structure nearby and the two families lived more or less communally. Beattie began to focus on painting, while also making collages and drawings. Paintings such as *George Herms (from footage of Finger-Water-Light)* (1964) were depictions of single frames taken from the films. With Herms, Beattie published several editions of illustrated, hand-printed poetrycards for Love Press. *Game for Angels* (1963)—made as a gift for Cameron's daughter, Crystal—is an elaborately decorated set of poems on loose-leaf cards. Beattie, who had a more classical education in art history than most of his friends, encouraged Herms to focus on assemblage, deeming that Herms's subtly patinaed sculptures enjoyed more of a painterly quality than his canvases and drawings.[2]

In the 1970s Beattie enrolled in graduate school at University of California, Berkeley, and received a Masters Degree in 1976. An interest in astronomy led to his most accomplished artworks: drawings and paintings based on planetary and galactic observations made with a telescope on his property. (His observations included the discovery of a star that was officially named and recorded.) Beattie's series of *Sky Paintings* (1975) were examples of what he called "abstract realism," depicting the experience of deep space from four to nine miles above the earth. The *Jet Trails* paintings were abstract fields violated by single marks that symbolically represented mankind's intervention in nature.

Drawings based on firsthand observations of outer space such as *Colliding Galaxies with a Plethora of Globular Clusters* (1976) describe cosmic occurrences with mystical connotations not unlike the *Mandala* drawings of Bruce Conner. Many of the galaxy paintings were small in scale, featuring complex masonite surfaces of paint with glued-on pieces of metal press type. These works were exhibited at San Jose Museum of Art in 1976 and 1982, and San Francisco Museum of Modern Art in 1980. Beattie was employed as director of Santa Rosa Art Center when he died of natural causes in 1987. *Michael Duncan*

1 Paul Beattie, "Summary of Career," April 22, 1975, Beattie Archive, Collection of Robyn Beattie, Petaluma.
2 Conversation with George Herms, November 3, 2004.

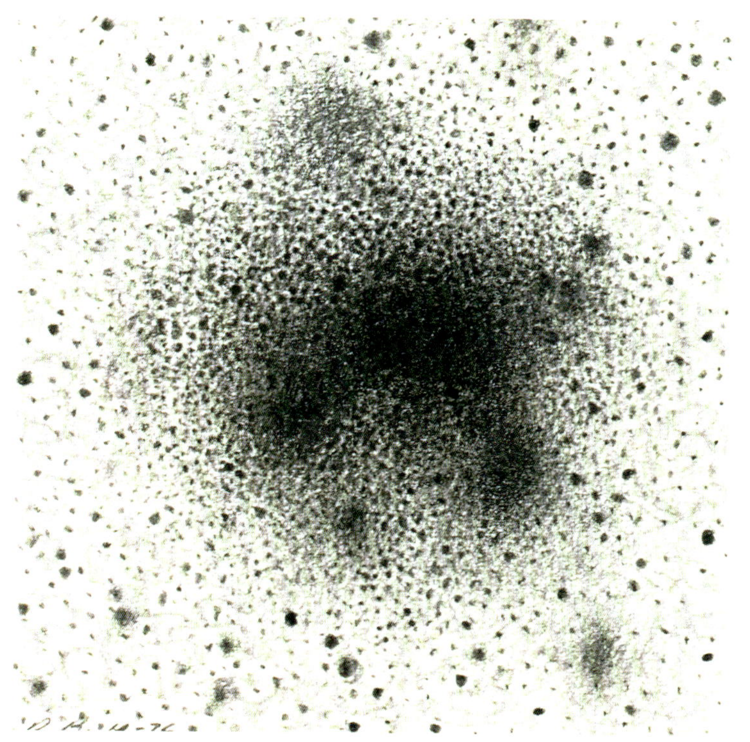

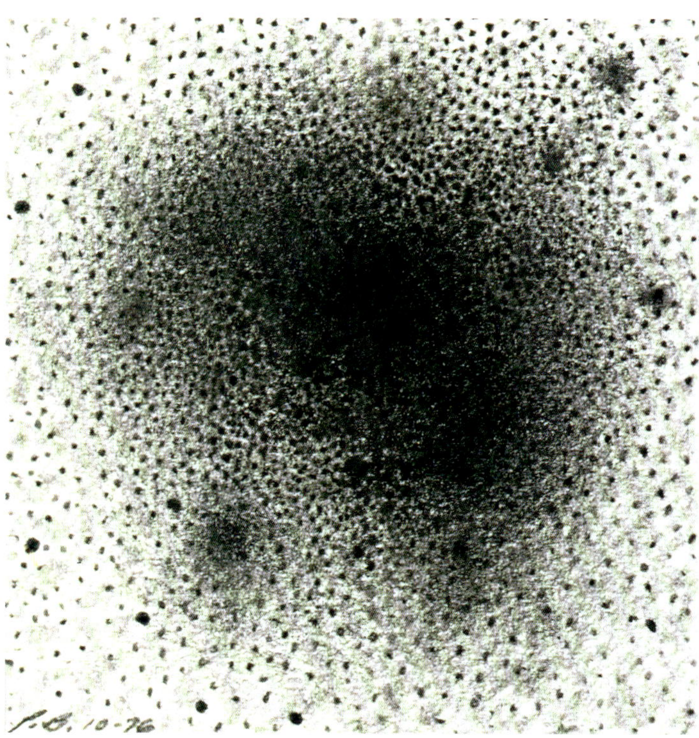

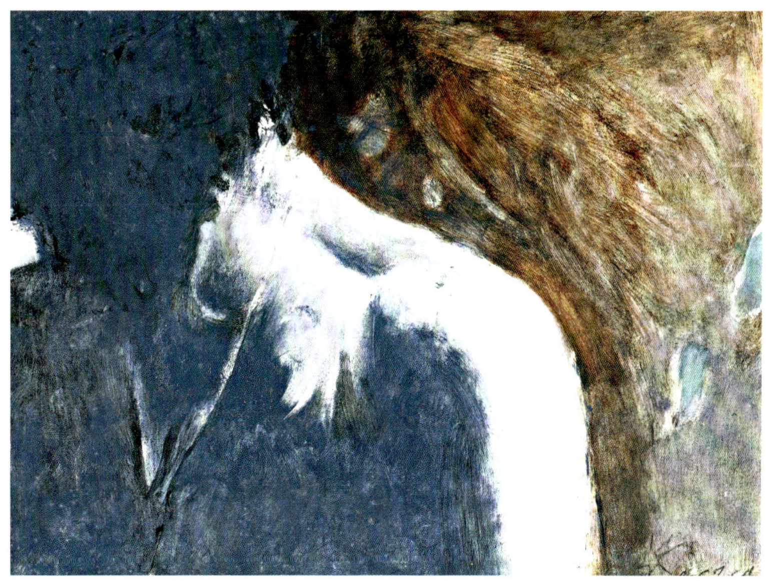

Ray & Bonnie Bremser

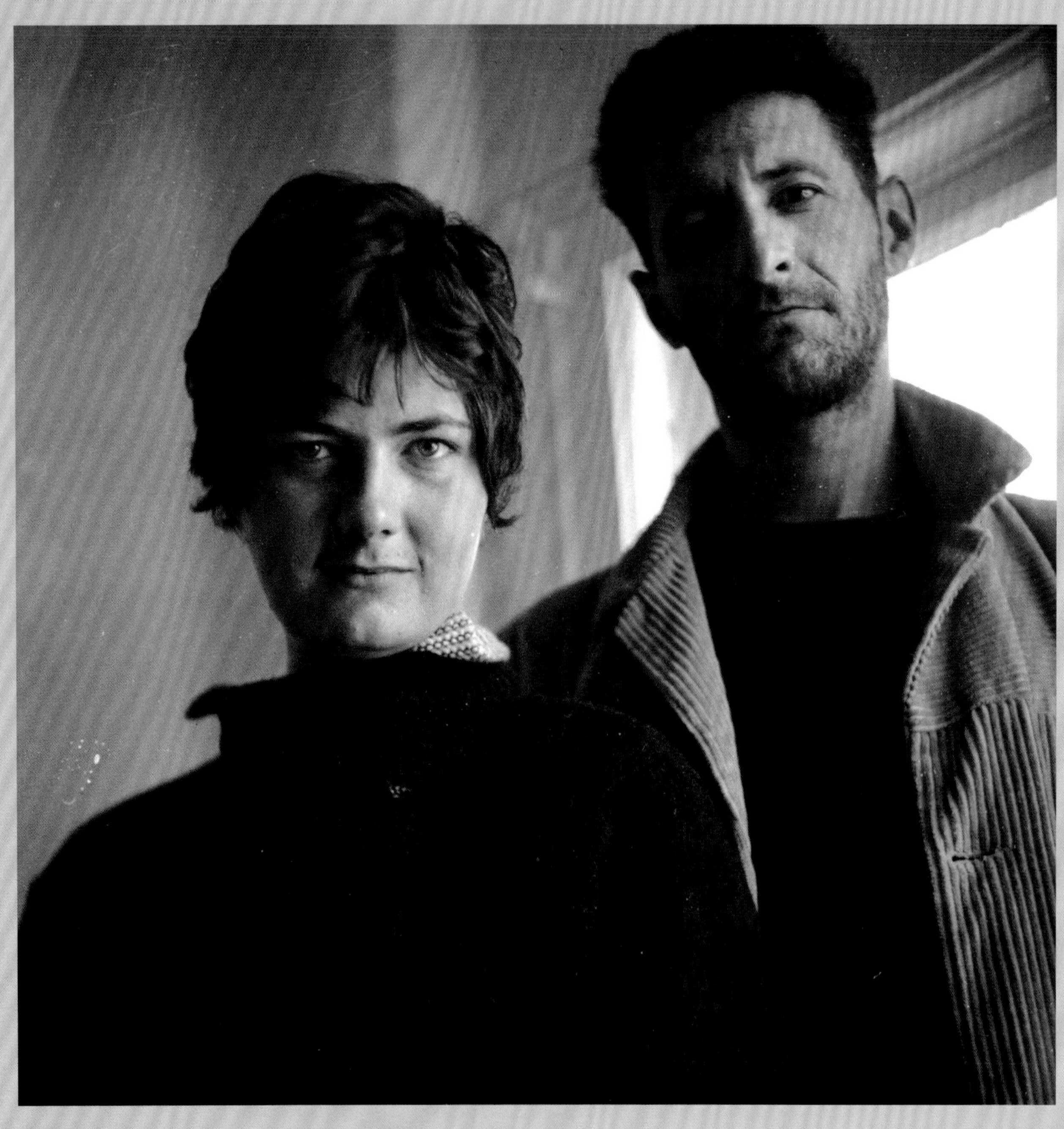

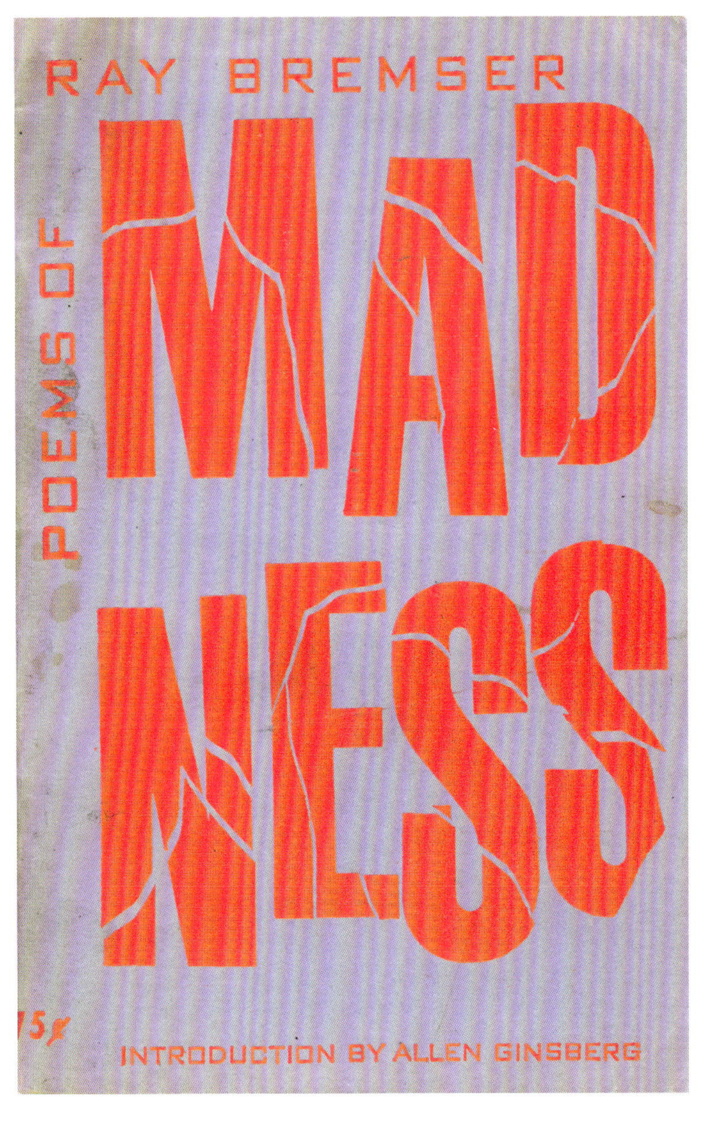
RAY BREMSER
POEMS OF
MAD
NESS
75¢
INTRODUCTION BY ALLEN GINSBERG

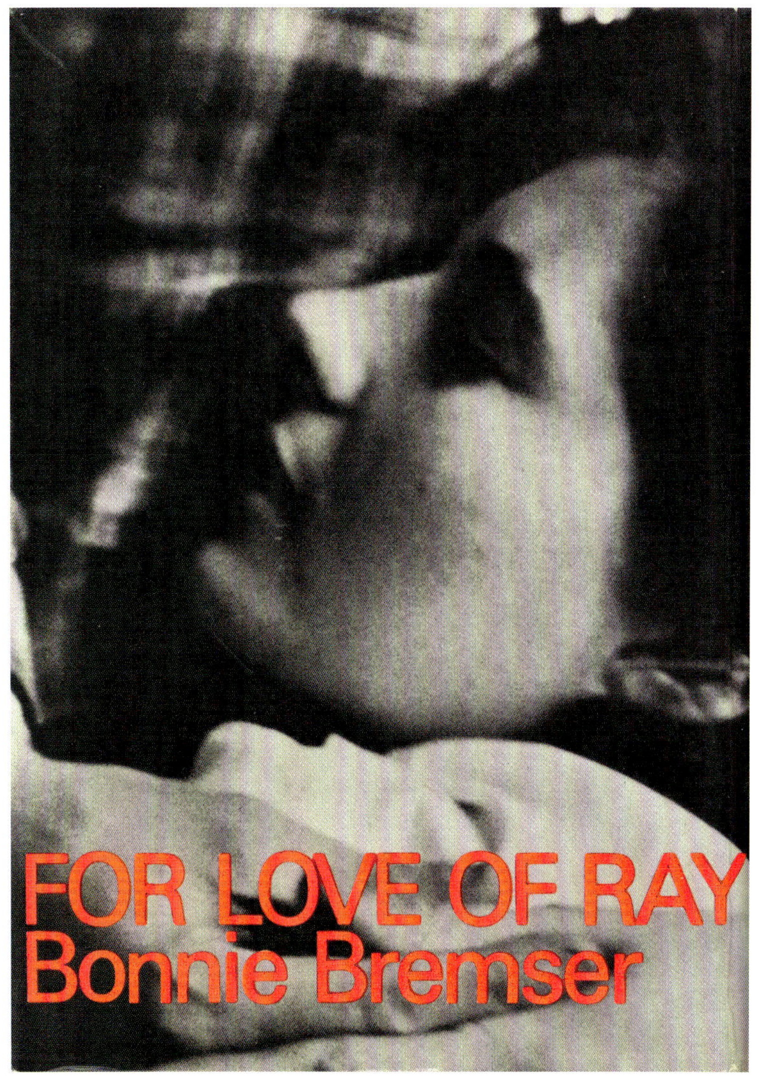
FOR LOVE OF RAY
Bonnie Bremser

The romantic myth of the outlaw poet is skewered by the downbeat experiences of Beat writers Ray and Bonnie Bremser. Born in 1934, from a middle-class New Jersey family, Ray Bremser was an early jazz aficionado with a grudge against authority. In 1951, during the height of the Korean War, he went AWOL on the fourth day of Air Force basic training.[1] After a short stay in the stockade, he managed to get an honorable discharge. Back in Jersey City, he quickly found himself in trouble again after robbing a gas station—an act he later interpreted as a kind of existential impulse. Having just turned eighteen, he was tried as an adult and sentenced to Bordentown Reformatory where he was incarcerated for six and a half years.

Bremser blossomed intellectually in prison, receiving his high-school diploma and discovering an interest in literature, especially the works of Shakespeare and Jean Genet. He began corresponding with poets, including Ezra Pound and Robert Graves. Turned on by the emerging Beat scene, he forwarded poems to Allen Ginsberg, Gregory Corso, and LeRoi Jones. Just before Bremser's parole in 1958, Jones agreed to publish his work in *Yugen*. In a letter to Ginsberg, Bremser could barely contain his excitement, "So happy, therefore, and ecstatic because a poem is in print, and more so because in YUGEN the company is all angels and madmen and prophets! Don't think I'm a jerk!"[2]

p. 86
Bonnie and Ray Bremser at 707 Scott Street, San Francisco, 1960. Photograph by Wallace Berman.

p. 87 left
Ray Bremser, *Poems of Madness* (New York: Paperback Gallery, 1965).

p. 87 right
Bonnie Bremser, *For Love of Ray* (London: London Magazine Editions, 1971).

p. 89 left
Alice Neel, *Bonnie Bremser*, 1963. Ink and paper, $29^{1}/_{2}$ x 22 inches. Courtesy Robert Miller Gallery.

p. 89 right
Ray and Bonnie Bremser, c. 1970
Photographer unknown.

Upon his release, Jones gave Bremser a party where he met many major players in the New York literary world, including Frank O'Hara, Diane DiPrima, and Jack Kerouac. Although his parole required him to reside in Jersey City, Bremser snuck away as often as possible, reading his poetry in New York venues such as the Five Spot, the Gaslight Café, and the Judson Church as well at nearby universities including Princeton, Vassar, and Brown. In 1959 after a Washington, D.C. reading with Ginsburg, Corso, Jones, and Peter Orlovsky, he met Bonnie Frazer, a nineteen-year-old Sweetbriar freshman and daughter of a State Department employee. She was immediately swept away by the misfit poet, and the couple married three weeks after they met.

Later that year, Bremser gave a radio interview in Philadelphia in which he denounced prison conditions and spoke on behalf of legalizing marijuana. Shortly thereafter, he was incarcerated for parole violation for six months. A letter to the court from William Carlos Williams helped facilitate his release. Back with Bonnie, who was now pregnant, Bremser ran into trouble again only two weeks later, when he was arrested on suspicion of armed robbery—a crime Bremser swore he did not commit. After a grand jury indicted him in late 1960, he and Bonnie borrowed money from Elaine de Kooning and other friends and took off with their baby, Rachel. En route to Mexico, they passed through the Bay Area where they met and were photographed by Wallace Berman.

The Bremsers' harrowing life in Mexico is chronicled in Bonnie Bremser's tersely poetic, sexually forthright memoirs, *Troia: Mexican Memoirs* (1959, later published as *For Love of Ray*, 1971). Narrated in present tense, the book presents a tough-minded account of their grim existence, including descriptions of Bonnie's stints as a prostitute, prompted as she put it, by "pure necessity." Finally, after about nine months on the lam, while Bonnie was in Mexico City earning money as a hooker, Ray was arrested by local police in Veracruz and extradited to Webb County Jail in Laredo, Texas. Miraculously, Bonnie was able to raise money for his bail and the couple again decided to flee to Mexico. Before they left, they gave their baby up for adoption, a decision that haunted them both.

Back in Mexico City, they lived with Philip Lamantia, while Bremser produced a cycle of "jazz poems," some of which were later collected in *Blowing Mouth/Jazz Poems, 1958–1970* (1978). Still barely eking out a living, the couple's relationship fell apart in 1961. Bonnie remained in Mexico City to pursue another relationship, while Ray risked a return to New York. Living in Manhattan's Lower East Side, he was introduced to some of his longtime jazz heroes, including John Coltrane, Elvin Jones, and McCoy Tyner. He also developed an addiction to cocaine and amphetamines.

After three months, Bonnie returned to Ray. Almost immediately, trouble struck again when Ray was arrested for possession of marijuana and identified as a fugitive from his past conviction. He was incarcerated until 1965, the year in which his first book, *Poems of Madness*, was published, featuring an introduction by Allen Ginsberg. In Ray's absence, Bonnie stayed in New York where she wrote him a series of letters that later became the manuscript for *Troia: Mexican Memoirs*. She was friendly with poets and artists in the New York scene and in 1963 sat for a portrait by Alice Neel.

On release from prison, where Ray had developed an addiction to heroin, he moved back to the Lower East Side

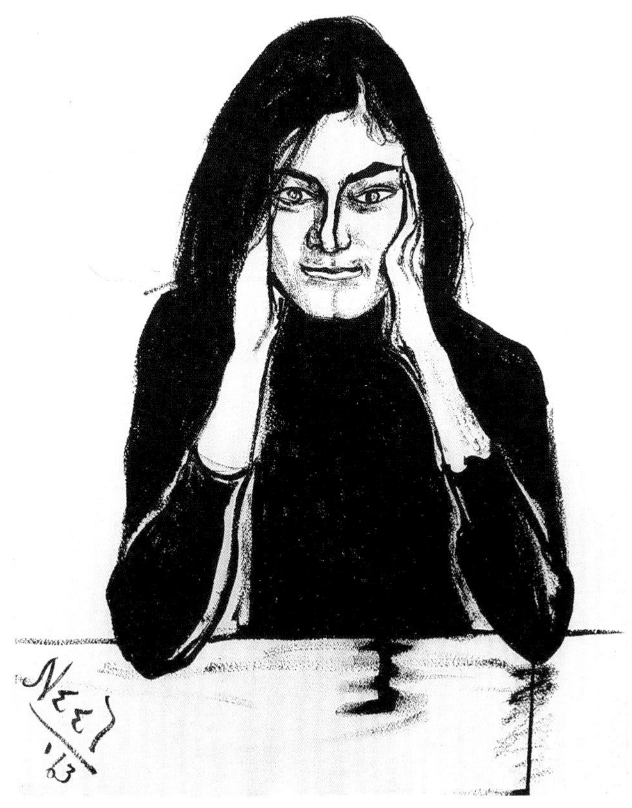

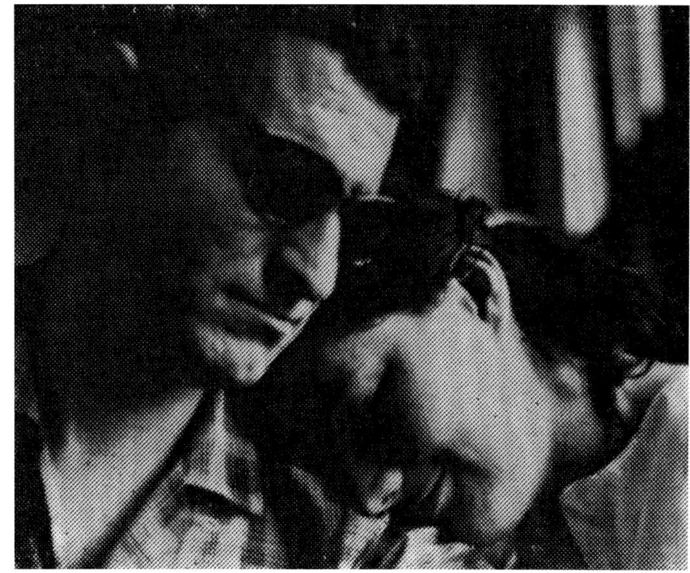

with Bonnie. After a year, he went cold turkey to break his habit. Written while he was in solitary confinement at Trenton State Prison, Bremser's second book, *Angel* (1967, Tompkins Square Press), featured an introduction by Lawrence Ferlinghetti. After Ray finished his term of parole, the couple left New York for Guatemala. Their second child, Georgia, was born in 1967.

Soon destitute and now alcoholic, Ray returned to New York in 1969. Bonnie stayed behind in Central America with a ballet dancer lover. Ray recuperated at Ginsberg's farm in Cherry Valley, New York and again dedicated himself to writing. Bonnie rejoined him the next year after he sent her the manuscript for *Black Is Black Blues* (1971), a series of long poems dedicated to her and their daughter.

While living on the farm, their relationship broke off for the final time. They both, however, continued to live in upstate New York. Ray continued to write and publish, and underwent intermittent treatment for alcoholism. His volume of collected poems, *Blowing Mouth* (1978, Cherry Valley Editions) won him a new cult audience. In the 1980s and 1990s, he took part in a variety of jazz and poetry reading events. He maintained an indigent, bohemian lifestyle in Utica, New York until his death in 1998.

Bonnie remained for years in Cherry Valley where she was transformed by rural life. While working on Ginsberg's farm, she began to study agricultural development, eventually earning a masters degree in biochemistry. In the 1990s Bonnie moved to Michigan where she worked for the Department of Agriculture as a soil surveyor, "having left her Beat life far behind."[3] Now retired, she has returned to writing. *Michael Duncan*

1 Biographical information taken from Arnold Moodnik and Mikhail Horowitz, "Ray Bremser," and Michael Perkins, "Bonnie Bremser," in Ann Charters, ed., *The Beats: Literary Bohemians in Postwar America—Dictionary of Literary Biography 16, Part 1:A–L* (Detroit: Bruccoli Clark/Gale Research, 1983) p. 33–42.

2 Ray Bremser letter to Allen Ginsberg, November 5, 1958, Allen Ginsberg Letters, Special Collections, Stanford University Libraries.

3 Brenda Knight, ed. *Women in the Beat Generation* (Berkeley: Conari Press, 1998), p. 270. Also see interview with Brenda Frazer (Bonnie Bremser) in Nancy M. Grace and Ronna C. Johnson, *Breaking the Rule of Cool: Interviewing and Reading Women Beat Writers* (Jackson: University Press of Mississippi, 2004), p. 109–133.

Charles Brittin

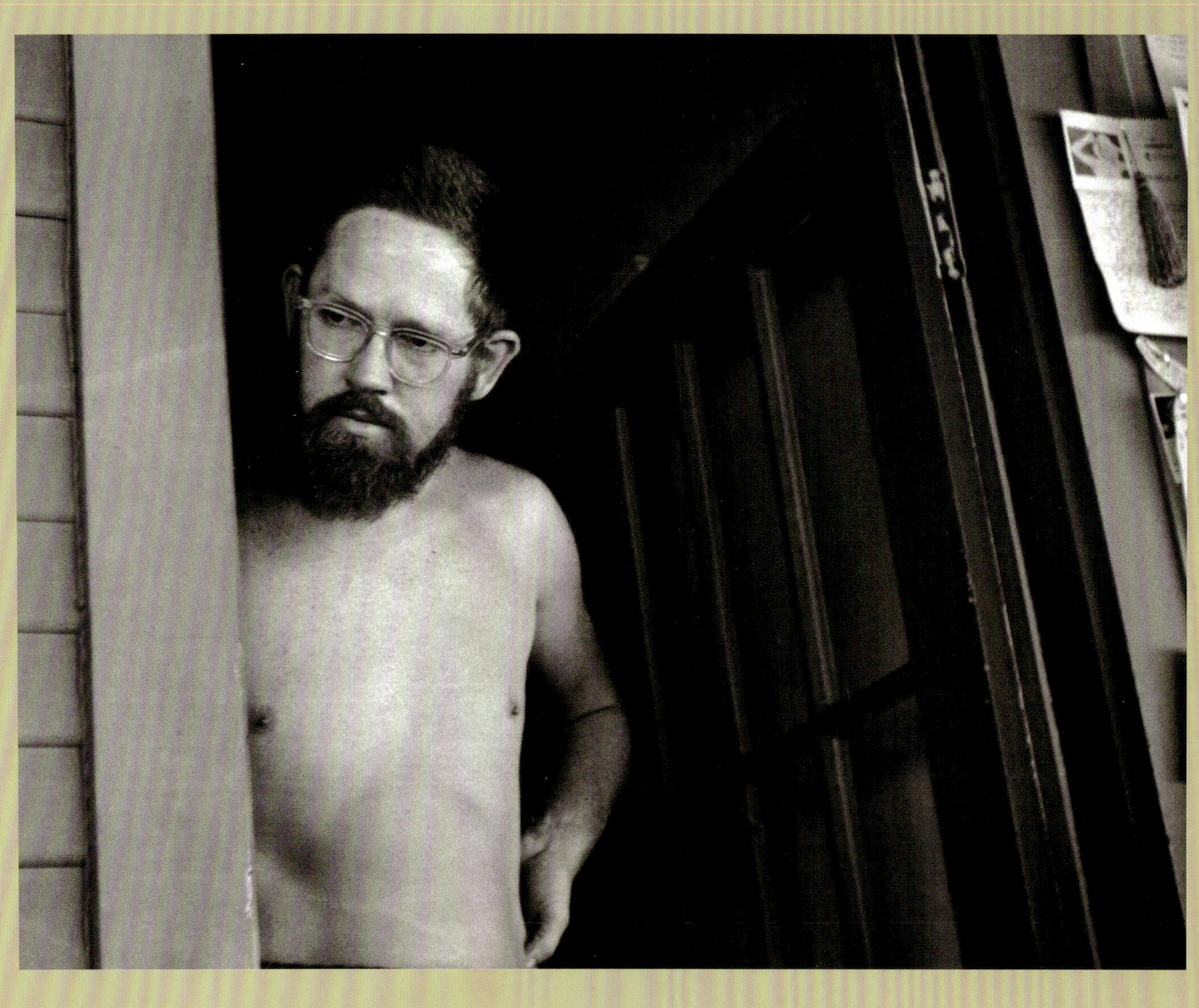

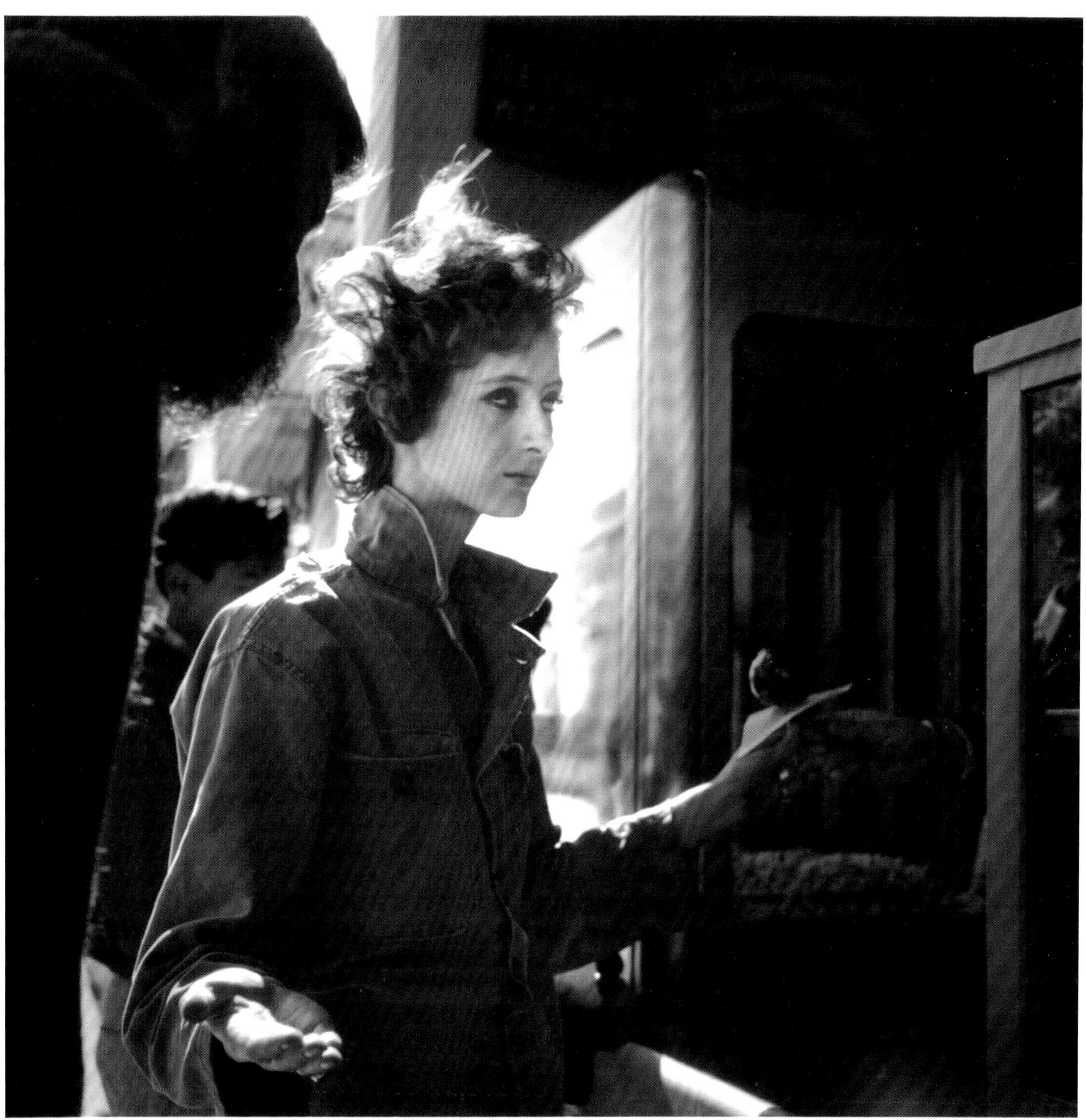

Throughout the 1950s, Charles Brittin was the unofficial house photographer for Wallace Berman and the community that coalesced around him. Born in Cedar Rapids, Iowa, in 1928, Brittin had two sisters who were much older, and he essentially grew up as an only child. When he was fifteen his father died, and the following year Brittin and his mother moved to Los Angeles where they spent their first year staying with family friends in the Fairfax district; that time was a period of huge transformation for Brittin. "It seemed like a foreign country to me," recalls Brittin of the largely Jewish neighborhood. "After six months at Fairfax High I was a Marxist, a radical, and I'd found the world culturally."[1]

In 1946 Brittin enrolled at UCLA and began hanging out at the Coronet Theater, which was the only place in town screening foreign, experimental and underground films. "The first time I was profoundly affected by a work of art was at the Coronet," says Brittin. "I saw Dreyer's *The Passion of Joan of Arc* and came out of the theater knowing something terrifying and wonderful had happened to me. That film showed me there was something to strive for, so I started taking film classes. By 1950 I knew I wasn't a filmmaker, because I didn't have the confidence to go out and make movies, but I liked shooting film so I started thinking about photography."

By 1951 Brittin was married to his first wife and living in Venice Beach, where he worked as a mailman and spent much of his free time wandering around with a camera. Venice was a sleepy, shabby little beach town back in the 1950s, and was largely the province of marginalized types and the poor. Brittin came to know it intimately, and his pictures from the period are freighted with the hushed beauty and forlorn sweetness particular to the past.

When Brittin's marriage ended in 1955 he found himself alone and adrift, and it was then that he wandered into the world of Wallace Berman. "Wally and Shirley became like family to me," recalls Brittin, who spent the next five years taking photographs of the Bermans and the people they knew. Brittin's Venice apartment became a hangout for the group, and Brittin shot hundreds of pictures of the artists, musicians, poets, models and writers who were forever dropping by. Brittin's friendship with Berman expanded into a collaboration in 1955 when Berman began publishing *Semina*. Because of Brittin's knowledge of darkroom technique, and his enthusiasm for Berman's aesthetic, he wound up doing "lots of darkroom work for Wally." Brittin also shot the covers for *Semina Two* and *5*.

Brittin married again in 1956, but that marriage ended after two years. By that point Berman and many of the people Brittin had befriended through him had decamped to Northern California, and Brittin's life began moving in another direction. He remained close to Berman—they corresponded regularly, and Berman mounted an exhibition of Brittin's pictures at the Semina Gallery in 1961—but he was becoming part of a different community.

In 1962 Brittin and his third wife, Barbara, joined CORE (the Congress of Racial Equality) and embarked on a decade of political activism. Brittin captured all of it with his camera, and his photographic archive came to include searing images of the deep South in the early 1960s, the myriad anti-war actions of the period, the 1967 march on the Pentagon, and the Black Panthers.

"In the early 1960s the Freedom Rides were happening, and the political turmoil of the Cold War and the aftermath of the atomic bomb were out there just waiting to affect me," says Brittin, who supported himself working as a photographer for Charles and Ray Eames from 1963 through 1970. "I suddenly realized I was compelled to do something because the times demanded it."

In the 1970s Brittin was forced to curtail his activities when his health began to fail; it wasn't until he underwent a 1990 liver transplant, then a kidney transplant in 1996, that he was able to resume his work as an artist. "Since I survived I feel I have the chance to do things I'd never thought of doing," says Brittin, whose work was the subject of an exhibition organized in 1999 by Walter Hopps for Santa Monica's Craig Krull Gallery. The following year Brittin began making video pieces, and in 2002 his photographs were featured in *Arthur* and *Mojo*. The Getty Research Institute acquired Brittin's photographic archive in 2005, and in 2006 Greybull Press will publish a monograph that includes images culled from fifty-four years of work. Brittin lives in Santa Monica, California.

Kristine Mckenna

p. 90
Charles Brittin, Venice Beach, 1956, Photograph
by Wallace Berman.

p. 91
Shirley Berman, Ocean Park Pier, 1957, Photograph
by Charles Brittin.

p. 93 left
John Reed, Venice, 1955, Photograph by Charles Brittin.

p. 93 right
Wallace Berman, Mailer to Charles Brittin, 1960.

p. 94 left
Wallace Berman, Ferus Gallery, 1957, Photograph
by Charles Brittin.

p. 94 right
Robert Alexander, Ferus Gallery, 1957, Photograph
by Charles Brittin.

p. 95
Arthur Richer, Syndell Studios, 1955, Photograph
by Charles Brittin.

1 All quotations from a conversation with Charles Brittin, December 5, 1999.

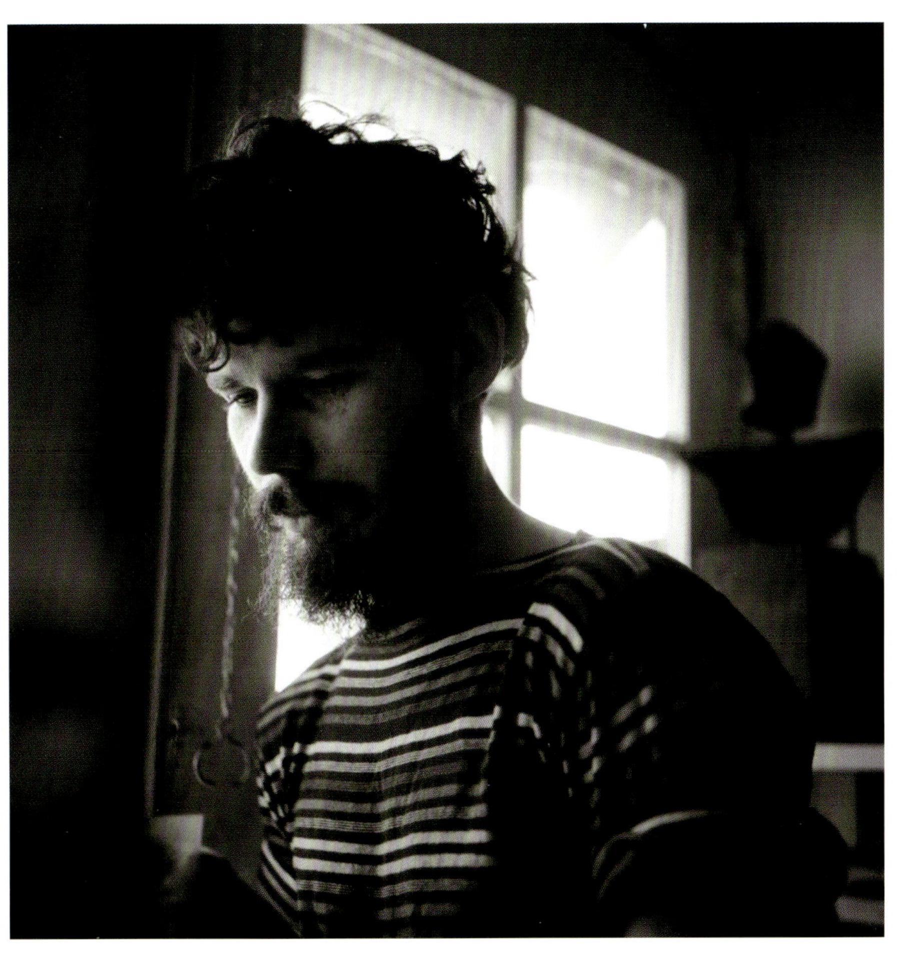

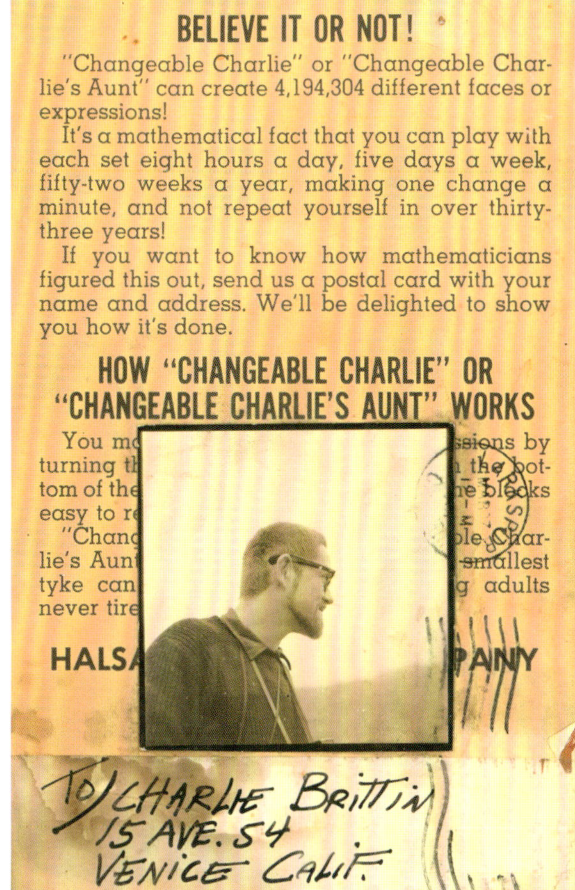
BELIEVE IT OR NOT!

"Changeable Charlie" or "Changeable Charlie's Aunt" can create 4,194,304 different faces or expressions!

It's a mathematical fact that you can play with each set eight hours a day, five days a week, fifty-two weeks a year, making one change a minute, and not repeat yourself in over thirty-three years!

If you want to know how mathematicians figured this out, send us a postal card with your name and address. We'll be delighted to show you how it's done.

HOW "CHANGEABLE CHARLIE" OR "CHANGEABLE CHARLIE'S AUNT" WORKS

You mo… …ssions by turning th… …n the bottom of the… …e blocks easy to r…

"Chang… …ble Charlie's Aunt… …smallest tyke can… …g adults never tire…

HALSA… …PANY

TO/ CHARLIE BRITTIN
15 AVE. 54
VENICE CALIF.

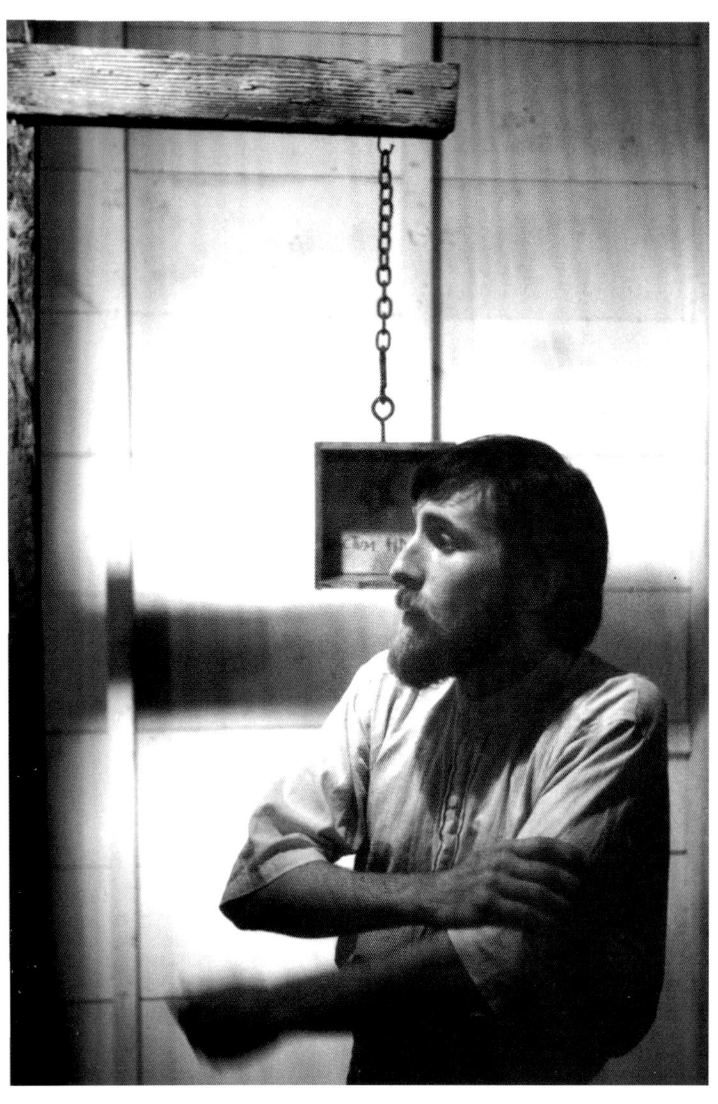

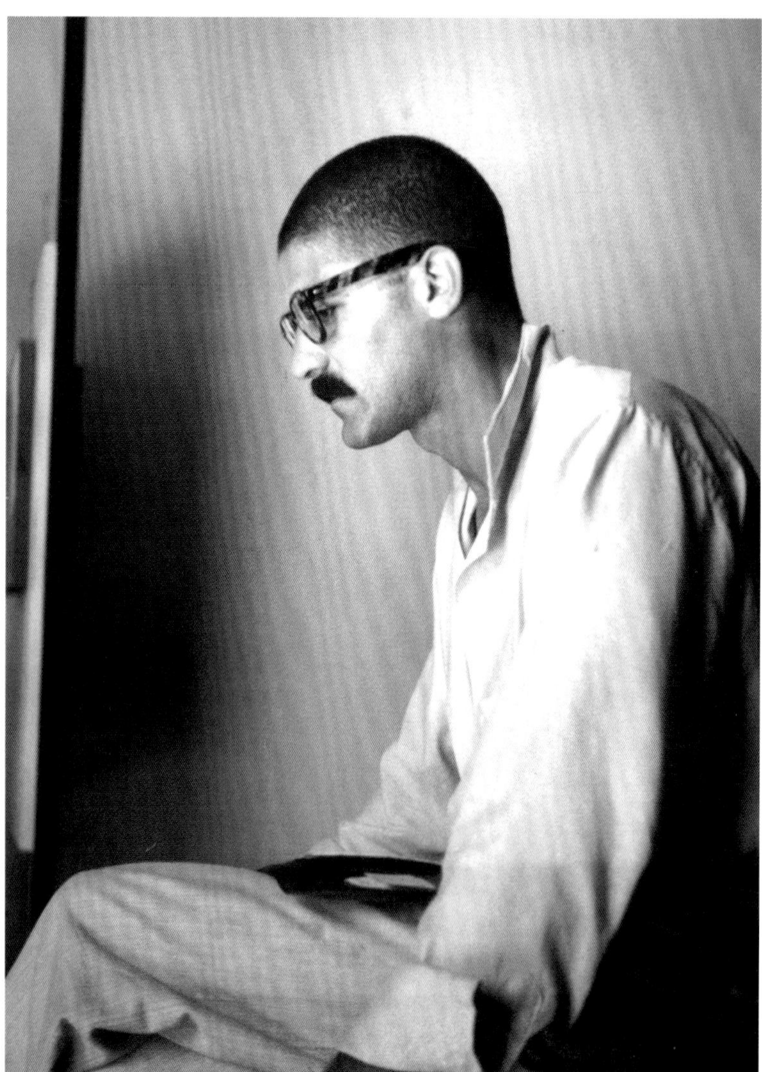

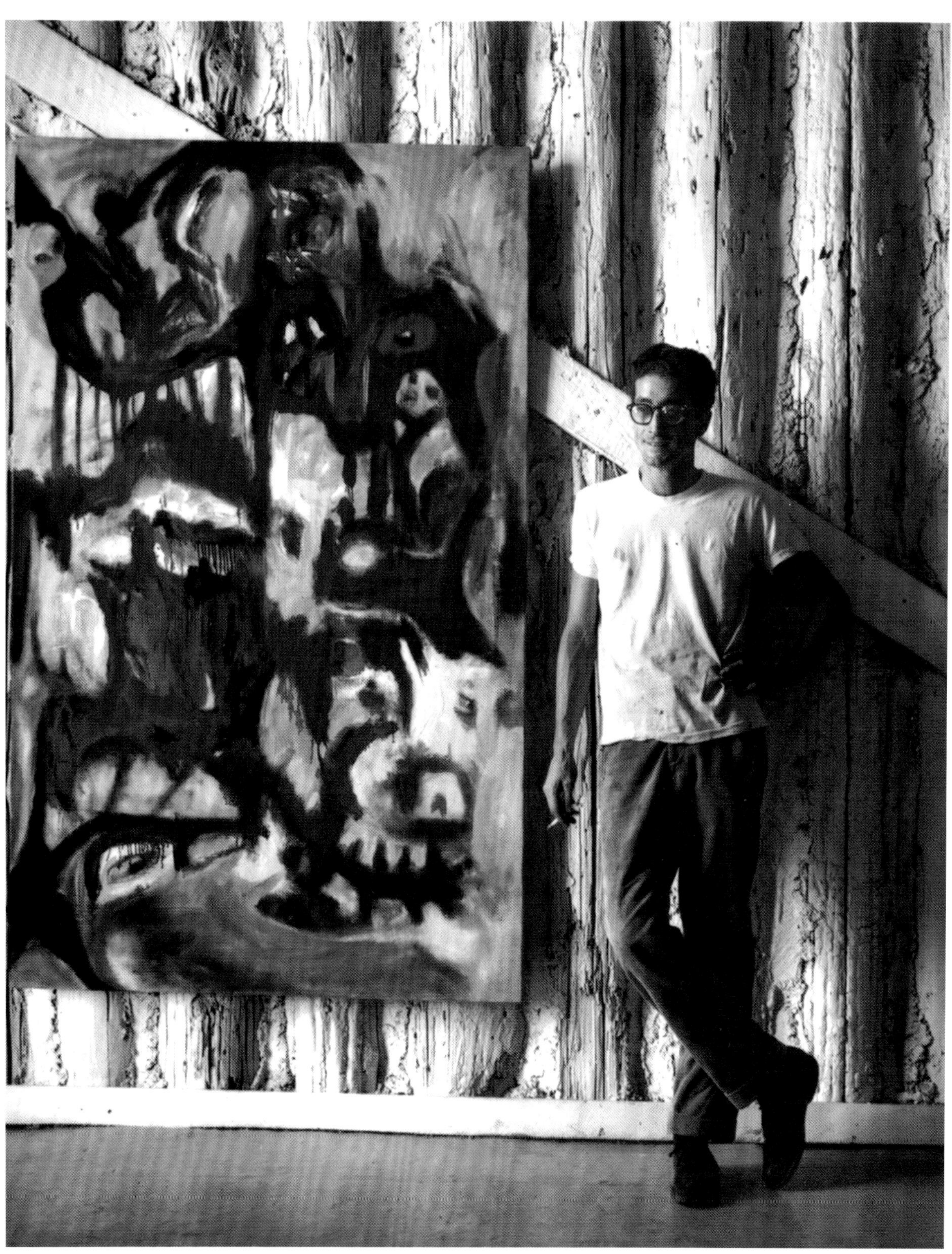

Joan Brown

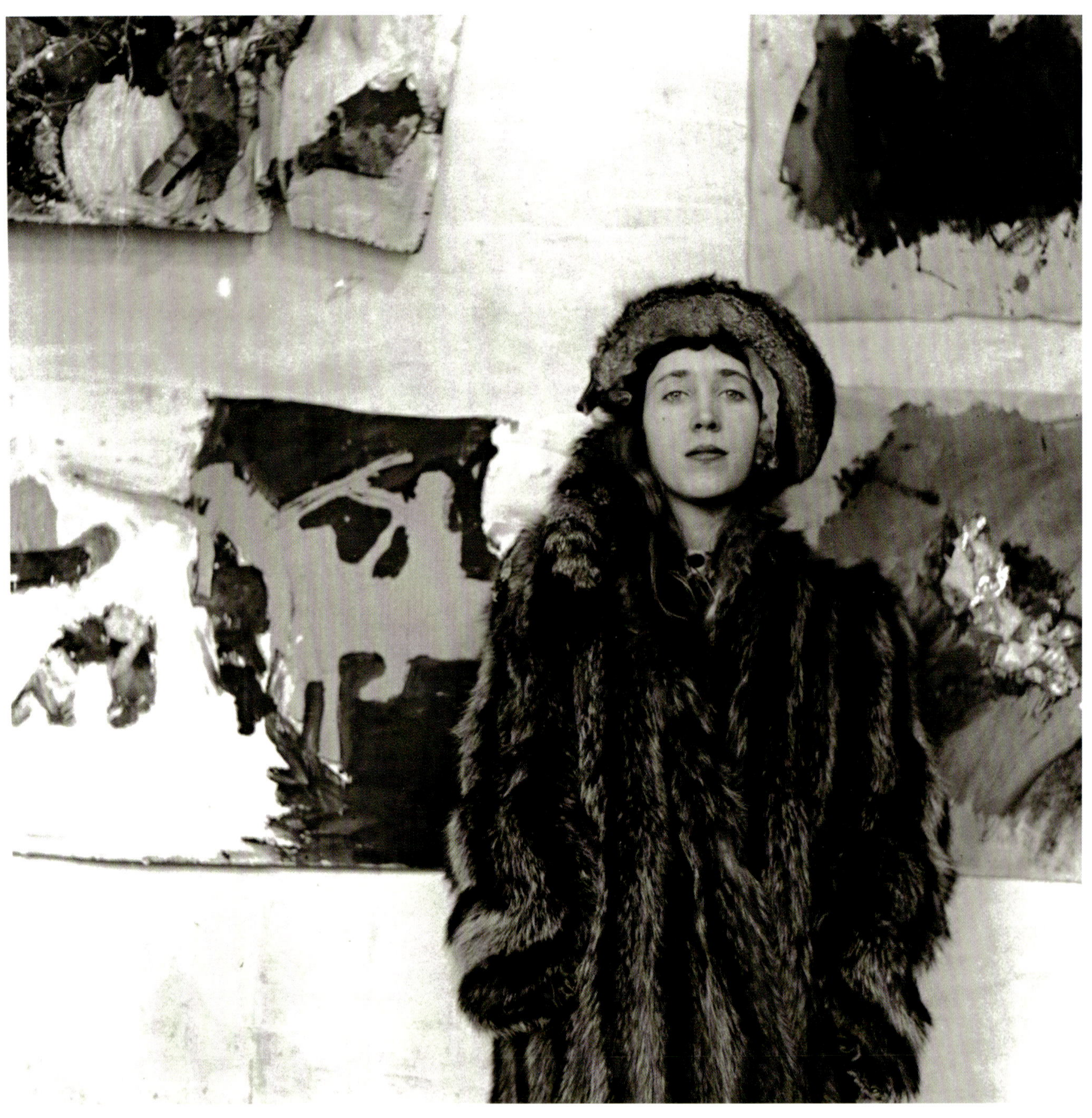

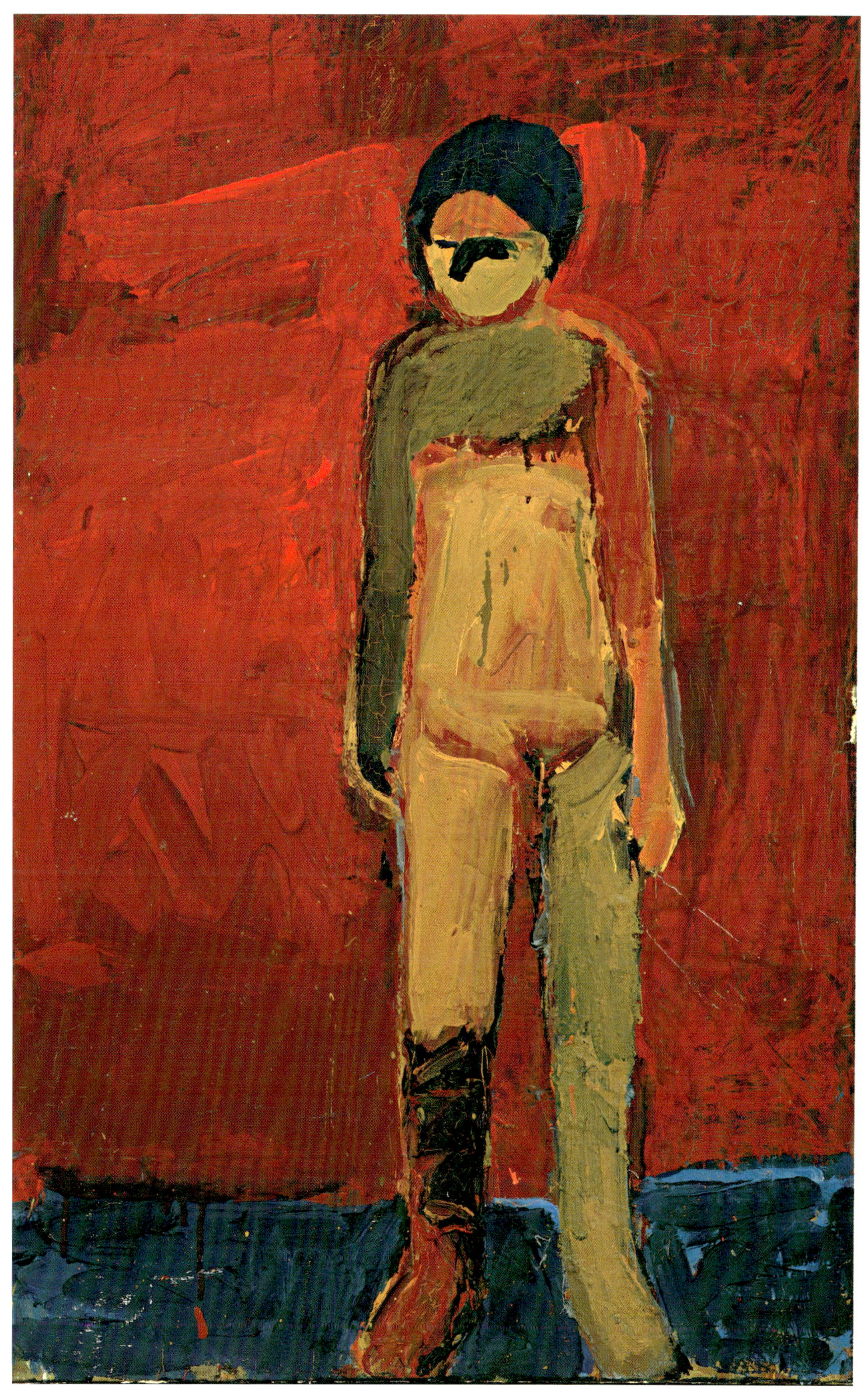

Bay Area painter Joan Brown applied Abstract Expressionism's emphasis on subjectivity and interior investigation to quirkily confessional self-portraits and narrative paintings of domestic scenes. Toying with traditions of self-portraiture as she mined her personal life for subject matter, her work provides a crucial link between Abstract Expressionism and the 1970s performance work of artists such as Eleanor Antin, Hannah Wilke, and Carolee Schneemann. By exploring confessional modes, Brown was able to probe social and psychological assumptions about gender and identity that presage ideas in much current figurative work. Her irreverent explorations of the conflicted roles associated with femininity make her seem a kind of god-mother of contemporary "Bad Girl" artists such as Karen Kilimnik and Nicole Eisenman.

Born in 1938 and a resident of the Bay Area all her life, Brown attended the San Francisco Art Institute (then called the California School of Fine Arts) in the wake of its Abstract Expressionist explosion (1955–59), studying with Elmer Bischoff, Nathan Olivera, and Richard Diebenkorn. Brown's stubborn independence and strong will was fostered by the fact that—unlike most young women artists of her generation—she experienced little difficulty in being recognized for her work. Discovering in art school a visceral facility with paint, Brown soon was keeping pace with her stellar group of teachers, showing at age twenty-two with New York's Staempfli Gallery. In 1962 she received the Merit Award for Art from *Mademoiselle*. Early works were purchased by the Albright-Knox Museum and the Museum of Modern Art.

p. 96
Joan Brown, Spatsa Gallery San Francisco, 1958. Photograph by Wallace Berman.

p. 99
Joan Brown, Self Portrait, 1958, oil on canvas.

p. 98
Joan Brown, *The Day Before the Wedding*, 1962. Oil on canvas, 72 x 81 inches. Minnesota Museum of American Art, Saint Paul.

p. 99
Joan Brown and Man on Horseback, 1957. Photograph by Wallace Berman.

Brown worked on a large, often human-sized scale with vivid colors, slathered impasto, and homespun comedy, flaunting a fearless gutsiness that rivaled that of any of the older generation of Bay Area paint-slingers. Her independent-thinking, action-packed life can be tracked in many self-portraits and repeated depictions of her four husbands, son, pets, and friends.

Brown's early work seems generated out of the collective energy of her extraordinary peer group. In 1958, while married to painter William Brown, she lived next door to Jay DeFeo and Wally Hedrick at 2330 Fillmore Street. While living with painter Manuel Neri from 1959

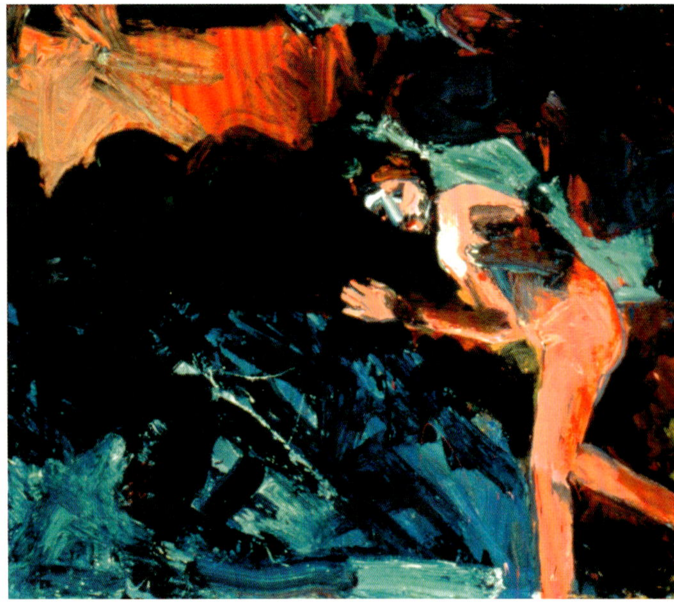

to 1966, Brown was neighbor and friend to artists Wallace Berman, Jess, George Herms, and Jean and Bruce Conner, most of whom she showed with at San Francisco's artist-run galleries. Early on, Brown enjoyed solo exhibitions at The Six Gallery (1957), Spatza Gallery (1958), and Batman Gallery (1961). In her 1975 interview in the Archives of American Art, Brown credited Berman with being a loose kind of spiritual center of their "moral group," whose attitude, for her, stood "for the whole idea of the individual."[1]

Brown's crude, rag-covered sculpture, *Man on Horseback* (1962) is indicative of the funky expressionism of this community of grunge-loving artists; their group was jokingly dubbed by Conner the "Rat-Bastard Protective Association." Brown clearly responded to the darkly comic beauty of Conner's assemblages, the sensitivity of Jess's early paintings, and the spontaneity of Neri's slapdash plaster sculptures. The intense brushwork of DeFeo's masterful early paintings also clearly made an indelible impact.

Embracing the iconoclasm, sincerity, and homespun funkiness of her peers, Brown shifted the energies and exploratory passions of Abstract Expressionism into the kitchen. By domesticating the movement's intensity, her paintings convey a kind of ipso-facto feminism. Her wild brushwork reveals not post-war angst or existential machismo but instead celebrates the physical presence of Brown's son, dog, and even her refrigerator.

But in 1965—just as Pop and the San Francisco Beat era were in full gear—Brown put the brakes on her career. Deciding that she could too easily fake spontaneity in her work, she retreated from her large-scale, showy expressionist style to labor for an entire year on a small, thinly worked painting depicting an arrangement of cucumbers and eggs, *Still Life #1*. This shift prompted Brown's break with her New York dealer and initiated the investigation of symbolic figuration that she would pursue for the rest of her life.

A variety of new interests and influences now occupied the artist. A series of drawings and cartoon-like paintings of animals reflected her enthusiasm for the imagery of Henri Rousseau. She endowed depictions of dogs and cats with mysterious inner lives; through them, she seemed to channel her own quest for identity. Similarly, Brown's remarkable 1970s self-portraits explored the notion of the self as an objectified icon. Although Brown was resistant to the organized feminist movement, her work offers a thorough critique of the social bonds and stereotypes that continue to constrain the female gender.

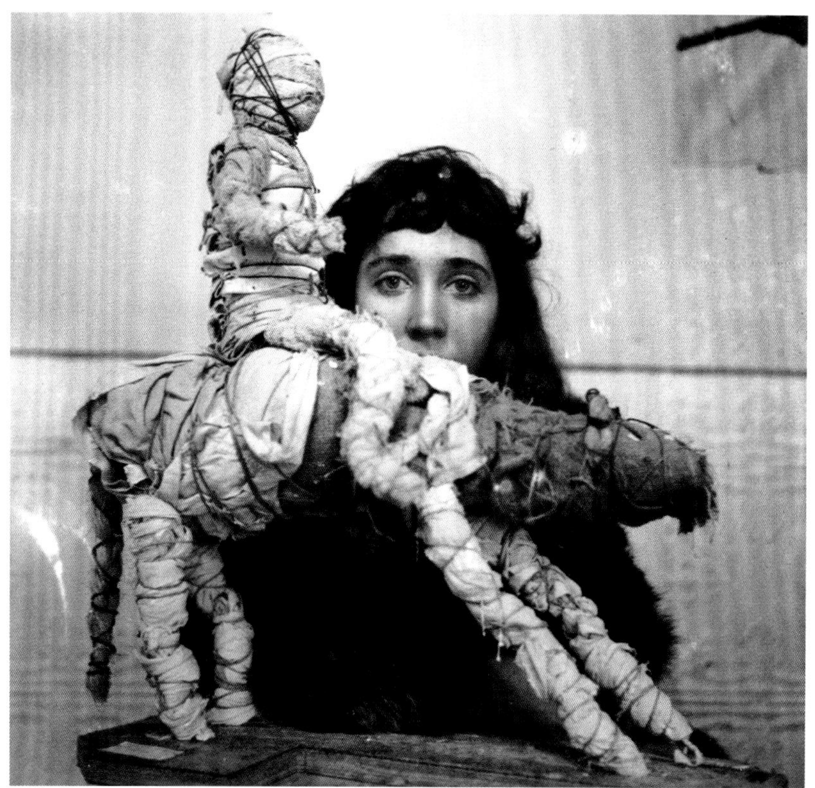

When Brown took up long-distance swimming, she embraced it as heroic, metaphysical subject matter for paintings. Swimming for Brown was an exercise in self-discipline that brought her face-to-face with her own physical limitations. In 1975 she nearly drowned in a group swim from Alcatraz Island to the San Francisco coast. In a series of remarkable works titled *After the Alcatraz Swim* (1975), she showed how difficult it was to comprehend her near-death experience.

In the late 1970s Brown continued to transform her life into art as she pursued a kind of open-jawed spiritual quest; at this point images drawn from ancient Egyptian religion, theosophy, and Hinduism began to appear in the paintings. Brown's late paintings draw on images from the arcane and outré teachings of Edgar Cayce, Paul Brunton, Madame Blavatsky, Jane Roberts' Seth, and the Egyptian pharaoh Akhenaton. These works have drawn a less than enthusiastic critical response.

In the last eight years of her life, Brown constructed eleven tiled, outdoor obelisks featuring iconic images of animals and nature. Modeled after Egyptian obelisks, some over forty feet high, these large-scale public works sampled symbols from a wide variety of cultures and religions in hopes of reaching a broad audience with a kind of all-purpose spiritual message. Brown's experiments in self-portraiture and symbolic figuration came to a tragic halt in 1990 with a fatal accident during the installation of an obelisk designed for Sathya Sai Baba's museum at his ashram in Puttaparthi, India.

Brown's death seems particularly unfortunate for the assessment of her work, since it occurred in a stylistic transition period when the artist had retreated from painting to search for a more direct means of symbol-making in public sculpture. Her work was surveyed by the Oakland Museum and Berkeley Art Museum in 1998.

Michael Duncan

1 "Joan Brown Interview," with Paul Karlstrom, July 1–September 9, 1975, Archives of American Art, Smithsonian Institution, Reel 3196, p. 27.

Cameron

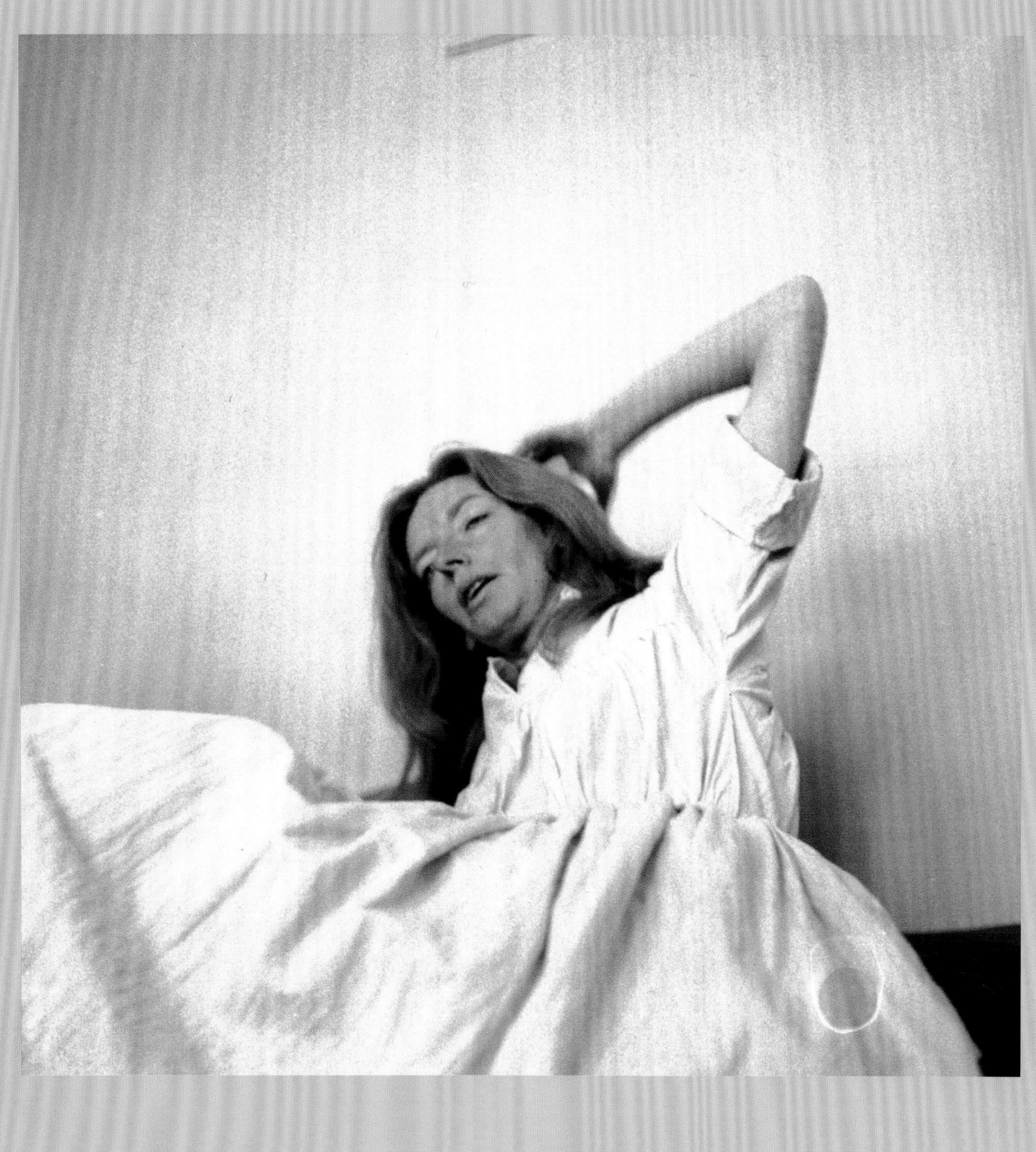

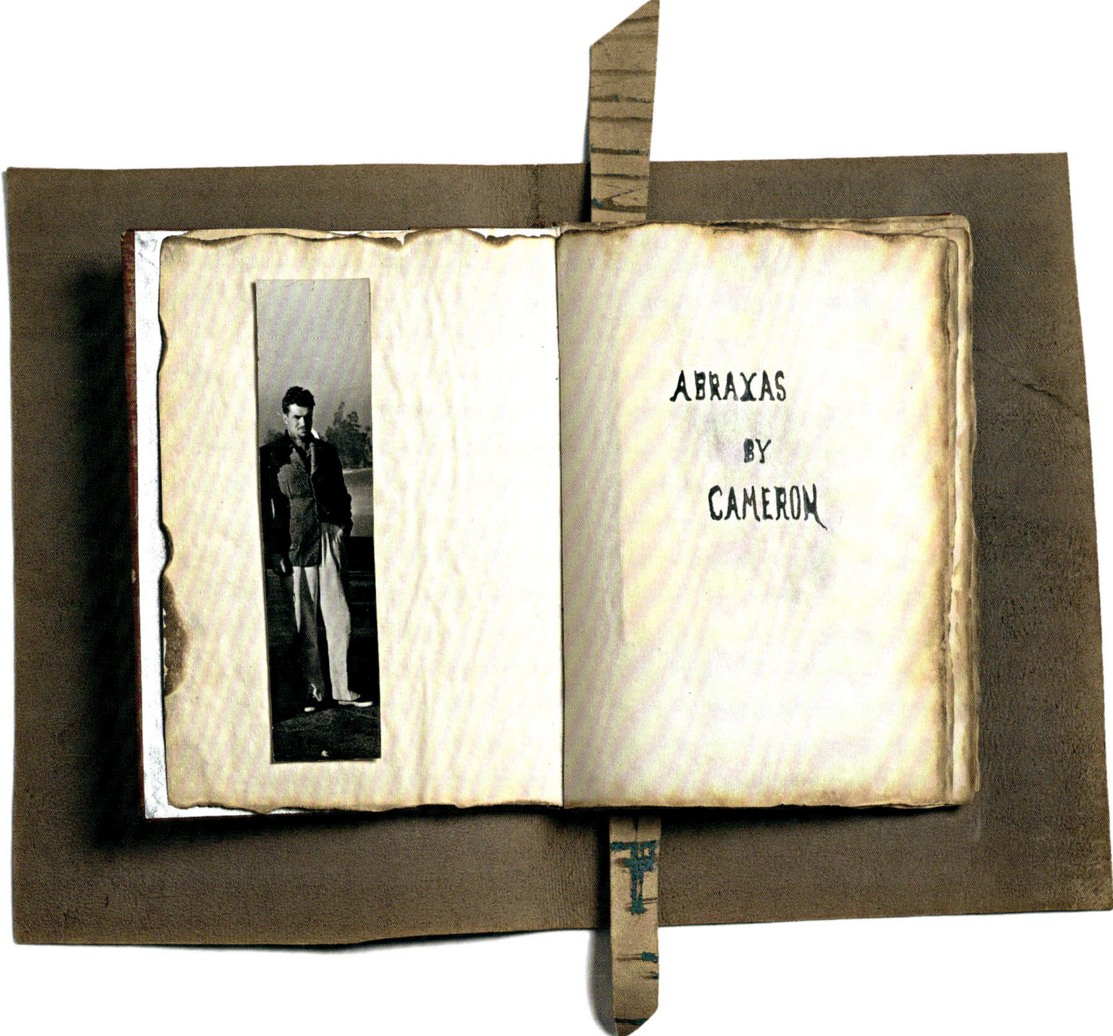

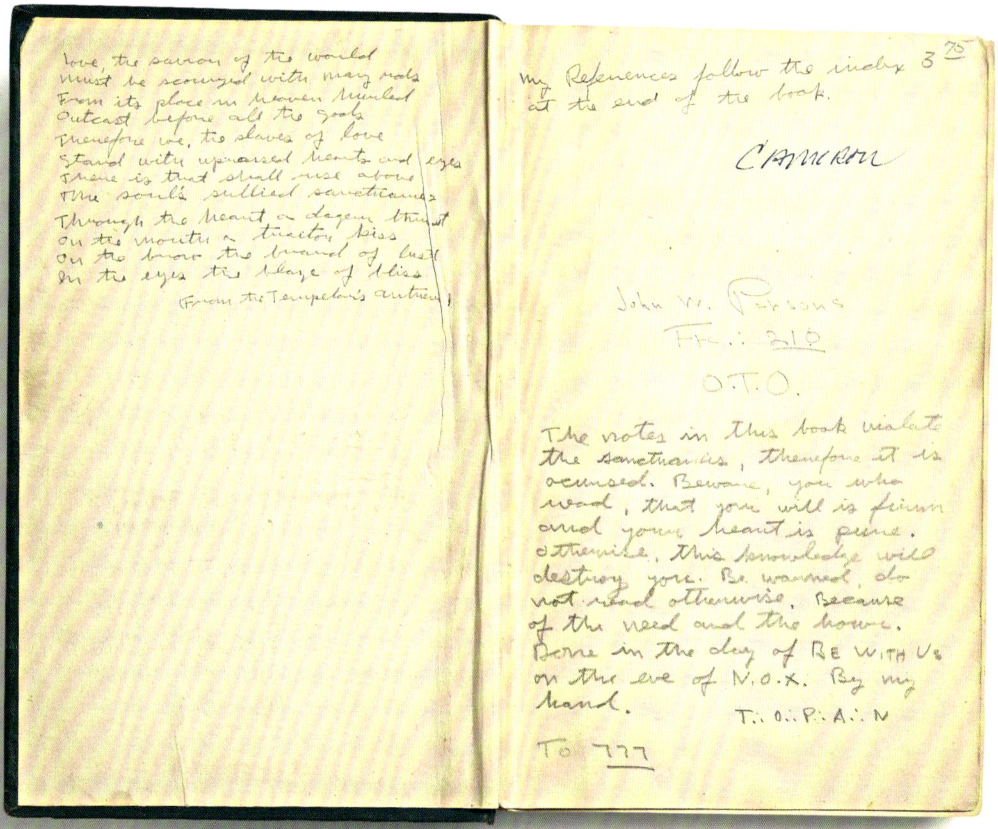

love, the saviour of the world
must be scourged with many rods
From its place in heaven hurled
Outcast before all the gods
Therefore we, the slaves of love
Stand with upraised hearts and eyes
There is that shall rise above
The soul's sullied sanctuaries
Through the heart a dagger thrust
On the mouth a traitor kiss
On the brow the brand of lust
In the eyes the blaze of bliss
(From the Templar's anthem)

My References follow the index at the end of the book. 3 75

CAMERON

John W. Parsons
Fr.: 210
O.T.O.

The notes in this book violate the sanctuaries, therefore it is accursed. Beware, you who read, that your will is firm and your heart is pure. otherwise, this knowledge will destroy you. Be warned, do not read otherwise. Because of the need and the hour. Done in the day of BE WITH US on the eve of N.O.X. By my hand.

T.: O.: P.: A.: N

To 777

Artist, performer, poet, and occult practitioner, Cameron (Marjorie Cameron Parsons Kimmel) is one of the most fascinating underground figures of her generation. A maverick follower of the esoteric mysticism of Aleister Crowley and his philosophical group, the O.T.O. (Ordo Templi Orientis), she was also an accomplished painter and draftsman and mentor to younger artists such as George Herms and Aya Tarlow. A powerful personality, she led a rebellious and troubled life fraught with hardship and poverty. Her sensitive drawings and paintings, however, delineate a magical realm of metamorphosis and protean transformation. Featuring symbolic creatures in imaginary landscapes, her delicately articulated artworks rival those by fellow surrealists such as Leonora Carrington, Remedios Varo, and Ithell Colquhoun.

p. 100
Cameron, 1962, Photograph by Wallace Berman.

p. 101 top
Cameron, *Abraxas* sketchbook, c. 1957.

p. 101 bottom
Cameron's annotated copy of Eliphas Lévi, *The History of Magic* (New York: E.P. Dutton, Third Edition, 1947), Collection of Temple of Man.

p. 102
Cameron, *Untitled (Lady in the Lake)*, 1962, Ink and gouache on paper.

p. 103 left
Cameron, *Hekas, Hskin Etoz Beahi I*, c. 1955, Gouache on paper on cardboard.

p. 103 right
Cameron, *Untitled (Winged Angel)*, c. 1960, Gouache on black paper.

p. 104
Cameron, *Untitled (Crystal)*, c. 1961, Ink on gouache on wood panel.

p. 105
Wallace Berman, Collage mailer to Cameron, 1962, Photograph of Cameron by Wallace Berman, 1955.

Cameron's biography is shrouded in mystery. Born in 1922 in Belle Plain, Iowa, she was a cantankerous child whose mystical, artistic nature went against the grain of her railroad-worker father, church-going family, and small town neighbors. Graduating from high school at the height of World War II, she enlisted in the Navy and was assigned the tasks of drawing maps and working in a photographic unit, jobs that she later regretted as her "karmic connection" to wartime deaths.[1] Despite her success in these jobs, when she learned that her brother, an Air Force tail gunner, had been injured in action, she fled to Iowa to see him. She was declared AWOL, court-martialed, and confined to the base for the remainder of the war.

Upon discharge from the service, she moved to Pasadena where her parents were then living and where she perhaps attended art classes.[2] Disillusioned with mainstream culture, she became an enthusiastic supporter of jazz, frequenting the black clubs on Central Avenue. Her life was forever changed, however, when an old Navy friend took her to the home of Jack Parsons (1914–1952), one of the founders of the Jet Propulsion Lab, and a star pupil of Crowley and the O.T.O. Instantly struck by Cameron's dramatic red hair and intriguing looks, Parsons was convinced she was his "Scarlet Woman," the incarnation of what he had been searching for in his "sexual magick" experiments.

Indoctrinating her in cult lore, Parsons dubbed her "Candida" and the couple married in 1946. Cameron wavered in her devotion to the occult with sojourns to a Swiss convent and, in 1948, to Mexico where she went to pursue her art. She settled for a time in San Miguel d'Allende where she met artists Leonora Carrington and David Siquieros and the Los Angeles performers Renate Druks and Paul Matheson. During her Mexico period, Parsons sent Cameron a remarkable series of letters instructing her further in magical practices.[3] In 1950 she returned to her husband who was working at that time in explosives research for Hughes Aircraft.

Parsons's occult practices led to extended investigations by the F.B.I. and the termination of his government defense work. The couple planned to leave the country for Mexico in 1952, but Parsons was killed in a freakish explosion in his Pasadena garage laboratory caused by his dropping a container of fulminate of mercury. (His death has caused much speculation by occult conspiracy theorists.) After Parsons's death, Cameron retreated to the desert of Beaumont, California, living for a while in an abandoned canyon without water or power. Returning to Los Angeles, she reintegrated herself with society by painting a series of works called the *Parchments*.[4] She gave birth to a daughter, Crystal, in 1955.

Cameron's romantic esthetic and commanding persona prompted filmmaker Curtis Harrington to commemorate her output as a visual artist in *Wormwood Star* (1955), a lyrical short film recording the art on the walls of her candlelit studio. Paul Mathison and the actor Samson Debrier introduced her to filmmaker Kenneth Anger, who

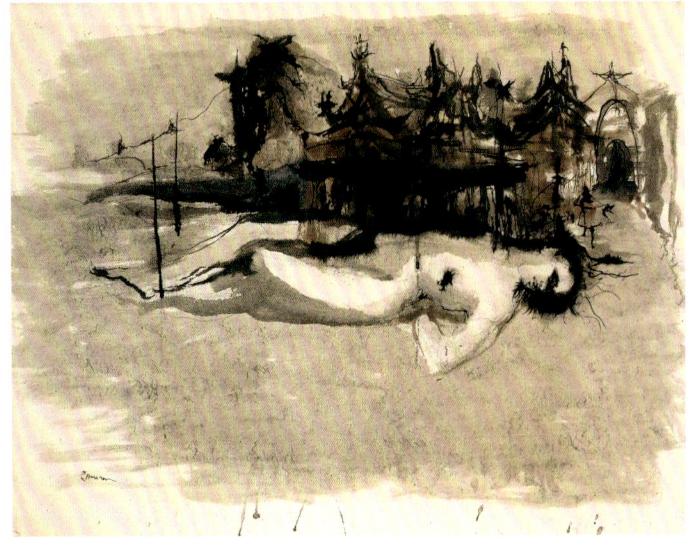

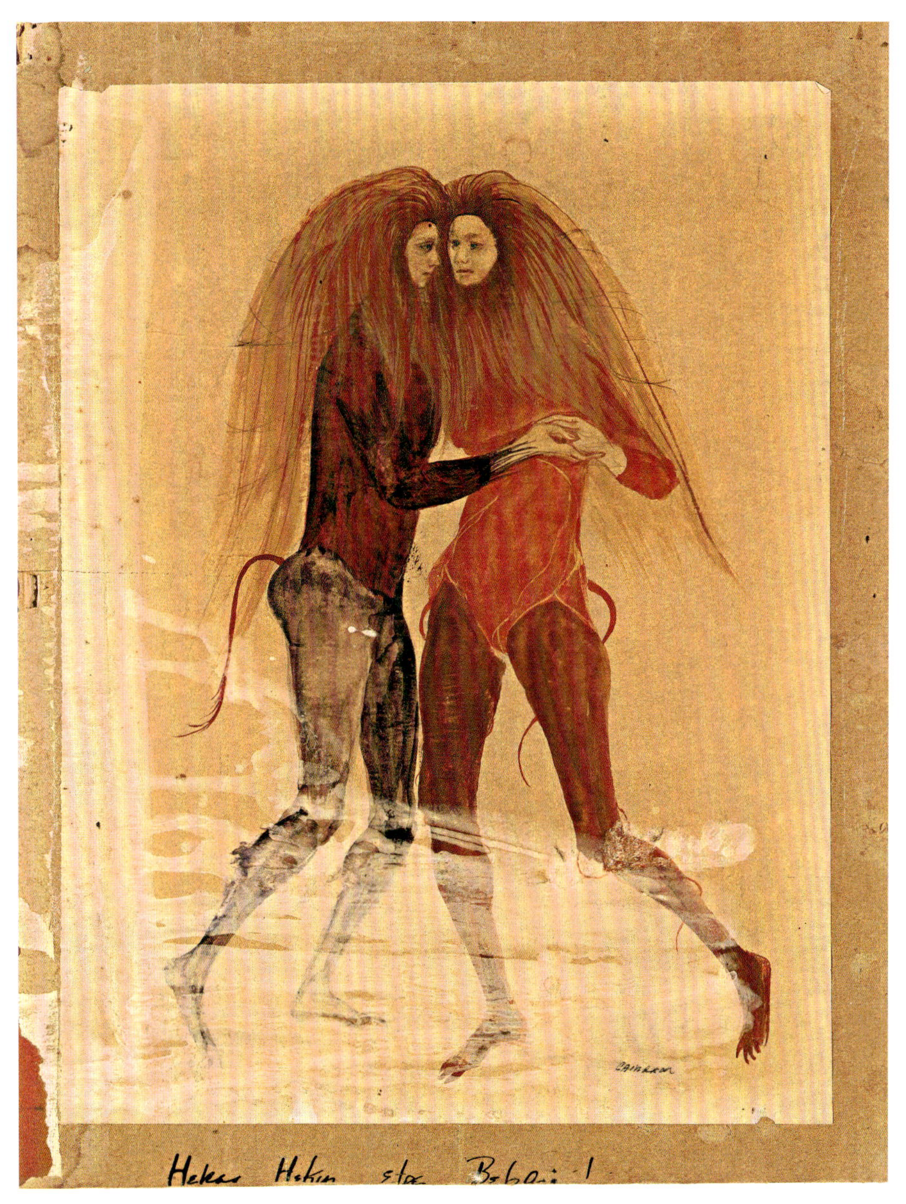

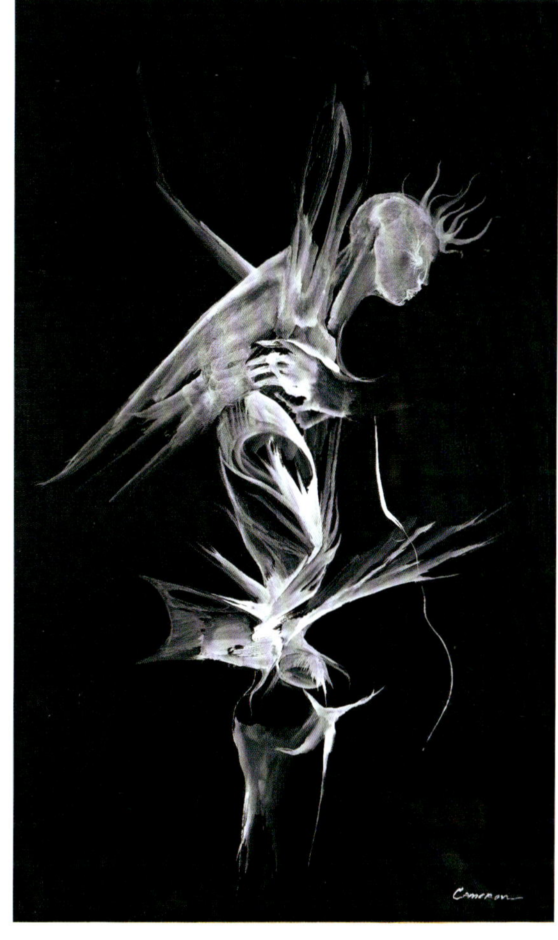
Cameron

cast her in a leading role opposite Anais Nin in his film *Inauguration of the Pleasure Dome* (1956). A striking presence in the film, she enjoyed a tempestuous relationship with Anger for the rest of her life. She also played a role alongside Dennis Hopper in Harrington's feature *Night Tide* (1961). In 1969 she appeared in the unreleased film, *Thumbsuck*, by artist John Chamberlain, filmed in Santa Fe.

In the early 1950s, Cameron met fellow jazz enthusiast Wallace Berman. She later recounted that she was impressed by the fact that, shortly after they were introduced, he gave her a copy of Hermann Hesse's *Steppenwolf*. Although steering clear of her occult activities, Berman was intrigued with her persona and, as she put it in her 1986 interview with Sandra Starr, "He seemed to be interested in somehow promoting me."[5] Berman used his photograph of Cameron on the cover of *Semina 1* and included in the issue a 1954 drawing she had made during her first experience with peyote, which she had taken after hearing a lecture by Aldous Huxley. The drawing became renowned as the image that the Los Angeles Police Department cited as "lewd" and used to shut down Berman's 1957 exhibition at Ferus Gallery. After this experience, Cameron, like Berman, refused to show her art in commercial galleries.

She devoted herself to writings and artworks that explored the ideas of mystical transcendence she had learned from Parsons. In 1964 she self-published *Black Pilgrimage*, a volume of dark poems and ink drawings. Her prose excerpt published in *Semina Two* is a kind of exhortation to her dead husband, invoking a spiritual power: "Rise up! I have surpassed the tomb you dreamed for me." Addressed to Myrha (Smyrna)—who, in Greek mythology, developed an incestuous passion for her father and gave birth to Adonis—Cameron's poem in *Semina 8*, titled *June 2, 1962*, finds no respite from the "dying world" except through the "grace and joy and sorrow" of a child. The kohl-eyed, wild-haired sphinx in the ink drawing accompanying the poem seems incapable of providing solace (see pg. 67).

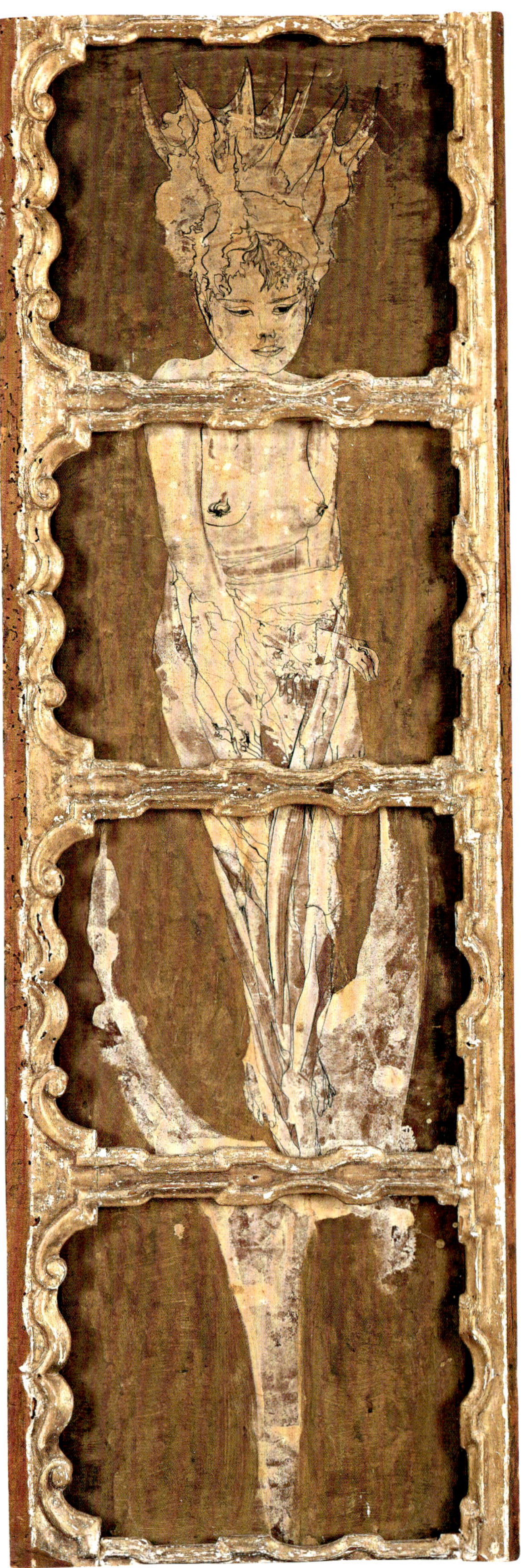

Despite the grim fatality of much of her writings, Cameron's artworks portray a fanciful lyricism. Her portrait panel of her daughter presents Crystal as an extenuated ephebe or sprite, seemingly the embodiment of a mythological figure. In the early 1960s she corresponded with Joseph Campbell, citing her interest in his book *The Hero with a Thousand Faces*, as well as in the fiction of Hermann Hesse and Isak Dinesen.[6]

With a brief sojourn in Santa Fe in the late 1960s, Cameron spent her last decades in a small house in West Hollywood. In 1989 Cameron co-edited with O.T.O. leader Hymenaeus Beta an edition of the occult writings of Parsons.[7] Also that year, Cameron's artworks were surveyed in an exhibition at the Los Angeles Municipal Art Gallery curated by Edward Leffingwell. Titled "The Pearl of Reprisal," that exhibition, her first, included watercolor, ink, and casein drawings from the series *Anatomy of Madness* (1956) and *Pluto Transiting the Twelfth House* (1978–86). Cameron died of cancer in Pasadena in 1995. Her work was included that year in the Whitney Museum of American Art exhibition, "Beat Culture and the New America 1950–1965." *Michael Duncan*

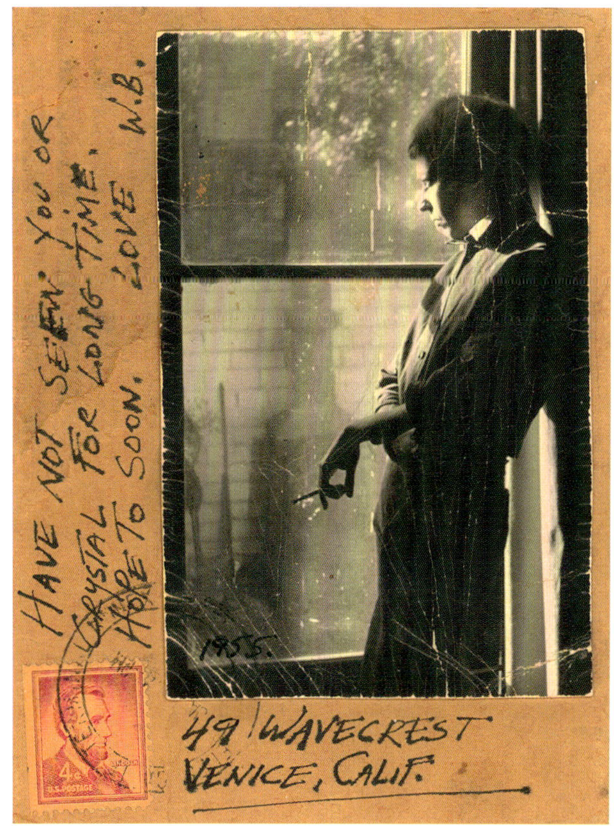

1 Brian Butler. "Cameron: The Wormwood Star," In Richard Metzger, ed. *Book of Lies* (New York: Disinformation, 2003), p. 205.
2 In the archive of Los Angeles artist, Lorser Feitelson, a June 12, 1947 letter from the director of the Académie de la Grande Chaumière in Paris acknowledges Feitelson's sponsorship for "Marjorie Cameron" as a potential pupil in the school. Feitelson taught at the time at Art Center School in Pasadena. Feitelson Archive, Archives of American Art, Smithsonian Institution. Cameron was in Paris in 1947 but there is no record of her attending classes at the Académie.
3 See http://www.bablon.net/jwp/camltrs.html
4 *Book of Lies*, p. 209.
5 Sandra Leonard Starr, *Lost and Found in California*, (Santa Monica: Corcoran, Shoshona Wayne and Pence Galleries), p. 70.
6 Letter from Cameron to Joseph Campbell, October 2, 1961, Cameron archive, collection of Scott Hobbs.
7 Cameron Parsons and Hymenaeus Beta, *Freedom is a Two-Edged Sword* (Tempe, Arizona: New Falcon Publications, 1989).

Bruce Conner

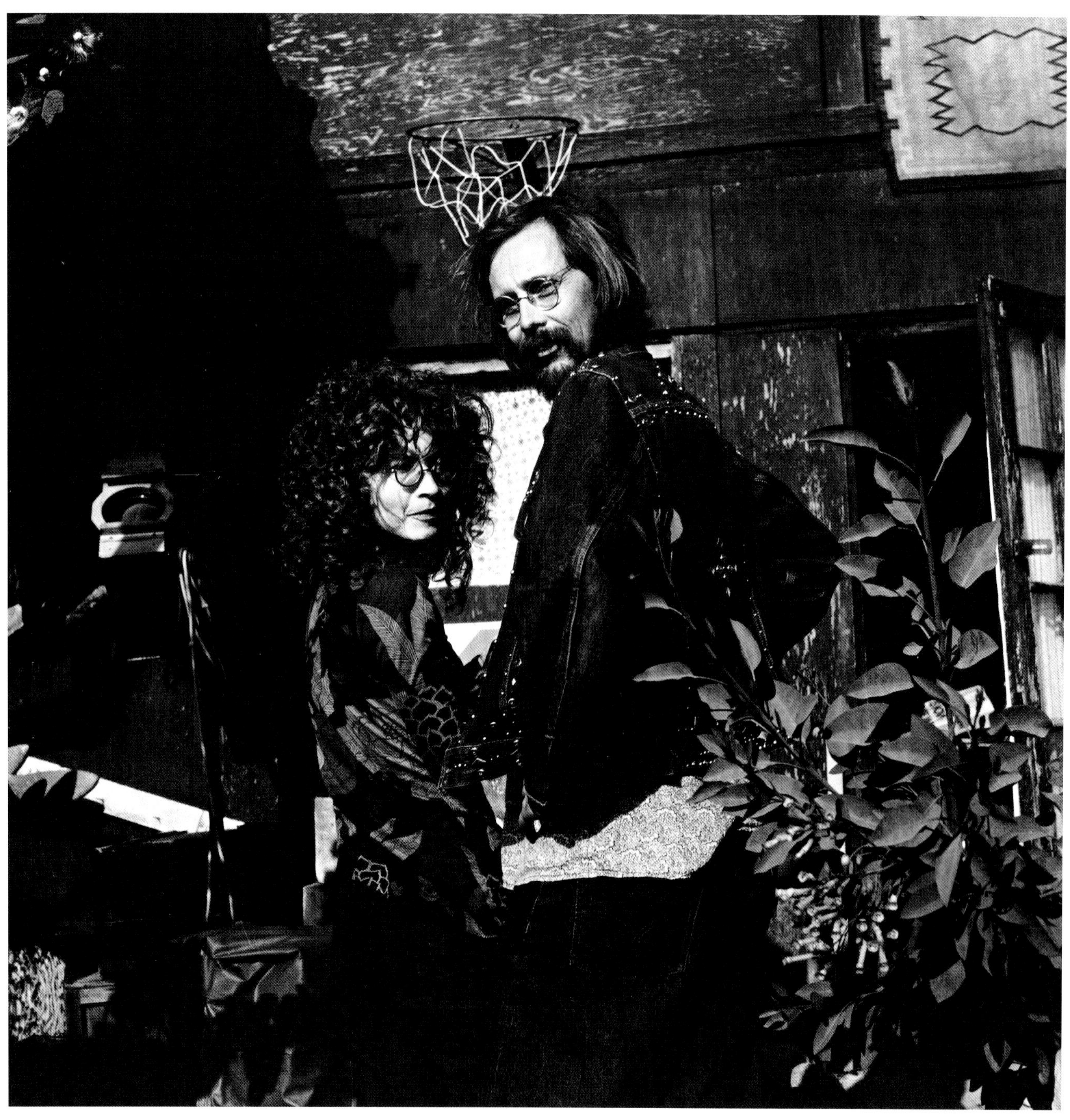

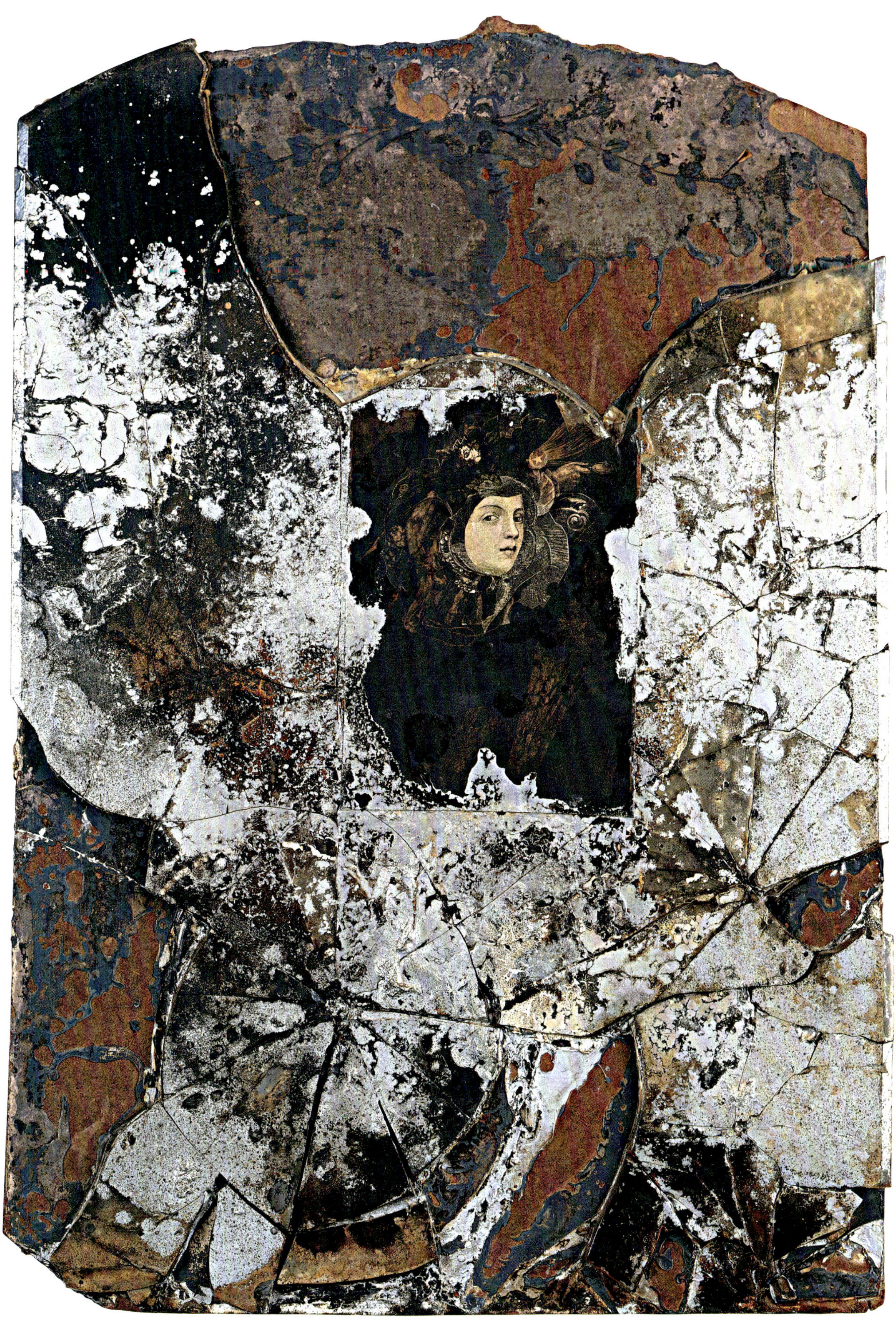

Long known only to cognoscenti, Bruce Conner's films, assemblages, drawings, paintings, collages, photographs, and conceptual stunts have recently gained widespread acclaim. Conner was born in McPherson, Kansas in 1933, grew up in Wichita, and attended the University of Nebraska (B.A., 1956). After short stints at the Brooklyn Museum Art School and the University of Colorado, he and his artist wife, Jean, moved to San Francisco in 1957, following the advice of poet Michael McClure, Conner's childhood friend. Living in a Jackson Street apartment only three blocks away from the Bermans, the Conners fell in with a stellar community of artists and writers that included Jay DeFeo, Wally Hedrick, Joan Brown, Jess, George Herms, and Robert Duncan.

The darker side of sex and romance animates Conner's assemblages of the early 1960s, which are among the most intense, haunted artworks of the past century. These fetishistic conglomerations of feathers, fabric, jewelry, wallpaper, and fur, usually encased in skeins of nylon stockings, suggest loose narratives of violence and unrequited desire.

Conner claims to have gotten the idea for the pendulous shapes of many of his assemblages from the burlap sacks used at the time by San Francisco garbagemen. He explained,

> *When the truck was full, they would hang them on the sides like big lumpy testicles. So they were using all the remnants, refuse, and outcasts of our society. The people themselves who were doing this were considered the lowest people employed in society.... I decided, we'll have the RAT-BASTARD PROTECTIVE ASSOCIATION: people who were making things with the detritus of society, who themselves were ostracized or alienated from full involvement with the society.*[1]

p. 106
Bruce Conner and friend,
Topanga Canyon, 1969,
Photograph by Wallace Berman.

p. 107
Bruce Conner, *Mirror Collage*,
1960, Assemblage on masonite.

p. 109
Bruce Conner, First "Love" Sign
in Haight-Ashbury, Photograph
of Bruce Conners' street graffiti,
San Francisco, 1961, Courtesy
of the artist.

p. 110 left
Bruce Conner, *Chou Rat*, c. 1960,
Mixed Media, 20 x 6 x 6 inches,
courtesy Michael Kohn Gallery.

p. 110 right
Bruce Conner, *Generic Rat Hand
Grenade*, 1960, Assemblage.

p. 111
Bruce Conner,
September 13, 1959, 1959,
Mixed-media assemblage.

For Conner's artist friends, the Rat-Bastard Protective Association was a counterculture version of the Pre-Raphaelite Brotherhood, celebrating their distance from mainstream values. Although they were open to the trashiest elements of pop culture, the Beat artists were inheritors of the introspection of Abstract Expressionism and were grounded in a search for meaning beyond the scope of mainstream Eisenhower America. The underlying earnestness of the Beat movement contrasts vividly with the cynicism of Pop art. As Conner makes the distinction, "We were interested in a spiritual quest. It was a time when people would die or go to jail for their art.... I get impassioned and that's not cool and cool was what Pop art was all about."[2]

Conner further explored the narrative and emotional ramifications of the collage esthetic in *A Movie* (1958), a 16mm film cobbled together from leftover footage bought in a local camera store. Its sequences include sections of newsreels featuring stunts and disasters, blue movies, a Hopalong Cassidy western, a German propaganda film, a compilation film of racing accidents, and various styles of film leader. Conner's zippy editing style, predicated on surreal comic juxtapositions, has been the model for the entire output of MTV and countless television commercials.

In 1961 Conner's dissatisfaction with the conventions of American society led him and Jean to leave the country for Mexico. Based in Mexico City, Conner began to make drawings featuring loosely penciled embryonic forms, patterned mushrooms, and organically blossoming maps. Mexico's third world culture, with its omnipresent Catholic and pre-Columbian imagery, broadened the spiritual base of his work.

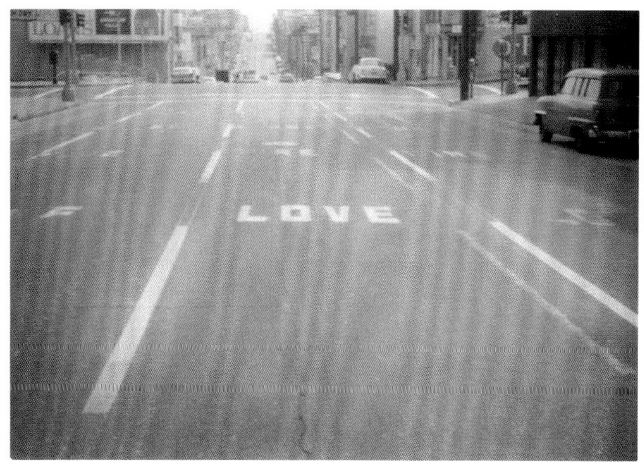

In 1962 the couple returned to the United States following the birth of their son, Robert. Soon Conner—as he put it—"decided not to glue the world down anymore," feeling that he was becoming too identified with assemblage. His ensuing works, the *Mandala Series* (1965), are tightly rendered ink drawings consisting of labyrinthine, meandering lines grouped to create an overall design of target-like concentric circles. The allover drawings function as records of obsessive performances. Conner used Pentel felt-tip watercolor pens that allowed him to keep drawing for hours without lifting pen from paper. The tones and chance wavering of lines create textures whose irregular effects are somewhat like those of the weathered patinas of the antique objects used in the assemblages.

Conner's inkblot drawings (1975–present) similarly explore the conflation of symmetry and chance. Conner arranges the blots in rows that conform to the folds of his pieces of paper. As Conner has noted, the inkblot drawings relate less to Rorschach blots than to the symmetrical forms found in wood grain, traditional ornamentation, and natural objects like snowflakes and crystals.

The mystery of form and the physical representation of the human spirit are manifested in Conner's stunning series of photograms referred to as *Angels* (1974–75). Conner variously positioned himself in front of full-length pieces of photosensitive paper and, with the help of photographer Edmund Shea, experimented with light exposures.

The life-enhancing power of light is raucously celebrated in the five-minute, black and white film *Breakaway* (1966). To the soundtrack of a Phil Spector-ish pop sigle written and performed by Toni Basil, Conner edited footage of the choreographer/singer dancing and cavorting with mod gyrations in various outfits and states of undress. The quick cuts transform Basil's image into swathes of moving light, reflecting the experience of liberation hoped for in the song's lyrics. Then, unexpectedly, when the two-and-a-half minute song is over, the film and soundtrack are reversed. The film describes a "breakaway" from ordinary life, time, and motion that is transcendental and psychedelic. It is one of the great lesser-known artworks of the 1960s, capturing the era's spiritual yearning and utopian vision.

But Conner's idealism is accompanied by extreme political skepticism. *Television Assassination* (1963–64/1995), a fourteen-minute black and white 8mm film projected onto a blank television screen, deconstructs footage of the Kennedy assassination using slow motion detail, repetition, and re-editing. Through stutter-like editing of key sequences, Conner creates a disturbing, numbing account of the traumatic event—and the media's crass collusion in its madness.

In his recent collages based on cutout sections of found engravings, Conner cobbles together surreal allegories, lyrically transforming esoteric and Christian imagery. Conner's surreal approach refurbishes shopworn biblical scenes, heightening their mystery. Conner's romantic faith in the pursuit of artistic truth has led him through a dizzying variety of forms and media. Light on his feet, he has tempered the grand aspirations and heavy themes of his work with humor, iconoclasm, and a healthy love for the absurd. He bypasses the pieties of postmodern thinking, and instead, with extraordinary subtlety and sophistication, rekindles old-fashioned mysteries.

Michael Duncan

1 Interview with Peter Boswell from June 15, 1983 cited in, "Theater of Light and Sound," *2000 BC—The Bruce Conner Story, Part II*, exh. cat. (Minneapolis: Walker Art Center, 1999), p. 41.

2 Remarks at Walker Art Center, October 10, 1999. Conner is clearly referring to Wallace Berman's arrest for obscenity at the 1957 opening of his Ferus Gallery show in Los Angeles.

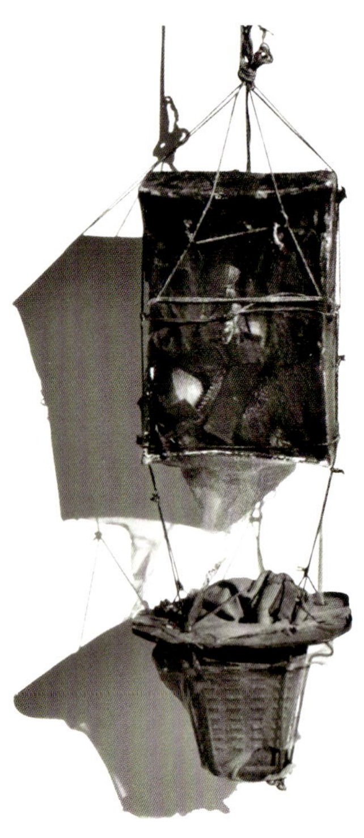

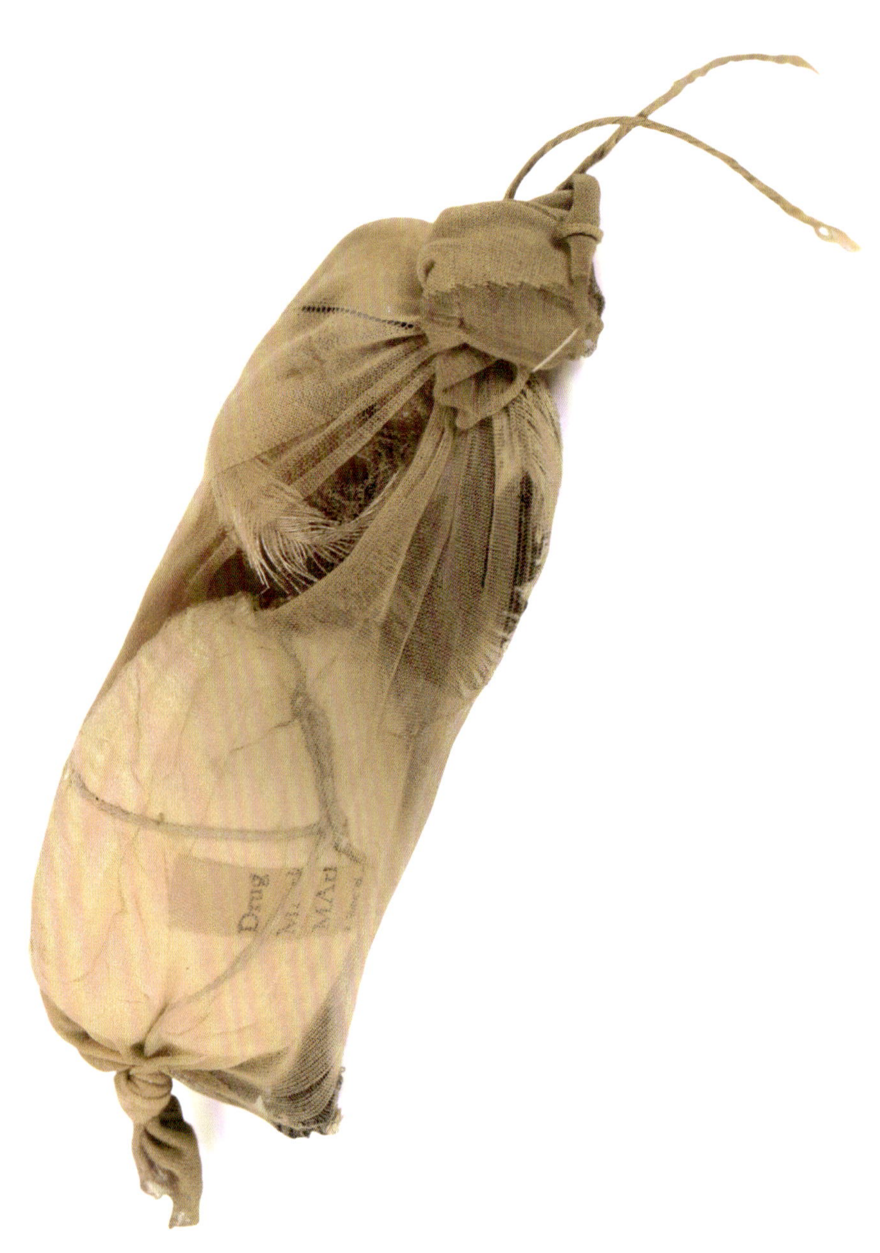

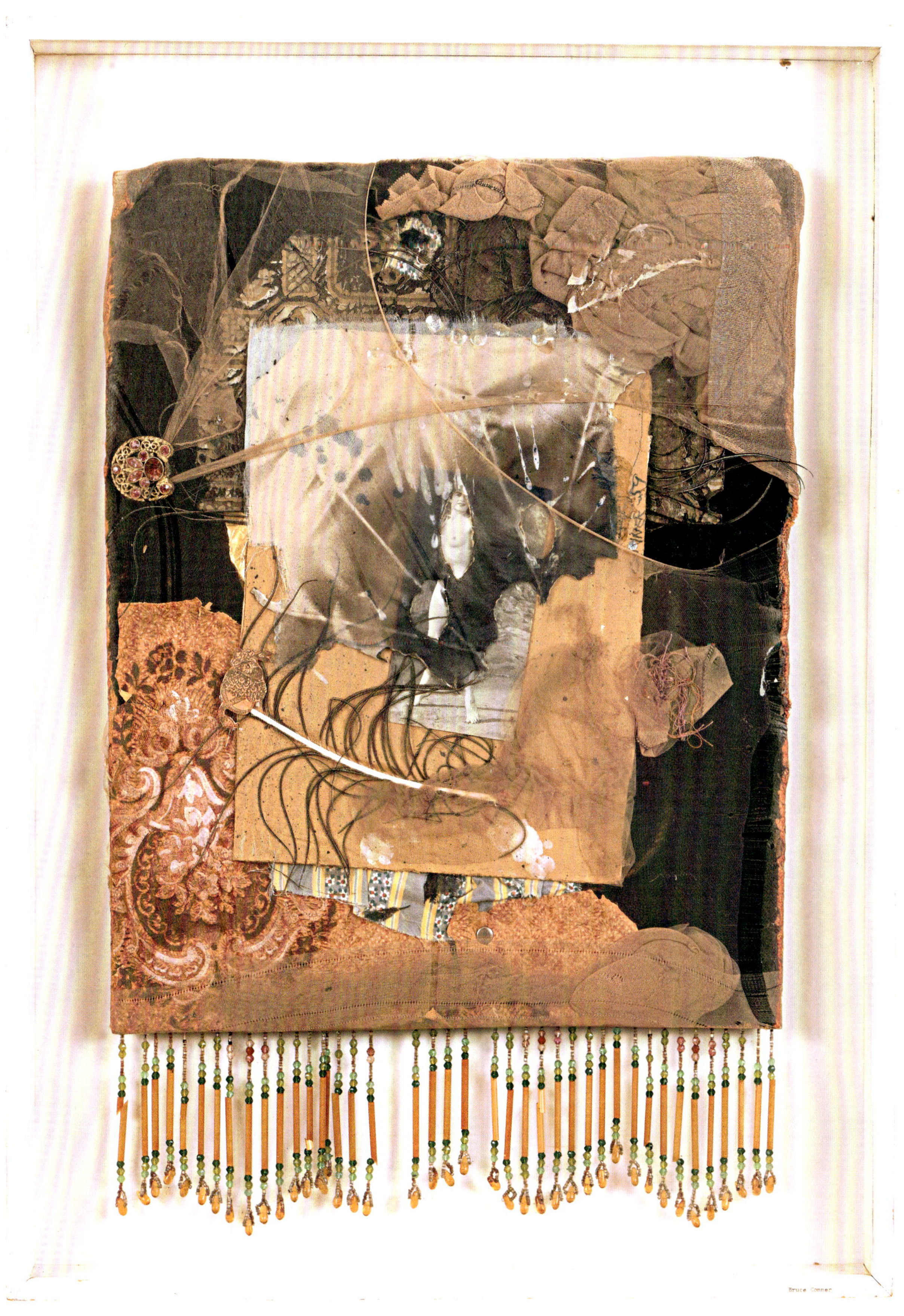

111 Bruce Conner

Jean Conner

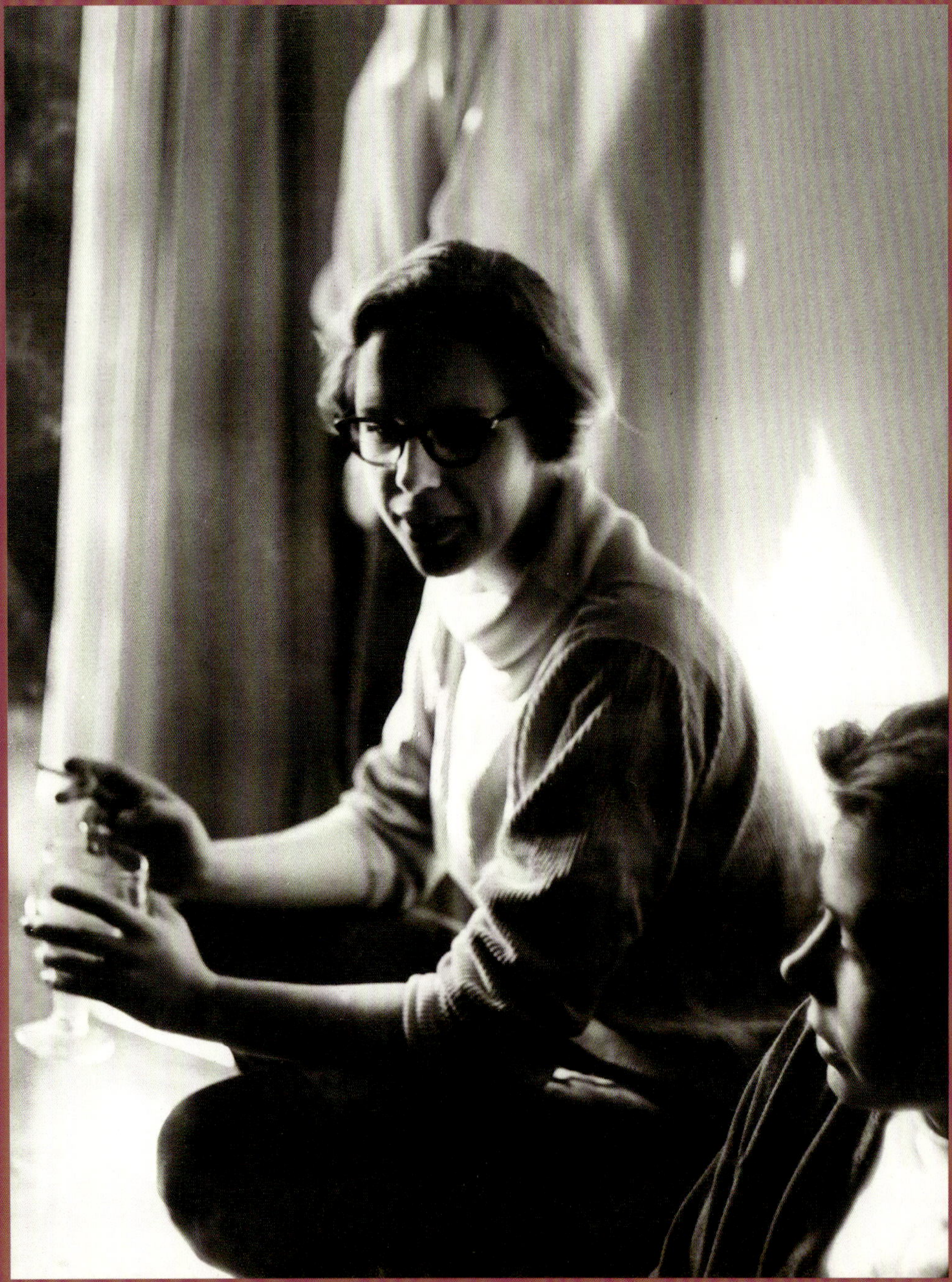

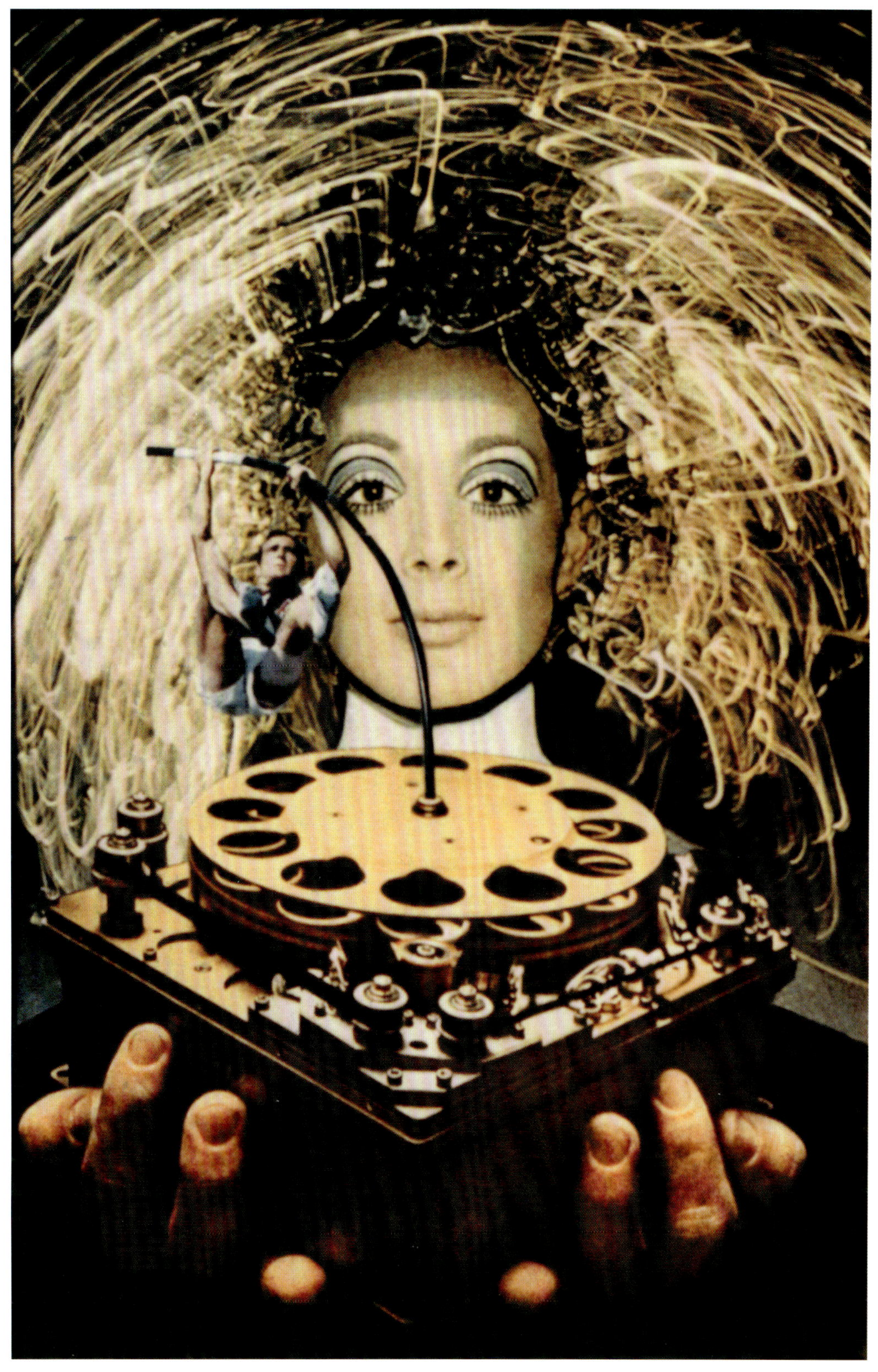

An accomplished artist whose subtle, handsome works deserve a wider audience, Jean Conner has been working quietly in the background throughout her husband Bruce's long career. She was born Jean Sandstedt in 1933 in Lincoln, Nebraska to a chemist father and housewife mother. Always loving to draw and paint, she attended the University of Nebraska (B.A., 1955) and the University of Colorado (M.F.A., 1957). While in school in Nebraska, she began experimenting with pastels, using them to highlight her watercolors. In graduate school, among other paintings and prints, she made a series of pastels influenced by the mystical still lifes of Odilon Redon. Her painting, *Floating Head* (1960) shows her allegiance to Redon with its mists of lush color and mysteriously rendered figure.

Jean met Bruce Conner at school in Nebraska where he was already involved in making collages and paintings. The couple married in 1957 and moved to San Francisco where they stayed briefly with Michael and Joanna McClure before moving to an apartment on Jackson Street near Wallace Berman, Jay DeFeo, and Joan Brown. Jean appears in a photograph as one of the friends who helped DeFeo transfer *The Rose* to a larger canvas backing in 1959.[1]

In San Francisco, Jean began making black and white collages from magazine photos before switching to color images in 1960. Developing from color and shape associations, her collages are conceived formally and often incorporate images layered within images. As she has stated, "I have always been fascinated by 'hidden objects' in childrens' activity books."[2] One of Jean's collages hung in the home of Wallace Berman and was one of the few works to be rescued from the Crater Lane house after it was destroyed in a mudslide in 1965.

p. 112
Jean Conner and Joanna McClure, c. 1959, Photograph courtesy estate of Jay DeFeo.

p. 113
Jean Conner, *Mz. Bell*, 1969, Collage.

p. 115 top
Jean Conner, *Floating Head*, 1960, Oil on canvas.

p. 115 bottom
Jean and Bruce Conner in Batman Gallery, 1964, Photograph by Edmund Shea.

In 1959 her works were in "Something Akin to Dada," a group show at the Spatsa Gallery put together by gallery owner Dimitri Grachis that also included work by Bruce Conner, Alvin Light, Wally Hedrick, and Art Grant. Over the years she has exhibited in a number of solo and group exhibitions. She was a member of Bruce Conner's and Michael McClure's Rat-Bastard Protective Association, a loose confab of artists including Joan Brown, Jay DeFeo, Wally Hedrick, Manuel Neri, and composer Terry Riley.

The couple experienced extreme financial hardships in the late 1950s, until Bruce's work began to sell after his 1960 exhibition at the Alan Gallery in New York. The next year, Jean and Bruce moved to Mexico City where they hoped to live cheaply, avoid the bomb, and concentrate on making art. Traveling through the countryside, Jean became fascinated by the country's rich visual culture. Her sumptuous depictions of a piñata and a Mexican funeral wreath demonstrate refined draftsmanship and an ability to convey spirituality through symbolic imagery. An impressionistic drawing of mushrooms evokes similar works by her husband from the time. Jean gave birth to the couple's son, Robert, in Mexico City in 1962. Soon thereafter, their savings ran out and they returned to the United States. They landed in Brookline, Massachusetts as guests of Timothy Leary, and remained on the East Coast until returning to San Francisco in 1965. Reassimilating herself into the art community, she became close to Joan Brown whose son, Noel, was approximately the same age as Robert.

A dark, moody symbolist style continued to haunt Jean's works of the early 1960s. In the pencil drawing *Young Woman with Skull* (1963), an emanating skull hovers like an aura above the depiction of a girl whose head emits a shadowy radiance. A submerged cross adds further portent to the depiction. Over the years, Jean has gravitated towards floral and other still-life subjects executed in a symbolist style. A sly humor permeates the collages. *Mz. Bell* (1969) depicts a fantastic telephone device offered up by a wild-haired, seemingly electrically charged goddess. Other collages from the 1960s toy with anthropomorphism and the invention of fantastic landscapes.

Conner has credited the undercurrent of spirituality in her work to growing up, as she puts it, "in a community centered around the local church. Though my collages have a feeling of celebration there is also an overtone of somberness. Perhaps that is my Nordic background appearing."[3] She has continued to make surreal collages in a variety of styles, using images taken from popular magazines. In recent years, she has been actively involved in a number of San Francisco environmental groups including Fort Point Environmental Club and Friends of Glen Canyon Park.

Michael Duncan

1 Jane Green and Leah Levy, ed. *Jay DeFeo and the Rose* (Berkeley: University of California Press, 2003), p. 76.
2 Jean Conner, *Collages by Jean Conner*, undated statement, artist's archive.
3 Ibid.

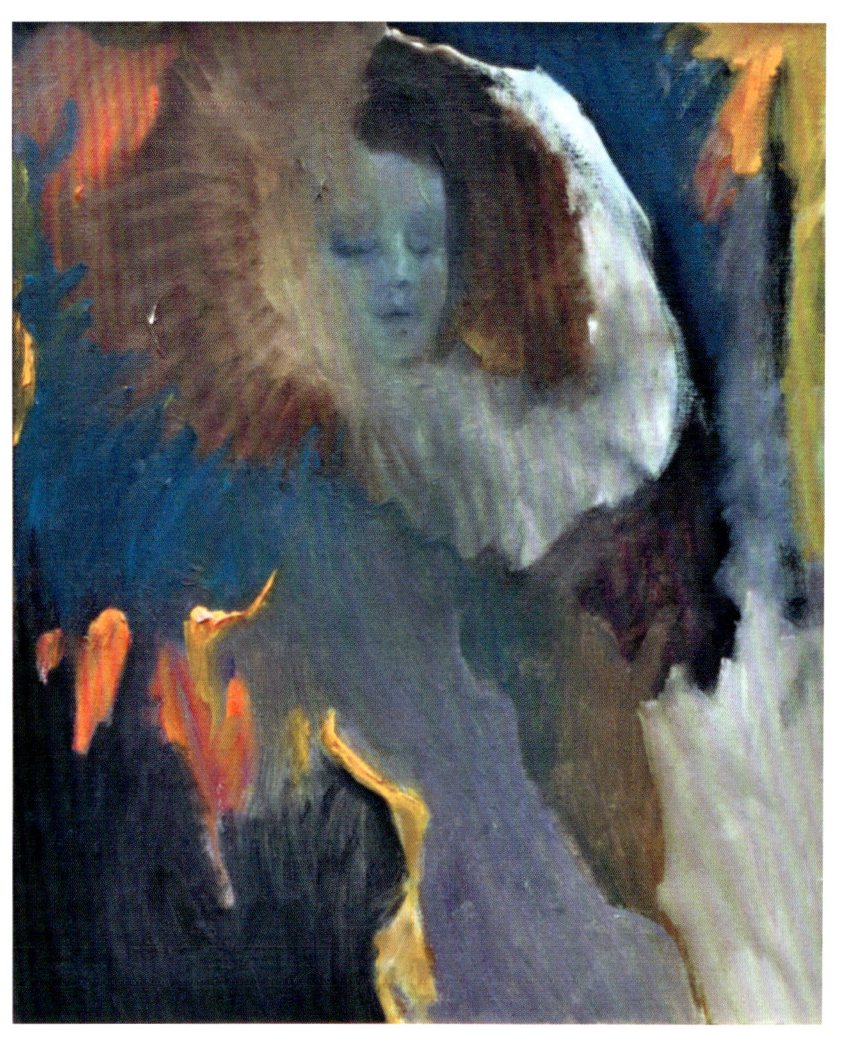

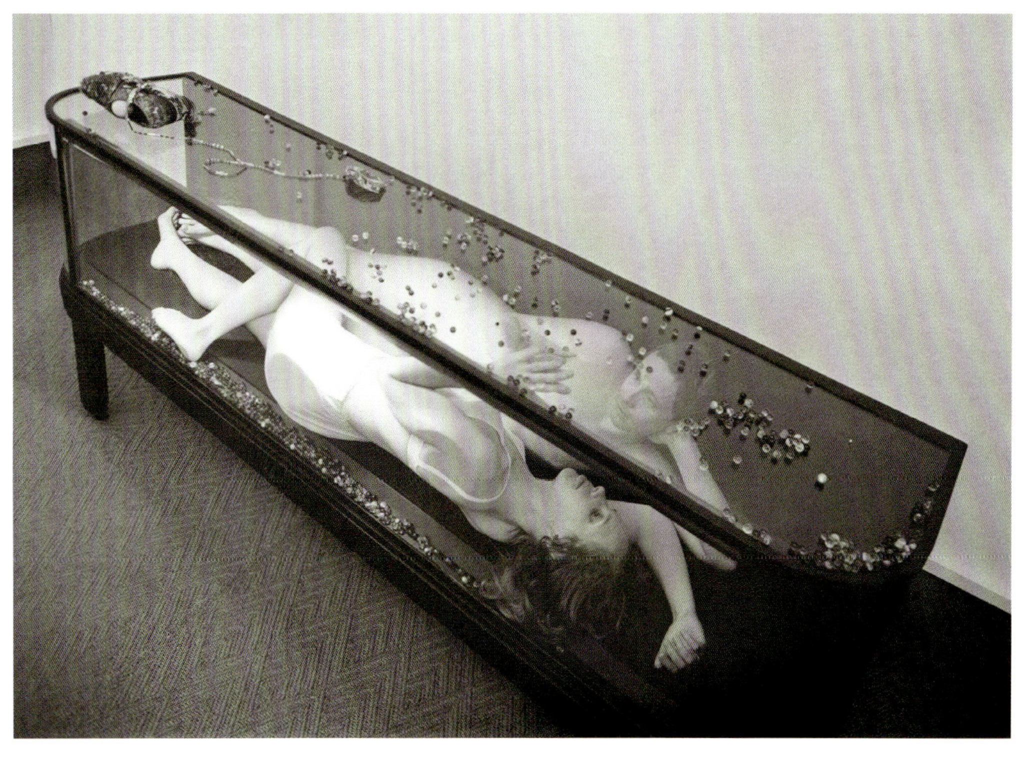

Jay DeFeo

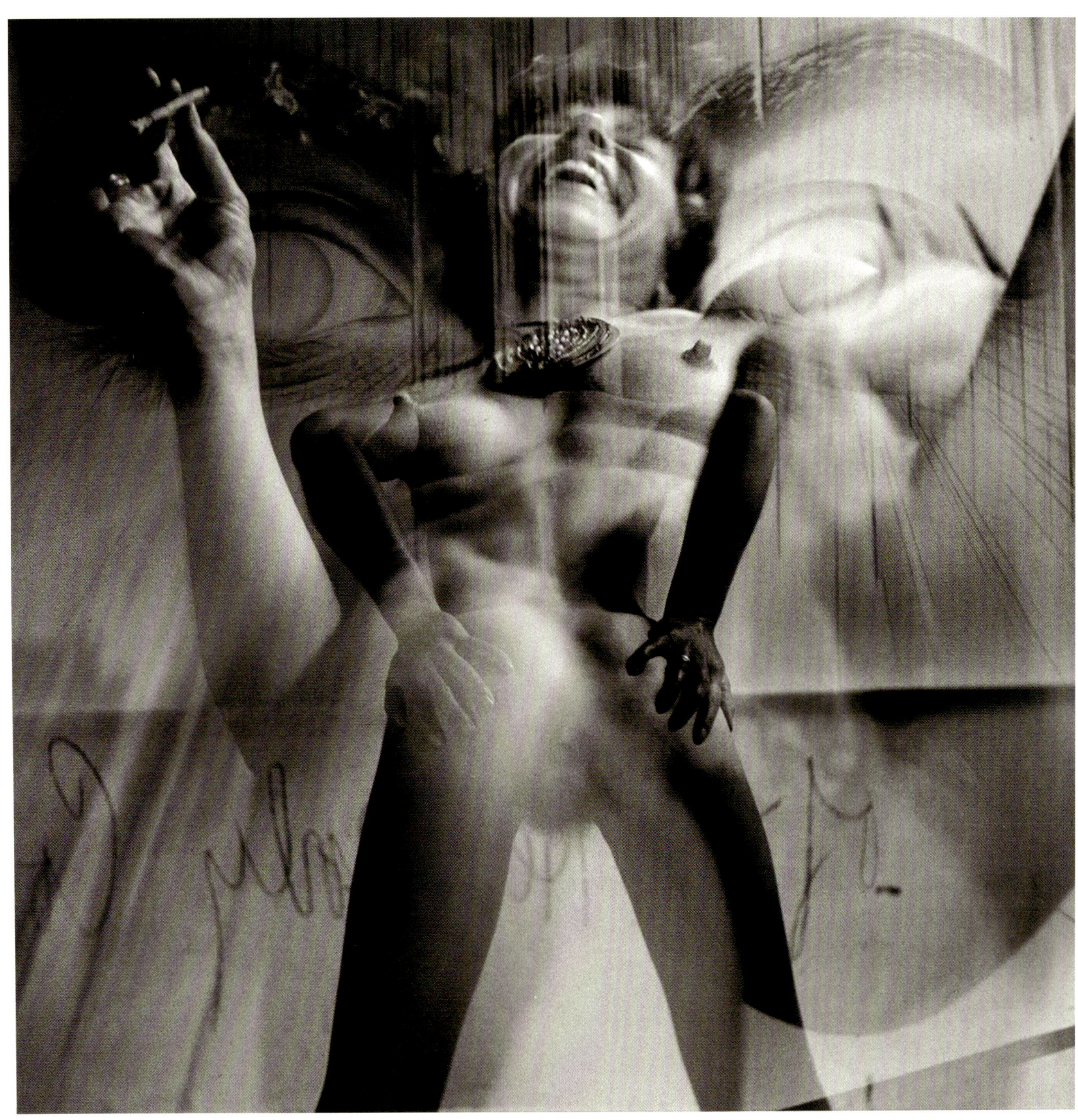

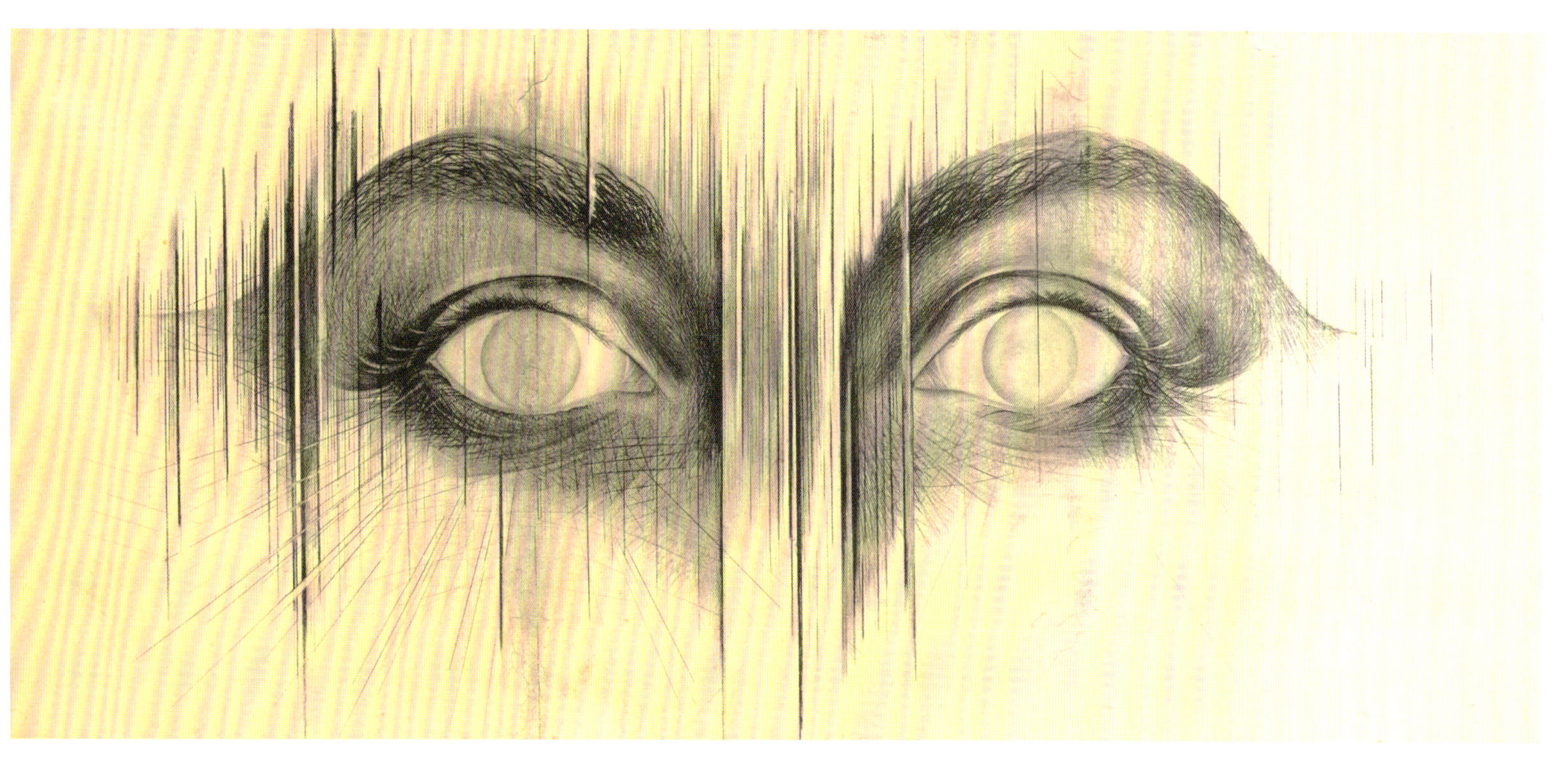

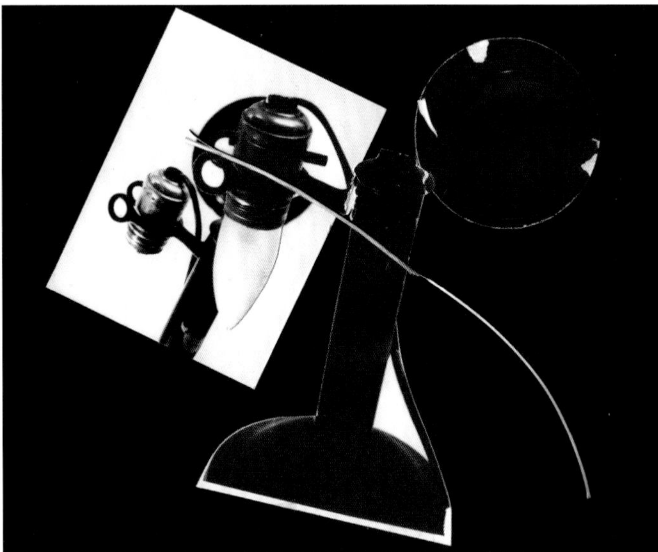

Fifteen years after her death, Jay DeFeo is finally being recognized as one of the premier artists of her generation. Long acclaimed by peers such as Bruce Conner, Wallace Berman, Michael McClure, and Joan Brown, DeFeo pursued a mode of symbolic expressionism with an unmatched fervor and intensity. *The Rose* (1958–65), a thickly incrusted impasto painting featuring a sculptured starburst motif, is the visual masterwork of the Beat era, a painting whose spiritual aura and commanding physical presence make it one of the greatest works of the twentieth century.

Born in Hanover, New Hampshire in 1929, DeFeo spent her entire life in the Bay Area after her family moved there when she was two. Upon receiving her master's degree in art from the University of California at Berkeley in 1951, she spent a year and half on a fellowship that enabled her to travel to art museums throughout Europe, before settling for six months in Florence. Working in her small pensione, she completed a large number of abstract paintings on paper using loosely rendered symbolic shapes—a cross, bird, torso, eye, and floating triangle and square—that remained important in her later work.

Back in San Francisco, DeFeo began making work in a variety of media, including small wire sculptures and jewelry that she later cited as sources for the image of *The Rose* (earlier titled *Deathrose* and *The White Rose*). She married fellow artist Wally Hedrick in 1954, and the next year moved with him to a building at 2322 Fillmore Street that also housed Joan and William Brown, Michael and Joanna McClure, Craig Kauffman, and Sonia Gechtoff and James Kelly. DeFeo realized that her obsessive, seven-year devotion to *The Rose* ruled out the typical exhibition schedules for emerging artists. She seemed to accept her devotion to the painting as something out of her control.

DeFeo clearly relished her friendships with poets such as McClure, who dedicated several poems to her. She inscribed a quotation from the Philip Lamantia poem reproduced in *Semina 4*—"Tell him I have eyes only for Heaven / as I look to you / Queen mirror / of the heavenly court"—on one of the end-pages of her copy of Lamantia's *Ekstasis*. On the next page of the book, she made an important working sketch for *The Rose*.[1] This quotation can also be seen painted on DeFeo's studio wall in one of Berman's 1959 photographic portraits of her.

In 1958 Wallace Berman took a series of provocative photographs of DeFeo posing in front of *The Rose* that he displayed the next year in a one-day exhibition at his nearby apartment on Scott Street. The photographs are clearly a kind of collaboration, with a nude DeFeo dramatically interacting with her epic painting and posing sensuously with Christmas tree tinsel. Their correspondence reveals a close friendship predicated on inside jokes, a passion for sports, and a mutual respect for the seriousness of their endeavors.

For example, on Berman's 1965 *Film-Makers Festival* poster—mailed back and forth from Wallace to Jay to Wallace—DeFeo wrote, "*The White Rose* is a fact painted somewhere on a slow curve between destinations. This is all I remember. This is all I know. It is all I can say about The Universal Pasttime and for all Giant fans who believe in the second coming of Casey Stengel."[2] In 1974 DeFeo made four abstracted gestural portraits of Berman's head, based rather literally on two self-portrait photographs he had sent her on a 1970 mailer.[3]

DeFeo exhibited the luminous works made while she was working on *The Rose* at Dilexi Gallery in 1959 and at Ferus Gallery in 1960. She was included in "Sixteen Americans," Dorothy Miller's prestigious exhibition at The Museum of Modern Art, but opted to skip the opening in favor of spending more time in her studio working on *The Rose*. In 1965 Walter Hopps convinced DeFeo to exhibit the painting at Pasadena Art Museum. Bruce Conner's short film, *The White Rose*, poignantly documents the removal of

p. 116
Jay DeFeo, San Francisco, 1959, Photograph by Wallace Berman.

p. 117
Jay DeFeo, Announcement for Dilexi Gallery exhibition featuring *The Eyes* (1958), 1959, Collection Charles Brittin.

p. 118
Jay DeFeo, *Collage for Bruce Conner*, 1973, Photocollage.

p. 119 top
Jay DeFeo, *Untitled (Portraits of Wallace Berman)*, 1974, Synthetic polymer on paper.

p. 119 bottom
Jay DeFeo, *Temple (for W.B.)*, 1980, Mixed-media on masonite.

p. 120
Footstool used during painting of *The Rose*, 1958–65.

p. 121
Jay DeFeo, Fragment of *The Rose* with note, c. 1970.

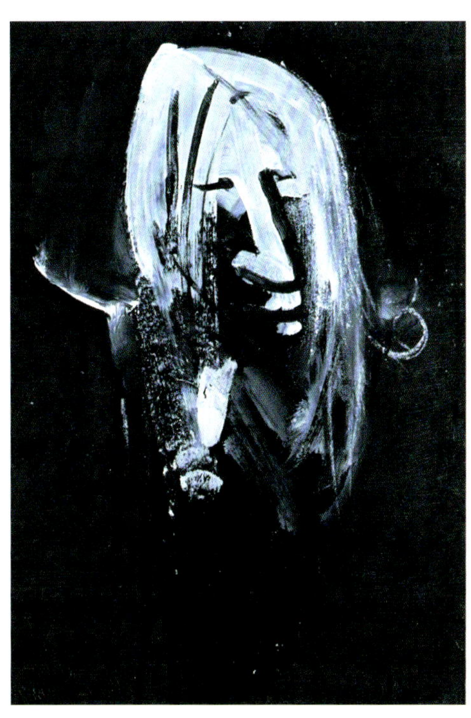

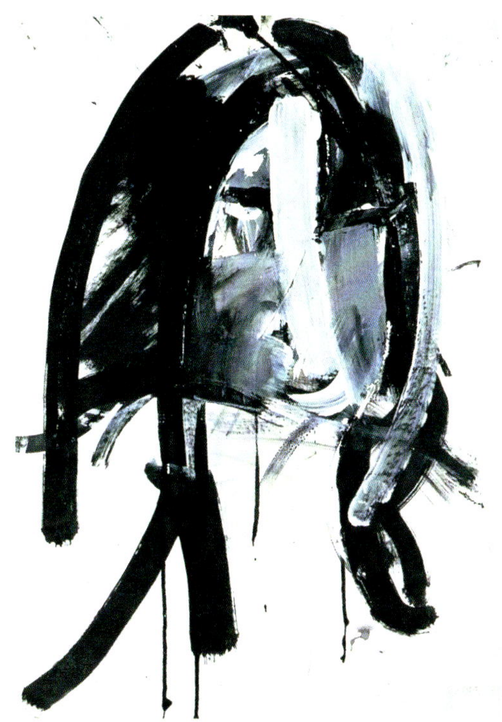

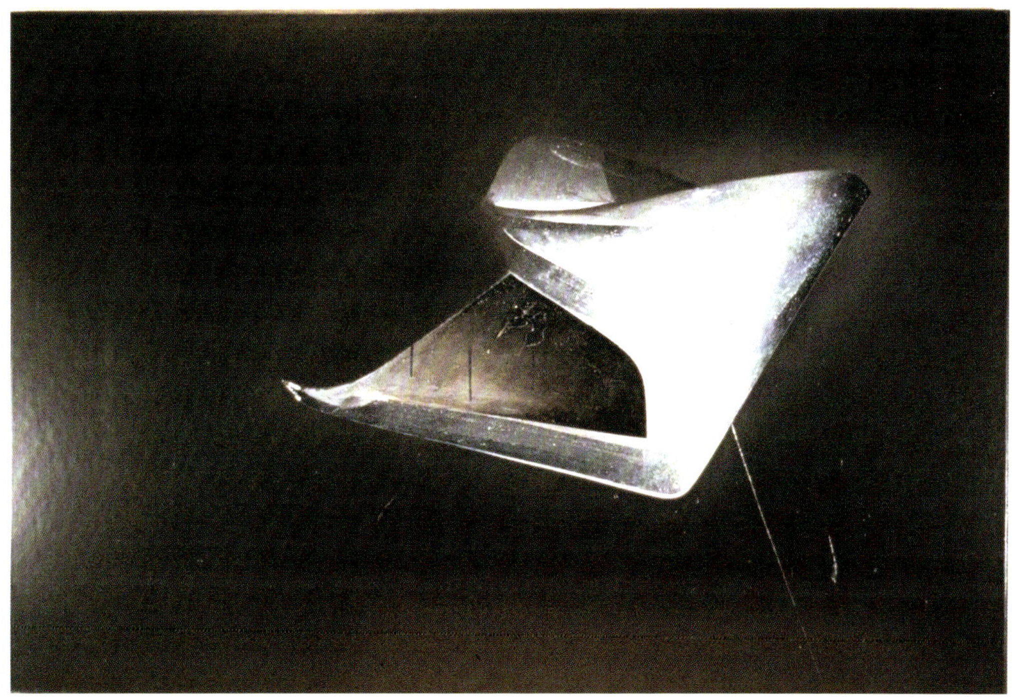

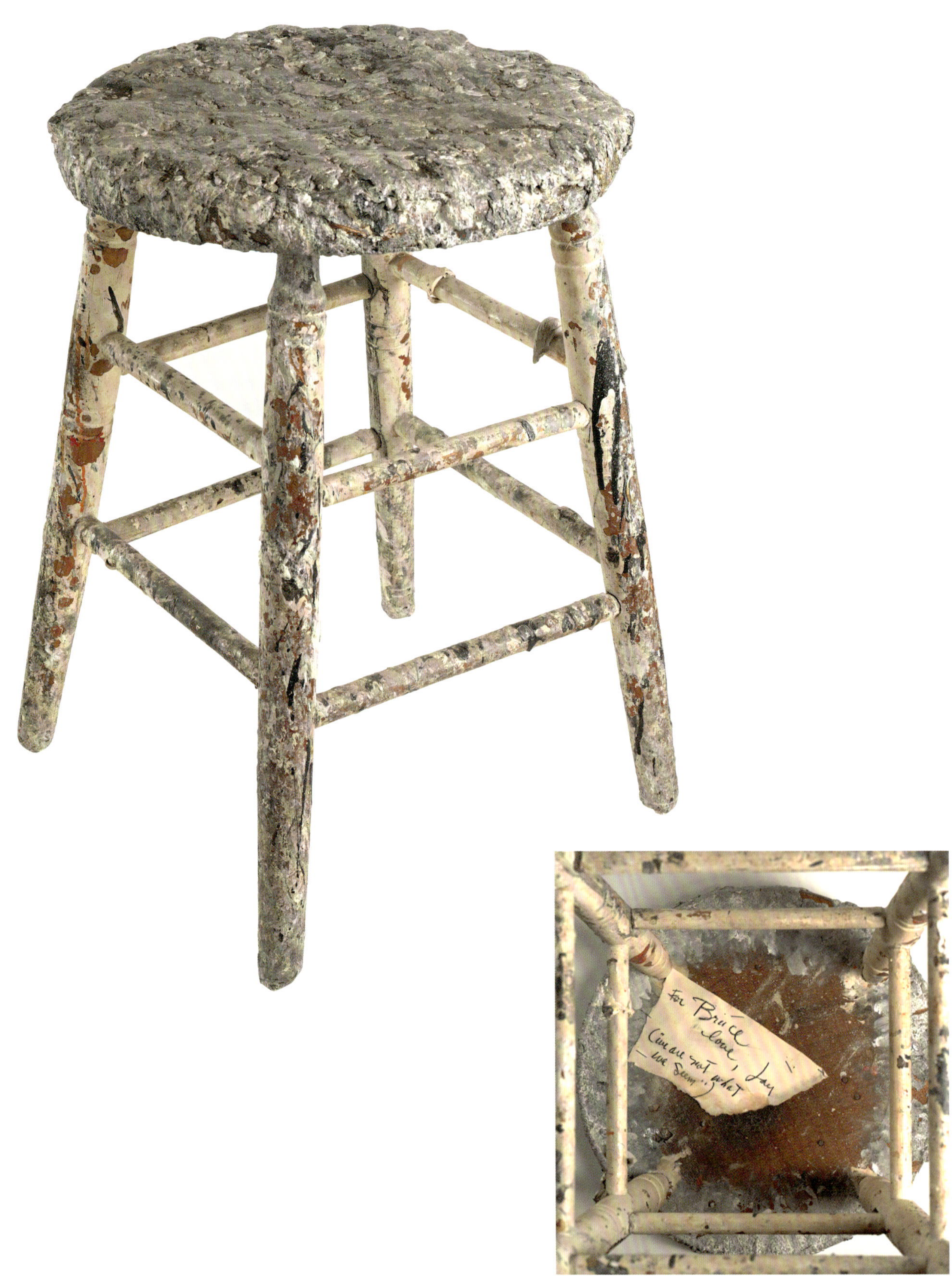
for Bruce
love, Jay
(we are not what
we seem)

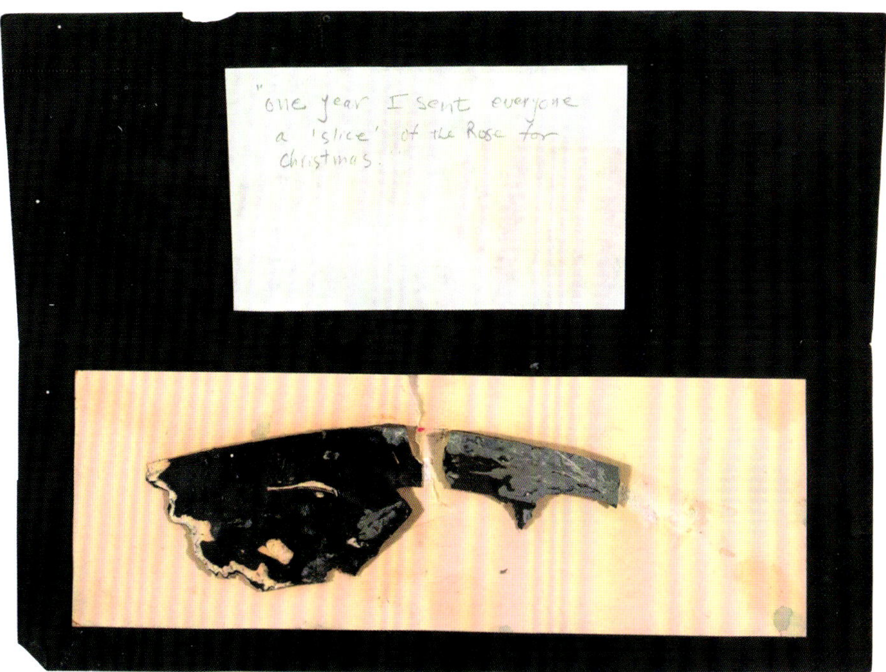

the eleven-foot high, twenty-three-hundred-pound, paint-encrusted piece from DeFeo's second-floor studio by a team of Bekins movers using a forklift.

After three years further delay, *The Rose* was finally exhibited in 1969 at the Pasadena Art Museum and the San Francisco Museum of Art, after which it was installed at the San Francisco Art Institute. It was in storage there, hidden behind a fiberboard panel until 1994, when it was finally uncovered, conserved, and purchased by the Whitney Museum of American Art.

After completing *The Rose*, DeFeo refrained from painting for three years, moving to a small house in Larkspur in 1969. In the 1970s she began to create paintings, drawings, and collages inspired by organic and mechanical forms. While teaching part-time at the San Francisco Art Institute, she became interested in photography and learned to make prints in her home darkroom. Odd formal relationships and resemblances in her photography sparked her new works. One series was based on the image of a camera tripod; another from 1973 was inspired by the marathon phone conversations she had with Bruce Conner.

As a token of friendship, DeFeo gave Conner the footstool she used when painting *The Rose* along with a note reading: "For Bruce / love, Jay / ("we are not what / we seem").[4] In DeFeo's paintings, simple shapes are isolated and elevated into deeply mysterious images. She described her process as "placing large single, rather organic forms of a provocative but unspecific nature in spaces that appear limitless beyond the boundaries of the panel."[5] Several paintings from this period stem from abstract-looking photographs she took of her dental bridge. In *Temple (for W.B.)* (1980), the shape of a used gum eraser is transmogrified into a spiritual portal or metaphysical vortex.

In 1981 DeFeo joined the faculty of the art department of Mills College and moved to Oakland where she began making large gestural paintings which were exhibited at Gallery Paule Anglim. In the last decade of her life, DeFeo visited Mexico, Japan, Hong Kong, New York, Europe, and Africa where she scaled Mount Kenya, a feat she had long wanted to accomplish. Several of her last works, made after she was diagnosed with lung cancer, employ mountain imagery, conjuring dramatic landscapes from angular brushwork. DeFeo died in 1989. In 1996 her works were surveyed in an exhibition curated by Constance Lewallen and organized by the Galleries at the Moore College of Art and Design, Philadelphia.

Michael Duncan

1 Reproduced in *Jay DeFeo and "The Rose,"* ed. Jane Green and Leah Levy (Berkeley: University of California Press, 2003) p. 159.
2 Wallace Berman Archive, Archives of American Art, Smithsonian Institution.
3 Marla Prather, "Foreword: Beside *The Rose:* DeFeo's Work at the Whitney Museum," *Jay DeFeo and "The Rose,"* p. xvii.
4 Bruce Conner, Brochure for "Jay DeFeo: Drawings and Photo Collages from the 1970's," Kohn Turner Gallery, October 1994.
5 DeFeo, 1972 Letter to Pat Adams, cited by Constance Lewellan, "Mountain Climbing," *Jay DeFeo: Selected Works 1959–1989* (Philadelphia: Moore College of Art and Design, 1996), p. 21.

Diane DiPrima

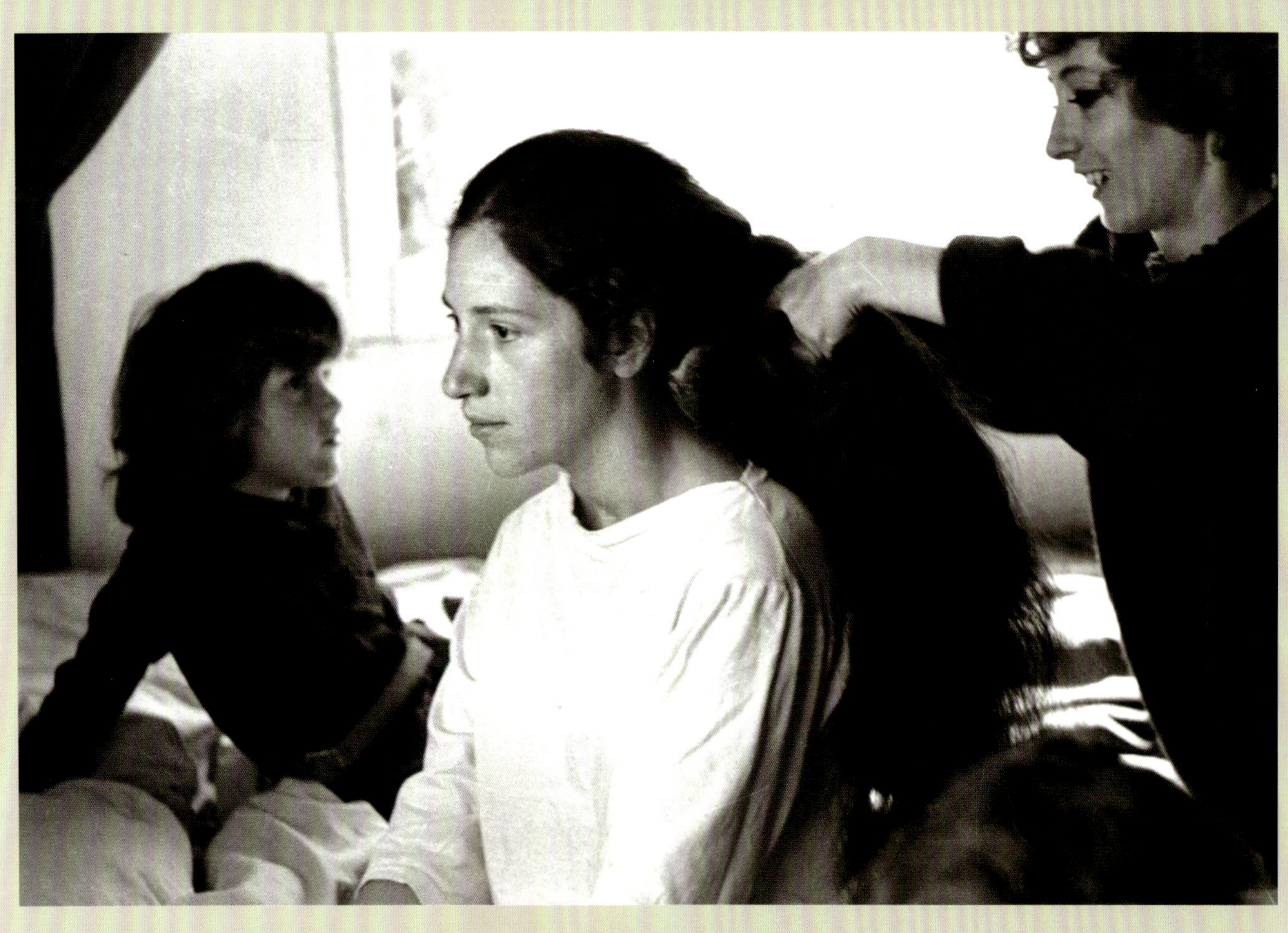

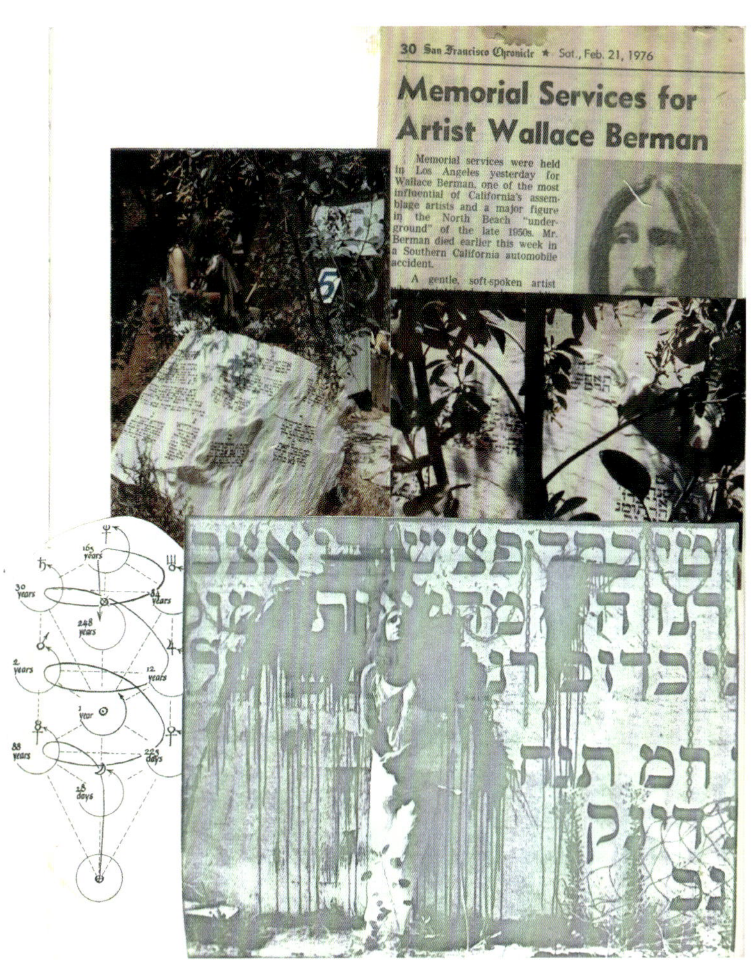

30 San Francisco Chronicle ★ Sat., Feb. 21, 1976

Memorial Services for Artist Wallace Berman

Memorial services were held in Los Angeles yesterday for Wallace Berman, one of the most influential of California's assemblage artists and a major figure in the North Beach "underground" of the late 1950s. Mr. Berman died earlier this week in a Southern California automobile accident.

A gentle, soft-spoken artist

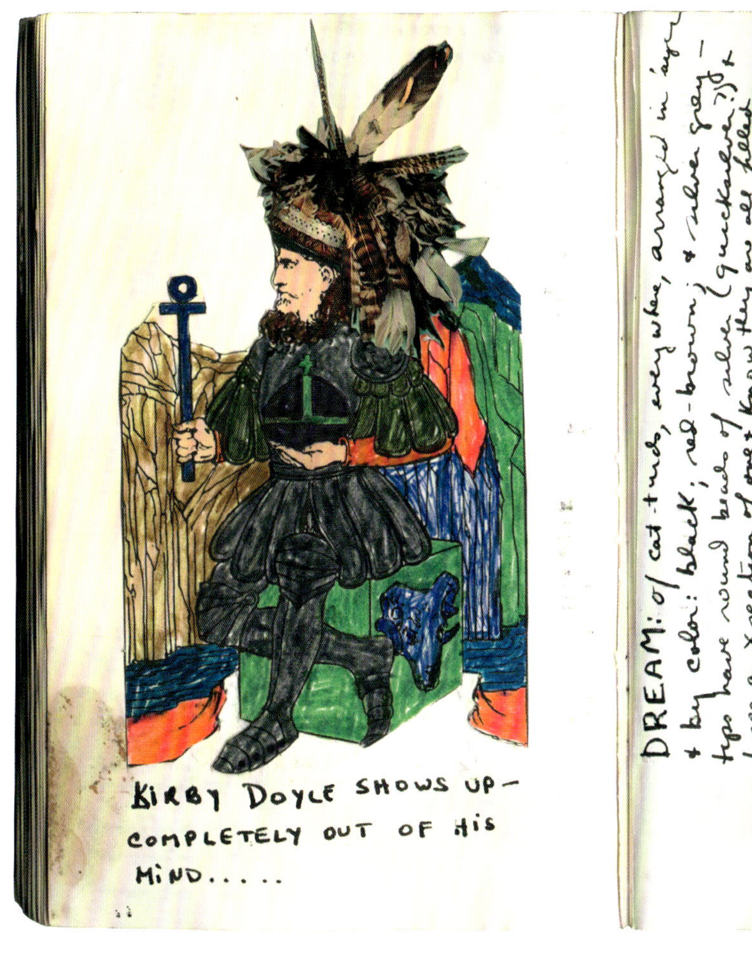

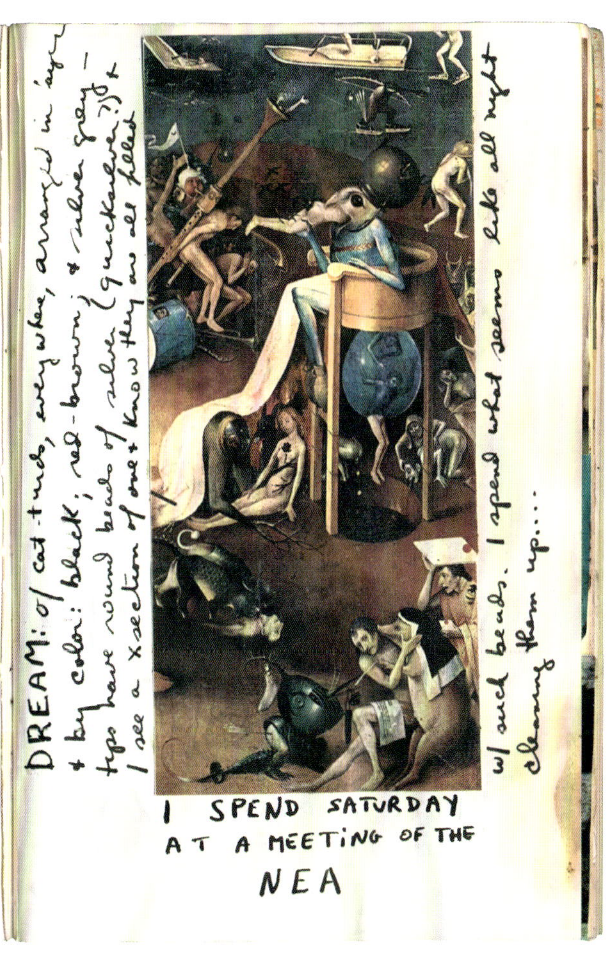

For over five decades, poet Diane DiPrima has chronicled her romantic, spiritual, and intellectual growth in writings rooted in personal experience. Early in her writing career she stated her poetic credo: "The requirements of our life is the form of our art."[1] Born in 1934 in Brooklyn to first-generation Italian parents, DiPrima decided at the age of fourteen to commit herself to a life as a poet. A free-thinking iconoclast, she proudly points out that her maternal grandfather, Domenico Mallozzi, was an anarchist associated with Emma Goldman and Carlo Tresca.[2] DiPrima attended Swarthmore College before dropping out to pursue a bohemian lifestyle in New York. Her first book of Beat-influenced lyrical poetry, *This Kind of Bird Flies Backward*, was published by LeRoi Jones's Totem Press in 1958.

Working on a mimeograph machine, DiPrima started the influential Beat newsletter *The Floating Bear* with Jones (Amiri Baraka) in 1959 and went on to edit and distribute it herself from 1963 to 1968. Named for Winnie the Pooh's upturned umbrella boat and beginning with a mailing list consisting of 120 names from Jones' address book, *Floating Bear* published works by Michael McClure, John Wieners, William Burroughs, David Meltzer, Frank O'Hara, Gary Snyder, and many others.

DiPrima's complex relationship with both male and female lovers and her growth as a young poet is documented in the lively and moving volumes, *Memoirs of a Beatnik* (Olympia Press, 1969) and *Recollections of My Life as a Woman* (Viking Penguin, 2001). These autobiographies stand as perhaps the most comprehensive account of the values and everyday life of a poet in the Beat era.

Energized by a do-it-yourself esthetic, DiPrima bought a small offset press and founded Poet's Press in 1964 to publish volumes by herself and writers such as Jean Genet, Kirby Doyle, Michael McClure, Audre Lorde, Timothy Leary, Robert Creeley, and Robert Duncan. Two Poets Press books written by DiPrima (*Earthsong: Poems 1957–1959* and *L.A. Odyssey*) featured cover drawings by George Herms. In the 1960s DiPrima also served as a contributing editor to the journals *Yugen* and *Kulchur*.

In 1961 DiPrima co-founded the New York Poets Theatre which over the next four years produced one-act plays by poets Frank O'Hara, James Schuyler, Michael McClure, and John Wieners. DiPrima met many of the West Coast Beat poets and artists when they came through New York for readings and exhibitions. In 1964 DiPrima paid the travel expenses for George Herms to come to New York to design sets for a production of McClure's *The Blossom, or Billy the Kid*. Herms also later designed the sets for an Intersection of the Arts production of DiPrima's play *Whale Honey* (1975).

In the early 1960s, DiPrima's friendships sparked several long visits to the West Coast. She had been corresponding with Wallace Berman and trading copies of *Floating Bear* for copies of *Semina*. In 1962 she stayed with the Bermans in Los Angeles and was impressed with their relaxed lifestyle. In her memoirs she described her first impressions of Wallace, "There was a softness about him—not a gay quality, just a soft female/maleness I couldn't place. I found it disorienting and attractive all at once."[3] On that trip, she also met Cameron and was impressed by her intensity and directness.

After a brief stint in the Bay Area where she married her companion Alan Marlowe, DiPrima settled in Topanga Canyon in a small house near that of George Herms. Before reacting against the laidback lifestyle, she received a steady stream of visitors from the Bay Area and New York, including Kirby Doyle, DiDi Morrill, Warhol

p. 122
Diane DiPrima with Tosh and Shirley Berman, Crater Lane, 1962. Photograph by Wallace Berman.

p. 123 top
Diane DiPrima, *West Coast Notebook 13: November 23, 1975–March 20, 1976*, Journal with collages and drawings.

p. 123 bottom
Diane DiPrima, *SF Notebook 5: November 22–March 31, 1973*, Journal with collages and drawings.

p. 124
Diane DiPrima, *Earthsong: Poems 1957–59* (New York: Poets Press, 1968). Cover drawing by George Herms.

p. 125
Diane DiPrima, Braid and note to Wallace Berman, c. 1968, Wallace Berman archive, Archive of American Art, Smithsonian Institution.

p. 126
Diane DiPrima, *Darkness Invocation*, 1976, Collage and poem on paper.

P. 127
Diane DiPrima, *Untitled*, 1975, Collage on paper.

EARTHSONG

Diane di Prima

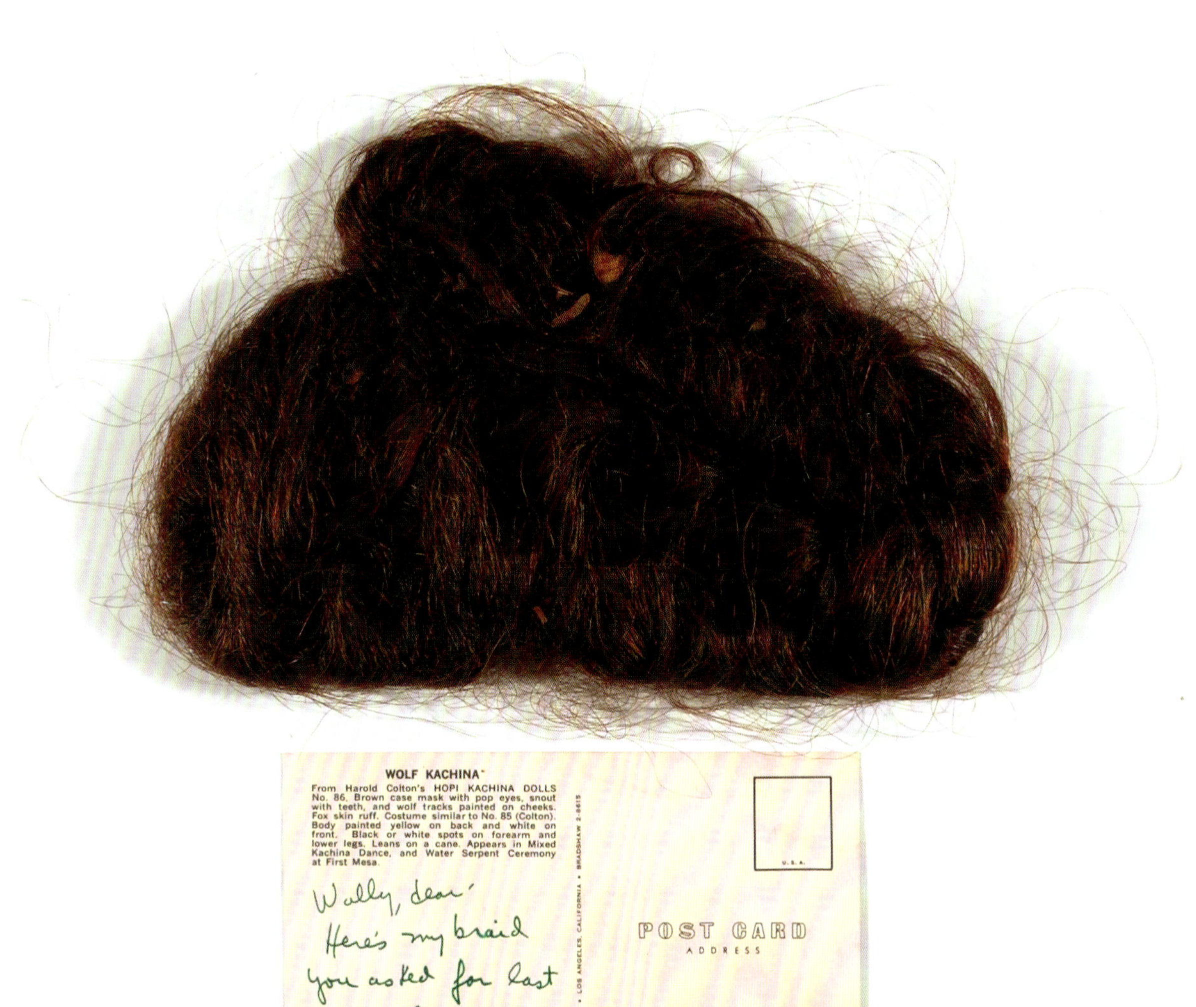

WOLF KACHINA
From Harold Colton's HOPI KACHINA DOLLS No. 86. Brown case mask with pop eyes, snout with teeth, and wolf tracks painted on cheeks. Fox skin ruff. Costume similar to No. 85 (Colton). Body painted yellow on back and white on front. Black or white spots on forearm and lower legs. Leans on a cane. Appears in Mixed Kachina Dance, and Water Serpent Ceremony at First Mesa.
© KOLOR VIEW • LOS ANGELES, CALIFORNIA • BRADSHAW 2-6615
POST CARD
ADDRESS
U.S.A.
Wally, dear'
Here's my braid
you asked for last
year - slightly beat
up - Love
Diane

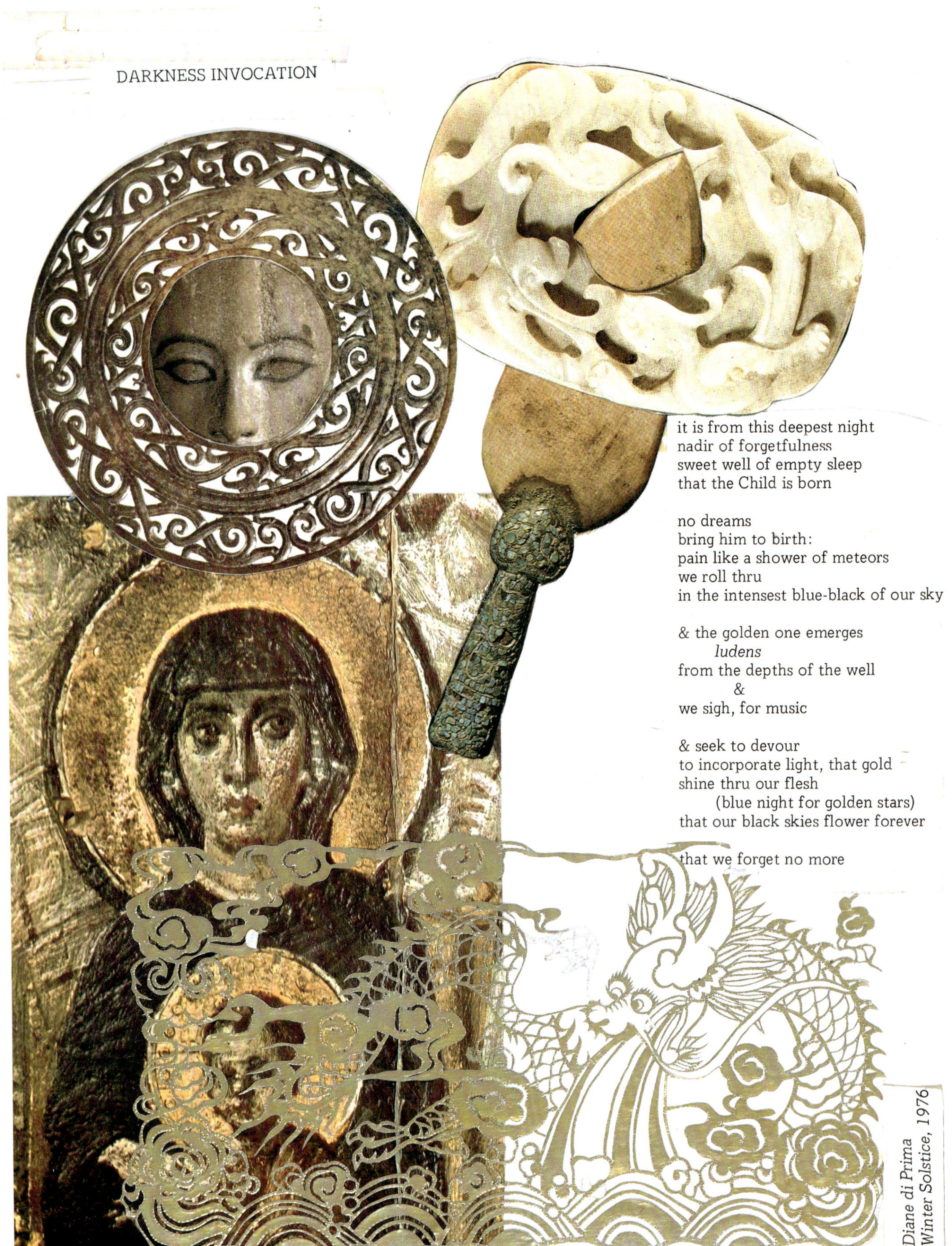
DARKNESS INVOCATION
it is from this deepest night
nadir of forgetfulness
sweet well of empty sleep
that the Child is born

no dreams
bring him to birth:
pain like a shower of meteors
we roll thru
in the intensest blue-black of our sky

& the golden one emerges
ludens
from the depths of the well
&
we sigh, for music

& seek to devour
to incorporate light, that gold
shine thru our flesh
(blue night for golden stars)
that our black skies flower forever

that we forget no more
Diane di Prima
Winter Solstice, 1976

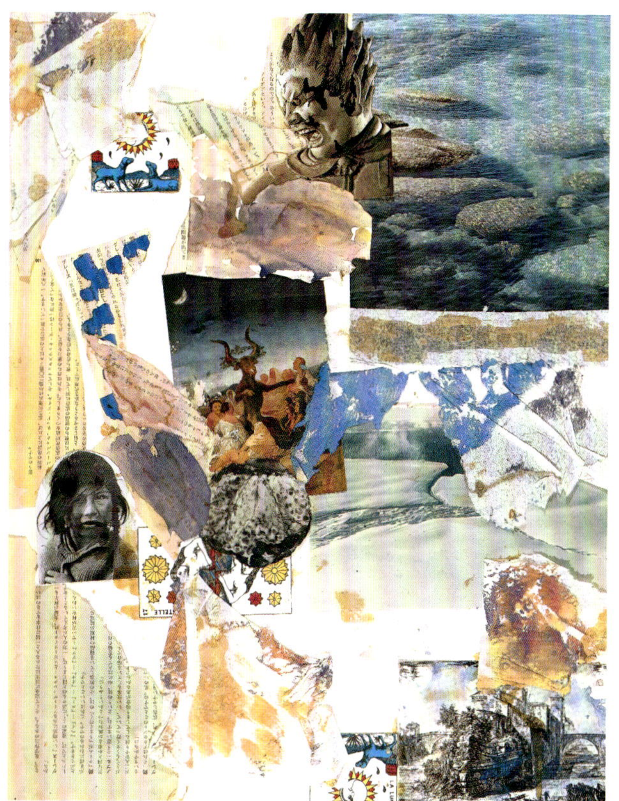

cohort Billy Name, and dancer Freddie Herko. Illustrated with sensitive drawings and collages, her personal journals meticulously describe her observations about differences in East and West Coast Beat bohemia.

Back in New York in 1963, just before the birth of her third child, Alexander, she appeared in Jack Smith's film *Normal Love* and, simultaneously, Andy Warhol's film *Andy Warhol Films Jack Smith Filming Normal Love*. In 1966, while her marriage to Marlowe was falling apart, she moved to Millbrook in upstate New York to Timothy Leary's psychedelic community. She then moved with her family to the Bay Area in 1968. In San Francisco, she was involved with the activities of the Diggers and other political causes.

In the late 1960s DiPrima was inspired by a number of spiritual and philosophic movements stemming from her study of the *I Ching*, the Kabbalah, alchemy, Buddhism, Zen, and esoteric thought. The interior ruminations of her poetry, however, have always been grounded by references to everyday life. Her responsibilities as a mother of five children have provided much of the tension and poignancy of her probing autobiographical writings.

DiPrima's writings of the 1970s track her outrage at the political injustices of the Vietnam War and her personal experiences in the budding feminist movement. Begun in the 1970s, *Loba* (New York: Penguin, 1998) is an epic poem in sixteen sections that serves as a cross-cultural investigation of the female spirit, seen through the figure of a she-wolf inspired by Navajo mythology.

DiPrima has taught writing at San Francisco's New College of California and founded the San Francisco Institute of Magical and Healing Arts where she taught from 1983 to 1992. She has written thirty-five books of poetry and prose and her writings have been translated into over twenty languages. In his introduction to DiPrima's *Pieces of a Song: Selected Poems* (City Lights, 1990), Robert Creeley stated,

> *Her search for a human center is among the most moving I have witnessed—and she took her friends with her, though often it would have been simpler indeed to have gone alone. God bless her toughness and the deep gentleness of her hand.*[4]

Michael Duncan

1 Diane DiPrima, *Recollections of My Life as a Woman: The New York Years* (New York: Penguin Books, 2002), p. 226.
2 Diane DiPrima, "Biography," www.dianediprima.com/bio.html
3 DiPrima, *Recollections*, p. 303.
4 Robert Creeley, "Foreword for Diane," in Diane DiPrima, *Pieces of a Song: Selected Poems* (San Francisco: City Lights, 1990), p. vii.

Kirby Doyle

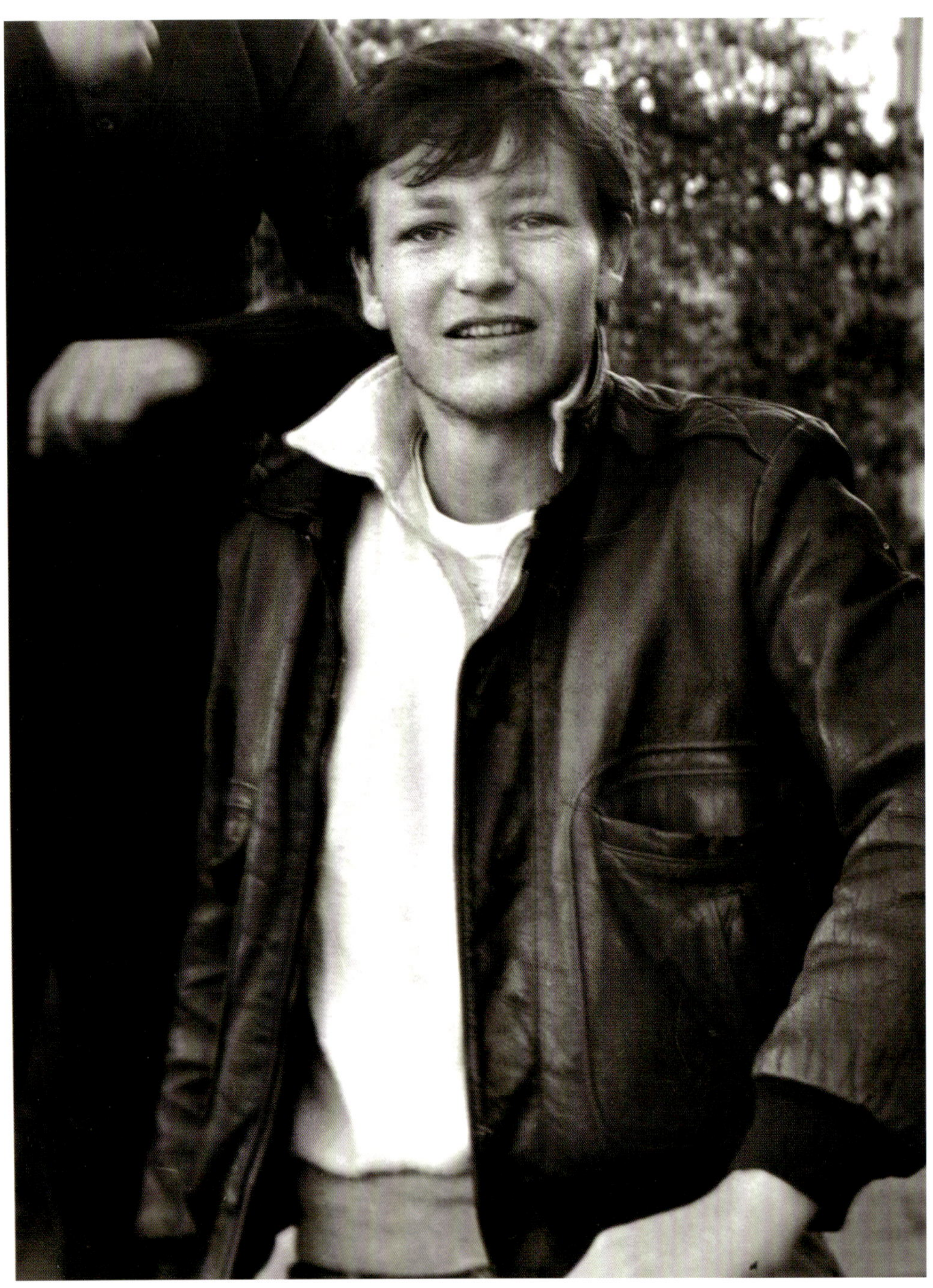

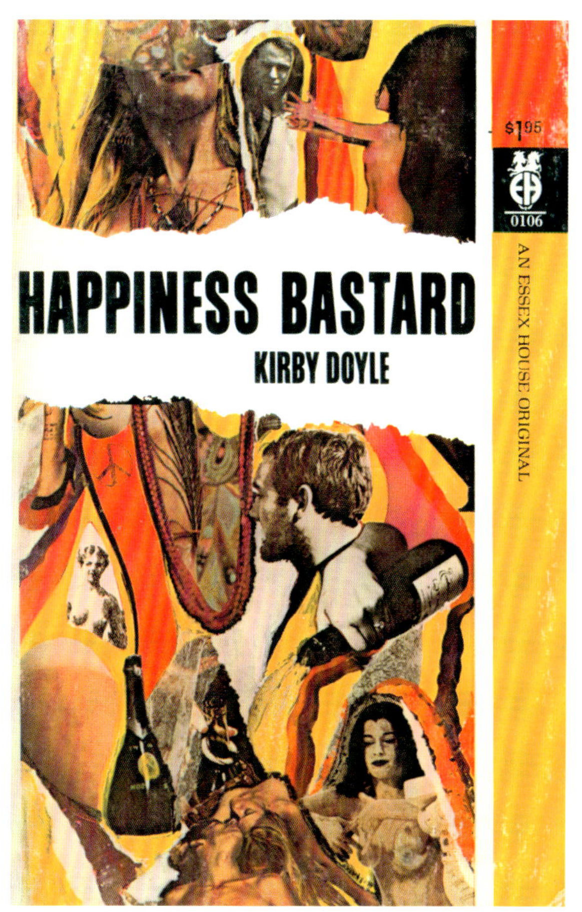
$1.95
EH
0106
HAPPINESS BASTARD
KIRBY DOYLE
AN ESSEX HOUSE ORIGINAL

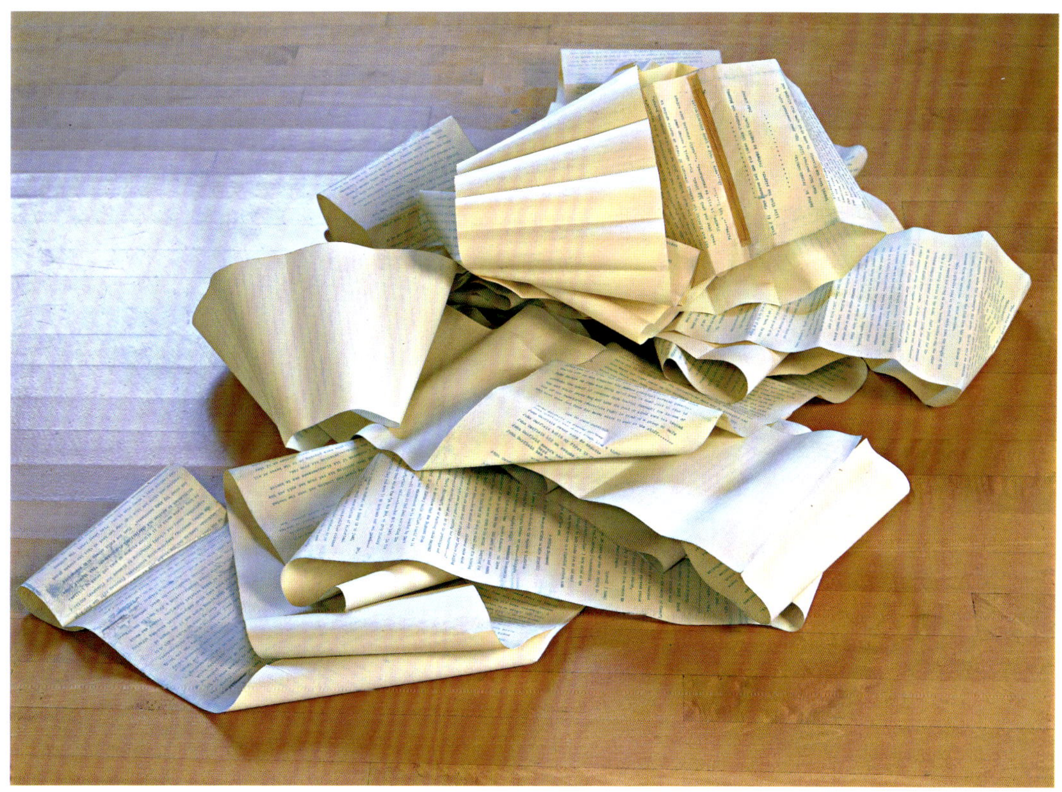

Kirby Doyle was master of both the brief lyric (after Sappho), and the modern epic (after Charles Olson). Doyle also wrote several novellas in a freewheeling prose style that chronicled his chaotic bohemian life. A hulking figure with rugged good looks, the youthful Doyle resembled Marlon Brando in *The Wild One*, replete with motorcycle and black leather jacket. In later years he aged into a shambling and craggy figure with elegant bearing, when he would live for solitary months in the woods of Mount Tamalpais, only to break his retreats with explosive appearances on the North Beach scene, sharing poetry, drink, and companionship with his fellow writers.

Nature was the constant in Doyle's poetry, especially in his later years. He belonged to the fraternity of California poets for whom wilderness was the great teacher. Like Gary Snyder and Lew Welch (Doyle's mentor), the profusion, intricacy and balance of the natural world set the pattern for his work. Unlike Snyder or Welch, whose works were informed by Zen, Doyle rejected all religions and philosophies in favor of a pantheism born of the natural world.

A native of San Francisco, Doyle attended private schools in Marin County and showed promise as an athlete. At sixteen Doyle falsified his birth certificate, joined the U.S. Army, and was stationed in Okinawa with the corps of engineers: "I learned poetics operating electrical power generators. It's how I learned to touch something too terrible to contemplate, too powerful for resistance, with a blind satisfaction for its own sake—at sixteen years of age." After his Army discharge he traveled throughout Europe as a transient laborer and wanderer: "After several years of journeymanship in what I call the 'fundamentals of art,' I returned to the U.S."

p. 128
Kirby Doyle, Larkspur, 1960,
Photograph by Wallace Berman.

p. 129 top
Kirby Doyle, *Happiness Bastard*
(North Hollywood: Essex House,
1968).

p. 129 bottom
Kirby Doyle, Typed single-scroll
manuscript for *Happiness Bastard*,
1967.

p. 130
Kirby Doyle, *Sapphobones*
(Kerhonkson, New York:
The Poets Press, 1966) with
illustrations by Kirby Doyle.

p. 131
*Kirby Doyle in the basement
of City Lights Books*,
San Francisco, 1959, Photograph
by Patricia Jordan.

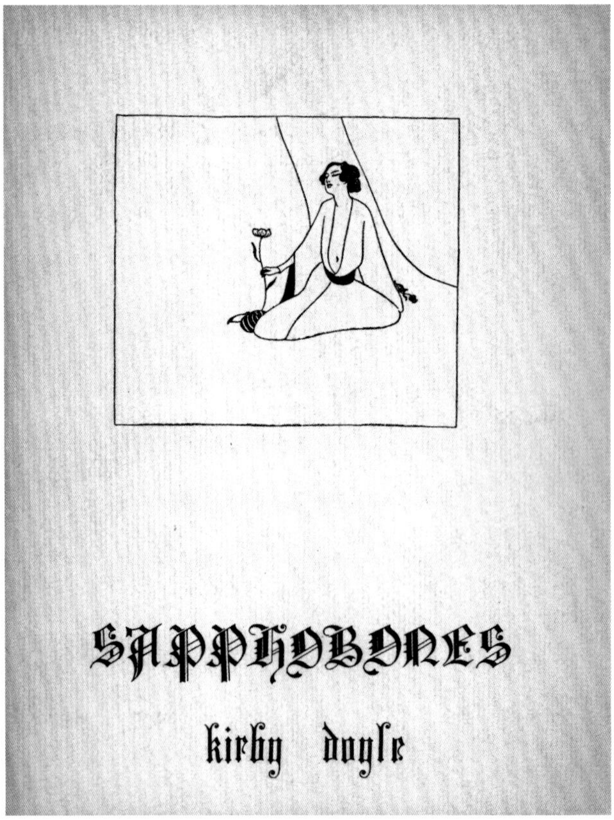

Doyle married in 1953, and he and his wife had two children in their first two years of marriage. They moved into married students' housing at San Francisco City College, where Doyle had enrolled in culinary school in 1955. A few months thereafter he transferred to San Francisco State College to become an art major, "not knowing what else to do." For Doyle, college life was filled with frustration, confusion, and a sense of waiting for something to happen. One day he showed a fellow student a four-line poem he had written. The student suggested Doyle sit in on a class sponsored by the Poetry Center at the college. To the young Doyle, who claims that by age nineteen he had read only two books, poetry was a revelation: "Suddenly the doors of plausibility swung wide open, for the first time in my life." The Poetry Center at San Francisco State College, run by Ruth Witt-Diamant, was an unusual institution in American academic life. Guest poets and lecturers included Charles Olson, Dylan Thomas, Marianne Moore, and Randall Jarrell. Doyle attended their lectures and readings and enrolled in a class taught by Kenneth Rexroth, conducted in Rexroth's home in the city's Fillmore district.

In 1956 Doyle's wife opened a bookstore on Fillmore Street called The Golden Bough. Through her bookshop and Rexroths's gatherings, Doyle met other poets—Lew Welch, Michael McClure, John Wieners, Philip Whalen, Robert Duncan, Philip Lamantia—and the artist Wallace Berman. Berman was the first champion of Doyle's work, and published some of the poet's earliest efforts in *Semina*. Doyle's ardent romantic imagery was rooted in the courtly love poems of the troubadours—the rose, the cup, and the lady—but skillfully updated in the vernacular of the streets. It was a combination perfectly tailored to Berman's aesthetic—in fact, their specific imagery often overlapped, as did an ever-present subtext of narcotics. Doyle's lyrics, often only six or eight lines in length, were also well suited to *Semina's* small-scale format. From 1957 to 1959, with encouragement from Berman, Doyle composed the thirty-six poems later published by Diane DiPrima's Poet's Press, under the title *Sapphobones* (1966). These lyrics, most often on the subject of refused or betrayed love, were occasionally set to ancient Anglo Saxon melodies and meant to be sung.

The sense of eroticism as a heightened mode of awareness that informed *Semina* likewise served as Doyle's method in his remarkable first novel, *Happiness Bastard* (1968). Like Kerouac's *On The Road*, it was written on a single roll of teletype paper, and tells the story of a squalid love affair, related in equally licentious prose. As Doyle recalls, it was "written on a sojourn that my lover post-wife and I took to New York in 1959–60." The work was published in butchered form nearly a decade after its composition by Essex House in North Hollywood, a publisher of soft core pornographic novels that folded the following year, making the book largely unavailable. *Happiness Bastard* is a brutal work of black humor born of Doyle's own struggle with poverty, drug addiction, and unhappy love affairs. Along with Irving Rosenthal's *Sheeper* (a book that exerted great influence on Doyle), it is one of the great lost novels of the Beat Generation; in fact both novels share the poet John Wieners as an eccentric main character.

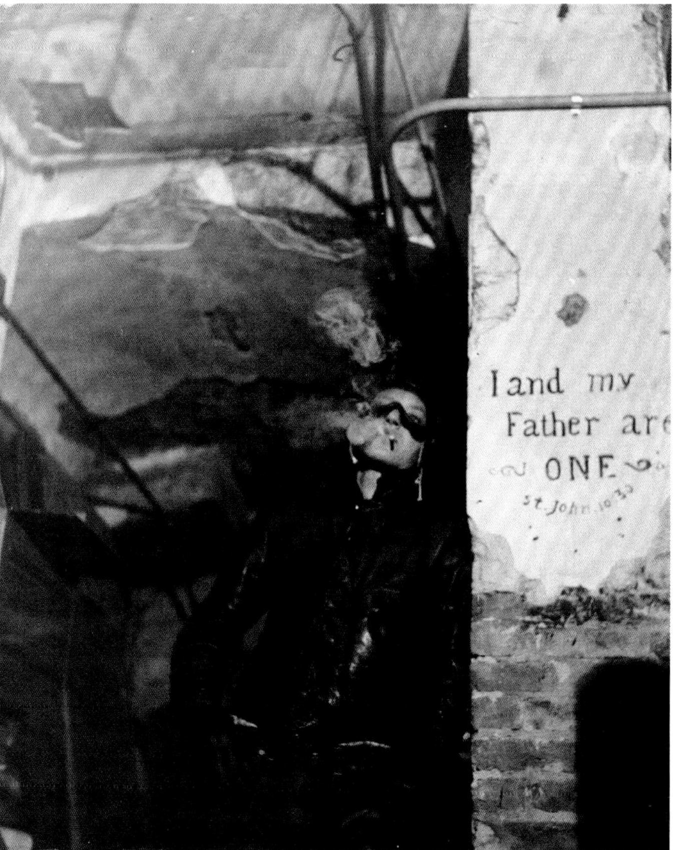

In the early 1960s Doyle returned to the West Coast from New York, and composed a book of approximately sixty poems, believed to be lost. It was during the period, from 1960 to 1965, that Doyle's drug addiction precluded any further writing. "I spent many years in Narcotica," Doyle confessed. "So urgent is the poetical expression that the poet is forced to the original urgency. Why should I dabble, attendant upon its announcement, when I can have the gist of my civilization in a needle?" In 1966 Doyle resumed writing, and the following year *Angel Faint*, the second volume of "Th' Couple" trilogy, was published and distributed for free by the Digger's Communication Company, the publishing cooperative of the Haight-Ashbury hippie community. According to its author, "*Angel Faint* was printed on a stolen mimeograph machine, in a limited edition, for underground purveyance." (A rare surviving copy was deposited by Robert Duncan in the Bancroft Library at Berkeley.)

Following the publication of *Angel Faint*, in disappointment and neglect, Doyle again stopped writing. The dozen years that Doyle lived outside of society (1968–80) were spent in small towns, communes, and camping in the wilderness in California. In 1977, after three years of solititude on Mt. Tamalpais, Doyle rejoined the community of poets in San Francisco. The next twelve years would prove among the happiest and most productive of his life. Doyle found himself an elder statesman of a thriving poetry scene, and discovered a devoted audience for his work in the circuit of North Beach poetry readings, and various small presses, including *Beatitude* magazine, Kaye McDonough's Greenlight Press, and Tisa Walden's Deep Forest (named after a Doyle poem).

In 1979 Doyle was inspired by a discarded photograph of a woman lying in a gutter. With her strange beauty as his muse, he began work on "Pre-American Ode," an epic poem which occupied him for the next decade. A parallel work from this period is the novella *White Flesh* (1980–82), a narrative of approximately one hundred pages that focuses on a single event—an encounter between the author and his lover in a city park at evening. Only portions of "Pre-American Ode" have been published, in pamphlet form. Kirby Doyle spent the last ten years of his life battling physical and mental illnesses in a California state hospital, where he died in 2002.

Raymond Foye

Bobby Driscoll

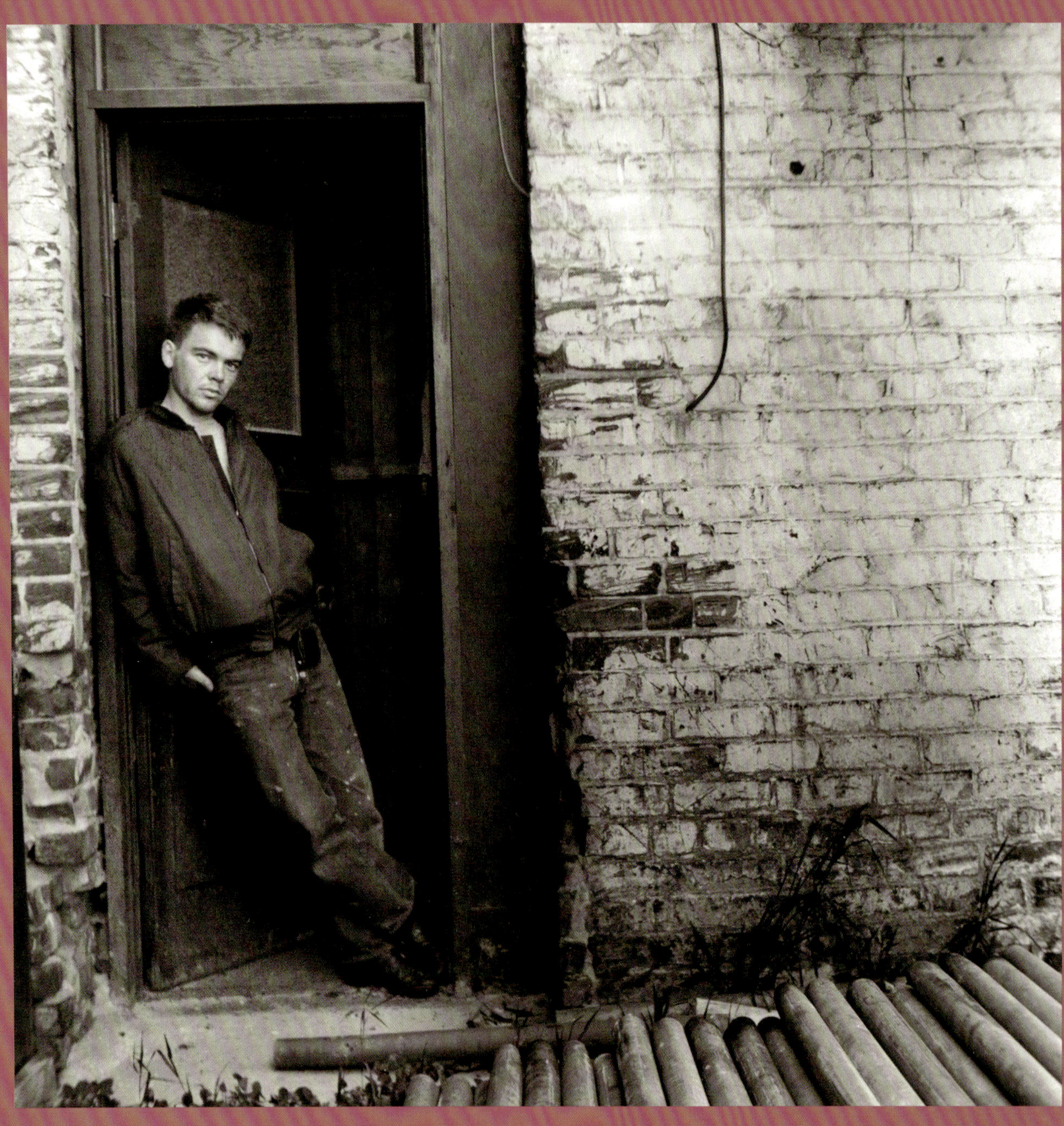

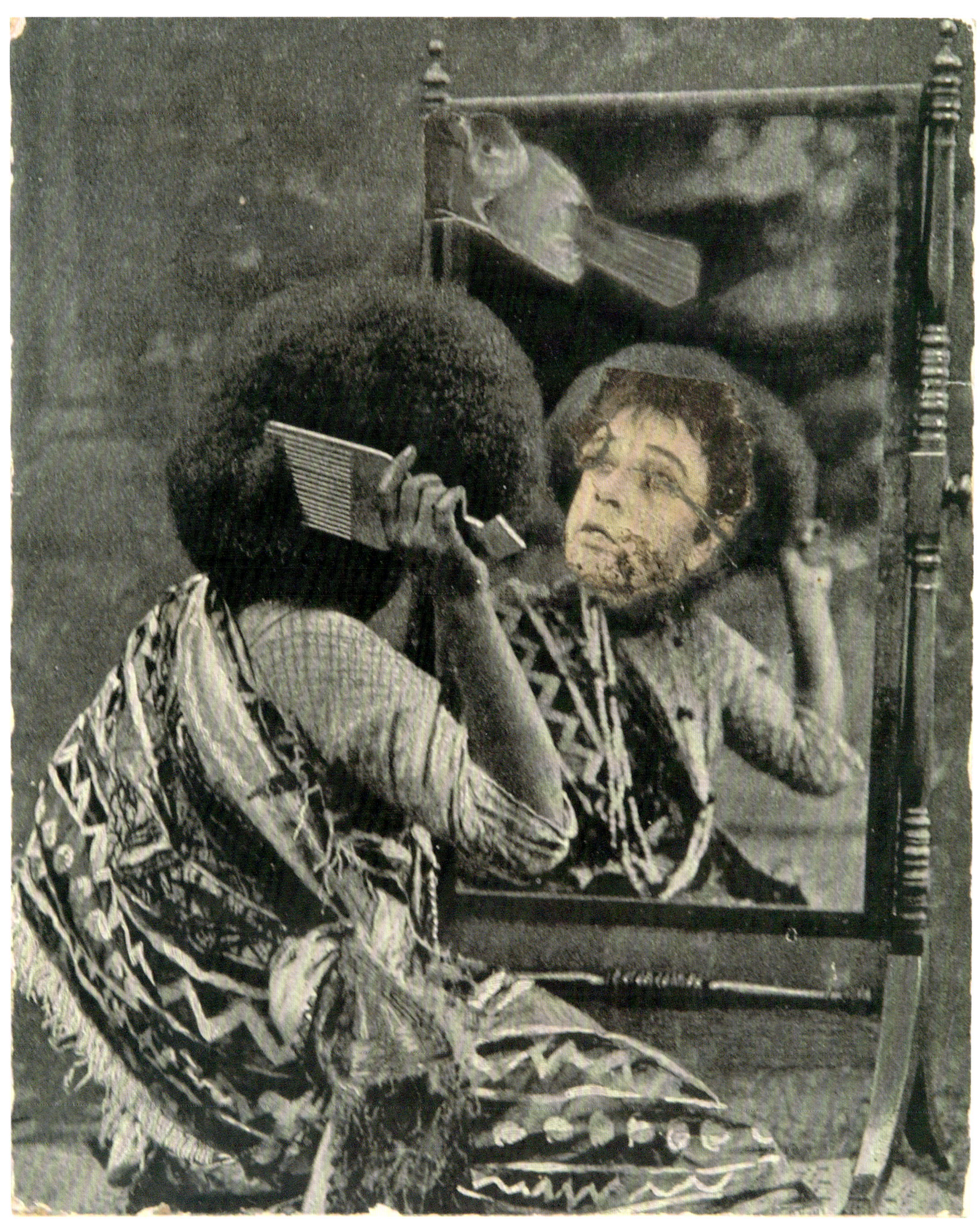

Bobby Driscoll is one of the most tragic figures in the Berman circle. A child star who had been used up and cast off by the entertainment industry by the time he was sixteen, Driscoll was ill-equipped to deal with life beyond the false reality of the studios, and he was dead of a drug overdose by the time he was thirty.

Born in Cedar Rapids, Iowa, in 1937, Driscoll was an only child who moved with his parents to Altadena, California in 1942. On the encouragement of the local barber, Driscoll's parents began taking him to auditions and within a year he was cast in MGM's *Lost Angel*, directed by Robert Rowland. Small parts in *The Sullivans*, *Miss Susie Slagle's*, and *O.S.S.* led to a starring role in Disney Studios' 1946 production of *Song of the South*. Disney was pleased enough with Driscoll's work to offer him an eight-year contract, so with his family, Driscoll relocated to Pacific Palisades and enrolled at The Hollywood Professional School. In 1949 he starred in *The Window*, a modest but effective suspense film produced by RKO, and roles in *Treasure Island* (1950), *When I Grow Up* (1951), and *The Happy Time* (1952) followed. Disney terminated his contract in 1953, shortly after he completed work on its animated production of *Peter Pan* (Driscoll provided the voice for the lead character), and by all accounts, Driscoll took his firing hard. It was during this period that he became involved with drugs, and by 1954 he was using heroin.

p. 132
Bobby Driscoll, San Francisco, 1959, Photograph by Wallace Berman.

p. 133
Bobby Driscoll, Untitled (for Wallace Berman), 1964, Mixed-media collage.

p.134
Bobby Driscoll, Mailer to George Herms, 1958, Collage on cardboard.

p. 135 top
Bobby Driscoll, Mailer to Joan and Billy Jahrmarkt, 1964, Mixed-media collage.

p. 135 bottom
Bobby Driscoll, Untitled, 1965, Mixed-media collage.

Movie offers became increasingly scarce as Driscoll approached the end of his teenage years; then finally they evaporated altogether and Driscoll began working in television. In 1956 Driscoll met the Bermans through his friends Dean Stockwell and Russel Tamblyn, both of whom had also been child stars. At that point Driscoll was living in Topanga—"Bobby lived in Topanga before any of us," George Herms points out—and he was trying to stay out of trouble. His success in that endeavor was variable.[1]

"When we saw Bobby he wasn't using drugs—that was part of Wallace's deal with him," Shirley Berman recalls. "Bobby was so cute—he was a little elf—and he was a very good artist, too. He made little collaged books that were just beautiful."[2]

During the years Driscoll was part of the Berman community (from 1956–63), he wrote verse and created collaged mailers and small artworks that reveal him as a poetic, tormented young man with a dark sense of humor. A handful of these pieces survive in the collections of Tamblyn, Herms, and the Archives of American Art, and they resonate today as haunting artifacts of a star-crossed life.

In December of 1956, Driscoll and Marilyn Jean Rush were married in Mexico, and over the next five years they had three children together. Driscoll's string of arrests caused severe stress to his relationship with his wife, however, and in 1961 their marriage ended.

When Driscoll was arrested in 1962, drug addiction was beginning to be regarded as an illness rather than a crime, and, according to George Herms, Driscoll was one of the first drug offenders to be sent to the Narcotics Rehabilitation Center at Chino State Prison. Apparently he failed to receive the help he'd hoped to find during his six months there. "In the first letter he sent me he said, 'There are no nurses here,'" Herms recalls.

Shortly after his release in 1963, Driscoll met and married DiDi Morrill, a former airline stewardess who had recently returned to L.A. from New York, where she had been involved with dancer Freddie Herko. Morrill's

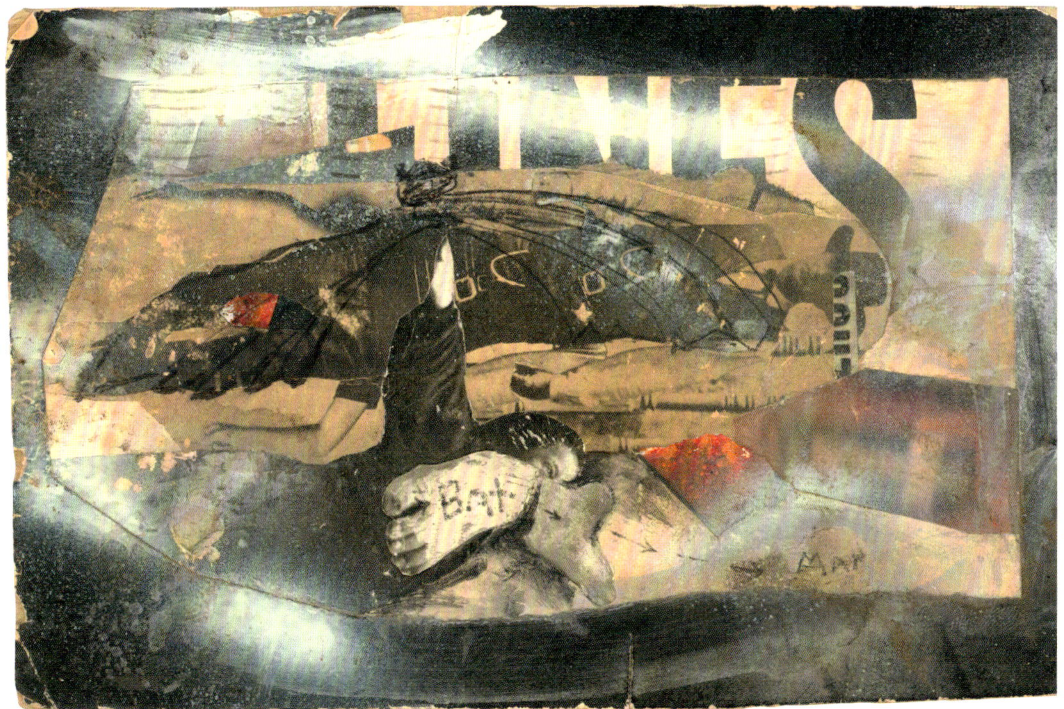

brother, Terry Morrill, has stated, "Nobody ever filed the paperwork, so although they had a nice wedding, it was never legalized.

"They were living in Beverly Glen, which was really happening back then," Morrill continues, "and they were both doing a lot of drugs. The three of us then decided to go to New York, planning to sell a bunch of pot, then fly to Crete, but we got ripped off and Bobby and DiDi fled to Montreal."[3]

After hiding out in Canada for a while, Morrill returned to L.A. and Driscoll went back to New York, where it is assumed he spent the next four years chasing his heroin habit. His friends in Los Angeles lost contact with him, but they weren't surprised when his badly decomposed body was discovered by children playing in an abandoned tenement in Greenwich Village in 1968. No one came forward to claim or identify the body, so Driscoll was buried in a pauper's grave. A year later his identity was revealed through fingerprints. *Kristine McKenna*

1 Conversation with George Herms, February 15, 1999.
2 Conversation with Shirley Berman, January 9, 1999.
3 Conversation with Terry Morrill, November 4, 2003.

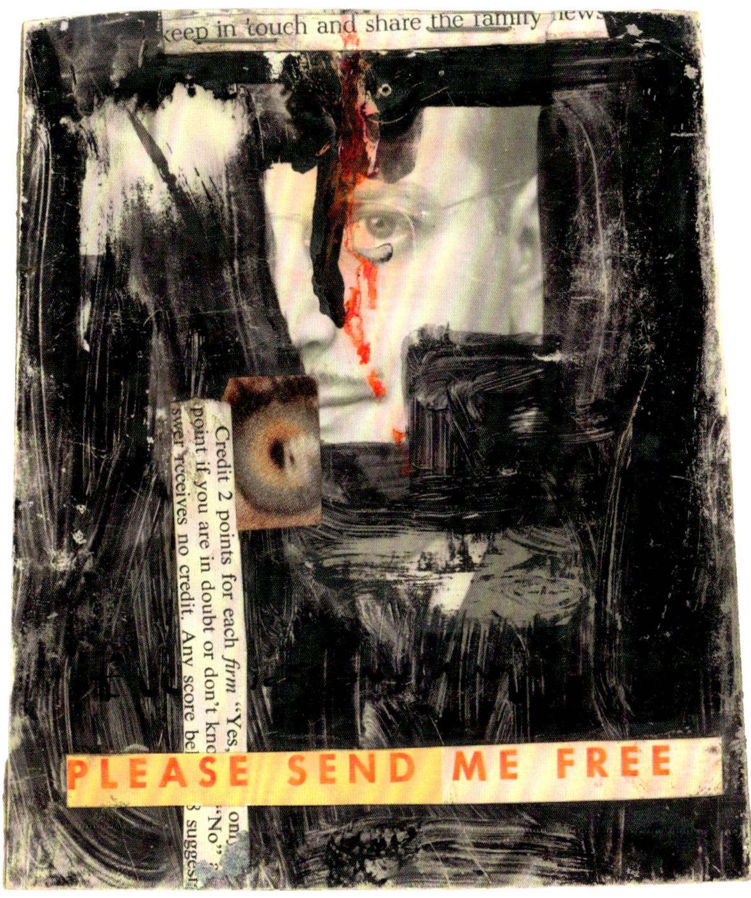

Robert Duncan

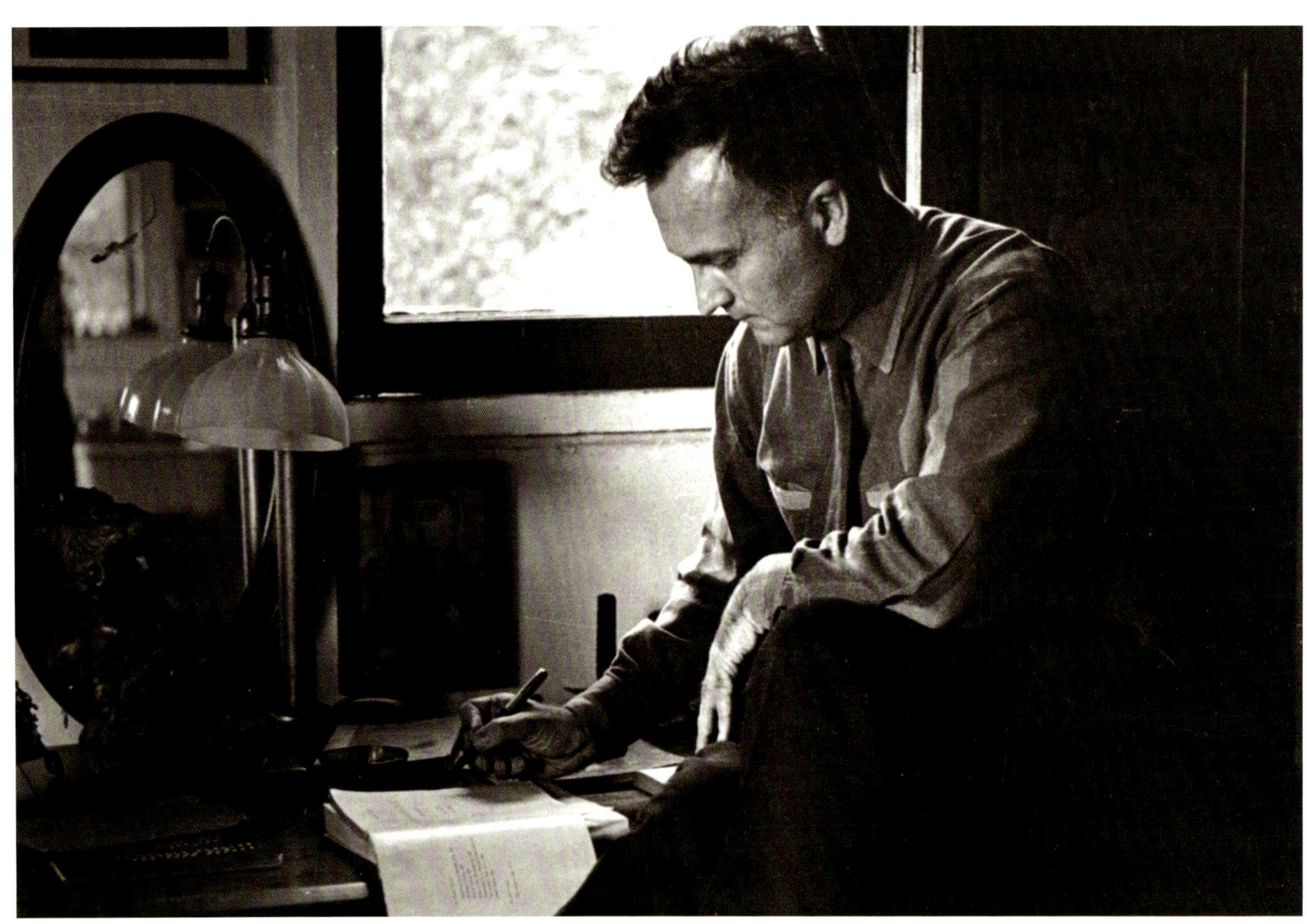

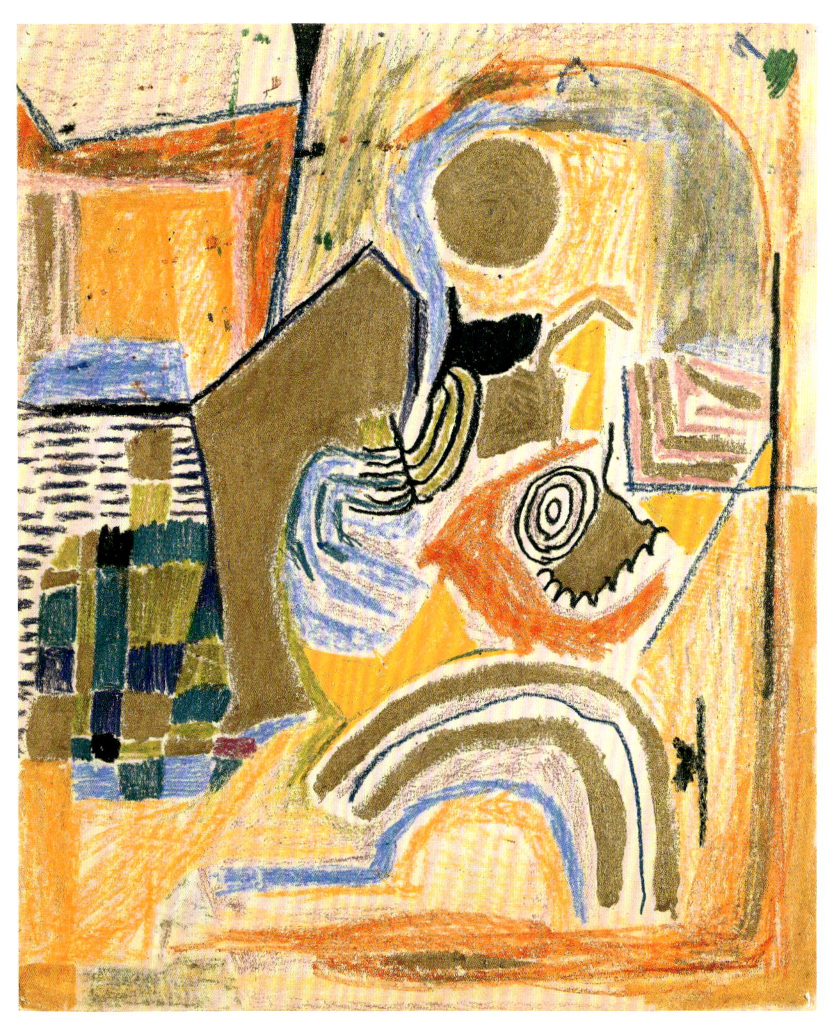

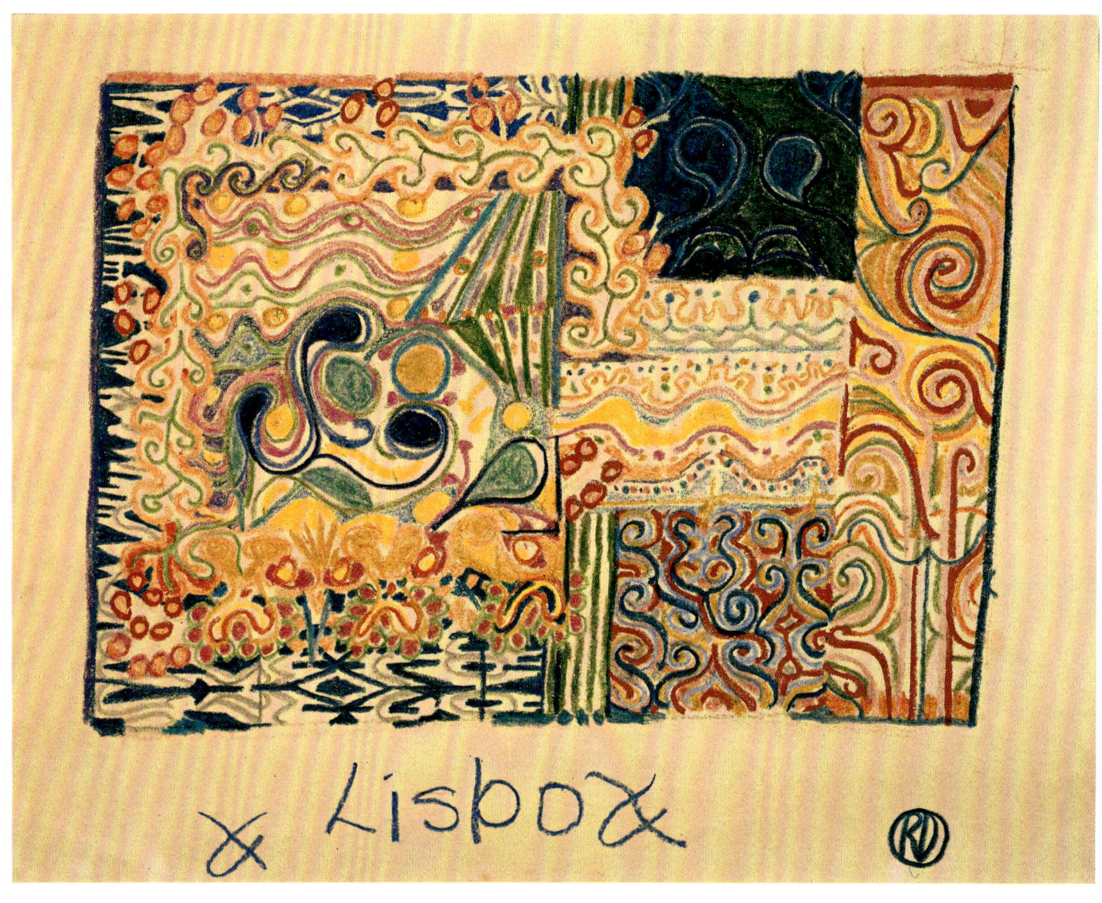
& Lisboa &

Robert Duncan is a uniquely towering figure in American poetry, offering in his writings a myth-obsessed appreciation for all forms of the poetic imagination. A voracious reader of everything from Paracelsus to the Oz books, Duncan published over forty volumes and has been acknowledged as one of the most erudite poets of his time. Duncan enjoyed a rich domestic and artistic life shared with his partner Jess whom he met in 1950.

Duncan and Jess came to artistic maturity together, ever expanding and refining their study of world literature and art. Duncan's method, inspired by Ezra Pound, was to bring together motifs and themes from all literary history; in his eclectic myth-laden verse, he took as his program "to emulate, to imitate, to reconstrue." The couple's quiet, esthetically enriched lifestyle served as an ideal for many West Coast artists and poets, particularly Wallace Berman.

p. 136
Robert Duncan, Crater Lane, 1962, Photograph by Wallace Berman.

p. 137 top
Robert Duncan, *A Winter Sun Yet Dark*, 1950, Wax crayon and gold paint on paper.

p. 137 bottom
Robert Duncan, *A Lisboa*, 1957, Wax crayon on paper.

p. 138
Robert Duncan, *Faust Foutu: A Comic Masque* (Stinson Beach: Enkidu Surrogate, 1959), cover drawing by Robert Duncan.

p. 139
Jess, *The Door of Many Colord Glass Opend: Imaginary Portrait #1: Robert Duncan*, 1952, Oil on canvas.

Born in Oakland in 1919 and adopted as an infant by Bakersfield followers of theosophy and hermetic thought, Duncan was from his youth steeped in myth and allegorical interpretation. He attended University of California at Berkeley for two years before heading to Woodstock and then Manhattan in 1938, where he fell under the spell of writer Anaïs Nin and her friends Henry Miller, Lawrence Durrell, and Kenneth Patchen. He was drafted in 1941 but managed to obtain a psychological discharge.

In 1944 he published a controversial essay in *Politics* magazine, "The Homosexual in Society," which forever marked him as an outsider from the East Coast mainstream literati. His writings of the 1940s probe his explorations of myth and romance and reflect his discovery of writers who would prove to be lifelong influences: Gertrude Stein, H.D., Pound, and James Joyce. Duncan returned to Berkeley in 1946, taking classes in medieval and Renaissance studies and connecting with a circle of poets associated with Kenneth Rexroth that included Jack Spicer and Robin Blaser. His experiences as part of the so-called "Berkeley Renaissance" provided the subtext for "The Venice Poem" (1948), a richly allusive investigation of the poetic spirit.

In the early 1950s Duncan published regularly in *Origin* and *Black Mountain Review* and corresponded with Charles Olson. Duncan's volume *Caesar's Gate Poems 1949–50* (Berkeley: Sand Dollar, 1972) was illustrated with collages by Jess, as were many of Duncan's later publica-

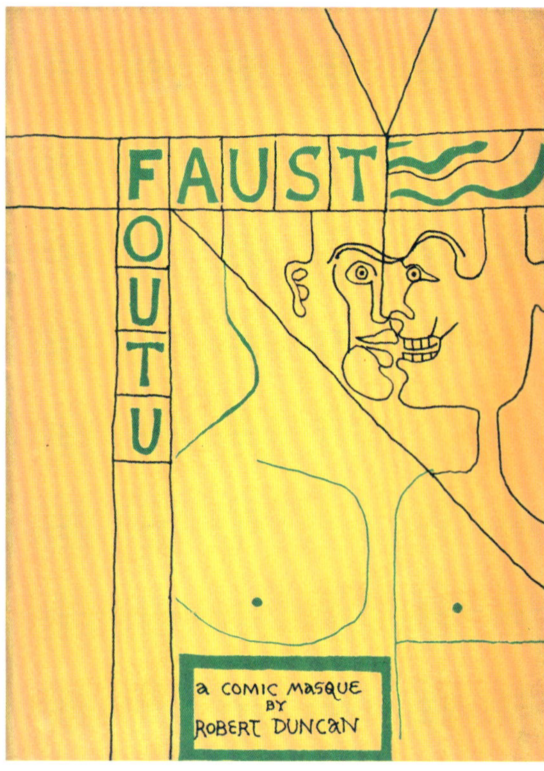

tions. *Letters* (Highlands, NC: Jargon Press, 1958) includes poems dedicated to those Duncan considered his poetic peers: Olson, Denise Levertov, Robert Creeley, Philip Lamantia, Michael and Joanna McClure, Helen Adam, and James Broughton.

One afternoon in 1954, on the recommendation of filmmaker Kenneth Anger, Wallace and Shirley Berman visited Duncan and Jess in their San Francisco apartment, resulting in what Duncan later called, "an unfolding recognition that we were possibly fellows in our feeling of what art was."[1] Berman began a correspondence, creating for Duncan and Jess some of his most playful and lyrical collage mailers. In 1963, Duncan sent the Bermans the manuscript of a poem that he had dedicated to them, "Structure of Rime XIX ("The artists of the survival..."')," later published in his volume *Roots and Branches* (New York: Scribner's, 1964).[2]

Duncan and Jess traveled in Europe in 1955, returning the next year to Black Mountain College in North Carolina where Duncan taught two classes alongside Olson. When the college was forced to close for financial reasons, the couple returned to San Francisco where Duncan immersed himself in completing his best-known

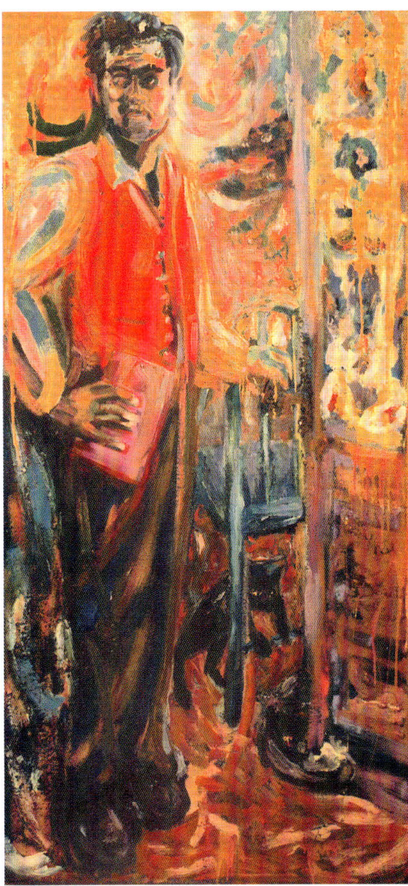

book, *The Opening of the Field* (New York: Grove, 1960), inspired by Olson's notion of "open field" verse.

A staged reading in 1955 at The Six Gallery of Duncan's verse play, *Faust Foutu*, featured performances by Duncan, Michael McClure, Helen Adam, Lawrence Jordan, and Jess, as Faust's mother. The published version of the play (Stinson Beach: Enkidu Sur, 1960) featured Duncan's stylized line drawings. Although not widely known, Duncan's visual art provides a fascinating backdrop to his writing.[3] In his college years, Duncan was interested in the automatic drawings of the Surrealists. Inspired by the activities of his painter friends Virginia Admiral and Lili Fabilli, he made spontaneous, colorful crayon designs, many on unpainted wood furniture.[4] As Admiral stated, these designs were made "without hesitation, self-doubt, theorizing, speculating, or calling it art."[5]

Christopher Wagstaff has pointed to the joyousness of Duncan's line drawings executed in a style similar to that of Picasso, Matisse, and Cocteau. Duncan had met Hans Hofmann in Provincetown and was clearly drawn to his use of bright colors. In 1951 Duncan began using a special crayon made of beeswax and oil that resisted fading from sunlight. Wagstaff has noted the special properties of crayon as a medium, "Less fluid than oils, crayons require a sense of working *into* and *with* a form rather than working *out* a predetermined form, a very important distinction for Duncan."[6]

For the homes he shared with Jess, Duncan assembled an art collection, featuring works by Edward Corbett, Dean Stockwell, Marjorie McKee, Admiral, Harry Jacobus, Lawrence and Patricia Jordan, Lynn Brown, and Jess. Guests to the house would often participate in crayon drawing sessions after dinner. In the spirit of the surrealists, Duncan, Jess, and Jacobus made a series of Exquisite Corpse drawings together in 1952 and 1953. In 1952, as a Christmas present to friends, Duncan made an edition of fifty copies of the hand printed book *Fragments of a Disorderd Devotion*, each with a watercolor or crayon decorated cover. He later made for friends many books, scrapbooks, poems, and cards decorated with drawings and abstract designs.

Duncan foreswore publishing for fifteen years while he was writing *Ground Work: Before the War* (New York: New Directions, 1984). This complex volume touching on all of his major themes was followed by *Ground Work II: In the Dark* (New York: New Directions, 1987), his last major book. Duncan received a Guggenheim Fellowship in 1963, the National Poetry Award in 1985, and three fellowships from the National Endowment for the Arts. He died in San Francisco in 1988 after a long struggle with kidney disease. *Michael Duncan*

1 Robert Duncan, "Wallace Berman: The Fashioning Spirit," *Wallace Berman: Retrospective*, exh. cat. (Los Angeles: Fellows of Contemporary Art, 1978), p. 19.
2 Robert Duncan, Letter to Wallace and Shirley Berman, March 15, 1963, Wallace Berman Archive, Archives of American Art, Smithsonian Institution.
3 See Robert L. Bertholf, *A Symposium of the Imagination: Robert Duncan in Word and Image*, exh. cat. (Buffalo: Poetry/Rare Books Collection, State University of Buffalo, 1993) and Christopher Wagstaff, *Robert Duncan: Drawings and Decorated Books*, exh. cat. (Berkeley: Rose Books, 1992).
4 Virginia Admiral, "Remembering Robert Duncan," in Wagstaff, p. 9.
5 Ibid., p. 11.
6 Christopher Wagstaff, "An Interior Light: A Note on Robert Duncan's Crayon Drawings," p. 14.

Joe Dunn

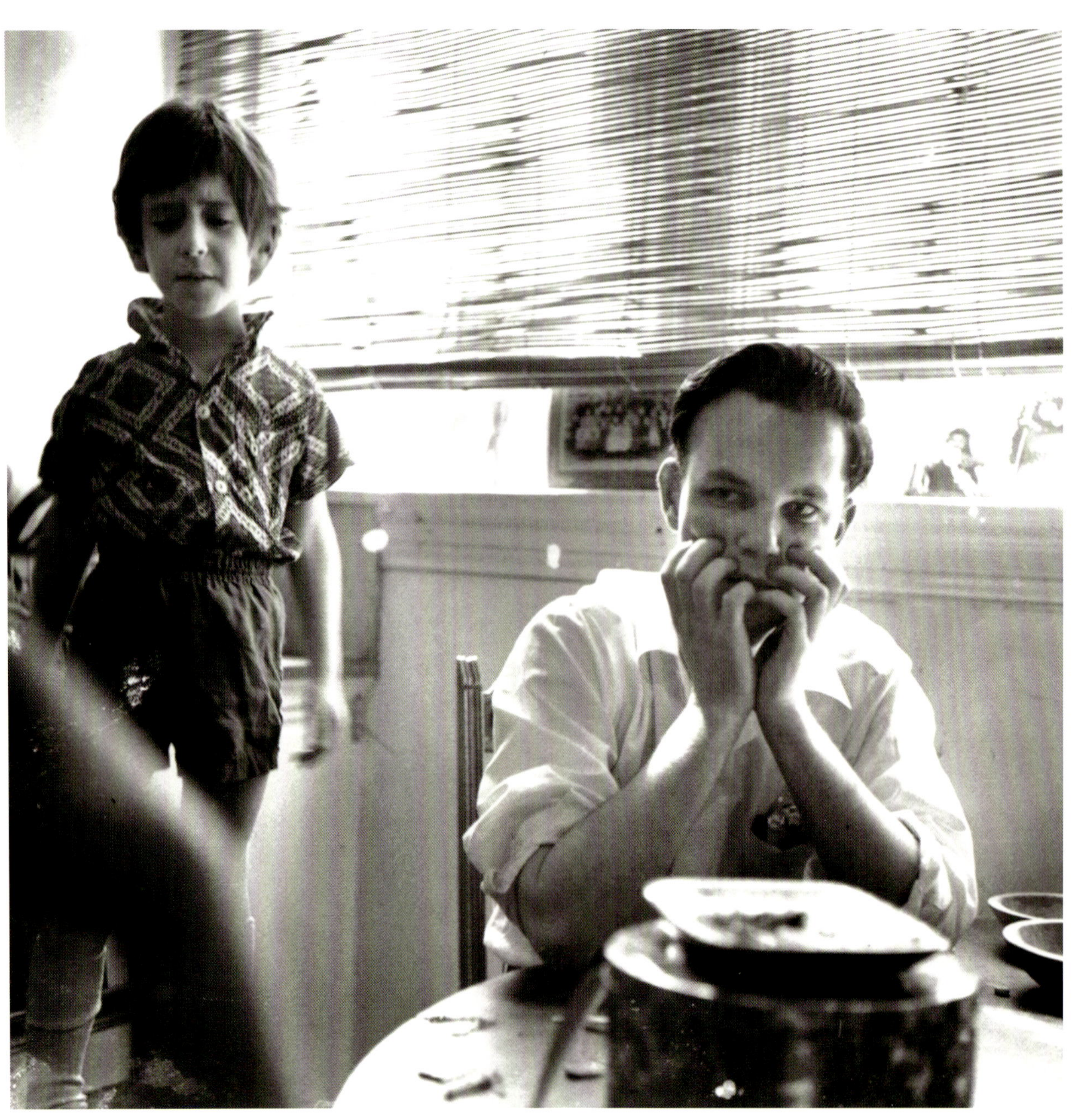

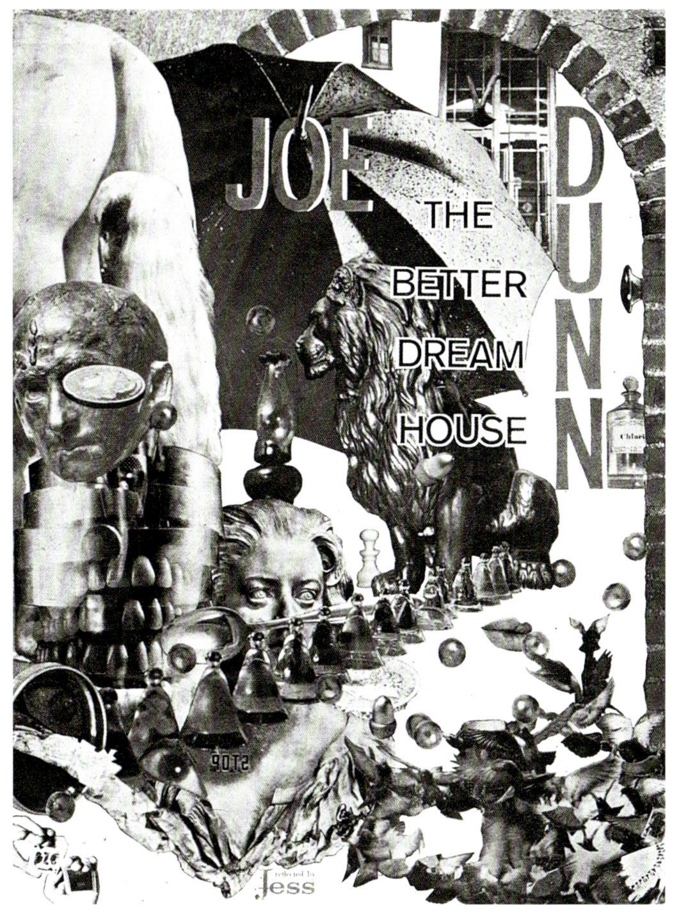

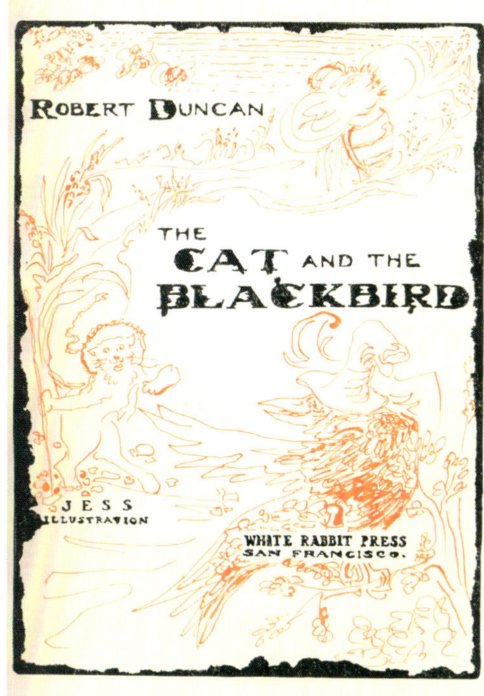

For poets of the 1950s, an underground rival to the "Berkeley Renaissance" scene was the so-called "Boston Renaissance," ruled by longtime friends John Wieners, Steve Jonas, and Joe Dunn. Dunn had attended Robert Duncan's writing class at Black Mountain College, where he also met Jess, with whom he later collaborated on several publications for White Rabbit Press.

An edgy, energetic character, Dunn—although married and allegedly straight—was for many years the obsessive love interest for poet Jack Spicer.[1] To silence Spicer's hatred for Boston, in 1956 Dunn and his wife Carolyn moved with him to San Francisco, where Spicer launched his Poetry as Magic workshop at the Public Library. For several years, this poetry circle frequently met at the Dunns' apartment on Jackson Street where the gatherings included figures such as Robert Duncan and James Broughton.

A poetry enthusiast found Dunn a job running the print department of the city's Greyhound Bus Company and Dunn was allowed to use the office press on off-hours and Saturday nights to pursue his own publishing ventures. Dunn applied himself to White Rabbit Press with feverish energy, publishing ten titles in the first year, including books by Jonas, Spicer, Denise Levertov, Richard Brautigan, Helen Adam, Robert Duncan, and Charles Olson. White Rabbit Press books were all lithographed in handsome editions from the authors' typescripts in a standard 8 1/2 x 6 1/2 inch size. A drawing of a rabbit by Robert Duncan was used as the press colophon. Jess provided illustrations and covers for several of their offerings.

The glory days of the press were short-lived. Dunn's addictive personality quickly led to problems with alcohol and Methedrine. Squandering his subscribers' funds on drugs, Dunn lost control of the business in 1958. Graham Macintosh reinstated the press from 1962 until 1972, continuing to publish important publications by authors such as Duncan, Spicer, Wieners, and Dunn.[2]

Michael Duncan

p. 140
Joe Dunn and Tosh Berman, 707 Scott Street, 1959, Photograph by Wallace Berman.

p. 141 left
Joe Dunn, *The Better Dream House* (San Francisco: White Rabbit Press, 1968).

p. 141 right
Robert Duncan, *The Cat and the Blackbird* (San Francisco: White Rabbit Press, 1967).

1 For a full account of this obsession, see Lewis Ellingham and Kevin Killian, *Poet Be Like God: Jack Spicer and the San Francisco Renaissance* (Hanover & London: Wesleyan University Press, 1998).

2 For further information on White Rabbit Press, see Steven Clay and Rodney Phillips, *A Secret Location on the Lower East Side* (New York: New York Public Library and Granary Books, 1998), p. 62 and Alastair M. Johnston, *A Bibliography of the White Rabbit Press* (Berkeley: Poltroon Press, 1985).

Llyn Foulkes

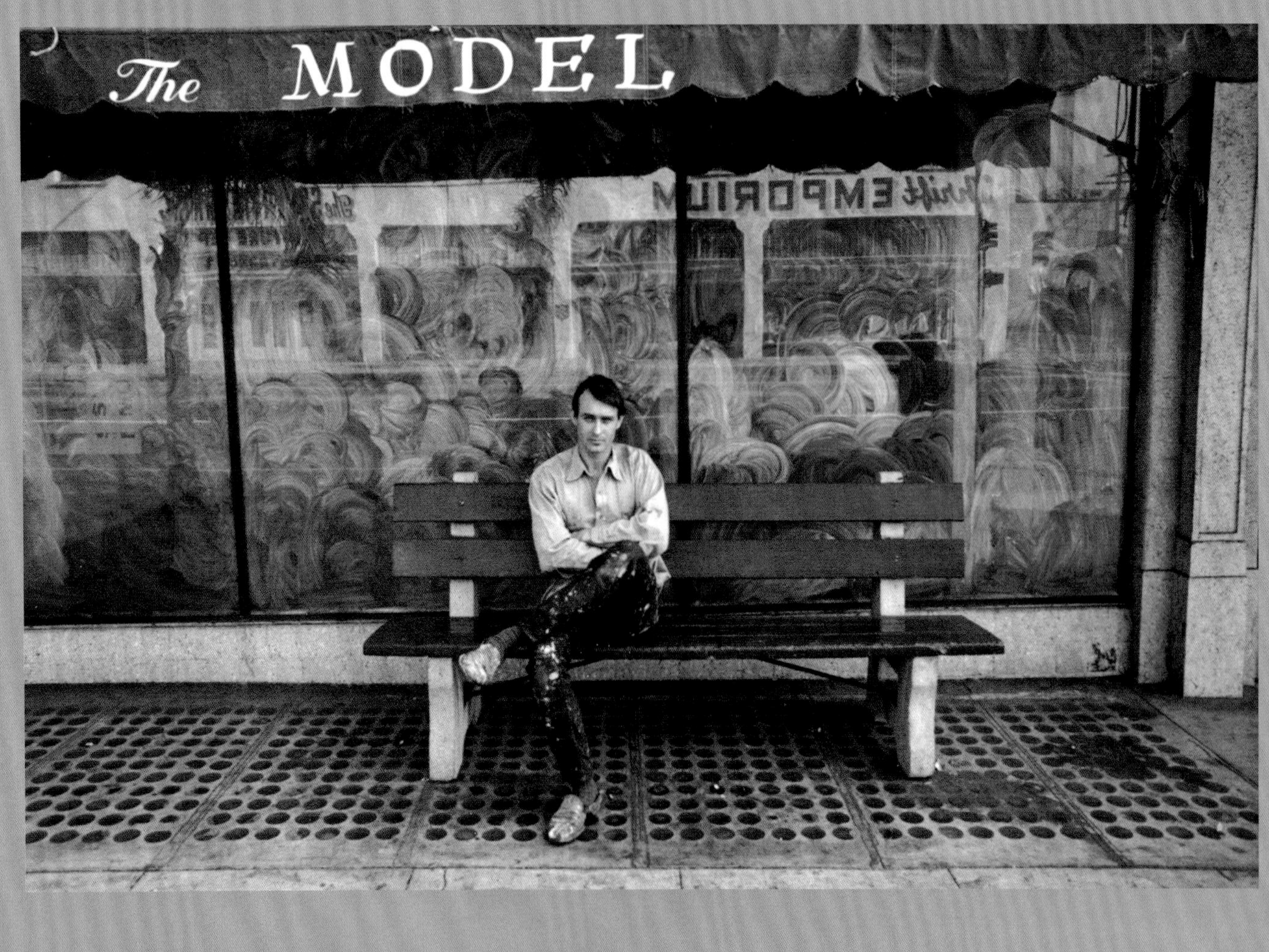

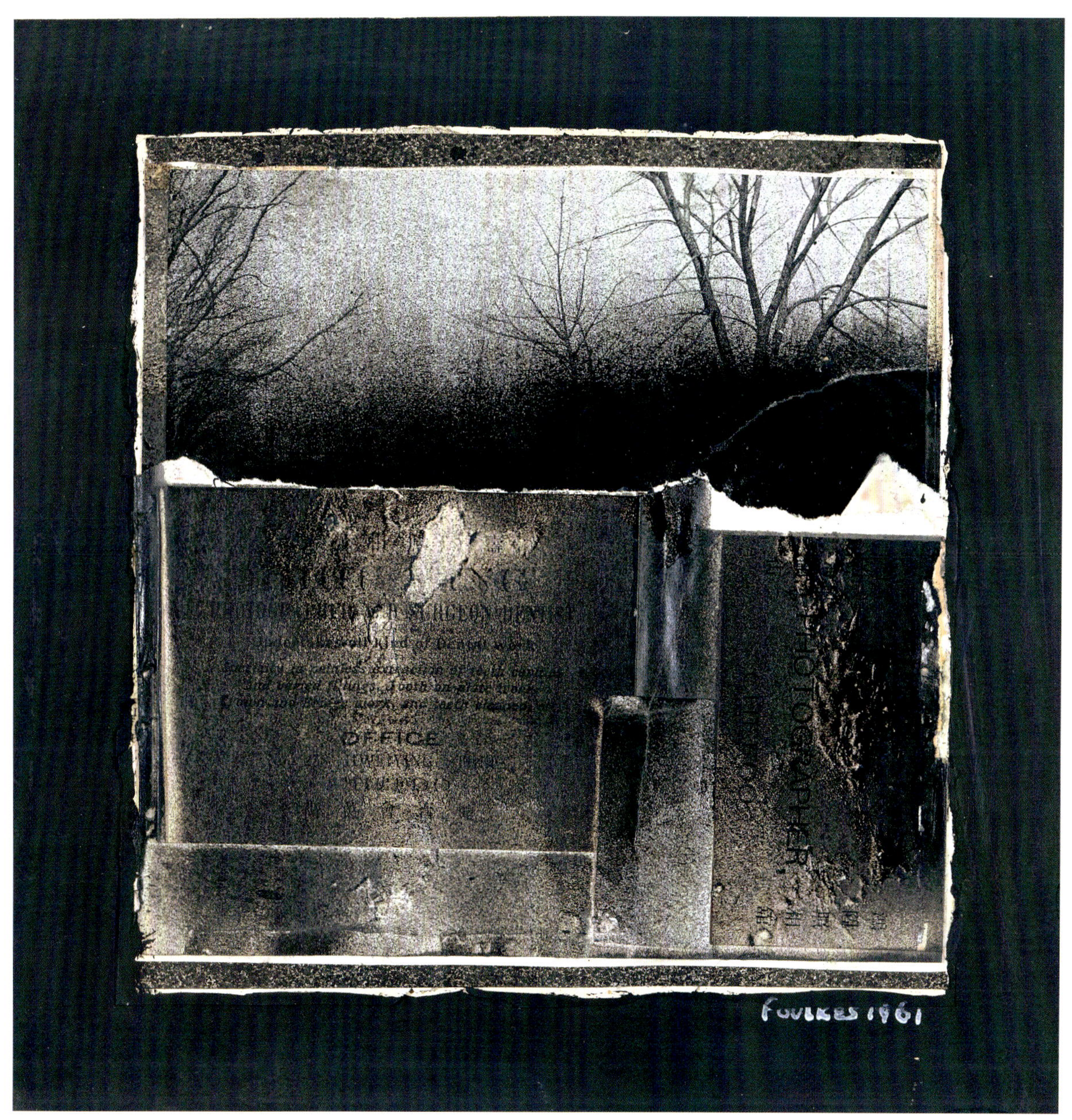
OFFICE
PHOTOGRAPHER
FOULKES 1961

Earnest, theatrical, and politically driven, Los Angeles artist Llyn Foulkes is a vastly underrated American master. His goals are serious, rigorous, and impossible to dismiss. Unabashed about seeking a popular audience for art, Foulkes pursues visceral effects and instantly recognizable imagery to convey his dark vision of American culture in trouble. Drawing from disparate sources that range from Dalí and Disney to Bellini and Donatello, he seeks nothing less than to reinvigorate painting with the moral seriousness of Renaissance religious art.

p. 142
Llyn Foulkes, 1964, Photograph by Dennis Hopper.

p. 143
Llyn Foulkes, *Untitled (Cabinet Series)*, 1961, Collage with photo.

p. 144
Llyn Foulkes home studio, 1964.

p. 145
Llyn Foulkes, *Sheep of Araby*, 1972, Mixed-media, 4 5/8 x 4 5/8 inches, Collection of Dean Stockwell.

Oddly, a natural gift for comic performing seems to have led Foulkes to his role as a moral arbiter of Pop culture. Born in Yakima, Washington in 1934, he was eleven years old when he discovered the satirical music of Spike Jones and developed the first incarnation of his One-Man-Band—a jerry-built musical contraption combining horns, washboard, drum, and vibraphone—on which he continues to improvise and play his sardonic compositions. In high school he was exposed to the works of Salvador Dalí, whose eccentricity, daring, and brilliant technique have been a lifelong inspiration.

After briefly attending the University of Washington, Foulkes joined the Army and was posted to Germany where he became absorbed in European art history and witnessed the devastating effects of World War II. After his release from the military in 1957, he moved to Los Angeles to study art at Chouinard Art Institute, which was then firmly entrenched in Abstract Expressionism.

Learning from the sophisticated abstract styles of teachers Richards Ruben and Emerson Woelffer, Foulkes emerged from school fully developed as an artist. Incorporating photographs as well as collaged objects with charred and molten textures, the paintings from his first one-man exhibition at Ferus Gallery (1961) remain remarkably inventive, conceptually varied, and fresh. With the anti-formalist esthetic of the times, Foulkes made use of the painterly qualities of found assemblage elements.

Foulkes was a self-described "anti-social loner," developing his work in isolation in his Highland Park studio. The dark lyricism of his work, however, clearly appealed to the sensibility of other Los Angeles artists. Foulkes's 1962 exhibition at the Pasadena Art Museum, curated by Walter Hopps, prompted Wallace Berman to visit his studio, bringing with him Dean Stockwell who later took Foulkes to visit George Herms. Berman and Stockwell sent Foulkes collaged mailers. Foulkes reciprocated with a small drawing of a hand with a cross on the palm that Berman reproduced in *Semina 8*. As Foulkes has pointed out, in several of Berman's later Verifax collages, he used the image of a cross within his hand-held radio frame.[1]

Like the rest of Berman's circle, Foulkes had a dark, lyrical sensibility, occasionally manifested in poetic text written directly on the works, such as that on *Ellensberg Canyon Landscape* (1962): "Let the sunless sky close around me, that I may not view the perpetual hue of sight—perchance within darkness to advance with oblivious fright from the sun." Although Foulkes was never Berman's intimate friend, he felt, as he later put it, "There was a certain kind of spirituality that was connecting us."[2] Later, while represented by Rolf Nelson Gallery in Los Angeles, Foulkes also came to know and appreciate fellow gallery-artist Jess, whom he visited in San Francisco and with whom he traded work.

Foulkes became well known in the late 1960s for Pop paintings structured as large-scale postcards of desert landscapes. In 1969, however, he repudiated the movement, railing against its flat, thin images and arid planes. Foulkes settled on the neglected medium of relief as the best way to lure viewers deep into the illusionistic space

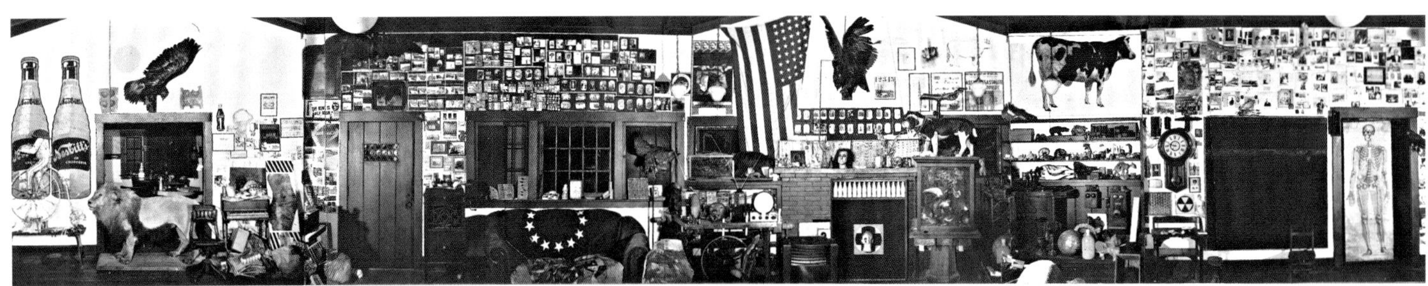

of pictures. With protruding architectural moldings and receding details dug into his wooden panels, Foulkes envelops viewers in his cartoon-like tableaux and self-portraits. The incorporation of real fabrics, objects, and photographs into the reliefs seems less a nod to assemblage than a desire for heightened realism and tactile immediacy.

Foulkes's best known Pop paintings were large-scale depictions of desert and rock landscapes that conjure an affectless existential angst. Although Foulkes's pop landscapes effectively captured a sense of new world anti-utopia, the artist felt constrained by their serial imagery and emptied content. He called a halt to such work, concentrating on the music of his rock group "The Rubber Band" (1973–77).

Experimenting in his studio in the early 1970s, Foulkes blotted out the face of a self-portrait with an angry swatch of blood-red paint. The ghoulish self-revelation of *Who's on Third* (1971–73) re-kindled Foulkes's interest in visual art. Foulkes's series of transgressive portraits skewered the sanctity of formal portraiture with a gory Dadaist energy. He exploded the public facades of patriarchal businessmen, military leaders, bureaucrats, and art officials, stripping away their faces to reveal the rot within.

In the 1980s Foulkes began exploring larger arenas for social commentary. With sprightly Puritanical fervor, he took on American corruption as a personal burden. His hair shirt is our national soullessness, epitomized in the squeaky clean, corporate symbol of Mickey Mouse. For Foulkes, Disney's mass-marketing of culture—as demonstrated in the world's millions of *Lion King* and *Pocahontas*-addled toddlers—is an insidious menace that permeates all levels of American society.

His tableaux twist pop culture heroes such as the Lone Ranger and Superman, pondering their hapless, hopeless roles as moral arbiters in an already blasted world. Although all of his portraits have autobiographical elements, self-portraiture has directly entered Foulkes's work in works that present suburban frustration, social corruption, corporate greed, and moral ambiguity. Los Angeles is the specific site for Foulkes's messianic mission.

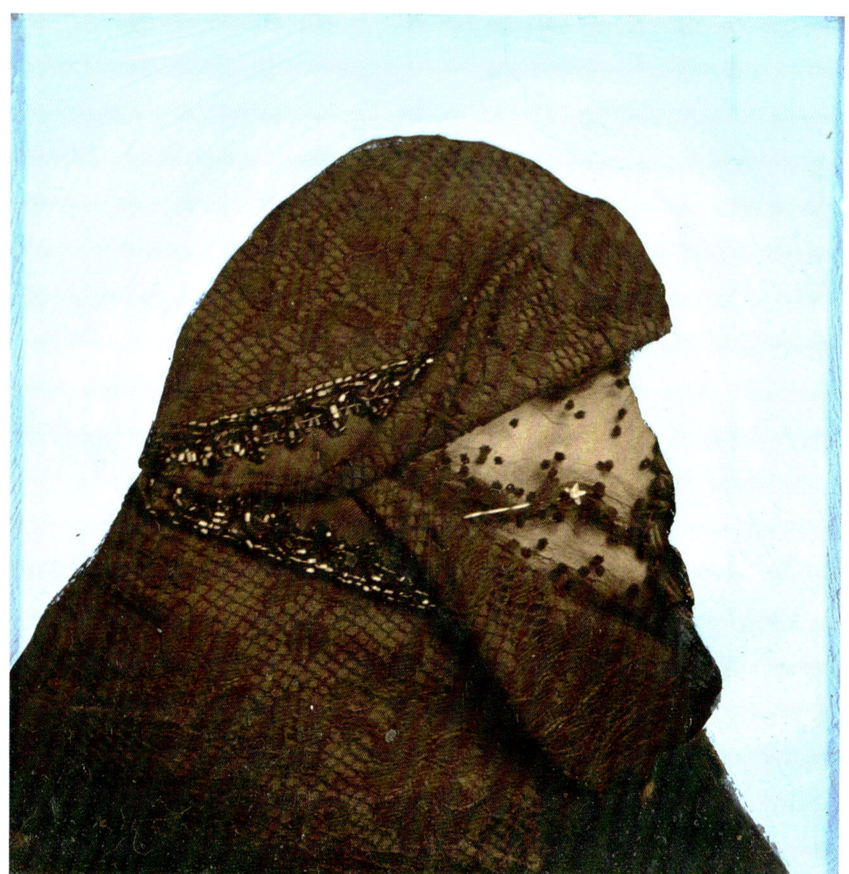

Foulkes has made many landscape reliefs that present the American frontier as a fenced-off, homogenized burlesque ruled by a demonic Mickey Mouse. Several 1990s self-portraits brilliantly combine the fiery anger of the earlier heads with the black comedy of the tableaux. Self-portraiture has deepened Foulkes's tragicomedy, making his cultural martyrdom into a winning emblem for the American outsider. Standing in opposition to Mickey Mouse, Foulkes readily states, "I am a spiritual person." In this age of inbred sellouts and mass-media acquiescence, his earnest desire to take on the burden of American culture makes Foulkes a brave and unique figure.

Michael Duncan

1 Interview with Llyn Foulkes by Paul Karlstrom, July 17, 1997, Archives of American Art, Smithsonian Institution, Tape 2, Side B.
2 Ibid.

Loree Foxx

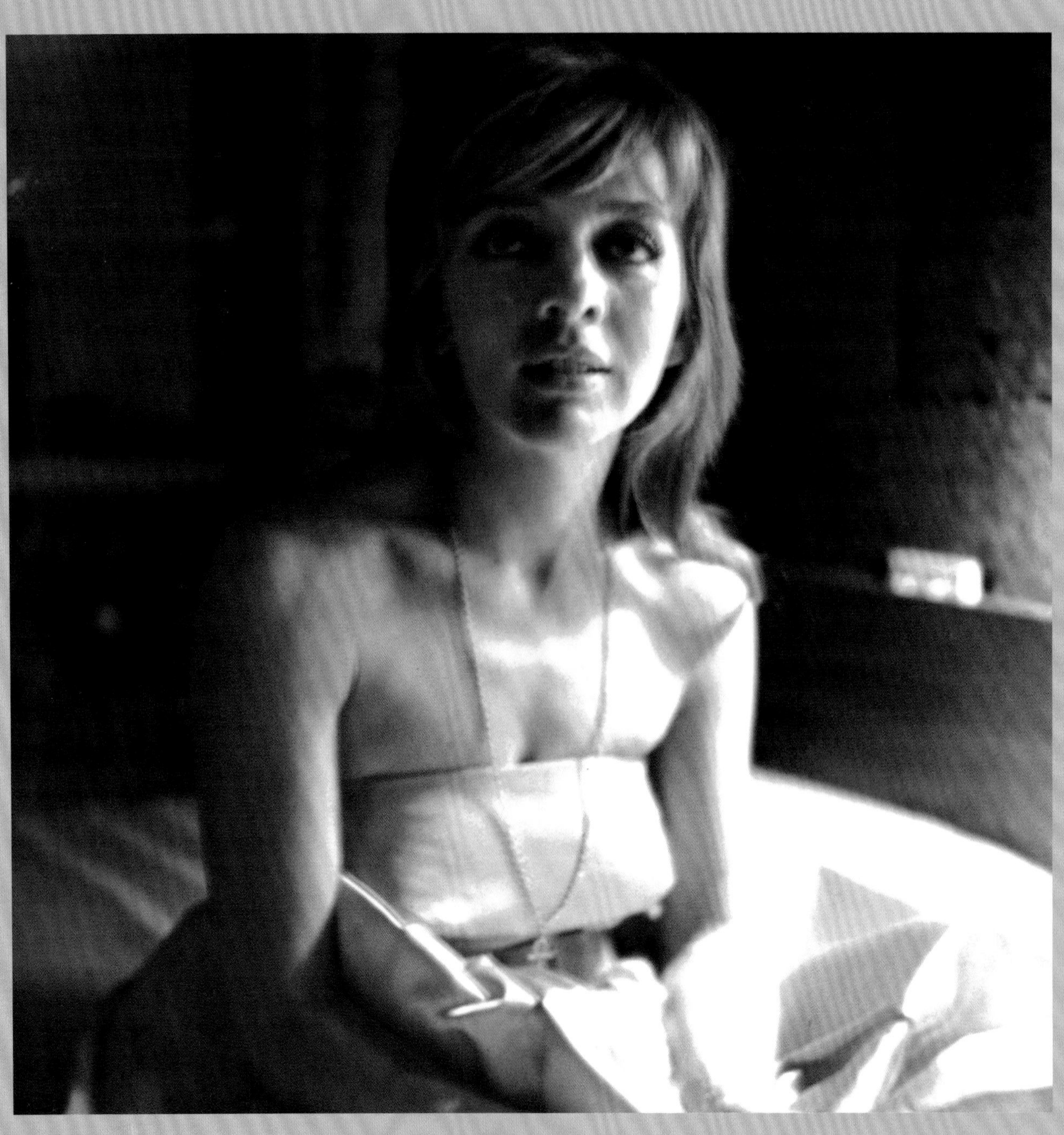

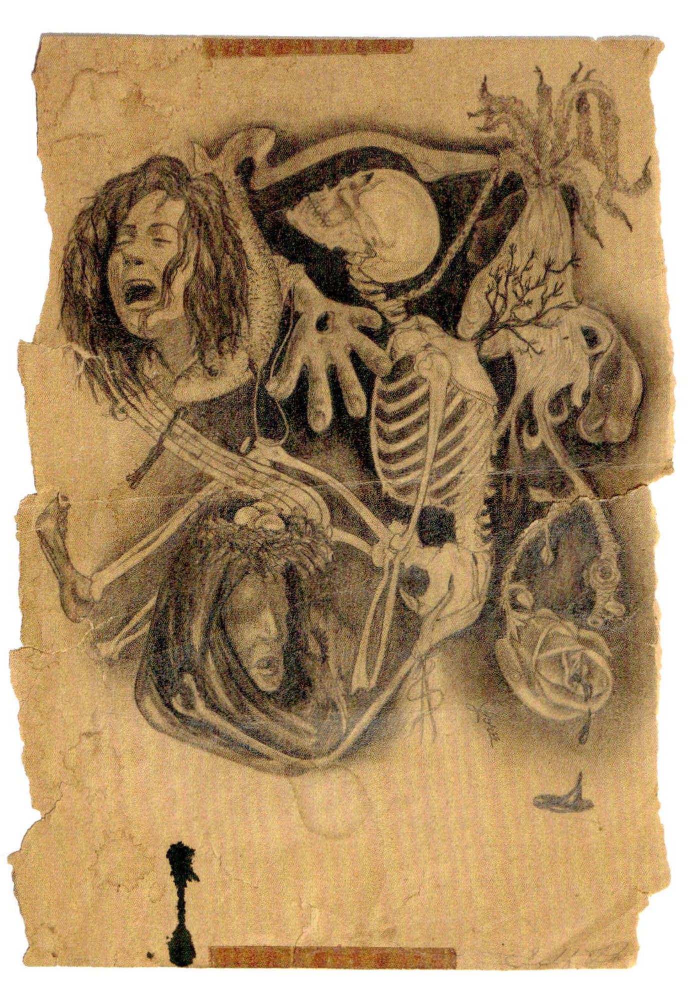

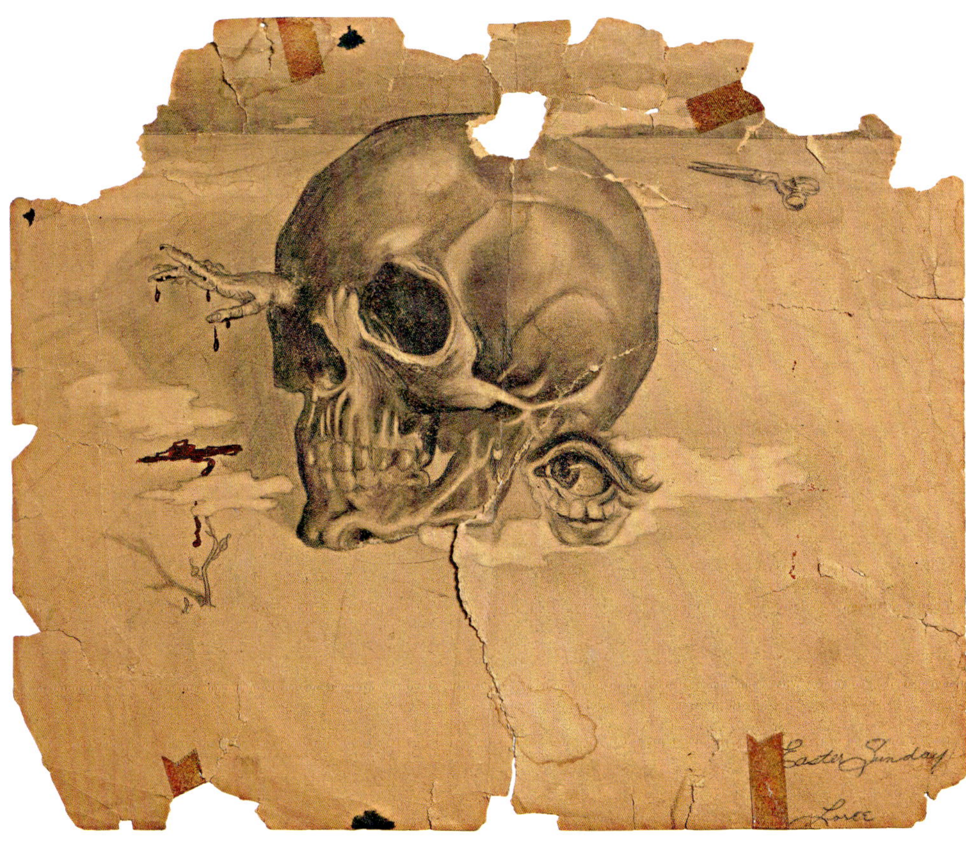
Easter Sunday
Loree

Loree Foxx was born Dolores Pitkin Fox, in Baltimore, in 1929. She was a pretty, self-possessed little girl, and as was the case with many pretty little girls of her generation, her mother had high hopes for her future as a film star. Toward that end, Foxx's mother left her husband, relocated to Los Angeles, changed her daughter's name, and sent her to the Hollywood Professional School. "Loree never went to public school," Foxx's niece, Suzi Hicks, recalls. "Her mother wouldn't allow her to go anywhere except where the child stars went."[1]

Foxx became a dancer for the Megland Kiddies when she was seven years old, and in 1939 she was cast as a ballerina in the Munchkinland sequence in *The Wizard of Oz*. As a teenager she dated Donald O'Connor, who'd been a classmate at the Hollywood Professional School, and in 1947 she landed a part in *The Bachelor and the Bobbysoxer*, starring Cary Grant. By that point, however, it had become clear to Foxx that she wasn't cut out for a career in the film industry. A strong personality who gravitated toward the hip street culture of 1940s Los Angeles, Foxx began dating Wallace Berman in 1948, and at that point she turned her back on the movie business entirely.

p. 146
Loree Foxx, Los Angeles, 1955, Photograph by Wallace Berman.

p. 147 top
Loree Foxx, *Self-Portrait*, 1949, Ink on paper.

p. 147 bottom
Loree Foxx, *Easter Sunday*, 1949, Ink on paper.

p. 149
Loree Foxx, *Untitled (Jody and boyfriend, Wallace and girlfriend, and Loree Foxx)*, 1950, Ink and gouache on paper.

Berman was in his zoot-suit period then, and he and Foxx were a dazzling couple who frequented the jazz clubs of Central Avenue and jitterbugging joints like the Palladium. By all accounts they were something to see on the dance floor, and they devoted a good deal of time and energy to local dance contests, which they frequently won. During that period Foxx befriended Lee Wilder, owner of Tempo Music Shop, which was the place to go for jazz records during the 1940s. Through Wilder, Foxx became part of the jazz community, which included Lenny Bruce, who became a close friend to Foxx.

During the 1940s Berman produced a series of surrealist pencil sketches made in homage to his jazz heroes. Foxx made drawings then, too, in a style identical to Berman's, however, the tone of her work is considerably darker. In *Easter Sunday*—a morbid work clearly influenced by Dalí—a skull is positioned at the center of a parched desert landscape next to a barren tree. A gnarled female hand juts from the brow of the skull, blood dripping from its fingers, as an eyeball surrounded by teeth floats nearby. Another work, *Self-Portrait*, is structured around an image of a skeleton with a chain around its neck. Woven into a nightmarish mass of imagery is the sleeping face of a weathered old woman with a bird's nest atop her head, a rose dripping blood, a few bars of musical notation, and a swollen hand pierced by a bullet hole. Dominating the composition is an image of a young woman, her face contorted in agony. An untitled work from 1950, executed in chalk and pastel, exploits a completely different and vaguely Cubist style evocative of Paul Klee. Presently in the collection of Donald Morand, the drawing depicts two couples juxtaposed with an isolated figure that looks on longingly from a distance; according to Morand, Foxx made the drawing at a point when she felt she'd been replaced by another woman in Berman's affections.

By 1950 Foxx's romance with Berman had evolved into a friendship, and in 1951 she married musician Gil Barrios. The marriage was annulled after five months, and a few months later she opened a short-lived arts and crafts shop on La Cienega Boulevard with friends Bill Rotsler and Donald Morand. By the end of 1951, Foxx and Morand had become a couple, and they moved to New York so Foxx could pursue a modeling career. "She was working at a theater on Fifty-seventh Street and was stealing several hundred dollars a night from the cash register—Loree was a terror," Morand recalls with a laugh. "There was no controlling her. She was a thief, a compulsive shoplifter and she was manipulative, but she was also very smart, and she was intensely alive."[2]

Foxx returned to Los Angeles with Morand at the end of 1952 and settled for two years in a house in Manhattan Beach, across the street from her mother. "Loree wor-

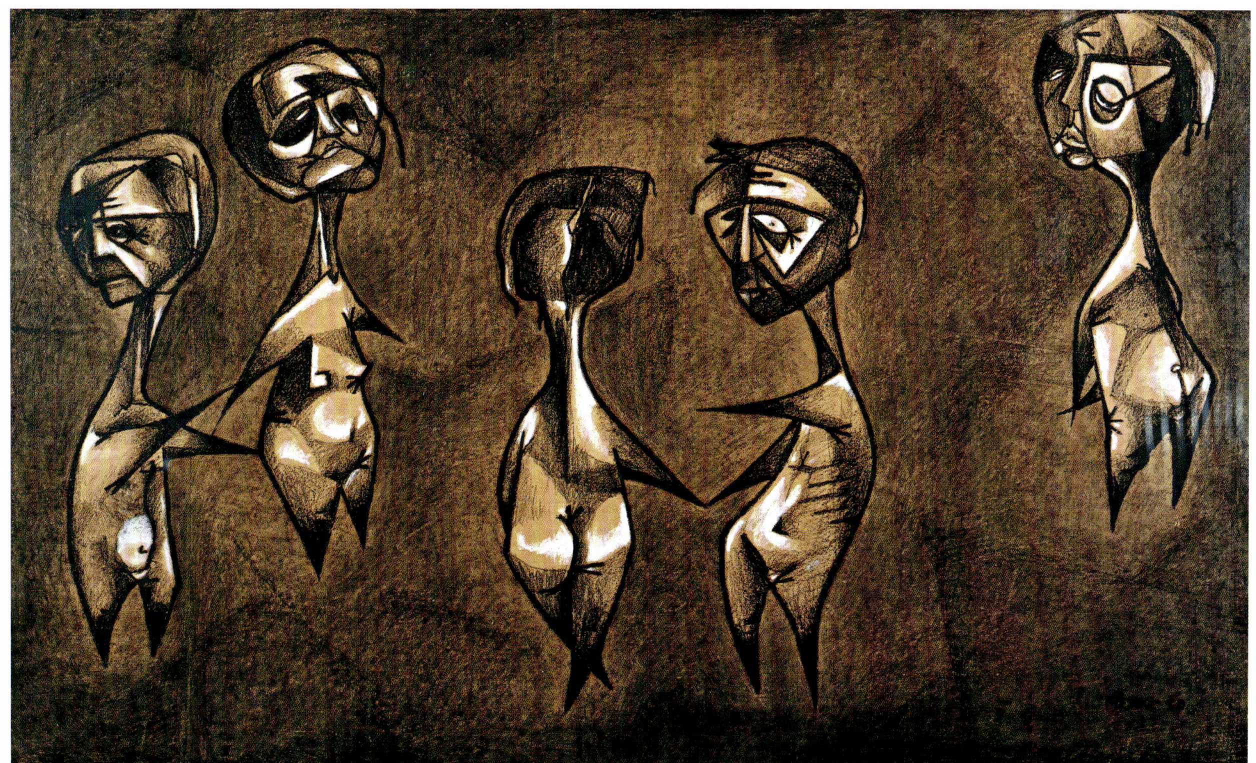

shipped her mother and she had a totally different, really sweet personality when she was with her," comments Morand, who remained close to Foxx for a decade after their affair ended. "She'd play cards with her and eat her terrible cookies. It's true that Loree hated being pushed into the movies, but she appreciated her mother's belief in her."

In 1954 Foxx moved to Desert Hot Springs where she took a job in a factory, and a year later she bought a place in Joshua Tree. "Loree had severe asthma, which is what took her out to the desert," Morand recalls. "After she moved to Joshua Tree a mutual friend of ours who was her lover at the time, Dick Constantino, moved out there with her. Then I moved there in 1959 and we all lived together."

"Loree was a very persuasive person and she was like the queen out there," Morand continues. "Richard and I worked, and we had a hired hand to care for Loree's animals—she had two lions, a couple of horses, donkeys, and some Nubian goats. She spent the day making beaded curtains, or drawing and painting. Loree was constantly drawing, but unfortunately some of her best work was destroyed. She made caricatures of all the people who hung out at Norman Rose's book store, and some people destroyed them while Norman had them up. Loree could really get people, and there were those who took offense at how she portrayed them."

Morand left Joshua Tree in 1964, while Foxx remained there for the rest of the decade, as her life became increasingly tumultuous. "She was not in good shape," Morand says. "Loree had a drug problem that began when she was very young and they gave her Benzedrine to boost her performance in films. She mostly took speed, which exacerbated the extreme aspects of her personality, but Loree would take anything."

In 1972 Foxx was arrested in Arizona as an indigent, and was sent to the Arizona State Penitentiary. "At that point I knew very little about what was going on in Loree's life," says Morand. "All I know is that she sold her place in the desert, she was on the road with Dick Constantino's ex-wife, Candy, and she was traveling in a van full of her stuff." Foxx had an asthma attack while she was in custody and was given medication she was allergic to which killed her. She was forty-two years old. *Kristine McKenna*

1 Conversation with Suzi Hicks, December 20, 1999.

2 All quotations by Donald Morand from a conversation on August 31, 2004.

Ralph Gibson

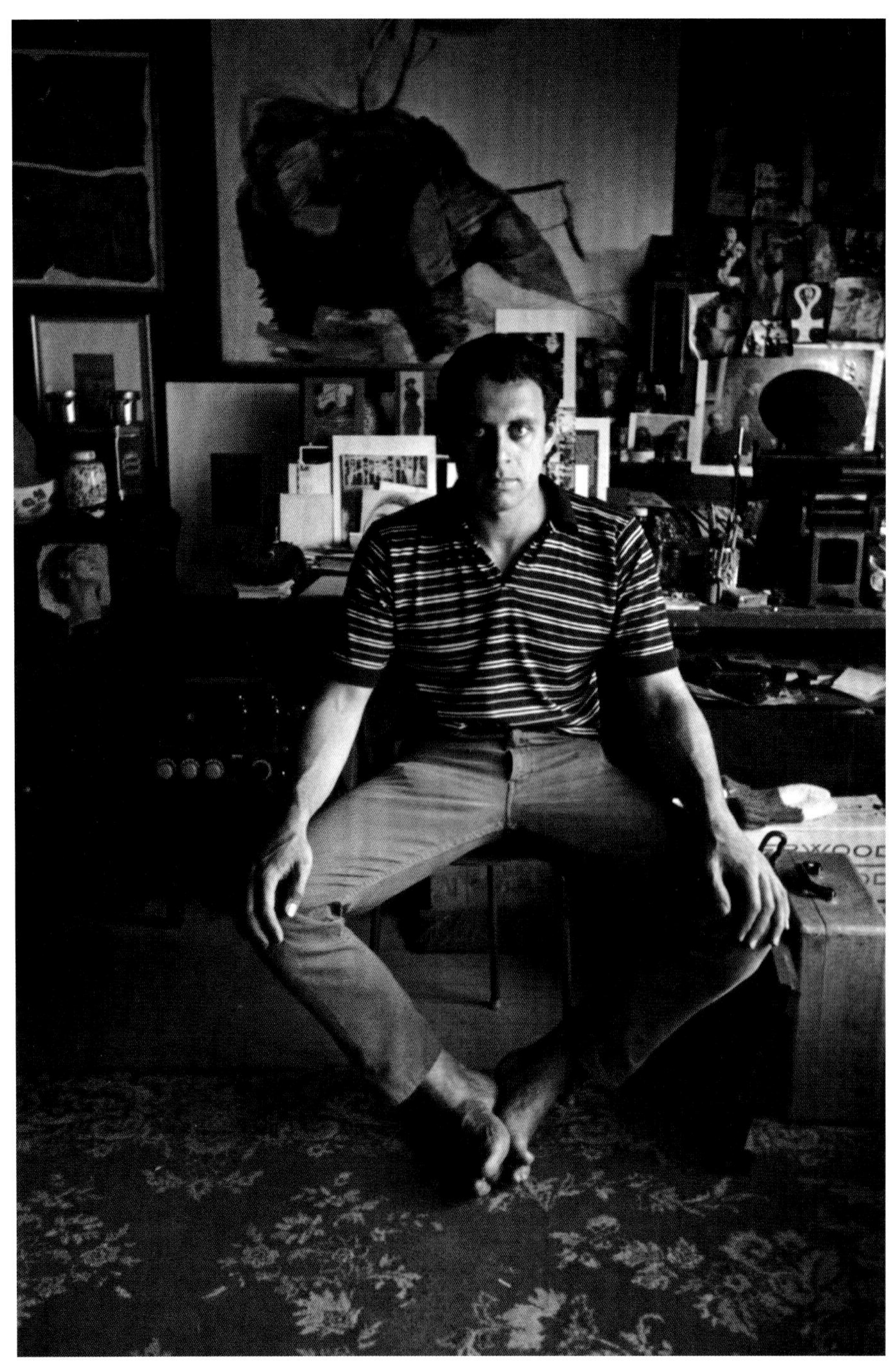

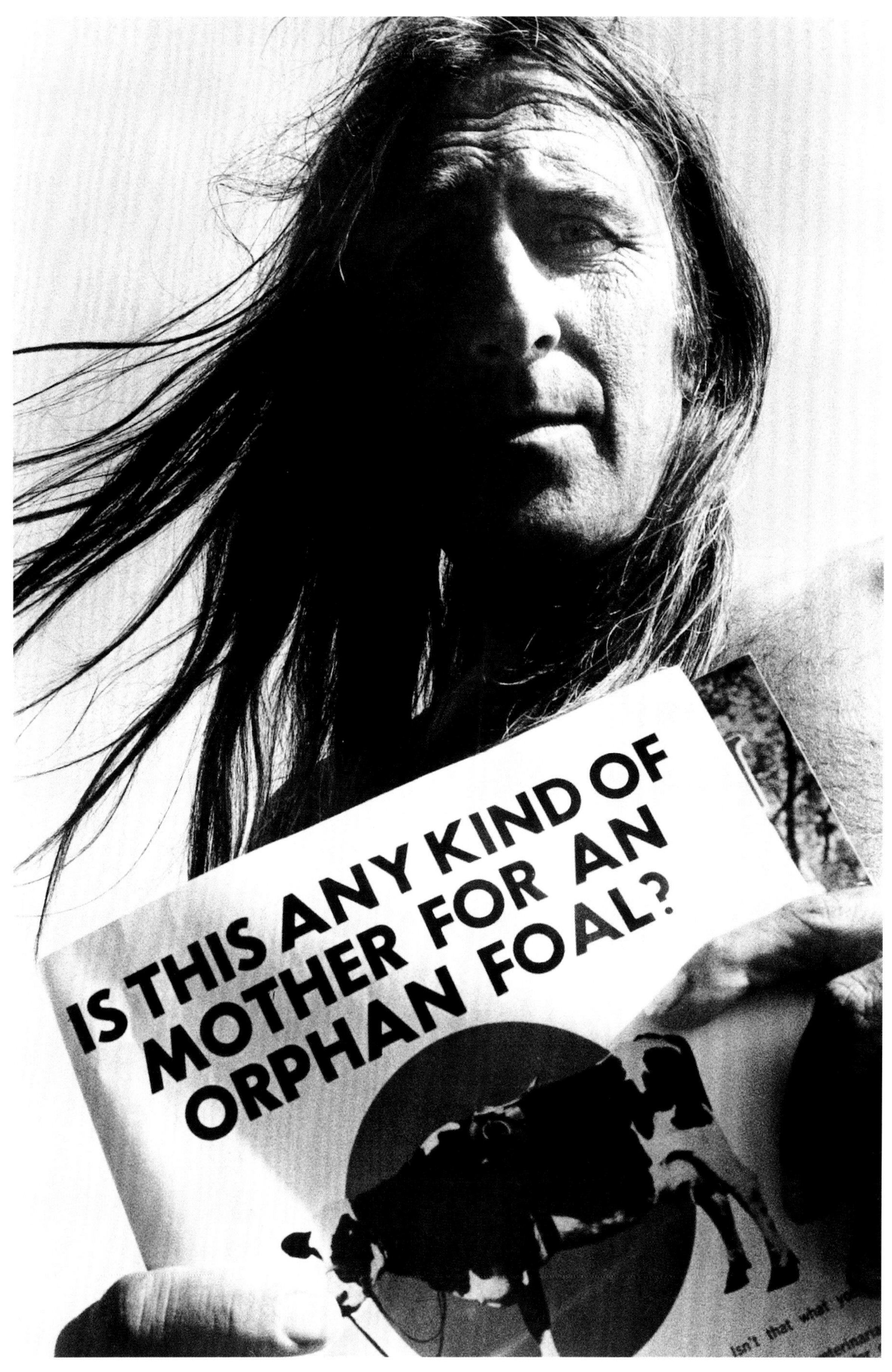
IS THIS ANY KIND OF MOTHER FOR AN ORPHAN FOAL?

Street photography was one of the great art forms of the twentieth century. As defined by Henri Cartier-Bresson, Diane Arbus, Robert Frank, and Walker Evans, among many others, it served as the foundation for the golden age of photojournalism, and it was the starting point for artist Ralph Gibson.

"I was really formed by *Life* magazine," recalls Gibson, who was born in Los Angeles in 1939. "On Friday afternoon I'd get out of school and I wouldn't walk, I'd run the mile or so from school to get to that new issue of *Life*. In those days it was largely black and white, and I know that from a purely subliminal point of view that's where I formed my proclivities. I don't know why I responded so intensely to photographs—in fact, I didn't even know I was responding at that point. It wasn't until I decided to be a photographer while I was in art school that some of those earlier childhood feelings coalesced into a clarified definition."[1]

Gibson was a complicated boy who flunked out of high school and wound up in the Navy, and that proved to be a lucky break for him. The Navy sent him to photography school, and by the time he left the service in 1959 he was a crack technician. "There was an enlightened aspect to naval photography at the time," Gibson says, "because naval photography was founded by Edward Steichen, who was a four-stripe captain during World War II."

p. 150
Ralph Gibson at the Berman home on Crater Lane, 1964, Photograph by Wallace Berman.

p. 151
Wallace Berman, Los Angeles, 1974, Photograph by Ralph Gibson.

p. 152
Whiskey a Go Go, Los Angeles, 1962, Photograph by Ralph Gibson.

p. 153
Billy Ferguson in Beverly Glen, 1963, Photograph by Ralph Gibson.

Gibson took all he had learned in the Navy and set out to become an artist; his first step in that direction was shooting photographs of San Francisco, where he settled after leaving the service. Gibson's pictures from this period reflect central themes of classic street photography: the ephemeral loveliness of the city street with its river of faces; the loneliness of the solitary individual and the comfort of the crowd; workers solemnly bent to their tasks; the ever-changing light capable of transforming the mood with a single passing cloud. Gibson's hand is muted in these pictures, and he continued working in that mode until the late 1960s.

Gibson went through an intense tutorial in 1960 when Dorothea Lange hired him to be her assistant. "Dorothea was an extremely difficult woman," recalls Gibson, who remained at the post through 1961. "She knew nothing about technique and I was this crackerjack technician from the Navy, so I worked in her darkroom. Dorothea wanted passionately to change social conditions, and the sheer force of her will made the materials obey. She was a messianic personality who wanted to change things, and she did. It often happens that work infused with the degree of passion Dorothea had is called art, but I don't think she ever set out to make art."

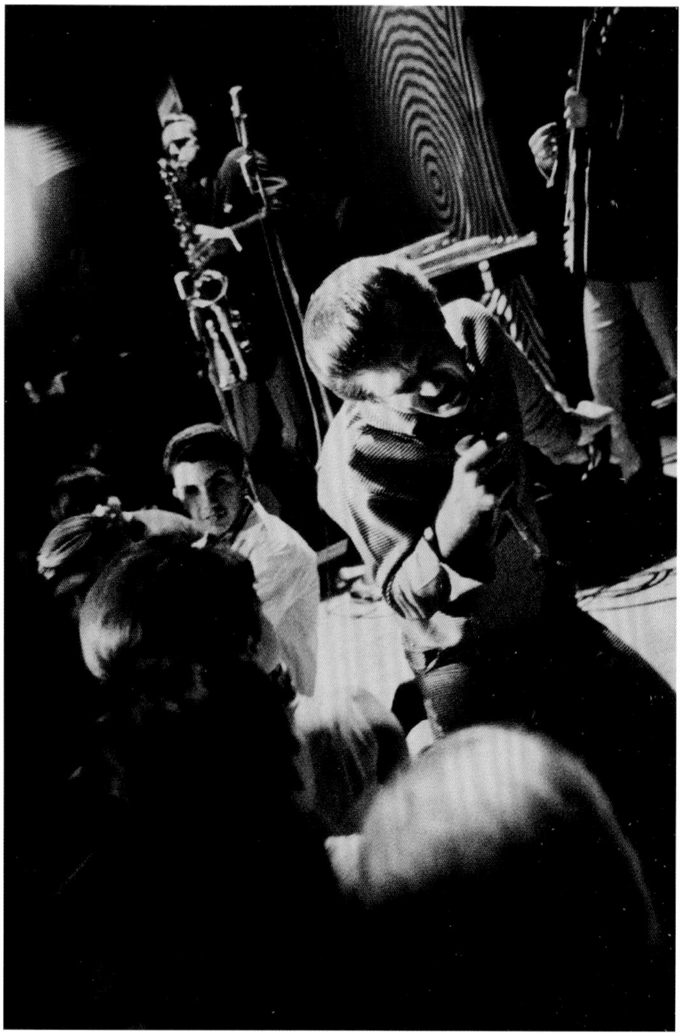

In 1962 Gibson moved to Los Angeles and settled in Beverly Glen, where he crossed paths with Berman. "I was extremely fortunate to fall in with Wallace Berman and get to know friends of his like Dean Stockwell—that was easily the best thing about the time I spent in L.A.," he recalls.

"Wallace was an inspiring person and he had a profound effect on everyone who came into contact with him." Gibson remained in Los Angeles for four years, and during that time he compiled a portfolio of photographs that create an indelible portrait of a specific time and place; his pictures of the Sunset Strip, strippers, girls in bikinis, and convertibles couldn't have been taken anywhere else.

Gibson's learning curve ramped up considerably in 1966 when he moved to New York and landed a gig as assistant to photographer Robert Frank. There were many brilliant photographers roaming the streets of Manhattan at that point, too, and Gibson made a point of meeting them all. "I got to know Diane Arbus and Louis Faure, who came over to my loft one day and dropped my camera, then gave me a lecture on how to drop a Leica," Gibson laughs. "In those days if you went up Fifth Avenue you'd probably run into Diane or Garry Winogrand, and Lee Friedlander was on the street, too. Larry Clark had just arrived in town from Vietnam and the minute Larry showed up he and I bonded—we just had a lot to say to one another."

It was during those years that Gibson began moving toward his signature style. The composition of his pictures became more graphic and dramatic, the subject matter grew increasingly surreal, and the objects and forms in his pictures took on a quality of mystery and portentousness; these stylistic advances culminated in his first book, *The Somnambulist*, published in 1970 by his own Lustrum Press. By that point Gibson had completely moved away from street photography in favor of impeccably composed images of people, places and things distilled to their essence. Over the past thirty-four years, he's published twenty-one books, including Clark's legendary book of 1971, *Tulsa*, and in the early 1970s, he initiated a book project with Wallace Berman that never came to fruition. Gibson has created photographic portraits of Berlin, Manhattan, San Francisco, Egypt, France, Italy and Japan, and shot hundreds of luminous pictures of women, many of which feature his companion of twenty-six years, Mary Jane Marcasiano. Gibson lives in New York, and is currently working on a series of portraits of jazz guitarists.
Kristine McKenna

1 All quotations by the artist from a conversation with Ralph Gibson, November 1, 2003.

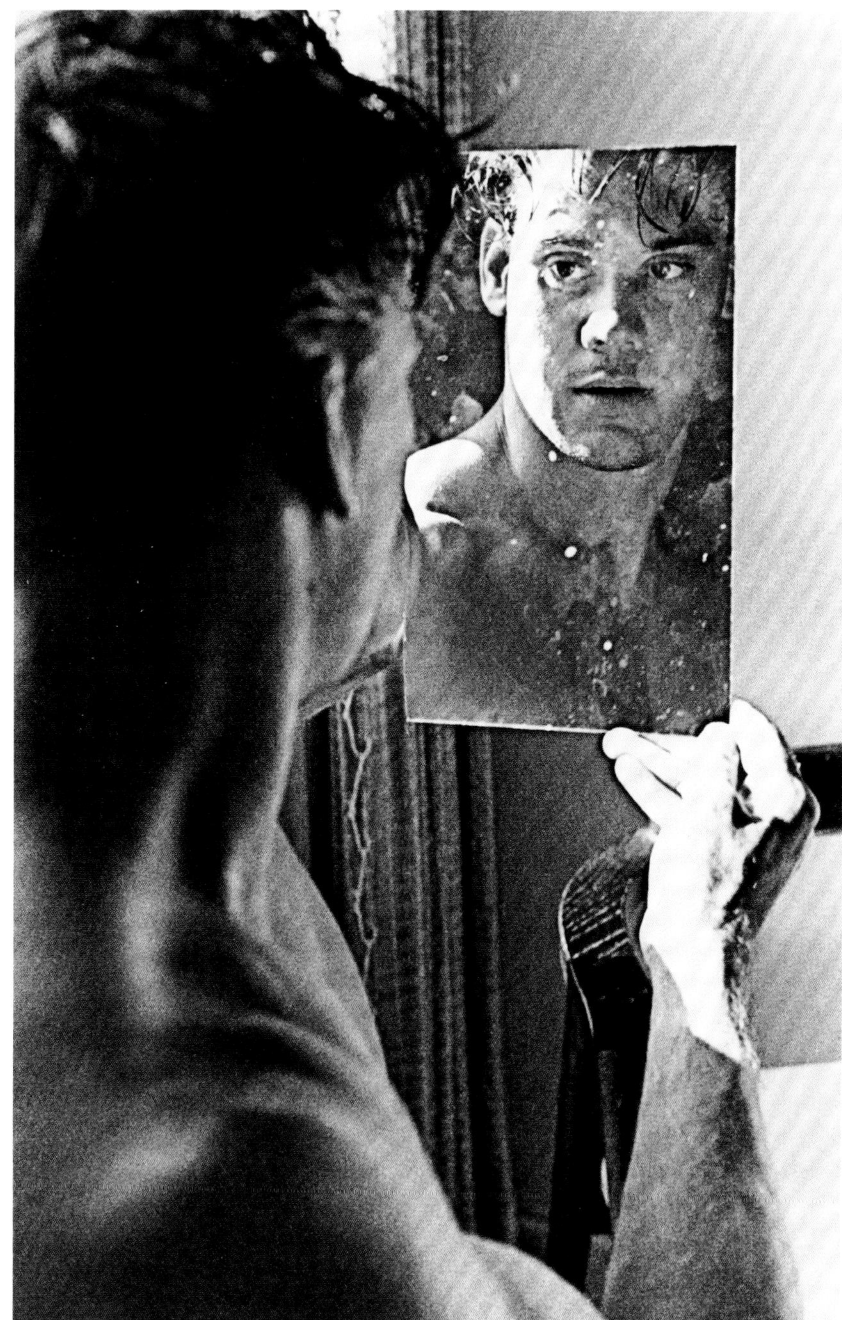

Allen Ginsberg

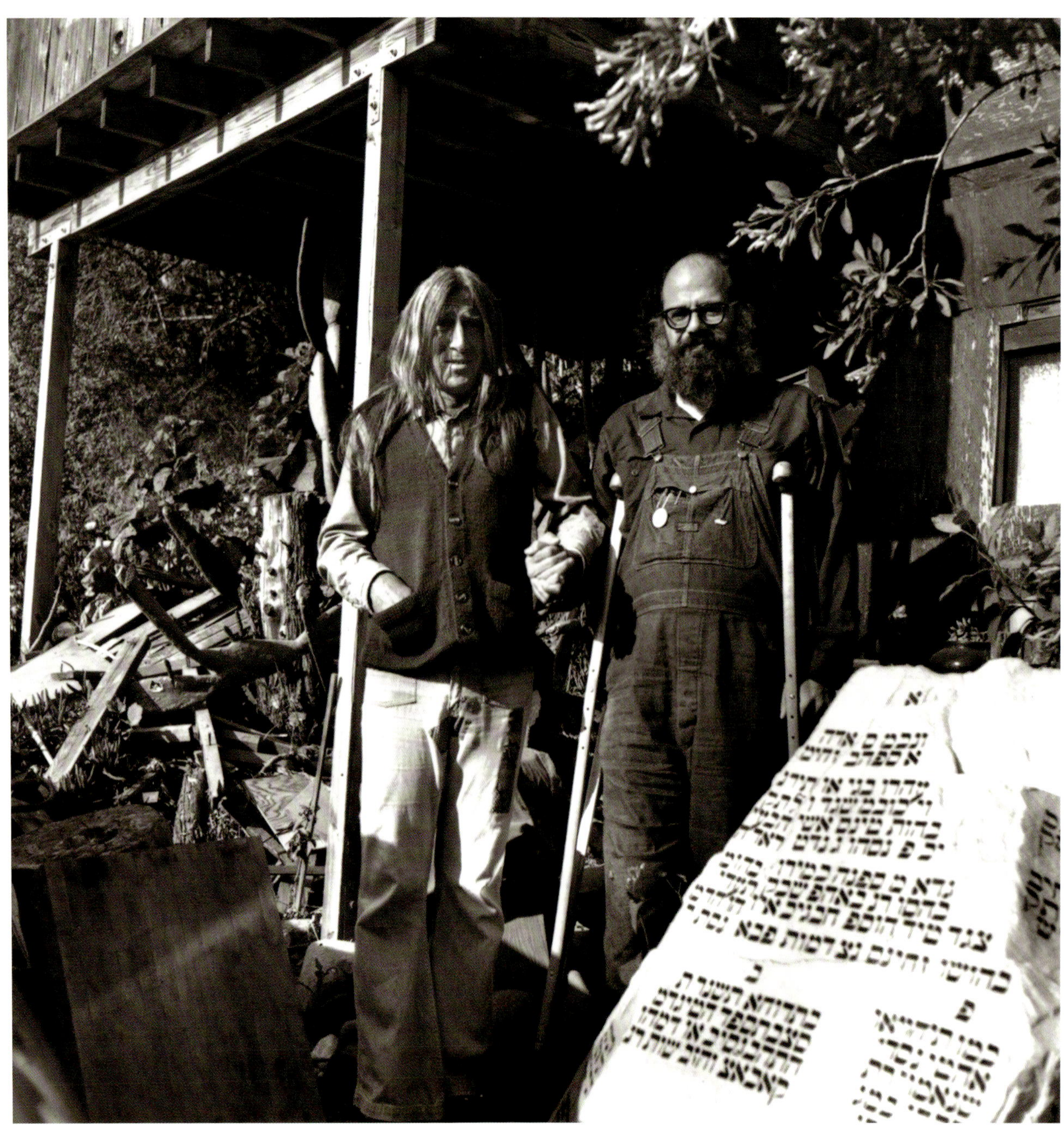

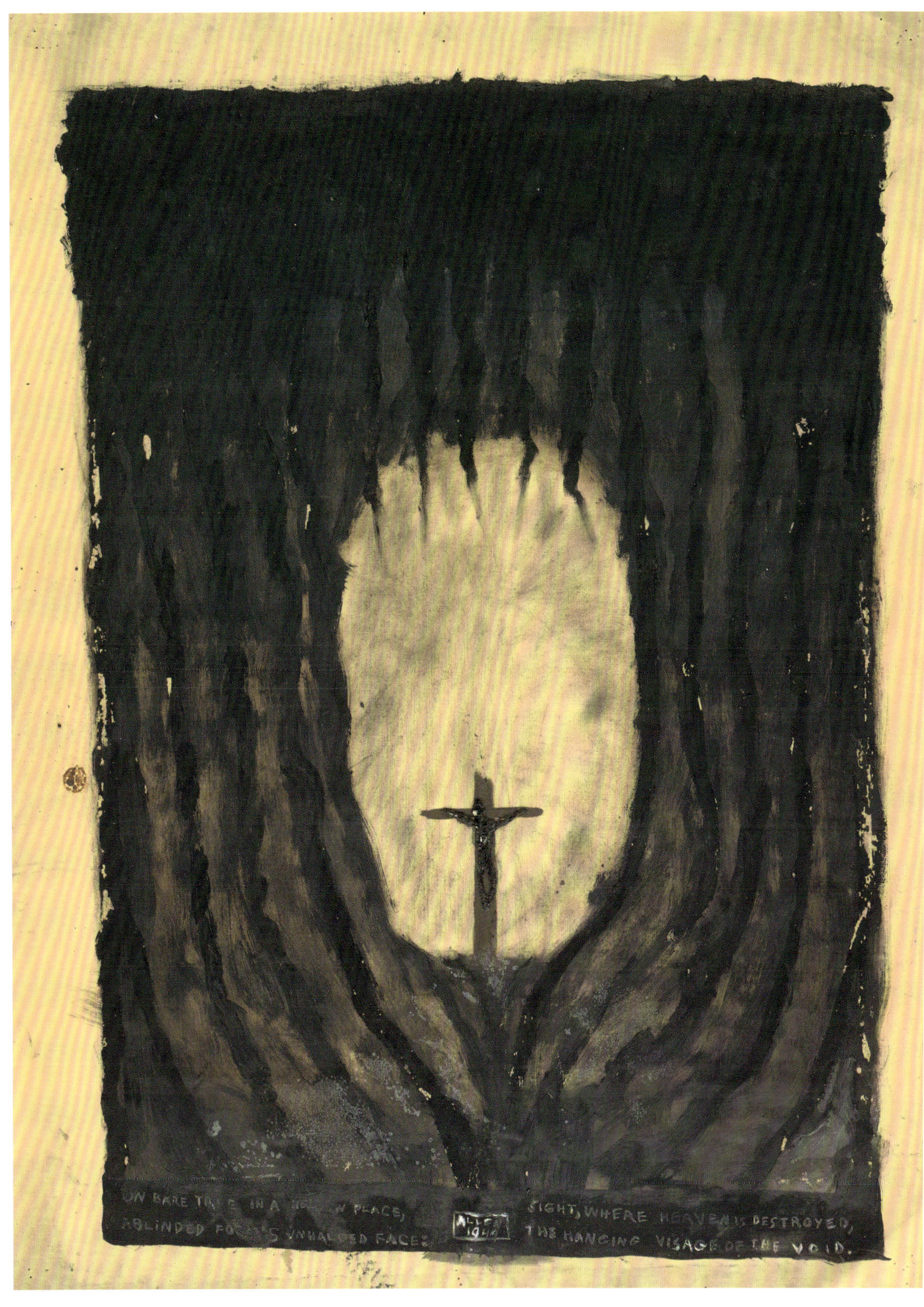
ALLEN
1944
SIGHT, WHERE HEAVEN IS DESTROYED,
THE HANGING VISAGE OF THE VOID.

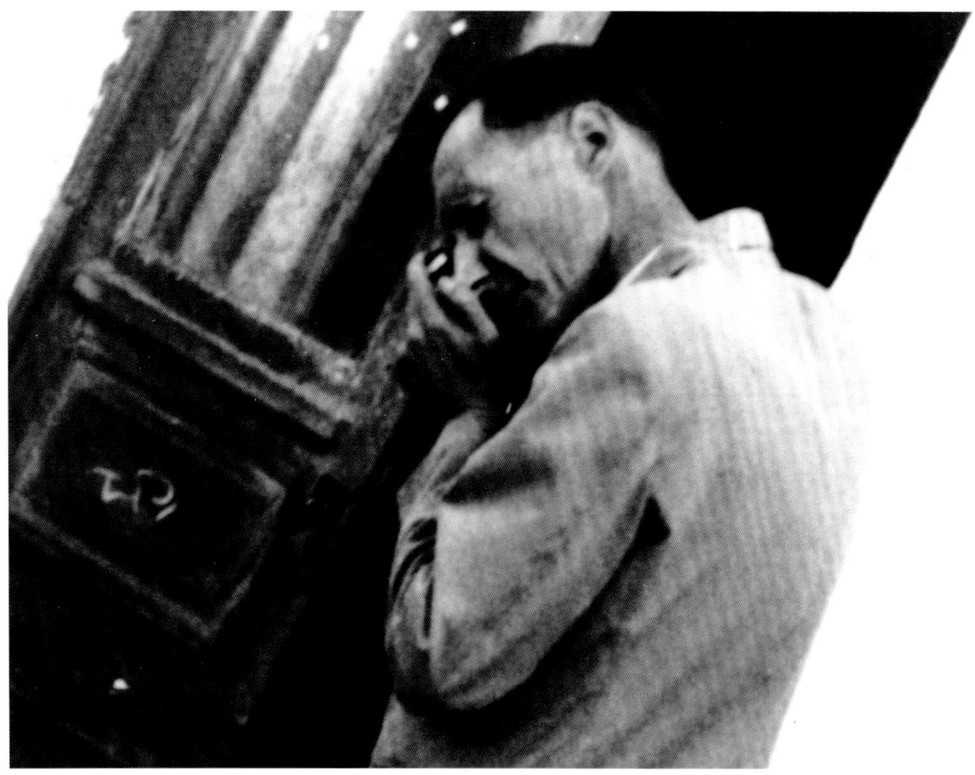

For over four decades the prominent voice of the Beat Generation, poet Allen Ginsberg had strong ties both to the East and West Coast. His volumes, *Howl and Other Poems* (1956), *Kaddish and Other Poems* (1961), *Planet News: 1961–1967* (1968), and *The Fall of America: Poems of these States, 1965–1971* (1972) continue to be widely read expressions of personal anguish and frustrations with mainstream America.

Besides Ginsberg's talent as an exuberant and passionate poetic force, he had a generous and congenial spirit, and was personally involved in the lives and careers of an astounding number of fellow poets and artists. In his archive at Stanford University Libraries, for example, are letters and correspondence from many in Wallace Berman's circle, including Berman, Ray Bremser, David Meltzer, Diane DiPrima, Jack Smith, John Chance, William Burroughs, Lew Welch, Bonnie Bremser, Alexander Trocchi, Henry Miller, Philip Lamantia, Ron Loewinsohn, John Wieners, Kenneth Anger, Jack Hirschman, Bob Kaufman, Taylor Mead, and Arthur Richer.

Born in New Jersey in 1926, the son of a Russian émigré mother and schoolteacher father, Ginsberg studied literature at Columbia University and graduated in 1948. While still in school, he met Jack Kerouac, William Burroughs, and Neal Cassady who became major influences and inspirations for his poetry. In 1948, Ginsberg experienced a vision of William Blake speaking to him, an event that led to the blossoming of his poetic voice.

In 1954, after traveling alone in Mexico for five months, Ginsberg moved to San Francisco, where he soon met Peter Orlovsky with whom he established a longtime relationship. Written the next year directly on the typewriter, the poem *Howl* translated the spontaneous jazz-like raps of Cassady and Kerouac into a sustained bardic utterance that struck a cultural nerve.

When Ginsberg first read the poem in 1955 at The Six Gallery, he received a boisterous ovation. The now-legendary evening also featured readings by Michael McClure, Philip Whalen, and Gary Snyder, with Philip Lamantia reading poems by the recently deceased poet John Hoffman (a contributor to *Semina 5*). After the publication of *Howl* by City Lights in 1956, several attempts were made to ban it for obscenity. William Carlos Williams and Robert Duncan, among many other writers, spoke out adamantly on its behalf.

After traveling in Europe and Northern Africa in 1957, Ginsberg resettled in a Manhattan Lower East Side apartment, where he resided until 1996. Throughout his

p. 154
Allen Ginsberg, Topanga Canyon, 1971, Photograph by Wallace Berman.

p. 155
Allen Ginsberg, *Untitled* (*"On bare tree in a hollow place...)*, 1949, painting on linen, Allen Ginsberg Archive, Stanford University Libraries.

p. 156
William Burroughs Photographing in New York, 1953, Photograph by Allen Ginsberg.

p. 157 left
Allen Ginsberg, *Self Portrait, Tangier*, 1961, 16 x 20 inches, Courtesy Howard Greenberg Gallery, New York.

p. 157 right
Self portrait in San Francisco, 1955, Photograph by Allen Ginsberg.

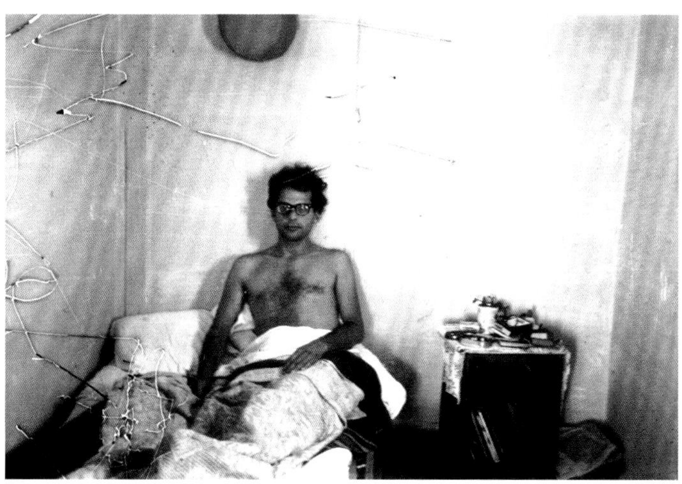

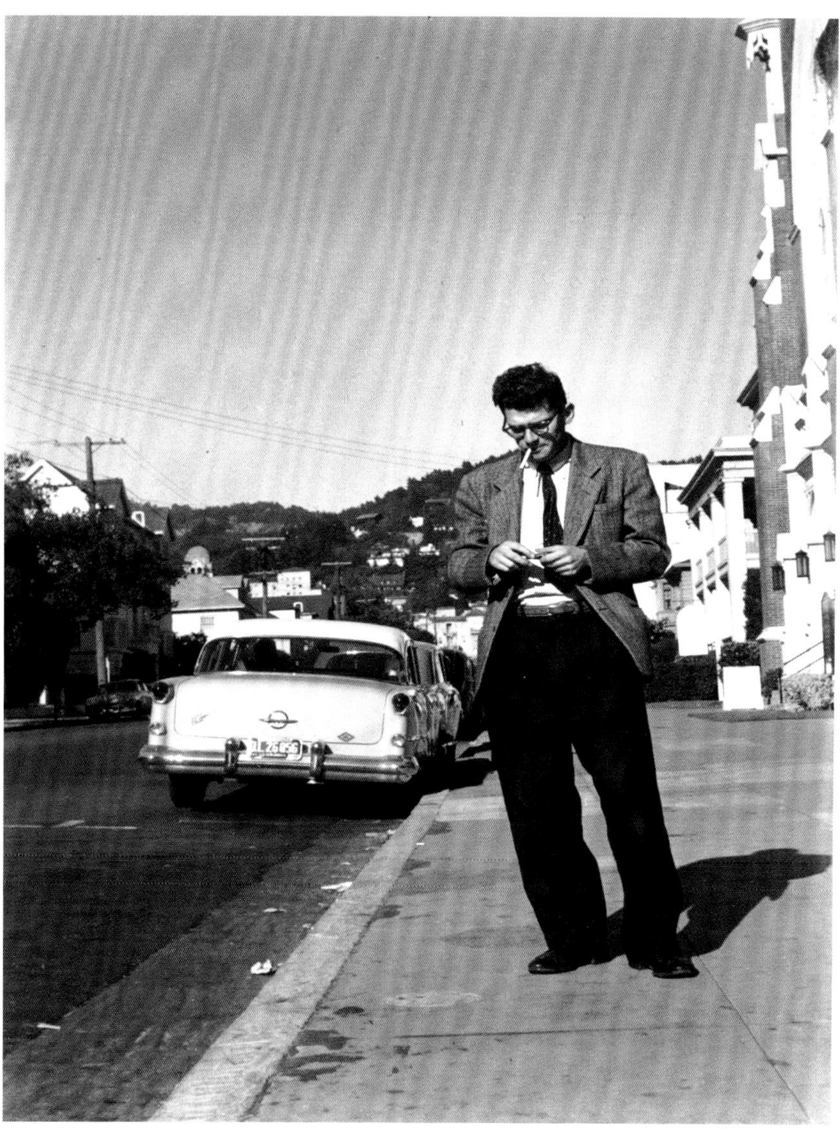

life, he continued to travel frequently to San Francisco and to maintain his West Coast friendships. Wallace Berman clearly identified with Ginsberg's troubles with censorship and greatly respected his writing. After including one of Ginsberg's poems in *Semina 4* (1959), Berman wrote him asking for a poem of "not more than ten lines" for the "Mexican issue" (*Semina 5*).[1]

In 1974, Ginsberg helped establish the Jack Kerouac School of Disembodied Poetics at the Naropa Institute in Boulder, Colorado, a Buddhist university where he taught courses in poetry and meditation. Encouraged by his friend Robert Frank, Ginsberg had begun taking photographs in 1953. His shots of travels and portraits of fellow artists were collected in two books, *Photographs* (1991) and *Snapshot Poetics* (1993). He taught at Brooklyn College from 1987 until his death of a heart attack in 1997.

Michael Duncan

1 Berman, Postcard mailer to "Alan Ginsberg," 1959, Allen Ginsberg Archive, Stanford University Libraries, Box 2, Folder 31. The postcard demonstrates the casual nature of Berman's requests for *Semina* submissions: "Also, if you have anything by Burroughs that hasn't been printed yet and Kerouac. Mexican subject matter doesn't have to dominate poem—a sentence or word in poem is cool."

Billy Gray

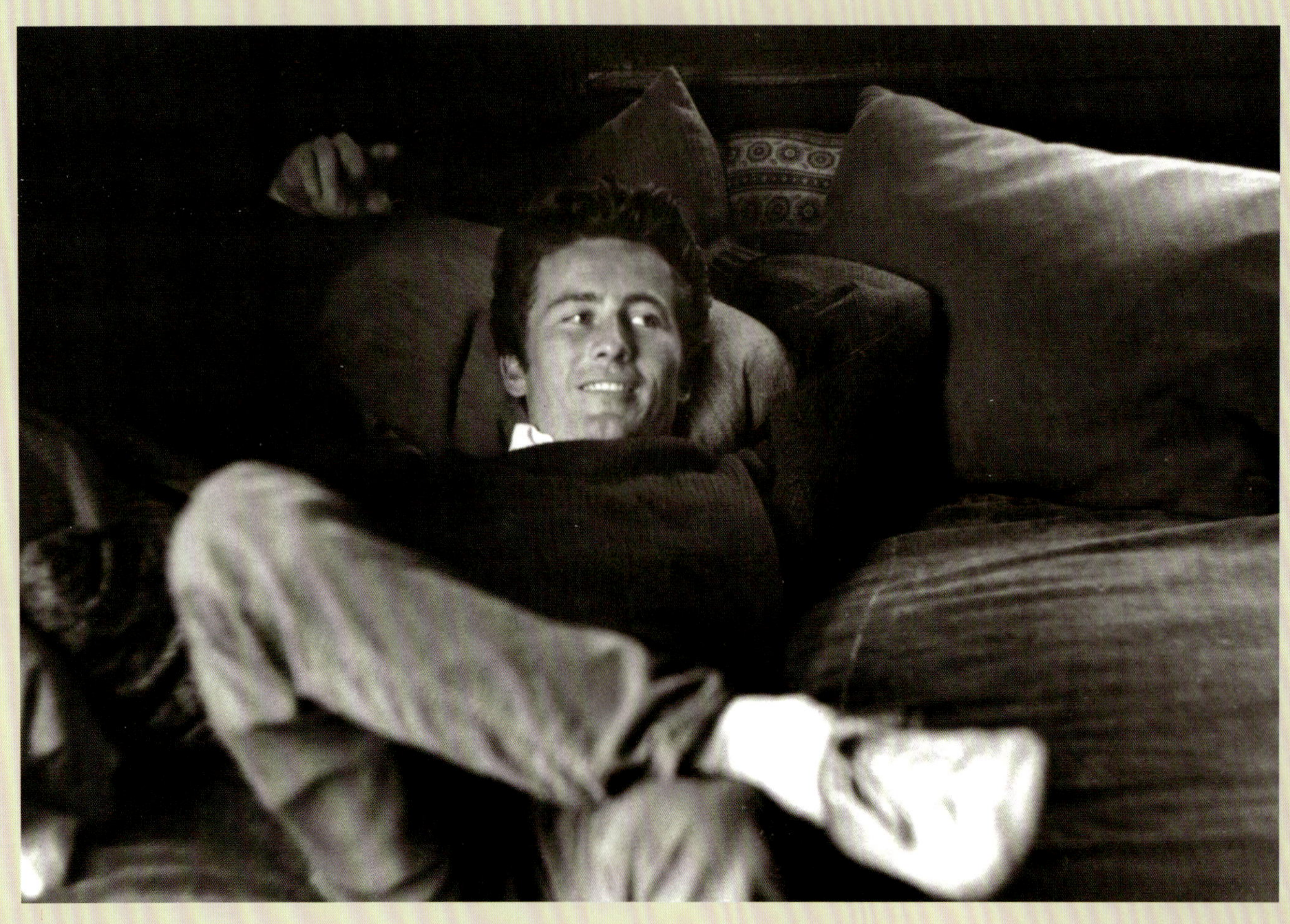

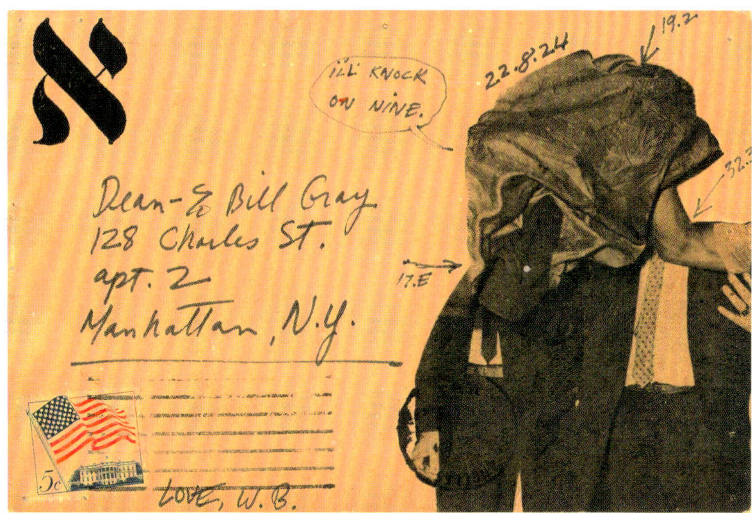

Billy Gray was born in Los Angeles in 1938, the son of western B-movie actress, Beatrice Gray. When Gray was six years old his mother's agent saw him in a school play and decided to represent him, too; Gray immediately began getting cast in movies, and between the years 1944 and 1953 he appeared in more than thirty-five films, including Robert Wise's 1951 sci-fi classic, *The Day the Earth Stood Still*. In 1954 Gray became a household name when he was cast as Bud Anderson on *Father Knows Best*, a hugely successful television series that aired until 1960. It was during those years—in 1957—that his friend Bobby Driscoll introduced him to Wallace Berman.

"I met Wallace right after his exhibition at the Ferus Gallery, then five months later he moved to San Francisco, so it wasn't until he returned to Los Angeles in 1961 that we really got to know each other," recalled Gray, who has lived in Topanga Canyon since 1954. [1]

"Wallace came into my life around the same time that I met George Herms, and before I met them I hadn't had much exposure to visual art; I just kind of followed the lead that both of them offered in that regard," added Gray, who began working with stained glass at that point.

Gray's acting career was derailed in 1962 when he was arrested on charges of possessing marijuana. "When I got busted for grass that was pretty much the end of it," Gray recalls. "Because I was tied up with 'Bud Anderson,' it just became too big an issue." Gray did have a starring role in Dennis Hopper's 1971 western, *The Last Movie*, but by the end of the 1960s he was devoting most of his attention to motorcycle speedway racing and developing his skills as an inventor; among his creations are the F-1 guitar pick and a utensil for removing corks from champagne bottles.

Kristine McKenna

1 Conversation with Billy Gray, October 13, 1999.

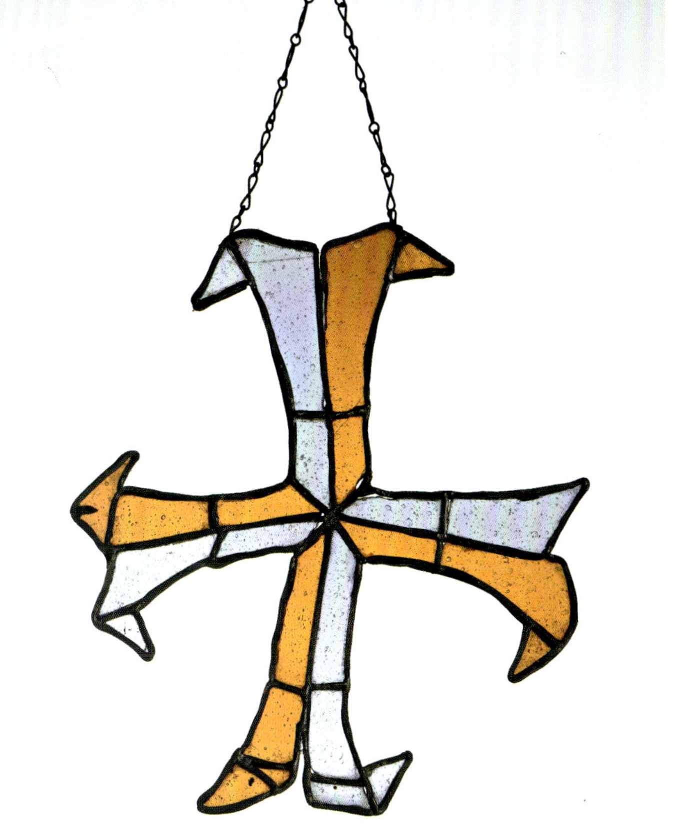

p. 158
Billy Gray in Beverly Glen, 1962.
Photograph by Wallace Berman.

p. 159 top
Wallace Berman. Untitled mailer to Billy Gray and Dean Stockwell.

p. 159 bottom
Billy Gray. Untitled medallion (cross). Leaded stained glass. 1962.

George Herms

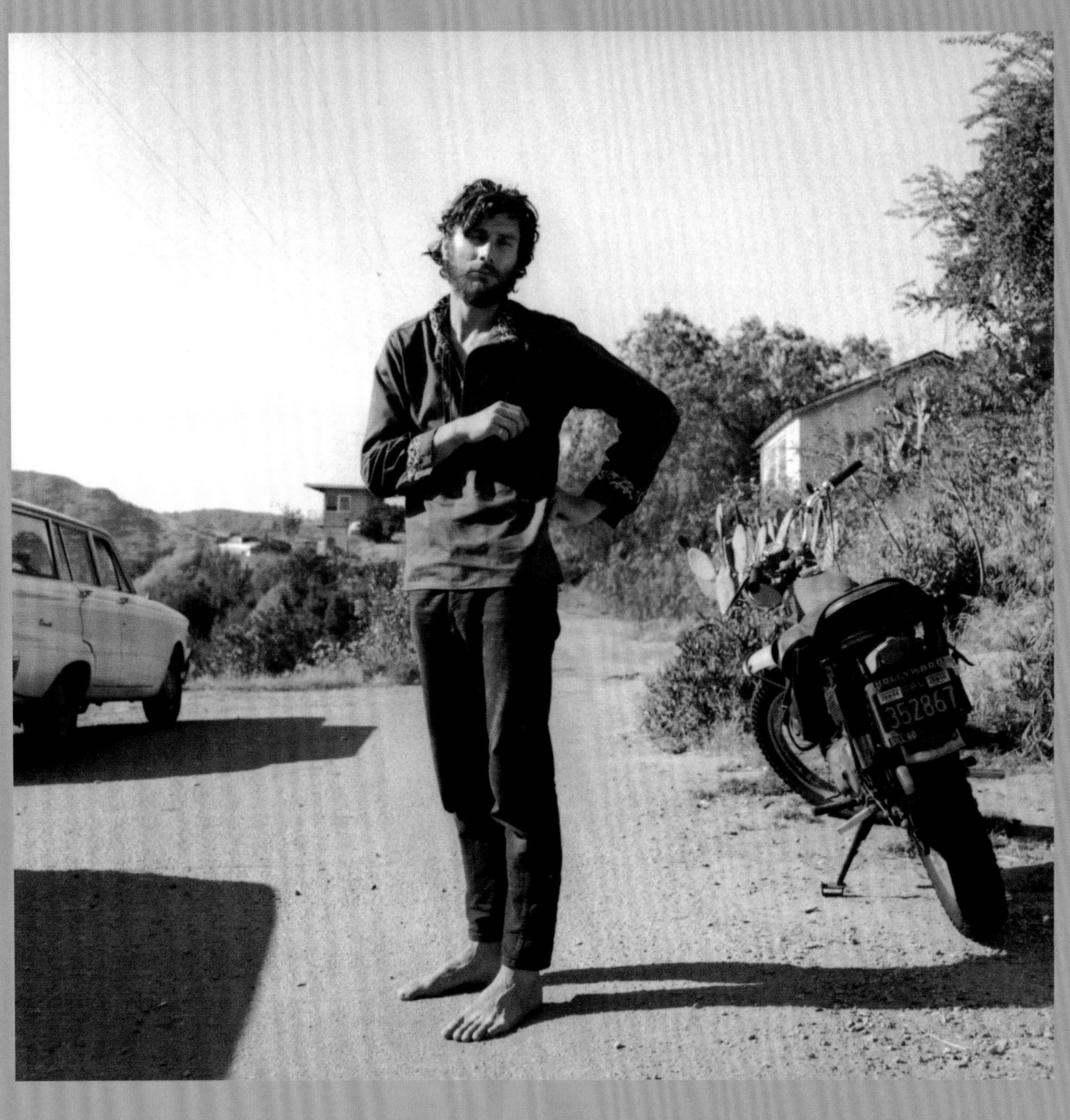

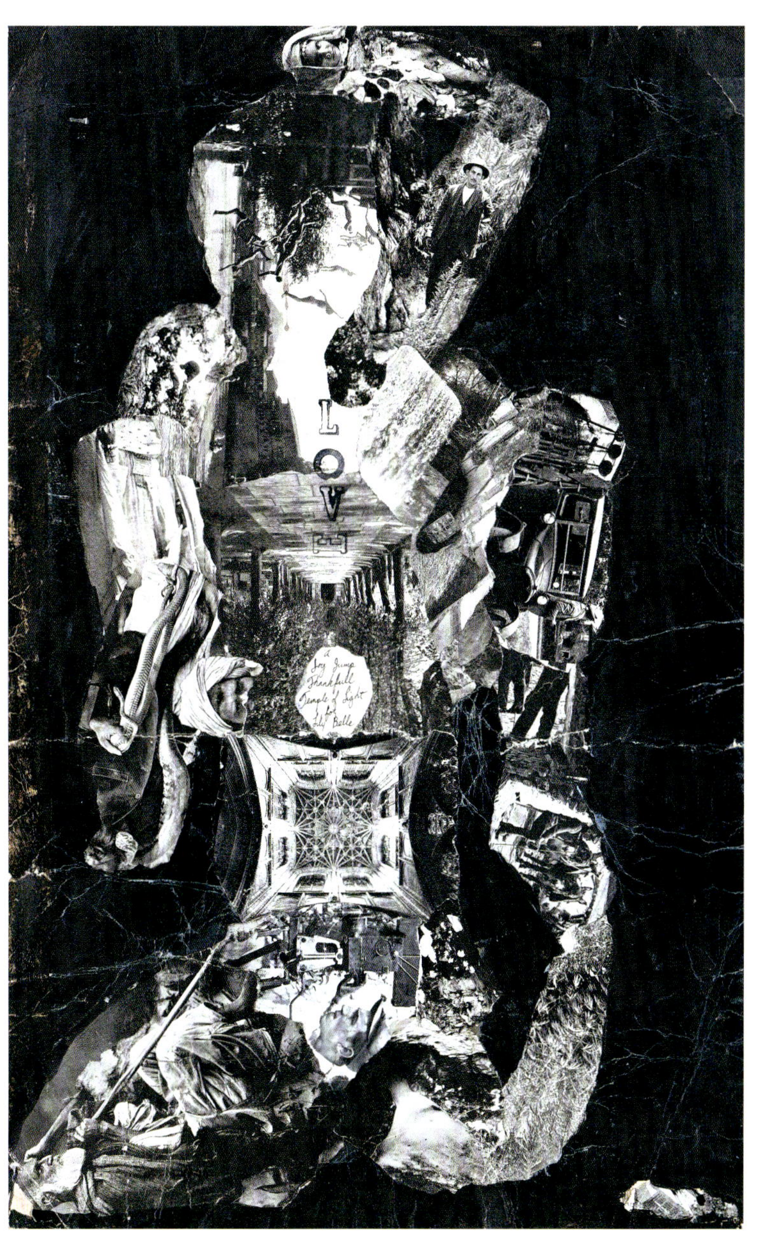

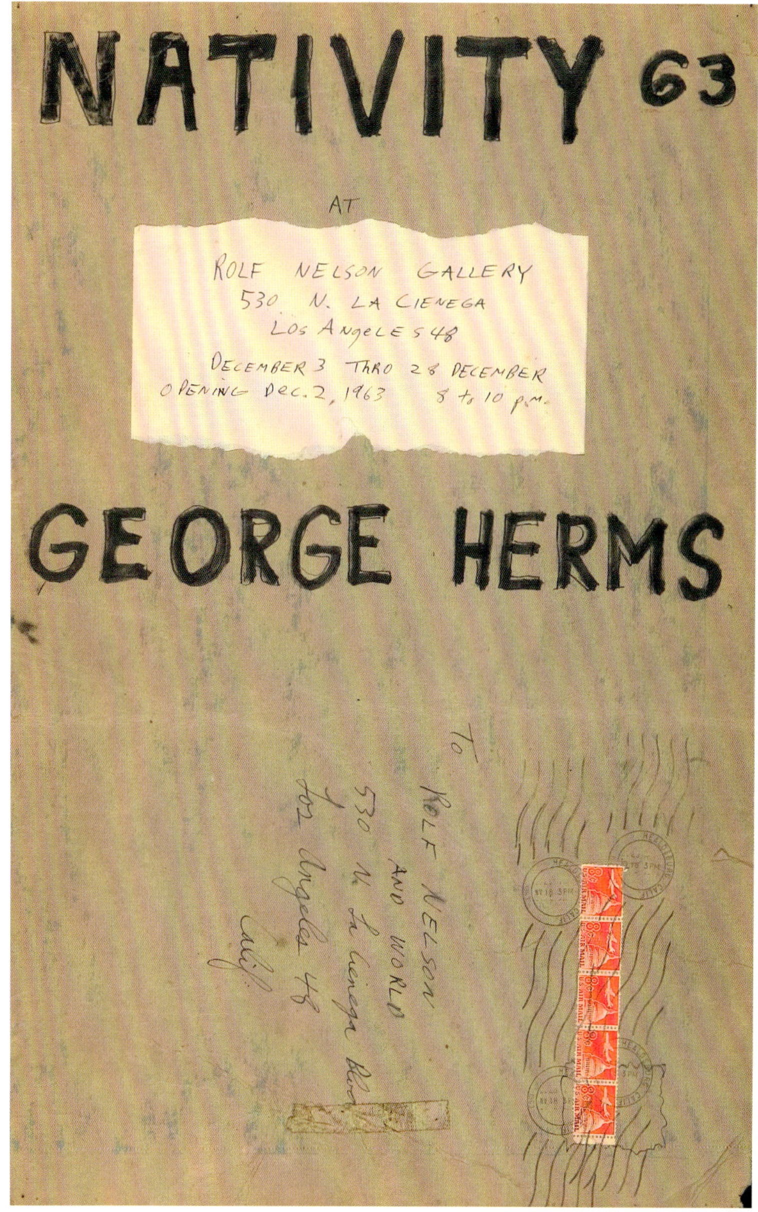
NATIVITY 63
AT
ROLF NELSON GALLERY
530 N. LA CIENEGA
LOS ANGELES 48
DECEMBER 3 THRO 28 DECEMBER
OPENING DEC. 2, 1963 8 to 10 p.m.
GEORGE HERMS
To
ROLF NELSON
AND WORLD
530 N. La Cienega Blvd
Los Angeles 48
Calif

One of the founders of West Coast assemblage art, George Herms keeps the flame alive in works that carry forward the radical, lyrical values of those he calls "The Poet Heroes of My Youth." From the onset of his career, Herms' highly esthetic sculptures, paintings, and drawings have operated on a poetic level, using visual puns, Pop culture references, and time-scarred materials to put an expressive spin on American culture. In assemblages of found objects and richly weathered discards, he seeks to reinterpret and reinvigorate the past, accruing new connotations for detritus. As Wallace Berman's most active acolyte, he has become the unofficial historian of the West Coast Beats, carrying on the tradition through works such as his 1992 facsimile edition of *Semina* (Love Press and LA Louver Gallery) and an ongoing series of sculptures commemorating individual poets, artists, and jazz musicians.

p. 160
George Herms, Topanga Canyon, 1965, Photograph by Wallace Berman.

p. 161
George Herms, *Nativity (for exhibition at Rolf Nelson Gallery)*, 1963, Mixed-media collage on board.

p. 162
George Herms, *Spring Vision*, 1965, Oil on canvas.

p. 163 top
George Herms, *Gold Seeds Revolve*, 1962, Mixed-media assemblage on wood.

p. 163 middle right
Wallace Berman, *Poster for George Herms Exhibition at Batman Gallery*, 1961, Lithograph.

p. 163 bottom
George Herms, 1961, Photograph by Wallace Berman.

p. 164
George Herms, *Pretender to the Throne*, 1965, Ink on paper.

p. 165 left
Diane DiPrima as Mary Shelley, Jackson Allen as Shelley in *Whale Honey* by Diane DiPrima, set by George Herms, Intersection for the Arts, 1975.

p. 165 right
George Herms, Sets for *Whale Honey*, 1975.

The son of an agronomist, Herms was born in 1935 in Woodland, California. While studying engineering at the University of California at Berkeley, Herms became turned on by jazz and literature. He left school in 1954 and moved to Los Angeles where he got a job as a tabulation operator for Douglas Aircraft and spent his evenings in jazz clubs. The next year he moved to Mexico to write and find himself, but after he was robbed and left penniless in the desolate countryside, he returned home. On his twentieth birthday, while babysitting for friends in Topanga Canyon, he met Robert Alexander and Wallace Berman. Berman impressed him by spontaneously giving him a copy of Thomas Merton's *Tears of the Blind Lions* as a birthday gift.

Returning to Berkeley, Herms spent a year taking courses in literature and music appreciation, until dropping out again in 1956 to move to Hermosa Beach with his girlfriend Polly Levee. Working at another aircraft parts facility, Herms immersed himself in the jazz and art scenes, while solidifying friendships with Berman, Alexander, Bobby Driscoll, Dean Stockwell, David Meltzer, and Cameron. Herms spent much time at the Bermans' house, helping assemble *Semina* and perusing Berman's *View* magazines and books such as Robert Motherwell's *The Dada Painters and Poets*.

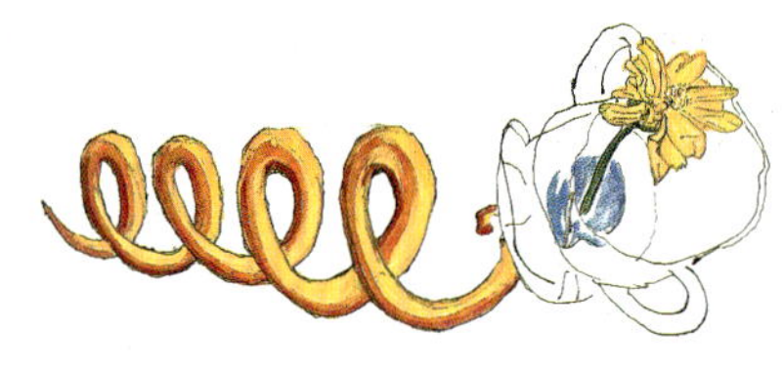

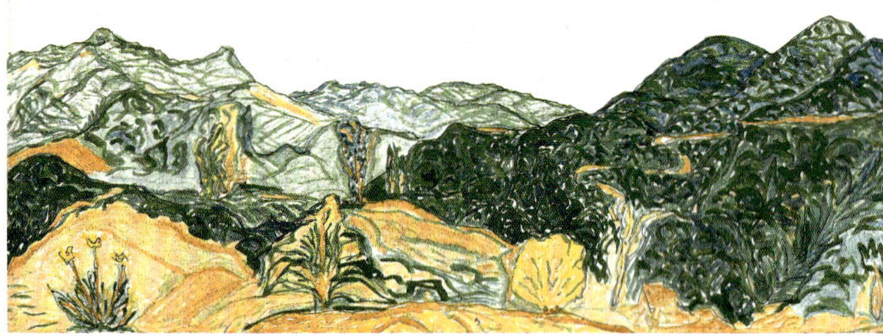

Emulating Berman, he bought a small hand-press and began printing poems. Herms also began to make assemblage collages from machine parts, punch-card detritus, and beach trash. In 1957 after the obscenity trial involving Berman's Ferus exhibition, Herms temporarily exchanged houses with the Bermans so that they could avoid the publicity generated by the trial. Later that fall, Polly—by then married to Herms—wanted to return to her studies at Berkeley. Before leaving Hermosa Beach, Herms took all the assemblages he had made to a vacant lot and invited Berman, Alexander, Reed, and Meltzer to see what he called "The Secret Exhibition." Herms's work reportedly emerged fully developed in this first grouping of assemblages, all of which were abandoned. As influences, Herms has credited Edmund Teske's photographs and the paintings of Yves Tanguy that he saw in *View*.[1]

When the Bermans moved to the Bay Area in 1957, they first stayed with Herms in Berkeley. There Berman finished editing *Semina Two*. Herms worked at Norman Rose's book warehouse along with Alexander, Meltzer, and Arthur Richer who had all moved north. He spent time at the Bermans' Scott Street apartment watching sports with Wallace and hung out at jazz clubs where he saw Thelonious Monk, the Modern Jazz Quartet, and Bud Shank. He learned painting techniques from Richer but things went awry when the two were arrested for selling a small amount of marijuana. Richer managed to avoid conviction, but Herms was sentenced to six months at Santa Rita Honor Farm. While there, most of his early work was destroyed in a Berkeley fire.

Upon his release in 1958, Herms moved to the mountain community Tuolumme where he painted, took peyote, and studied astrology and esoteric practices by corresponding

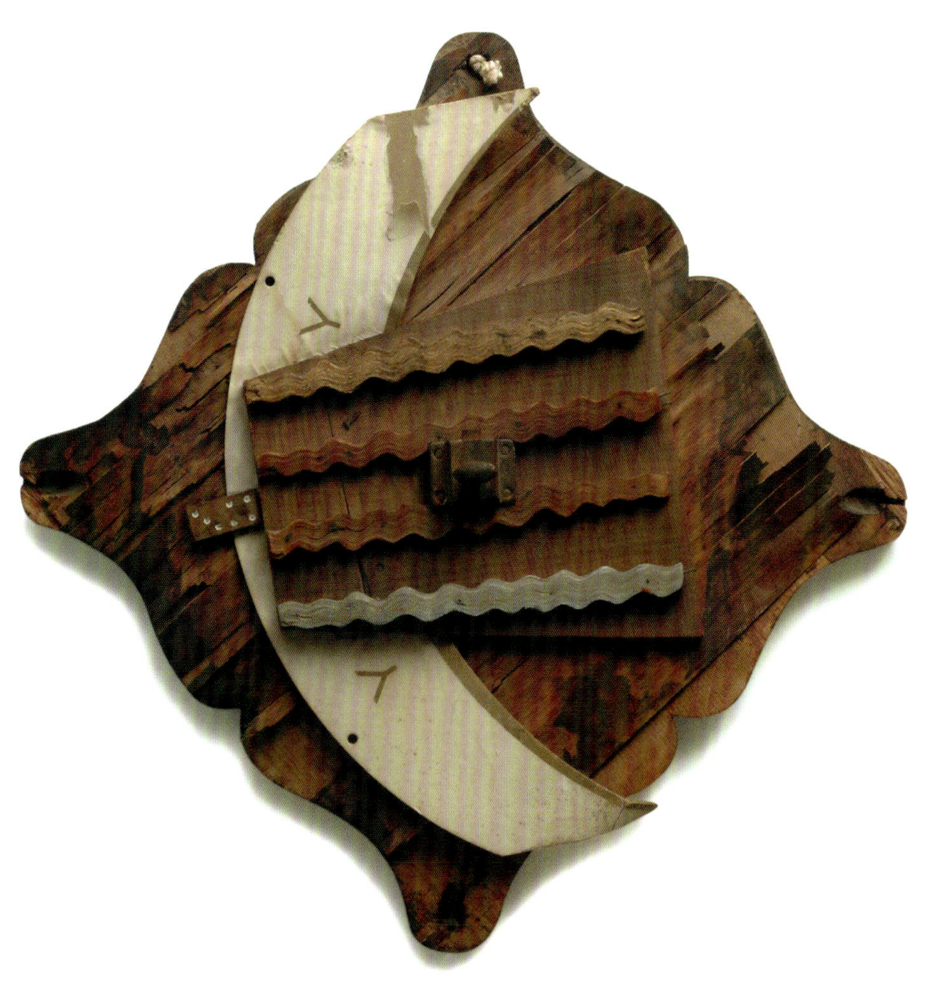

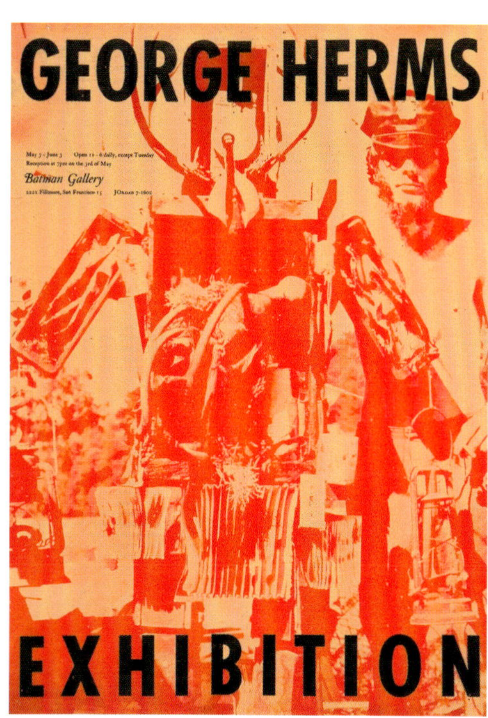
GEORGE HERMS
May 3 - June 3 Open 12 - 6 daily, except Tuesday
Reception at 7pm on the 3rd of May
Batman Gallery
EXHIBITION

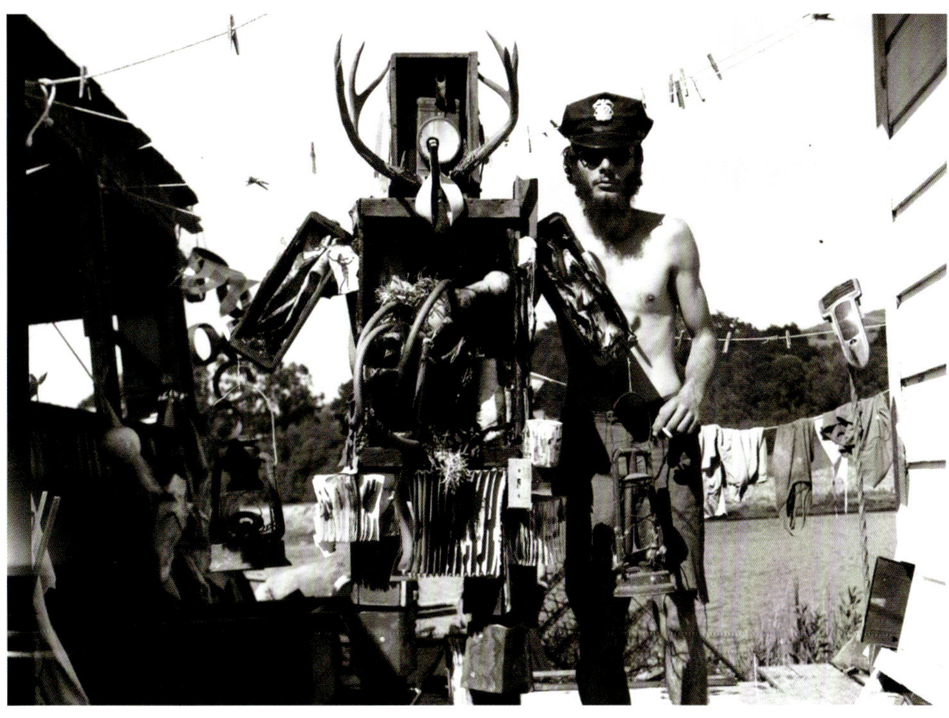

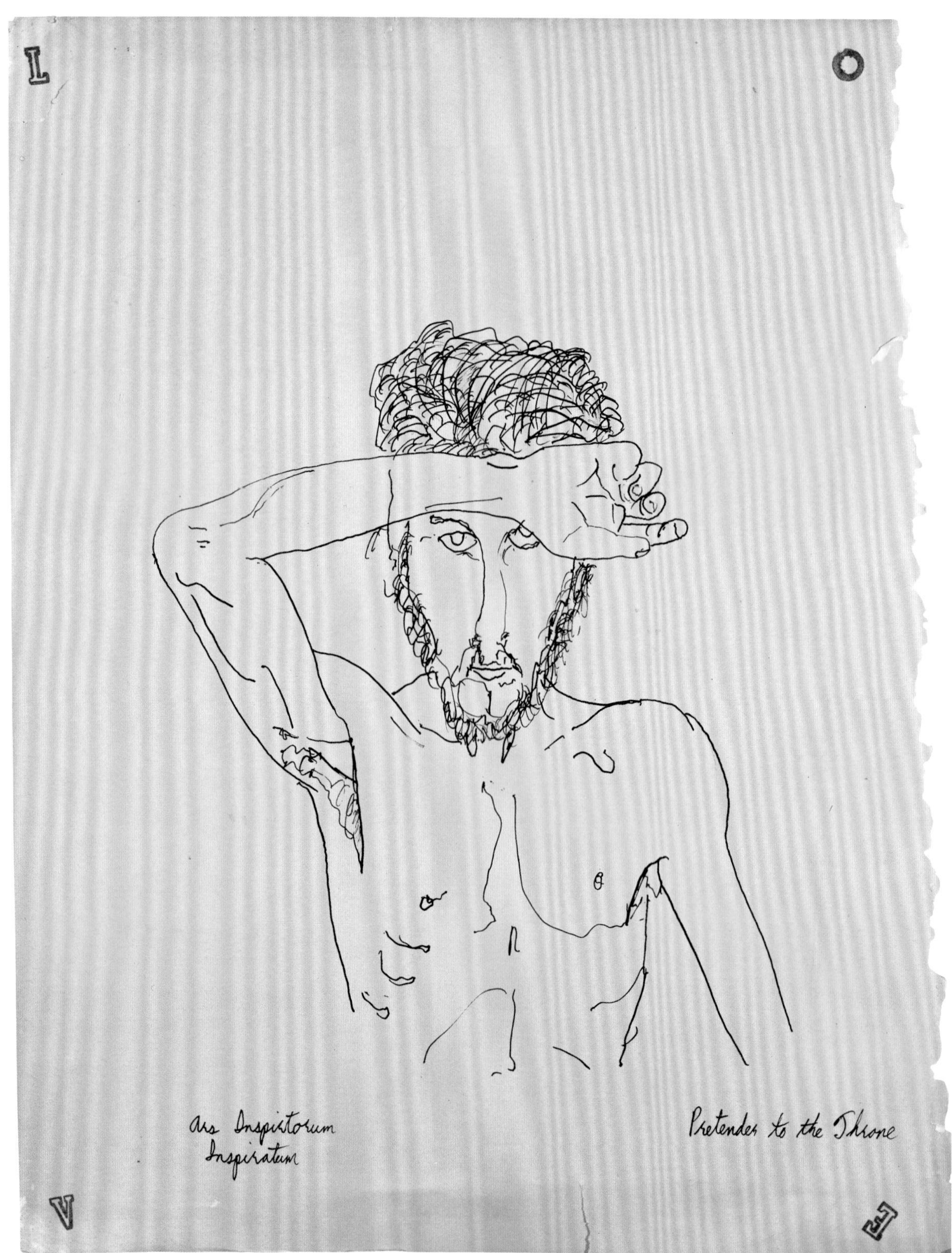
L
O
Ars Inspistorum
Inspiratum
Pretender to the Throne
V
E

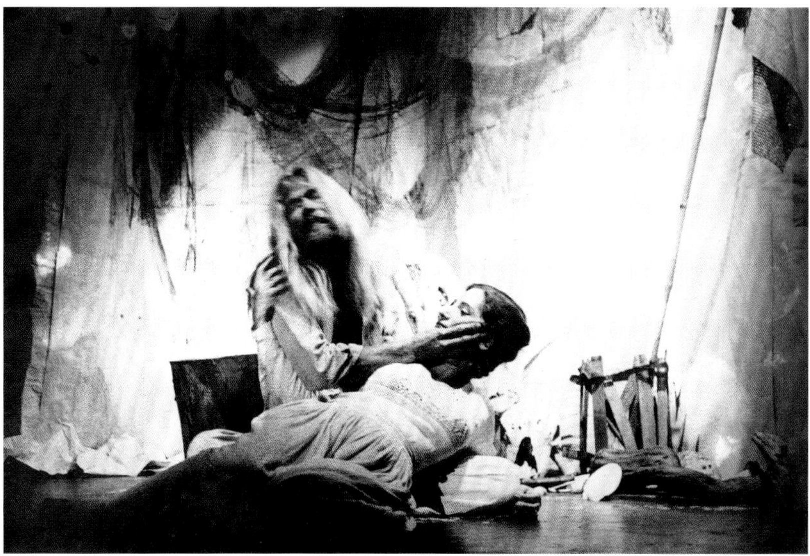

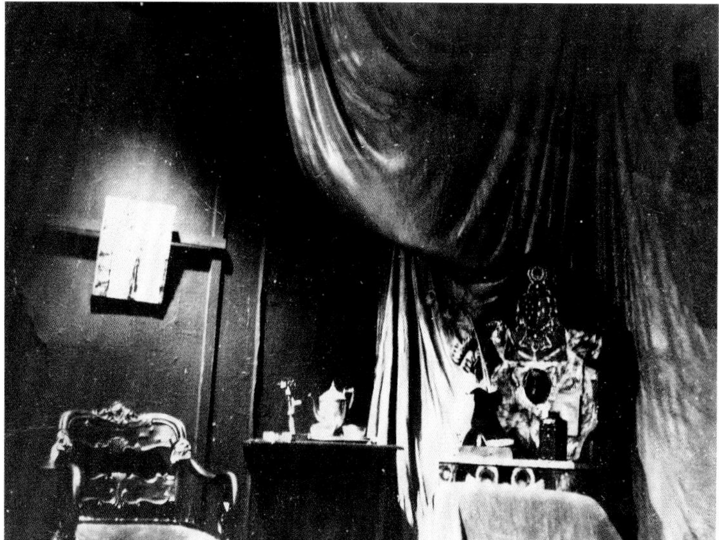

with Cameron, Elias Romero, and Aya (Tarlow). Herms moved back to San Francisco late the next year, where he helped Robert Alexander renovate The Cellar, a short-lived jazz and poetry club.

Herms and his second wife Louise followed the Bermans and the Jahrmarkts to Larkspur, living near their houseboats in a boat house without running water or electricity. Continuing to make work, Herms had exhibitions at Berman's Semina Gallery (1960) and then at Batman Gallery (1961). The Batman show featured Herms's first tableaux including *The Meat Market*, made from refuse from the local Larkspur dump. Berman designed the publicity poster for that exhibition.

When the Bermans left Larkspur to return to Los Angeles, Herms moved to Topanga Canyon where he worked on the film *Jewelface* with Lawrence Jordan. In an exhibition at the Pasadena Art Museum, one of Herms's assemblages featuring an American flag prompted a protest by the American Legion and was vandalized by an irate patron. In 1963 Dean Stockwell filmed Herms making work for his film *Moonstone*. Throughout his adult life, Herms has experienced financial difficulties, prompting many cycles of eviction notices, rent parties (dubbed *Tap City* performances), and complicated living arrangements.

Herms moved to Mill Creek in Northern California where he and Paul Beattie built a ramshackle communal house for their two families. Herms and Beattie collaborated on several films and handmade publications of poetry and drawings. In 1964 Herms lived in New York for three months designing sets for Michael McClure's play *The Blossom or Billy the Kid*. He returned to make a film with Billy Jahrmarkt before again moving back to Topanga Canyon where he began his *Zodiac Behind Glass* series and began publishing books on his hand-press under the name Love Press.

Throughout the 1960s Herms continued to collaborate with artist friends, providing the poster for Aya's *Magic Theater* and a set for McClure's *The Beard*. Teaching stints in the 1970s led him up and down the West Coast while he produced work for a constant stream of exhibitions. In 1984 he was awarded the Prix de Rome and created the stunning series of assemblages using local cast-offs, *Rome Poem*. Retrospectives of his work have been held at the Los Angeles Municipal Art Gallery, curated by Edward Leffingwell in 1992, and at the Santa Monica Museum of Art, curated by Walter Hopps in 2005.
Michael Duncan

1 Sandra Leonard Starr, *Lost and Found in California* (Santa Monica: Corcoran, Shoshana Wayne, and Pence Galleries, 1988) p. 93.

Jack Hirschman

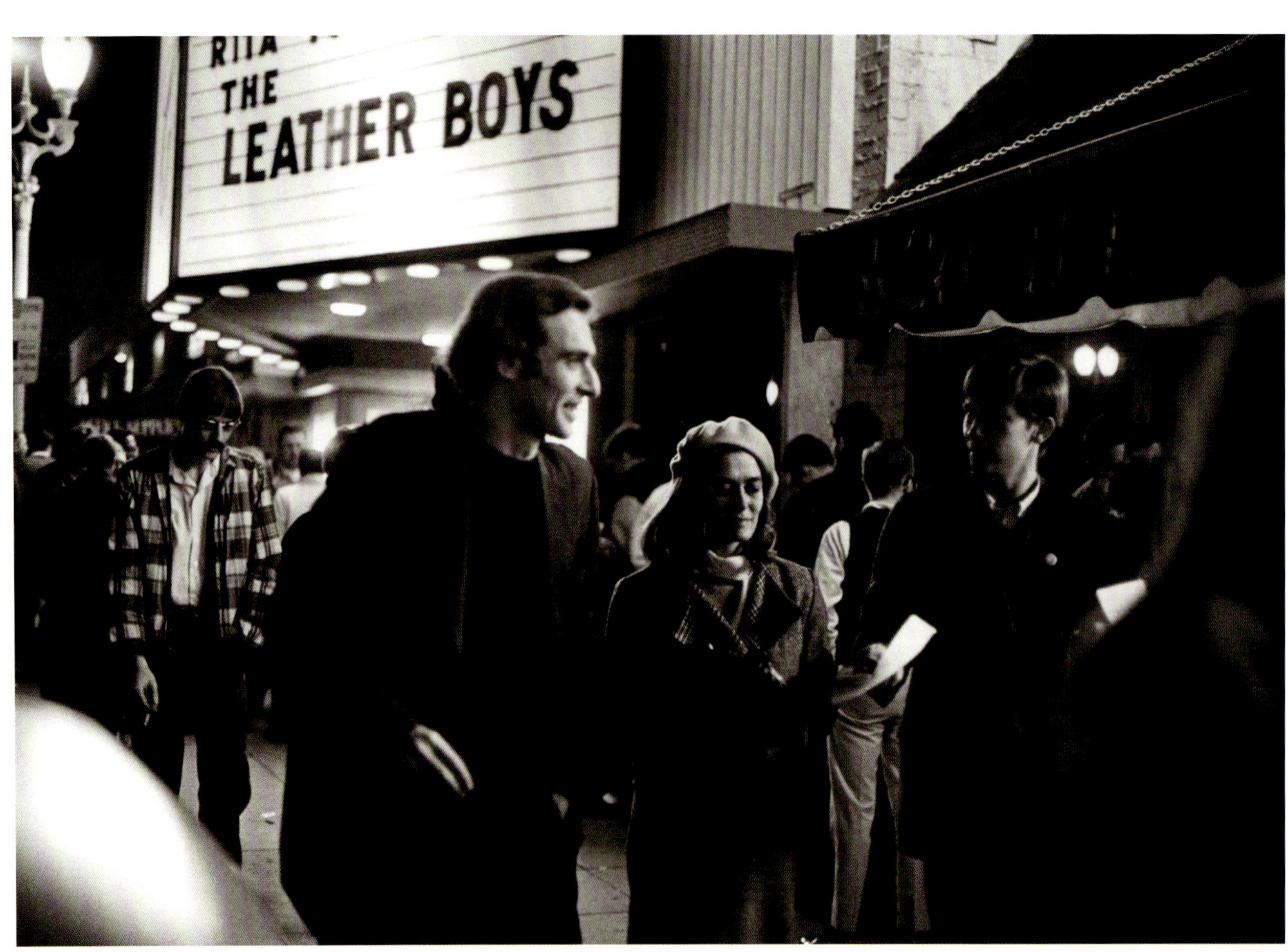

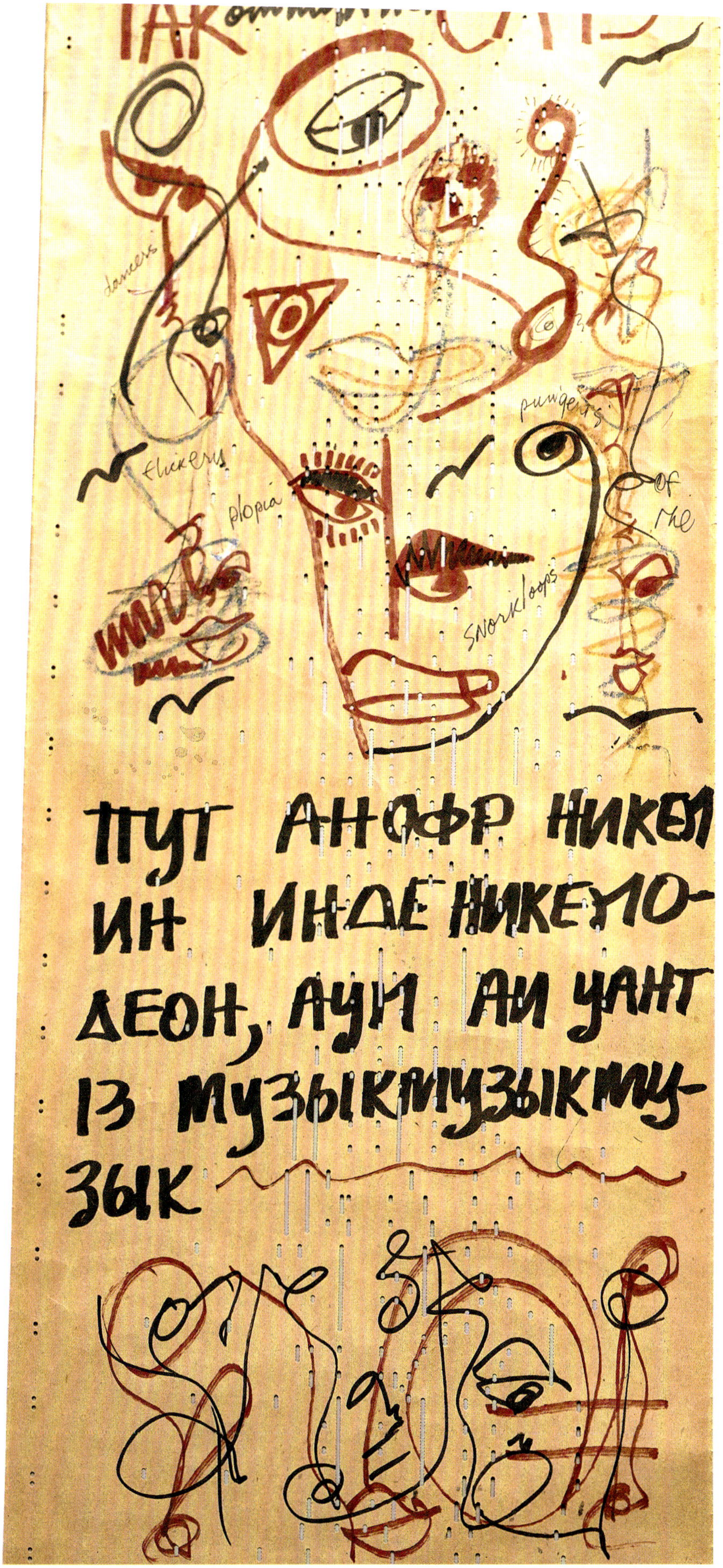

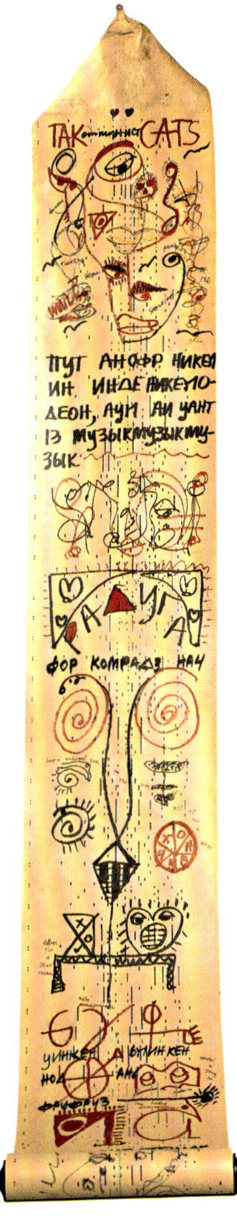
TAK CATS
ПУТ АНОФР НИКЕЛ
ИН ИНДЕ НИКЕЛО-
ДЕОН, АУИ АИ УАНТ
13 МУЗЫКМУЗЫКМУ-
ЗЫК
ФОР КОМРАДЗ НАЧ

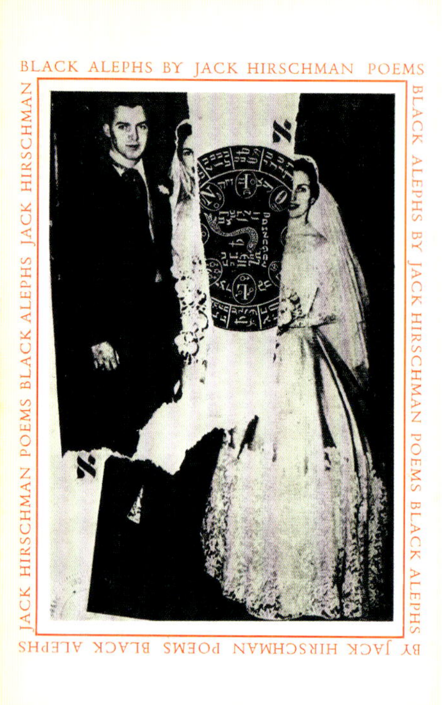

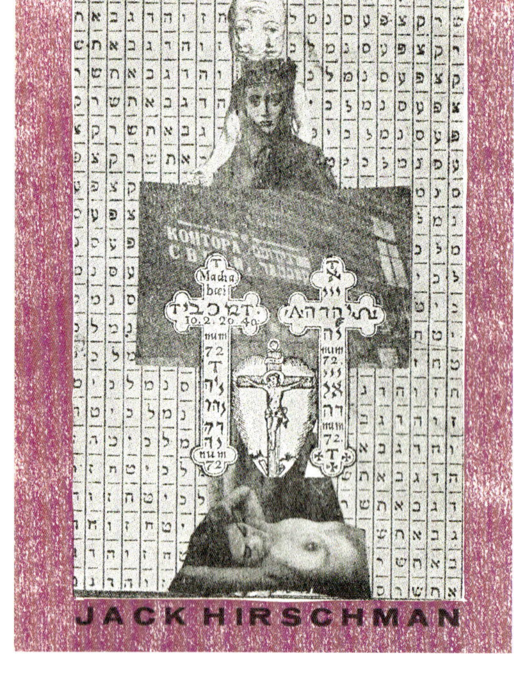

David Meltzer has aptly described poet and translator Jack Hirschman as "an immensely present yet hidden figure in the cultural politics and life of American poetry."[1] Born in 1933 to a middle-class family in the Bronx, Hirschman worked on city newspapers as a teenager and studied journalism and English literature at the City College of New York. His earliest poems were formal experiments dealing with leftist political themes. He married fellow student Ruth Epstein in 1954 and began graduate studies at Indiana University the next year.

p. 166
Jack Hirschman and Ruth Hirschman Seymour outside the Cinema Theater on Western Avenue, 1963. Photograph by Charles Brittin.

p. 167
Jack Hirschman, *Old Timer's Waltz*, 1970, Drawings and poem on roll for player piano, collection of Bonnie and Russel Tamblyn.

p. 168 left
Jack Hirschman, *Black Alephs* (New York: Phoenix Book Shop, 1969), Cover by Wallace Berman.

p. 168 right
Jack Hirschman, *Cantillations* (Santa Barbara: Capra Press, 1974), Cover by Wallace Berman.

P. 169
Jack Hirschman, *Yod* (London: Trigram Press, 1966).

In Bloomington he met Clayton Eshleman who later, as editor of the journal *Caterpillar*, published his work and that of many in Wallace Berman's circle. Following his own tastes beyond the confines of academia, Hirschman began corresponding with Allen Ginsberg after the publication of *Howl* and sent him his translations of poems by Russian poet Vladimir Mayakovsky in 1957. Hirschman received a doctorate in comparative literature from Indiana University in 1959 with a thesis devoted to the novels of Djuna Barnes and Hermann Broch.

Soon with a family of two children, he began teaching at Dartmouth College where he met a number of visiting poets, including Robert Duncan, Lawrence Ferlinghetti, and Robert Creeley. Under the spell of Ginsberg, Creeley, and Charles Olson in the early 1960s, Hirschman's poetry began loosening up. For the *Village Voice*, he wrote the first major review of John Wieners's *The Hotel Wentley Poems*.

He began teaching at the University of California Los Angeles in 1961 and his wife, Ruth became cultural program director of the influential radio station KPFK. The station regularly featured poetry readings and avant-garde programming such as a weeklong tribute to Antonin Artaud. For the 1962 tribute, Wallace Berman organized a reading of Artaud's "To Have Done With the Judgement of God."[2] Hirschman provided Berman with the short poem by Artaud which was published in *Semina 8*.[3]

In Los Angeles, the Hirshmans socialized with many of the poets and artists in Berman's circle, including George Herms, Dean Stockwell, Robert Alexander, William Margolis, Stuart Perkoff, and Russel Tamblyn. Hirschman received a writing grant from UCLA in 1964 and traveled to France, Greece, and England. He edited a selection of Artaud's writings (City Lights Books, 1965) that introduced the French writer to an English-speaking readership.

Hirschman's volume of poems and calligraphic drawings, *Yod* (Trigram Press, 1966) demonstrated his interest in the Kabbalah. *Yod* featured short poems that play off shaped typography and calligraphic drawings that refer to the letters of the Hebrew alphabet. His later essay, *KS (Kabbala Surrealism)* serves as a kind of manifesto for art

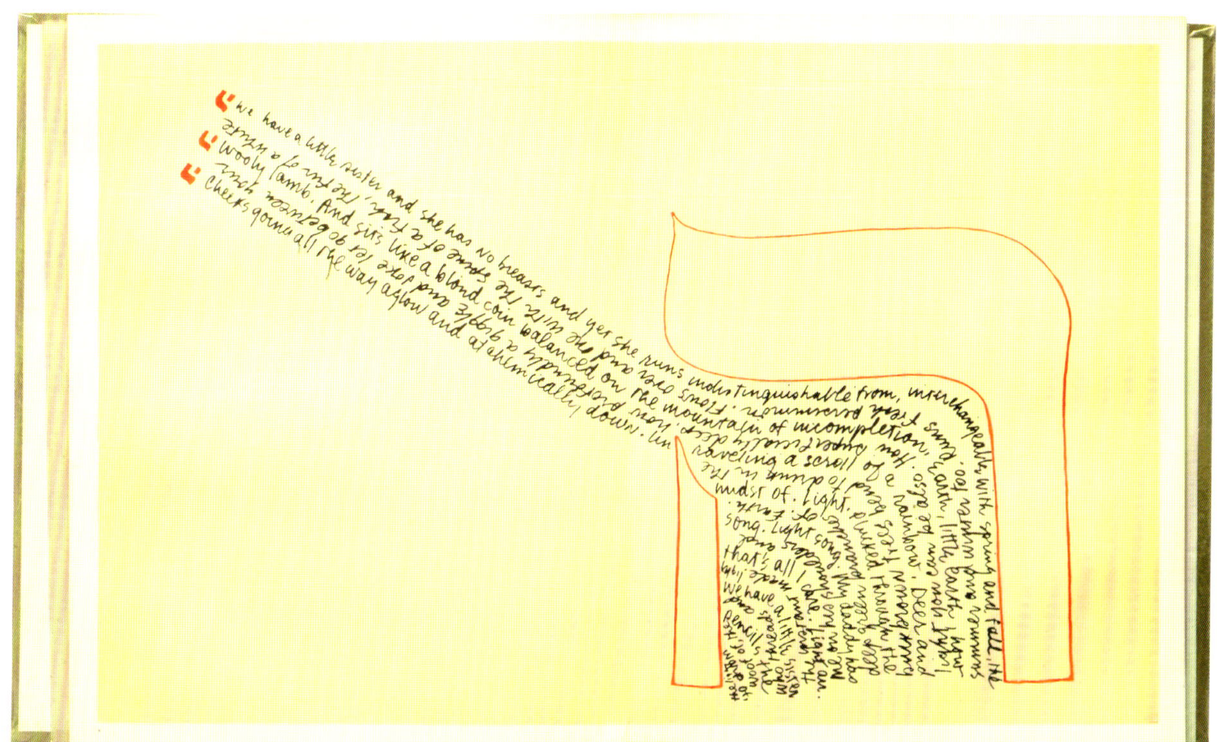

that explores the wordplay and all-inclusive symbolism of the Kabbalah, as well as what he called, "the mythic confirmation of art-as-life-as-purest-friendship" asserted in the works of Artaud, Berman, and David Meltzer.[4] Including poems dedicated to his wife Ruth, Kirby Doyle, George Herms, and singer Ray Charles, Hirschman's volume *Black Alephs* (Phoenix Bookshop/Trigram Press, 1969) related Kabbalistic symbology to the plight of contemporary African Americans. The book also featured Verifax collages by Berman.[5]

Hirschman was very active in the antiwar movement and was fired by UCLA in 1966 for giving high grades to all draft-eligible students to aid them in avoiding conscription.[6] Giving up academia, he devoted himself to writing and translating, publishing over fifty volumes in the past four decades. After his marriage ended in 1972, he moved to San Francisco, establishing a base from which he has traveled extensively. In the 1970s he was associated with a group of North Beach poets that included Bob Kaufman, Kirby Doyle, Gregory Corso, Tisa Walden, and David Meltzer. After translating *A Rainbow for the Christian West* (Los Angeles/Fairfax: The Red Hill Press, 1972) by the Haitian writer Rene Depestre, Hirschman was led to explore Marxist philosophy. He became a member of the Communist Labor Party in 1980 and has continued to be involved with a number of progressive political groups in the United States, Haiti, and Central America.

From the 1970s to the present, Hirschman has made thousands of drawings with politically charged texts in Russian and English that he calls "talking leaves," in the tradition of the American Sequoia tribe.[7] His visual work has been extensively collected by the Marvin and Ruth Sackner Archive of Concrete and Visual Poetry in Miami Beach. Since his marriage to poet Agneta Falk in 1999, he has maintained dual residences in San Francisco and Yorkshire, England. *Michael Duncan*

1 Jack Hirschman and Matt Gonzalez, "Chorosho! An Auto/Biographical Sketch of Jack Hirschman," *San Francisco Call*, May 24, 2002, www.sfcall.com/issues%202002/5.24.02/hirschman_bio_5_24_02.htm.

2 June 26, 1962 Berman letter to David Meltzer, collection of Phil Aarons.

3 Undated correspondence, c. 1963 from Hirschman to Berman, Wallace Berman Archive, Archive of American Art, Smithsonian Institution.

4 Jack Hirschman, *KS (Kabbala Surrealism)*, (Venice, California: Beyond Baroque Foundation, 1972), p. 10.

5 See Marco Nieli, "Interview with Jack Hirschman," *Left Curve*, No. 25, 2002, www.leftcurve.com.

6 Jack Hirschman and Matt Gonzalez, ibid.

7 Nieli, ibid.

Dennis Hopper

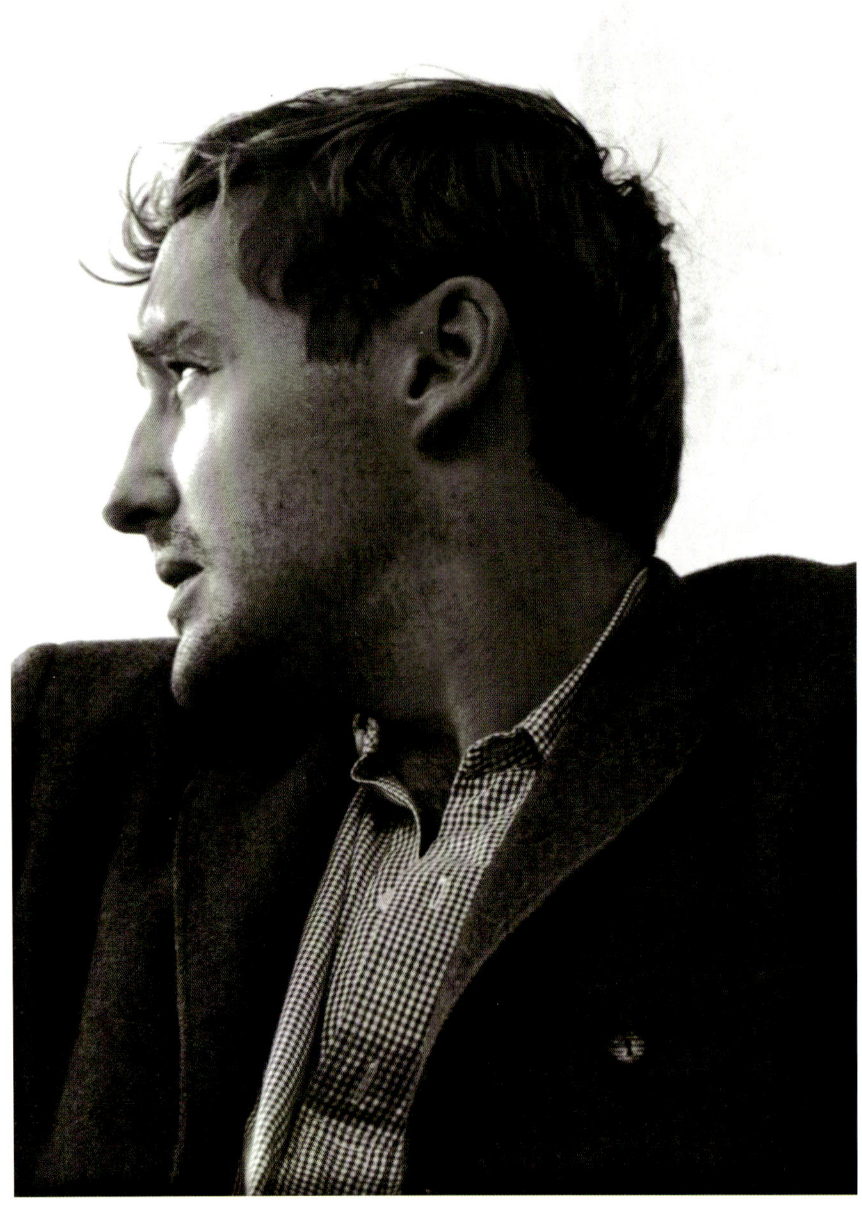

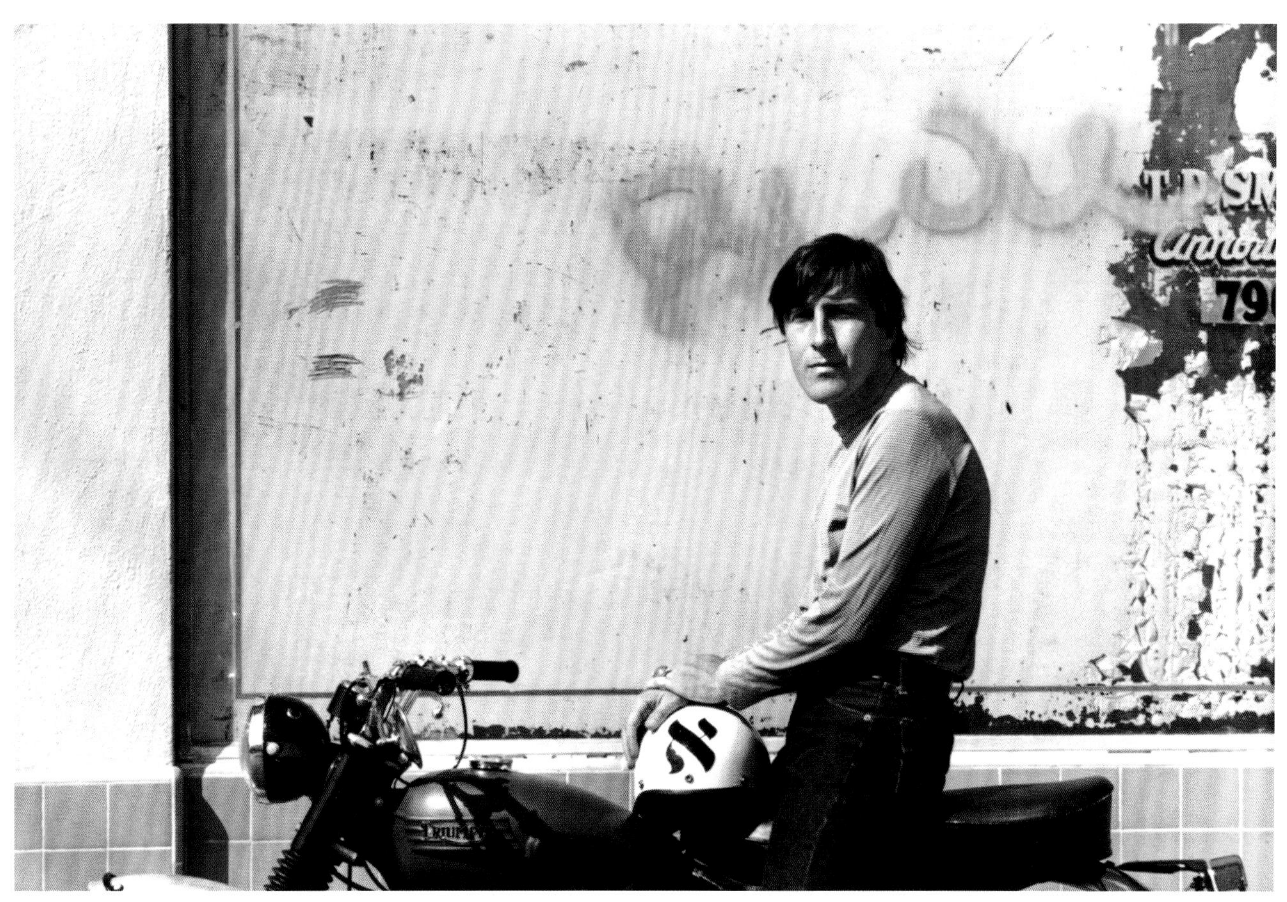

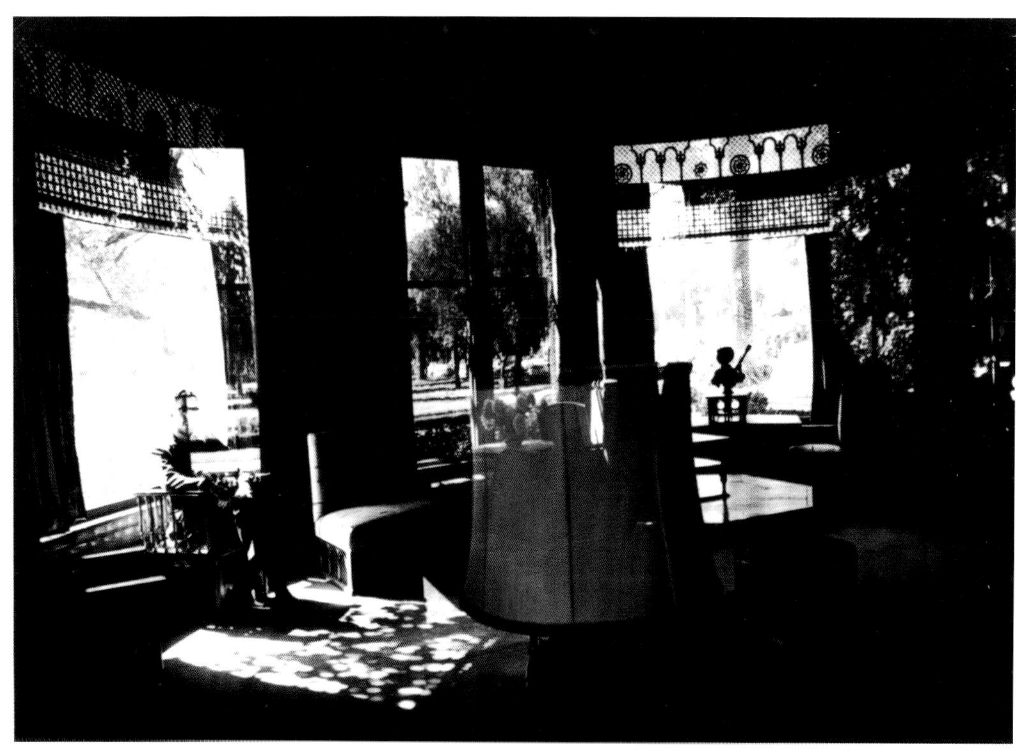

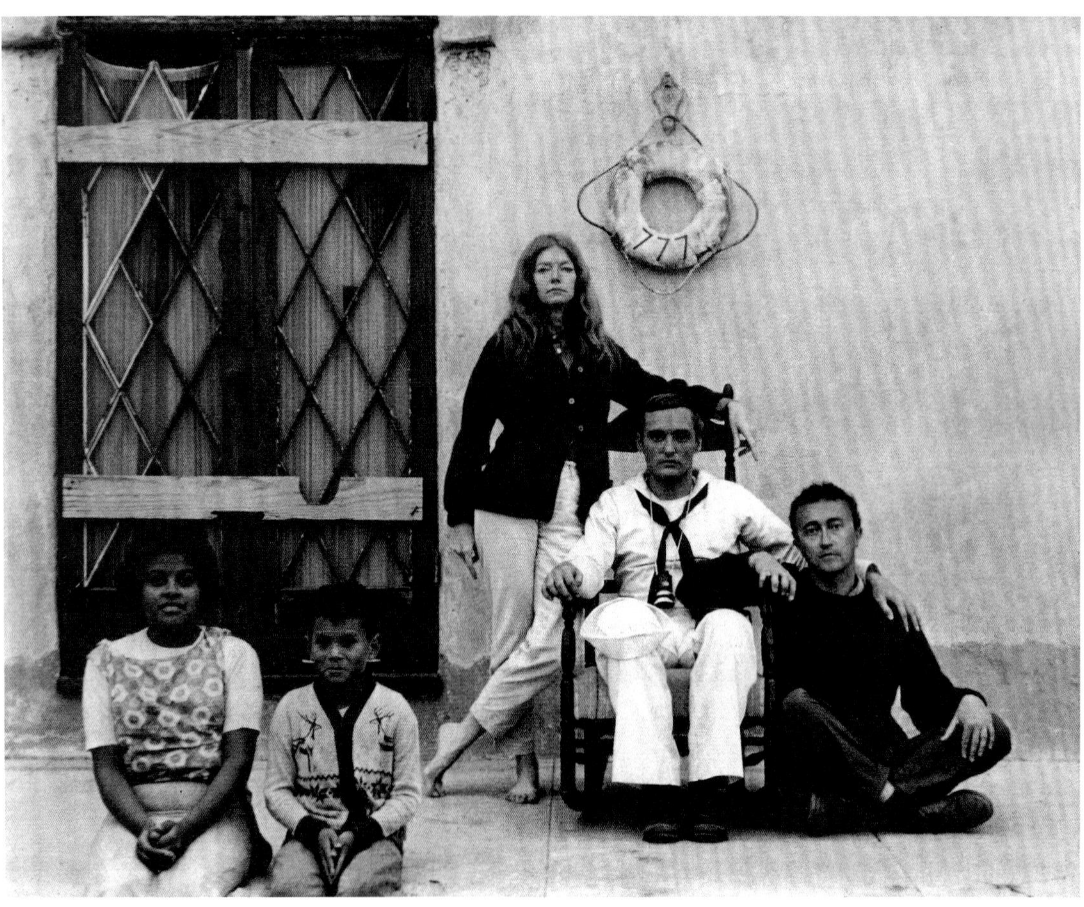

Actor, photographer, filmmaker, and painter Dennis Hopper is a jack-of-all-trades, managing intermittent yet long-term careers in a variety of media. Born in 1936 in Dodge City, Kansas, Hopper took art classes as a child at the Nelson Atkins Museum of Art in Kansas City. When he was thirteen, his family moved to San Diego where he acted in Shakespeare productions at the Old Globe Theatre and apprenticed at La Jolla Playhouse. Hopper graduated from high school in Los Angeles in 1955 and immediately was signed by Warner Brothers Studio.

He soon met actor/collector Vincent Price who showed him his collection of contemporary works that included paintings by Abstract Expressionists such as Richard Diebenkorn and Emerson Woelffer. Attracted to the dense, abstract surfaces of mottled paint, Hopper began painting in earnest. (A fire in his Bel Air studio in 1961 destroyed much of his early work, including over three hundred paintings.)

Hopper credits James Dean, alongside whom he acted in *Rebel Without a Cause* (1955) and *Giant* (1956), with the advice to take up photography, a medium that suited Hopper's energetic and inquisitive eye. He attended Los Angeles gallery shows and at a 1957 poetry reading at Stone Brothers was introduced to Wallace Berman by Dean Stockwell. When disagreements with the director Henry Hathaway on the set of *From Hell to Texas* (1958) stalled Hopper's rising acting career, he moved to New York where he studied acting with Lee Strasberg and regularly visited the Museum of Modern Art. Hopper began to experiment with black and white photography using Tri-X film, which was especially effective for night shooting. These early photographs reveal an eye for background street detail such as graffiti and billboards.

Back in Hollywood, Hopper began collecting art, purchasing the first Andy Warhol soup can painting from

p. 170
Self-portrait, 1966, Photograph by Dennis Hopper.

p. 171 top
Wallace Berman, 1964, Photograph by Dennis Hopper.

p. 171 bottom
Walter Hopps, Waiting for Marcel Duchamp, Green Hotel, Pasadena, 1962, Photograph by Dennis Hopper.

p. 172
Cameron, Dennis Hopper, and Curtis Harrington on the set of Night Tide, directed by Curtis Harrington, 1961, Collection of Dennis Hopper.

p. 173
George and Nalota Herms, 1961, Photograph by Dennis Hopper.

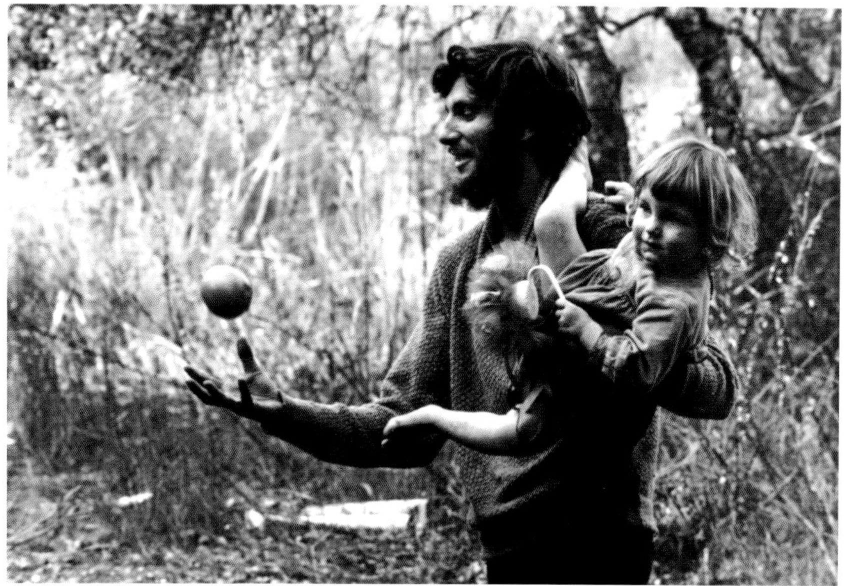

Virginia Dwan Gallery. He got to know the cutting-edge local artists of the Ferus scene and purchased important early works by Berman, Bruce Conner, George Herms, Dean Stockwell, and Ed Kienholz. The Marcel Duchamp retrospective at the Pasadena Art Museum in 1963 made a deep impression on him, opening his eyes to chance encounters and the idea of the readymade. Also that year, Hopper starred in Curtis Harrington's strangely poetic film *Night Tide*, which featured Cameron in a supporting role.

Hopper's 1960s photographic portraits of artists are his best-known works, capturing their subjects' active essences. As his acting career again began to take off, he took his camera wherever he traveled, recording pop stars, artists, and the Civil Rights March of 1963. He documented performance artist Allen Kaprow's *Ice Palace* project with still photographs and film. Marrying actress Brooke Hayward in 1961, Hopper documented their life together in photographs later published as *1712 North Crescent Heights* (Los Angeles: Greybull Press, 2001). These images create a sparkling record of the burgeoning of pop Los Angeles and the counterculture.

Curator Rudi Fuchs has written about the painterly quality of Hopper's photographs:

> *The motifs are set down sharply, observed from a close perspective in a generally shallow, confined space. The background is often filled with additional motifs such as posters, inscriptions, ornaments.... There is hardly room for airiness and atmosphere. The photographs are dark and compact in form. In their visual aspect, they have a dense weight which is reminiscent of assemblage.*[1]

Long wanting to direct a film, Hopper was able to make *Easy Rider* (1969), a wildly successful low-budget feature that launched the independent film movement. The film's examination of drug and hippie culture seems to depict the dissolution of many of the ideals that originated in the beat era. Playing off Wallace Berman's role as the maker of *Semina*, Hopper cast him in a small role as a hippie seed-sower. Formally, Hopper credited Bruce Conner's quick-cut editing style as an important influence.

Hopper's next film project, *The Last Movie* (1971), a self-reflexive story of a star-crossed feature being shot in Peru, featured small roles for Toni Basil, Dean Stockwell, Russel Tamblyn, and Billy Gray. Its experimental nature caused trouble at the box office and brought a temporary halt to Hopper's directing career. Temporarily abandoning painting and photography, Hopper spent the remainder of the 1970s largely secluded in Taos indulging in self-destructive drug use.

Hopper reemerged in 1980, directing the film *Out of the Blue* and giving up drugs and alcohol in 1984. He created perhaps his most memorable film performance in David Lynch's *Blue Velvet* (1986). He began again to make Abstract Expressionist paintings in the early 1980s, and created a series of graffiti-inspired works on the heels of directing *Colors* (1988), a film about Los Angeles gangs. Traveling around the world for his renewed acting career, he made large, color, close-up photographs of walls, remarkable for their clarity and painterly effects. The found designs and patterns on the walls led him in turn to experiment with more rough-hewn, geometric paintings.

In the 1980s Hopper began collecting Neo-Expressionist art, including works by Julian Schnabel, David Salle, Jean-Michel Basquiat, and Kenny Scharf. Hopper's works were surveyed in an international traveling exhibition in 2001, organized by the Stedelijk Museum, Amsterdam and the MAK Museum, Vienna. *Michael Duncan*

1 Rudi Fuchs, "Back and Forth," *Dennis Hopper (A Keen Eye)* (Amsterdam: Stedelijk Museum, 2001) p. 12–13.

Walter Hopps

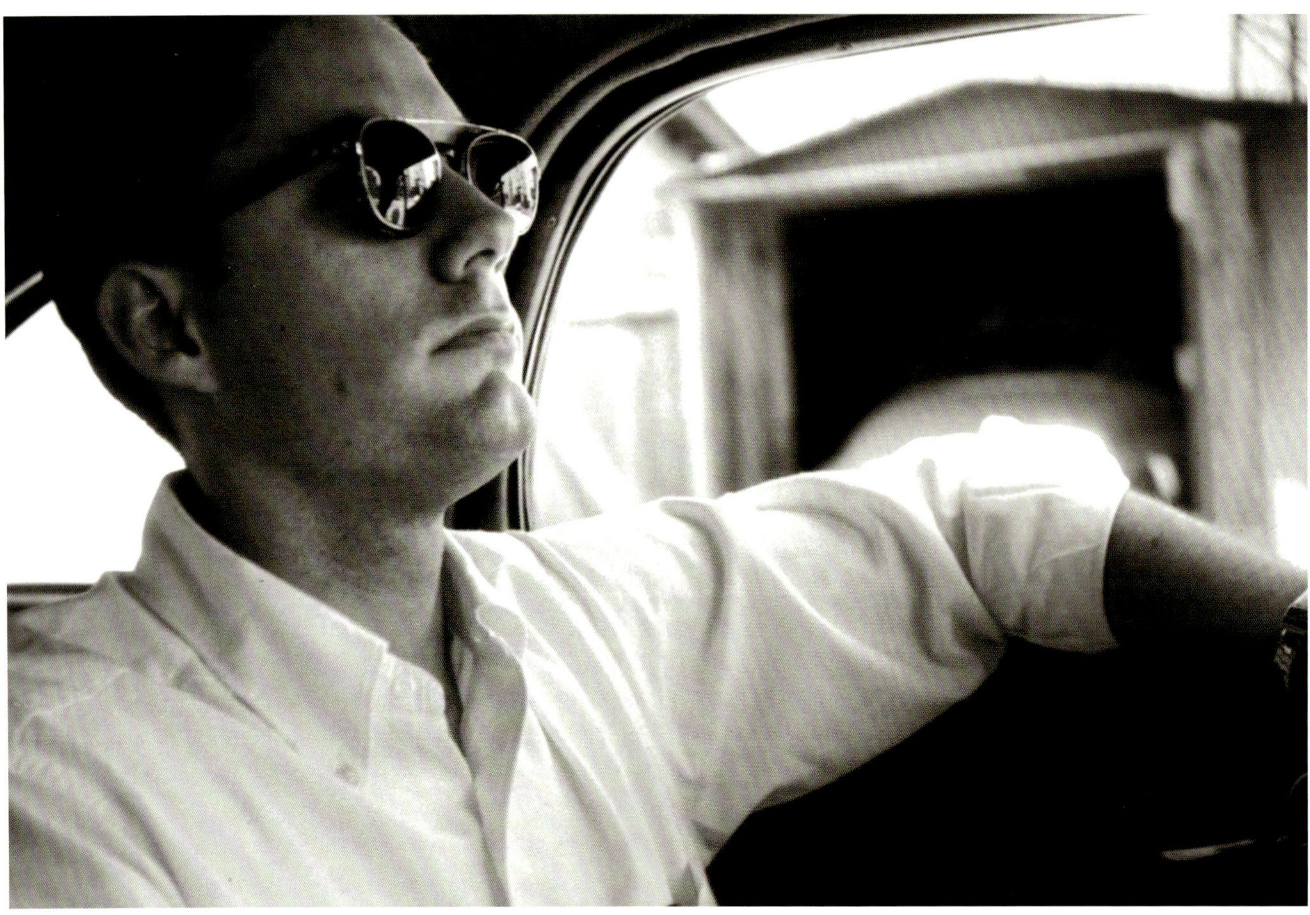

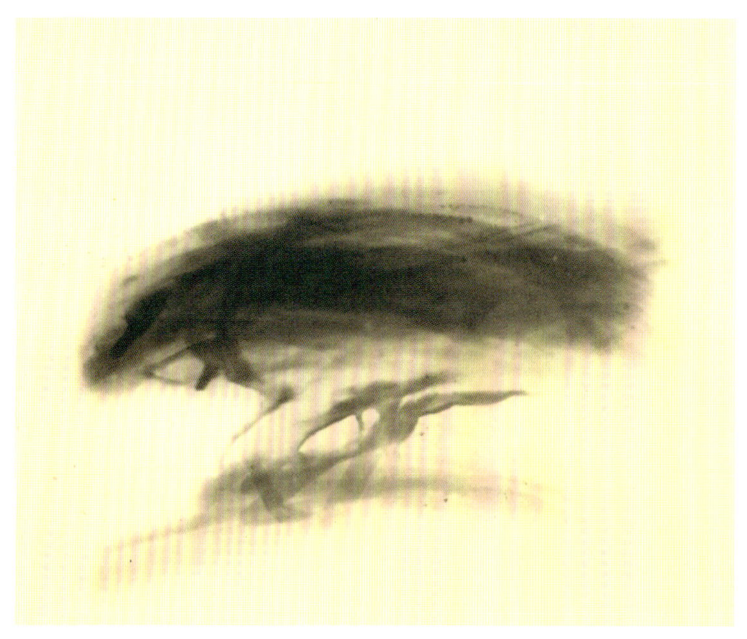

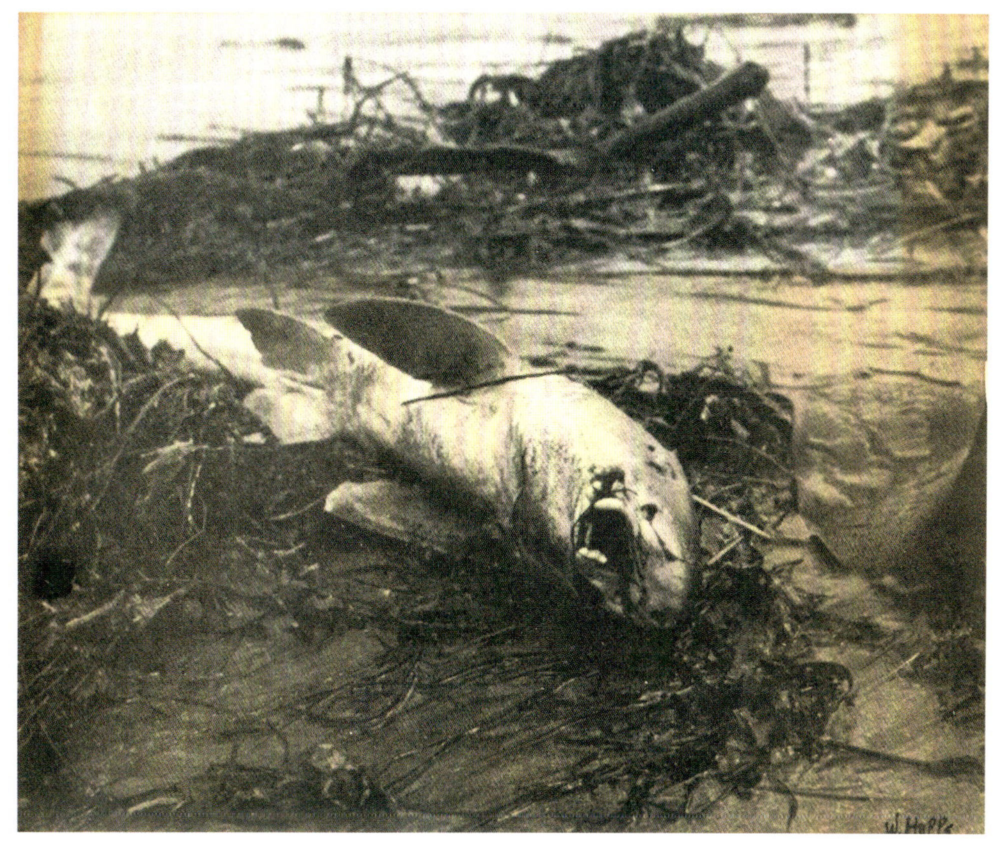

Walter Hopps was born in 1932 to a middle-class family in Eagle Rock, California. As a child he fell ill with rheumatic fever, and during a lengthy convalescence he began taking photographs; although he never exhibited them, he continued to take pictures throughout his life. Hopps was still in high school when he met Walter and Louise Arensberg, legendary collectors of Surrealist art who were the primary patrons of Marcel Duchamp. The Arensbergs owned many of Duchamp's key pieces, and seeing that revolutionary work set Hopps's course in life. There were, however, several fascinating detours along the way.

In 1950, while in his freshman year at Stanford, Hopps teamed up with Jim Newman to form Concert Hall Workshop, an agency devoted to the promotion and booking of jazz, which Hopps loved. By 1954, however, he'd put music aside and opened his first gallery, Syndell Studios, in Brentwood, California. During that year at Stanford, Hopps had become deeply enamored with the abstract painting then flourishing in the Bay area, and one thing he hoped to achieve in opening a Los Angeles gallery was to introduce that work to a wider audience.

"During the late 1940s and into the 1950s, the real action in art was in the Bay area, and an awful lot of what I was interested in I had to import from San Francisco," recalled Hopps, who lived behind the Syndell with his first wife, art historian Shirley Neilsen. "Then, as it got deeper into the 1950s and the 1960s, it became increasingly intractable to do anything in the Bay area."[1]

p. 174
Walter Hopps, Los Angeles, 1956. Photograph by Wallace Berman.

p. 175 top
Walter Hopps, Untitled drawing published in *Semina 1*, 1955.

p. 175 bottom
Walter Hopps, Untitled photograph published in *Semina Two*, 1957.

p. 177
Walter Hopps at Ferus Gallery, Los Angeles, 1957. Photograph by Charles Brittin.

As the energy in the Bay area was dissipating, things were picking up steam in Los Angeles; among those leading the charge into the future was Wallace Berman, who had begun publishing *Semina* in 1955. "*Semina* was a strange mix of rough, secular stuff and bits of ethereal transcendence," said Hopps, who contributed two photographs to *Semina 1*, and one photograph to *Semina Two*. "Berman was the first artist I knew to create a literary and visual arts portfolio that included beautiful things from the past, and taken together, it pointed to a world beyond."

In 1955 Hopps teamed up with Jim Newman and artist Craig Kauffman to organize Action 1, a group exhibition presented in the merry-go-round building on the Santa Monica Pier. The following year, Hopps collaborated with artist Robert Alexander and Ed Kienholz on Action 2, a survey show presented at the Coronet Louvre Theater on La Cienega Boulevard. Hopps and Kienholz enjoyed working together, so in 1957 they joined forces to open the Ferus Gallery, which is widely acknowledged as the first significant Los Angeles gallery to showcase the work of young artists. Among those who received support from Ferus early in their careers are Ed Ruscha, Bruce Conner, Robert Irwin, Jay DeFeo, Andy Warhol, Roy Lichtenstein, Ken Price, Peter Voulkos, Wallace Berman, Jasper Johns, and Frank Stella.

Kienholz quickly discovered he'd rather be making art than running a gallery, so Hopps bought out Kienholz's share of Ferus shortly after it opened. Hopps wasn't cut out to be a salesman either, however, and he soon found himself organizing exhibitions for the Pasadena Museum of Art; Hopps early curatorial projects there included a show of drawings by Richard Diebenkorn and Frank Lobdell, an exhibition of abstract paintings by Robert Irwin, and the first museum exhibition of work by Kienholz. In 1962 Hopps was hired as a full-time curator at Pasadena, and he gave his share of Ferus to dealer Irving Blum.

In 1963 Hopps was made Director at Pasadena. From the earliest days of his career, it was widely acknowledged that Hopps possessed an extraordinary eye and had an intuitive grasp of how to hang a show; during the 1960s he was also significantly ahead of the curve. His exhibition, "New Paintings of Common Objects," mounted at the Pasadena Museum in 1962, was an early excursion into Pop; he gave Frank Stella his first museum show; and he organized the first retrospective exhibitions of work by Joseph Cornell and Marcel Duchamp. Dazzlingly brilliant though he was, Hopps was also extremely mercurial, and in 1966 the Pasadena Museum let him go after he suffered a psychological breakdown that required several weeks of hospitalization.

After he got back on his feet, a fellowship at the Institute for Policy Studies took Hopps to Washington, D.C., where he was named Director of Special Projects for the Corcoran Gallery in 1967. During his tenure at the Corcoran he presented exhibitions of work by Barnett Newman, Tony Smith, David Smith, and Robert Morris, among others. In 1972 he became embroiled in a conflict surrounding the museum staff's efforts to unionize, and his tenure at the Corcoran ended.

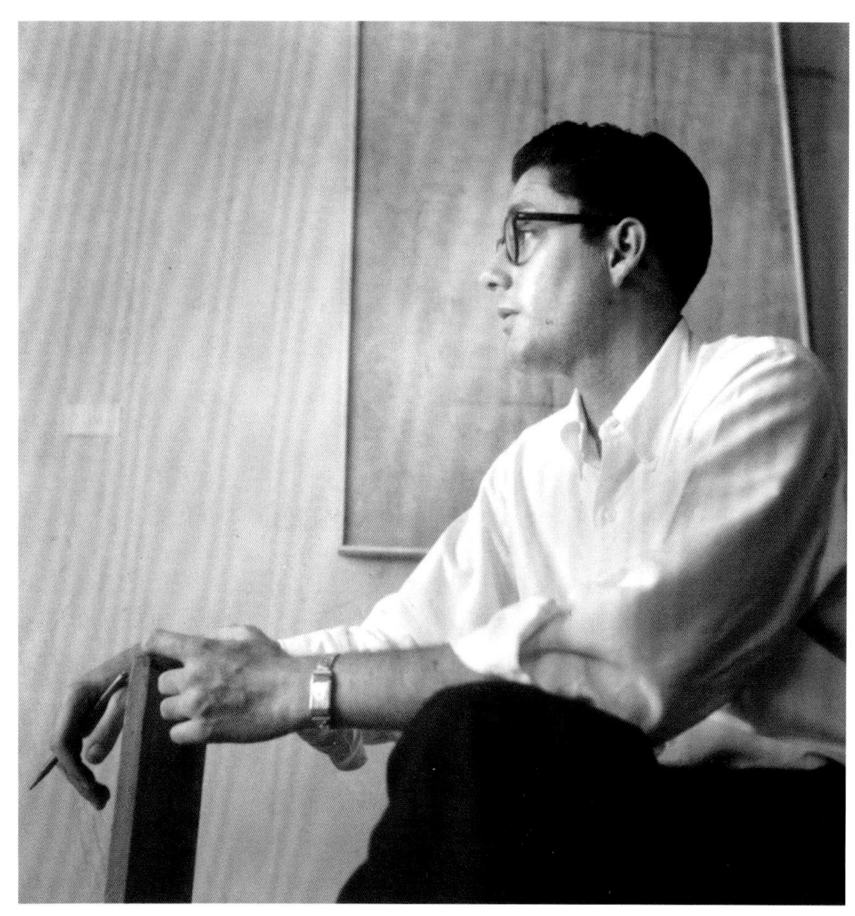

The following year the Smithsonian named him Senior Curator for Twentieth-Century Art at the National Collection of Fine Arts, and he immediately began working on a landmark retrospective of work by Robert Rauschenberg, which opened in 1976. The show was hugely successful, but Hopps had alienated many of his co-workers during his tenure at the National, and by 1979 it was clear to him the time had come to resign.

In 1980 Hopps began a long and fruitful partnership with art patron Dominique de Menil, who hired him as a consultant to the Menil Foundation in 1980, and then named him Founding Director of The Menil Collection when it opened in Houston in 1987. By 1989 it was clear to all involved that Hopps's gifts were as a curator rather than a museum director, and he was made consulting curator for The Menil, a title that allowed him a great deal of flexibility.

During the 1990s, Hopps worked with various museums organizing traveling exhibitions of work by Ed Kienholz, Robert Rauschenberg, Joseph Cornell, and Marcel Duchamp, among others. In 2001 he was appointed Adjunct Senior Curator of Twentieth-Century Art at the Guggenheim, where he organized a retrospective exhibition of work by James Rosenquist that opened in 2003 at The Menil. In 2005 he organized a retrospective of work by George Herms for the Santa Monica Museum of Art. Hopps died in Los Angeles of congestive heart failure in March 2005. *Kristine McKenna*

1 All quotations from a conversation with Walter Hopps, July, 1993

Billy Jahrmarkt

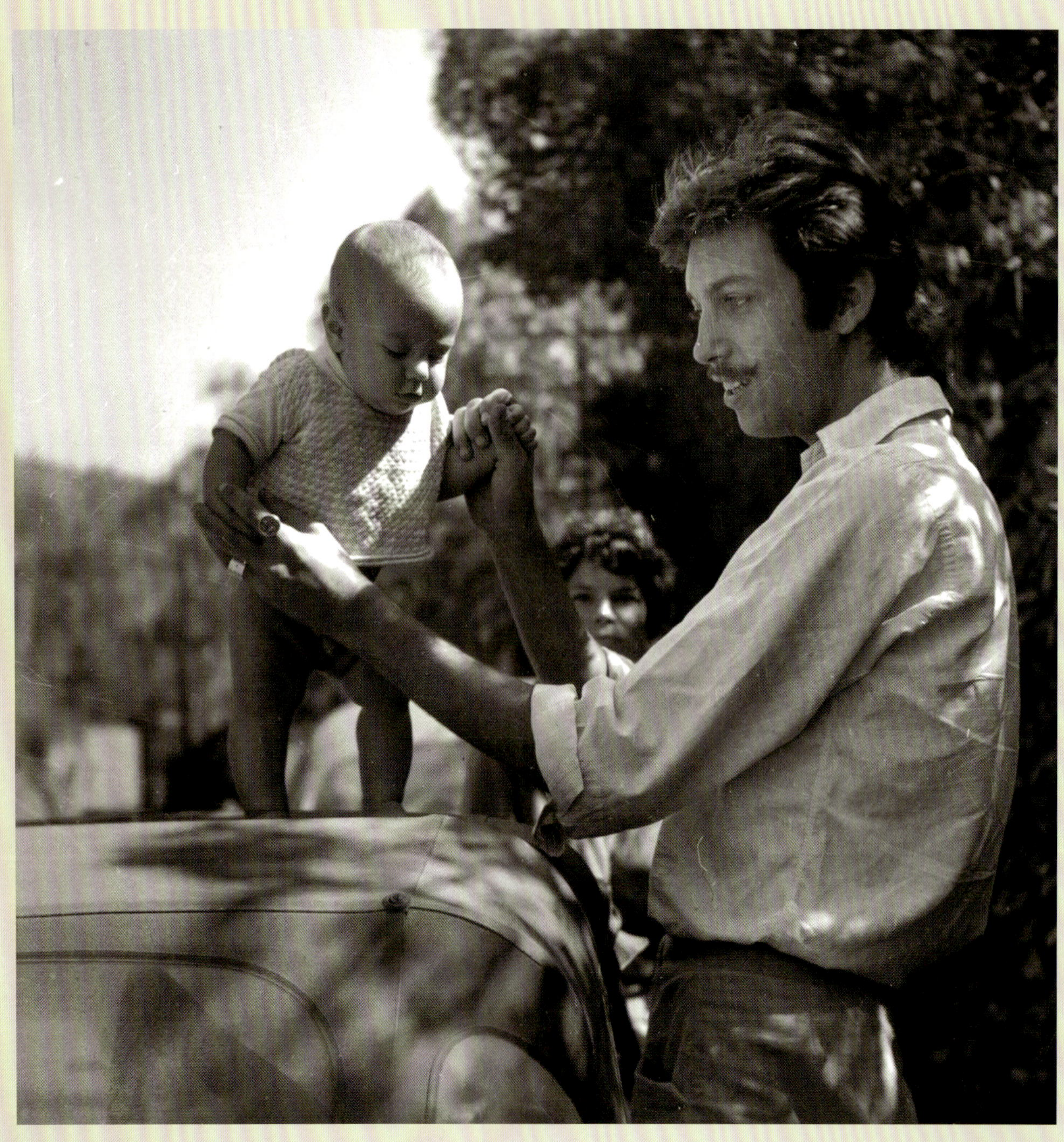

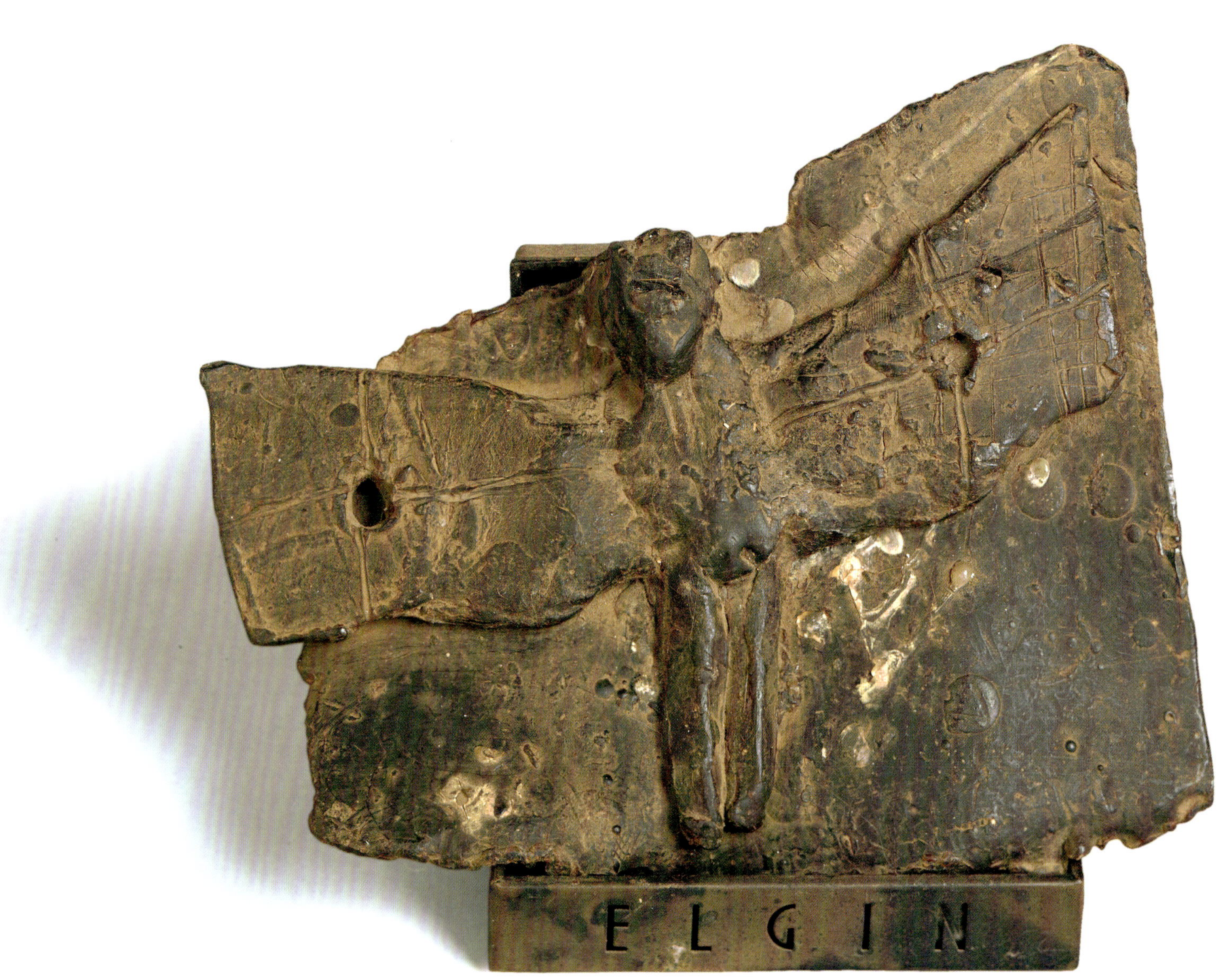
ELGIN

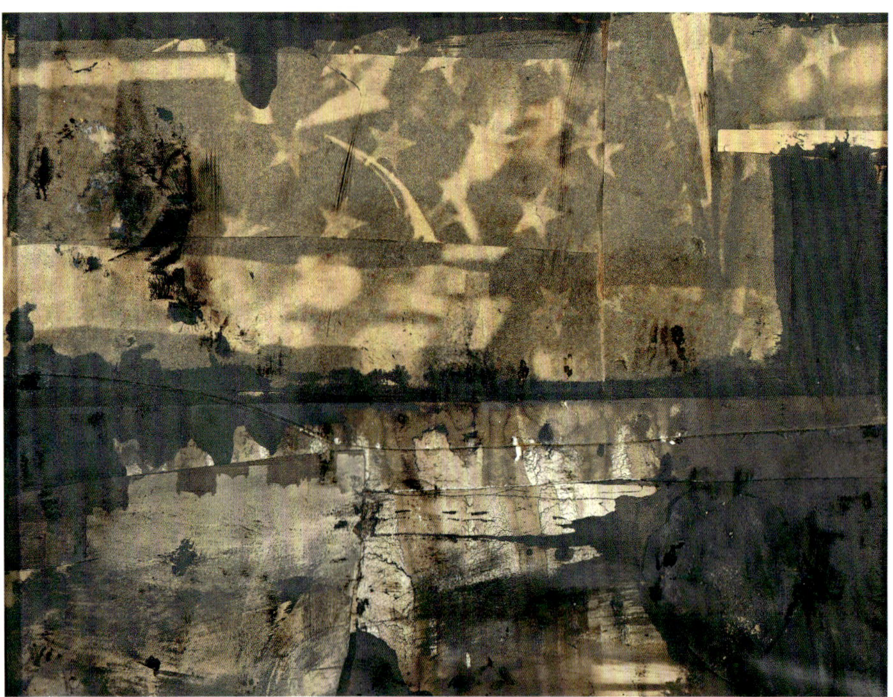

Billy Jahrmarkt was born in New York in 1936, the son of a successful businessman in the garment trade. Jahrmarkt's entrée into Los Angeles's underground art community came through Wallace Berman's brother-in-law, Donald Morand, who lived in Manhattan in the early 1950s with his girlfriend, Loree Foxx.

"We had an apartment on Fifty-fourth Street, and Billy was a rich kid who was attending an art school in our neighborhood," Morand comments. "He was only around sixteen then but he was already kind of fancy, and he ran with a bunch of guys we used to call the Eighty-fifth Street gang who hung out around Needle Park. They were a fun bunch of kids who were really into jazz, and they hung out at our apartment and smoked pot. Billy was already a junkie when we met him."[1]

Sometime in the mid-1950s, Jahrmarkt moved to Los Angeles, and his first destination was the Beverly Glen home of Morand, who put him up for the first few weeks he was in town. While he was living in Los Angeles, Jahrmarkt met a young girl from Beverly Hills whom he married. In 1959 he and his wife Joan moved to San Francisco where they met the McClures and the Conners, among others. "My husband, who had a very keen eye for art and was in fact an artist himself, realized that more exposure was needed for this highly creative bunch of people," recalls Joan Jahrmarkt.[2]

p. 178
Billy Jahrmarkt, Crater Lane, 1964, Photograph by Wallace Berman.

p. 179
Billy Jahrmarkt, *Watch Bat for George Herms*, 1961, Clay sculpture on found metal stand.

p. 180
Billy Jahrmarkt, *Homage to McClure*, 1960, Collage and paint.

p. 181
Billy Jahrmarkt, Untitled (face), 1964, verifax follage.

Thus was born the Batman Gallery, an exhibition space Jahrmarkt opened with financial assistance from his father. Located at 2222 Fillmore Street in a defunct dress shop scouted out by Bruce Conner, the gallery opened in November of 1960 with an exhibition of work by Conner, who also designed the gallery space. The walls were black, the lighting was dramatic, and a system of movable panels was installed that allowed the space to be divided up in different ways.

"Billy's skills as an artist were an important part of that gallery," says George Herms of the Batman, which also hosted poetry readings, film screenings, and plays. "Billy was always really ahead of everything, and when he came to Los Angeles from New York he was a very well-informed artist. But from the time he was a teenager he'd had a narcotics problem, and he loved guns. He slept with a gun under his pillow."[3]

The most pressing manifestation of Jahrmarkt's narcotics problem, as regarded his gallery, was that he had a difficult time maintaining regular business hours. The situation was exacerbated by the fact that the Jahrmarkts were living alongside the Herms and the Bermans in Larkspur, which was a world unto itself far removed from the affairs of San Francisco. In the fourteen months that followed the gallery's opening, Jahrmarkt mounted nine exhibitions at the Batman; among them were solo shows of work by Joan Brown, George Herms, Dean Fleming, George Abend, and Bernice Bin. However, sales were spotty at best, and

Conner wound up taking Jahrmarkt to court for his failure to pay the artist for a work sold by the gallery.

In February of 1962, Jahrmarkt sold the gallery to psychiatrist Michael Agron, and he and his family—which now included three children—returned to Beverly Glen, where they lived down the hill from the Bermans. Shortly after returning to Los Angeles, Jahrmarkt acquired a Verifax machine and began experimenting with it as an art making tool. An untitled work from 1964, in the collection of Dennis Hopper, is among the few surviving works from this period of production. A fascinatingly strange distortion of a female face, the piece has the ghoulish allure of work by Hans Bellmer, and it leaves one hungry to see more work by Jahrmarkt. Apparently he lost interest in the process in fairly short order, and in 1964 he gave the Verifax machine to Berman.

The Bermans were close to the Jahrmarkts during those years in the early 1960s—in fact, the Bermans lived with them for a short time after their house was destroyed in a mud slide—but when the Bermans moved to Topanga in 1966, the two couples began to drift apart. As is often the case in lives dominated by the need for heroin, Jahrmarkt allowed friendships and his art making practice to fall by the wayside, and toward the end of his life, many longtime friends lost track of him and most of his art disappeared.

In the early 1970s the Jahrmarkts moved to Afghanistan "because junk was legal there and you could walk around packing a gun," as George Herms has explained it. In 1973, Jahrmarkt dropped a gun that went off and shot him in the stomach. Apparently unaware of the gravity of his wound, he bled to death by the following morning. "Nobody expected Billy to live very long," says Michael McClure of Jahrmarkt, who was thirty-seven years old at the time of his death.[4] *Kristine McKenna*

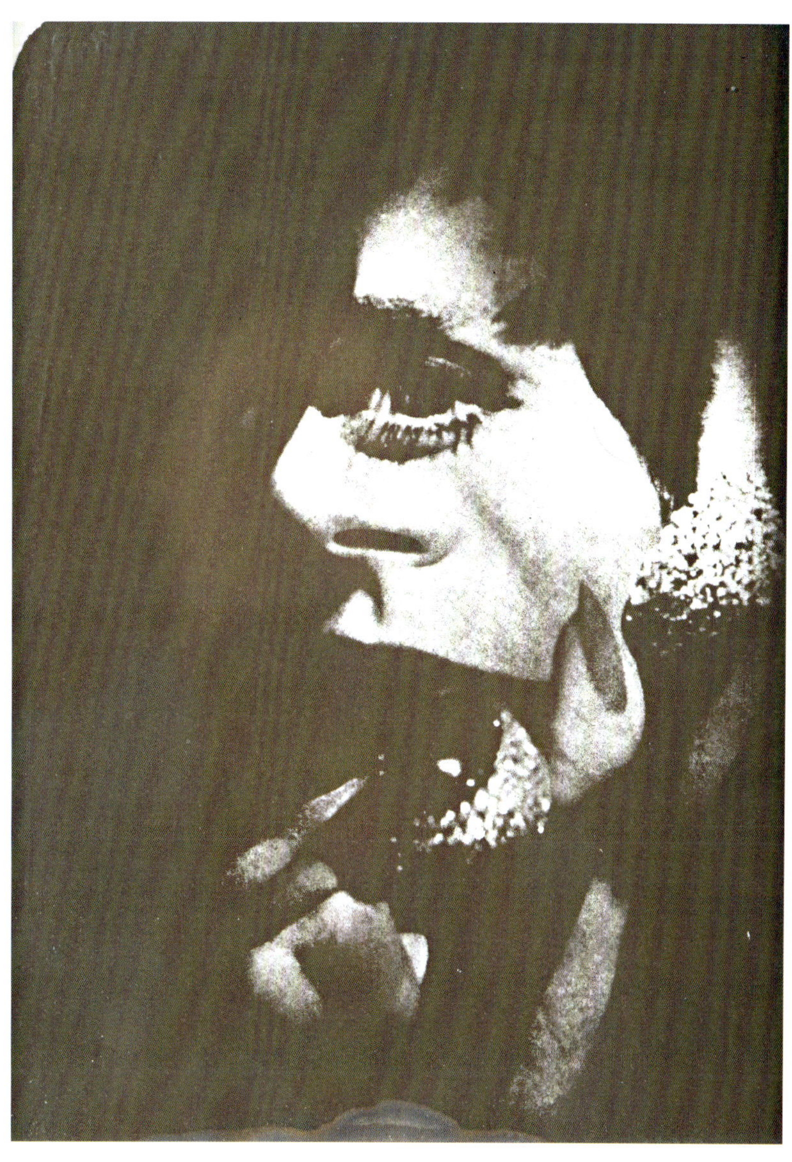

1 Conversation with Donald Morand, August 31, 2004.

2 Sandra Leonard Starr, *Lost and Found in California: Four Decades of Assemblage Art*, (Los Angeles: Corcoran, Shoshana Wayne, and Pence Galleries, 1988), p.104.

3 Conversation with George Herms, February 15, 1999.

4 Jack Foley, *O Her Blackness Sparkles!: The Life and Times of the Batman Art Gallery, San Francisco 1960–65* (San Francisco, 3300 Press: 1996), p. 5.

Jess

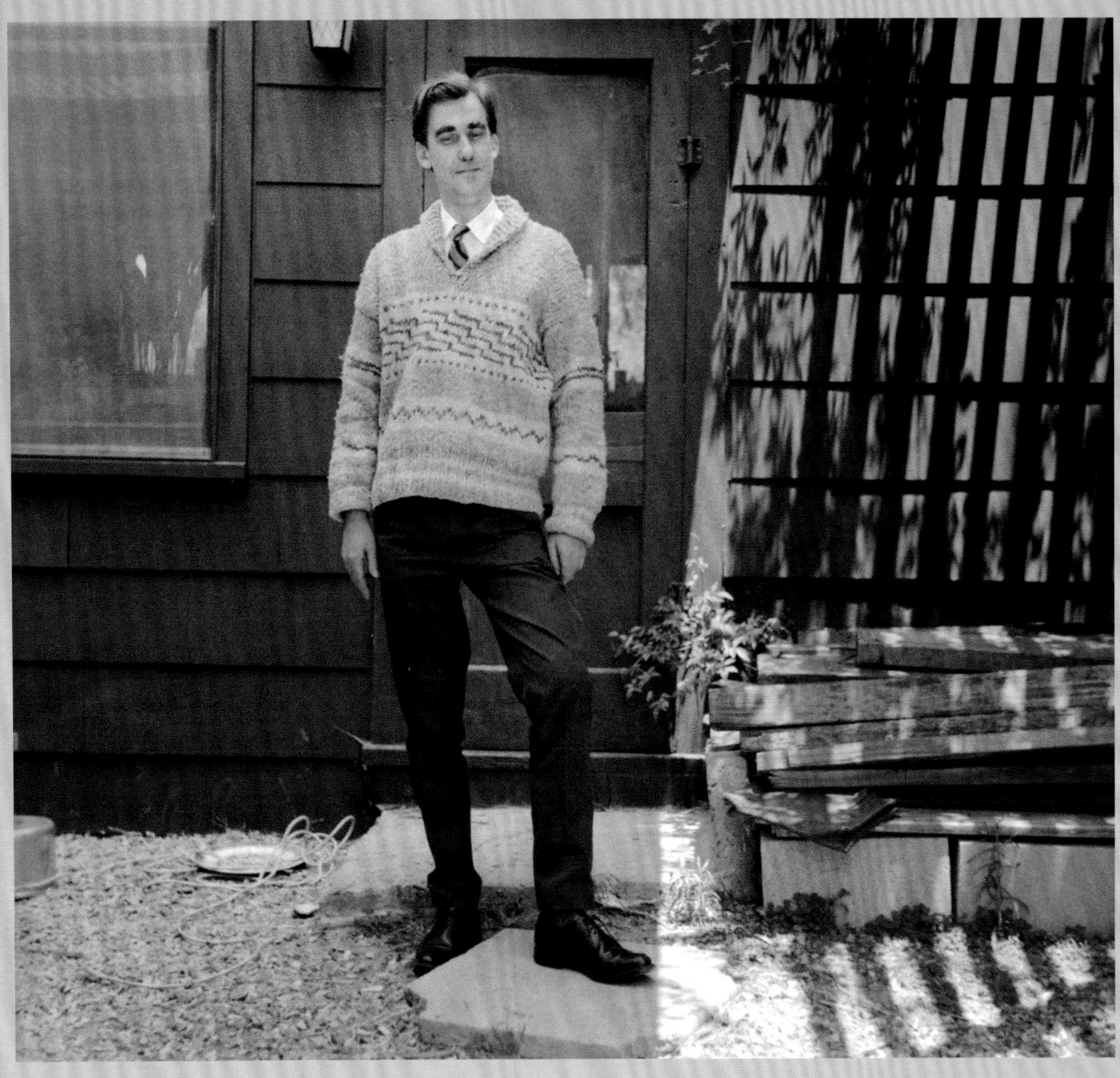

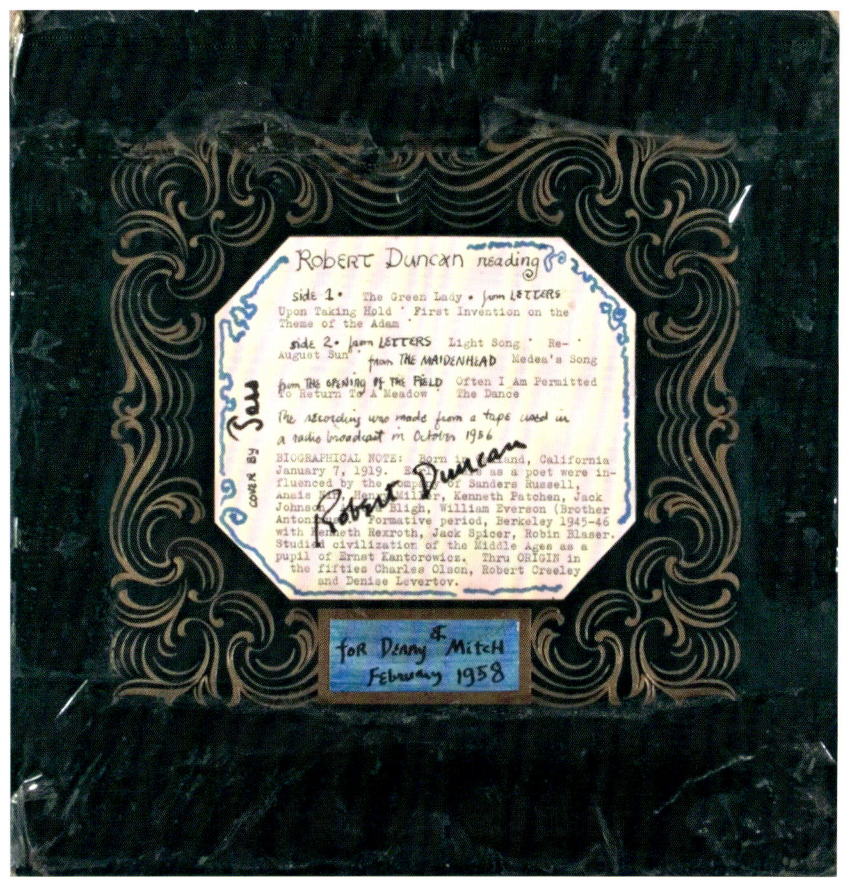
Robert Duncan reading
side 1. The Green Lady · from LETTERS
Upon Taking Hold · First Invention on the
Theme of the Adam ·
side 2. from LETTERS Light Song · Re-
August Sun · from THE MAIDENHEAD Medea's Song
from THE OPENING OF THE FIELD Often I Am Permitted
To Return To A Meadow · The Dance
The recording was made from a tape used in
a radio broadcast in October 1956
BIOGRAPHICAL NOTE: Born in
California
January 7, 1919.
as a poet were in-
fluenced by the
of Sanders Russell,
Miller, Kenneth Patchen, Jack
Bligh, William Everson (Brother
Formative period, Berkeley 1945-46
with
Rexroth, Jack Spicer, Robin Blaser.
civilization of the Middle Ages as a
pupil of Ernst Kantorowicz. Thru ORIGIN in
the fifties Charles Olson, Robert Creeley
and Denise Levertov.
COVER BY Jess
Robert Duncan
for Denny & Mitch
February 1958

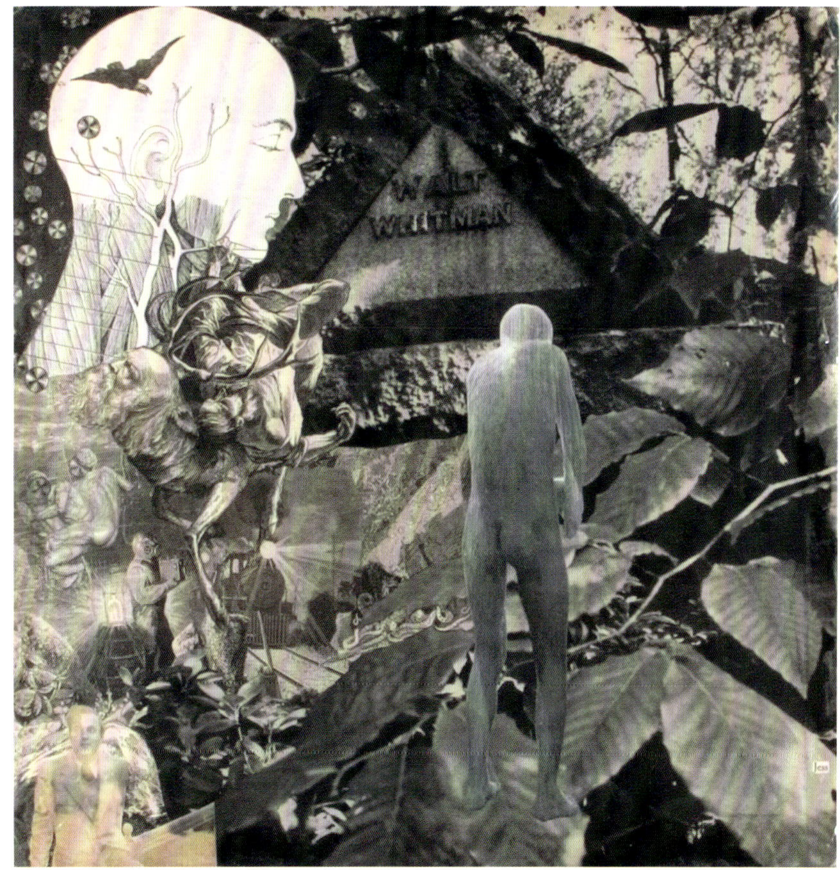
WALT
WHITMAN
Jess

Jess was a quietly independent artist and poet who developed a complex synthesis of art and literary history in his paintings, collages, and sculptures. Born Burgess Collins in 1923 in Long Beach, California, Jess was trained as a chemist and worked during World War II on the production of plutonium for the Manhattan Project. Experiencing extreme anxiety over the ramifications of his atomic-energy work, Jess had a dream in 1949 that prophesied the devastation of the world in 1975. Eight weeks after the dream, Jess abandoned science and his surname and moved to San Francisco to enroll in the California School of Fine Arts, then in its heyday with a faculty that included Clyfford Still and Edward Corbett. In 1951 Jess met poet Robert Duncan and embarked on a domestic relationship of shared esthetic concerns that lasted until Duncan's death in 1988.

Duncan and Jess came to artistic maturity together, ever expanding and refining a study of world literature and art focused on myths, symbols, and archetypes. In *Caesar's Gate*, their first important collaboration, Jess's collages provide a direct visual complement to a group of Duncan's poems completed in 1955 while the couple was on an extended visit to Majorca.

At home, Duncan and Jess became crucial participants in the burgeoning Bay Area poetry and art scenes, developing particularly close friendships with Helen Adam, Pauline Kael, Patricia and Lawrence Jordan, Jay DeFeo, Michael McClure, Bruce Conner, and George Herms. Along with painter Harry Jacobus, Jess and Duncan ran the King Ubu Gallery in 1952–53, hosting exhibitions of work by Elmer Bischoff, David Park, Hassel Smith, and Jess himself.

p. 182
Jess, Topanga Canyon, 1968,
Photograph by Wallace Berman.

p. 183
Robert Duncan, *Robert Duncan Reading from Letters, The Opening of the Field*, 1958, (Recordings of radio broadcasts from October 1956), Collaged record jacket by Jess, 1958, Mixed-media on fiberboard, vinyl.

p. 185
Jess, *Armageddon*, 1960, Mixed-media collage on paper.

p. 186
Jess and Robert Duncan,
A Book for Patty, 1959,
Mixed-media handmade book.

p. 187
Jess, *Untitled*, 1961–63,
Ink on paper.

The couple set up their homes as havens dedicated to their collections of books, esoteric lore, and the art of their friends. In 1967 Jess and Duncan moved to their ultimate home, a rambling 1890s Victorian house in the Mission district. Jess and Duncan had met Wallace and Shirley Berman in 1954 and began a close friendship based on the couples' similar mix of domesticity and artistic pursuits. In his collaged mailers to the couple, Berman tapped into their mutual love for the absurdities of Pop culture.

The threat of nuclear apocalypse is a recurring motif in Jess's work, often symbolized by the mushroom-cloud shape of the Omega symbol. Just as so much of Surrealism can be seen as a response to the horrors of World War I, Jess's work can be read as a reaction to the nuclear threat. Rejecting the world of twisted science, Jess sought a kind of redemption by entering the realm of myth and the imagination. His early paintings are moody tone poems in shades of green and brown, influenced by the dark lyricism of Corbett.

Jess's mature art is about the retrieval of images from a culture overflowing with them. Fully embracing a collage esthetic, he created odd interminglings and fantastic juxtapositions, using images taken from sources ranging from Dick Tracy to Dürer, from a Beatles bubblegum card to medical textbook drawings, from 1887 *Scientific American* line engravings to frames from George Herriman's *Krazy Kat*. Jess filtered these far-flung references through a self-described Romantic sensibility, one that valued the transforming power of the imagination above all else.

Jess's guides to the realm of fantasy and the spirit were a forgotten group of recondite writers and artists from the nineteenth and twentieth centuries. To study Jess's work is to discover an alternate literary universe

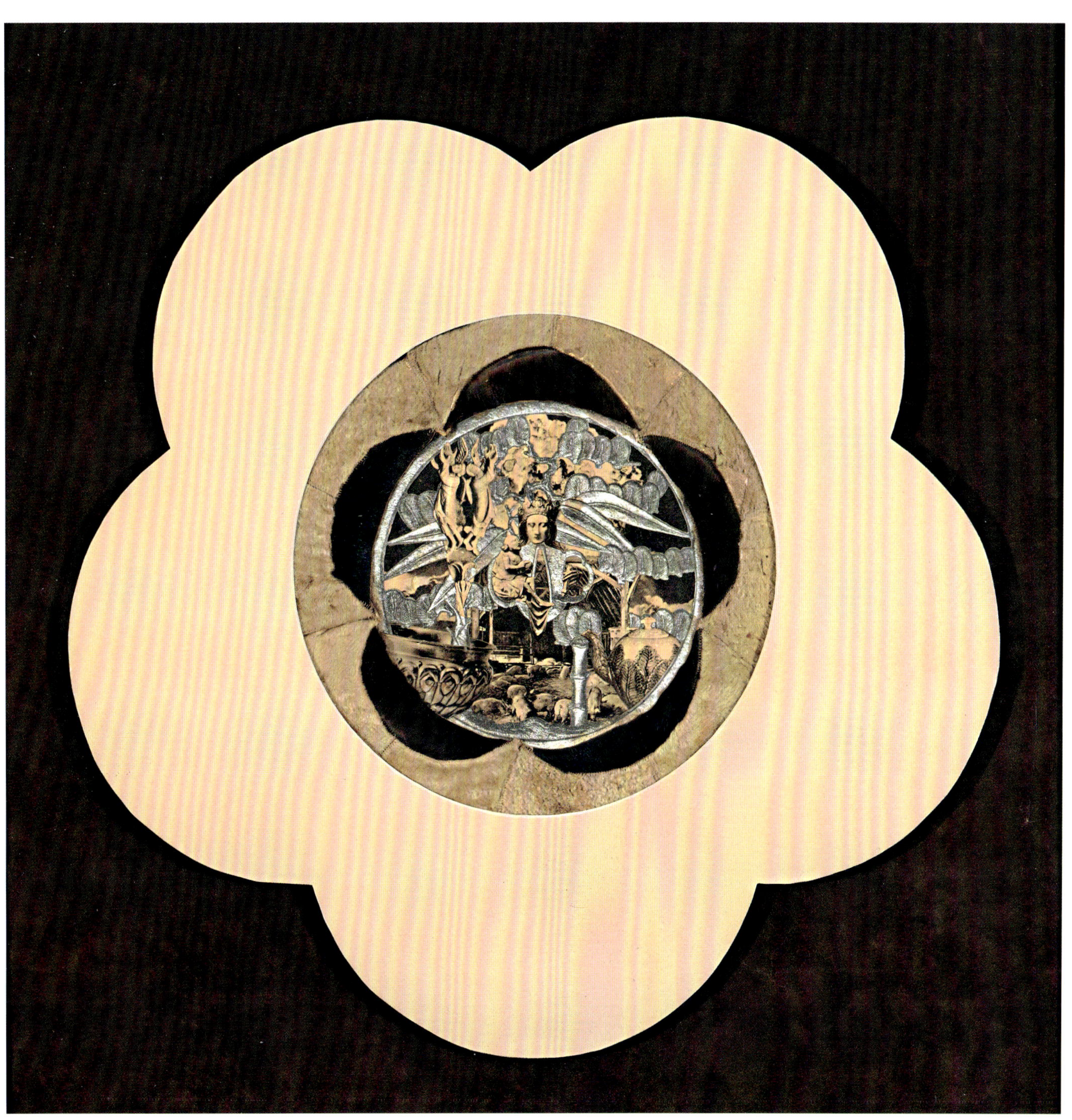

185 Jess

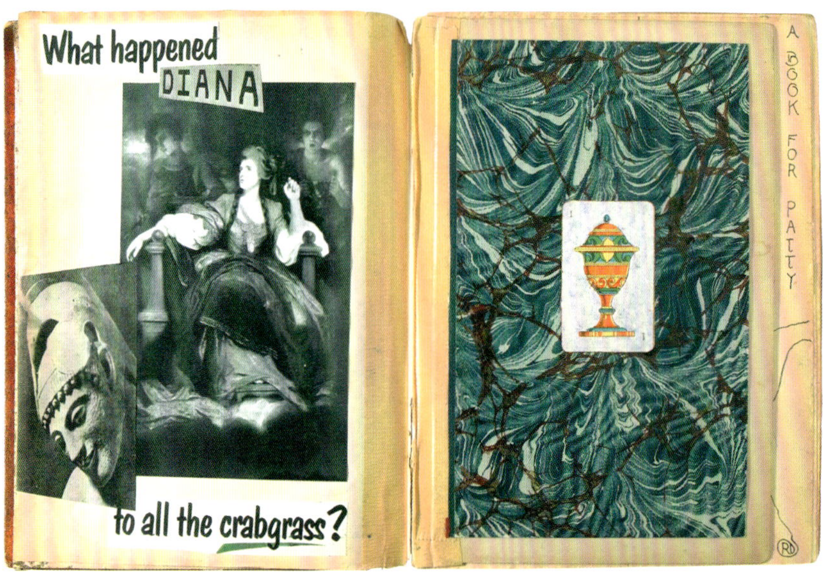
What happened
DIANA
to all the crabgrass?
A BOOK FOR PATTY

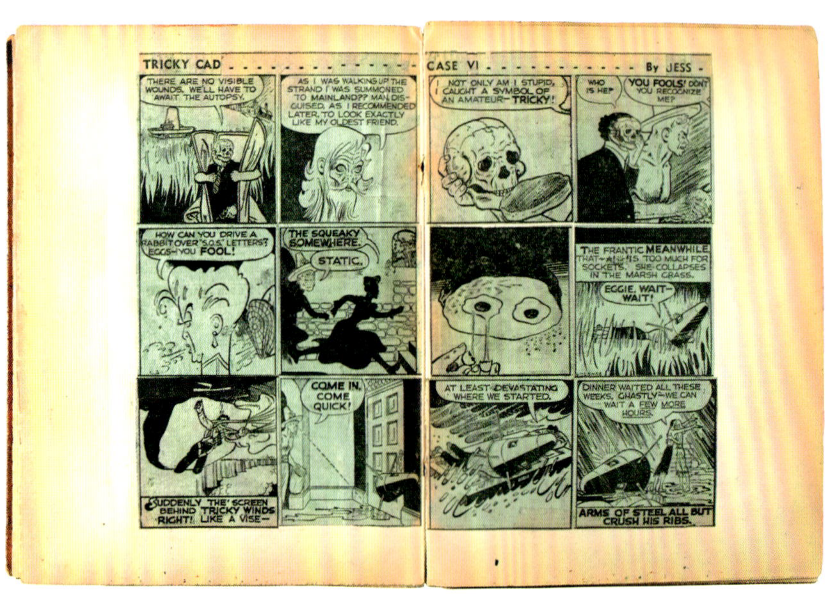
TRICKY CAD
CASE VI
By JESS
THERE ARE NO VISIBLE WOUNDS. WE'LL HAVE TO AWAIT THE AUTOPSY.
AS I WAS WALKING UP THE STRAND I WAS SUMMONED TO MAINLAND?? MAN, DISGUISED, AS I RECOMMENDED LATER, TO LOOK EXACTLY LIKE MY OLDEST FRIEND.
I NOT ONLY AM I STUPID, I CAUGHT A SYMBOL OF AN AMATEUR—TRICKY!
WHO IS HE?
YOU FOOLS! DON'T YOU RECOGNIZE ME?
HOW CAN YOU DRIVE A RABBIT OVER "S.O.S." LETTERS? EGGS—YOU FOOL!
THE SQUEAKY SOMEWHERE.
STATIC.
THE FRANTIC MEANWHILE
IS TOO MUCH FOR SOCKETS. SHE COLLAPSES IN THE MARSH GRASS.
EGGIE, WAIT—WAIT!
SUDDENLY THE SCREEN BEHIND TRICKY WINDS RIGHT! LIKE A VISE—
COME IN, COME QUICK!
AT LEAST DEVASTATING WHERE WE STARTED.
DINNER WAITED ALL THESE WEEKS, GHASTLY—WE CAN WAIT A FEW MORE HOURS.
ARMS OF STEEL ALL BUT CRUSH HIS RIBS.

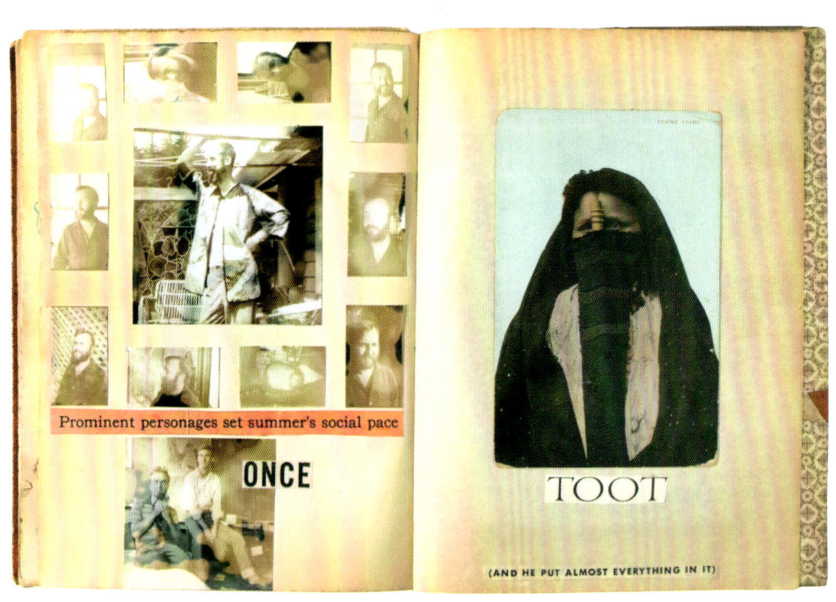
Prominent personages set summer's social pace
ONCE
TOOT
(AND HE PUT ALMOST EVERYTHING IN IT)

that encompasses the loopy fairy-tale allegories of George MacDonald, the fey, mysterious stories of Mary Butts, and the apocalyptic gothic fiction of Charles Williams. Jess found their art-history counterparts in equally obscure sources: the whimsical turn-of-the-century illustrations of Gelett Burgess, the Pre-Raphaelite painting of Herbert James Draper, and Egyptian papyrus illustrations from the twenty-first dynasty.

Jess's early collages—which he called *Paste-Ups*—used cutout advertising images and slogans to present a satirical, absurdist view of sexuality and politics. Inspired by Max Ernst's *Une Semaine de Bonté,* Jess's earliest collages reshuffle magazine advertisements and captions. The *Tricky Cad* series of the mid-1950s presents tongue-in-cheek rearrangements of the terse dialogue and posturing he-man imagery of Chester Gould's *Dick Tracy* comic strip.

As Jess grew obsessed with myth and archetype, his collages became intricate fields of clotted and amalgamated images that convey what he called "a network of stories." Increasing to sizes of up to four by six feet, the collages often took the form of giant landscapes or seascapes, sometimes with posters of mountains or oceans serving as backdrops. Exuberantly juxtaposing cutout images and layers of jigsaw puzzle pieces, Jess filled his landscapes with a host of symbolic images that are all spun out of the natural world. Here, metaphors are literalized and glued in place: Swimmers are clouds, red kittens are autumn leaves, Michelangelo's Sistine Chapel ceiling is the bark of a very well-decorated tree. The *Paste-Ups* are created worlds to get lost in; they are Jess's visual translation of fiction's narrative spell. At the same time, Jess presents not one but many stories simultaneously in the fashion of Brueghel or Bosch.

Jess's self-reflexive style of image-making was most powerfully conveyed in the *Translations* (1959–76), a group of thirty-two paintings of appropriated images from unusual photographs, prints, and drawings, rendered in the manner of schematically outlined and colored paint-by-number canvases. In reworking the black-and-white source images, he employed his unusual Abstract Expressionist palette, giving the paintings a color scheme that doesn't necessarily coincide with their graphic images and that often yields an abstract visual effect.

Jess also correlated each found image with a pertinent text—from Plato, William Blake, Gertrude Stein, and others—which he inscribed on the back of the canvas. Through the slow elaborate layering of pigment, the images were gradually imbued with Jess's sensibility; as he once stated, "I wanted to make myself aware of what I felt about this image. And this intense meditative process that I had undertaken allowed those feelings to come forth." This quirky, sumptuous body of work conceptually presaged the ideas of many postmodernist image manipulators.

Inactive in the last years before his death in 2004, Jess's final project was the six-by-five foot drawing *Narkissos* (1976–91), an intricate tableau of dense imagery spun off from the symbolic meanings of the Greek myth. In reexamining myths through a synthesis of art and literature, Jess's work remains a crucial assemblage of the meaning of our time. His career was last surveyed in a traveling exhibition organized by the Albright-Knox Art Gallery, Buffalo (1993–94). *Michael Duncan*

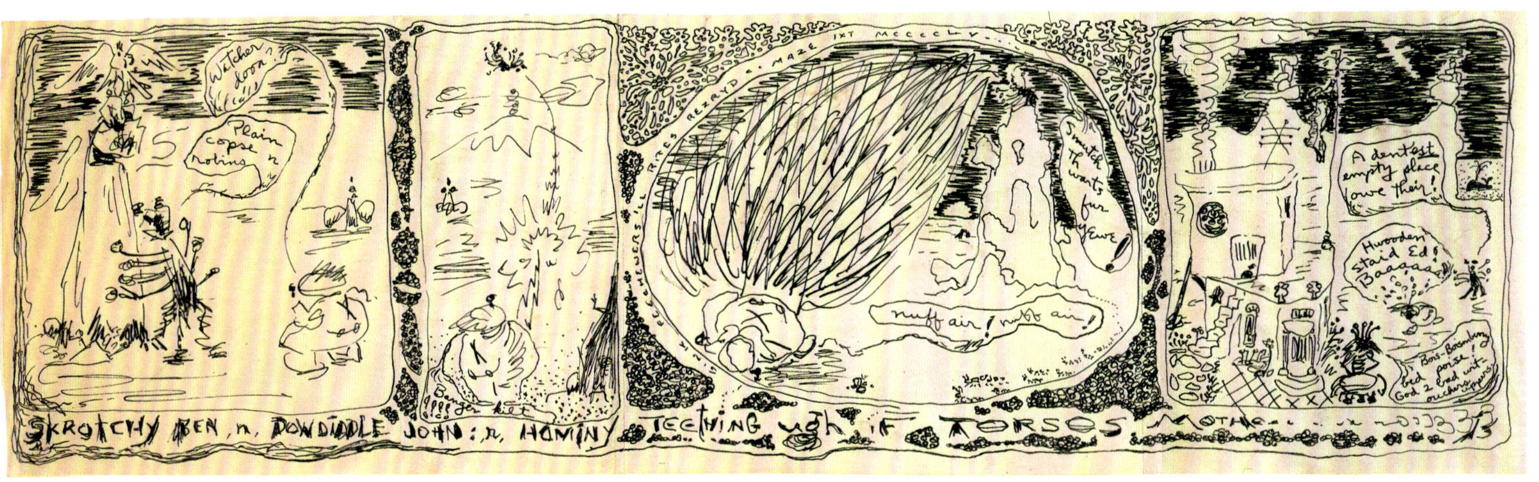

Lawrence Jordan

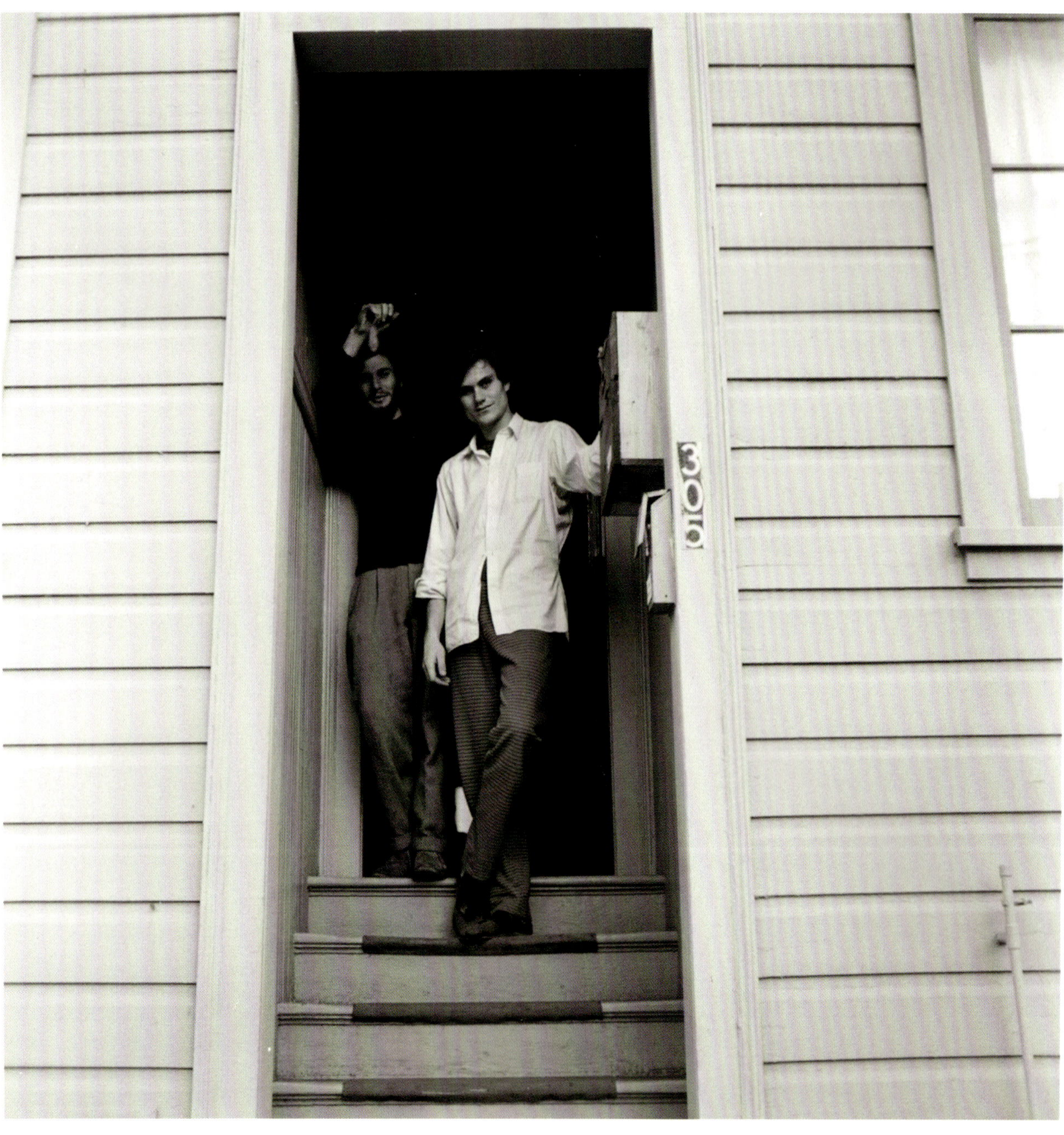

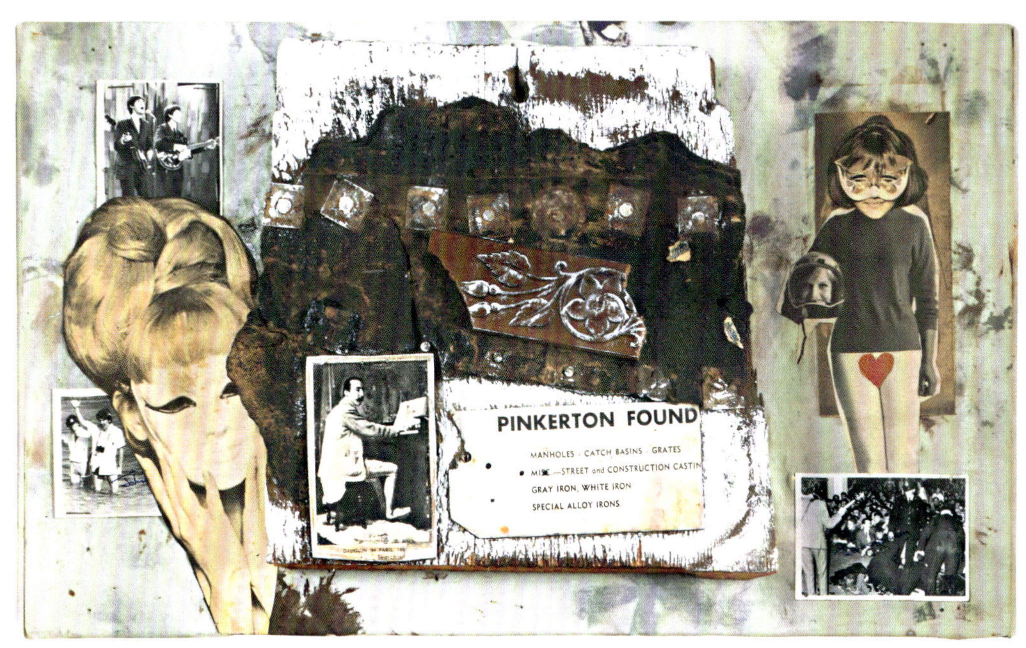
PINKERTON FOUND
MANHOLES · CATCH BASINS · GRATES
MISC.—STREET and CONSTRUCTION CASTIN
GRAY IRON, WHITE IRON
SPECIAL ALLOY IRONS

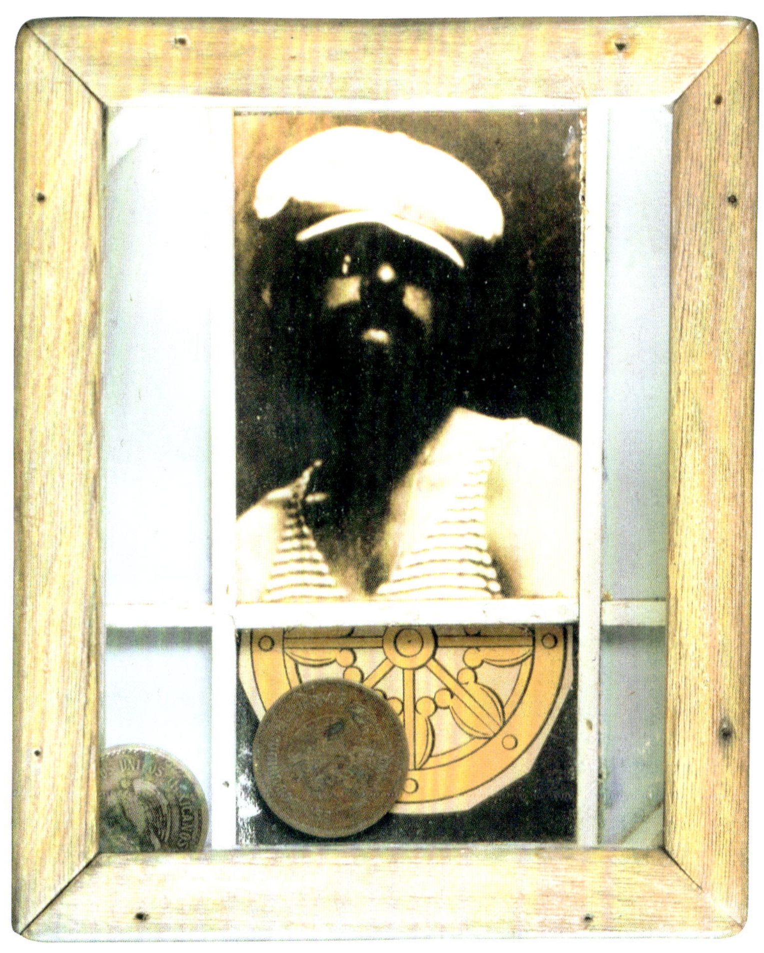

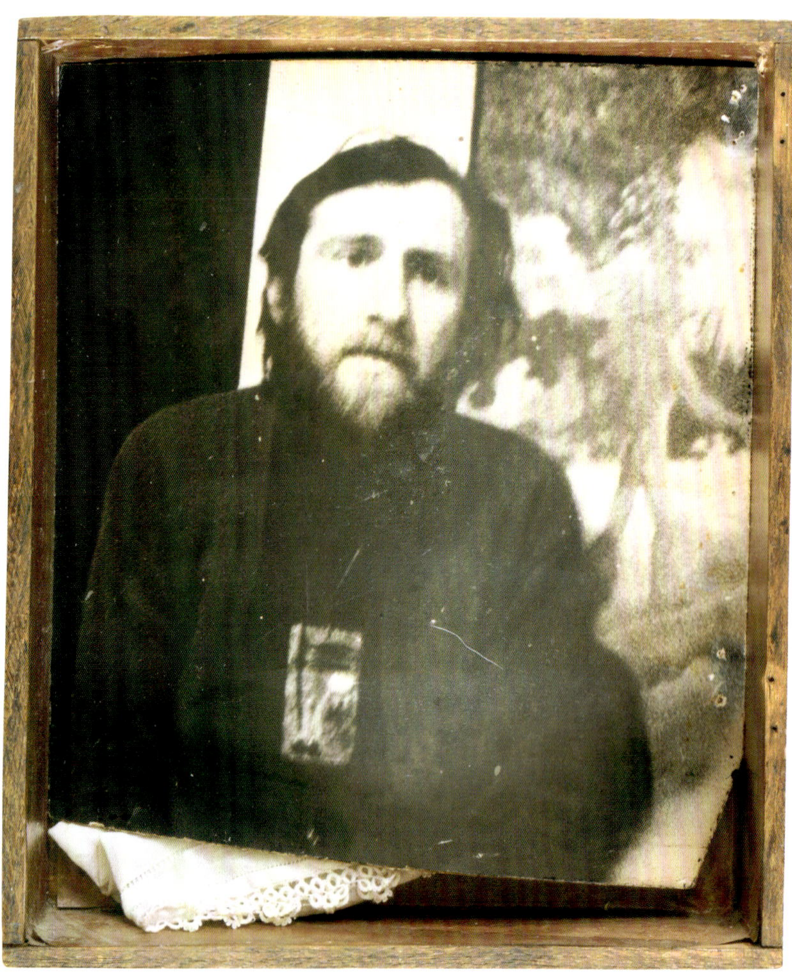

Known principally as a maverick spirit in the world of avant-garde American cinema, Lawrence Jordan played an important role in the late 1950s and early 1960s San Francisco art scene. Jordan has made over fifty experimental films, including a number of fanciful, filmic animations made from collaged cut-outs of Victorian engravings. The animations extend the dreamlike imagery of collaged landscape into a cinematic realm of transformation and free-form symbolism. Jordan seeks to delve into the deep structures and Jungian connotations of the mythological images his films reference. His alchemical approach to imagery creates what he has called the "theater of the mind, which you construct. That is the *Underworld*...the realm of the imagination. You have to have your theater. You have to have a place to work with images."[1]

p. 188
Lawrence Jordan and George Herms, Venice, 1961, Photograph by Charles Brittin.

p. 189 top
Lawrence Jordan, *Pinkerton Found*, 1963, Assemblage.

p. 189 bottom
Lawrence Jordan, *Portrait of John Reed*, 1964, Assemblage.

p. 190
Lawrence Jordan, *Portrait of Wallace Berman*, 1959, Mixed-media.

p. 191
Lawrence Jordan, *Rex in Eternum Vive*, 1961, Watercolor on paper.

Born in Denver in 1934 to schoolteacher parents, Jordan was a stellar student at South Denver High School, winning a scholarship to Harvard University. There he quickly lost interest in science after discovering the works of Sergei Eisenstein and other experimental European filmmakers. He began making films at the University Film Club but suffered a kind of breakdown and returned to Denver after a year. With highschool friend Stan Brakhage, he continued to experiment with film, and with other friends set up a little theater in Central City, Colorado in the summer of 1953.

Hearing about Kenneth Rexroth and the poetry scene of San Francisco, Jordan and his friends went to the West Coast, intending to find an audience for their films. Working as a hospital orderly, Jordan managed to become acquainted with the artistic community, soon finding himself playing Faust in Robert Duncan's *Faust Foutu* at The Six Gallery, performing alongside Jess, Duncan, Michael McClure, Helen Adam, and Jack Spicer. Still primarily interested in filmmaking, Jordan followed Brakhage to New York in 1955, where he was introduced to Maya Deren and Joseph Cornell—both of whom would become major influences on his work.

Returning the next year to San Francisco, he ended up living in the apartment of Michael and Joanna McClure, above Jay DeFeo and Wally Hedrick, and next door to Joan

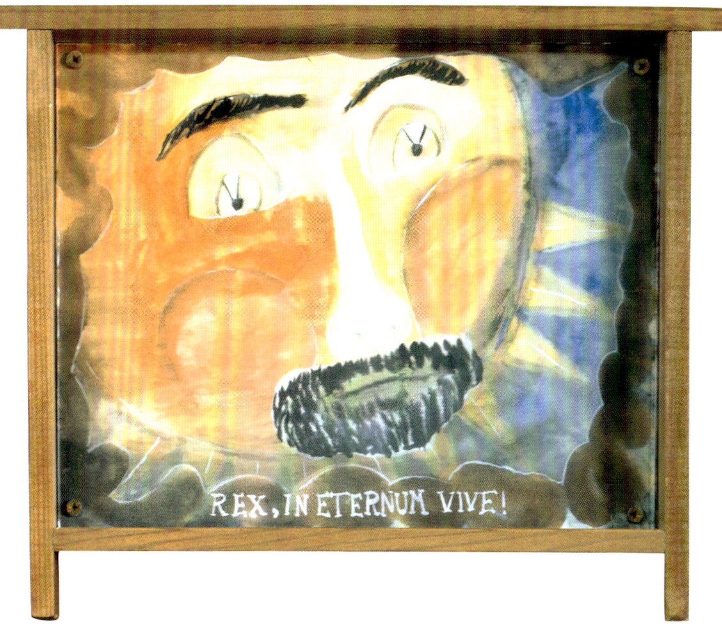

and William Brown. Over the next three years, between stints as a seaman in the Merchant Marines and travels in the Far East, Jordan met Philip Lamantia, Wallace Berman, George Herms, and Bruce Conner, with whom he started Camera Obscura, a film society that ran for a number of years. Jordan also established The Movie, San Francisco's first 16mm experimental film theater in 1958. His seven-minute film *Visions of a City* (1957) featured Michael McClure walking the shimmering streets of San Francisco, while *Triptych in Four Parts* (1957) included footage of John Reed and the Berman family, as well as a reverie devoted to peyote. Jordan's poem "Rockets," which Berman included in *Semina 5*, also celebrated the explosive, revelatory power of the ancient drug.

In the late 1950s Jess introduced Jordan to the collage novels of Max Ernst. These works inspired Jordan to begin making collages from cutout engravings and soon led to cinematic experiments with animated collage. Film writer P. Adams Sitney has distinguished Jordan's films from the contemporaneous animations of Harry Smith in their use of a static engraved backdrop that enables them to achieve a greater narrative illusion.[2]

In 1959 Jordan sent Joseph Cornell a copy of his handmade book of stills taken from Eisenstein's *Ivan the Terrible* and the two began a correspondence.[3] Over the next few years, Cornell commissioned Jordan to provide photographs and film sequences for him by mail. Jordan married Patricia Topalian in 1960 and, after the birth of their daughter Lorna, they moved to Larkspur, not far from the Bermans' houseboat. Cornell soon was corresponding with the entire family, commissioning provocative photos of Patty and sending Lorna collages and trinkets. In 1965 Cornell asked Jordan to come east to be his assistant. Living for a month in Cornell's house in Flushing, Jordan worked on box assemblages, edited Cornell's film *Legend of Fountains*, and shot new footage for him, in addition to making the only film of Cornell at work.

As the 1960s progressed, Jordan became well-known for animated shorts such as *Duo Concertantes* (1964) and *Gymnopedies* (1966) that used freely associated streams of engraved images. The second part of the former film featured a fixed photographic image of Patricia Topalian Jordan looking out on a tree-lined lake while animated woodcuts and etchings appear in the distance. Jordan spent nearly a half-decade making the eighty-seven-minute animated feature *Sophie's Place* (1983–87) in which 129,600 single-framed images envelop the mosque of Saint Sophia in Istanbul. The film, dubbed by Jordan "an alchemical autobiography," explores a variety of manifestations of Sophia, the Greek and Gnostic embodiment of wisdom. Another major effort, Jordan's 1990 collage animation, *The Visible Compendium*, tracks the mysterious and metaphorically rich voyage of a hot air balloon.

Jordan started the film department of the San Francisco Art Institute in 1969 and taught there for over thirty years. He has made his own box assemblages in Cornell's lyrically evocative style since the mid-1960s. Many feature ingenious mechanical and kinetic effects. He continues to make films and box collages at his home and studio in Petaluma where has lived since 1978. Among other ongoing projects, Jordan is collecting engravings for a forthcoming film dealing with the imagery of the Kabbalah. *Michael Duncan*

1 G.T. Collins, "Larry Jordan's Underworld," *Animation Journal*, Vol.6, No. 1, Fall 1997, p. 58.

2 P. Adams Sitney, *Larry Jordan* (St.Paul: Film in the Cities, 1980), p. 5.

3 See correspondence in Mary Ann Caws, ed., *Joseph Cornell: Theater of the Mind: Selected Diaries, Letters, and Files* (New York: Thames & Hudson, 1993).

Patricia Jordan

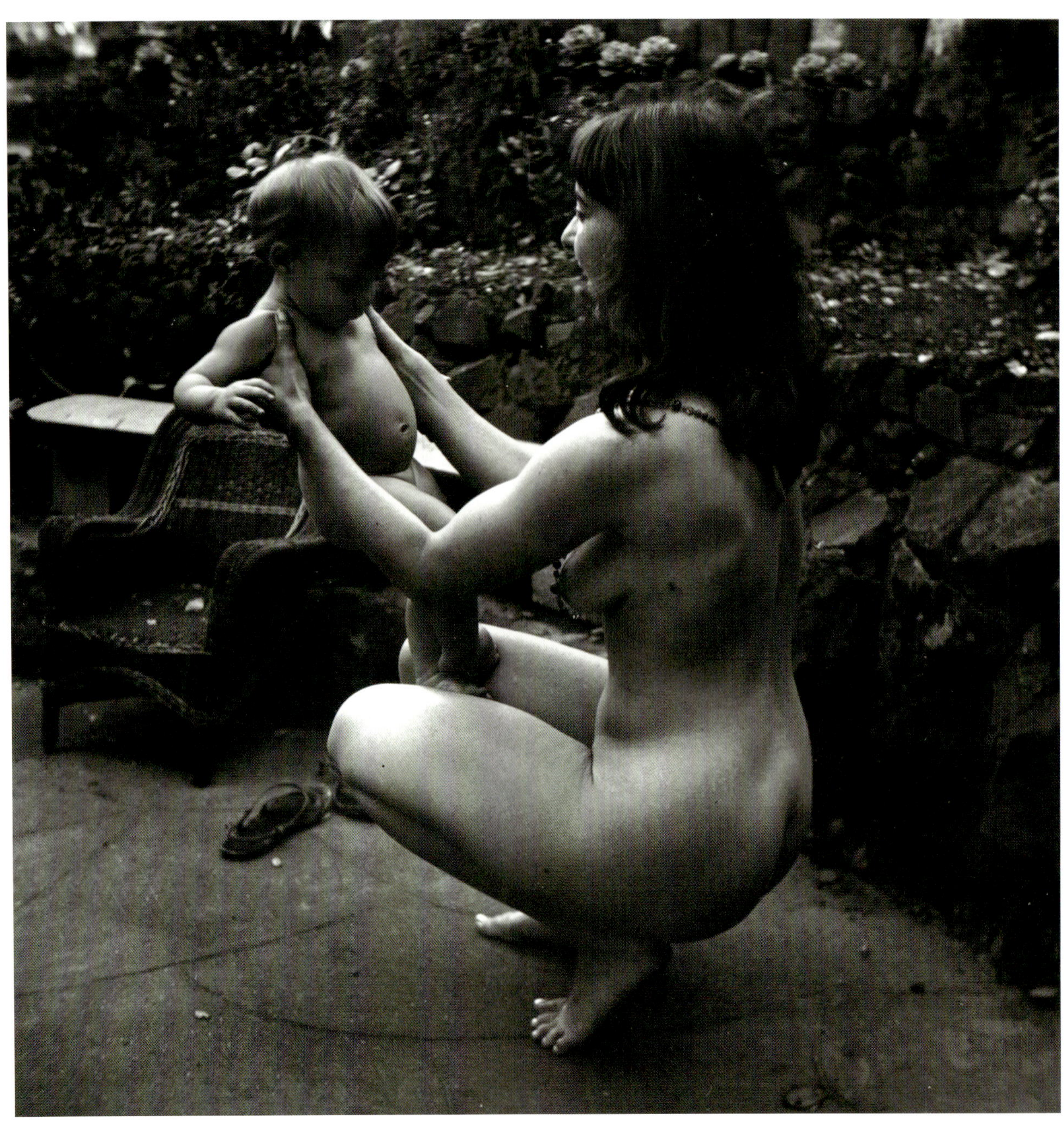

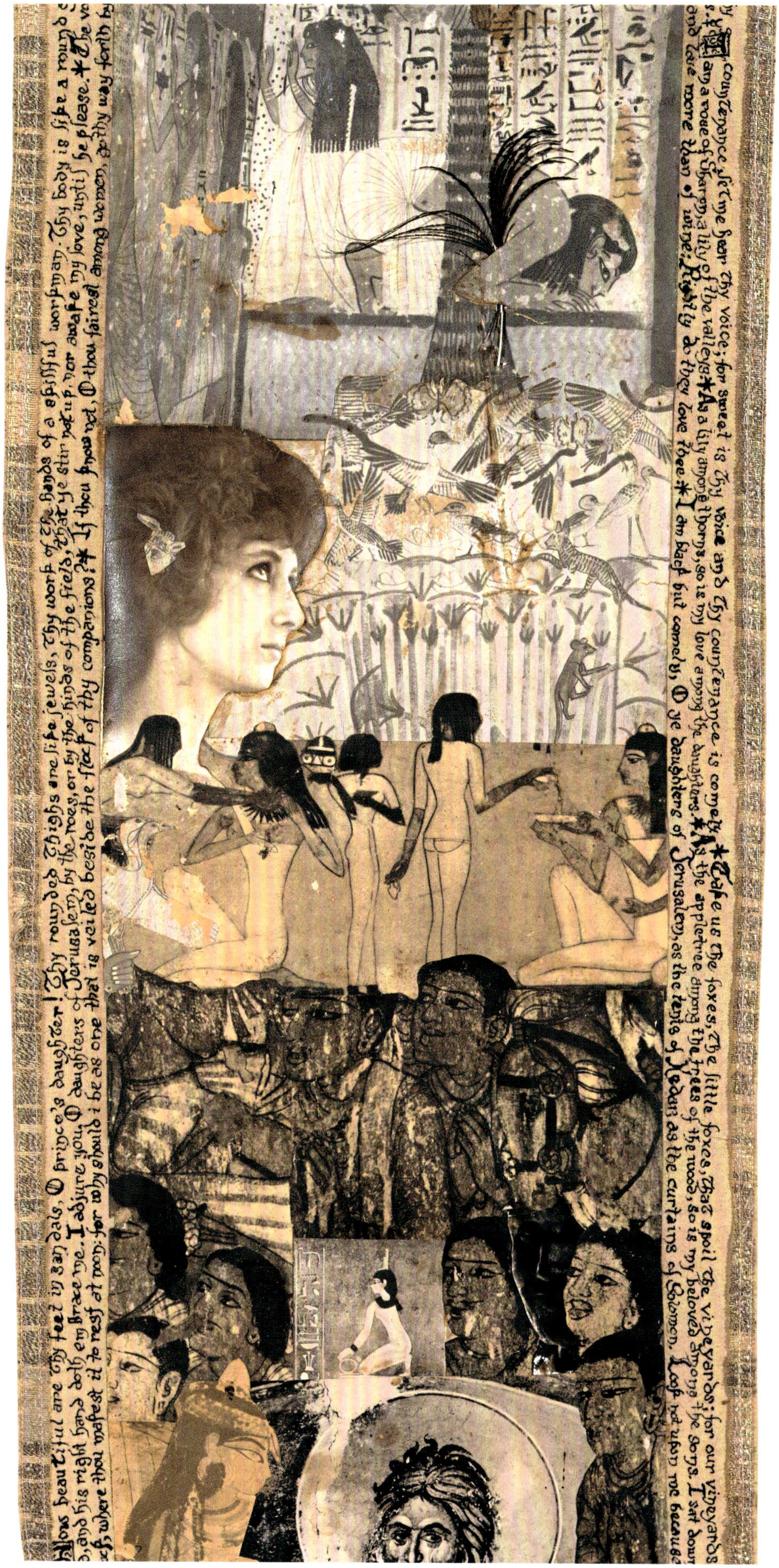

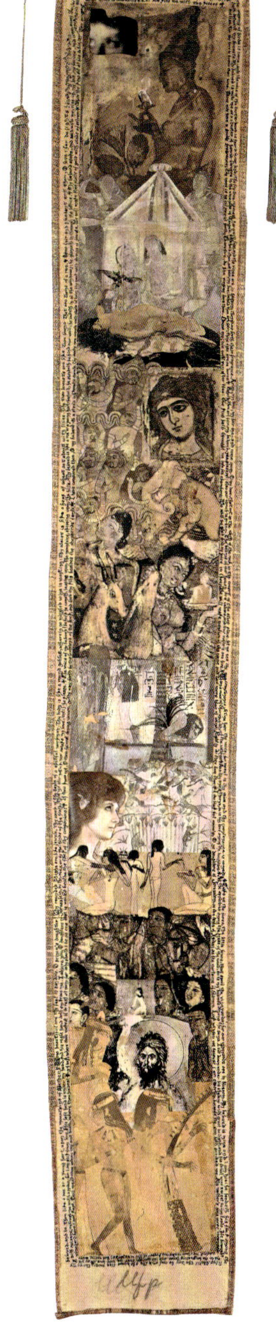

Patty Jordan's period of production as an artist was relatively brief, but she created some extraordinary things during the few years she was active.

Born Patricia Merle Topalian in Knoxville, Tennessee, in 1934, she was the only child of Eleanor Henry and Yervant Topalian. Jordan's father was an Armenian immigrant who fled his homeland during the Turkish genocide that began in 1915, and her mother was the daughter of Lt. Col. Ziba Lindley Henry, a doctor in the military. Jordan's parents met while attending the same college in Tennessee, and shortly after they married Patricia was born. When Jordan was two years old, her parents moved to San Francisco, where her father worked as a waiter at Vanesi's Restaurant and her mother became a teacher.

p. 192
Patricia Jordan with her daughter, Lorna, Larkspur, California, 1961, Photograph by Wallace Berman.

p. 193
Patricia Jordan, *Golden Damsels Descending from the Clouds*, 1960–61, Collage, embroidery, feathers, ink and photographs on linen.

p. 195
Kirby Doyle, Lawrence Jordan and Wallace Berman in San Francisco, 1959, Photograph by Patricia Jordan.

p. 196 and 197
Patricia Jordan contact sheets, c. 1960, with images of Jess, Wallace Berman Robert Duncan, Louise Herms, James Broughton, Michael McClure, and Tosh Berman.

Jordan's parents divorced in 1943. As was the custom during the war years, Jordan's mother began renting an extra room in their home to servicemen, which led to her becoming romantically involved with a Dutch soldier whom she married in 1949. Shortly after her wedding she asked Patty, then fifteen, to move out of the house, and Jordan got her own apartment.

Because she was a gifted student well ahead of her classmates, Jordan graduated high school at the age of fifteen and enrolled at San Francisco State College, which she attended from 1949 to 1959. Majoring in theater and dance, Jordan paid her way through college working as a life-drawing model and became one of the most sought after models in Northern California. She sat for Joan Brown, among others, and posed for a photograph commissioned by Joseph Cornell in what he referred to as "the Cavalier costume," as he found it evocative of Joan of Arc.[1]

In the early 1950s Jordan began taking photographs of her friends in the San Francisco art community, and over the course of the decade she shot hundreds of pictures of Wallace and Shirley Berman, Michael and Joanna McClure, Jess and Robert Duncan, and Kirby Doyle, among others. Jordan printed her own photographs and often worked in sepia tone, which lent her images a muted, dreamy quality that becomes increasingly potent as the 1950s recede further into the past. Many of her pictures have the slightly mannered self-consciousness of formal portraiture, and all of her work is heavily perfumed with the bohemian sensibility that pervaded San Francisco during the 1950s. In a shot of Kirby Doyle, posed in the basement of City Lights Books in 1959, the twenty-seven-year-old poet looks like nothing less than the poster child for the Beat Generation. Black leather jacket, shades, cigarette dangling from his mouth, head cocked back defiantly, an insolent look on his face—Doyle didn't miss a note, and Jordan didn't either. She framed and composed the picture exquisitely, right down the to the swirl of cigarette smoke that floats like a halo above Doyle's head.

Jordan forged an especially strong friendship with Duncan and Jess, and during the 1950s she created intensely romantic collages which, like those by Jess, integrate elements of the ancient and modern. For *Golden Damsels Descending from the Clouds*, a stunning work on fabric, Jordan combined found images of Byzantine religious icons, Pre-Raphaelite nudes, Egyptian hieroglyphs, Aztec gods and Hindu deities, with embroidery, feathers, and five of her own photographs of Shirley Berman. The

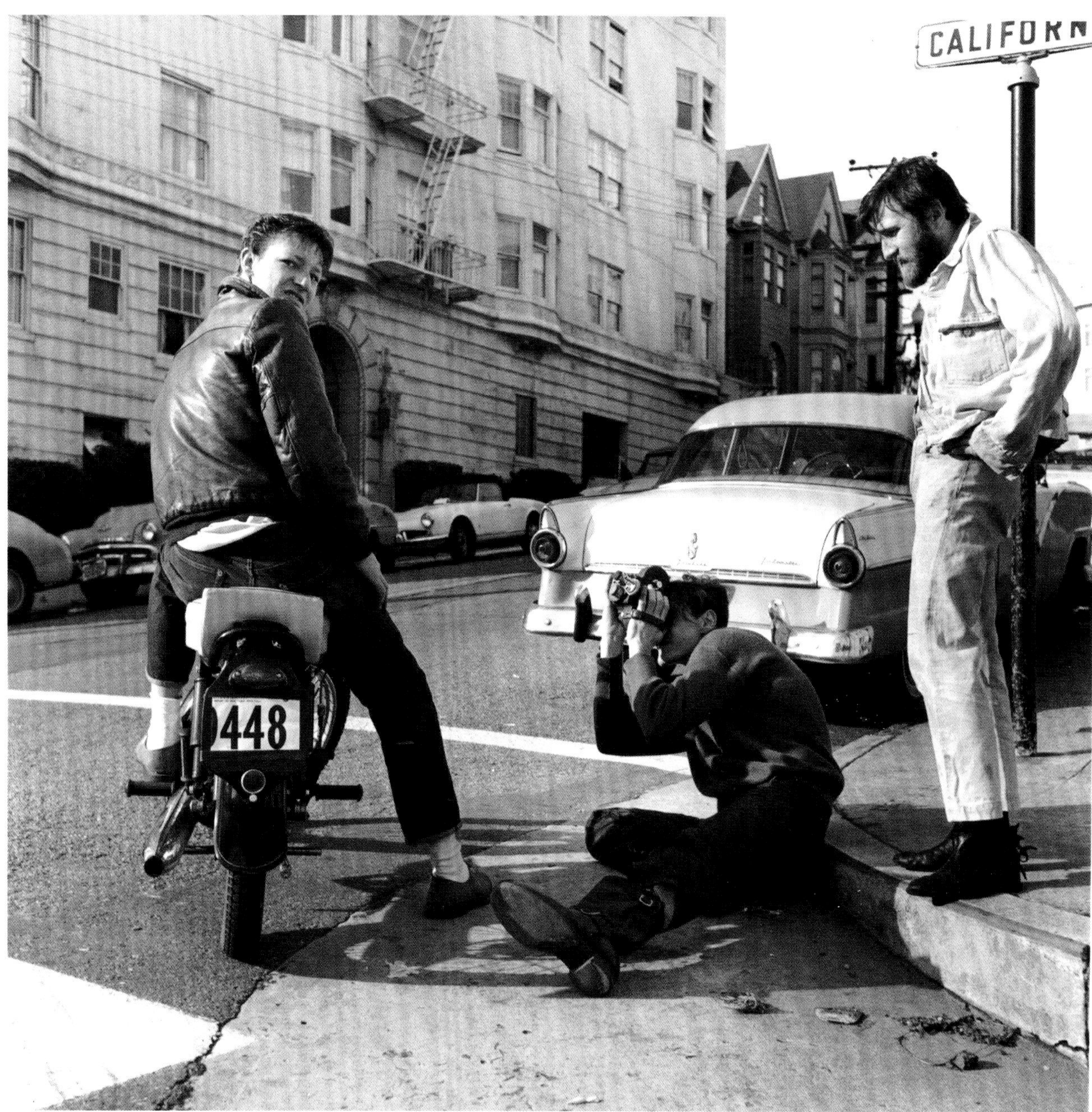

composition is bordered with a love sonnet, written in ink in a beautiful calligraphic hand.

In 1959 Topalian met artist Lawrence Jordan, whom she married in 1960. Their daughter, Lorna, was born the same year, and at that point the demands of motherhood took precedence over artmaking for Jordan. Berman included a portrait of Jordan taken shortly after the birth of her child in *Semina 7*, however, the San Francisco art community was beginning to play a less prominent role in her life. In 1962 the Jordans moved to San Anselmo, and she dropped further out of sight. (Jordan did, however, always remain close to Jess.) By the mid-1970s, when her marriage ended, Jordan had stopped taking pictures entirely and had begun to channel her creative energies into the healing arts.

"My mother taught dance and body movement on and off during the years I was growing up, and over a period of twenty years dance metamorphosed for her," says Lorna Jordan. "She created a life and a work environment at home and she taught a movement class for elderly women. That, in turn, transitioned into body work, counseling and massage. She was a very intuitive person and she became a mentor to many people."[2]

In September of 1988 Jordan was diagnosed with liver cancer. She died three months later at the age of fifty-four. *Kristine McKenna*

1 Mary Ann Caws, ed. *Joseph Cornell: Theater of the Mind: Selected Diaries, Letters, and Files* (New York: Thames and Hudson, 1993), p. 41.
2 Conversation with Lorna Jordan, February 3, 2002.

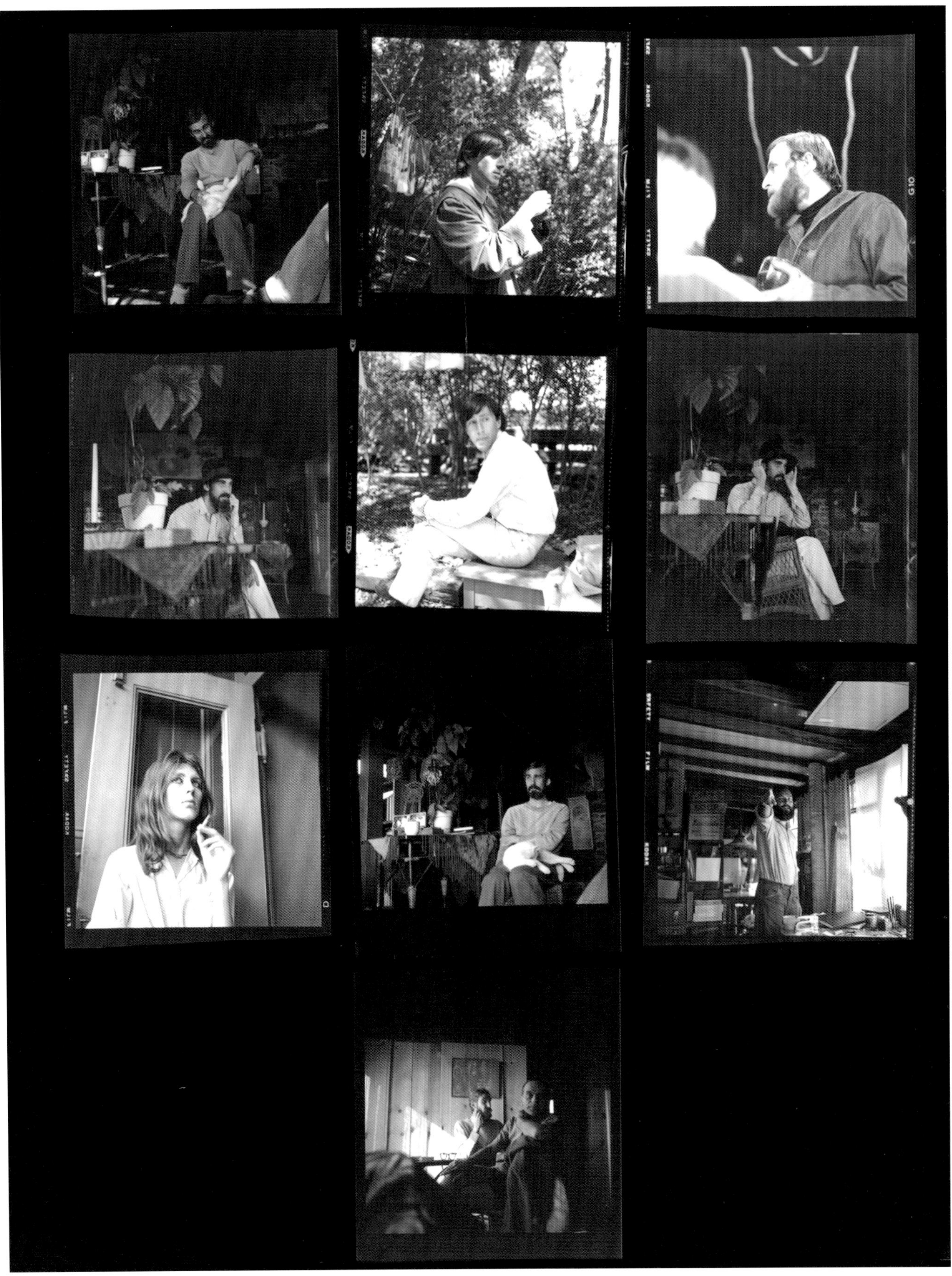

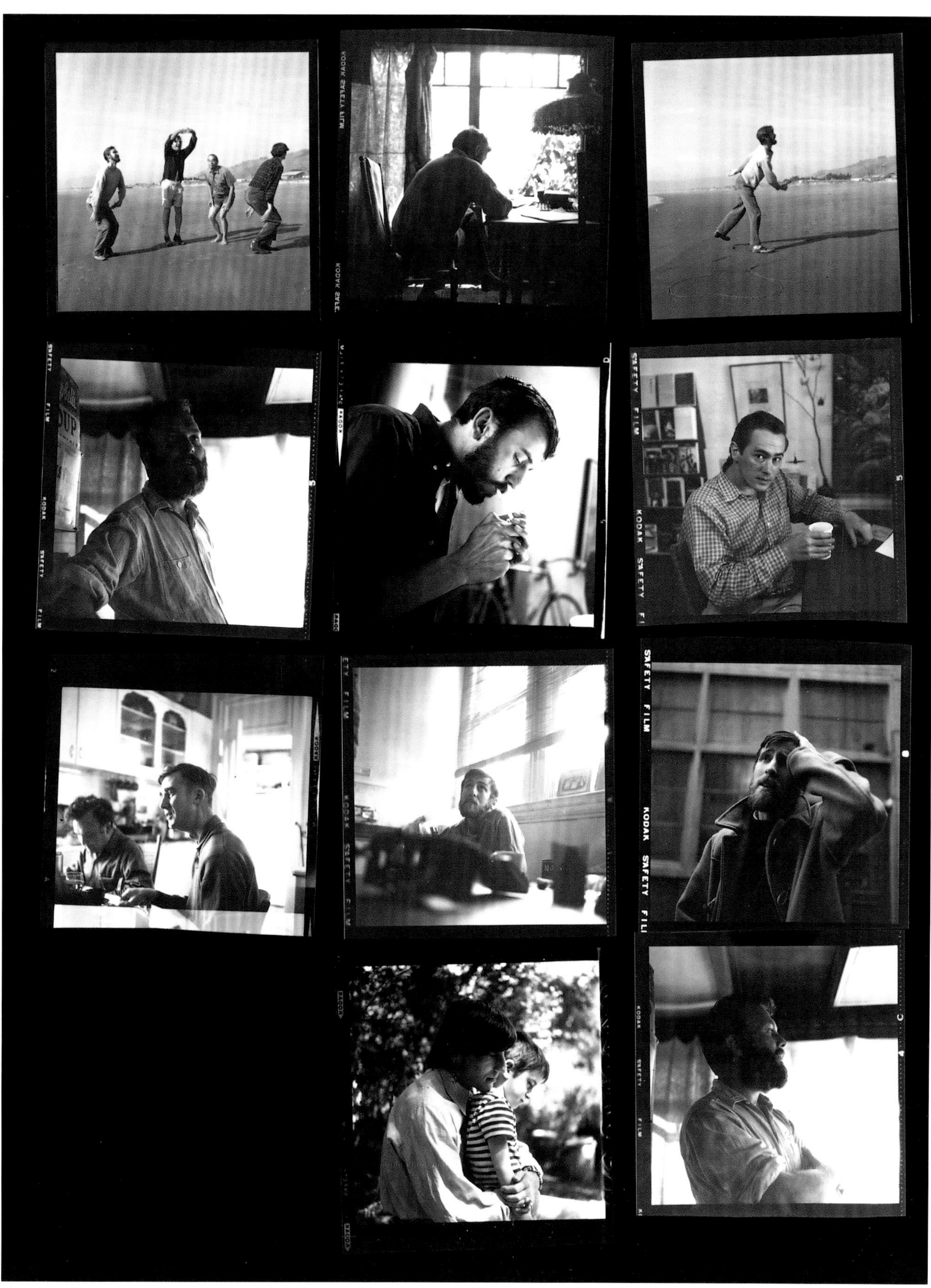

Bob Kaufman

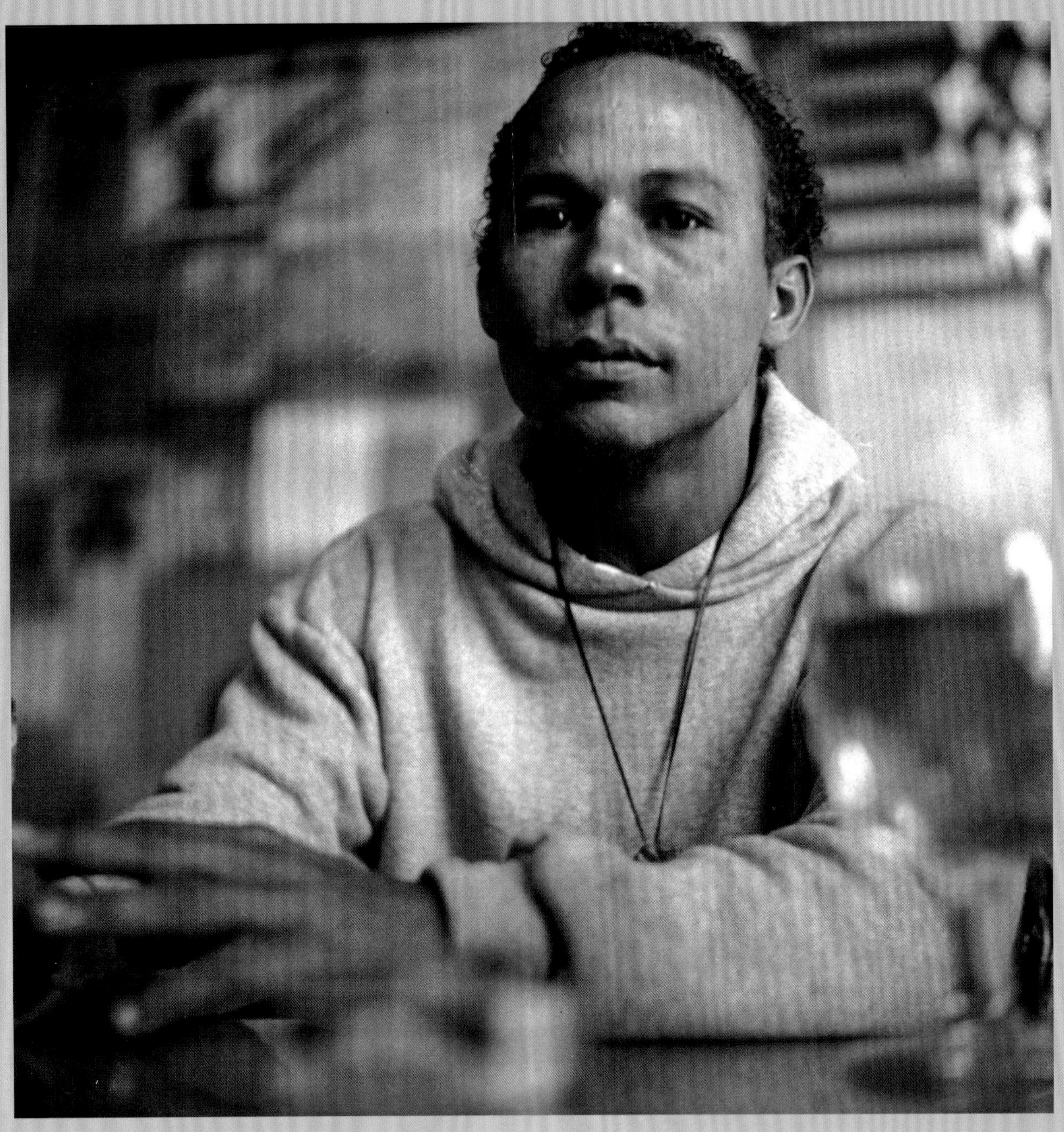

Blues For Hal Waters

My Head, My Secret Cranial Guitar, Strung with Myths
Plucked From yesterdays Transits, Buried in Robes of Echoes
My Eyes, Breezeless Flags, Lacquered To Present A Glint
My Marble Lips, Entrance To That Cave, Where Visions Renunciation,
Eternity Has Wet Sidewalks, Angels are Busted For Drunk Flying.
I only want Privacy To Create an illusion of me Blotted Out,
His High Hopes Were Placed in His Coffin, Long Paddles of Esteem For His Symbolic Canoe
If I Move To The Stars, Foward My Mail C/O. God, Heaven, Lower East Side
Too Late For Skin Diving and other Modern Philosophies, Put My Ego in Storage.
The Moon is Too Near my Family, + The Craters are Cold in Winter,
Lets Move To The Sun, Hot Water, Radiant Heating, Spacial Colors,
Knife Handle Convenience, Adjacent To God, Community Meeting Free.
Eskimo's Have Frozen Secrets in Thier Noses + Have Chopped Down The North Pole
The Last Buffalo Will Be Torpedoed By an Atomic Submarine, Firing Hydrogen Tiepins
God is my Favorite Dictater, Even Though He Refuses To Hold Free Elections
That Around me will Hold, I Worry about The Padlock i painted on
My Hair is overrun with Crabgrass, Parts of My Anatomy are Still Unexplored
No More Hard Sessions For Me, I am Going To Hell and Hear Some Good Jazz
Did you Hear The Good News, Terry + The Pirates are Not Really Real
If you Value The Comfort of your Fellow Worshipers, Dont Die in Church.
Why Ruin our Eyes With T.V, Lets Design Freeways after Dinner Tonight
He Might Have Lost Some Friends, But Jesus Could Have Made a Fortune on That Water To Wine Formula
History is The Only Diary God Keeps, + Somebody Threw it on The Bonfire
The Day of The Big Game at Hiroshima, The Moon is A Double Agent
This Year The Animals are Holding Thier First "Be Kind To People Week",
The Siamese Cats Will Not Participate + Will Hold Thier own Convention in Egypt,
The Civilized World Fears They May Attempt To Put Pharoah Back in Power
For God Sakes Hal, Jam The Radio Trip Them With your Guitar.

Born Robert Grenell Kaufman in New Orleans, Louisiana, in 1925, Bob Kaufman is a largely mysterious figure; the little that's known of his life is based on stories he told his wife, Eileen, interviews conducted during the 1980s by his brother George, and occasional biographical notes contributed over the years by fellow sailors, poets, and jazz musicians. Myths surrounding Kaufman are great and frequently embroidered, however, the facts, when discovered, usually support what is known of his remarkable life.

One of thirteen children, Kaufman grew up in Bayou St. John, a region of woods and swamps that had been a navigable waterway in the nineteenth century, connecting New Orleans with Lake Ponchartrain. The swampy environs of the Mississippi bayou, the spoken patois, the Dixieland bands heard on the streets, and the mixed racial background of his family (African, Caribbean, and Jewish) all combined to give his work its lush imagery and complex cadence. Kaufman spent much of his childhood in the company of his maternal grandmother, the daughter of a slave who had fled America to Martinique. A practitioner of voodoo and animist religions, she fed the young poet's imagination with Afro-Caribbean lore of spirits and sorcery. In his early teens Kaufman frequented New Orleans's French Quarter, where he absorbed the life of jazz and the river, and earned spare change shining shoes and tap dancing—a talent he'd occasionally amuse friends with later in life.

Kaufman was a restless and independent young man and when he was sixteen he joined the Merchant Marines, starting as kitchen help and working his way up to first mate. He shipped out regularly over the next twenty years, traveling around the world nine times, and surviving numerous shipwrecks. In India he helped a young acquaintance emigrate as a stowaway, and following World War II he ran guns to Israel. His fellow sailors recalled Kaufman as an exceptional seaman who always volunteered for dangerous assignments, such as climbing the masts during storms to tie down riggings. From a young age Kaufman read voraciously: Melville, Dostoevsky, Langston Hughes, Garcia Lorca, T.S. Eliot, and Wallace Stevens were favorite authors during his years at sea. In the mid 1950s, between trips to sea, he took classes in sociology and communist labor practices at the New School for Social Research in New York, and soon thereafter began a series of precarious visits to the deep South to organize Negro mine workers. (Eileen Kaufman recalls that when she met him he had recently returned from such a trip, and was still unable to eat solid food as a result of a police beating.) In the late 1950s Kaufman left the ships, possibly blacklisted because of his communist affiliations.

Working a kitchen job in the Hilton Hotel in downtown Los Angeles in 1957, Kaufman read a magazine article about the new bohemians living in San Francisco's North Beach. The following day he quit his job and drove north; when his car broke down in Big Sur he abandoned it, and continued his journey hitchhiking. On arriving in San Francisco, Kaufman found a thriving scene of poetry and jazz, and within days this intense and explosive figure had become an indispensable fixture in the community. In May of 1958 Kaufman met his wife, Eileen, and they married the following month. At that point Kaufman only recited his poems and he often made them up on the spot; it was Eileen who encouraged him to write down his poems, and she often transcribed—and always preserved—them herself. Were it not for Eileen Kaufman's determined intervention, the work of Bob Kaufman would probably be little more than an urban myth today.

The term "jazz poet" is often applied to Kaufman. This is appropriate, as he consciously sought to adapt the harmonic complexities and spontaneity of be-bop as exemplified by his hero Charlie Parker (after whom he named his son, Parker) into his writing. However, the term should not be used to pigeonhole the remarkable body of work he produced, which is rich in inspired imagery, wisdom, humor, linguistic daring, and lyric exuberance. Many of Kaufman's poems from this period were published as broadsides and were frequently printed entirely in capital letters, which lent a sense of urgency to his message. Like poetic bulletins, they contained the "news" of the day: babies being born, parties convened, poets getting arrested. So much was happening so quickly that *Beatitude* magazine, co-founded by Kaufman in 1959, actually began as a weekly poetry magazine.

Kaufman was a gentle man but he could also be angry and provocative, particularly when he was confronting authority. His unconventional appearance and interracial marriage made him a target for the local police, and he was arrested, beaten, and jailed on many occasions.

p. 198
Bob Kaufman at the Co-Existence Bagel Shop in San Francisco, 1958, Photograph by Wallace Berman.

p. 199
Bob Kaufman, Original manuscript for *Blues for Hal Waters*, (published in *Miscellaneous Man*, edited by William Margolis, No. 1, Summer 1968).

p. 201
Bob Kaufman, *Abomunist Manifesto* (San Francisco: City Lights Books, 1959).

p. 202
Bob Kaufman, *Second April* (San Francisco: City Lights Books, 1959), inscribed to Bill Margolis by Kaufman.

p. 203 top
Eileen and Bob Kaufman in San Francisco, 1958, Photograph by William Margolis.

p. 203 bottom left
Bob Kaufman, San Francisco, 1958, Photograph by William Margolis.

p. 203 bottom right
Bob Kaufman and William Margolis in San Francisco, 1958, Photographer unknown.

ABoMUNIST MANIFESTo

ABOMUNISTS JOIN NOTHING BUT THEIR HANDS OR LEGS, OR OTHER SAME.

ABOMUNISTS SPIT ANTI-POETRY FOR POETIC REASONS AND FRINK.

ABOMUNISTS DO NOT LOOK AT PICTURES PAINTED BY PRESIDENTS AND UNEMPLOYED PRIME MINISTERS.

IN TIMES OF NATIONAL PERIL, ABOMUNISTS, AS REALITY AMERICANS, STAND READY TO DRINK THEMSELVES TO DEATH FOR THEIR COUNTRY.

ABOMUNISTS DO NOT FEEL PAIN, NO MATTER HOW MUCH IT HURTS.

ABOMUNISTS DO NOT USE THE WORD SQUARE EXCEPT WHEN TALKING TO SQUARES.

ABOMUNISTS READ NEWSPAPERS ONLY TO ASCERTAIN THEIR ABOMINUBILITY.

ABOMUNISTS NEVER CARRY MORE THAN FIFTY DOLLARS IN DEBTS ON THEM.

ABOMUNISTS BELIEVE THAT THE SOLUTION TO PROBLEMS OF RELIGIOUS BIGOTRY IS, TO HAVE A CATHOLIC CANDIDATE FOR PRESIDENT AND A PROTESTANT CANDIDATE FOR POPE.

ABOMUNISTS DO NOT WRITE FOR MONEY; THEY WRITE THE MONEY ITSELF.

ABOMUNISTS BELIEVE ONLY WHAT THEY DREAM ONLY AFTER IT COMES TRUE.

ABOMUNIST CHILDREN MUST BE REARED ABOMINUBLY.

ABOMUNIST POETS, CONFIDENT THAT THE NEW LITERARY FORM "FOOT-PRINTISM" HAS FREED THE ARTIST OF OUTMODED RESTRICTIONS, SUCH AS: THE ABILITY TO READ AND WRITE, OR THE DESIRE TO COMMUNICATE, MUST BE PREPARED TO READ THEIR WORK AT DENTAL COLLEGES, EMBALMING SCHOOLS, HOMES FOR UNWED MOTHERS, HOMES FOR WED MOTHERS, INSANE ASYLUMS, SANE ASYLUMS, U. S. O. CANTEENS, KINDERGARTENS, AND COUNTY JAILS. ABOMUNISTS NEVER COMPROMISE THEIR REJECTIONARY PHILOSOPHY.

ABOMUNISTS REJECT EVERYTHING EXCEPT SNOWMEN.

By 1960 the harassment had become so intolerable that he accepted an invitation to read at Harvard University and resettled in New York City. The New York years (1960–63) were largely filled with poverty and addiction, although it was during this period that Kaufman did manage to assemble his first book of poems, *Solitudes Crowded with Loneliness* (1965), with his editors at New Directions. In 1963 he was arrested for walking on the grass in Washington Square Park, was imprisoned in the infamous Tombs, and narrowly escaped a forced lobotomy at Bellevue Hospital. Deeply shaken by the experience, he returned to San Francisco, only to confront the news of the Kennedy assassination. Wracked by visions of despair and destruction, he took a ten-year Buddhist vow of silence.

Kaufman moved out of North Beach and settled in a welfare hotel south of Market Street, where his drug use (largely methamphetamine) continued. One day Kaufman wordlessly deposited at the publishing offices of City Lights a leather binder filled with poems written on scraps of paper, napkins, and paper bags. This formed his second collection, *Golden Sardine* (1965). The book's editors, Claude Pelieu and Mary Beach, translated Kaufman's work into French, and he became known there as an American Rimbaud. Kaufman's message of freedom, liberation against all forms of oppression, and his celebrations of jazz, earned him an enormous audience, especially in Eastern Europe, and translations of his works followed in twenty two languages. In later years his foreign readers frequently turned up in the bars and cafes of North Beach hoping to meet him.

In 1973, a group of Kaufman's friends gathered at Malvina's Coffehouse to watch a television documentary about him directed by Kenneth Tynan titled *Dissent in the Arts in America*. Kaufman stumbled on the gathering by accident, and it was then that he broke his silence by reciting a poem to his wife. They renewed their vows and moved to a small house in Mill Valley where Kaufman began writing again. In 1977 a community of young poets gathered in North Beach once more, and *Beatitude* magazine was revived. "What am I, the local hero?" he asked a young poet one day, and indeed he was. He occasionally participated in readings, and continued to write. His poems from this period were collected in *The Ancient Rain* (New Directions, 1981). Many of these late poems reflect on the African-American experience, while others are preoccupied with an impending sense of nuclear doom and the encroachment of fascism in political and social life. In 1983 Kaufman became re-engaged with Zen Buddhism, an area of study that had always attracted him. In his final poems, written on the threshold of death, Kaufman was still a restless man searching for meaning, but he seemed overtaken by an uncharacteristic sense of peacefulness and light. Kaufman died in Northern California in 1986.

Raymond Foye

For Bill Margolis My Friend who Gives all of Himself for Love and Enriches My Existence This is Both of our Aprils Bobby.

SECOND APRIL

bob kaufman

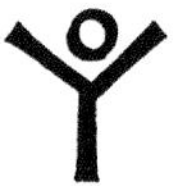

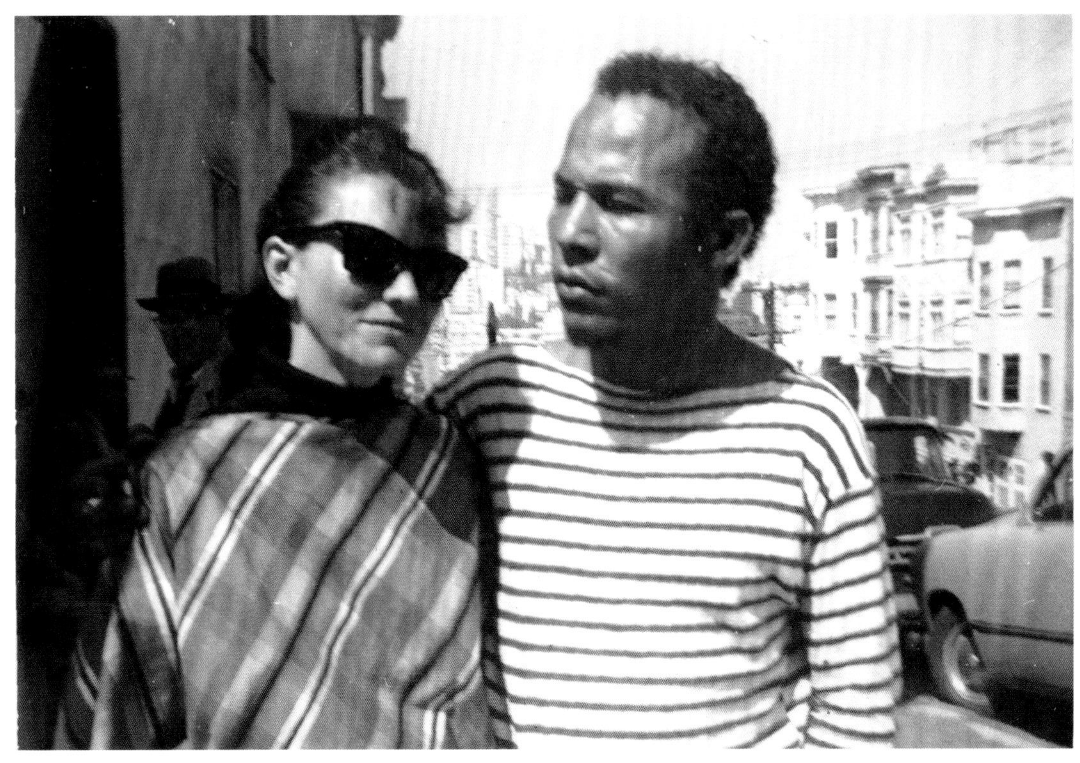

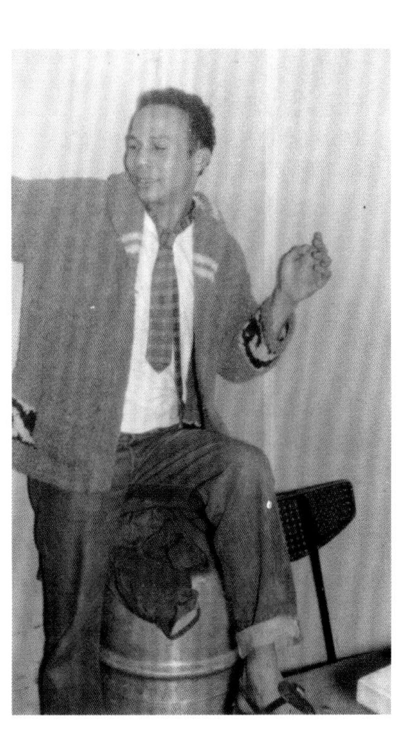

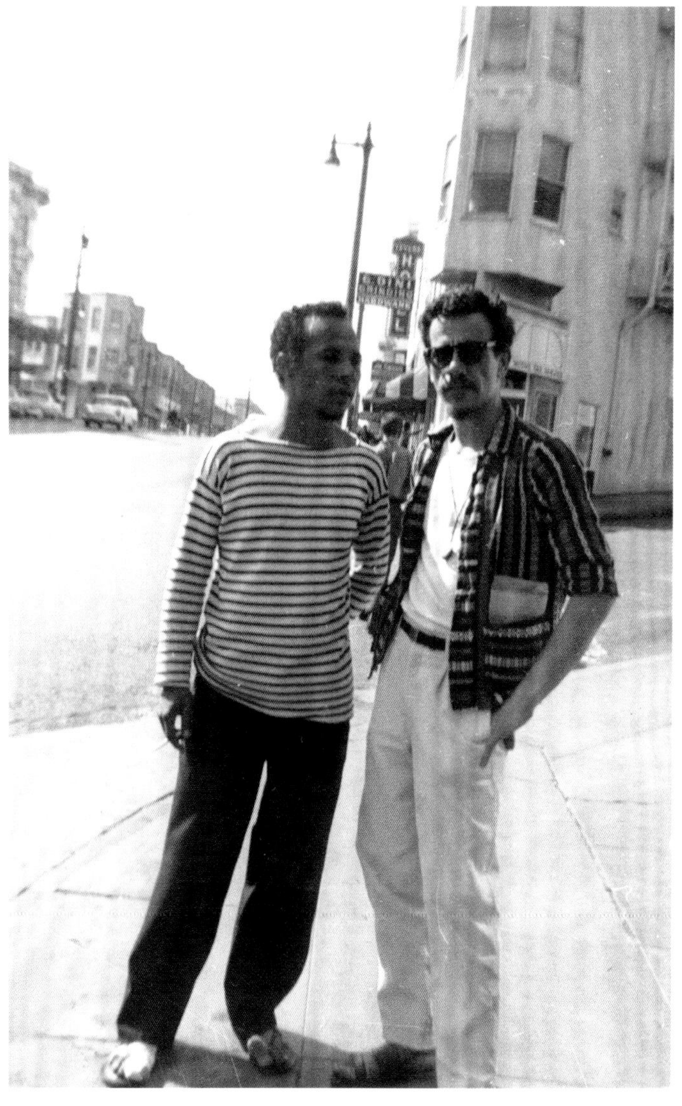

Philip Lamantia

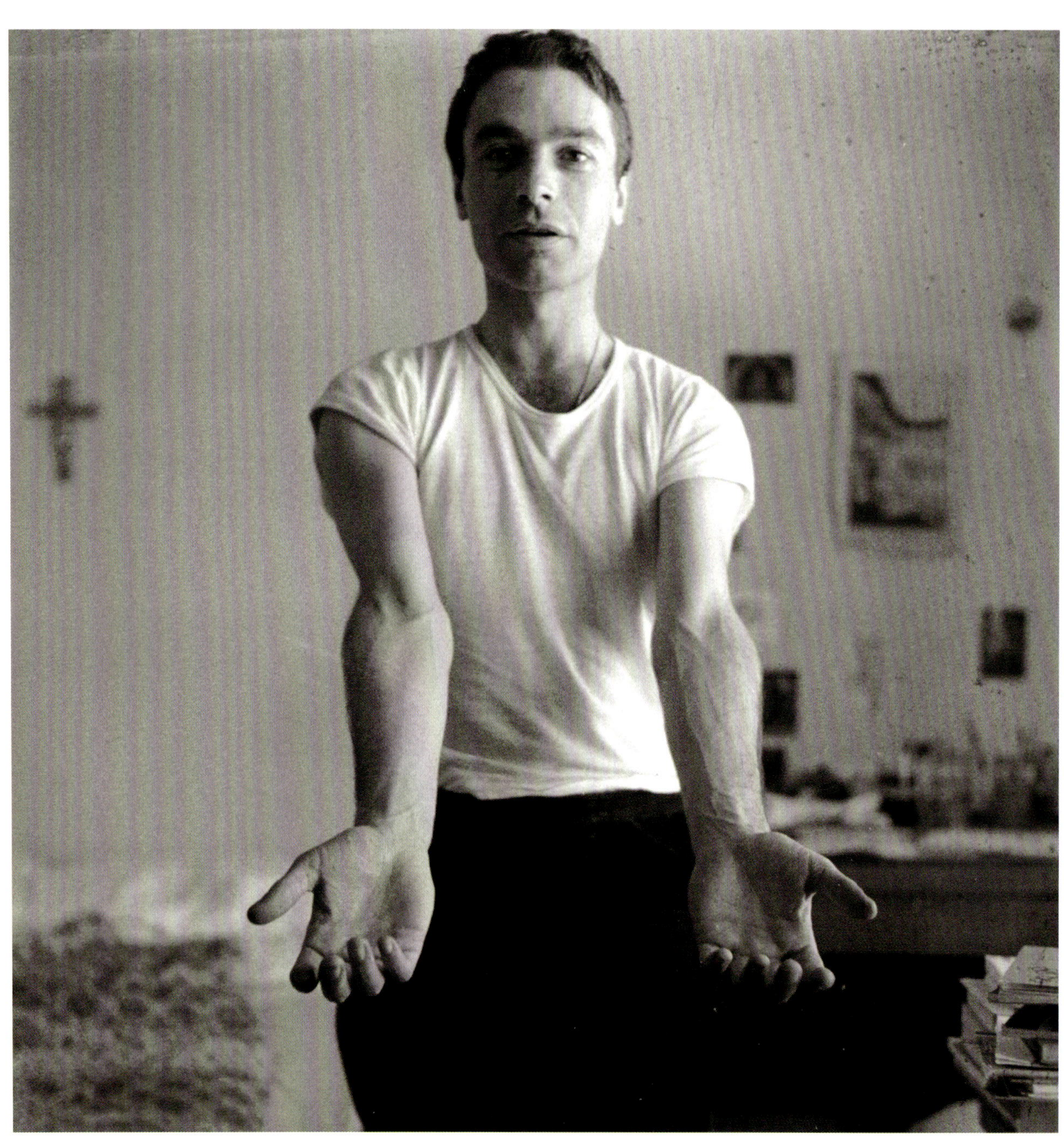

.: : EKSTASIS : :.

by

-Philip Lamantia-

His First Book
since *Erotic Poems*
Cosmic turn-on ! Theogonies & stars
- These ARE Poems
Are MYSTERIES
K
N
O
W
1334 Franklin N San Francisco
$1.25 THE AUERHAHN PRESS $1.25

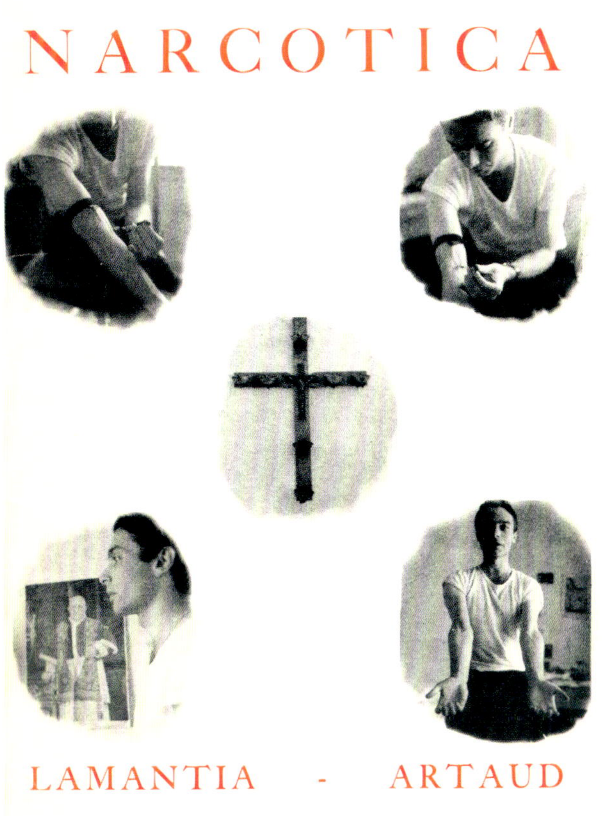

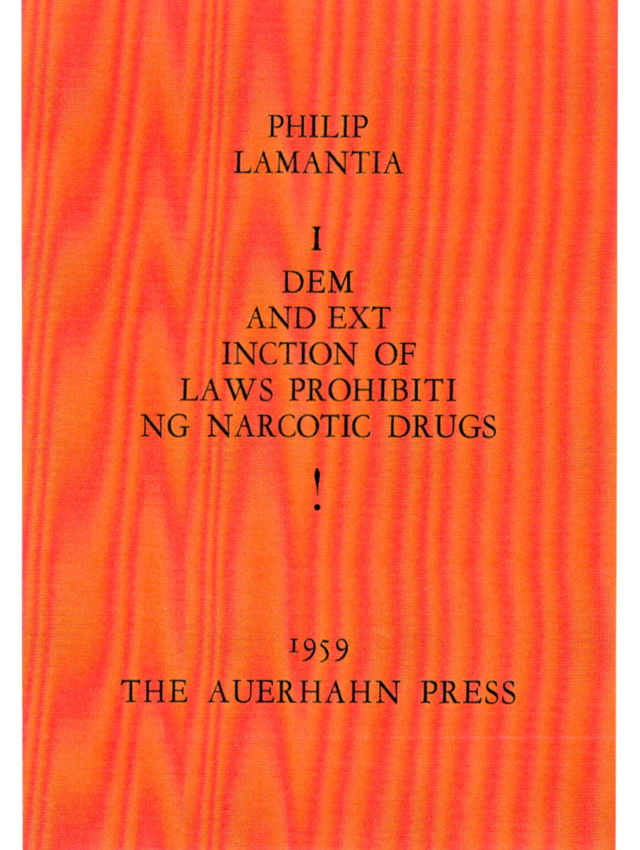

For California's poetry community of the 1950s and 1960s—and for Wallace Berman, in particular—Philip Lamantia served as a direct link to European Surrealism. More than any poet of his generation, Lamantia shared the Surrealists' enchantment with the irrational and he hungered for ecstatic experience. Lamantia was willing to pay the full price of admission for experiences demanding a conscious disordering of the senses, too, and his life was marked by drug addiction and the periodic bouts of depression that invariably afflict those who fly too close to the sun.

Born in San Francisco, in 1927, to a Sicilian immigrant family, Lamantia fell under the spell of Edgar Allan Poe and H.P. Lovecraft as a young boy, and began writing poetry in junior high school. He had his first direct exposure to Surrealism as a teenager when the San Francisco Museum of Art mounted retrospectives of work by Salvador Dalí and Joan Miro; on seeing those shows, Lamantia realized that "the purely revolutionary nature of Surrealism was part of my own individual temperament."[1] He began submitting poems to legendary Surrealist publication *View*, which published several of his poems in 1943, and offered him a job the following year. Lamantia was just sixteen at the time, but he didn't hesitate for a second.

p. 204
Philip Lamantia, San Francisco, 1958, Photograph by Wallace Berman.

p. 205 top
Philip Lamantia, Publication announcement for *Ekstásis*, with photograph of Lamantia by Pantale Xantos (Wallace Berman), 1959.

p. 205 bottom left
Philip Lamantia, *Narcotica* (San Francisco: Auerhahn Press, 1959), Cover photographs and art by Wallace Berman.

p. 205 bottom right
Philip Lamantia, Title page from *Narcotica*.

p. 206
Philip Lamantia, *The Blood of the Air* (San Francisco: Four Seasons Foundation, 1970) with illustrations by the author.

p. 207
Philip Lamantia, *Destroyed Works* (San Francisco: Auerhahn Press, 1962) with cover art, *Superhuman Devotion*, a 1962 collage by Bruce Conner.

"New York was the cultural center of the world at that point and was full of European émigrés who'd left Europe because of the war," Lamantia has recalled.[2] "Because I had a little job with *View*—I was sort of their office boy—I was wined and dined. I met everyone, including Max Ernst, Yves Tanguy, and André Breton, who was a charming man of enormous magnetism. I was only there for six months, but when you're that young each year is like a thousand."

Lamantia missed very little during his time in Manhattan—he even put in a brief appearance in Maya Deren's landmark experimental film, *Meshes of the Afternoon*—but when the war ended in 1945 the émigré community dispersed. Following an argument with *View* editor, Charles Henri Ford, Lamantia returned to San Francisco and finished high school. In 1946 he published his first book, *Erotic Poems* (Berkeley: Bern Porter Books), and from 1947 through 1949 he attended classes at the University of California at Berkeley.

Philip Lamantia

THE BLOOD OF THE AIR

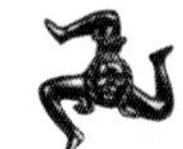

Four Seasons Foundation

San Francisco 1970

A highly educated man well versed in all manner of esotericism, Lamantia immersed himself in erotic mysticism, alchemy, and gnosticism at Berkeley as his writing style approached maturity. In a manner evocative of Lautréamont's *Chants de Maldoror*, Lamantia's poetry is rooted in extremes and swings between states of exaltation and debasement. During this period Lamantia also became involved with San Francisco's libertarian community which gave birth to the anarchist publication, *The Ark*, which Lamantia helped edit.

In 1949 Lamantia embarked on a decade of nomadic wandering which he referred to as his eclipse. "I went to New York in 1950 shortly after the Mafia decided to get into the heroin business, and I became an addict in two weeks,"[3] recalled Lamantia, who spent most of the 1950s in France, Morocco, and Mexico. "Mexico City was wonderfully habitable during the 1950s and I perched for long stretches with the Cora in the Sierra Madre Mountains," Lamantia has stated. "It was there that I began to return to my own roots, inspired by their vision and ritual."[4]

Lamantia periodically returned to San Francisco during those years, and he happened to be in town in October of 1955 for Allen Ginsberg's legendary reading of *Howl* at The Six Gallery. Lamantia was on the bill that night, too, and he used the opportunity to read work by John Hoffmann, a poet who'd recently died at the age of twenty-five in Mexico. Lamantia was back in San Francisco again in 1958, and it was then that he crossed paths with Wallace Berman.

"The connection between Wally Berman and Surrealism was definite, as far as I'm concerned," Lamantia has said of Berman, who included a Lamantia poem in *Semina 4*, and took photographs of Lamantia shooting heroin for the cover of Lamantia's book, *Narcotica*. "He had all the same books on alchemy and magic that I have, and was interested in the same subjects I've been interested in since I was fifteen. We had many long, up-until-dawn discussions about poetry and the relationship between the oracles."[5]

Lamantia published his second volume of verse in 1959 (*Ekstasis*, San Francisco: Auerhahn Press), but by 1960 his excessive lifestyle began to take a toll and he fell into a deep depression. He decided to stop writing and in 1963 he moved to Europe to study philosophy, mathematics, and esotericism. During this sabbatical from writing, three books by Lamantia were published: *Destroyed Works* (San Francisco: Auerhahn Press, 1962); *Touch of the Marvelous* (Berkeley: Oyez, 1966); and *Selected Poems 1943–1966* (San Francisco: City Lights Books, 1967).

Lamantia spent 1965 through 1968 living in Spain, and in 1970 he resettled in San Francisco where he married writer Nancy Peters. That same year he published his sixth book, *The Blood of the Air* (San Francisco: Four Seasons Foundation). The Lamantias spent much of the next twelve years exploring Native American sites along the Pacific Coast, from British Columbia through California. In the late 1970s Lamantia found himself drawn to San Francisco's thriving punk community and he frequented the punk club Mabuhay Gardens, which he found "perfectly in line with the revolutionary heart of Surrealism."[6]

Lamantia's *Becoming Visible* was published in 1981 (San Francisco: City Lights Books), but health problems forced him to slow down his writing practice during the 1990s. Lamantia died of heart failure at his home in North Beach in 2005. *Kristine McKenna*

1 Peters, Nancy J., "Philip Lamantia," *Dictionary of Literary Biography, Volume 16: The Beats: Literary Bohemians in Postwar America* (Detroit: Gale Research Company, 1983), p. 330.
2 From a conversation with Kristine McKenna, August 2, 2000.
3 Ibid.
4 Meltzer, David, editor, *San Francisco Beat: Talking With the Poets* (San Francisco: City Lights Books, 2001), p. 143.
5 Conversation with Kristine McKenna, August 2, 2000.
6 Meltzer, David, editor, *San Francisco Beat: Talking With the Poets* (San Francisco: City Lights Books, 2001), p. 148.

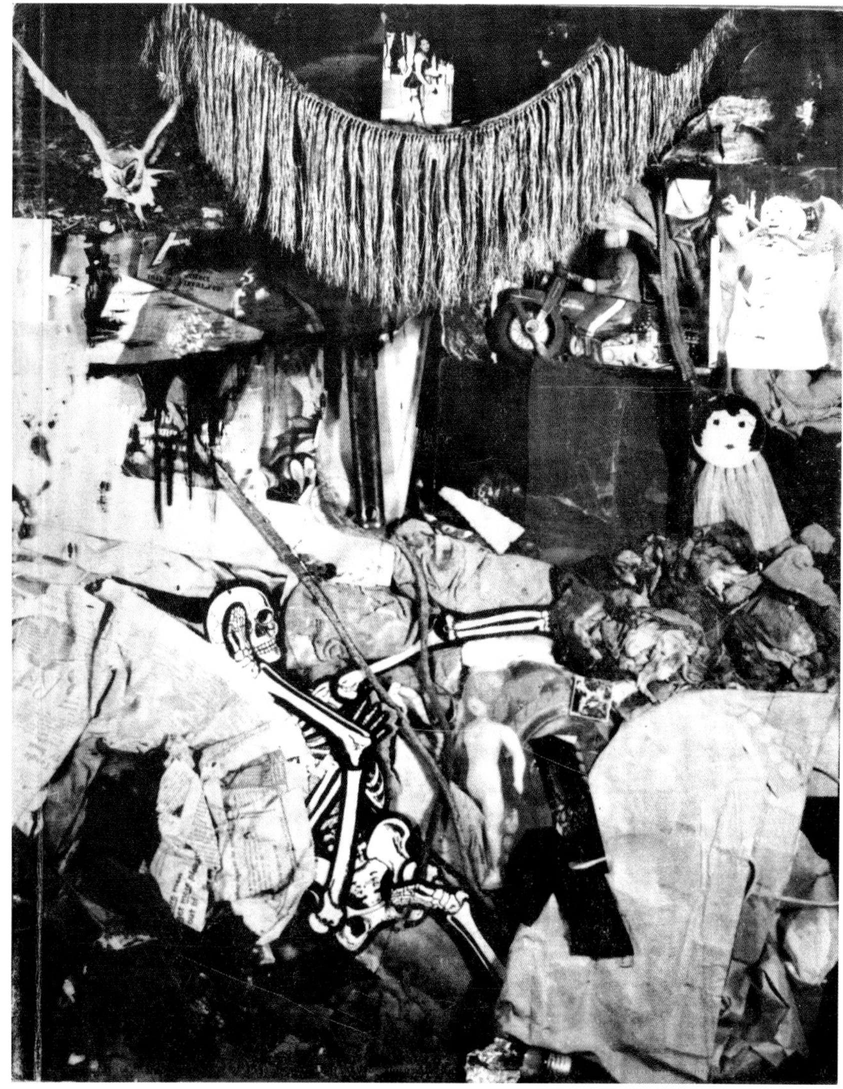

William Margolis

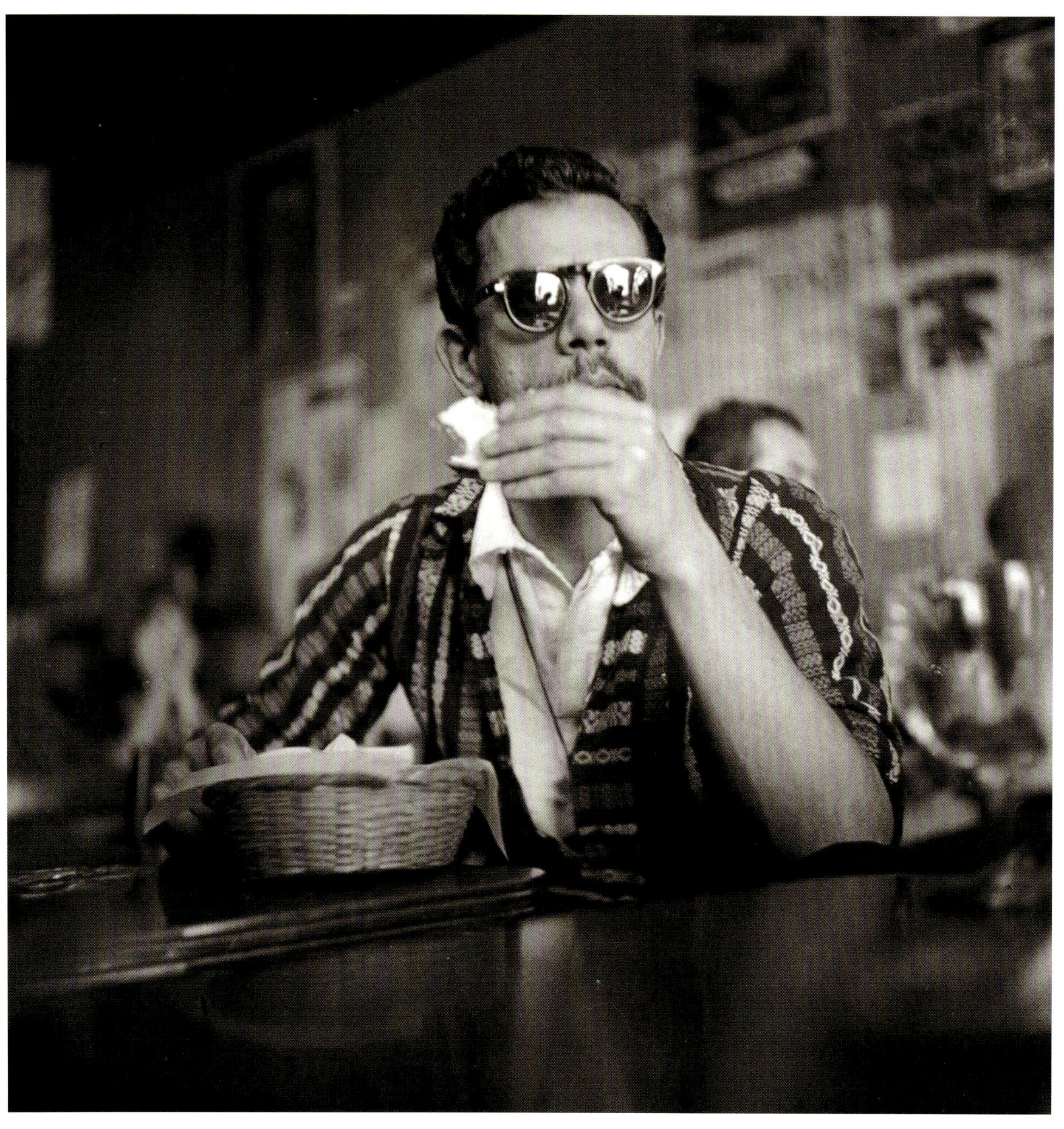

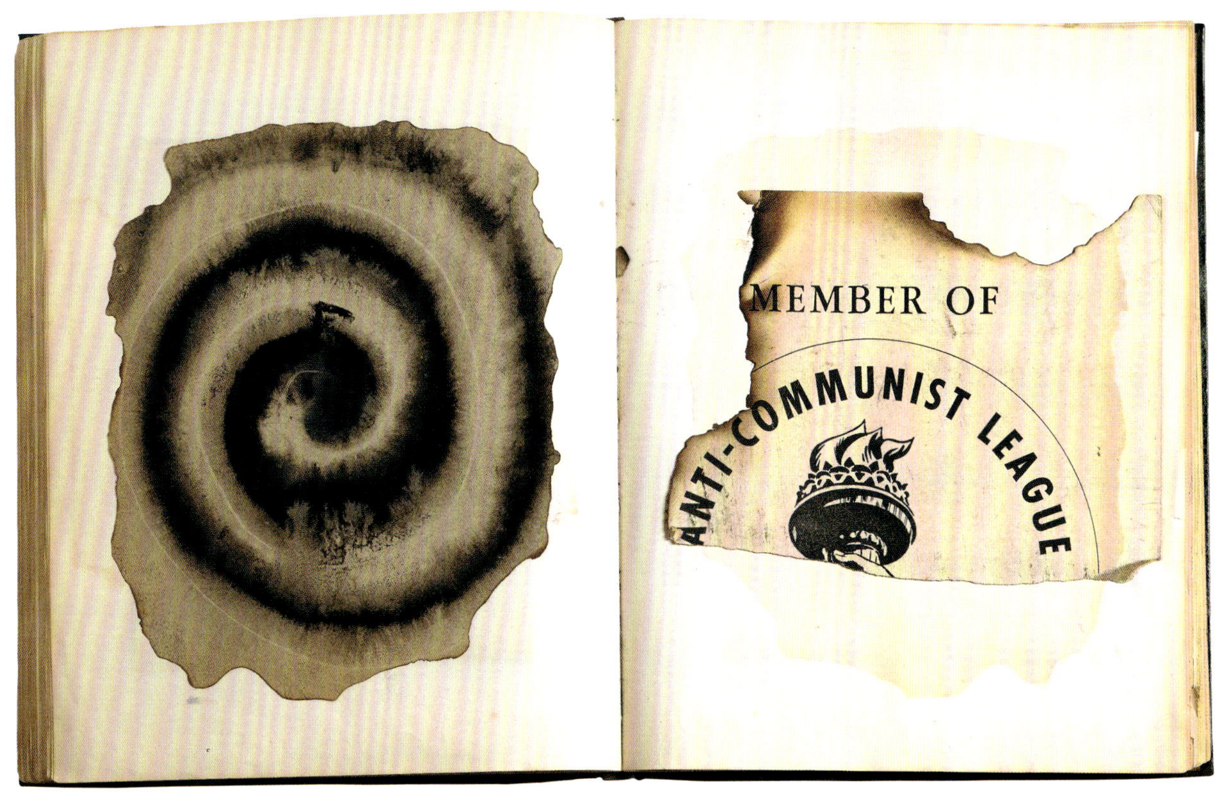

i ache with
tangled words
& nerves

raw with longing
for hills
& her touch...

i know you—
...pierced my
heart
with your eyes....

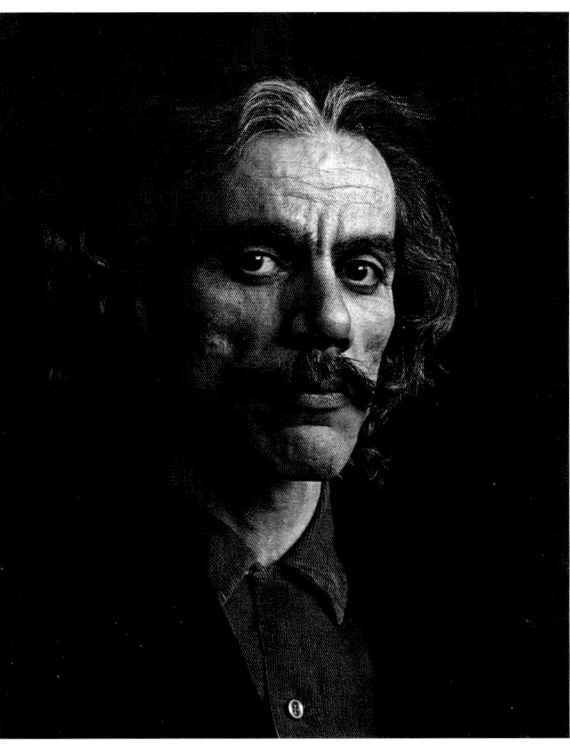

William Margolis was a stalwart member of the North Beach and Venice poetry scenes whose life was forever stamped by an impulsive romantic act. In 1960 during a lovers' quarrel, he leapt from his North Beach second-story window and was left paralyzed from the waist down. He was confined to a wheelchair for the remaining decades of his life. Born in 1927 in Chicago, Margolis served in the Navy after high school and attended Roosevelt College on the G.I. Bill. In school he developed an interest in abstract painting and photography. In 1950 he left college and drove down the East Coast in a camper van converted from an old bakery truck.

Drifting west, Margolis became involved in the formation of the literary journal *The Miscellaneous Man,* which was published in Berkeley from 1954 to 1959. Gradually shifting its focus from formal to freeform poetry, *Miscellaneous Man* featured works by Bern Porter, Lawrence Lipton, Stuart Perkoff, Lawrence Ferlinghetti, and Kenneth Patchen. In a case that rivaled the censorship trials of Ginsberg's *Howl,* the journal and City Lights Bookstore were accused of publishing and selling obscene writings due to the inclusion in issues 11 and 12 of Gil Orlovitz's "Statement of Erica Keith." The case was finally dismissed in October 1957.

In 1955, Margolis became the manager of 707 Scott Street, a San Francisco building inhabited by Lawrence Jordan and later by John Wieners and Wallace and Shirley Berman. Through his poet and artist friends, Margolis got a job in 1957 at the book distributor Paper Editions, working alongside Robert Alexander, John Reed, and Arthur Richer. In 1958 Margolis moved briefly to New York, and Wallace Berman took over the management of the Scott Street building. Berman included Margolis's poem "Morning" in *Semina 5*, the "Mexico" issue.

Returning the next year to North Beach, Margolis was able to make use of his publishing experience when his friend Bob Kaufman decided to start up *Beatitude*. Co-editing along with Kaufman and John Kelly, Margolis organized the effort, manning the mimeograph machine at the Bread and Wine Mission in North Beach and managing the magazine's distribution. In its heyday until 1961 (the magazine was re-started in 1969 and continued its run of thirty-four issues until 1987), *Beatitude* proved to be one of the quintessential publications of the Beat era, including selections from Allen Ginsberg, Jack Kerouac, Kaufman, Margolis, Michael McClure, Philip Lamantia, Richard Brautigan, Gregory Corso, Lenore Kandel, and Philip Whalen. At this time Margolis held a day job at the *Wall Street Journal*.

After what David Meltzer has called Margolis's "leap of faith and lost love" in 1960,[1] he was sent to Long Beach Hospital for a long period of recuperation and physical therapy. In the hospital he continued writing, using the hospital print shop to make copies of his self-published volume, *The Little Love of Our Yearning*. After his release from the hospital, he moved to Venice where he became involved with the Venice West poetry scene, reading often at Venice West Café and recording the readings of other poets.

Largely surviving on disability payments, he continued writing and editing, publishing journalistic pieces occasionally in *The LA Free Press* and *The Oracle*. Margolis edited the sole issue of the journal *Mendicant* in 1961 which featured works by Kenneth Patchen and James Boyer May as well as an excerpt from an essay by Stuart Perkoff about Aleister Crowley.

In the late 1960s Margolis moved to Guadalajara looking for an inexpensive place to live and write. There, he was tracked down by a female fan of his writing with whom he ended up living for several years.[2] Returning to Venice, he settled near the Temple of Man, Robert Alexander's irrepressible center and hangout for poets and artists. In

p. 208
William Margolis, Co-Existence Bagel Shop, San Francisco, 1958, Photograph by Wallace Berman.

p. 209 top
William Margolis, Untitled journal, 1955–59, Mixed-media

p. 209 bottom
William Margolis, Paste up galley for *The Anteroom of Hell*, (San Francisco: Inferno Press, 1957).

p. 210
William Margolis, 1971, Photograph by William Warren, Collection Temple of Man.

p. 211 left
William Margolis, *Untitled (Self-portrait)*, 1959, Pastel on paper.

p. 211 top
William Margolis, *The Little Love of Our Yearning* (San Francisco: Mendicant Editions, 1960), Author's pasteup.

p. 211 right
William Margolis, *The Anteroom of Hell* (San Francisco: Inferno Press, 1957).

p. 212 top left
Flyer for William Margolis reading at The Cellar, c. 1959, Margolis journal, Collection of Temple of Man.

p. 212 top right
Flyer for poetry reading at Threadbare, Pacific Grove, c. 1959, Margolis journal, Collection of Temple of Man.

p. 212 bottom
William Margolis, *(Three Ways) Out*, 1962, Handwritten manuscript

p. 213
Exterior of Margolis' North Beach apartment from whose second story window the poet leapt, 1960, Photograph by William Margolis.

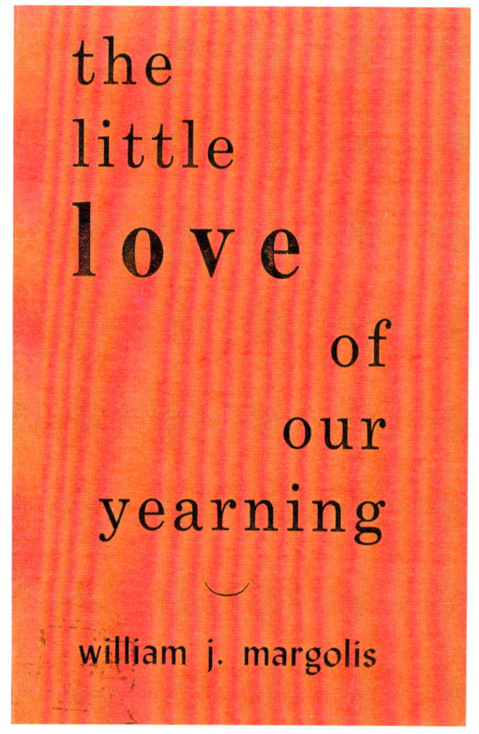
the
little
love
of
our
yearning
william j. margolis

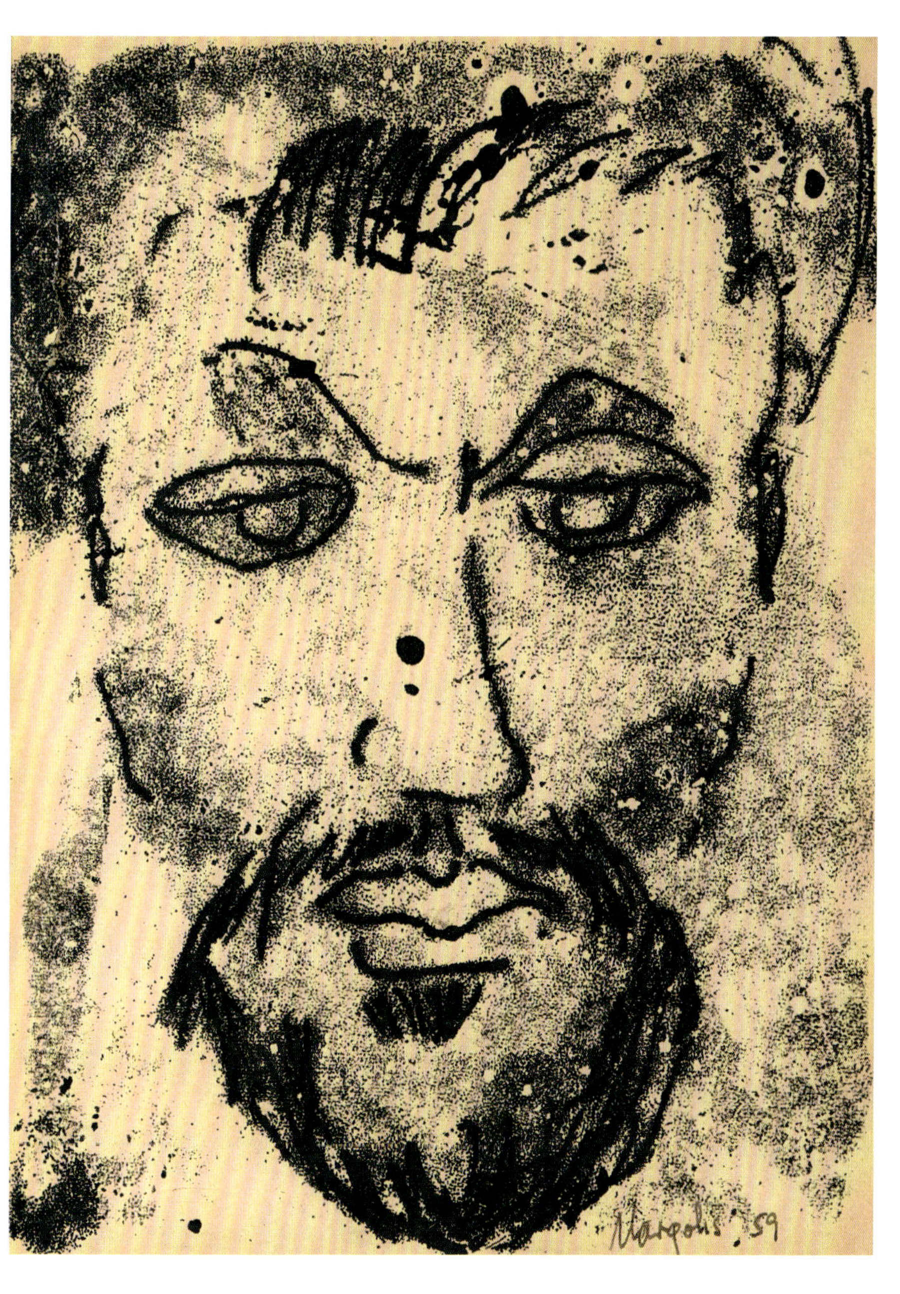
Margolis '59

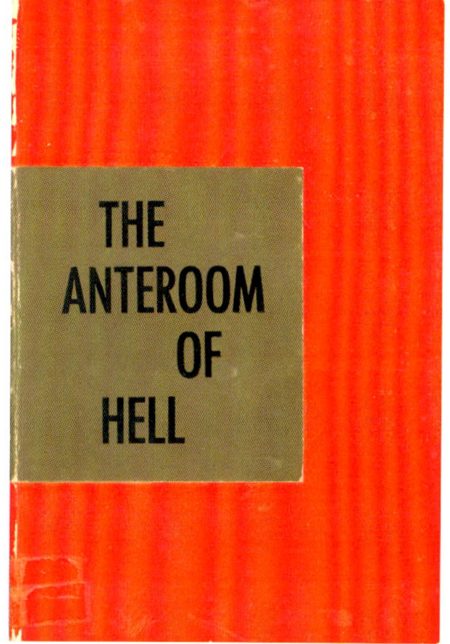
THE
ANTEROOM
OF
HELL

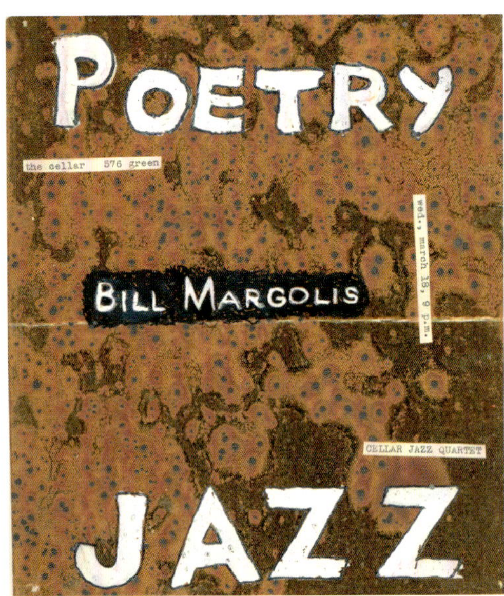

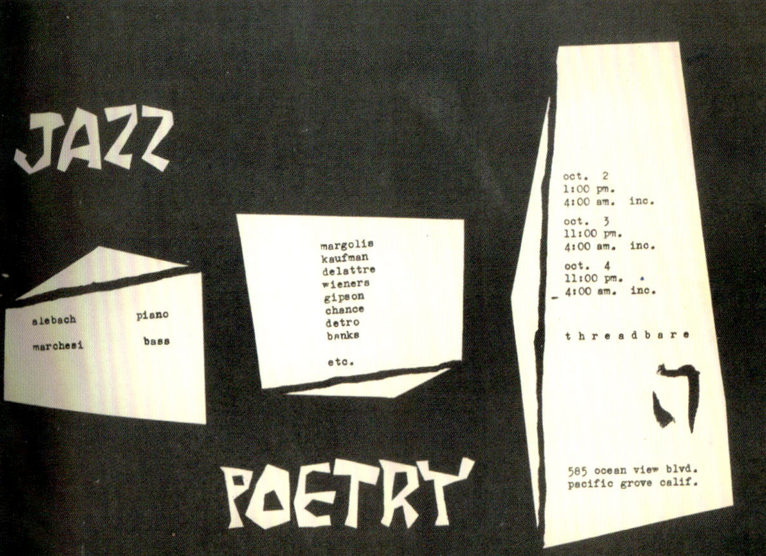

1968 Margolis revived *The Miscellaneous Man* for a single lively issue that featured selections from Antonin Artaud, Ruth Weiss, Dean Stockwell, Bob Kaufman, David Meltzer, Stuart Perkoff, Elias Romero, Jack Hirschman, George Herms, Fred Mason, and Vladimir Mayakovsky. The second issue, to be guest-edited by Jack Hirschman, was cancelled after a mishap with the printer.

Margolis continued to self-publish his writings under the imprint of the Temple of Man, using an early computer to print out his poetry volumes on eight-by-ten-inch dot matrix paper. He distributed copies of these works to friends and libraries. In the 1990s, he read his works at several Venice West evenings organized by the Venice Historical Society. Margolis died after infectious complications from a routine hospital examination in 1998.

Michael Duncan

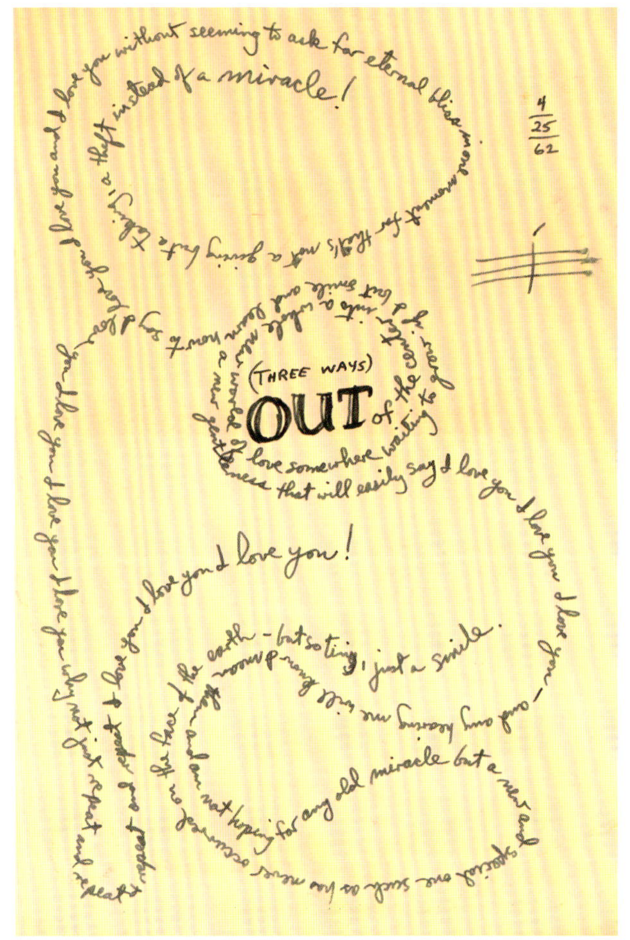

1 David Meltzer correspondence, December 2, 2004.

2 Telephone conversation with Marsha Getzler, December 29, 2004.

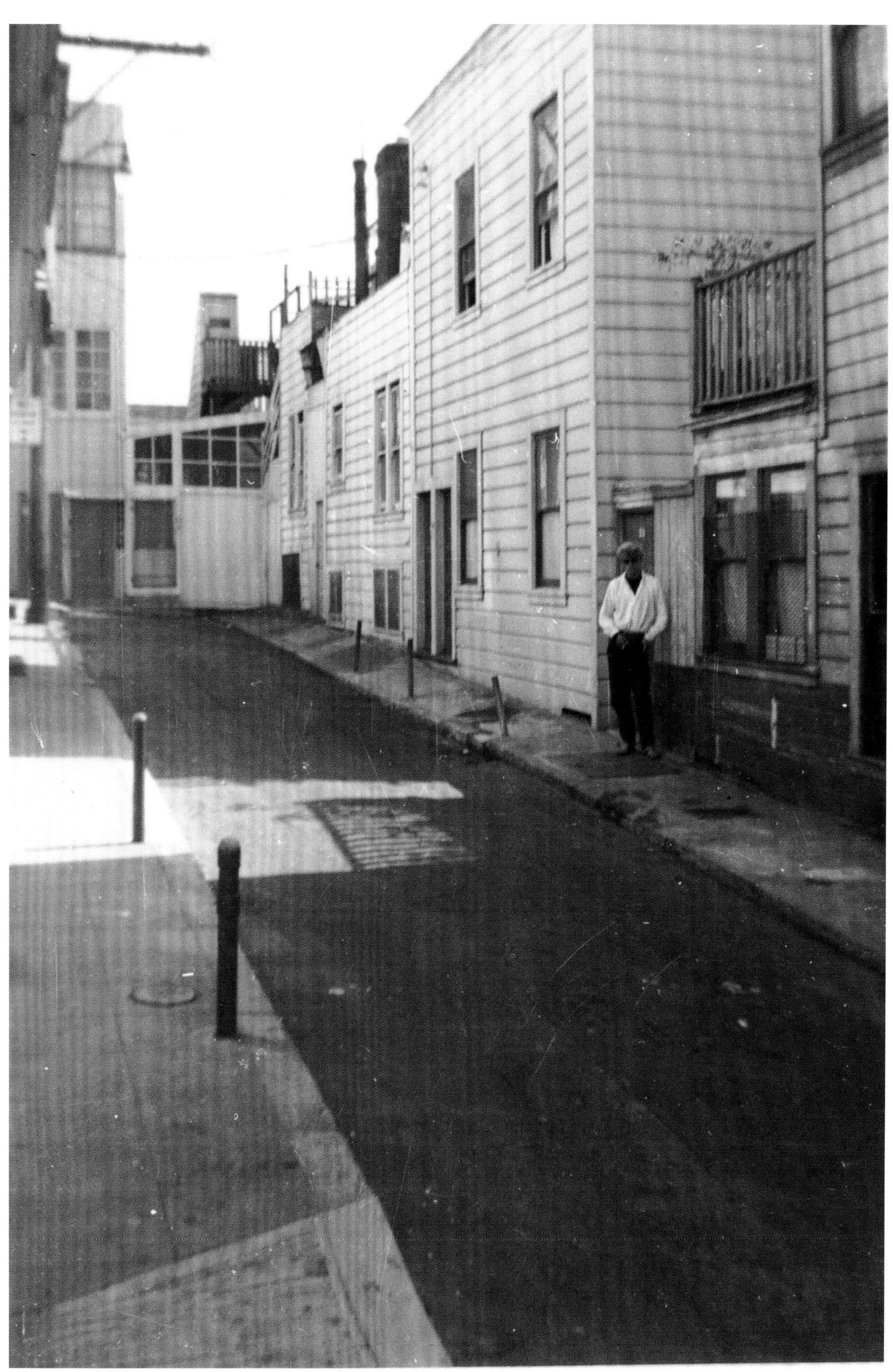

213 William Margolis

Michael McClure

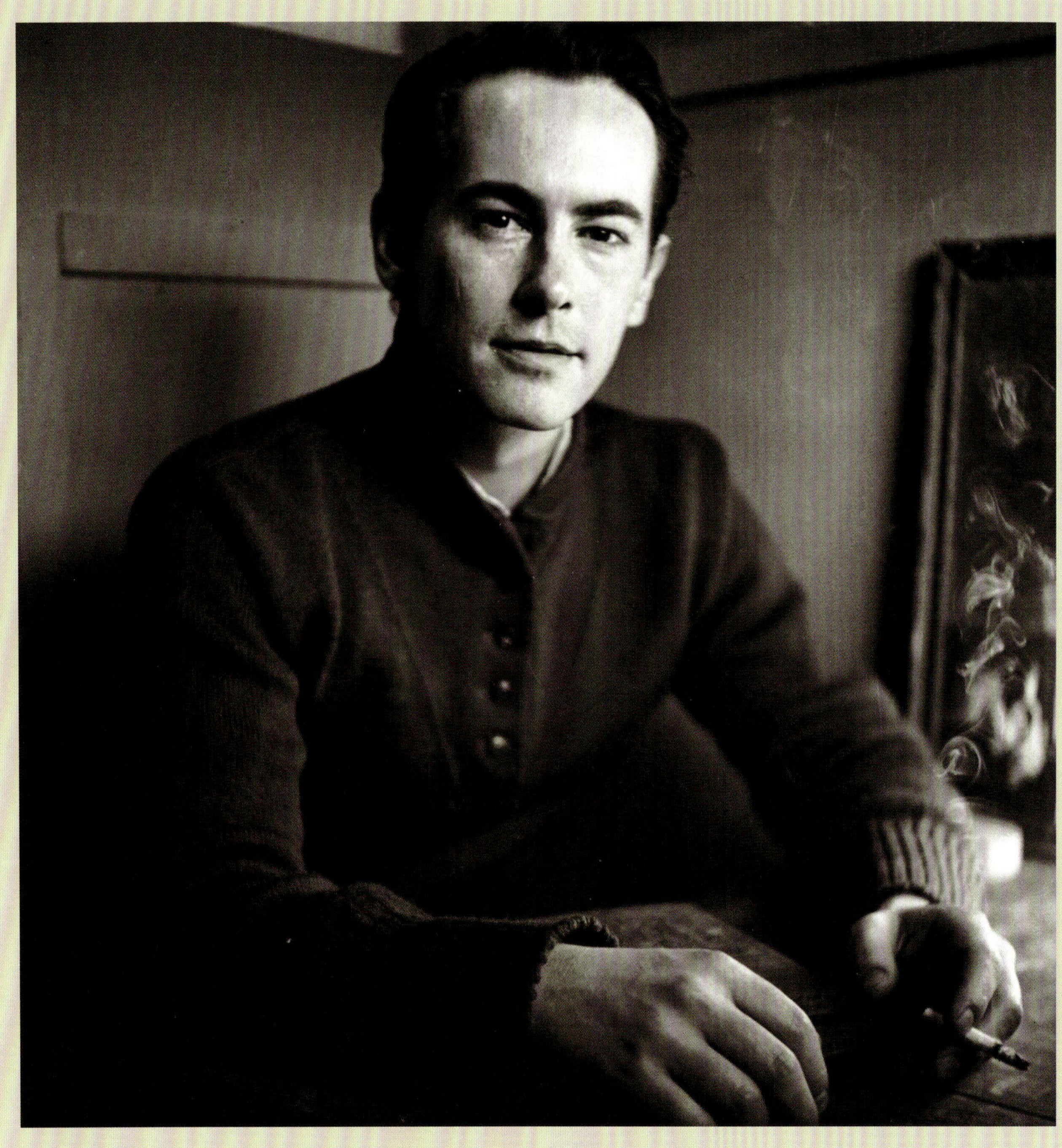

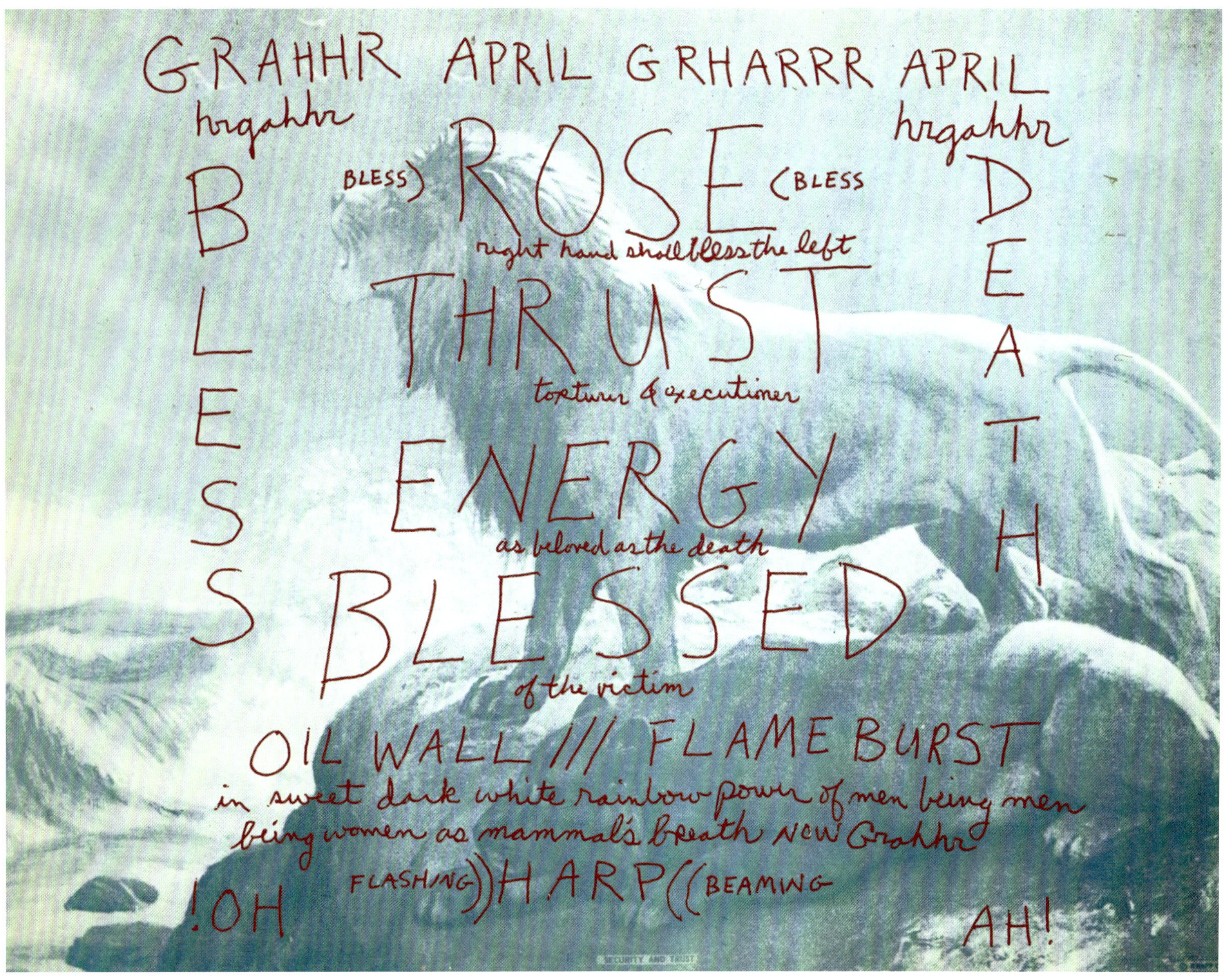
GRAHHR APRIL GRHARRR APRIL
hrgahhr
hrgahhr
BLESS) ROSE (BLESS
right hand shall bless the left
THRUST
torturer & executioner
ENERGY
as beloved as the death
BLESSED
of the victim
BLESS
DEATH
OIL WALL /// FLAME BURST
in sweet dark white rainbow power of men being men
being women as mammal's breath NOW Grahhr
!OH FLASHING)) HARP ((BEAMING AH!
SECURITY AND TRUST

"The poetry of the Beats is the first literary wing of the environmental movement,"[1] Michael McClure has observed; along with work by his colleague, Gary Snyder, McClure's poetry has embodied this belief with tremendous potency.

Born in Marysville, Kansas, in 1932, McClure was a child of divorce and spent his youth shuttling between Marysville, Seattle, and Wichita. It was in Kansas that he attended high school and befriended artist Bruce Conner, who was a classmate there. McClure had an abiding interest in nature from an early age, and although he began writing free verse as a teenager, he planned to become a naturalist.

In 1954 McClure moved to San Francisco hoping to study painting with Clyfford Still and Mark Rothko. Arriving there, he found they were no longer teaching in the Bay Area, but simultaneously realized that his interests in art and nature could be combined into a single creative practice. Enrolling in poetry workshops at San Francisco State College taught by Robert Duncan and Ruth Witt-Diamant, McClure discovered a "divine milieu," and became part of the Bay Area's burgeoning community of young poets. The seeds of McClure's notable work as a playwright also took root in San Francisco when he participated in a reading at The Six Gallery of Duncan's play, *Faust Foutu*, in 1955. McClure's career as a poet was officially launched that same year when he was included in the legendary Six Gallery reading that marked Allen Ginsberg's official unveiling of his signature poem, *Howl*. It was McClure's first time onstage as a poet, and the piece he read was "For the Death of 100 Whales."

McClure was married at the time to his first wife, poet Joanna McClure, and the couple was living on Fillmore Street where their neighbors included the Conners, Jay DeFeo, and Joan Brown. McClure has always maintained ties with disparate communities—musicians, Hell's Angels, actors, and playwrights—and he got on particularly well with visual artists. "McClure would go out of his way to look at things," Joan Brown recalled. "He was really genuinely interested in art."[2]

Concurrent with the birth of his daughter in 1956, McClure published his first volume of poetry, *Passage* (Big Sur: Jonathan Williams), while maintaining a day job running an addressograph machine in the mail room at the San Francisco Museum of Art. During this period he also teamed up with James Harmon and took over the editorship of anarchist magazine *Ark*, which morphed into *Ark II-Moby I* with their infusion of themes of pacifism and environmentalism. He also starred that year in Lawrence Jordan's experimental film, *Visions of a City*.

After seeing a copy of the first issue of *Semina*, McClure contacted Wallace Berman who immediately responded; Berman included McClure in *Semina Two*, and *4*, and devoted the entirety of *Semina 3* to McClure's "Peyote Poem."

"I'd been wanting to take peyote for a long time," McClure has recalled of the genesis of the poem, "and Wallace said 'I'll get you some.' It was mysterious to me how Wallace knew about so many things, just on a gut level, but I suppose it was knowledge he gathered on the streets of L.A. during the 1940s and early 1950s. He told me the specific way to take it, that I shouldn't eat the day before, and came by with five dried buttons. So I prepared it and ate it, and shortly after, the effects began to come on. I wrote the poem the next day."[3]

p. 214
Michael McClure in San Francisco, 1958, Photograph by Wallace Berman.

p. 215
Michael McClure, *Rose Thrust Energy Blessed*, 1968, Poster.

p. 216
Michael McClure, *Ghost Tantras* (San Francisco: City Lights Press, 1964) with cover photograph of McClure by Wallace Berman.

p. 217 top
Michael McClure, Collaged boxed mailer with untitled audio tape of McClure reading at the Lion House of the San Francisco Zoo in 1964, sound recording by Bruce "Kansas" Conner. Photograph by Wallace Berman.

p. 217 bottom
Michael McClure, Announcement for reading at the Cinema Theater, Los Angeles, with photographs of McClure by Wallace Berman.

p. 218 top
Michael McClure, Flyer for McClure's play, *The Beard*, 1966, Lithograph on paper.

p. 218 bottom
Michael McClure, *Poisoned Wheat* (San Francisco: privately published, 1965).

p. 219
Michael McClure, *Love Lion Lioness*, 1964, Lithograph on posterboard.

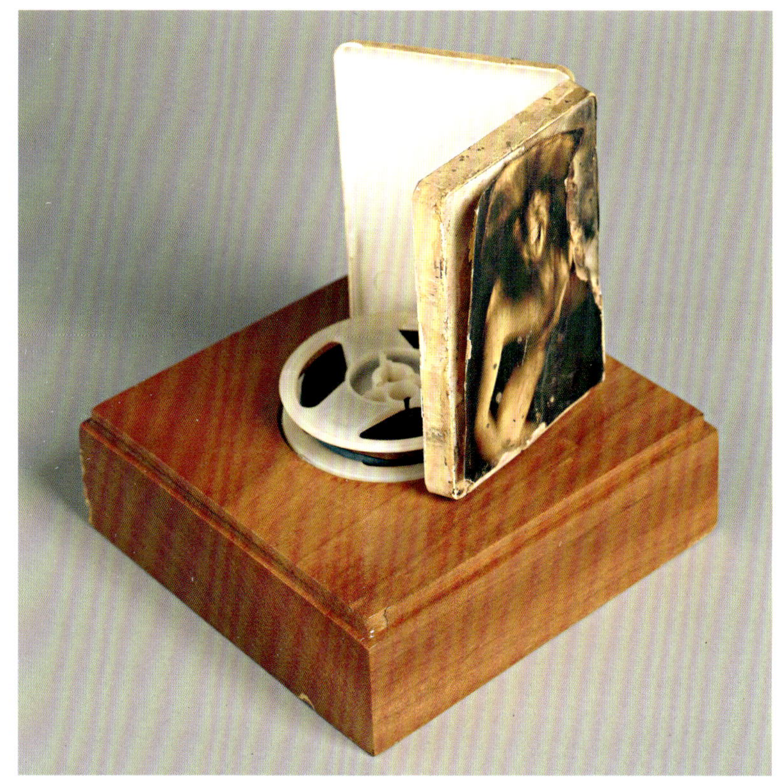

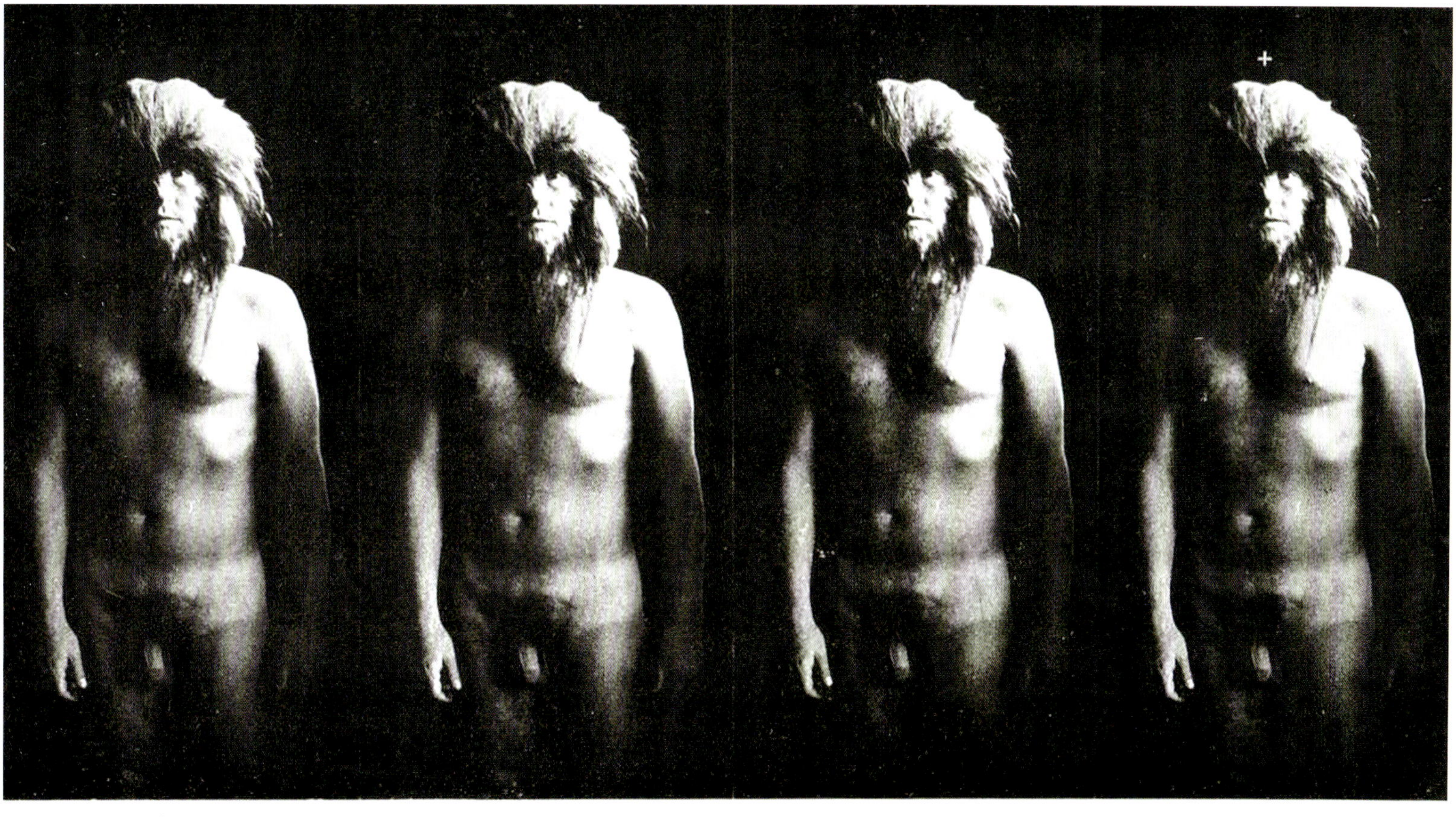

Poetry is a muscular principle and a revolution for the body-spirit and intellect and ear. Making images and pictures, even when speaking with melody, is not enough. There must be a poetry of pure beauty and energy that does not mimic but joins and exhorts reality and states the daily higher vision. To dim the senses and listen to inner energies a-roar is sometimes called the religious experience. It does not matter what it is called. Laughter as well as love is passion. The loveliness the nose snuffs in air may be translated to sound by interior perceptive organs. The touch of velvet on the fingertips may become a cry when time is stopped. Speed like calmness may become a pleasure or gentle muffled sound. A dahlia or fern might become pure speech in meditation. A woman's body might become the sound of worship. A goddess lies coiled at the base of man's body, and pure tantric sound might awaken her. There are no laws but living changing ones, and any system is a touch of death.

My eyes are intense dark brown and sometimes insane. I believe in LIBERTY, BEAUTY, FREEDOM, AND THE CREATION OF MY SOUL AND HELPING OTHERS IN THE CREATION OF THEIRS through poetry. —Michael McClure. The poet will read recent works Friday evening midnight May 15th at the Cinema Theatre.

CORRECTION: MAY 17 SUNDAY 8:30 P.M.
[illegible] 366 [illegible] CIENEGA ADM. 1.50

Photo of poet by Wallace Berman

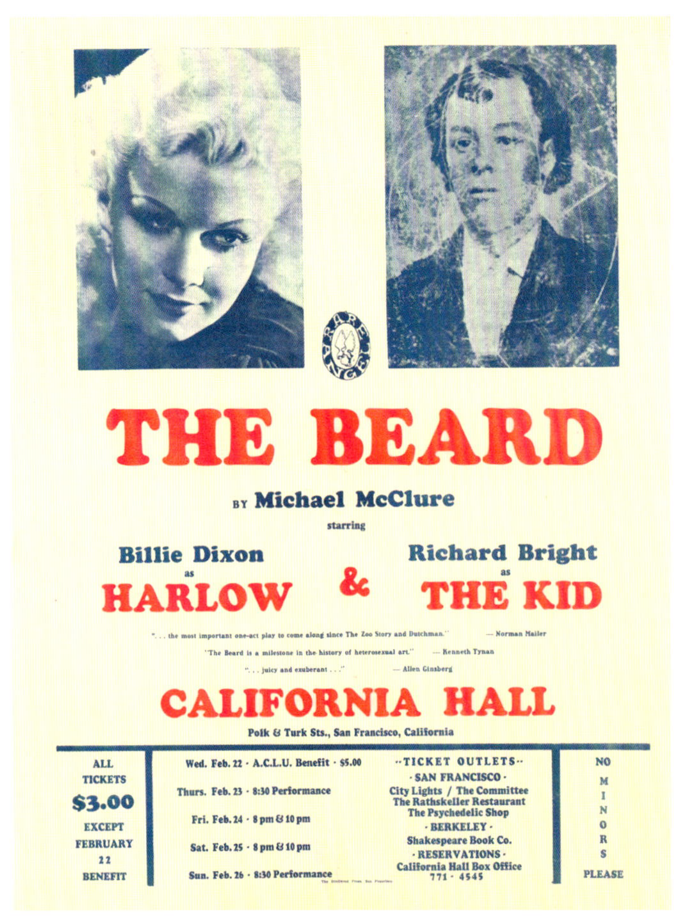
THE BEARD
BY Michael McClure
starring
Billie Dixon
as
HARLOW
&
Richard Bright
as
THE KID
". . . the most important one-act play to come along since The Zoo Story and Dutchman." — Norman Mailer
"The Beard is a milestone in the history of heterosexual art." — Kenneth Tynan
". . . juicy and exuberant . . ." — Allen Ginsberg
CALIFORNIA HALL
Polk & Turk Sts., San Francisco, California
ALL TICKETS $3.00 EXCEPT FEBRUARY 22 BENEFIT
Wed. Feb. 22 · A.C.L.U. Benefit · $5.00
Thurs. Feb. 23 · 8:30 Performance
Fri. Feb. 24 · 8 pm & 10 pm
Sat. Feb. 25 · 8 pm & 10 pm
Sun. Feb. 26 · 8:30 Performance
··TICKET OUTLETS··
· SAN FRANCISCO ·
City Lights / The Committee
The Rathskeller Restaurant
The Psychedelic Shop
· BERKELEY ·
Shakespeare Book Co.
· RESERVATIONS ·
California Hall Box Office
771 · 4545
NO MINORS PLEASE

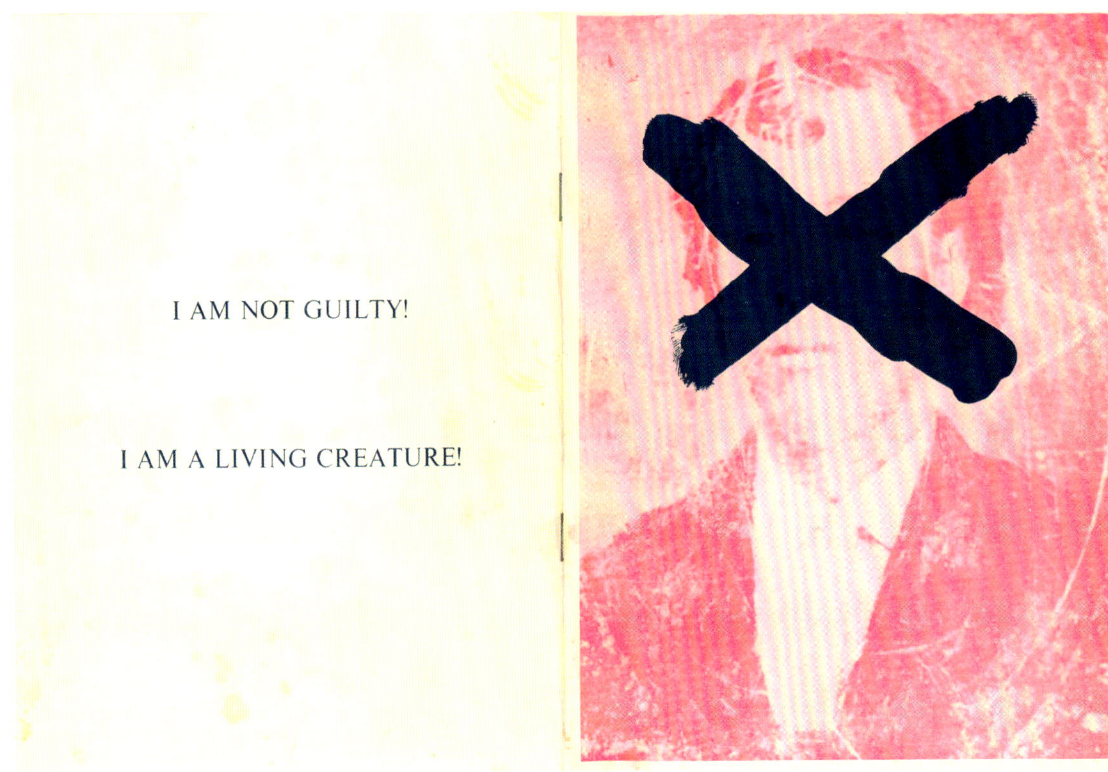
I AM NOT GUILTY!
I AM A LIVING CREATURE!

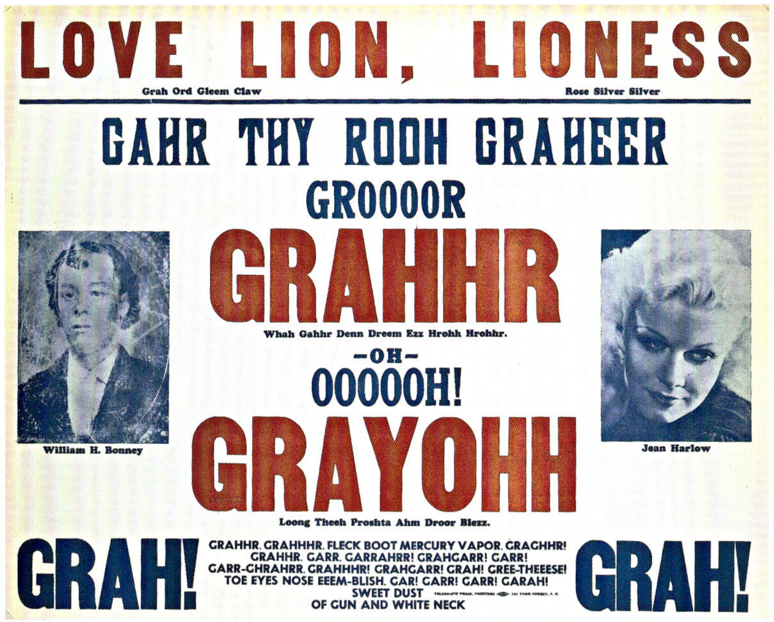

McClure has written a series of theater pieces he describes as "visionary comedies": The first, written in 1959, was titled *Raptors*, and the third, *The Feast*, was staged in 1960 at Billy Jahrmarkt's Batman Gallery. McClure became close to Joan and Billy Jahrmarkt, and often ran the gallery for them in the mornings. In 1961 McClure joined up with David Meltzer and Lawrence Ferlinghetti to launch the *Journal for the Protection of All Beings: A Visionary and Revolutionary Review*, which they continued to publish until 1978.

During the 1960s McClure saw a lot of Berman, who included a section of McClure's poem of 1963, "Ghost Tantra," in *Semina 8*. Berman created cover art for the poem when it was published as a book the following year, and in 1964, the ninth and final issue of *Semina* was comprised of a McClure poem written in response to the assassination of John Kennedy.

In 1964 Diane DiPrima's American Theater for Poets staged a production in New York of McClure's *The Blossom or Billy the Kid*, with sets by George Herms, who also created a lobby environment for the Los Angeles debut of McClure's play, *The Beard*, in 1967. McClure was spending a good deal of time in Southern California then, and in 1968 he became acquainted with the members of rock group, The Doors; nineteen years later he and Doors's keyboardist, Ray Manzarek, began collaborating on stage. Their performing partnership continues to be a significant aspect of McClure's life, as does his interest in nature. In 1972 he was part of a contingent of poets and intellectuals who attended the U.N. Environmental Conference in Stockholm.

McClure's first marriage ended in the early 1980s, and in 1986 he met artist Amy Evans, whom he married in 1998. The couple live in Oakland, where McClure teaches at the California College of Arts and Crafts. He continues to write regularly, and at this point has published more than sixty volumes of poetry. *Kristine McKenna*

1 David Meltzer, ed., *San Francisco Beat: Talking With the Poets* (San Francisco: City Lights Books, 2001), p. 185
2 Sandra Leonard Starr, *Lost and Found in California: Four Decades of Assemblage Art* (Los Angeles: Corcoran, Shoshona Wayne, and Pence Galleries, 1988), p. 95.
3 From a conversation with Michael McClure, January 29, 2000.

Taylor Mead

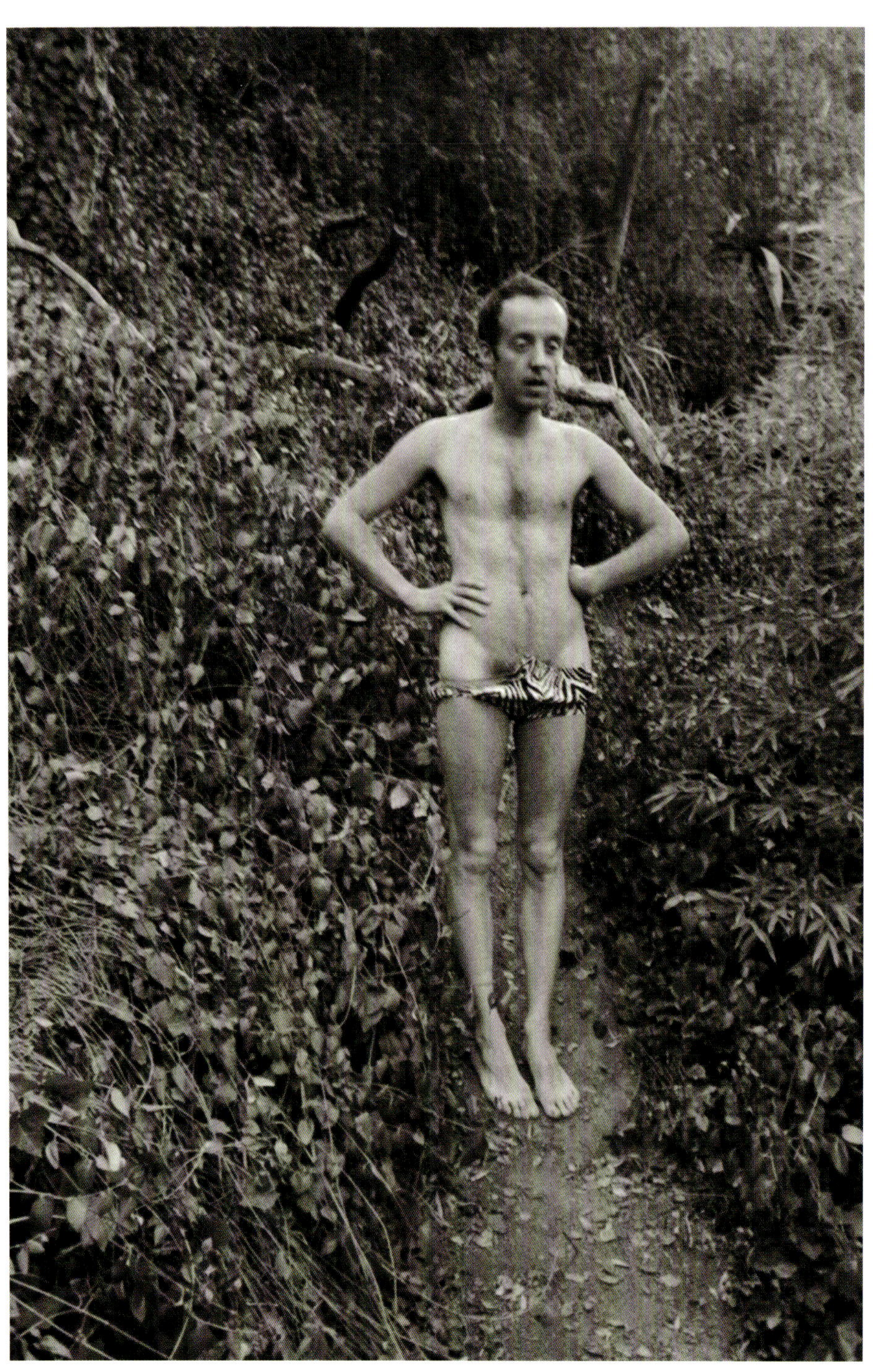

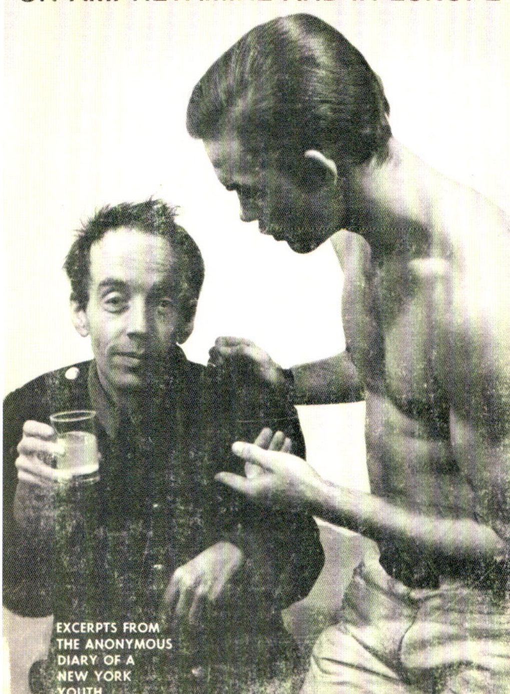

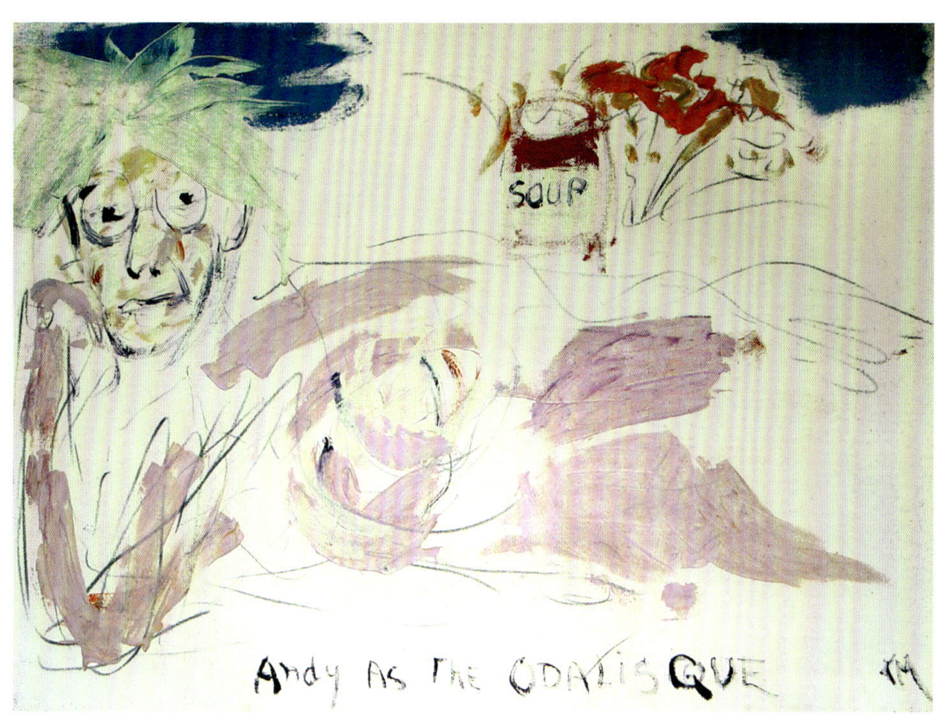

Taylor Mead was born in 1937 to a prominent family in Detroit, Michigan. As a child Mead led a life of privilege, and he was a popular student who excelled in theater and the arts at the various private schools he attended. As Mead moved into his teenage years he began to lose his bearings, however, and he embarked on a decade spent hitch-hiking around the country, drifting and in search of something. During those years he spent nine months at the Pasadena Playhouse; he was drafted into the army then rejected for medical reasons; and he held various desk jobs at Merrill Lynch in Detroit.

Because Mead was a gay man with a penchant for challenging authority, Detroit wasn't the most hospitable place for him, so in 1956 he moved to New York. He immediately began making a name for himself as an actor and landed the starring role in Ron Rice's cult film of 1960, *The Flower Thief.* At approximately the same time, Mead became a fixture on Manhattan's coffeehouse circuit, where his readings from his witty diary, *Excerpts From the Anonymous Diary of a New York Youth* were met with enthusiasm. (The third and concluding volume of Mead's diaries, *On Amphetamine and in Europe*, was published in 1968). During those early years in New York, Mead began making paintings, and he continues to produce them today, albeit at a very slow pace.

Mead's life underwent a significant transformation in 1962 when he met Andy Warhol, who took him under his wing as a protégée and cast him in several films, including *Lonesome Cowboys* in 1968. It was through Warhol that Mead met Wallace Berman, who appeared with him in Warhol's 1964 film, *Tarzan and Jane Regained, Sort Of...* Mead has collaborated with several notable underground filmmakers, performed extensively onstage, and won an Obie Award for his work in Frank O'Hara's *The General Returns From One Place to Another*. Mead continues to act, write and paint in New York City.

Kristine McKenna

p. 220
Taylor Mead in a scene from Andy Warhol's Tarzan and Jane Regained, Sort of... shot in the backyard of the Berman home in Beverly Glen, 1963. Photograph by Wallace Berman.

p. 221 top left
Taylor Mead, *Andy as the Odalisque*, n.d., Oil and acrylic on canvas.

p. 221 top right
Taylor Mead, *On Amphetamine in Europe: Excerpts from the Anonymous Diary of a New York Youth, Vol. 3* (New York: Boss Books, 1968). Cover photograph by John Chamberlain.

David Meltzer

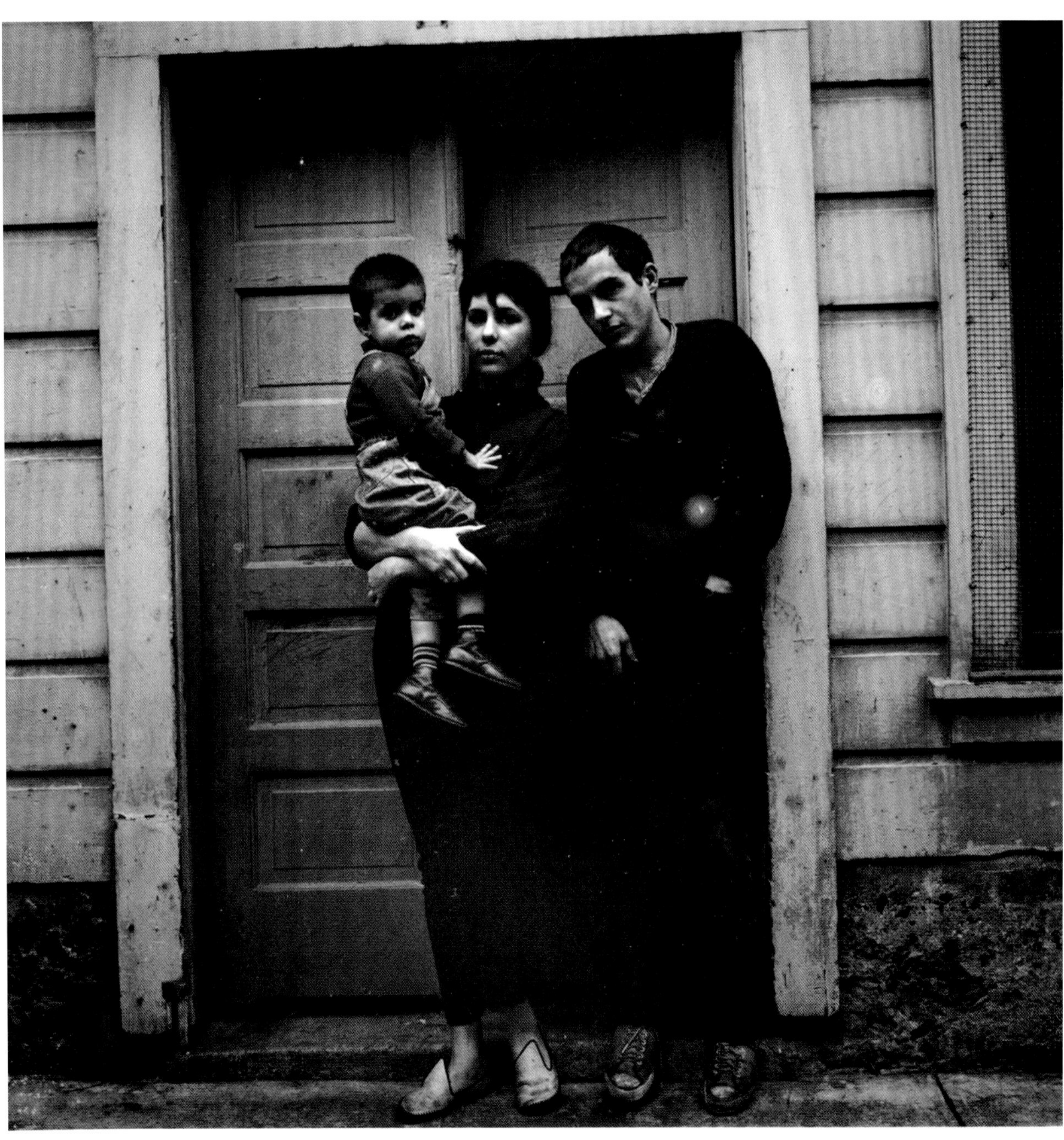

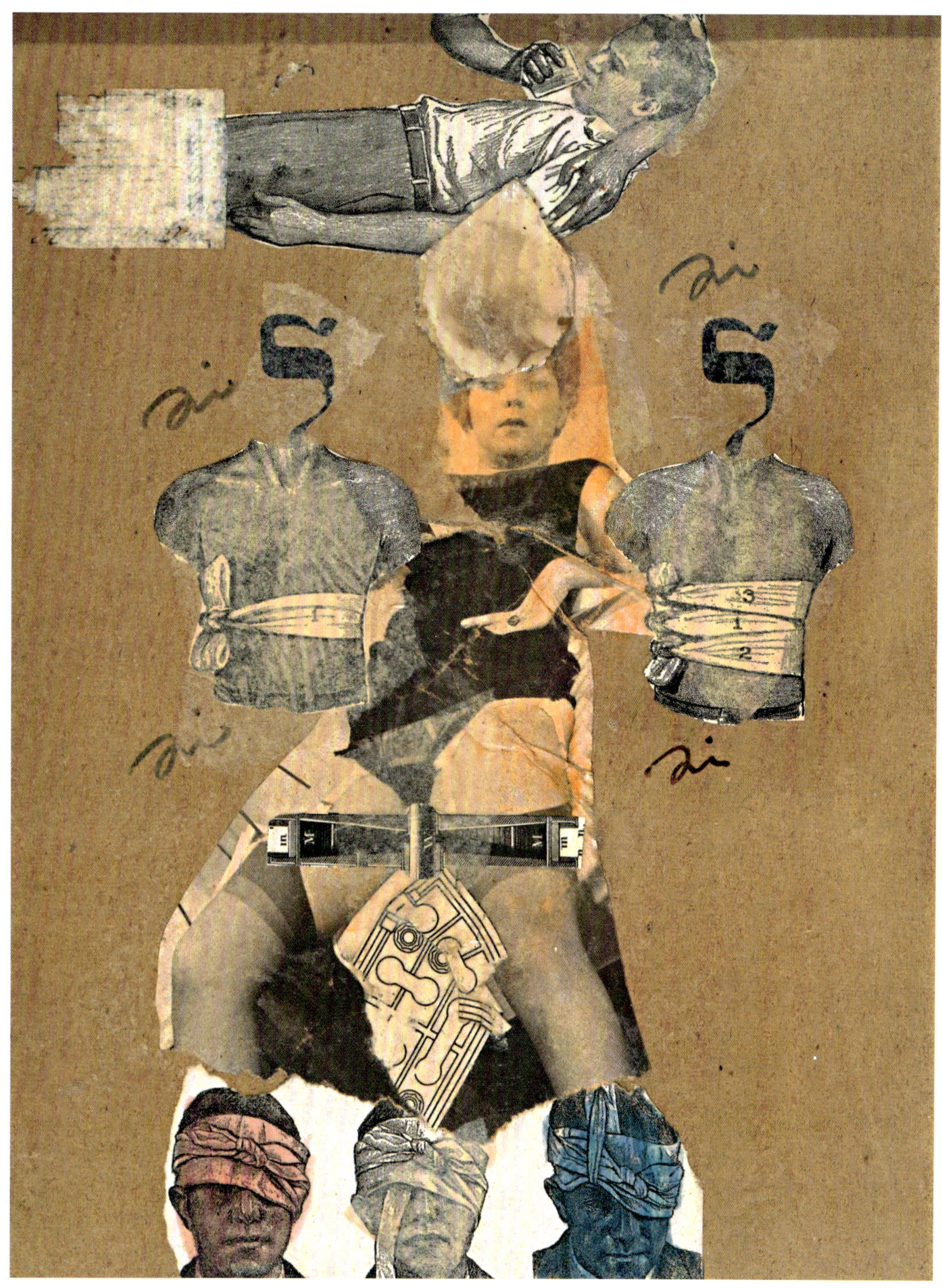

The die was cast for David Meltzer when he was nine years old and his father took him to see Charlie Parker at the Royal Roost in Manhattan; Meltzer realized then that the hipster's life was for him. "I liked the way they wore their clothes," Meltzer has recalled,[1] and he began fulfilling his destiny at the age of eleven when he wrote his first poem.

Born in Rochester, New York in 1937, Meltzer moved to Los Angeles in 1954 with his father following his parents' divorce. A precocious child who was reading Éluard, Aragon and Lorca by the age of thirteen, Meltzer had begun performing on *The Horn & Hardart Children's Hour* as a child in New York, and on arriving in Southern California his father, who was a musician and writer, encouraged him to pursue a career in show business. Meltzer had no interest in Hollywood, however, as he was already determined to be a poet. Just seventeen when he arrived in Southern California, Meltzer briefly split his time between classes at Fairfax High School and Los Angeles City College. However, it didn't take him long to deduce that his time would be better spent dispensing with school and devoting his time to reading, which is what he did.

At the time, Meltzer was dating artist Peggy Halper, who rented her studio on Santa Monica Boulevard to Ed Kienholz, who had recently arrived from Washington. Kienholz's studio quickly became a hangout for the local art community, and Meltzer immediately recognized them as his tribe. He formed a particularly strong bond with Wallace Berman, who took poetry as seriously as he did; Berman included Meltzer's writing in several issues of *Semina*, and devoted the entirety of *Semina 6* to Meltzer's poem, "The Clown." Meltzer admired Berman for his ability to

> *...combine and construct the images of a culture that was becoming increasingly mass-mediated and one dimensional into artworks that contained elements of an ongoing mystery. Wallace was the ultimate metaphysical confidence man, but his con was a good one. How many cons can you think of where everyone winds up feeling good about it?*[2]

In 1957 Meltzer moved to San Francisco where he met Christina Meyer, whom he married in 1959. The Meltzers had four children together, and formed a musical duo, the Mighty Mountain String Band, that performed throughout the Bay area during the 1960s and 1970s. A gifted musician, Meltzer fronted the psychedelic band Serpent Power during the 1960s, and often read his poetry accompanied by live jazz. Several critics have noted the distinctive musicality characteristic of Meltzer's poetry, which is also marked by a witty and generous view of the complexities of human relationships, a gentle lyricism, and profound belief in the power of the written word.

p. 222
David and Tina Meltzer with their son, Robert in San Francisco, 1958. Photograph by Wallace Berman.

p. 223
David Meltzer, Untitled (bandages). Mixed-media collage, 1969.

p. 224
David Meltzer, *Luna* (Los Angeles: Black Sparrow Press, 1970). Cover art by Wallace Berman.

p. 225
David Meltzer, *Amulet (Mandala)*. Mixed-media collage, 1969.

p. 226
David Meltzer, *Amulet (Menorah)*. Acrylic and ink on canvas, 1969.

p. 227
David Meltzer, *Hero/Lil* (Los Angeles: Black Sparrow Press, 1973). Cover art by Wallace Berman.

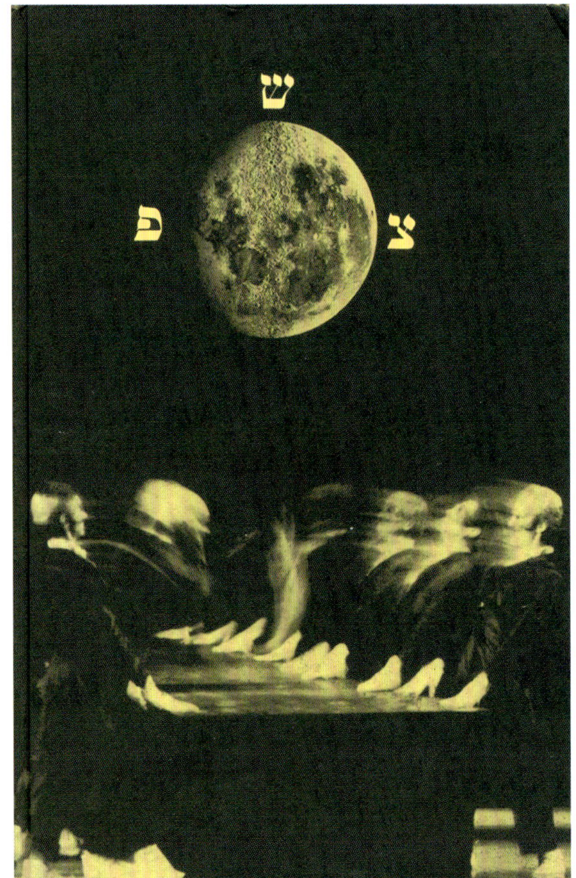

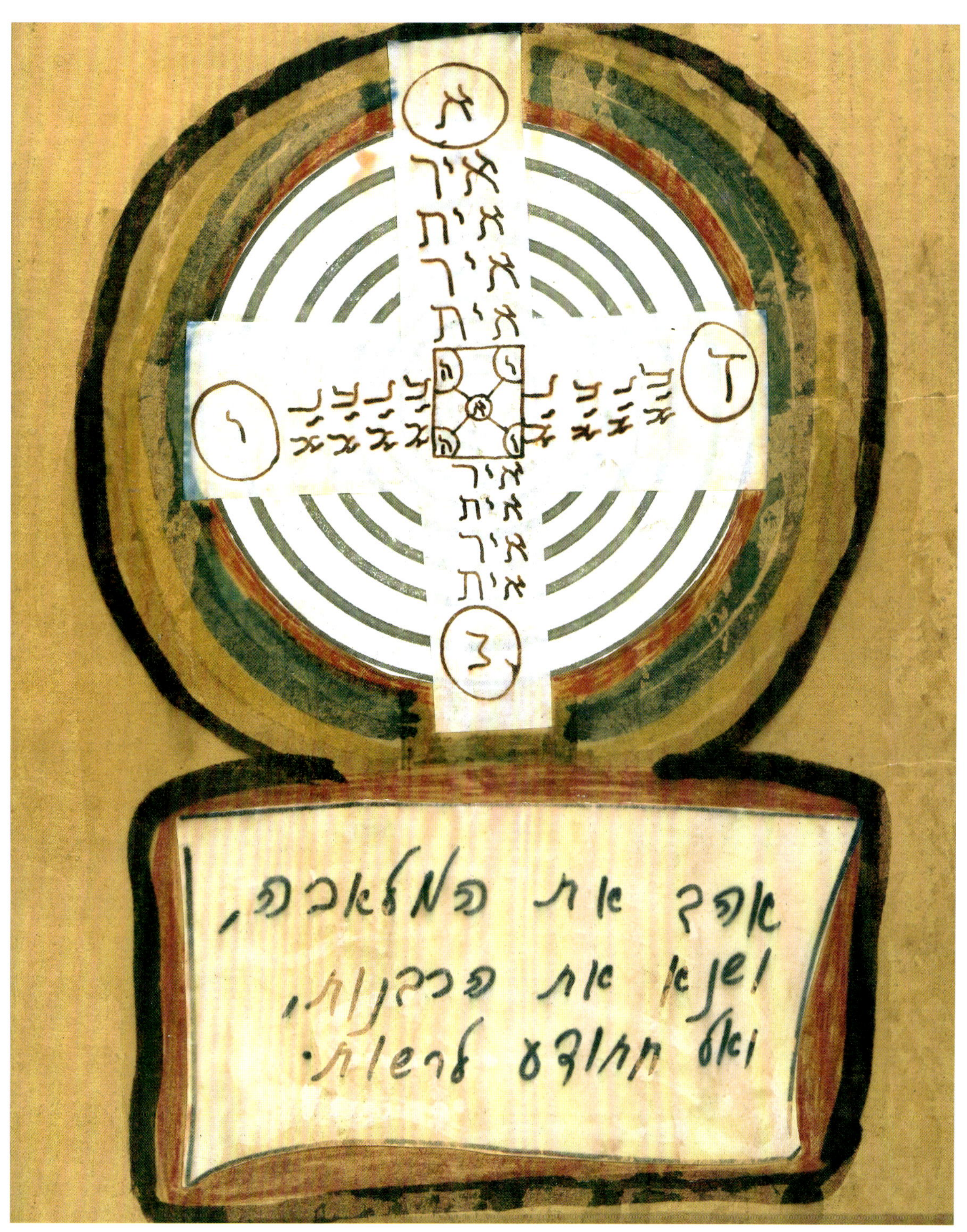
אהב את המלאכה,
ושנא את הרבנות,
ואל תתודע לרשות.

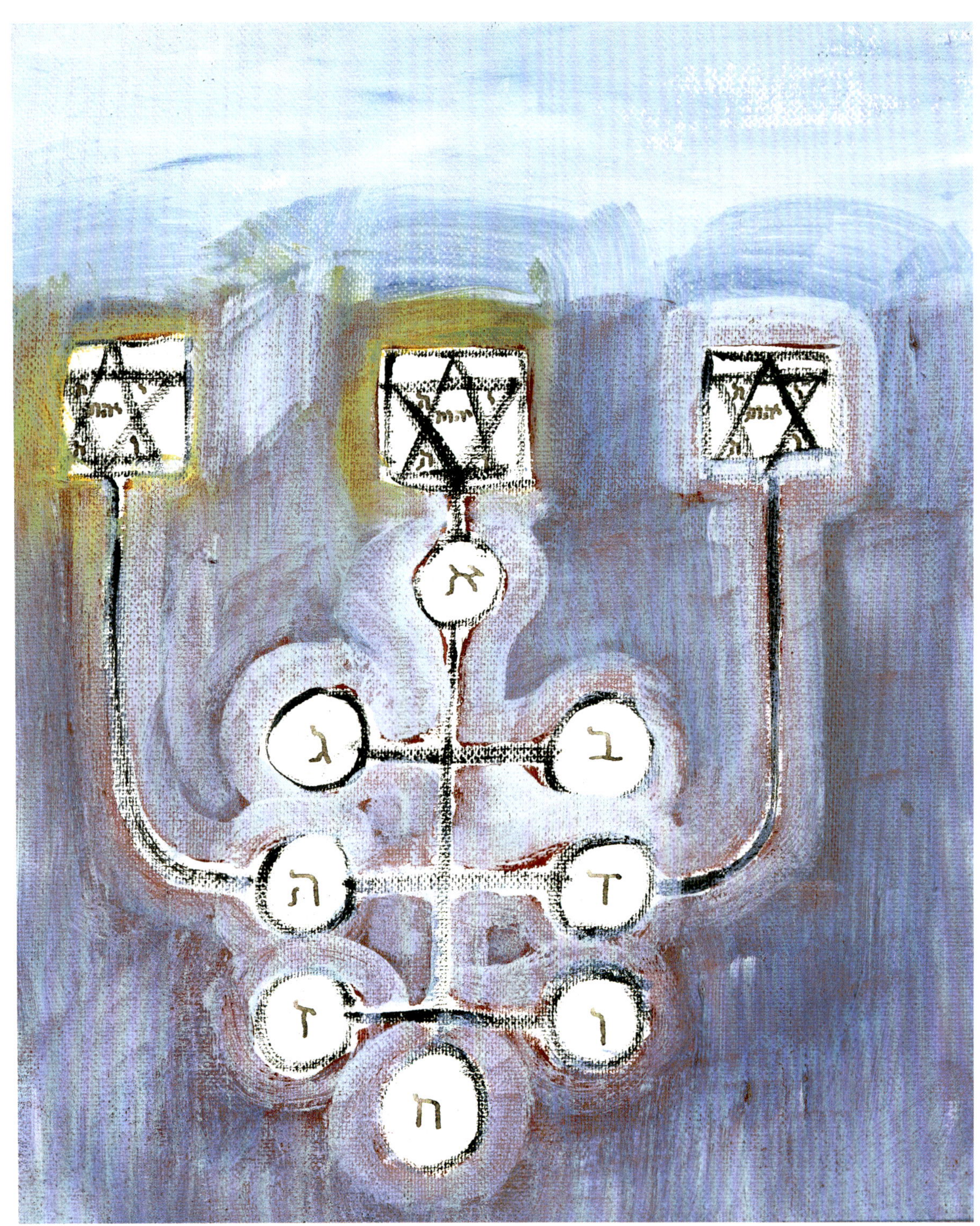
א
ג
ב
ה
ד
ז
ו
ח

"The poet is a revolutionary because he is constantly subverting corrupt institutional languages with his art," Meltzer has said. "He can make the life-denying rhetoric of power politics void by singing one coherent, true song. ...A poem can snap the lights on. That's how revolution begins."[3]

San Francisco was in the midst of a poetry renaissance when Meltzer arrived there, and he became part of a community of writers that included Michael McClure, Philip Lamantia, and Lew Welch. After settling in San Francisco, Meltzer went to work for his friend Robert Alexander, who was warehouse foreman for the book distribution outfit Paper Editions, and shortly thereafter he landed a job at The Discovery Book Store in North Beach, where he worked for nine years. During that period he launched the mail order distribution company Minotaur Books, along with Tree Books, a publishing house devoted to writings on Jewish mysticism.

In 1964 Meltzer became a serious student of the Kabbalah, and his interest in esoteric Judaism fostered an enduring friendship with poet Jack Hirschman, who has long been known for his great knowledge of the subject. Tree Books was the first American press to publish work by twentieth-century Kabbalist Edmund Jabes, and published the first complete English translation of the writings of thirteenth-century Kabbalist Abraham ben Samual Abulafia.

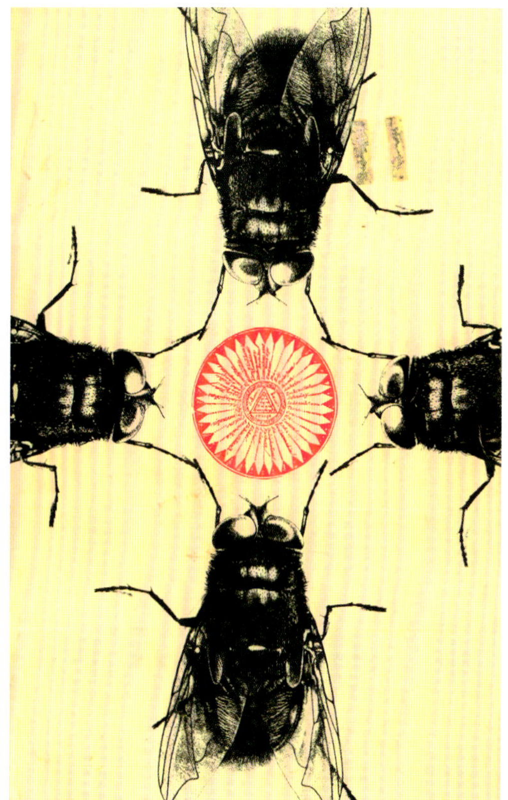

Between 1968 and 1970 Meltzer wrote a series of ten pornographic novels published by Essex House that he refers to as "agit-smut." Meltzer was an ardent feminist long before that point of view became commonplace, and the agit-smut books were his response to pornography and its subtexts of misogyny, exploitation, and imperialism. These themes can also be detected as a subtle through-line in several of his volumes of poetry, including *Bark: A Polemic* (Santa Barbara: Capra Press, 1973) and *Hero/Lil* (Los Angeles: Black Sparrow Press, 1973).

During the 1970s Meltzer taught at the Urban School in San Francisco, and developed a writing program for the California State penal institution at Vacaville. In 1971 he edited *The San Francisco Poets*, a collection of interviews with his peers, and in 2001 he compiled a second volume of interviews, *San Francisco Beat: Talking with the Poets*. (San Francisco: City Lights Books). Meltzer has edited a collection of folkloristic writings on birth (*Birth*, New York: Ballantine Books, 1973; revised edition, Berkeley: North Point Press, 1981), along with anthologies of writings on jazz and Kabbalism. He has published more than a dozen volumes of poetry, including an homage to all forms of music, *Harps* (Berkeley: Oyez, 1975), and *Two-Way Mirror*, (Berkeley: Oyez, 1977), an inquiry into the act of writing poetry which is structured as a children's primer. Meltzer's most recent book is *Beat Thing* (Albuquerque: La Alameda Press, 2004), an epic poem about the commercialization of the Beat Generation. Meltzer continues to teach and write in the Bay Area.

Kristine McKenna

1 From a conversation with Kristine McKenna on December 18, 1998.

2 Ibid.

3 Robert Hawley and Ann Charters, "David Meltzer," in Ann Charters, ed., *Dictionary of Literary Biography 16* (Detroit: Bruccoli Clark/Gale, 1983), p. 409.

Henry Miller

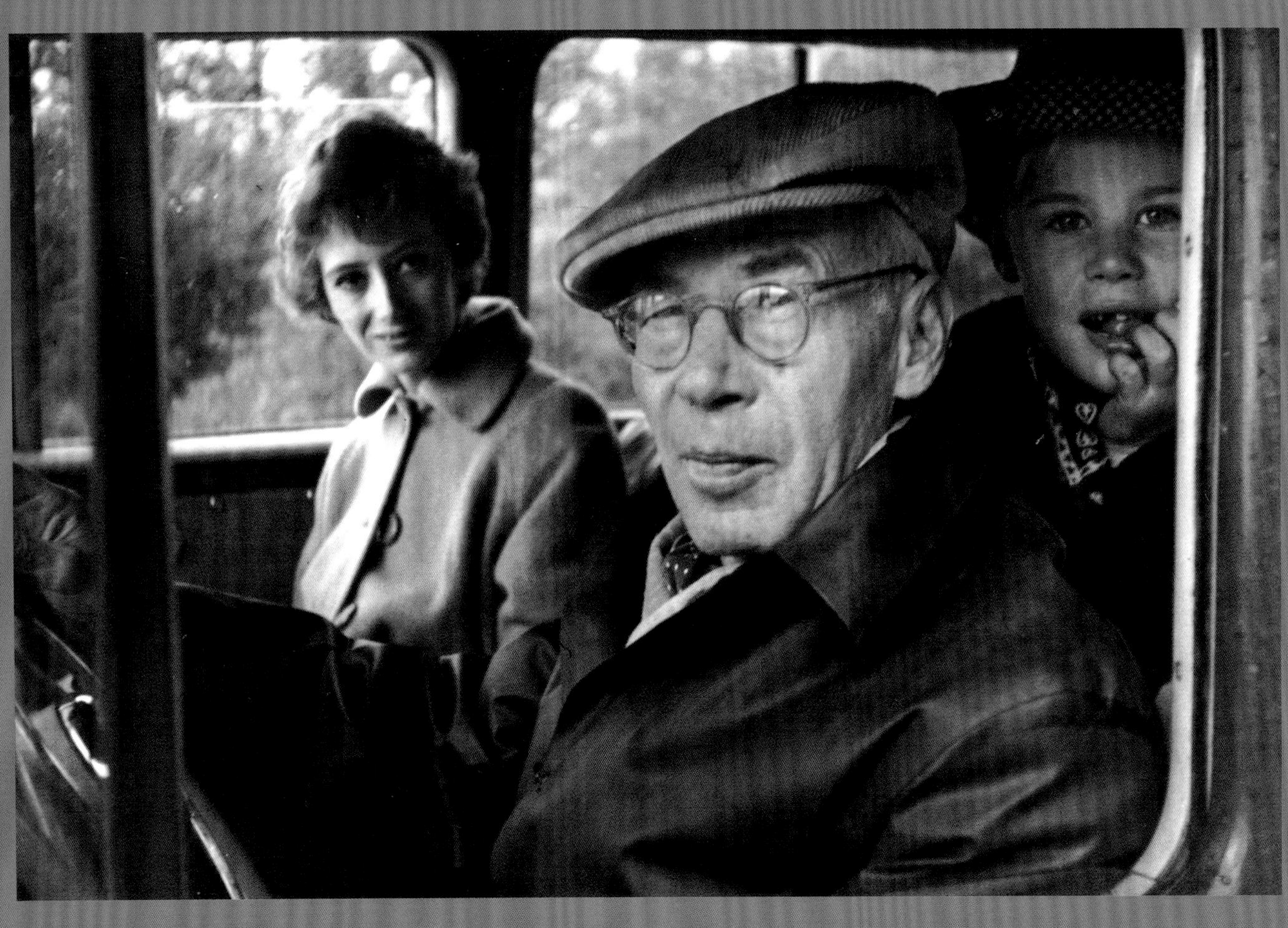

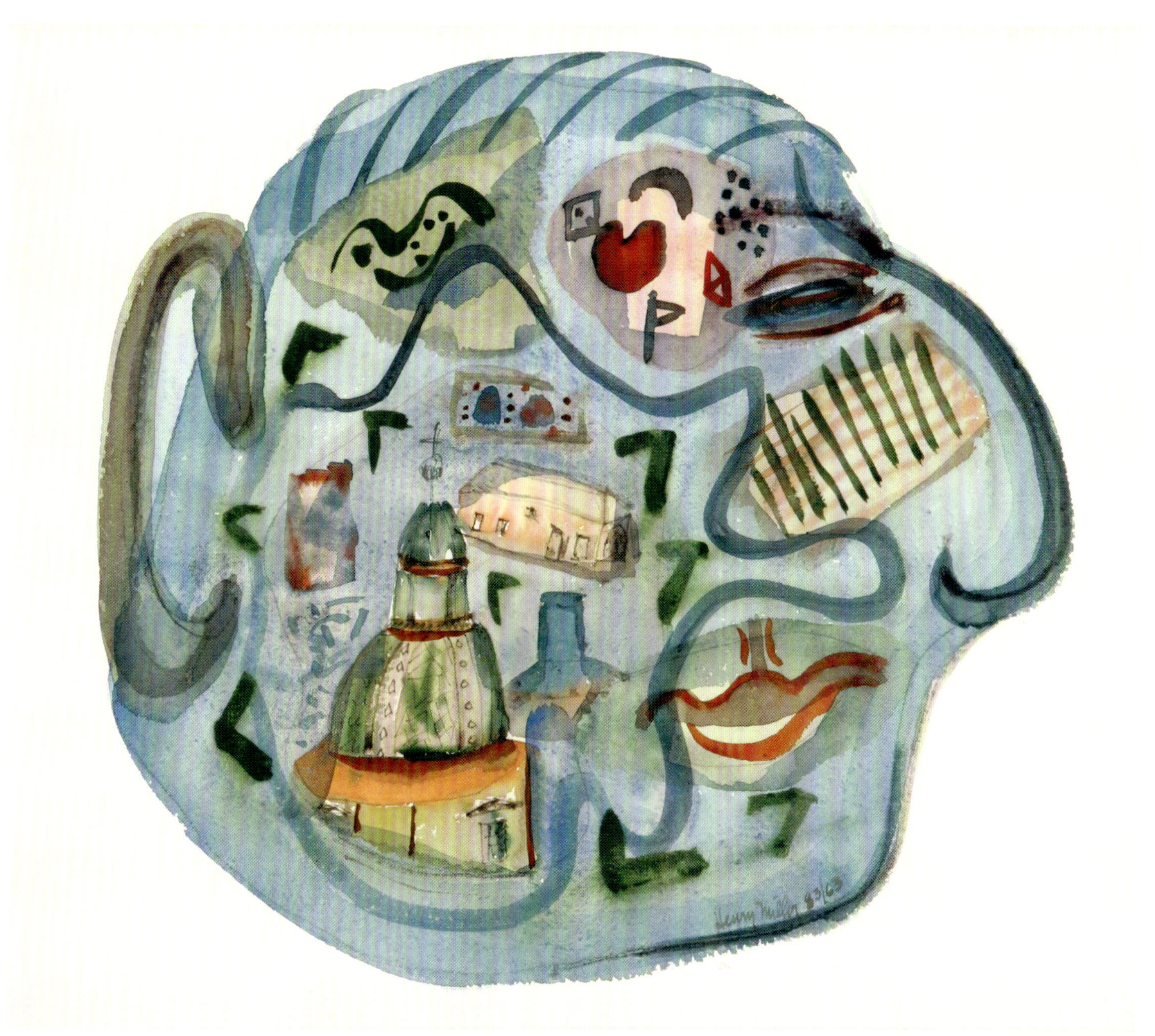

Henry Miller crossed paths with Wallace Berman just a few times, but he was regarded as a mentor and a hero by Berman and his peers. A bridge figure in American letters poised between Walt Whitman and Allen Ginsberg, Miller was a writer of tremendous generosity and breadth. The candid portrayal of sexuality in Miller's writing caused the subtler aspects of his aesthetic to go largely overlooked, however, and he lost considerable cultural currency with the advent of the feminist movement in the 1960s. Miller was widely attacked as a misogynist during that heady decade, but a close reading of his work shows him to be a writer of enormous humanism and complexity.

Born in New York City in 1891, Miller was the only child of German immigrants. Miller's father was a tailor and his mother was a controlling woman with bourgeois values Miller rejected from an early age. After high school Miller enrolled in City College of New York, but he dropped out after two months and worked a series of odd jobs. In 1917 he married the first of his five wives, Beatrice Sylvas Wickens, with whom he had a daughter. In 1920 he was hired by Western Union to work as a messenger, a job that left him sufficient free time to write. During the 1920s Miller turned out dozens of essays and short stories, most of which were rejected by the magazines he submitted them to.

p. 228
Henry Miller and Valentine Miller with Shirley Berman, Big Sur, 1954, Photograph by Wallace Berman.

p. 229
Henry Miller, *Blue Head*, 1963, Watercolor on paper.

p. 230
Henry Miller, Postcard to Wallace Berman, 1964.

p. 231
Henry Miller, *Womanish Dreams*, 1951, Watercolor on paper.

By 1923 Miller's first marriage had eroded, and, after a brief affair with his mother-in-law, he left Beatrice for June Mansfield, a taxi dancer he married in 1924. In 1930 he moved to Paris, and during his years there he devoured the writings of Rimbaud and Hesse, and developed an appreciation for the Surrealists—Miller listed André Breton's *Nadja* as one of his favorite books.

Miller's turbulent relationship with Mansfield, which continued for eight stormy years, opened the floodgates for him as a writer; Mansfield, in fact, was the catalyst for Miller's first and most notorious book, *Tropic of Cancer*, which was published in 1934 with funds supplied by Miller's friend and former lover, Anaïs Nin. *Tropic of Cancer* was followed two years later by *Tropic of Capricorn*, at which point Miller's reputation as a writer of dirty books was irrevocably established. Both books were banned in the United States for three decades, and were at the center of a landmark ruling on censorship made by the U.S. Supreme Court in 1964. For Berman, whose first art exhibition had been closed on grounds of obscenity, this was no small thing.

Oct. 1, 1964

Dear Wally,

On Oct. 7 my interview with Steve Allen will broadcast in the last third of his program (34 minutes) on channel 5.

My best, Henry

PS: Where is that Semina?

Miller never let the legal problems his books generated slow him down, and, by 1939, when the approach of World War II prompted him to return to the States, he'd completed three more books and dozens of essays. Arriving back in America, Miller spent two years traveling the country reacquainting himself with his homeland. The journey resulted in *The Air-Conditioned Nightmare* (1945), a book that can be summarized in Miller's observation that "the American way of life has created a spiritual and cultural wasteland." The Beat Generation, still gestating when Miller wrote the book, would agree.

Deciding he'd had enough of New York, Miller settled in Beverly Glen, California in 1942, and then, at the end of 1943, he moved to Big Sur. In 1944 he married a young philosophy student named Janina Martha Lepska with whom he had two children. The marriage ended after seven years, but Miller remained in Big Sur with his fourth wife, Eve McClure, whom he married in 1953. Miller's years in Big Sur were productive ones. In 1949 he completed *Sexus*, the first part of a planned trilogy deconstructing his years with June Mansfield titled *The Rosy Crucifixion* (he completed *Nexus* in 1960 and then abandoned the project). He also deepened his painting practice dramatically. Miller began making watercolors during his years in Paris, but it wasn't until he settled in Big Sur that he really devoted himself to it; he turned out hundreds of watercolors during his eighteen years there.

Time to paint—or do anything else—grew scarce for Miller during the 1950s, as his modest home became an increasingly popular site of pilgrimage for bohemians of every stripe. By 1960 the traffic had become unbearable and Miller moved again, this time to Pacific Palisades, a small beach community in southern California. His fourth marriage dissolved the year he moved, and his drive to write was leaving him; for the remainder of his life, painting was his central creative outlet. In 1967 he married a young Japanese cabaret singer, Hiroko Tokuda, whom he divorced ten years later. Miller died in Pacific Palisades in 1980. *Kristine McKenna*

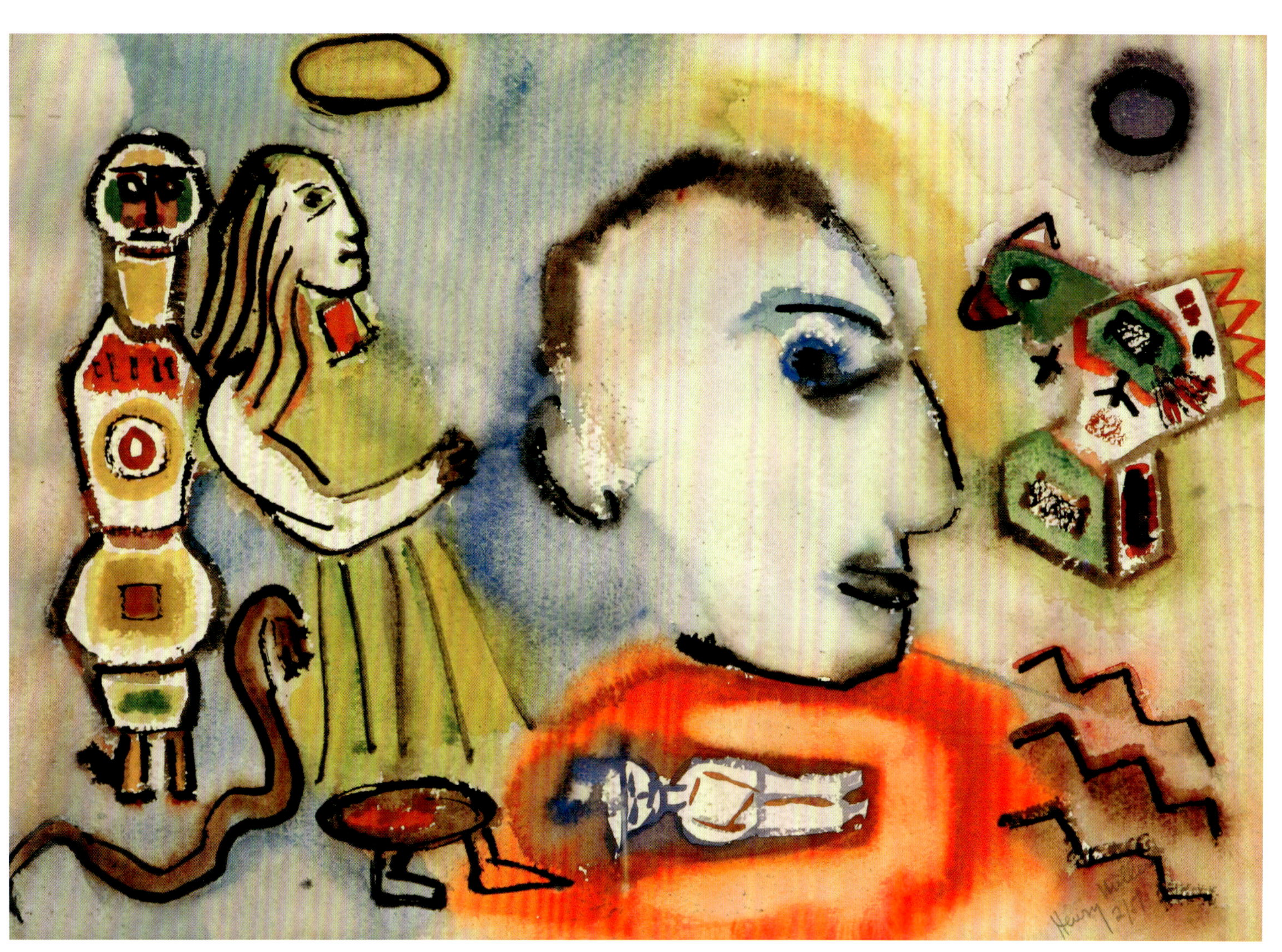

DiDi Morrill

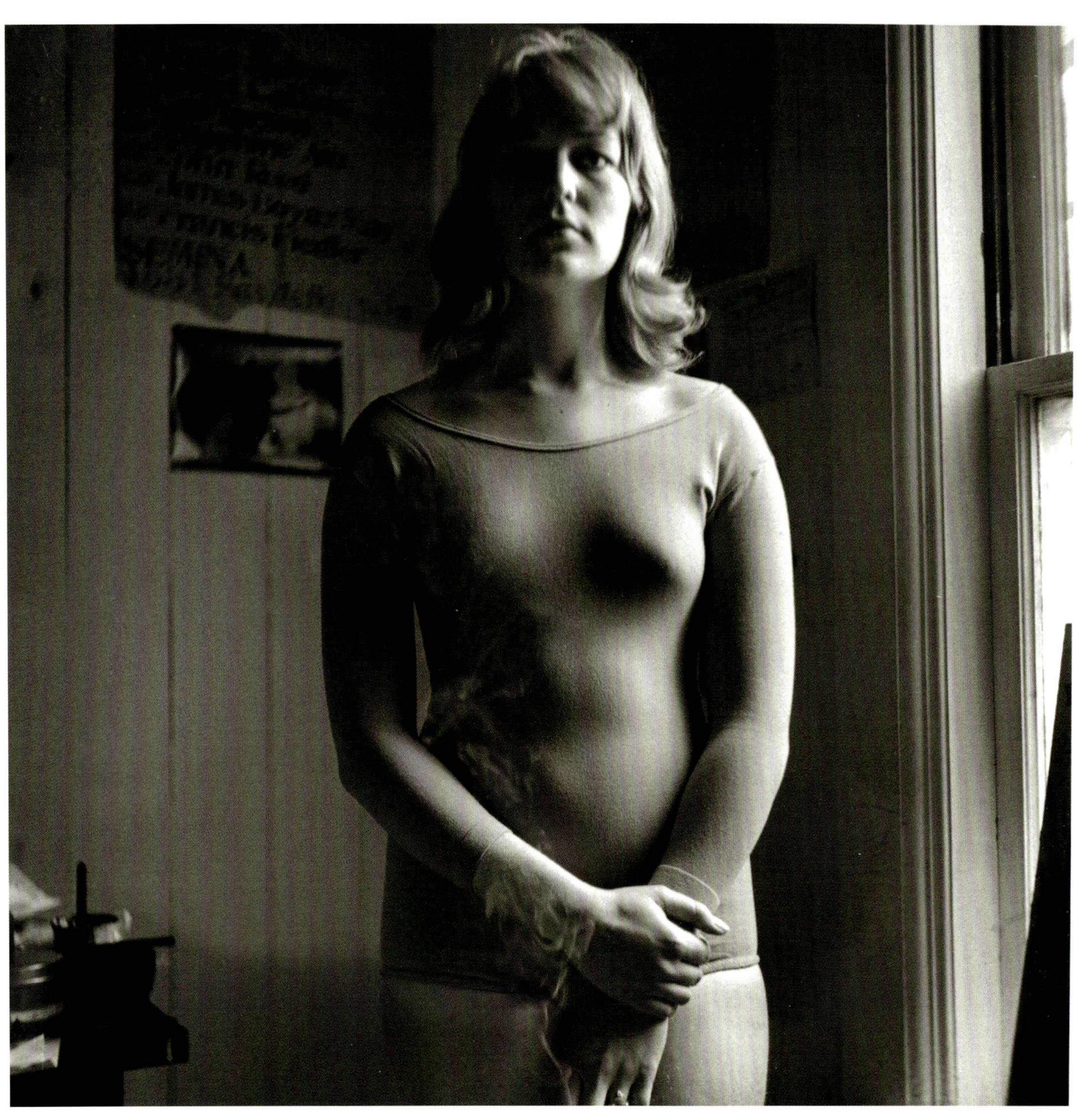

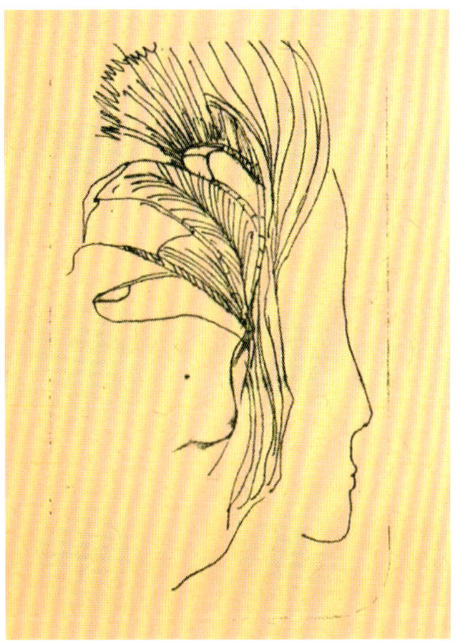

DiDi Morrill was born Sharon Diane Morrill in 1938, in San Leandro, California. Her father was a welder, and she had one brother, Terry Morrill, who was born in 1945. When she was a teenager she began hanging out on the North Beach Beat scene, and when she was eighteen she became a stewardess for United Airlines. She didn't enjoy the regimentation of the job, however, and left it after a year and became involved with musician Gerry Mulligan. In 1957 she began living with poet Kirby Doyle, who wrote two books—*Happiness Bastard* and *Angel Faint*—that were inspired by her.

"My sister had a big heart, but she was also a criminal," comments Terry Morrill of his sister, who supported herself through the late 1950s and 1960s with various acts of petty crime. "That started early; then after she left home she began stealing and using drugs—she was quite an addict. She was also fearless, and she spent a lot of time smuggling drugs in false-bottomed suitcases that she made herself. She dug the action and adrenalin of criminal activity."[1]

By 1963 Morrill had left Doyle and was living in Beverly Glen Canyon with Bobby Driscoll, whom she married shortly after they met. In 1964 they traveled to New York for a drug deal that went bad, and Morrill fled to Canada where she spent the next fifteen years on Canada's wanted list. She spent the remainder of her life in and out of various penitentiaries, on charges of drugs, credit card fraud, and racketeering. She was living alone in Hemet, California, at the time of her death, in 1999, from a heart attack at the age of sixty. *Kristine McKenna*

1 Conversation with Terry Morrill, November 4, 2003

DIDO

**Dido – US Citizen – Never Married – No children – Thief, fraud,
Con – educated by masters – on the street – travel – prison –**

**Dido – I am looking for the great man. To offer my services to. To
Serve in any way I can. I am a thief, a fraud, a con, but one who
Takes only from the enemy. And then, only to give back, for those
Who must be taken care of. I am a lioness who loves the hunt.**

**My value is my extreme mobility. I have no one. I am a
Wanderer. Who never travels on her own name. A master forger.
A provider of documents. Who has a fascination for plastics. A
Master false-bottom suitcase maker, a molder of fiberglass, one who
Can infiltrate the headquarters of the beast.**

**A protector of friends, of benefactors, who has been blessed with
Fortunes and has squandered them. Who is ready to retire to the
Cave. Who has no need of material things –**

**One who has learned her ax, her instrument. One who is
incorruptible – thank God! – who has no desire for power over
anyone. Adept with weapons, with no fear of violence if used
sparingly, specifically, to set an example, only to instruct –**

**With knowledge of airports, of smuggling; Afghanistan, Pakistan,
India, Indonesia, Australia, Canada, the US of A
Who has knowledge of the enemy's methods, of drugs; is an expert
on heroin and the effects thereof, of morphine, amphetamine,
hallucinogens, hashish –
One who can keep a secret**

**One who loves life, loves music, art, literature, philosophy, the
Ancestors and God. But
Most of all, loves God.**

p. 232
DiDi Morrill, San Francisco, 1959.
Photograph by Wallace Berman.

p. 233 top left
DiDi Morrill, drawing for the poem "Sunday Bonnet," by Bobby Driscoll, *Floating Bear*, Issue 33, 1967.

p. 233 top right
DiDi Morrill, *DIDO*, Poem published in *Black Ace Book 7* (Los Angeles: Temple of Man, ed. Marsha Getzler, 2002).

Stuart Perkoff

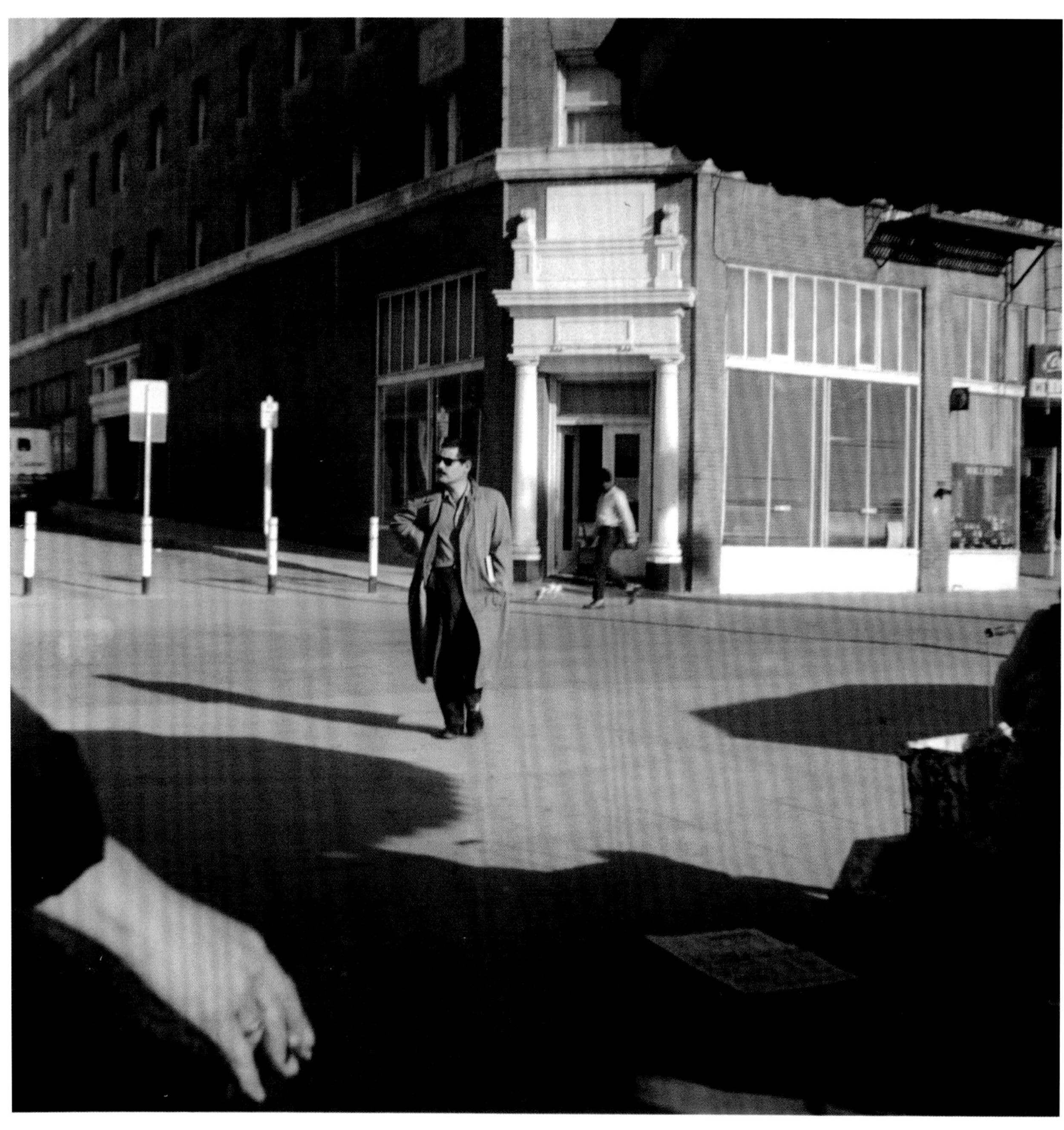

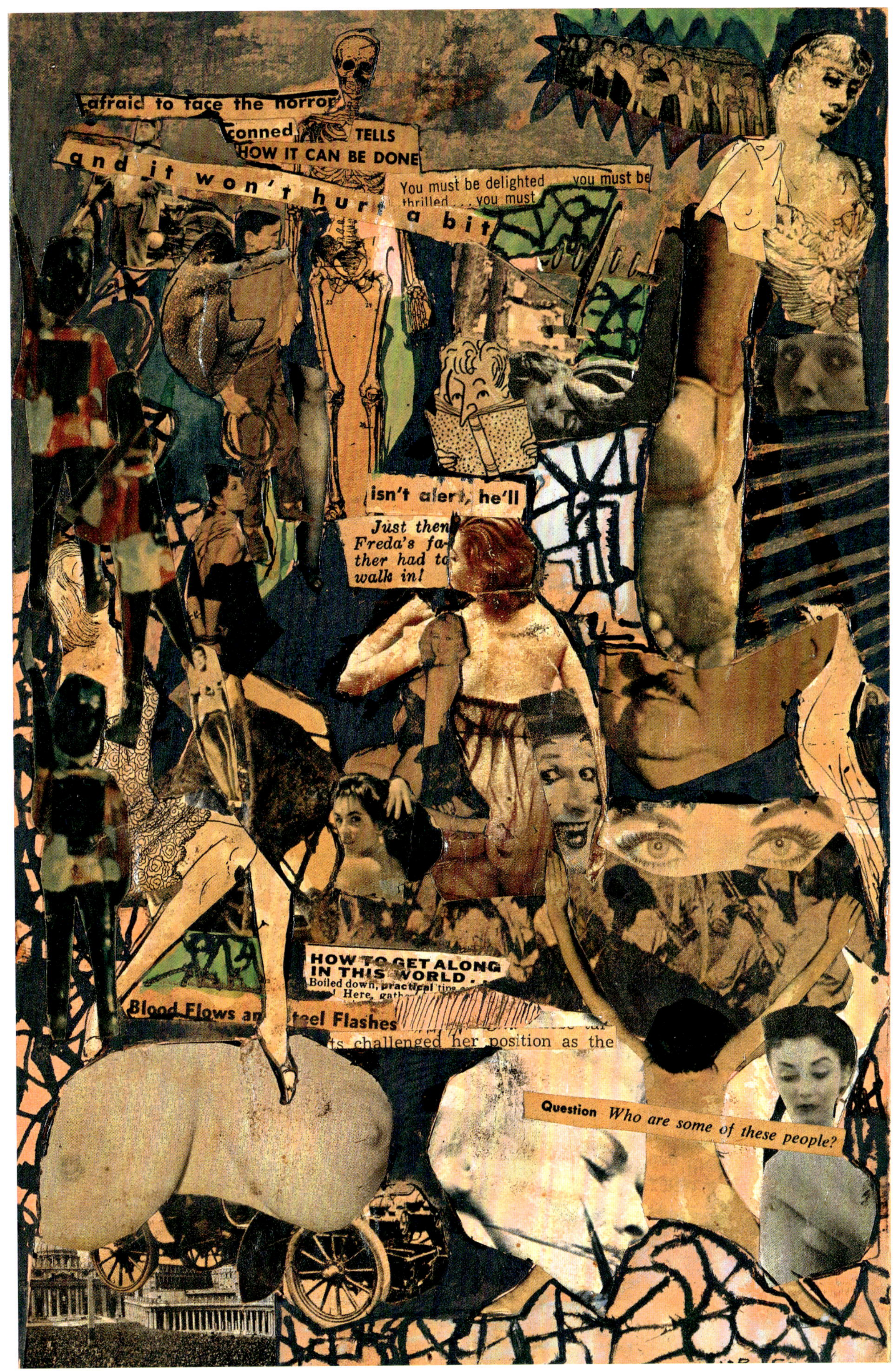
afraid to face the horror
conned
TELLS
HOW IT CAN BE DONE
and it won't hurt a bit
You must be delighted
you must be
isn't alert, he'll
Just then
Freda's fa-
ther had to
walk in!
HOW TO GET ALONG
IN THIS WORLD.
Boiled down, practical
Blood Flows
Flashes
challenged her position as the
Question Who are some of these people?

Stuart Perkoff has achieved cult status as the most accomplished poet associated with the "Venice West" group, even though many of his poems were allegedly destroyed or have been lost. Perkoff's compulsive behavior and drug addiction were counterbalanced by a genuine devotion to writing and a poetic voice of sophisticated urgency. Although he was infrequently published in his lifetime, several hundred unpublished poems have recently been collected, published along with those from his eight books in a 473-page volume, *Voices of the Lady: Collected Poems*, edited by the poet's brother.

Perkoff was well-known in Wallace Berman's circle, writing works dedicated to Allen Ginsberg, Ben Talbert, Kirby Doyle, and Bob Alexander. Berman included his poem, "Boplicity," in *Semina 4*. In an essay on Perkoff, Robert Creeley praised his "ability to take on the scale and fact of social despair and make of it a statement specific to what it was literally, not the usual conversion to charitable understanding or distancing social judgment."[2] Creeley alludes to Perkoff's writings about his heroin addiction as an accepted matter of fact: "It was part of himself and he took it therefore as real."

Born in 1930 in St. Louis to a Jewish bookmaker father and art-enthusiast mother, Perkoff became interested in politics as a bookish yet charismatic teenager, associating himself with anarchist rabble-rousers in the city slums. He joined the Communist Party, spent evenings in a bar called Little Bohemia, and began to write poetry in the style of Kenneth Patchen.[3] When Party leaders didn't take kindly to his lyrical love poems, he gave up membership and, impulsively, at age seventeen, left home for New York.

In the city he led a bohemian life, working in a drill press shop, writing poetry, and reading voraciously. In 1948, when the peacetime draft law went into effect, Perkoff turned himself in for failing to register--and later proudly claimed to be the first postwar draft resister. His father flew east to get him out of jail and brought him back to the West Coast where his family had moved. While working at a hamburger stand in Santa Barbara, Perkoff fell in love with a literate University of California student named Suzan Blanchard. The two married, and fled to New York. Shortly with a newborn and economically strapped, they were forced to return west, settling in Venice Beach, which was beginning to blossom as a haven for poets.

Soon they had two more children to support and were nearly destitute, but, despite the hardships, Perkoff's writing was on track. His first book, *The Suicide Room* (Karlsruhe: Jonathan Williams, 1956), which included poems written for Luis Buñuel, poet Jackson MacLow, and San Francisco abstract painter John Hultberg, was accepted by New York publisher and poet Jonathan Williams. He quickly became a primary figure in the living room salon of Lawrence Lipton, the self-proclaimed literary lion of what he dubbed "Venice West." These gatherings encouraged Perkoff to investigate literary history and apply more discipline to his work. Lipton recorded the poetry readings at soirees that regularly featured Perkoff's gravelly voiced, growling recitations.

While Perkoff attempted to earn a living through a string of low-paying day jobs, his family struggled to survive. Suffering from the pressures, Suzan began a decline into delusional schizophrenia that was later recounted in Lipton's book, *The Holy Barbarians* (New York: Julian Messner, 1959). After his wife was released from the state hospital in Camarillo, the Perkoffs borrowed money from their parents to open a coffeehouse, Venice West Café Expresso, whose wall Perkoff painted with an inscription by Wallace Berman taken from *Semina Two*, "Art is love is God."

While his marriage continued to deteriorate, Perkoff pledged allegiance to a mysterious female muse—the "Lady"—whom he claimed literally provided him with poems. Perkoff's 1950s and 1960s journals include entries

p. 234
Stuart Perkoff, Venice, 1965, Photograph by Wallace Berman.

p. 235
Stuart Perkoff, Untitled *("Afraid to face the horror")*, 1960, Ink, gouache, and collage on paper.

p. 236
Stuart Perkoff, *Alphabet* (Los Angeles & Fairfax: Red Hill Press, 1973), cover by Wallace Berman

p. 237 top
Stuart Perkoff, Loose page from Journal, May 1965, Ink and gouache on paper.

p. 237 bottom
Journal, April 1960, Mixed-media bound manuscript.

p. 238
Stuart Perkoff, Untitled *("Their skulls are of lead")*, Mixed-media collage on paper.

p. 239
Untitled, Journal, 1965, Collaged Cover.

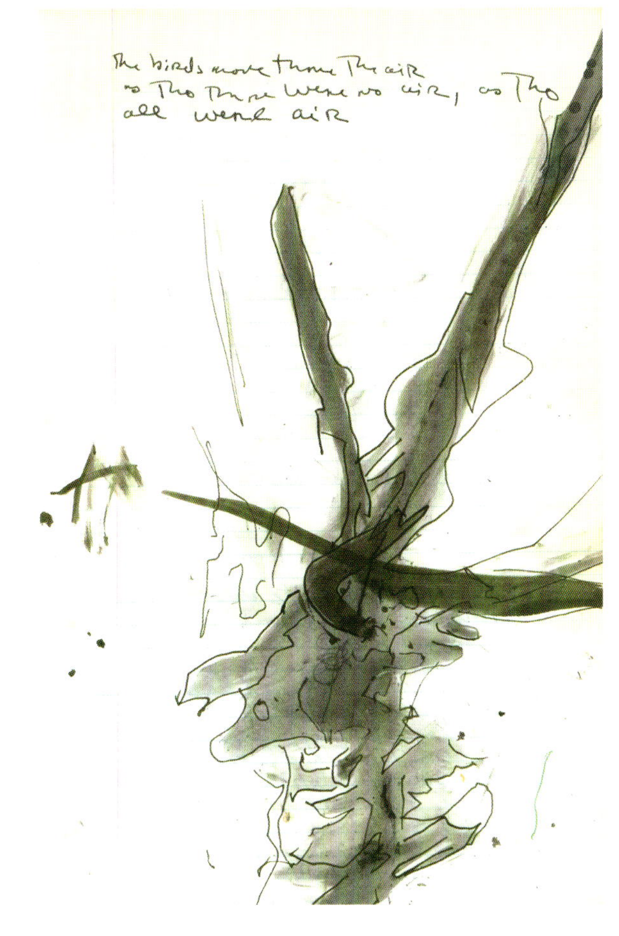
The birds move thru the air
as tho there were no air, as tho
all were air

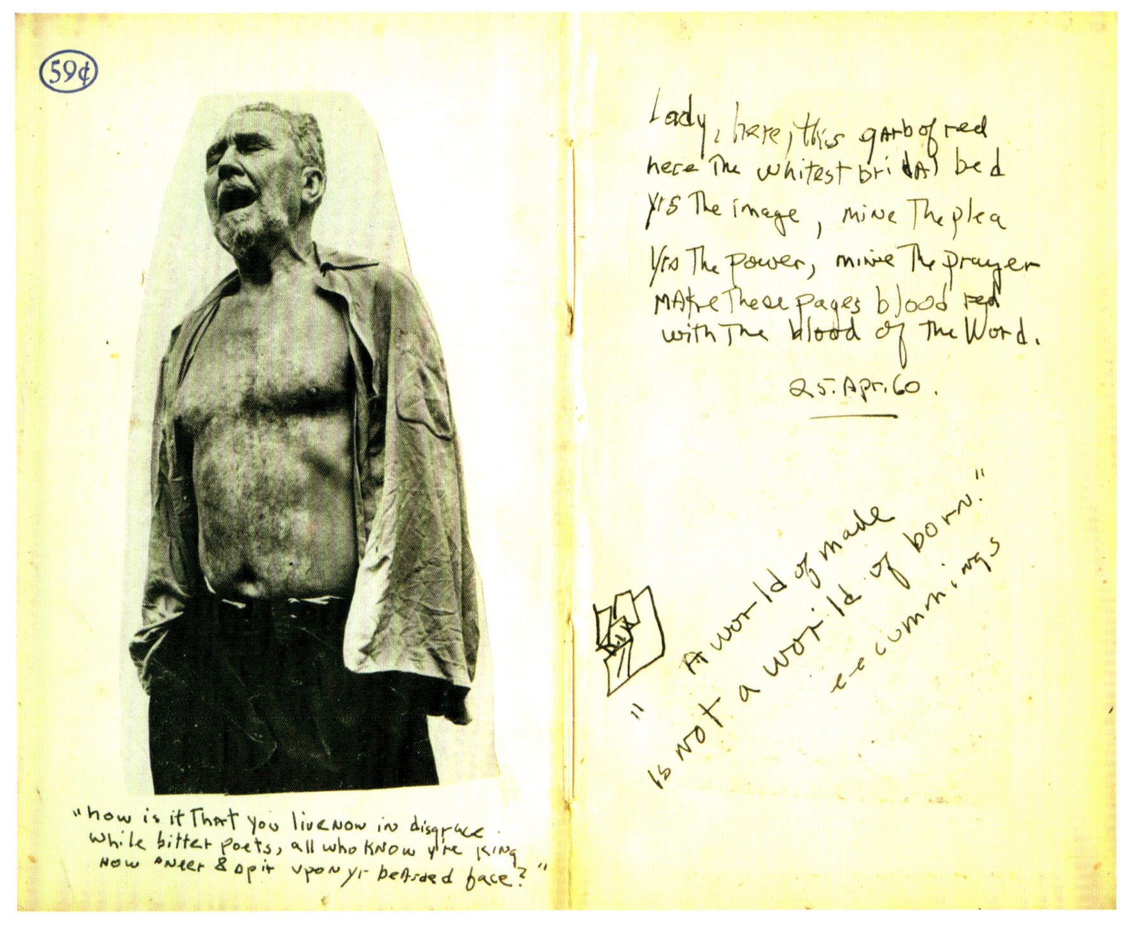
59¢
Lady, here, this garb of red
here the whitest bridal bed
yrs the image, mine the plea
yrs the power, mine the prayer
make these pages blood red
with the blood of the Word.
25. Apr. 60.
"A world of made
is not a world of born."
e e cummings
"how is it that you live now in disgrace
while bitter poets, all who know y're king
now sneer & spit upon yr bearded face?"

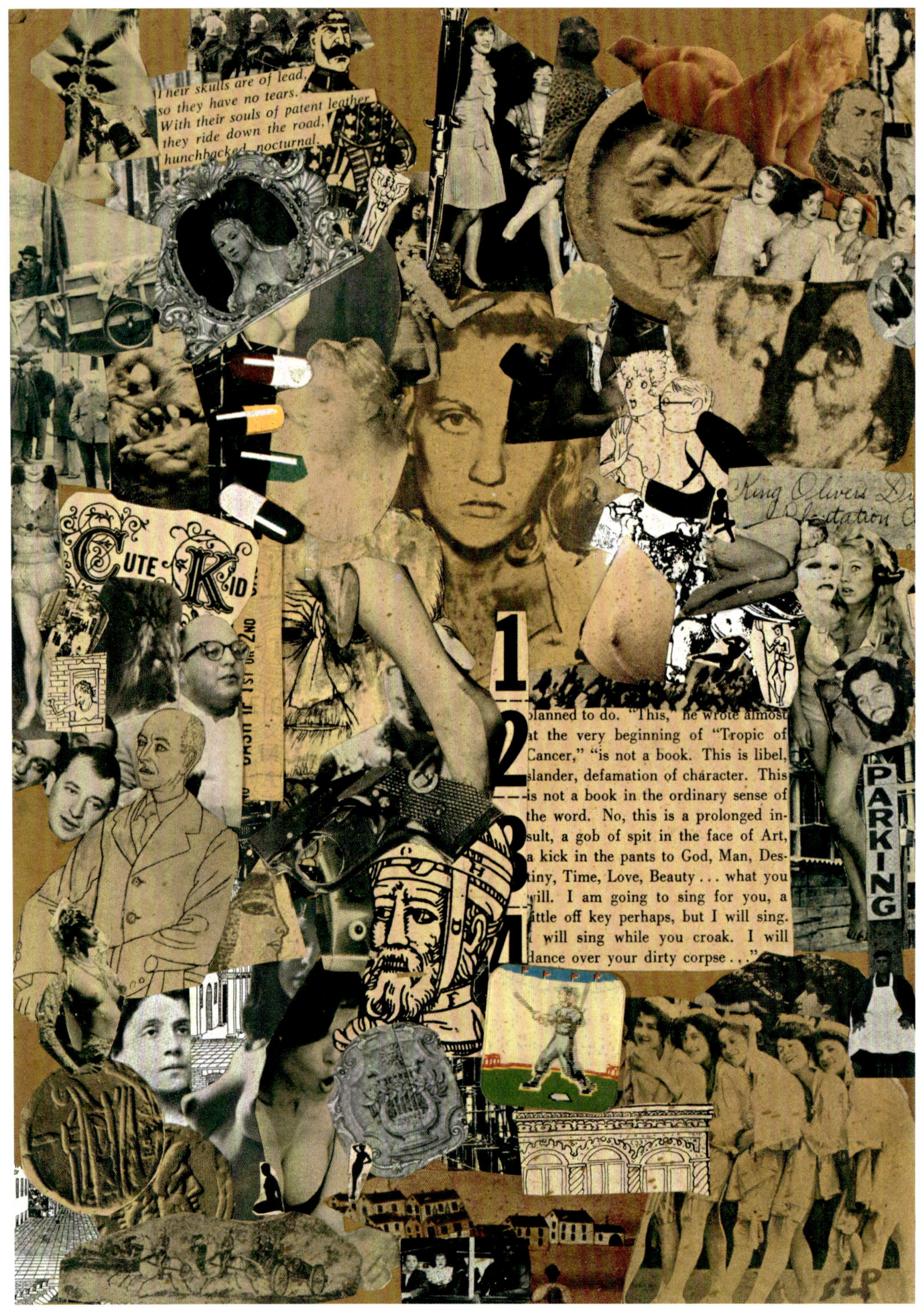
Their skulls are of lead,
so they have no tears.
With their souls of patent leather,
they ride down the road,
hunchbacked, nocturnal.
CUTE KID
1
2
3
planned to do. "This," he wrote almost
at the very beginning of "Tropic of
Cancer," "is not a book. This is libel,
slander, defamation of character. This
is not a book in the ordinary sense of
the word. No, this is a prolonged in-
sult, a gob of spit in the face of Art,
a kick in the pants to God, Man, Destiny, Time, Love, Beauty . . . what you
will. I am going to sing for you, a
little off key perhaps, but I will sing.
I will sing while you croak. I will
dance over your dirty corpse . . ."
PARKING

revealing his anxieties about providing for his family, as well as quotations from literary heroes such as Ezra Pound and Charles Olson. The journals' covers were often decorated with collages made from the comic books he devoured and collected. Other collages from around 1960 juxtapose comic book heroes with fragments of poetry.

After Perkoff's coffeehouse failed financially in 1959, he drifted into abuse of codeine-laced cough syrup and heroin and separated from his wife. When Lipton's book attracted mass-media attention, bringing busloads of posers to the Venice scene, Perkoff decided to escape to Guadalajara to begin a novel. His plans went awry when he was arrested in 1960 for drug possession and deported.

Back home, he continued to take drugs and write, convinced that withdrawal from heroin might block his creativity. For a brief period, his poetry seemed to flourish. Several of his poems were included in Donald Allen's 1960 Grove Press anthology, *American Poetry in the Twentieth Century*, and he even appeared as a contestant on Groucho Marx's game show *You Bet Your Life*. Perkoff spent much of the 1960s, however, indulging in the itinerant lifestyle of a heroin addict, with numerous scrapes with other users and the law. He was finally arrested on a drug charge in 1968 and sentenced to Terminal Island Federal Penitentiary.

Upon his release in 1971, he settled in Northern California with his ex-wife Suzan and their children. He attempted to lead a normal life, finally earning enough money to open a bookstore in Larkspur. He began *Alphabet* (Los Angeles and Fairfax, California: Red Hill Press, 1973), a cycle of poems based on Hebrew letters, which featured a cover designed by Wallace Berman. When Perkoff's relationship with Suzan again disintegrated, he abandoned his new life for Venice, crashing at the house of Bob and Anita Alexander. Perkoff had been hesitant about returning to Venice; as he stated in a note to Berman that accompanied the *Alphabet* poems: "I don't know if I'm coming down there or not. An awful lot of people running the beach w/ needles in hands—We'll see."[4]

Perkoff managed to receive a small Social Security pension, devote himself to writing, and find new acolytes on the scene. *Alphabet* had prompted an extended poetic investigation of Moses and the strength of the Jewish people. This relatively stable period was cut short when Perkoff was stricken with health problems in 1974 and died at age forty-three of complications from lung cancer.

Michael Duncan

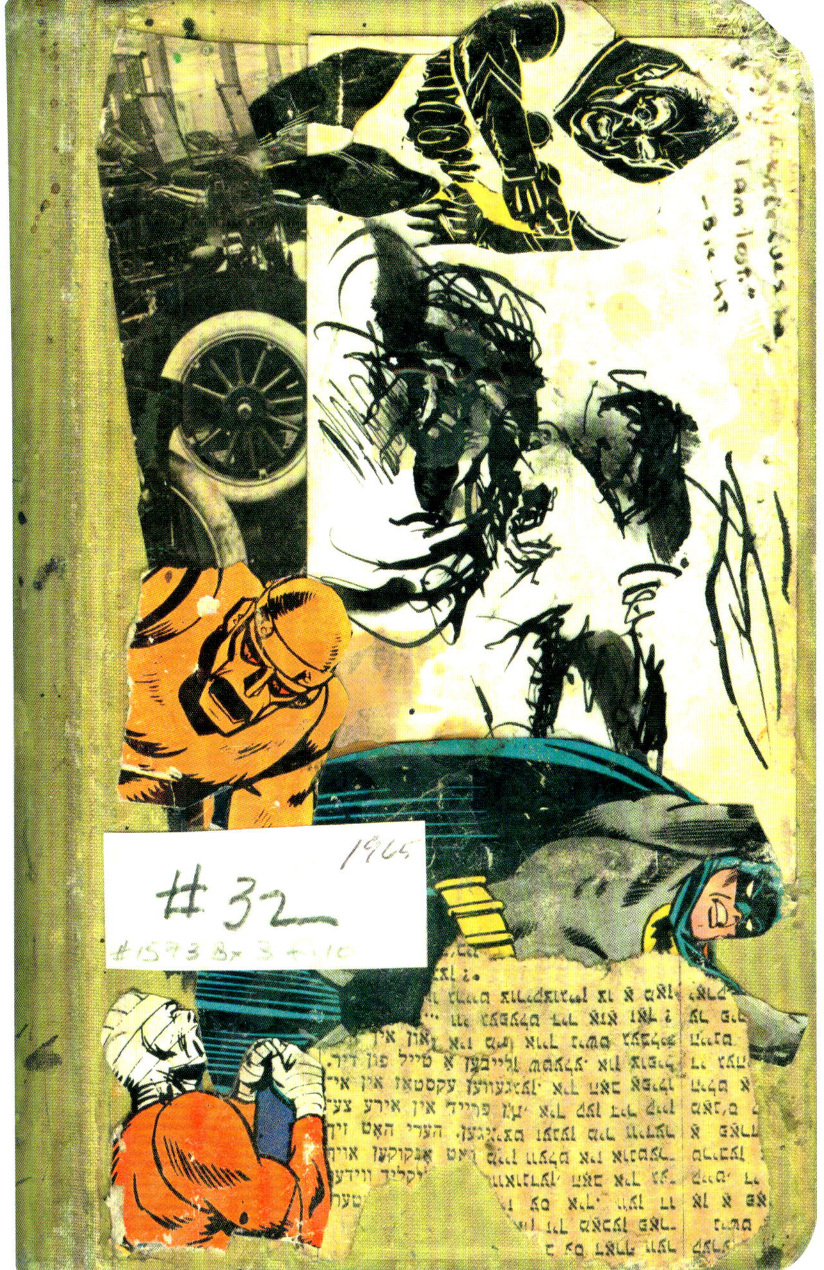

1 *Voices of the Lady: Collected Poems*, edited by Gerald T. Perkoff, M.D. (Orono, Maine: National Poetry Foundation, 1998).

2 Ibid., Robert Creeley, "For Stuart," p. 11.

3 See John Arthur Maynard, *Venice West: The Beat Generation in Southern California* (New Brunswick: Rutgers University Press, 1991), p. 62.

4 Perkoff letter to Wallace Berman, May 11, 1973, Wallace Berman Archive, Archives of American Art, Smithsonian Institution.

John Reed

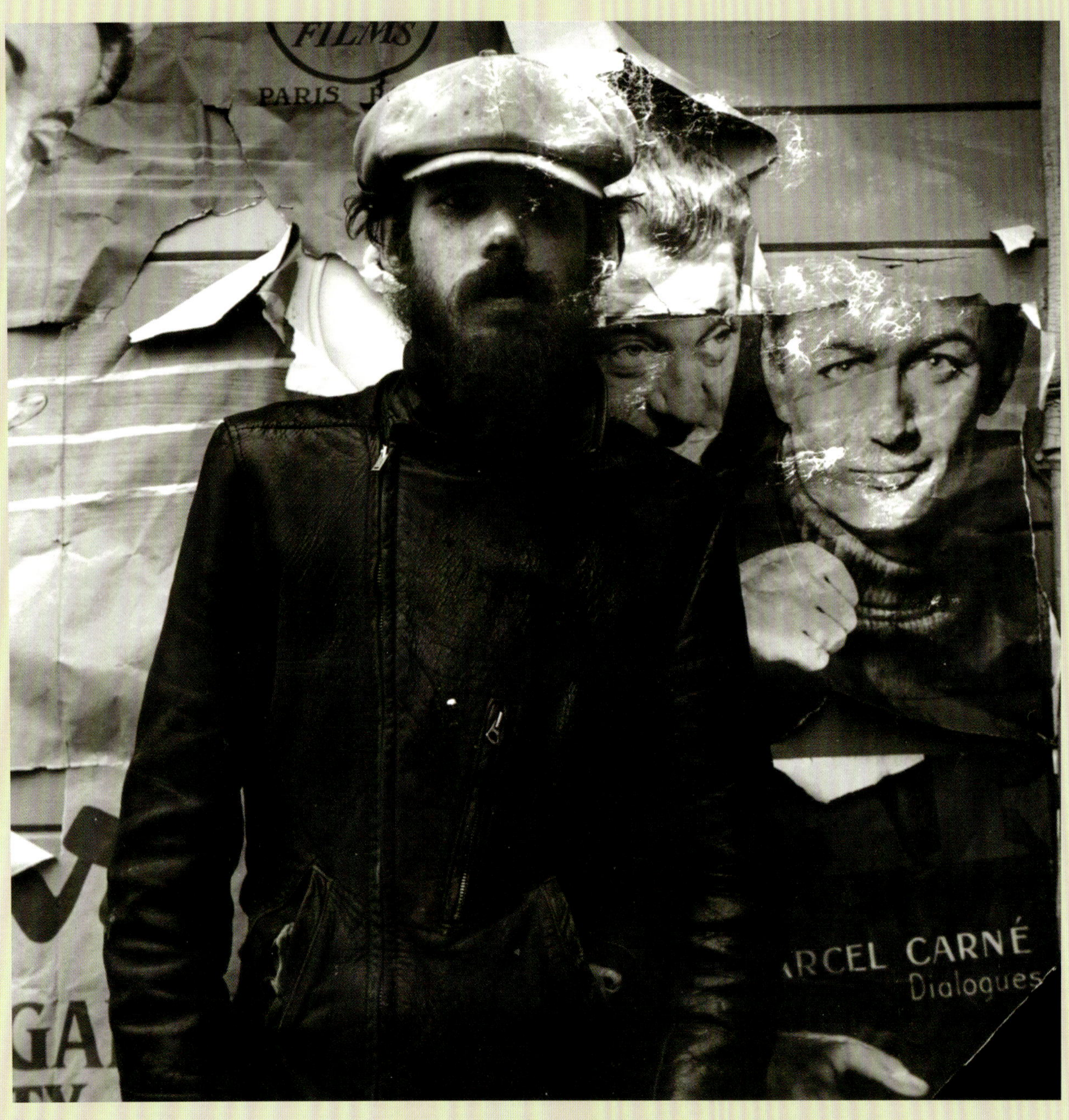

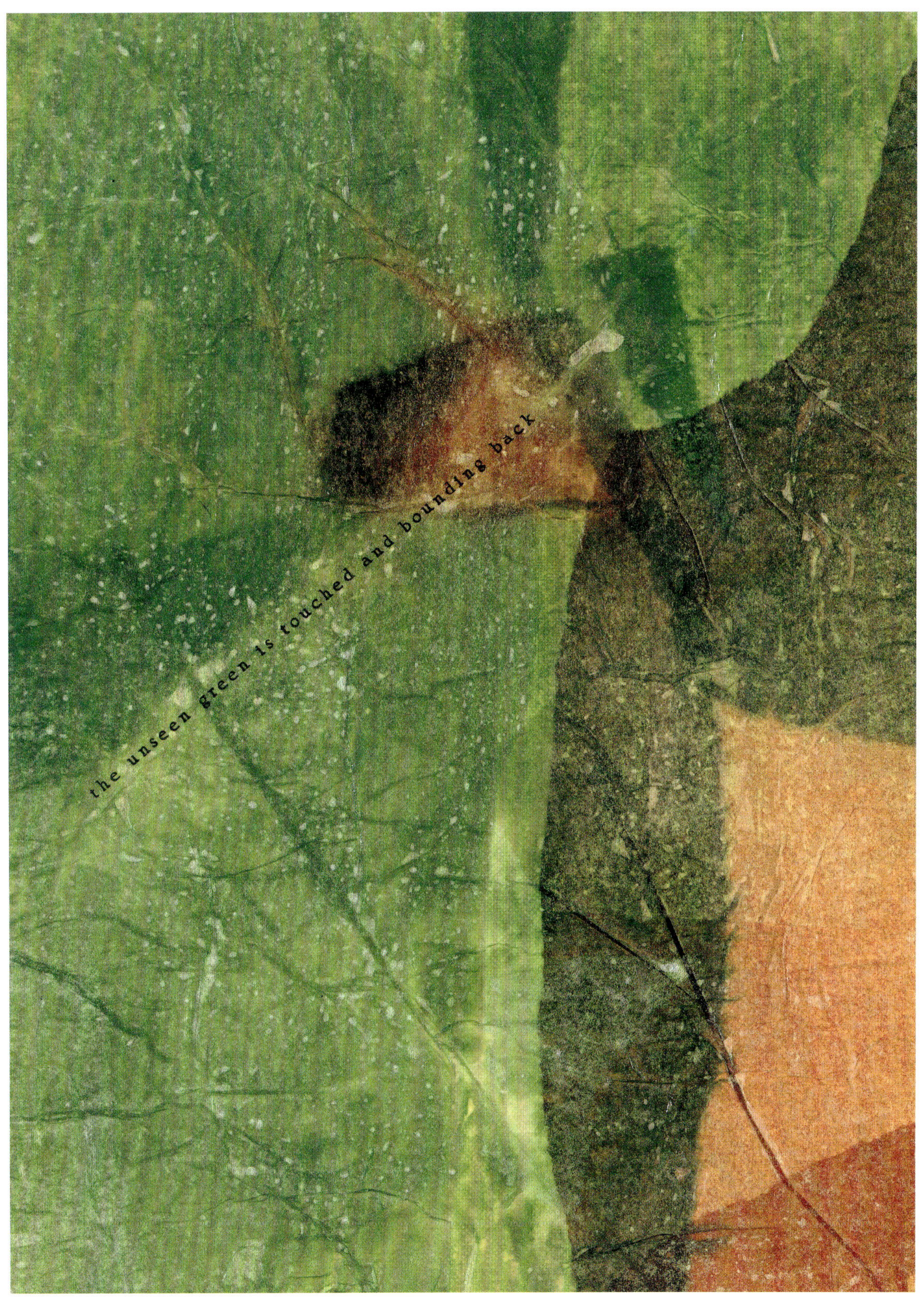
the unseen green is touched and bounding back

One of the key yet lesser-known figures in Wallace Berman's circle, John Reed was an accomplished artist and tragic misfit, dying homeless and indigent. Born in 1933 in Salt Lake City, he grew up in San Francisco and lived in California throughout his life. One of his longtime friends, George Herms, called him "one of the most mysterious characters on the scene."[1]

Close friends with Ed Kienholz, Reed lived in the back of Ferus Gallery for a period in the late 1950s. On the move throughout his life, he later lived with Kienholz in Topanga Canyon. In 1957 Reed gave Kienholz a book on Kurt Schwitters that provided the inspiration for Kienholz's earliest relief paintings.[2] An active member of the Los Angeles art community, he constructed sets for a production of Rachel Rosenthal's Instant Theatre from newspapers strung over clothesline and ladders. A jazz enthusiast, he played the clarinet and piano and was adept at improvisation.

p. 240
John Reed on Berman houseboat, Larkspur, 1961, Photograph by Wallace Berman.

p. 241
John Reed, *Untitled (The Unseen Green is Touched and Bounding Back…)*, 1955, Gouache on paper.

p. 242
John Reed, *SWOT*, c. 1960, Mixed-media book.

p. 243
John Reed, *Untitled*, c. 1960, Mixed-media book.

p. 244 top
John Reed, *Untitled*, 1955, Painting on canvas.

p. 244 bottom
John Reed, *Untitled*, c. 1960, Woodblock print, Collection of Temple of Man.

p. 245 left
John Reed, *Poster for Eric Nord Benefit*, 1957, Woodblock print.

p. 245 right
John Reed, from "Three Poems," 1958, *Floating Bear #33*.

In Los Angeles, Reed became close with Cameron. A number of his drawings and woodblocks featuring macabre mythical figures resemble the style of her artwork. He also made abstract paintings and collages that were delicate color studies, sometimes featuring textual fragments of poems glued to the surfaces in the style of works by Robert Alexander. Reed and Alexander made assemblages in the mid-1950s, working contemporaneously with Wallace Berman.[3]

Berman published two poems and three drawings by Reed in *Semina*. Reed also experimented with poetry made from collaged text cut out from Victorian novels and arranged as comical, sophisticated pictograms. Reed, however, never promoted his talents and had a very relaxed attitude about art and proprietorship. Charles Brittin recalled that in the early 1950s he casually deposited interesting found objects and other artists' unidentified sculptures at the Bermans' Crater Lane house for their perusal.[4]

In 1957 Reed moved to San Francisco along with Bob Alexander and Arthur Richer to work for the paperback book distributor Paper Editions. Berman organized a show of Reed's assemblages and collages at the Semina Gallery in 1960. Around that time, Lawrence Jordan shot a short film featuring Reed. He became friends with the poets Joe Dunn and John Wieners and like them his dependence on

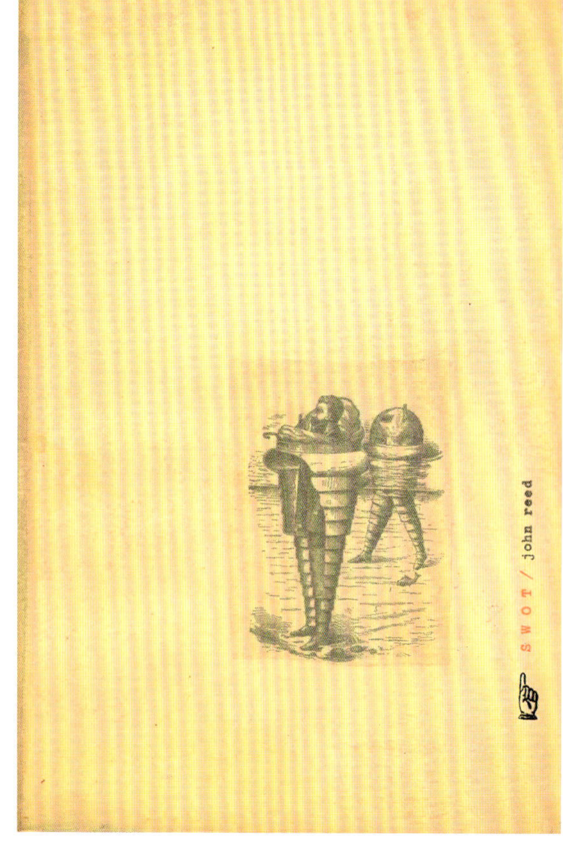

methamphetamines resulted in increasingly manic activity. In 1963 Reed was involved in the looting of brass fixtures and ornaments from San Francisco's baroque movie theatre, the Fox, just before it was demolished by the wrecking ball. Working at night, Reed holed up in the theatre for weeks, hiding and sleeping among a network of catwalks in the massive structure. Evading arrest, he was dubbed the "Phantom of the Fox Theatre" by the local press.[5]

Largely dropping out of circulation from his artist and poet friends in the late 1960s, Reed is remembered for his gentleness and sense of humor. His artwork was featured in the 1988 exhibition "Lost and Found in California: Four Decades of Assemblage Art." Homeless for many years, finally living on the grounds of the Pasadena Public Library, Reed was a genuinely underground figure. He died in 2001. *Michael Duncan*

1 Phone conversation with George Herms, January 2, 2005.
2 Sandra Leonard Starr, "Assemblage Art in California: A Collective Memoir 1940–1969," exh. cat. *Lost and Found in California: Four Decades of Assemblage Art* (Santa Monica: Corcoran, Shoshana Wayne, and Pence Galleries 1988, p. 89.
3 Conversation with Herms.
4 Charles Britten interview in Starr, p. 73–74.
5 Conversation with Herms.

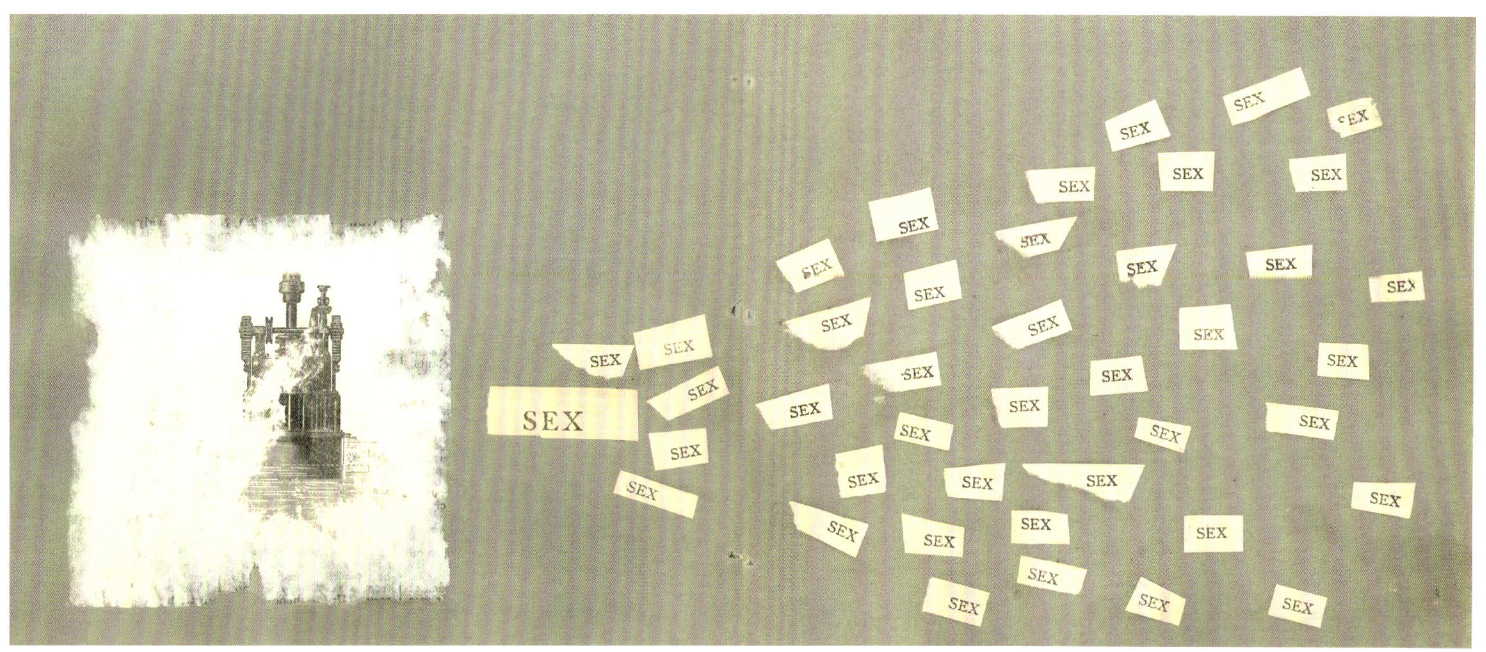
SEX
SEX
SEX
SEX
SEX
SEX
SEX
SEX
SEX
SEX
SEX
SEX
SEX
SEX
SEX
SEX
SEX
SEX
SEX
SEX
SEX
SEX
SEX
SEX
SEX
SEX
SEX
SEX
SEX
SEX
SEX
SEX
SEX
SEX
SEX
SEX
SEX
SEX
SEX
SEX
SEX
SEX

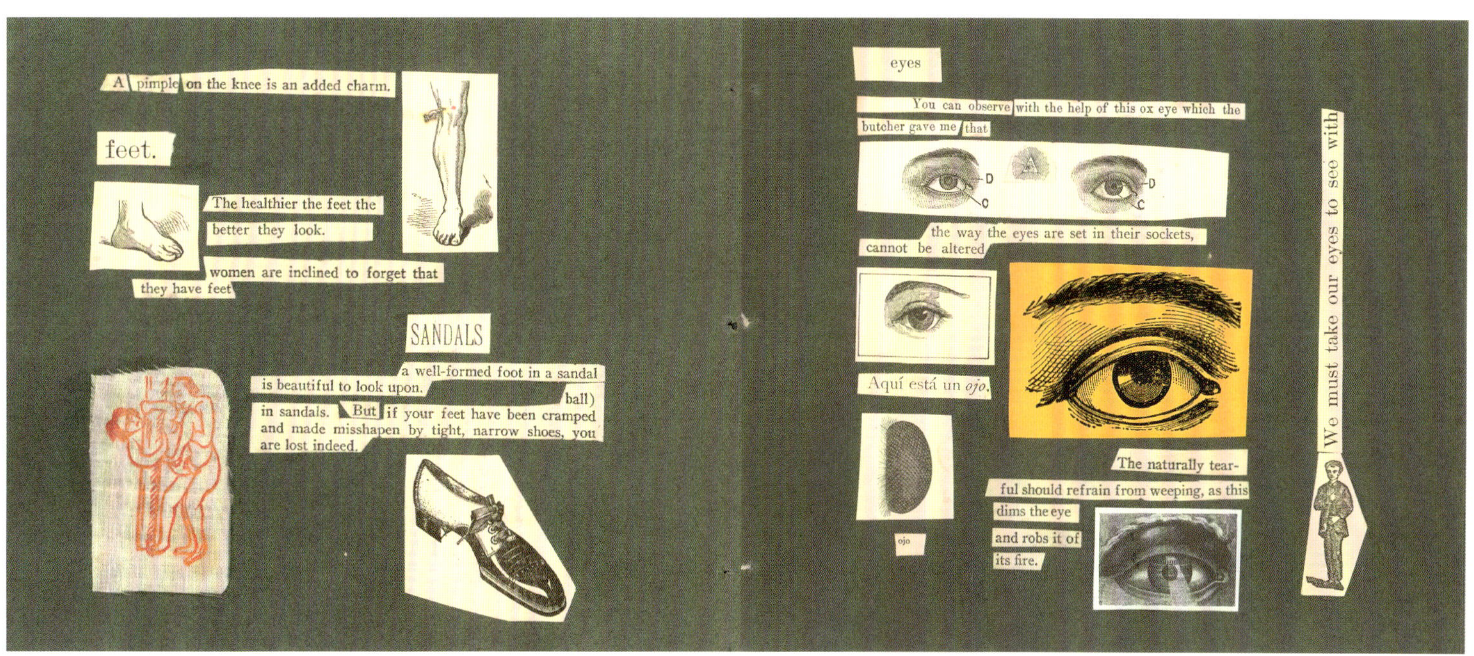
A pimple on the knee is an added charm.
feet.
The healthier the feet the better they look.
women are inclined to forget that they have feet
SANDALS
a well-formed foot in a sandal is beautiful to look upon.
ball)
in sandals. But if your feet have been cramped and made misshapen by tight, narrow shoes, you are lost indeed.
eyes
You can observe with the help of this ox eye which the butcher gave me that
the way the eyes are set in their sockets, cannot be altered
Aquí está un ojo.
ojo
The naturally tear-ful should refrain from weeping, as this dims the eye and robs it of its fire.
We must take our eyes to see with

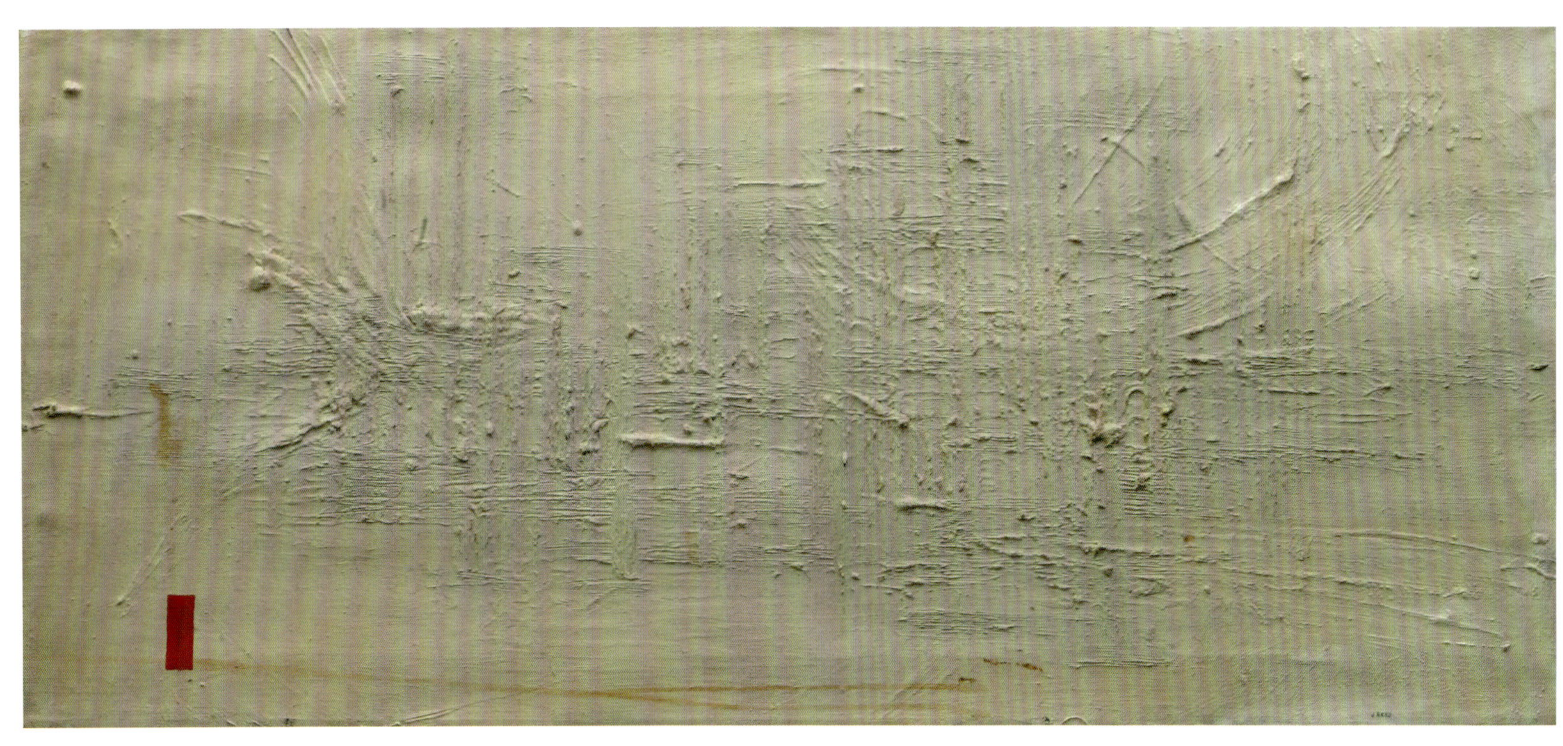

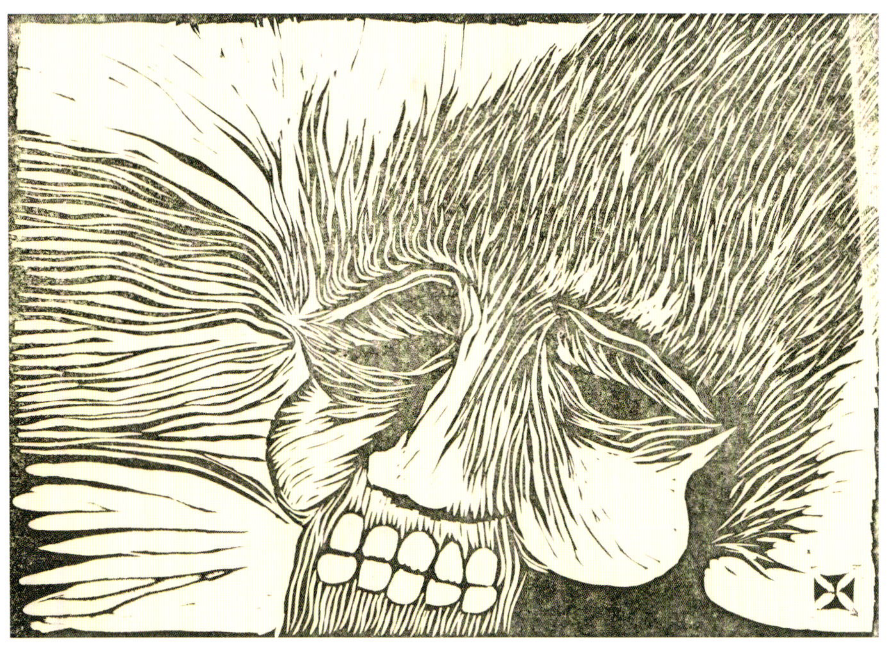

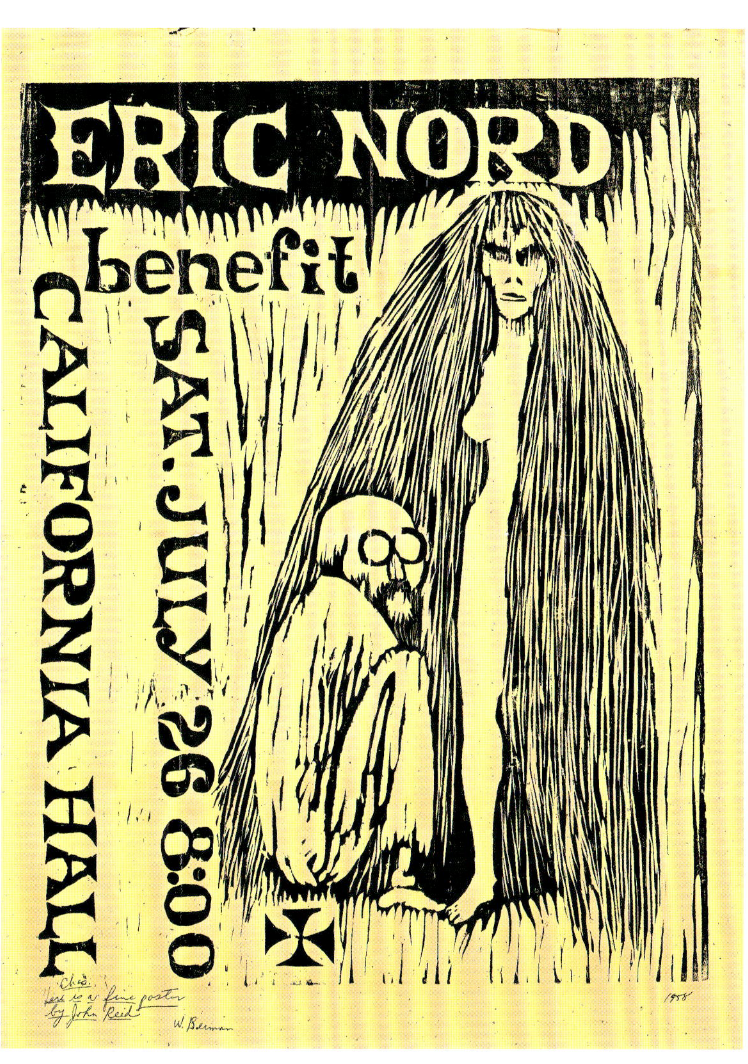

From Three Poems

1.

If the rats
Take over
Where
Love left off –
Am I
Supposed to pull up
My beauty?
Or
Wade in
And let them
Gnaw off my toes?

And never ship out
Again?

Arthur Richer

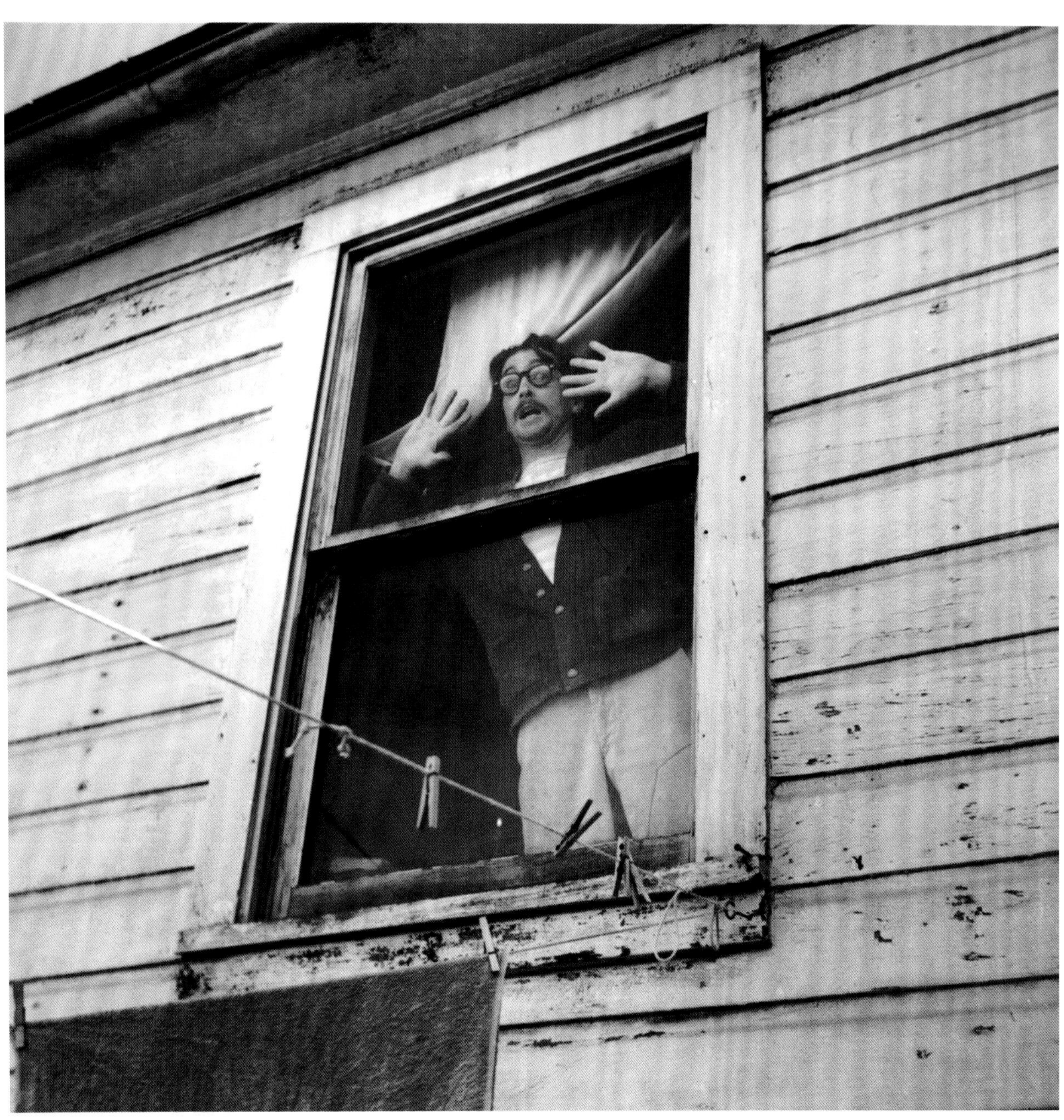

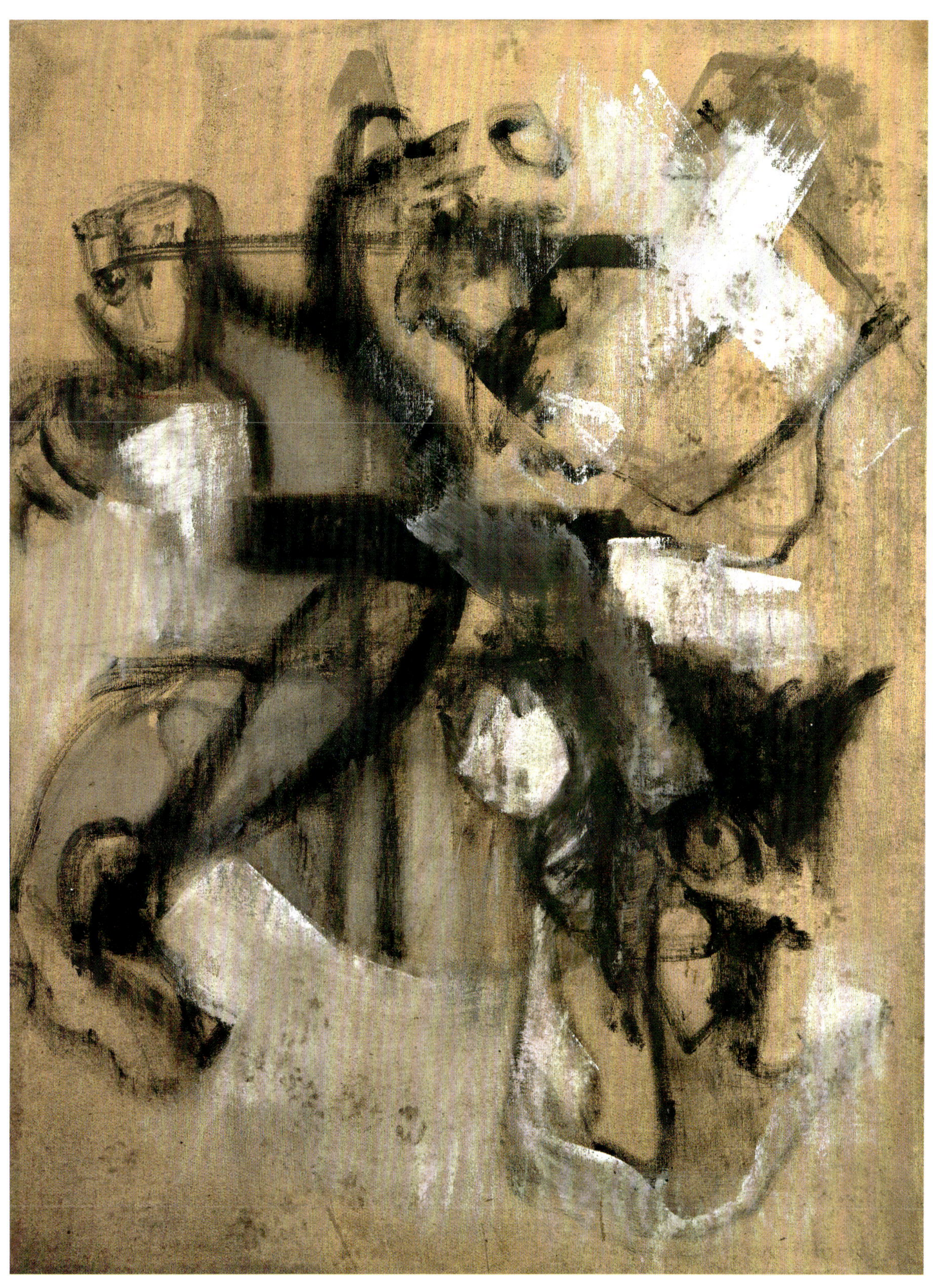

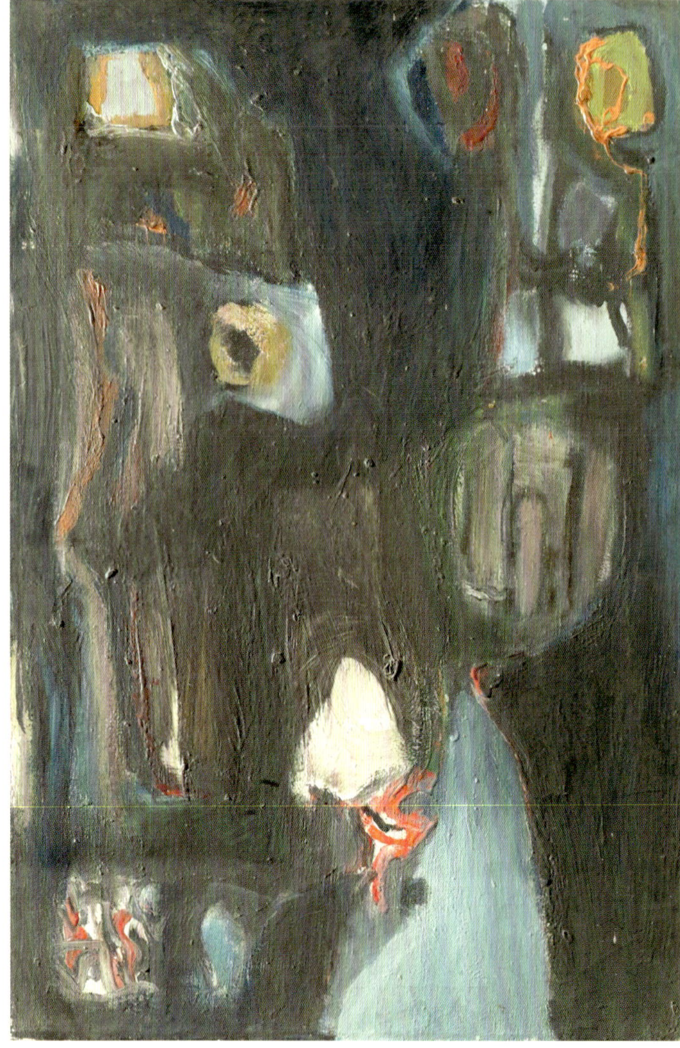

A legendary, larger-than-life personality of the Los Angeles Beat scene, painter Arthur Richer was one of the group's early casualties, dying at the age of thirty-seven. Born in New York in 1928, Richer moved to Los Angeles in the early 1950s after a stint in the Navy. In 1955 his drawing skills earned him a scholarship at Finch-Warshaw Art School, a private school established by Los Angeles painters Keith Finch and Howard Warshaw, located-first next door to Felix Landau Gallery on La Cienega and later in Brentwood. Both school founders were admirers of the work of Rico Lebrun, Southern California's most celebrated figurative artist of the time, known for his virtuosic draftsmanship and dark subject matter.

p. 246
Arthur Richer, Potrero Street, San Francisco, 1960, Photograph by Wallace Berman.

p. 247
Arthur Richer, *Samurai*, 1958, Oil on canvas.

p. 248
Arthur Richer, Untitled, 1956, Oil on canvas.

p. 249
Arthur Richer, *Nuro Muscliar #1*, 1956, Oil on canvas.

p. 250 and 251 top
Arthur Richer and Wallace Berman at Richer opening, Ferus Gallery, 1959, Ed Kienholz scrapbook, Collection of Nancy Reddin Kienholz.

p. 251 right
Unattributed review of Richer's Ferus exhibition, Ed Kienholz scrapbook, Collection of Nancy Reddin Kienholz.

Friend and fellow student Tom Eatherton has recalled how Richer tested the boundaries of his instructors, pushing his paintings in the direction of spontaneous Abstract Expressionism. Eatherton has described Richer as an outspoken advocate of painting above all other forms, notably collage or assemblage.[1] Richer's early works often employed crudely painted renditions of birds, animals, and human figures, used as launching pads for vigorous abstract brushwork and violent strokes of color. Featuring dark lumbering shapes juxtaposed with lyrical gestures, Richer's rhythmic compositions hint at his devotion to jazz which he pursued as a saxophonist. In New York, he had met many of the jazz greats, including Charlie Parker.

George Herms has described Richer's approach to painting as jazz-inspired, reporting that watching Richer paint was like feeling the energy of, "say, Count Basie's band when all the horns are blowing and you're standing right in front of it. The energy's coming off of you. That's what it was like. That was what was coming off this one skinny New York painter."[2]

On the recommendation of Wallace Berman, Walter Hopps visited Richer's studio and organized an exhibition of his work at Syndell Studio in 1955. Hopps also included works by Richer in a 1957 group show at Ferus Gallery and organized a solo exhibition of his black paintings there in 1959. Berman gave Richer a solo exhibition at Semina Gallery in Larkspur in 1961.

Richer's action painting seemed to emerge from his volatile personality. He was known as a wild card individual whose antics disrupted art openings, especially his own. Of Richer's painting *Clown* (1957), Billy Al Bengston commented, "An apt title, for that is more or less the way

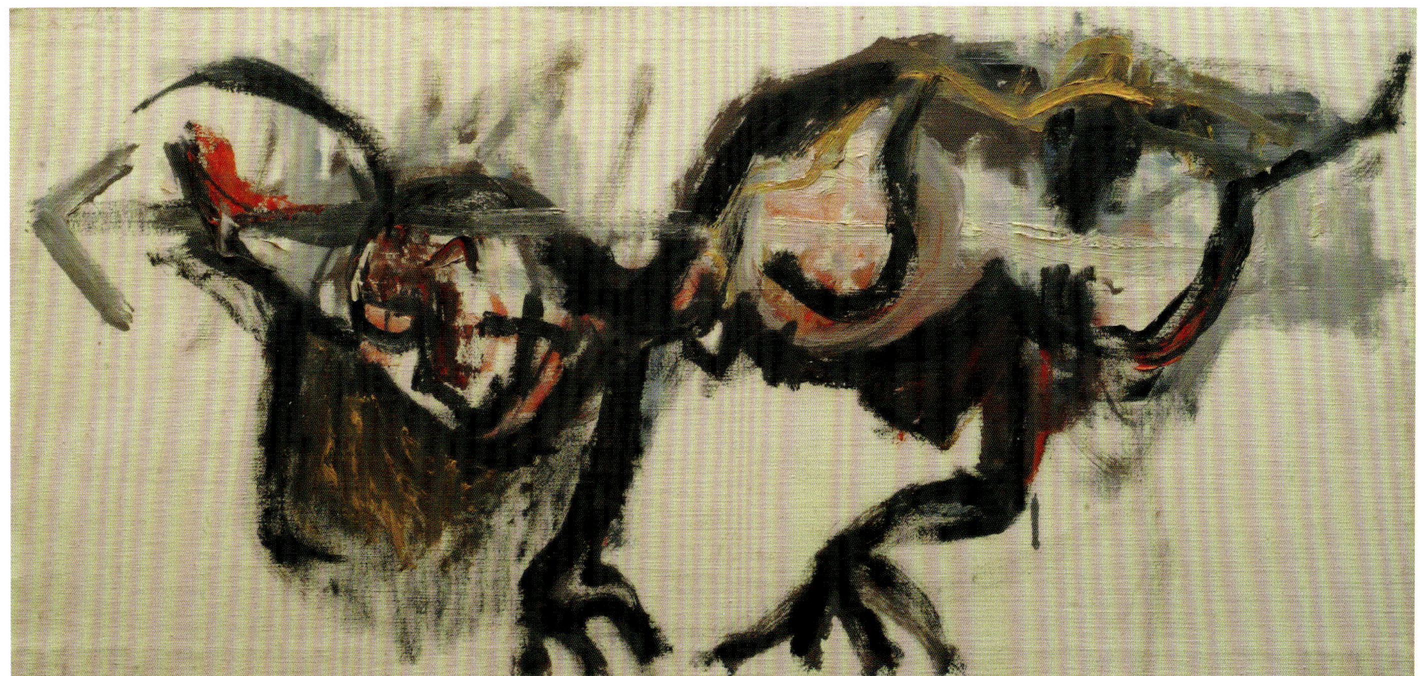

Artie was considered."[3] In the 1950s Los Angeles art scene, Richer's impulsive nature and penchant for dissention was only rivaled by John Altoon, the other masterful abstract painter in the Ferus Gallery stable. Rather than rivalry, the two seemed to share mutual respect. Herms recalled being at Altoon's studio with Richer when the two painters spontaneously began to collaborate on a painting, both flinging paint, Jackson Pollock-style, on a huge canvas.[4]

Richer's personal life was troubled. Severe back problems gradually led to his addiction to barbiturates, augmented by abuse of alcohol and heroin. Married to Betty Hertz—who under the name "Betty Bly" had sung with the Tommy Dorsey Band—Richer barely provided for their family of four children. For a 1959 article on the beatnik phenomenon, Lawrence Lipton, the author of *The Holy Barbarians,* directed a team from *Life* magazine to document the Richer family in their $75 a month "pad" in Venice. Photographed sitting underneath one of his huge abstract canvases, Richer is quoted as saying, "I would enjoy serenity, but I am called to the frontier of so-called civilization, as bizarre as it is. I must find chaos. My expression drives me."[5]

In the late 1950s, Richer taught Herms to stretch canvases, encouraging him to paint and draw as an alternative to assemblage and sculpture.[6] Briefly working together in a paperback book warehouse in San Francisco, Herms and Richer were arrested on a minor drug charge in 1958. Although Herms was sentenced to six months in prison, Richer was released. In 1959, Richer and his family moved to a cottage on the Potrero Hill property of Dr. Reidar Wennesland, an eccentric collector who was his biggest supporter. Richer also worked in 1960 with Robert Alexander on the renovation of the San Francisco jazz club, the Cellar.

In 1963 Richer and his family briefly moved in with the families of Herms and Paul Beattie in Mill Creek. A fire at the property prompted Richer to find alternative housing in a partially subsidized, migrant farmer's house on a vineyard in Healdsberg. Richer died there suddenly in 1965 from an accidental drug overdose. Six months later his wife Betty died of complications from an ulcer. As a tribute to his friend, Berman included a photograph of Richer playing the tenor saxophone in *Semina 7.* Herms's large assemblage, *Drug Store for Artie* (1991–92), is a salute to an artist whom Herms credits as a crucial inspiration.[7] The Wennesland collection, now housed in Kristiansand, Norway at Kristiansand Katedralskole and Agder College, includes nine large Richer paintings dating from 1952 to 1962. *Michael Duncan*

1 Conversation with Tom Eatherton, June 16, 2004.

2 Edward Leffingwell, "A Drug Store for Artie," *George Herms: The Secret Archives* (Los Angeles: Los Angeles Municipal Art Gallery, 1992), p. 6.

3 Billy Al Bengston, "Late Fifties at the Ferus," *Artforum*, January 1969, p. 35.

4 Conversation with Herms, June 29, 2004.

5 "Squaresville U.S.A. vs. Beatsville," *Life*, September 21, 1959, p. 33.

6 Conversation with Herms, June 29, 2004.

7 Leffingwell, p. 5.

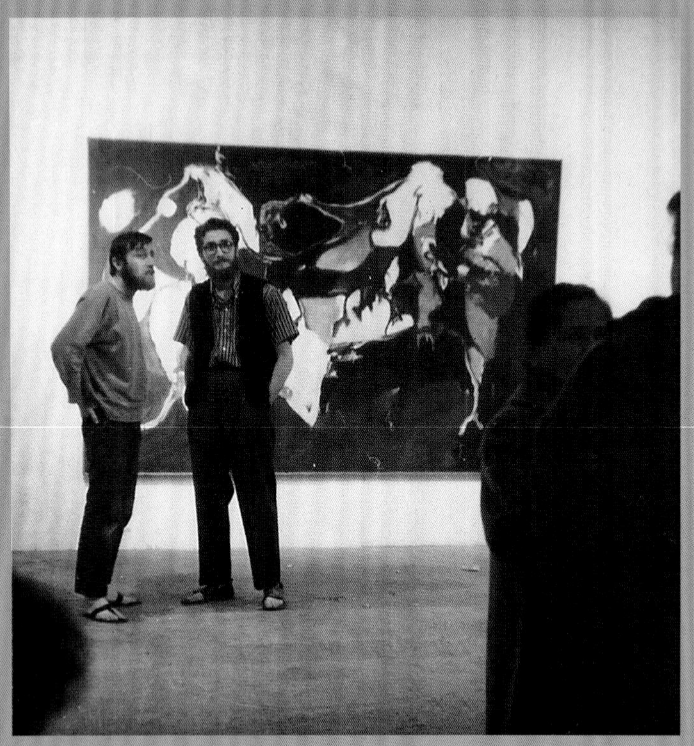

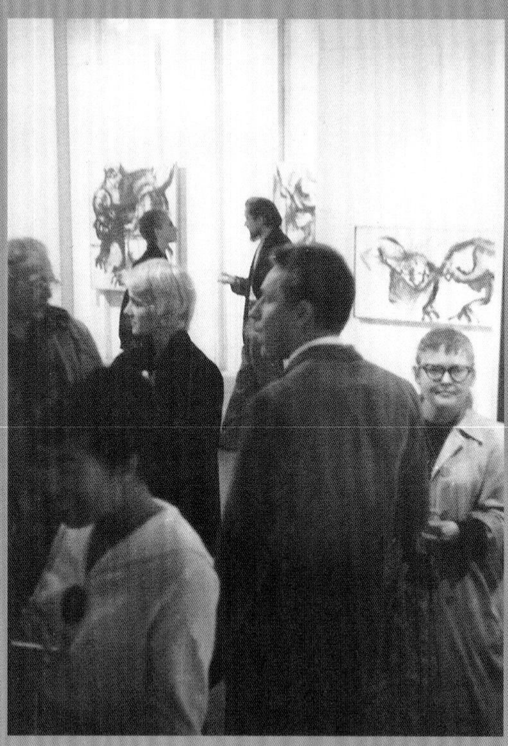

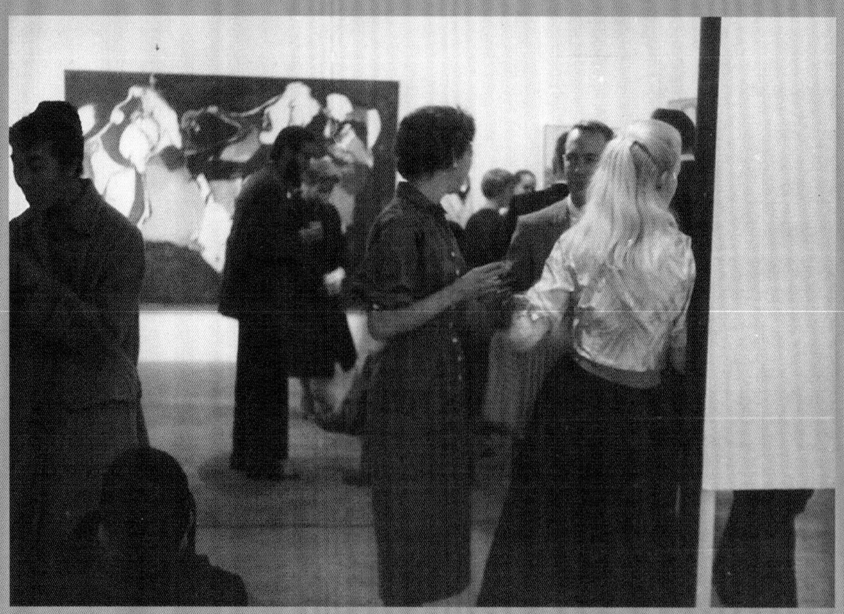

Arthur Richer

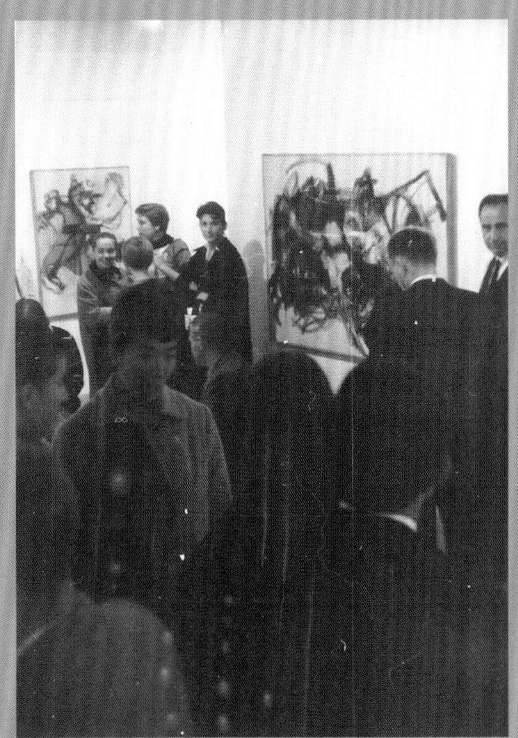

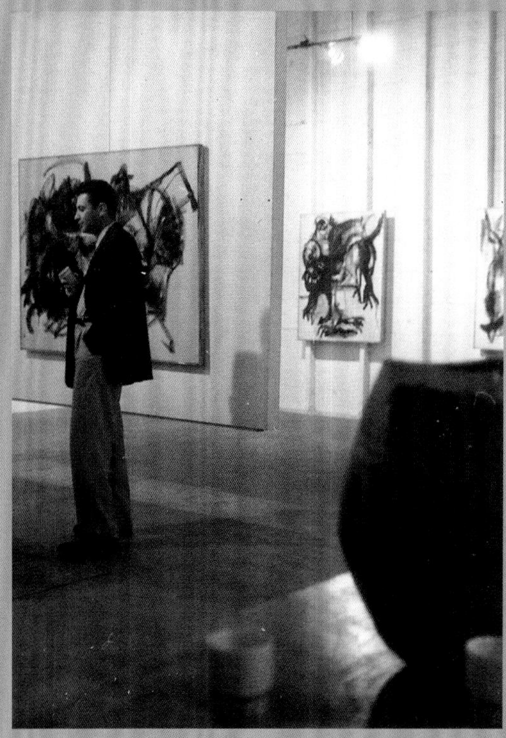

BLACK PAINTINGS

A few doors up La Cienega at the Ferus Gallery, 736-A North, paintings by Arthur Richer plunge one into night and mystification. Most of these black paintings seem to have something to do with bulls. I must have been born too soon for them.

Rachel Rosenthal

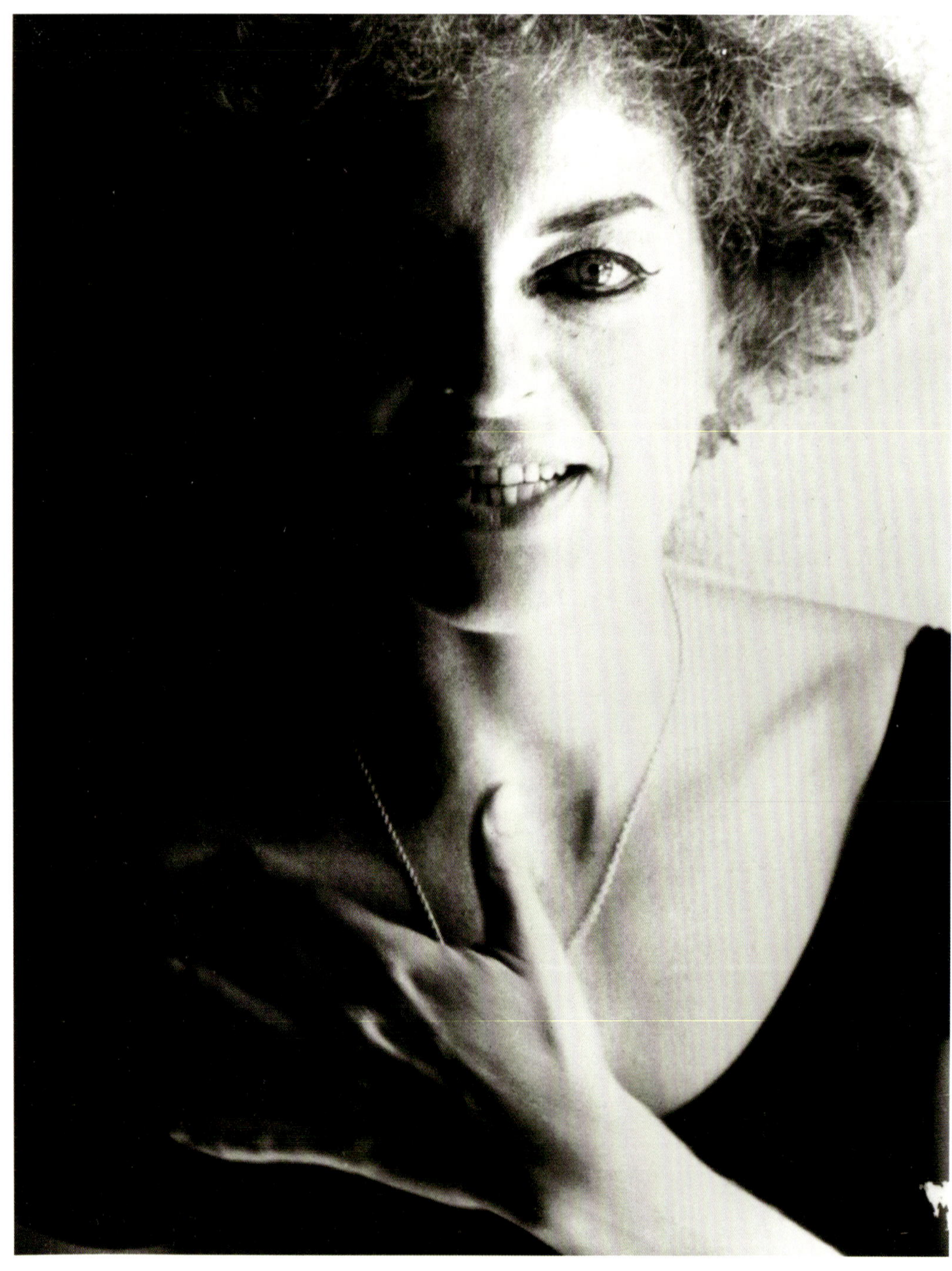

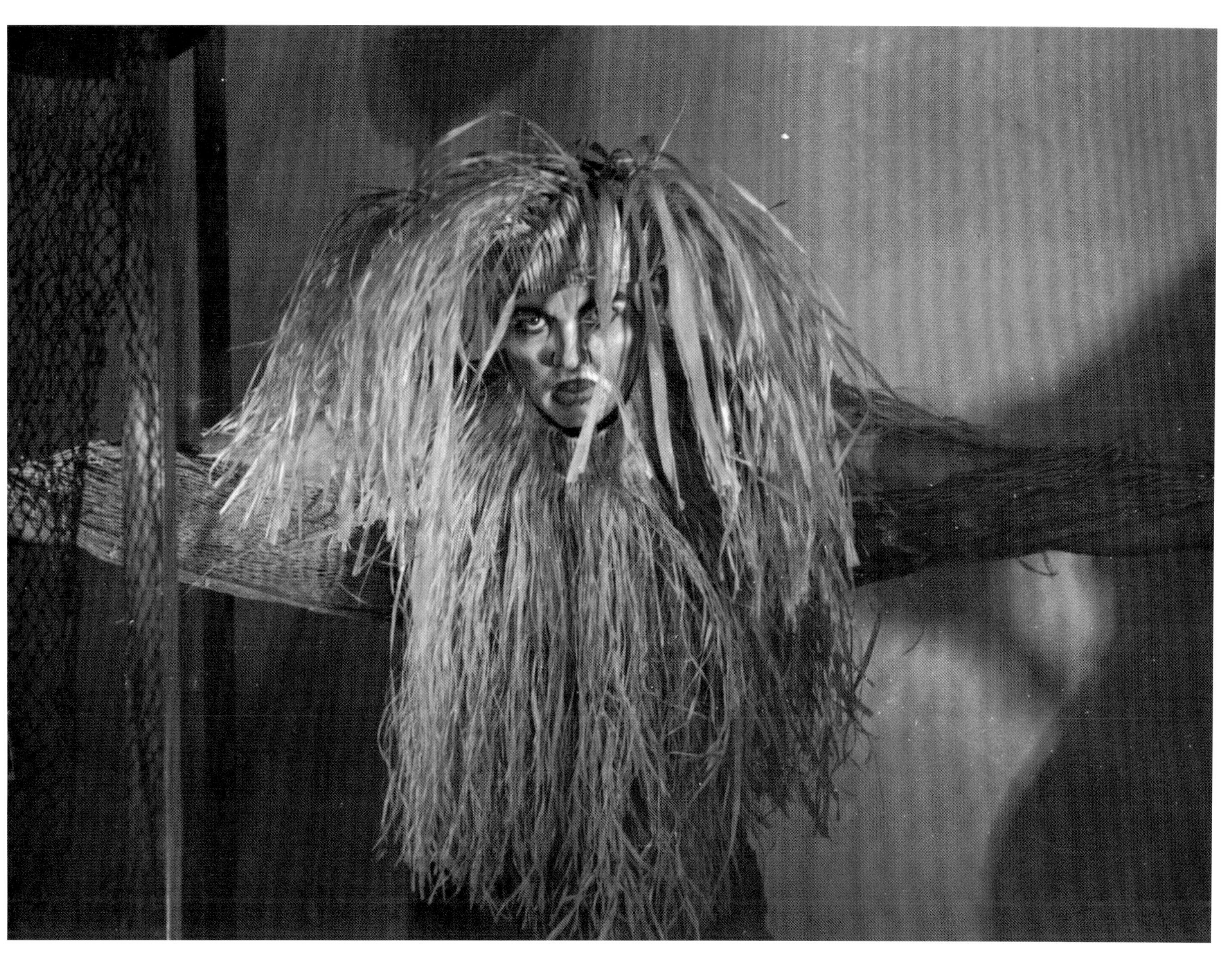

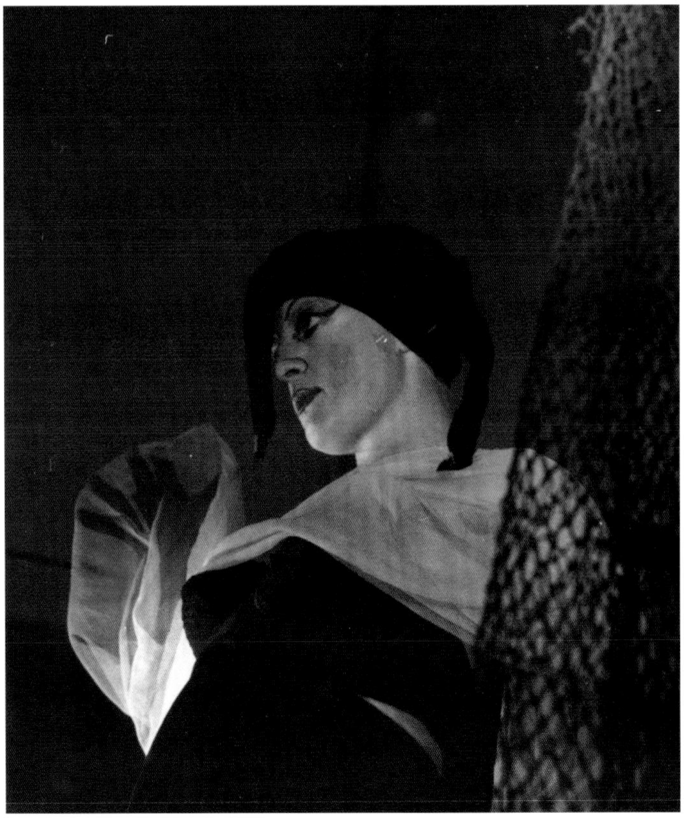

Performer and artist Rachel Rosenthal isn't usually mentioned as part of the community of European émigré artists who came to America during World War II, but that was, in fact, the path she traveled. All the art Rosenthal has created in various media over the past sixty years has been infused with her familiarity with the European avant-garde, and her roots there played a central role in shaping her persona as an artist.

Rosenthal was born into an upper class family of assimilated Russian Jews in Paris in 1926. She was fourteen when her family was abruptly forced to flee the city on the eve of the Nazi invasion. After a brief stop in Portugal, the family spent a year in Brazil, and then settled in 1941 in New York, where Rosenthal was exposed to all the city had to offer in terms of culture. She attended Manhattan's High School of Music and Art, where her classmates included Allen Kaprow and Morton Feldman, and her parents' circle of friends included Fyodor Chaliapin, Marc Chagall, Akim Tamiroff, Vladimir Horowitz, and Leonard Bernstein. After graduating from high school, Rosenthal studied painting with Hans Hoffman and attended the New School for Social Research where she took classes with Meyer Shapiro and Rudolf Arnheim.

Between 1946 and 1954, Rosenthal commuted regularly between New York and Paris, and during her time abroad she attended lectures by Maurice Merleau-Ponty, saw the original production of *Waiting For Godot*, and exhibited her engravings (in 1953, at the Salon de Mai in Paris). In New York she became part of John Cage and Merce Cunningham's circle, which included Cy Twombly, Robert Rauschenberg, Jasper Johns, David Tudor, and Ray Johnson. (It was Johnson, in fact, who gave Rosenthal her first cat, igniting her life-long commitment to animal rights.) Rosenthal was a dancer in Cunningham's junior company; she directed Ben Gazzara and Anthony Franciosa in off-Broadway plays and worked as an assistant to Heinz Condell, set designer for the Metropolitan Opera. During those years she was also making abstract sculptures out of metal and tar, which she exhibited in 1954 at New York's Tanager Gallery.

Rosenthal moved to Los Angeles in 1955, and a year later she launched Instant Theater. Largely inspired by Antonin Artaud's treatise of 1938, *Theater and Its Double*, Instant Theater was an experimental entity devoted to expanding and exploring the outer limits of dance, improvisation, and psycho-drama. Under Rosenthal's visionary stewardship, Instant Theater contained the seeds that would blossom into performance art during the 1970s.

Wallace Berman was among the first wave of people to attend and support Instant Theater, and he made a lasting impression on Rosenthal. "Whether he encouraged it or not, Wallace was a bit of a Christ figure to the group that coalesced around him," Rosenthal recalls. "He looked like a guru for starters, which always helps, and his work was spiritual. So much materialism had arisen in America during the 1950s and 1960s, and Wallace had philosophies that inspired people who were searching for alternative values."[1]

Instant Theater operated for approximately a decade, and during those years Rosenthal's production of static visual art was mostly limited to the creation of sets, props and costumes. In 1960 she married actor King Moody who became her partner in Instant Theater, and in 1962 they converted their Laurel Canyon home into a theater for the company.

Following the demise of Instant Theater in 1966, Rosenthal resumed her work as a sculptor and studied for two years with ground-breaking ceramicist John Mason. She exhibited her clay sculptures with increasing frequency during the late 1960s, customarily placing the sculpture in sand piles in wooden crates. Then, in the 1970s, her work abruptly took another sharp turn.

p. 252
Rachel Rosenthal, Los Angeles, 1956, Photograph by Wallace Berman.

p. 253
Lee Mullican in a production of Instant Theater, c. 1957, Photograph by Rachel Rosenthal.

p. 254
Rachel Rosenthal in a production of Instant Theater, c.1957, Photograph by King Moody.

p. 255 left
Ben Talbert, Announcement for Instant Theater, undated, Robert Alexander Archive, Archives of American Art, Smithsonian Institution.

p. 255 right
Rachel Rosenthal and Lee Mullican in a production of Instant Theater, c. 1957.

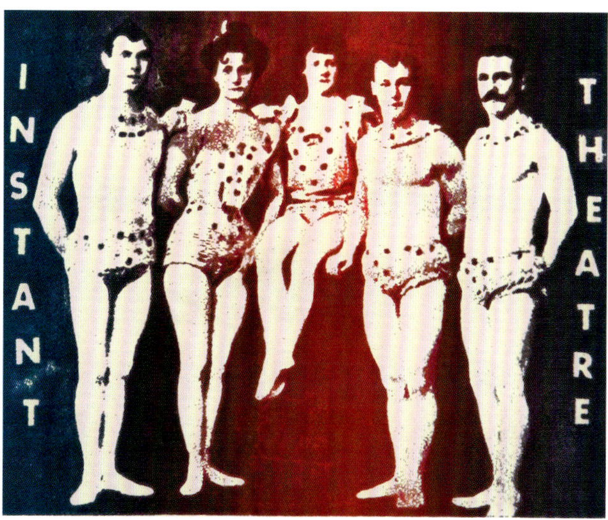

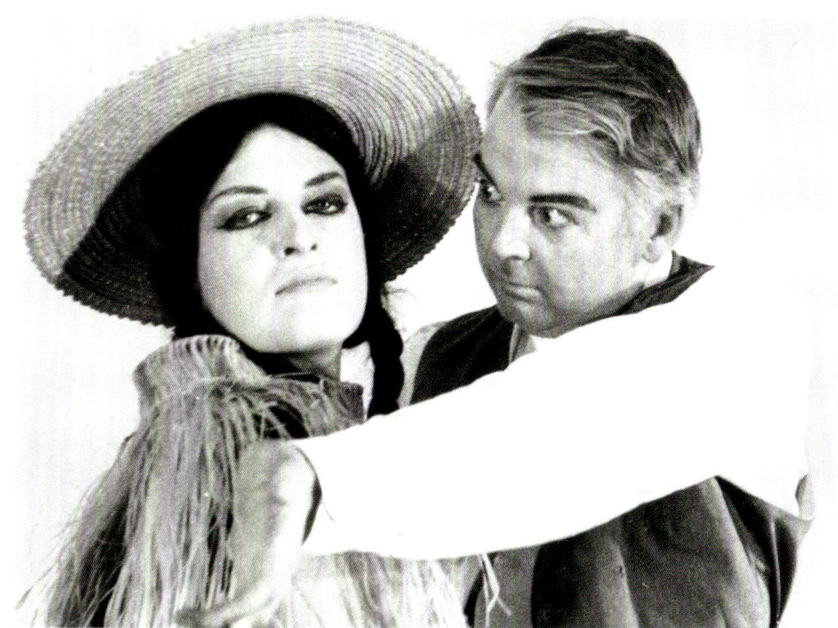

In 1972 Rosenthal was a participant in California School of the Arts' "West Coast Conference on Women Artists," and became part of the advance guard for Southern California's feminist art movement. In 1973 she served as a founding board member for the exhibition venue, Womanspace, and was also involved with Grandview (a collective gallery for women), the Woman's Building, and the women's art collective, Double X. In 1975 Rosenthal premiered her first piece as a performance artist, a mode of working that she continued to develop for the next twenty-five years; during those years she presented thirty-two discrete performance works at venues throughout the U.S. and Europe.

Following the end of her marriage in 1978, Rosenthal began regularly teaching classes in her storefront studio and residence in West Los Angeles. Her piece, *Rachel's Brain*, was included in Documenta 8 in Kassel, Germany, and in 1989 the piece received an Obie Award. During the 1980s, the focus of Rosenthal's work shifted increasingly from the personal to the political, and in 1993 she taught a performance workshop for people with HIV/AIDS. In 1994 she taught a workshop for battered women and was featured on the cover of *Ms. Magazine*. Rosenthal has been the recipient of more than twenty grants and awards, and has been a guest lecturer at hundreds of museums and schools throughout the world. Rosenthal lives and works in Los Angeles. *Kristine McKenna*

1 Conversation with Rachel Rosenthal, May 24, 2002.

Jack Smith

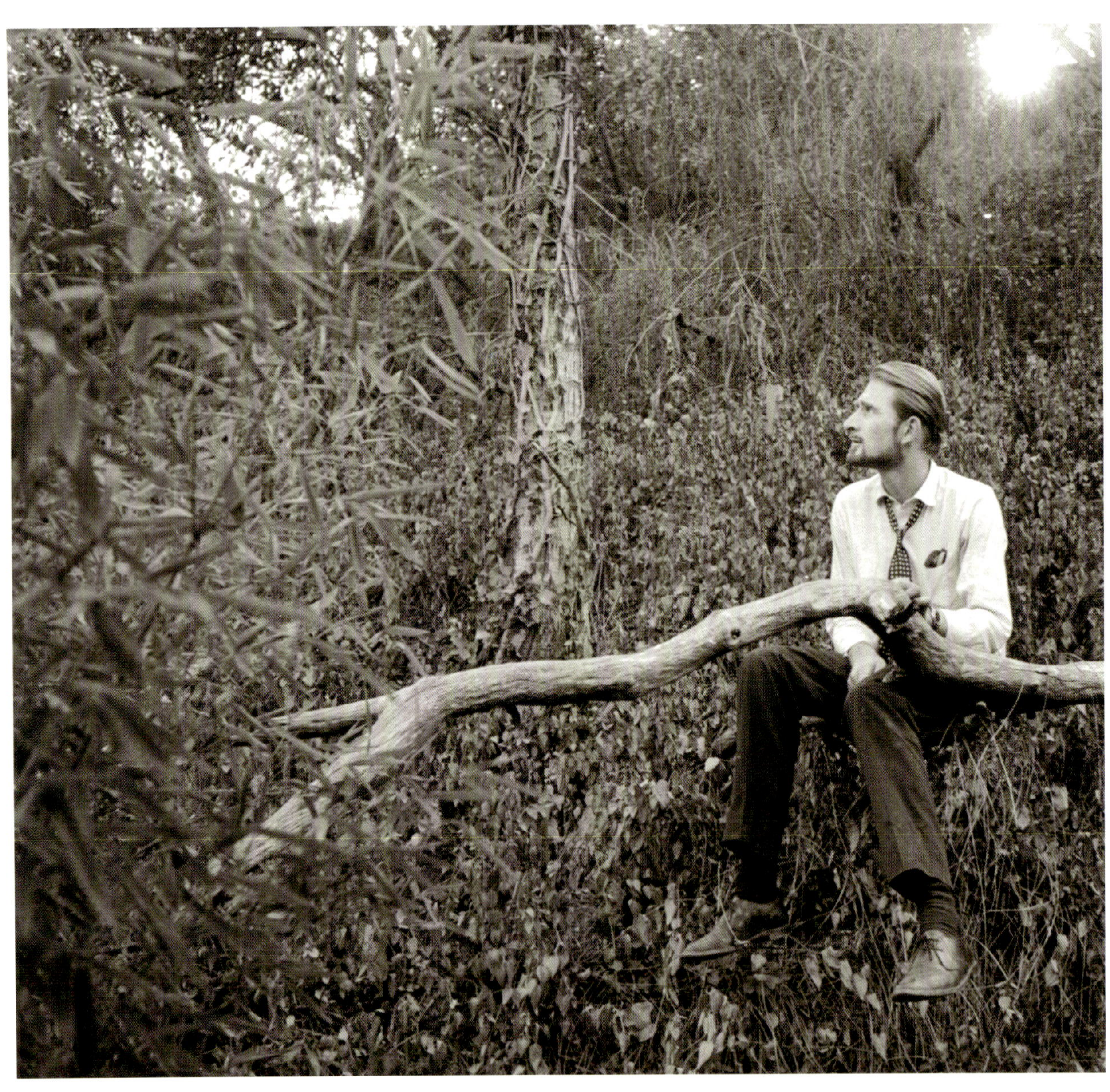

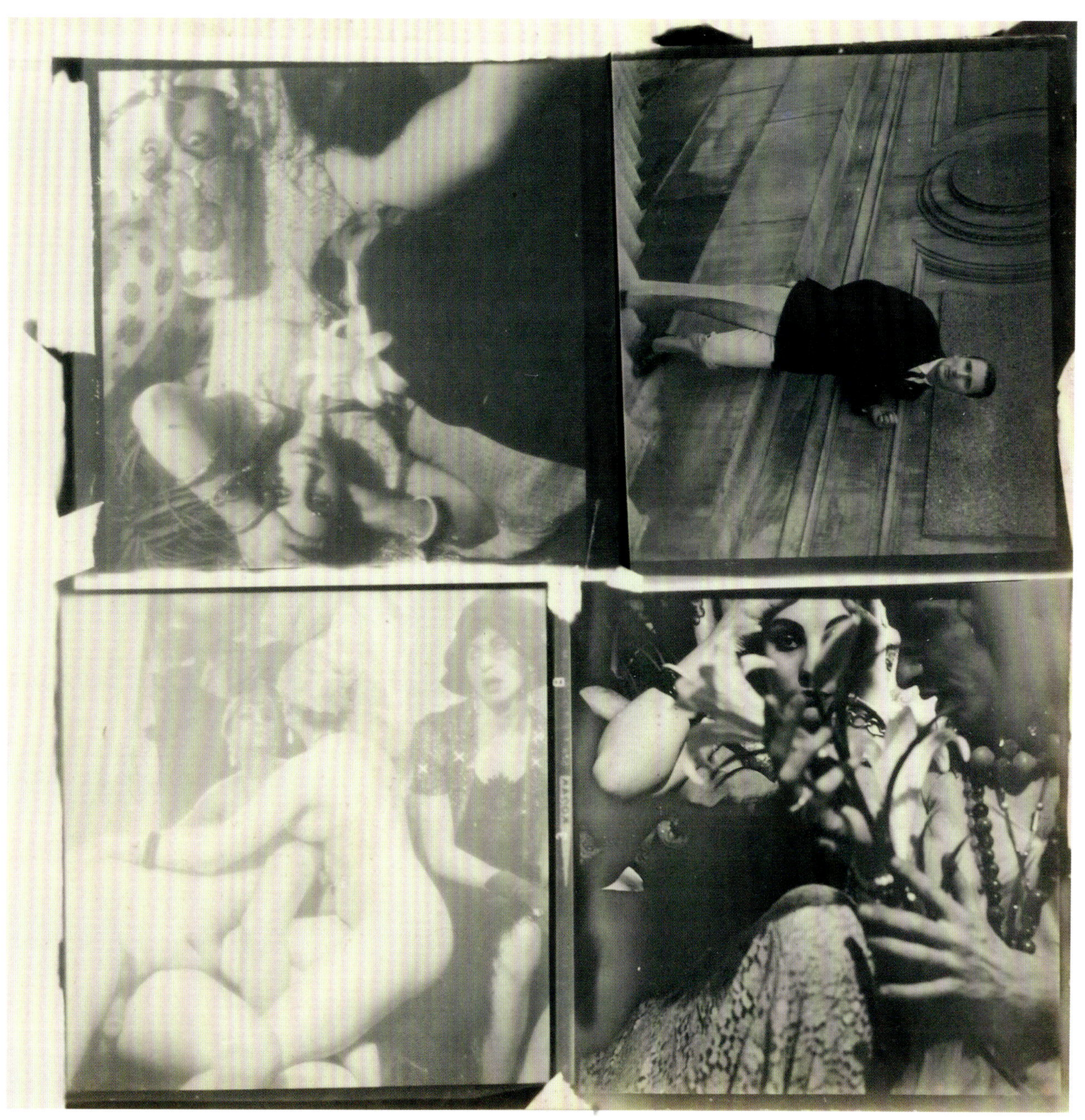

The extravagantly sexual, flamboyant, avant-garde film, *Flaming Creatures* (1963), immediately established its director Jack Smith as one of the quintessential underground artists of New York. His reputation spread quickly, buoyed by two visits to the West Coast shortly after release of the film. Born in Columbus, Ohio in 1932, Smith had moved to New York in 1953 determined to find a place for himself in the arts. In 1956 he met the underground filmmakers Ken Jacobs and Bob Fleischner and soon began acting. Using a camera borrowed from Jacobs, he shot his first film, *Scotch Tape* (1959), on a single, hundred-foot roll of Kodachrome film.

Celebrated for its swooning camera work and hallucinogenic atmosphere of befrilled drag and orgiastic indulgence, *Flaming Creatures* earned Smith the Fifth Annual Independent Film Award, sponsored by Jonas Mekas's influential journal *Film Culture*. Smith accompanied the film to Los Angeles when it was screened in October 1963 at the Coronet Theater. Earlier that year at Diane DiPrima's apartment in New York, he had met George Herms who in California introduced him to Wallace Berman. A fan of experimental cinema and steady patron of the Coronet, Berman invited Smith to screen *Scotch Tape* at his Beverly Glen home. Shirley Berman has fondly recalled Smith's visit, especially his "winning ways" with her son Tosh.[1] In the backyard on Crater Lane, Berman took photographs of a serene, dignified-looking Smith.

p. 256
Jack Smith, Los Angeles, 1963, Photograph by Wallace Berman.

p. 257
Jack Smith, from *The Beautiful Book*, 1962, Composite silver print.

p. 259 top
Jack Smith, *Octopus in Skirt*, 1969, Ink on screenprint on paper.

p. 259 bottom
Jack Smith, *The Miracle of Farblonjet, Technicolor Sunset Easter Pageant*, 1969, Ink on paper, collage.

In 1964, a screening of *Flaming Creatures* was shut down at the New Bowery Theater in New York and the film was later declared obscene in New York Criminal Court. On the heels of this notoriety, Smith was invited back to Los Angeles to join filmmaker Gregory Markopoulos and poet Michael McClure as judges for the Third Los Angeles Film-Makers' Festival. The festival was disrupted when filmmaker Kenneth Anger staged a protest over what he claimed was an unauthorized screening of his film *Inauguration of the Pleasure Dome* (1954). At the awards ceremony, Smith, in trademark style, presented the ever-dramatic Anger with the "Maria Montez Award," named for Smith's favorite actress-diva, the 1940s star of *Cobra Woman* and *Ali Baba and the Forty Thieves*.

Throughout the 1960s, appeals of the obscenity conviction for *Flaming Creatures* continued in the courts, climaxing in a 1968 screening in Senate offices arranged by Strom Thurmond. Stills from the movie allegedly "shocked Washington's hardened press corps."[2] Thoroughout the 1970s, Smith continued writing and performing in theater pieces while intermittently shooting footage for film projects. Smith created several loose narratives conceived as slide show projections, including *Moses* (1974), *Horror of the Rented World* (1975), and *How Can Uncle Fishhook Have a Free Bicentennial Zombie Underground?* (1976). He also acted in several early productions by theatrical impresario Robert Wilson.

In 1978 Smith received a ten thousand dollar grant from the National Endowment for the Arts for production costs of *Sinbad in the Rented World*, a much beloved project that he was never able to finish. He began to suffer from the effects of AIDS in 1988 and died the next year in New York. A full-scale traveling retrospective of Smith's works was organized by Edward Leffingwell for The Institute for Contemporary Art/P.S.1 New York in 1997. *Michael Duncan*

1 All information about Smith's visits to Los Angeles is derived from Edward Leffingwell's manuscript for his unpublished, full-length assessment of Smith's career, *The Only Normal Man in Baghdad*. Shirley Berman's comment was taken from Leffingwell's conversation with her, May 10, 1997.
2 Edward Leffingwell, "An Anecdoted Chronology," *Jack Smith: Flaming Creature: His Amazing Life and Times*, (London and New York: Serpent's Tail & Institute for Contemporary Art/P.S.1, 1997), p. 259.

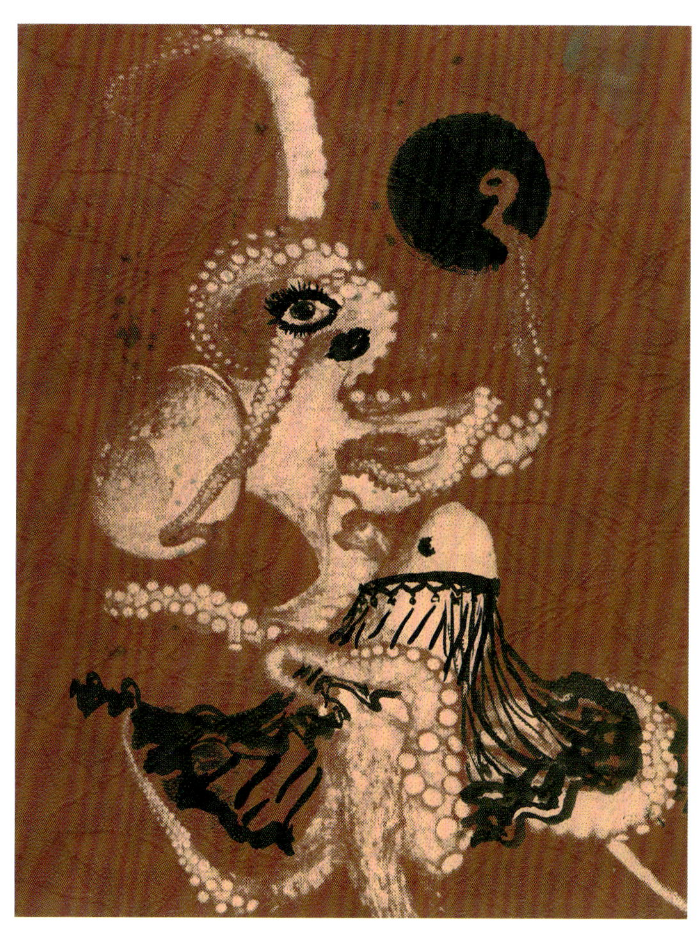

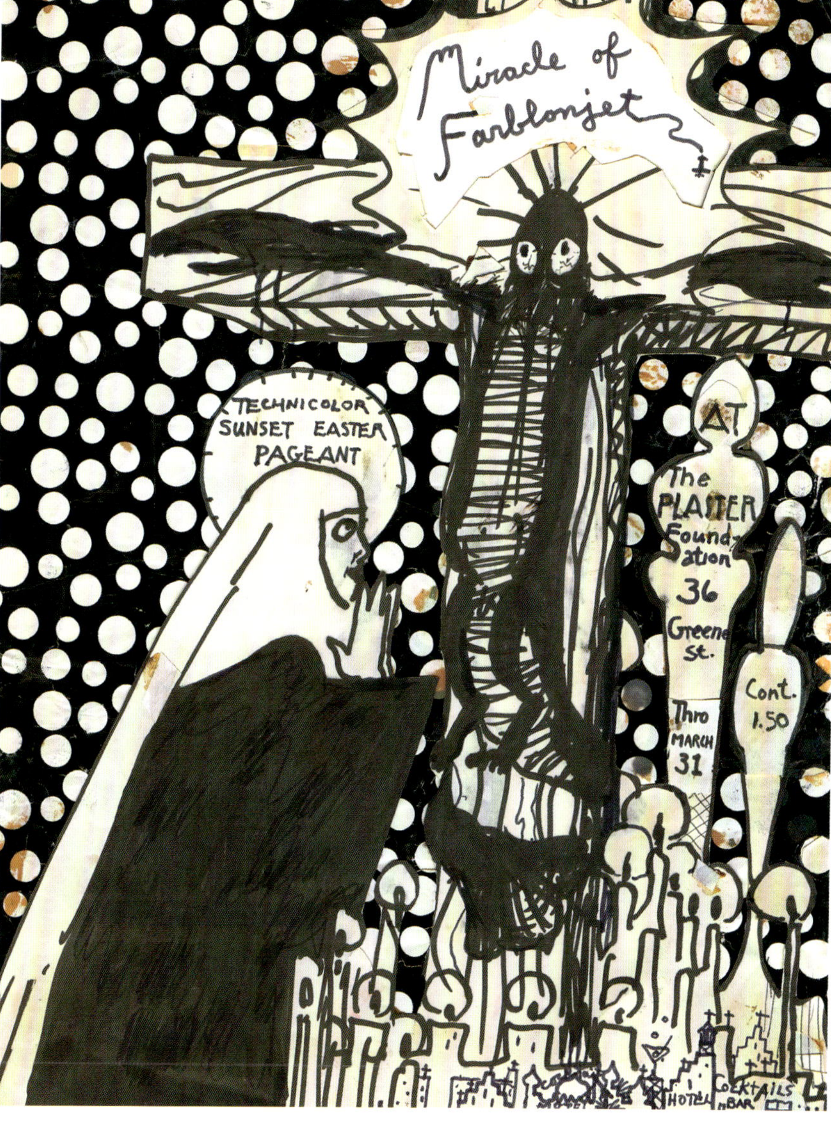
Miracle of Farblonjet
TECHNICOLOR SUNSET EASTER PAGEANT
AT The PLASTER Foundation 36 Greene St.
Thro MARCH 31
Cont. 1.50
HOTEL
COCKTAILS BAR

Dean Stockwell

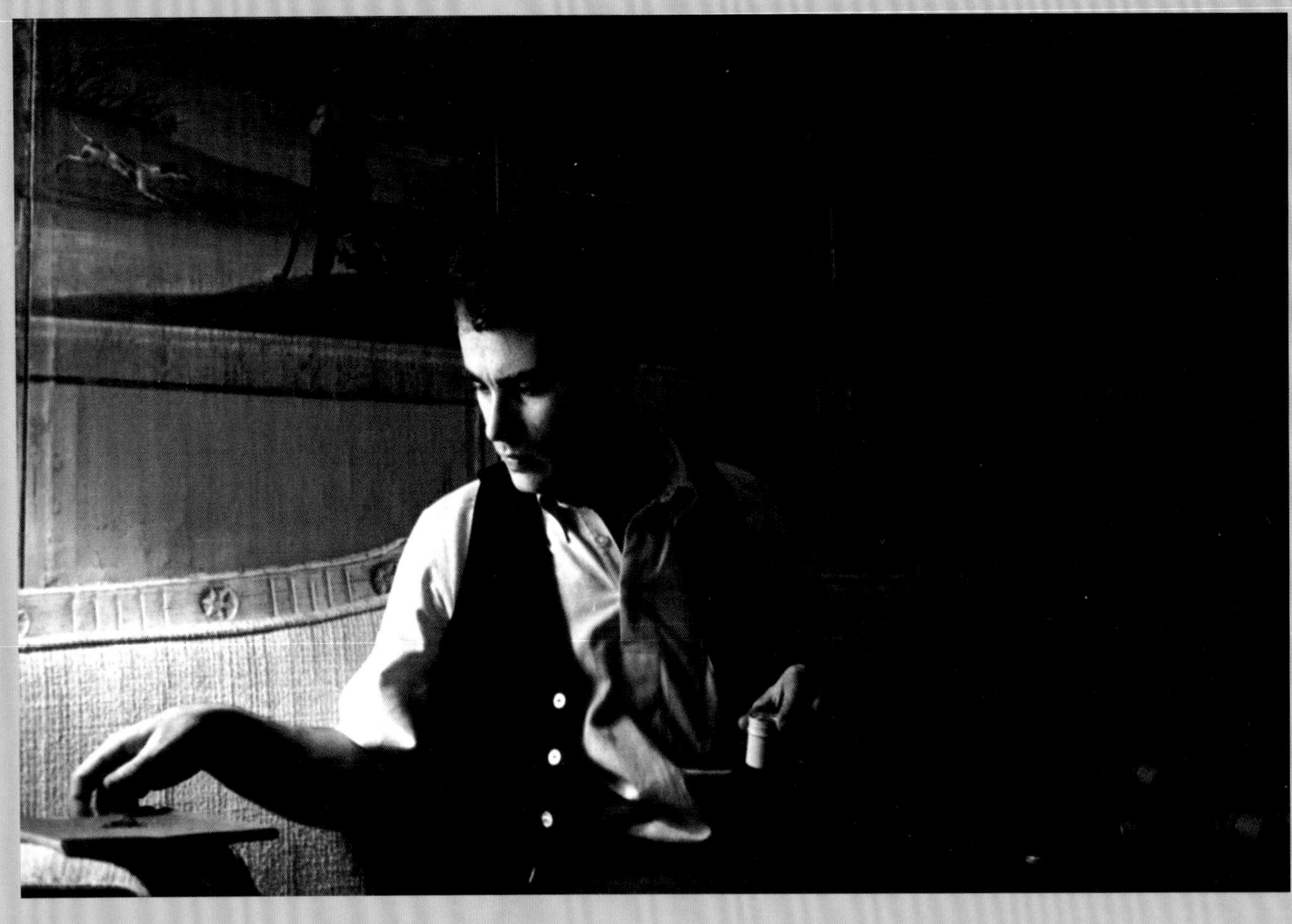

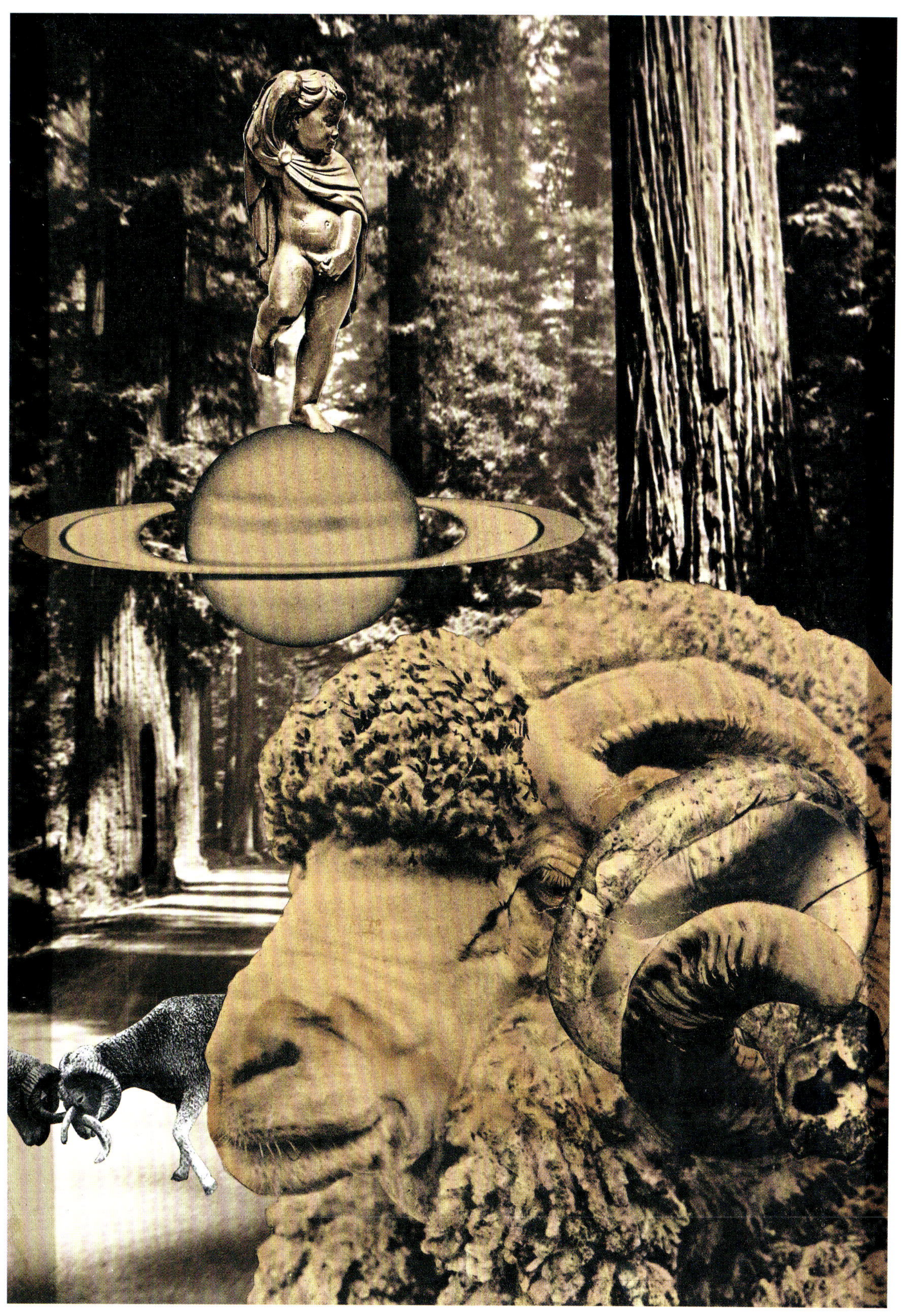

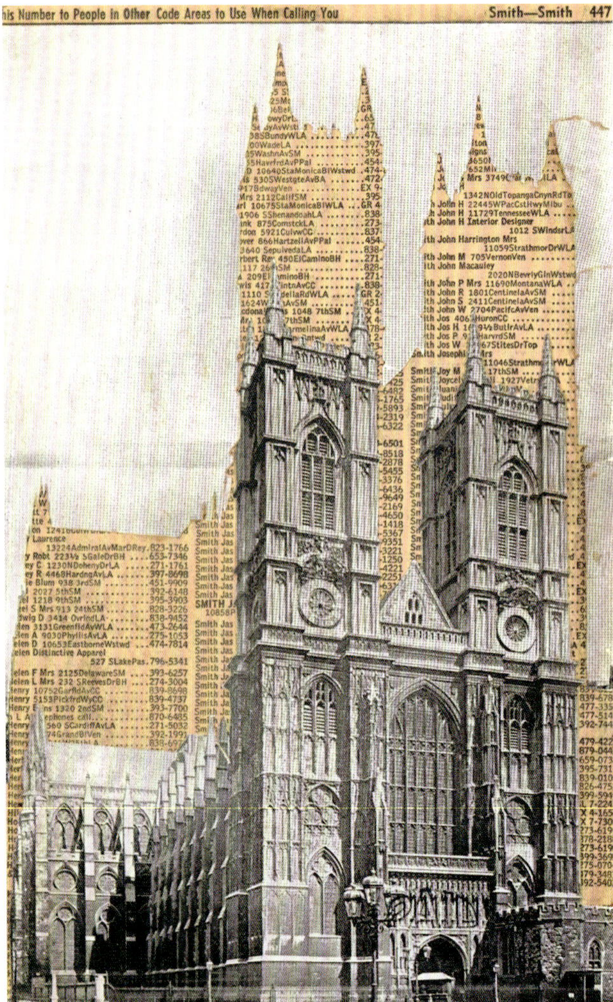

Dean Stockwell was born in Hollywood in 1935 and established himself as an actor as a child. In 1955 he met Wallace Berman and began a second career as an artist. Berman introduced the young actor to an anti-materialist community of visual artists that Stockwell immediately responded to, and he became an important early supporter and collector of works by Bruce Conner, George Herms, Jess, and Wallace Berman, among others.

Berman also familiarized Stockwell with collage, experimental film, and photography, and led him to the artmaking practice that has been a part of his life ever since. During the early years of their friendship, Stockwell developed a visual art vocabulary combining metaphysical symbols with surreal juxtapositions, which he continues to mine today. Working primarily in collage, Stockwell produced a large body of work in the 1950s that is at turns romantic, apocalyptic, and droll. Images of celestial bodies, Greek statuary, gothic architecture, advertising, and photography clipped from old *Life* magazines ricochet across the picture plane in collages that initially appear to be random, but on closer examination resonate with a strange portentousness. Working in this mode, Stockwell created the cover for *Semina 8*, and designed the cover for his friend Neil Young's album of 1977, *American Stars 'n Bars*.

From the mid-1950s until Berman's death in 1976, Stockwell worked in periodic bursts of activity, and among his output was a series of experimental films, one of which was an intimate portrait of George Herms at work in his studio. Unfortunately, most of Stockwell's films were either destroyed or lost. For most of the 1980s and 1990s Stockwell produced relatively little visual art, but that changed in 2002 when he began creating collages using found images, his own photographs, and computer technologies. In 2003 he commenced work on a series of collages titled *The Spagyric Eye* (spagyric refers to a form of plant alchemy), and in 2004 he exhibited the completed cycle of forty works at the RB Ravens Gallery in Taos. These recent works are very much in keeping with Stockwell's Surrealist-inspired art of the 1950s. *The Spagyric Eye* revolves around variations on two central images—an abandoned house and a human eye. Interwoven into each of them are images of feathers, jewels, dolls, thorns, snakes, astronauts, eggs, leopards, statuary of Hindu gods and figures from Greek mythology. Stockwell continues to work on computer-generated collages at his home in Taos, New Mexico.

Stockwell is also a gifted poet who has maintained an intermittent writing practice over the years. Many of his poems were inscribed onto postcards and sent to friends; as can be seen in the accompanying illustrations, his poems were intensely personal and dramatic. *Kristine McKenna*

p. 260
Dean Stockwell in Beverly Glen Canyon, 1963, Photograph by Wallace Berman.

p. 261
Dean Stockwell, Untitled (Ram's head), Collage, 1965.

p. 262
Dean Stockwell, *Smith*, 1958, Collage on cardboard.

p. 263 top
Dean Stockwell, Announcement for screening of three Stockwell films in Topanga Canyon.

p. 263 bottom
Dean Stockwell, Untitled note and poem sent to David Meltzer (written on his 21st birthday), 1956.

p. 264 top
Dean Stockwell, Untitled, Collage, 1957, Collection of the Artist.

p. 264 bottom
Dean Stockwell, *Suffragette*, 1965, Collage on posterboard.

p. 265 top right
Mailer to Ben and Shirley Talbot (Goodbye party for George Herms), 1963.

p. 265 bottom
Dean Stockwell, Stills from the film, *For Crazy Horse*, 1958, Letraset collage on found photos.

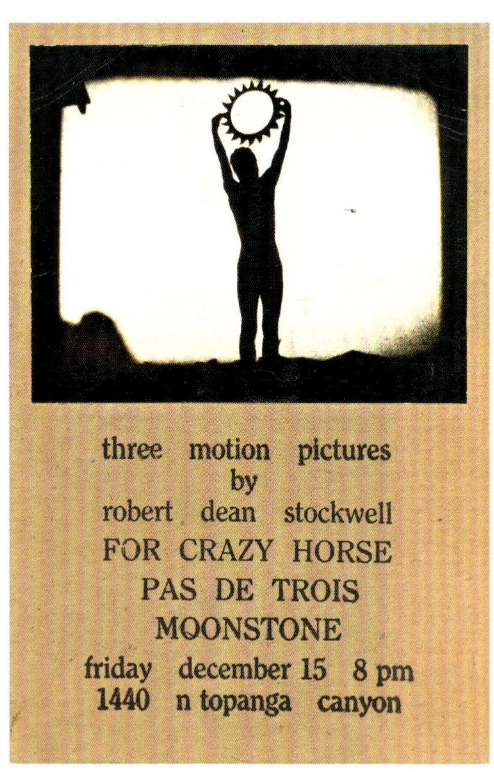

at wirley's 11:50 am

i have been sad tonight and i write to
you and that is just so...there is a
ghost singing in this room...did i
forsake..take my blood..
it is my birthday 21 and shirley made
a lovely cake for me and tosh blew the
candles quiet..bach is playing and that
too is just so..write to me..tell me
you are well if you are dying, in joy
if [illegible]g..words die in the m

over yes over

tonight tonight, i shall lay
me down to sleep down to...
i shall find a fine bed of lov
ing rocks loving rocks and lay
me down to sleep..soon..and
pull up about me a warm quilt
of soil about my frozen body
quilt of soil..tonight tonight
i promise i shall..then over
me to hide me from too many
stars i shall pull a beautiful
green blanket of loving grass
loving grass..and for my pill
ow i shall have a gentle stone
gentle stone with numbers on
it 21

5630 cartwright
n. hollywood

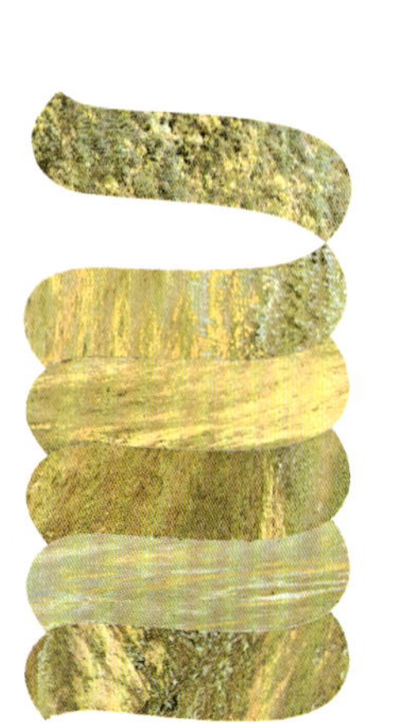
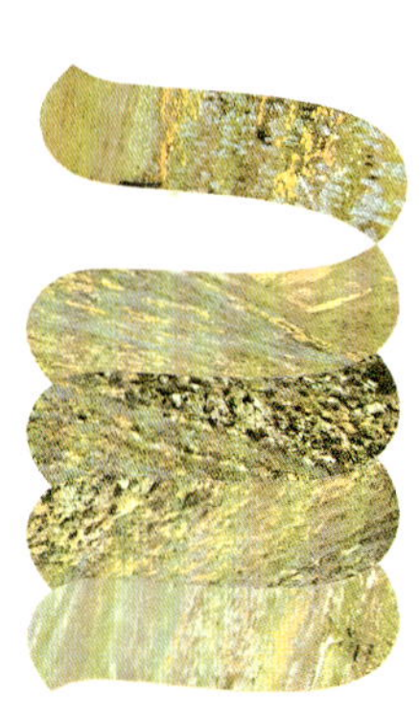
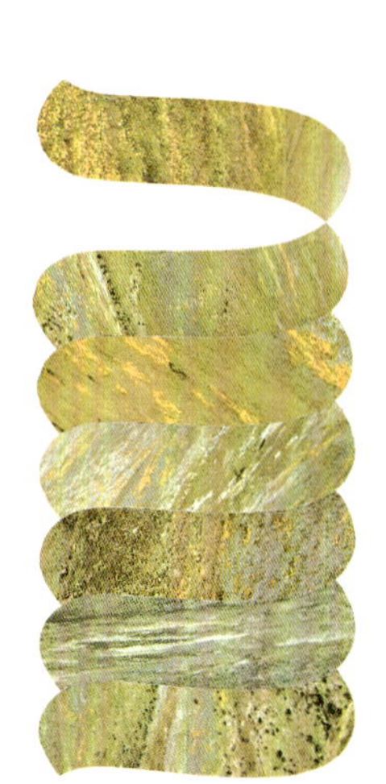
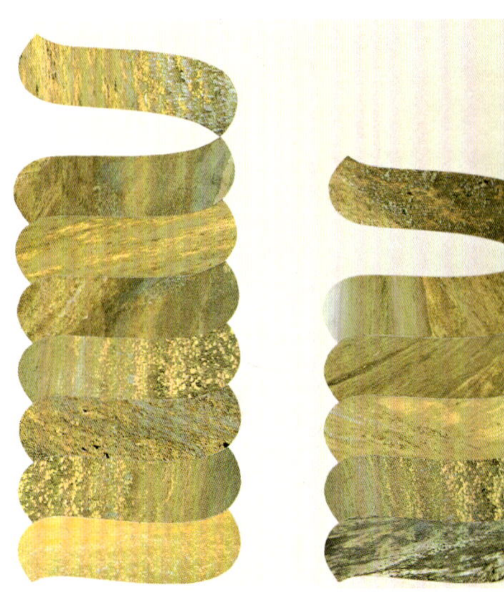
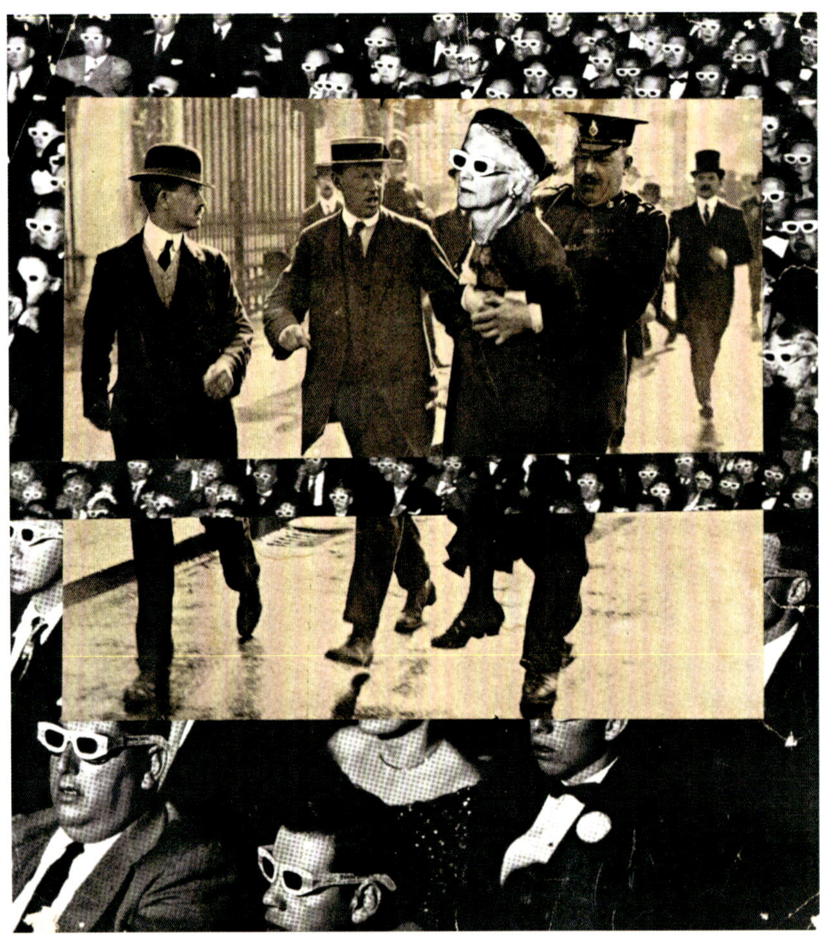

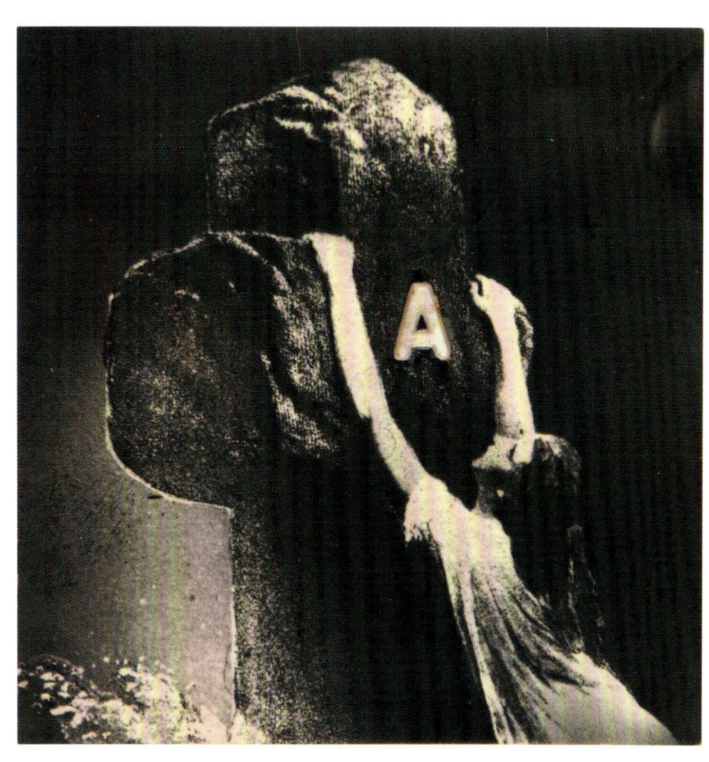
A

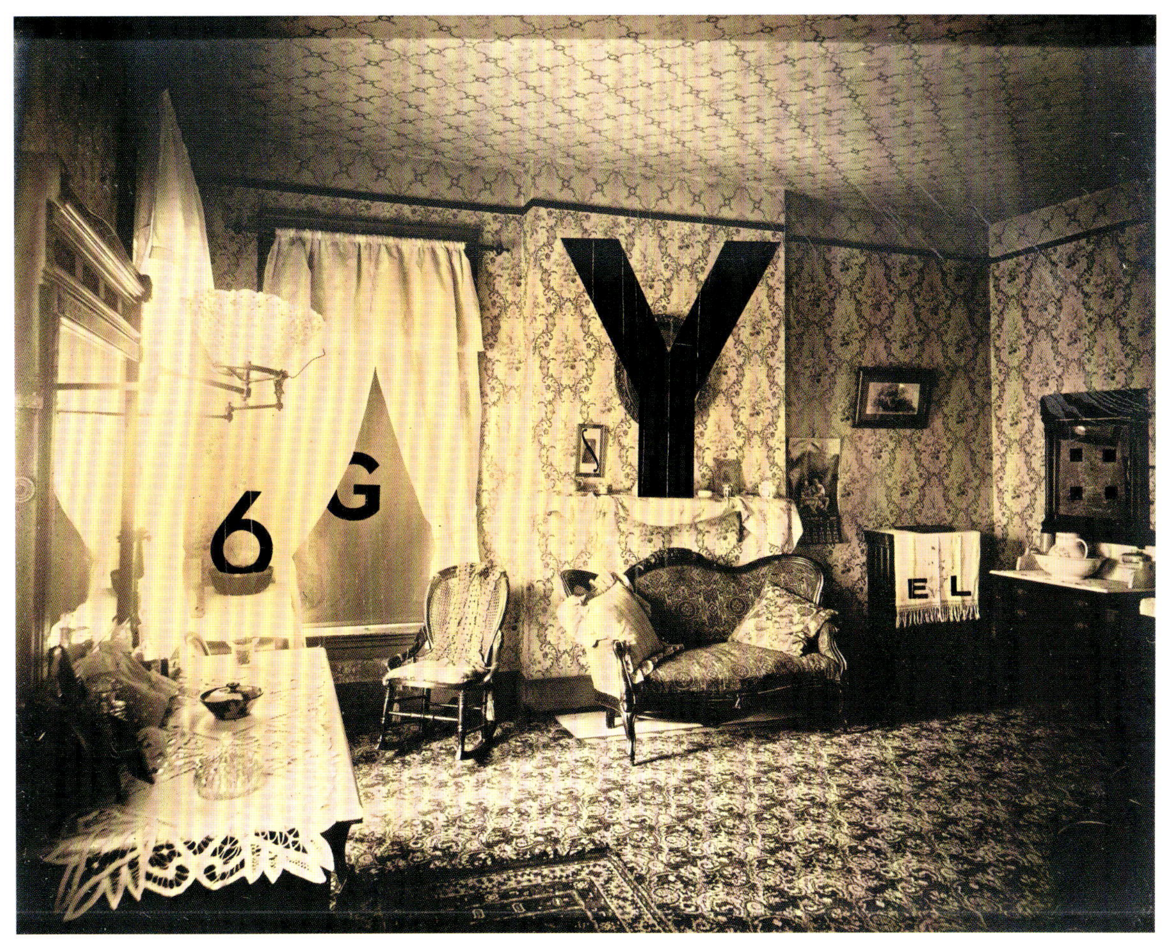
6
G
Y
EL

Ben Talbert

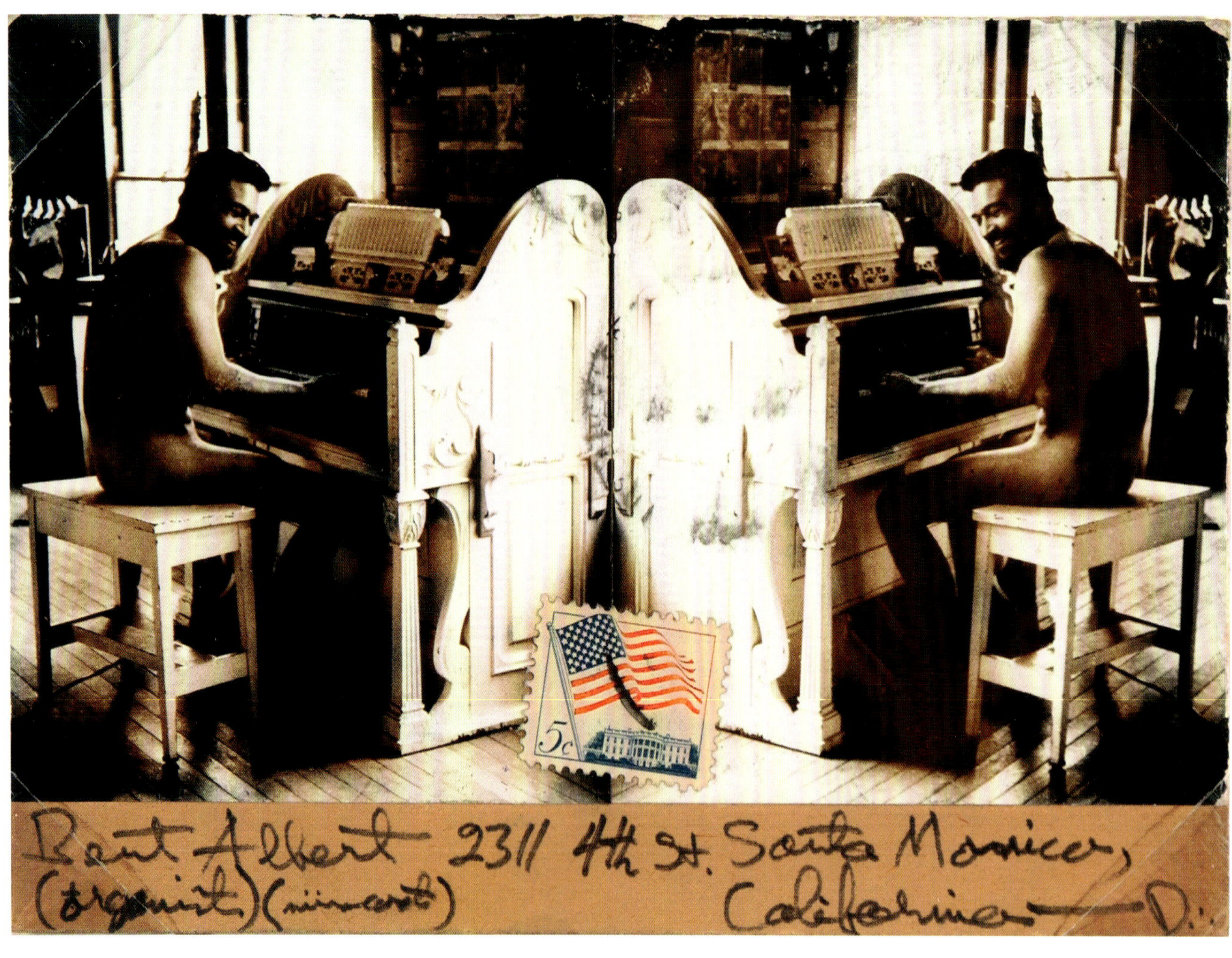

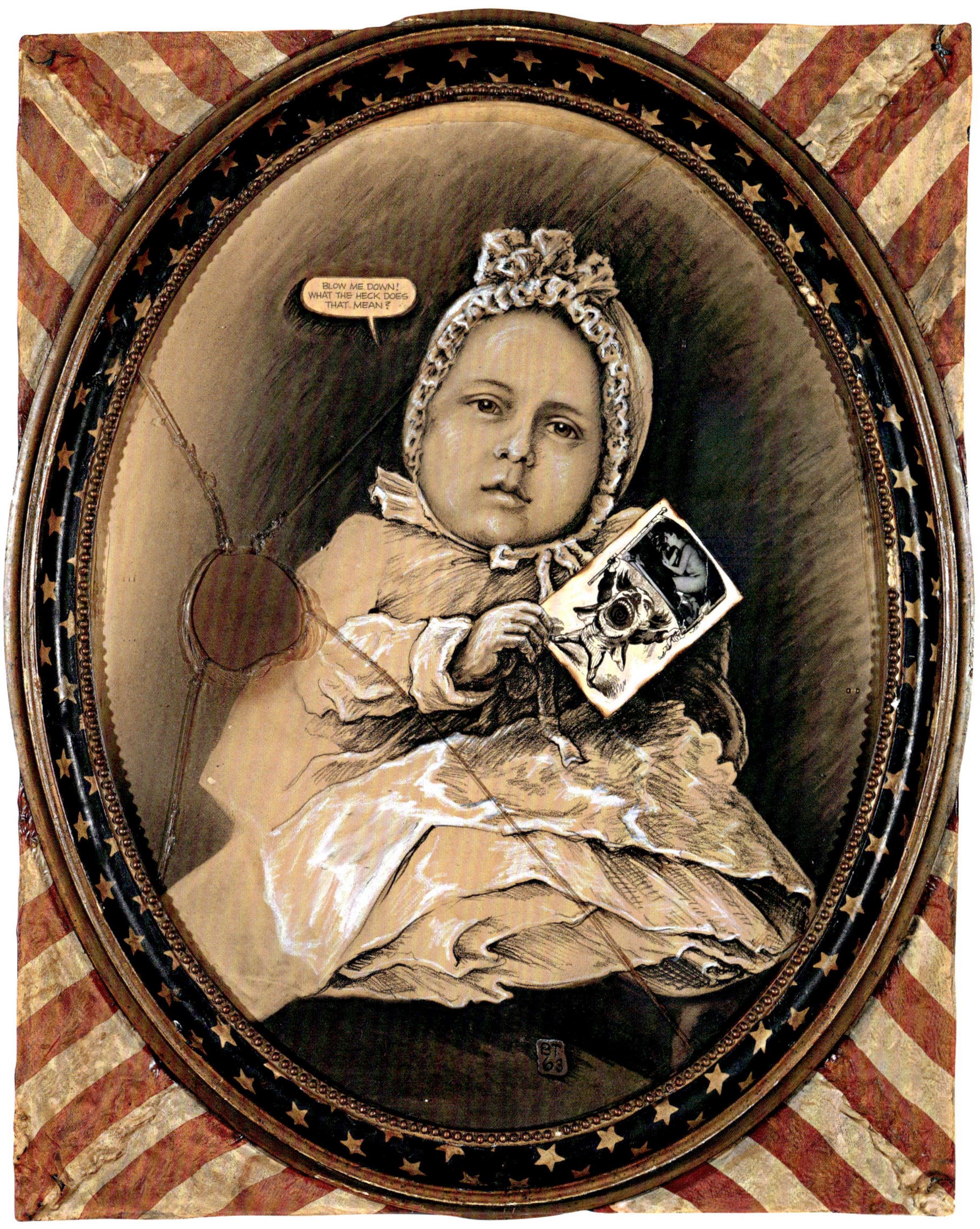

Bent Albert 2311 4th St. Santa Monica,
(organist)
California
5c

BLOW ME DOWN! WHAT THE HECK DOES THAT MEAN?
BT 63

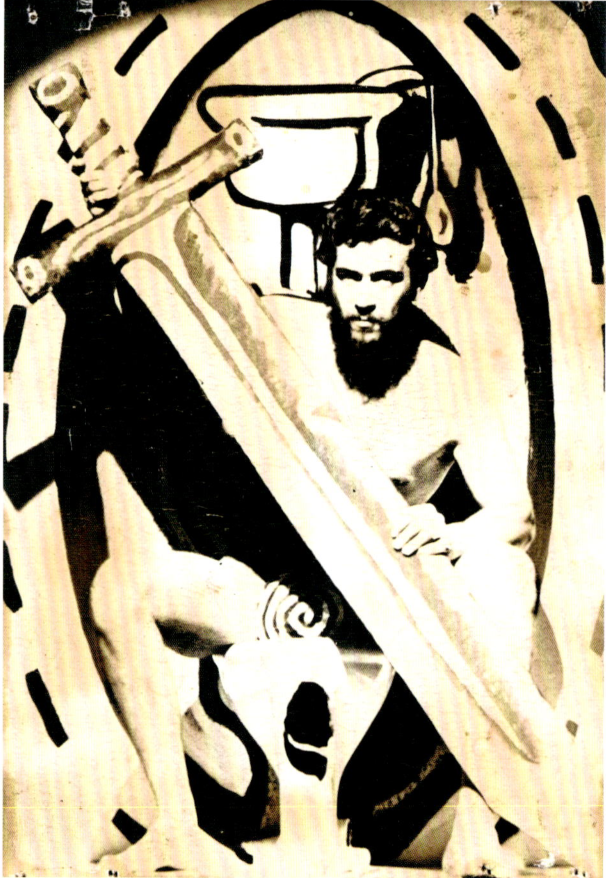

Ben Talbert was one of the promising talents of Los Angeles's postwar generation whose career in art was ended prematurely by his addictions. Born in Los Angeles in 1933, Talbert was the son of a truck driver, but, from the time he was young, great things were expected for him. Handsome, charismatic, and smart, Talbert was a natural leader who became the center of attention in any room he entered. "Ben was extremely macho," Tosh Berman recalls, "but he was a very funny guy who could really make my father laugh. They had a similar spirit and got along really well."[1]

Groomed for a career in the military, Talbert enrolled at Texas A&M to train as a pilot, but when he was disqualified from a flying career he changed his focus of study to aeronautical engineering. He dropped out of school after a year, though, and married his high school sweetheart, Shirley, in 1952. The following year Talbert was drafted and he served in the Army from 1953 to 1957.

p. 266
Ben Talbert at the piano, 1958. Photographed mailer mounted on posterboard by Dean Stockwell.

p. 267
Ben Talbert, *Tar Baby*, 1963. Mixed-media collage.

p. 268
Ben Talbert in Ubu Roi, 1964. Collaged photograph by Dean Stockwell.

p. 269
Ben Talbert, *Shrine of the Great American Weaner*, 1962–63. Assemblage with table, clock case, antlers, baby pacifier, fur, and oil (front view and back view).

p. 270
Ben Talbert, *Stamp Freak*, 1963. Mixed-media.

p. 271
Ben Talbert, *Ladies' All*, 1963. Mixed-media.

Upon his discharge from the service, Talbert turned his back on the military and enrolled at UCLA as a student in the urban land economics department. He lost interest in the subject after one semester, however, and transferred to the art department where his native gifts immediately became apparent. Talbert was a skilled draughtsman with a loose, breezy touch, and everything he made was freighted with his bawdy sense of humor and love of the perverse. Talbert delighted in playing with media and would, for instance, combine painted images of torn paper executed with trompe l'oeil accuracy with actual torn paper, photographs, and other collage elements.

Much of Talbert's work was erotic to such an intense degree that it was deemed too pornographic to exhibit by most art dealers. This would prove to be a huge obstacle for Talbert's art. Also working against him was the fact that Talbert had a voracious appetite for life and a reckless streak that would prove his undoing. According to Talbert's friend, curator Hal Glicksman, Talbert believed that Abstract Expressionism was "driven by emotions liberated by wine, pot, and lack of sleep."[2] Those were a few of the basic elements of Talbert's daily regimen, and, considering how he lived, he was astonishingly prolific.

Like Ed Kienholz, Talbert was a social critic, but he worked with a considerably lighter hand, and his concerns were almost exclusively sexual. Talbert's sensibility was clearly shaped by the pornography of the 1950s, which often presented voluptuous, all-American girls engaged in graphic sexual acts; Talbert was drawn to that thematic territory, and he developed a juicy, overripe way of handling paint that was well-suited to his subject matter. Pop motifs—imagery plucked from the funny papers, soldiers and guns, American flags—turn up repeatedly in Talbert's work, but the cool associated with East Coast Pop held no allure for him; he preferred his Pop lurid and overheated, and that's how he painted it.

Talbert's assemblages were a little more chaste than his paintings, but not much. For *Shrine of the Great American Weaner*, Talbert painted the face of a clock with red stripes, affixed a pacifier at its center, and glued a pair of stag antlers atop it. On the reverse side of the piece, a three-dimensional female breast juts from the back of the clock. Talbert completed the piece in 1962, during the three-year period he worked on *The Ace*, which is widely acknowledged to be his greatest work.

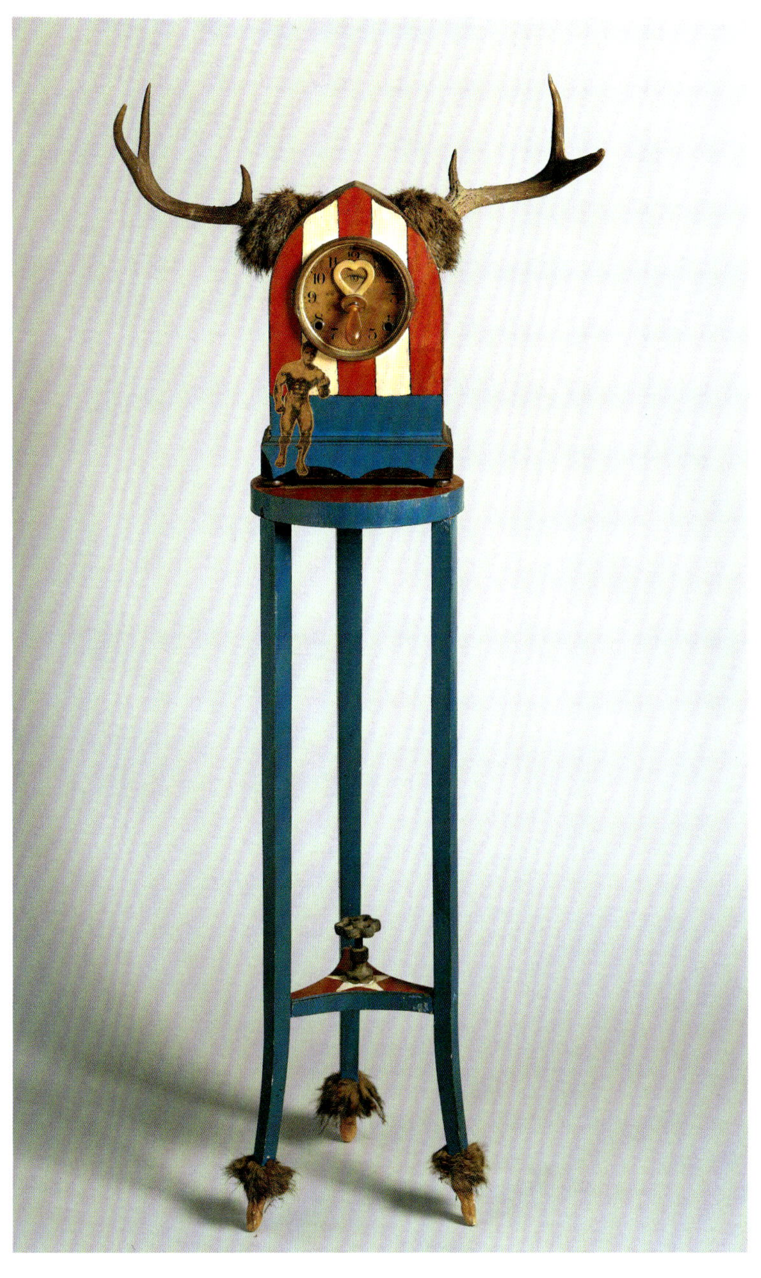

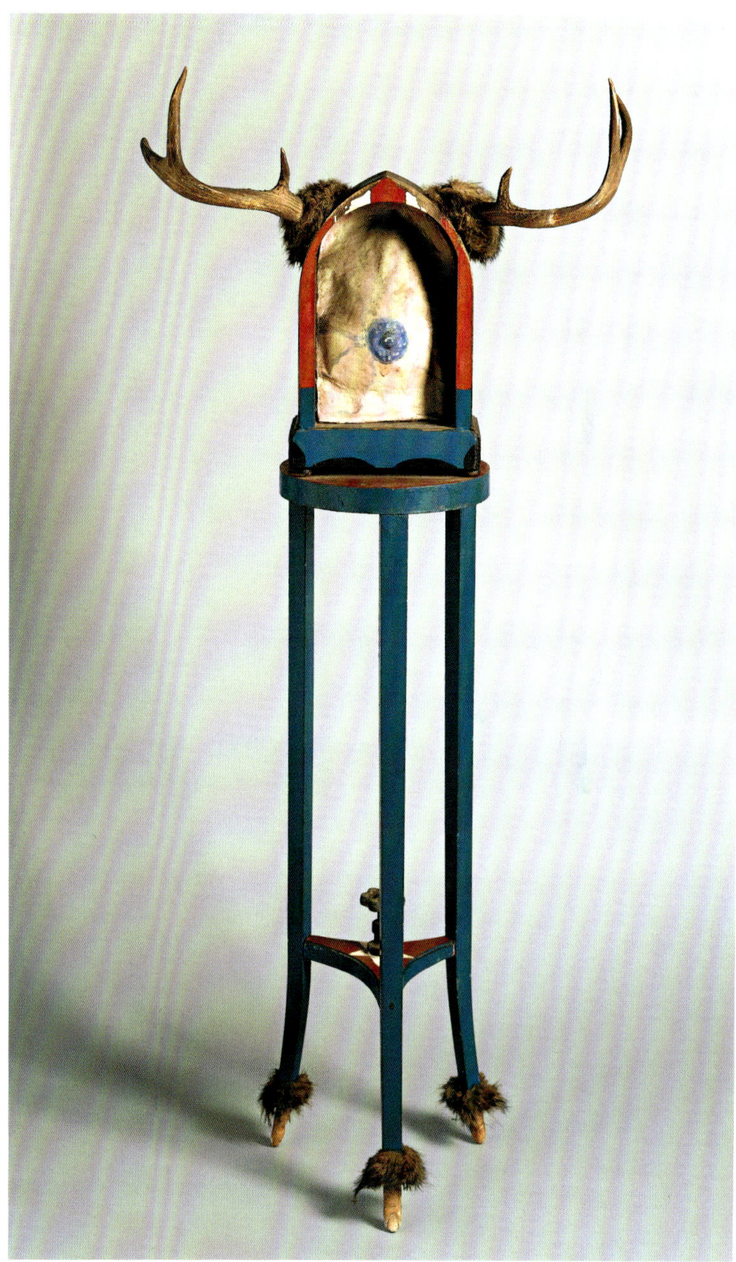

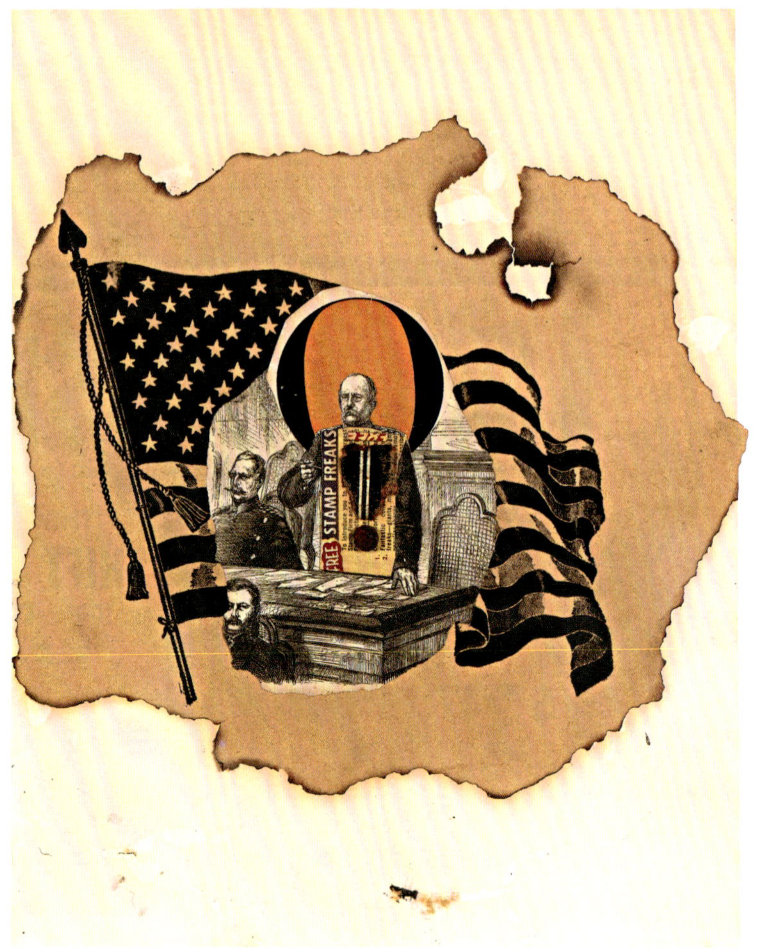

Incorporating the collection of aviation memorabilia Talbert began acquiring as a child, *The Ace* is a multi-layered work that deconstructs Talbert's boyhood dream of being a hero of the air age. *The Ace* is constructed on a painting easel, and at its center is a collage juxtaposing found images of war heroes with pictures of beautiful girls, which revolve around the first of the four aces, the ace of hearts. The ace of clubs—traditionally regarded as the death card—is represented by a tiny human skeleton. At the top of the piece is a one-way traffic sign, its arrow pointing up, and on the arrow is the ace of spades; on the playing card is an image of Ray Charles and text that reads "The ace is high." The fourth ace is hidden beneath a cover on the side of the easel which opens to reveal a mirror with the image of an eye affixed at the center, and the inscription, "You are the Ace of Diamonds." The front of the piece alludes to romantic associations with flying and is the affirmative side. An image of an atomic-bomb blast dominates the rear, nihilistic side, which has a dummy bomb inscribed with the names of cities destroyed by aerial attack. Presently in the permanent collection of the Nora Eccles Harrison Museum of Art, *The Ace* has been a centerpiece in numerous assemblage surveys of the past forty years.

Talbert had his debut as an exhibiting artist five years after he began making work in "Object Makers," a 1961 group show at Pomona College. Later the same year Walter Hopps organized Talbert's first one-man show at

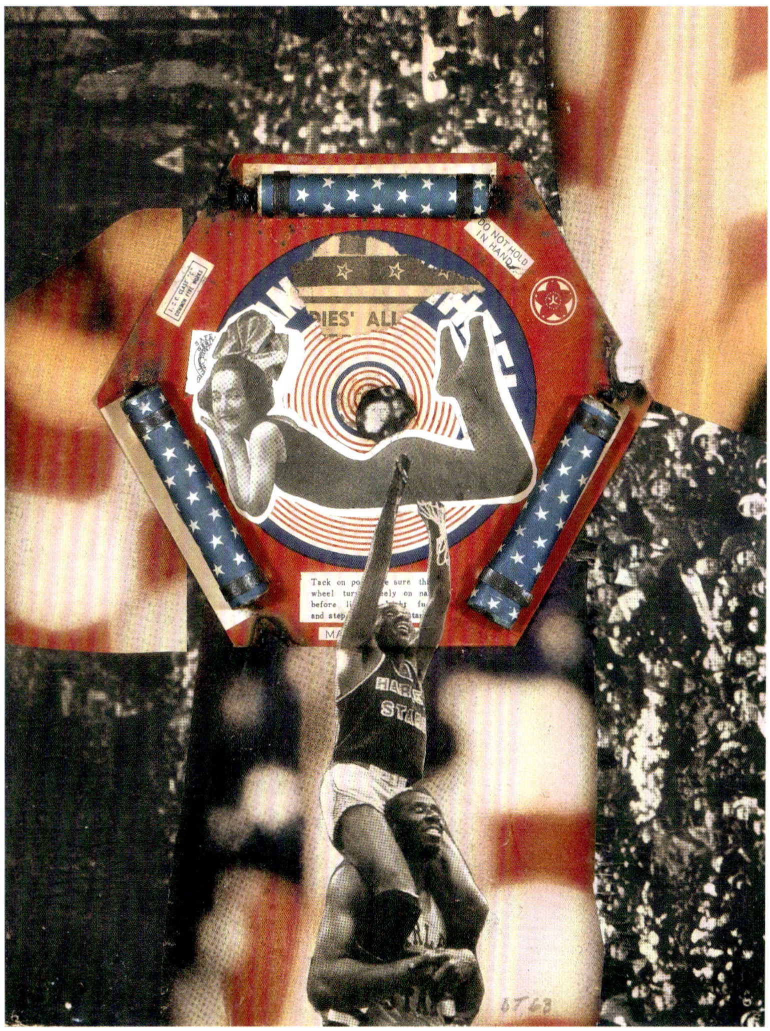

the Pasadena Art Museum. Hopps also included Talbert in "Directions in Collage: California," a group show at Pasadena in 1962. In 1964 Talbert designed sets and costumes for a staging of Alfred Jarry's *Ubu Roi* presented at the Coronet Theater, and beginning in 1965 he was in a series of three group shows ("The Arena of Love," "Boxes," "Drawings") at L.A.'s prestigious Dwan Gallery.

By the mid 1960s, Talbert's substance abuse began to take its toll. Shirley Talbert, who'd supported Talbert throughout their marriage so he could work in his Venice studio full-time, left him, and he was hospitalized several times for various drug-related health problems. In 1969 he began living with Gayle Davis, an exotic dancer whom he met at a rehabilitation center in Topanga run by Dr. Rosenberg, a psychiatrist who was an expert on alcoholism and did pioneering work in the use of art as a therapeutic tool. Together Davis and Talbert catalogued his work and mounted a retrospective exhibition in 1973 at the Mermaid Tavern in Topanga. Unfortunately, Talberts' drinking accelerated during the 1970s, and he died of an accidental overdose in 1974. *Kristine McKenna*

1 Conversation with Tosh Berman, January 11, 1999.

2 See Hal Glicksman, *Assemblage in California*, exh. cat (Irvine: The Art Gallery of the University of California, Irvine, 1968), p. 48–55.

Russel Tamblyn

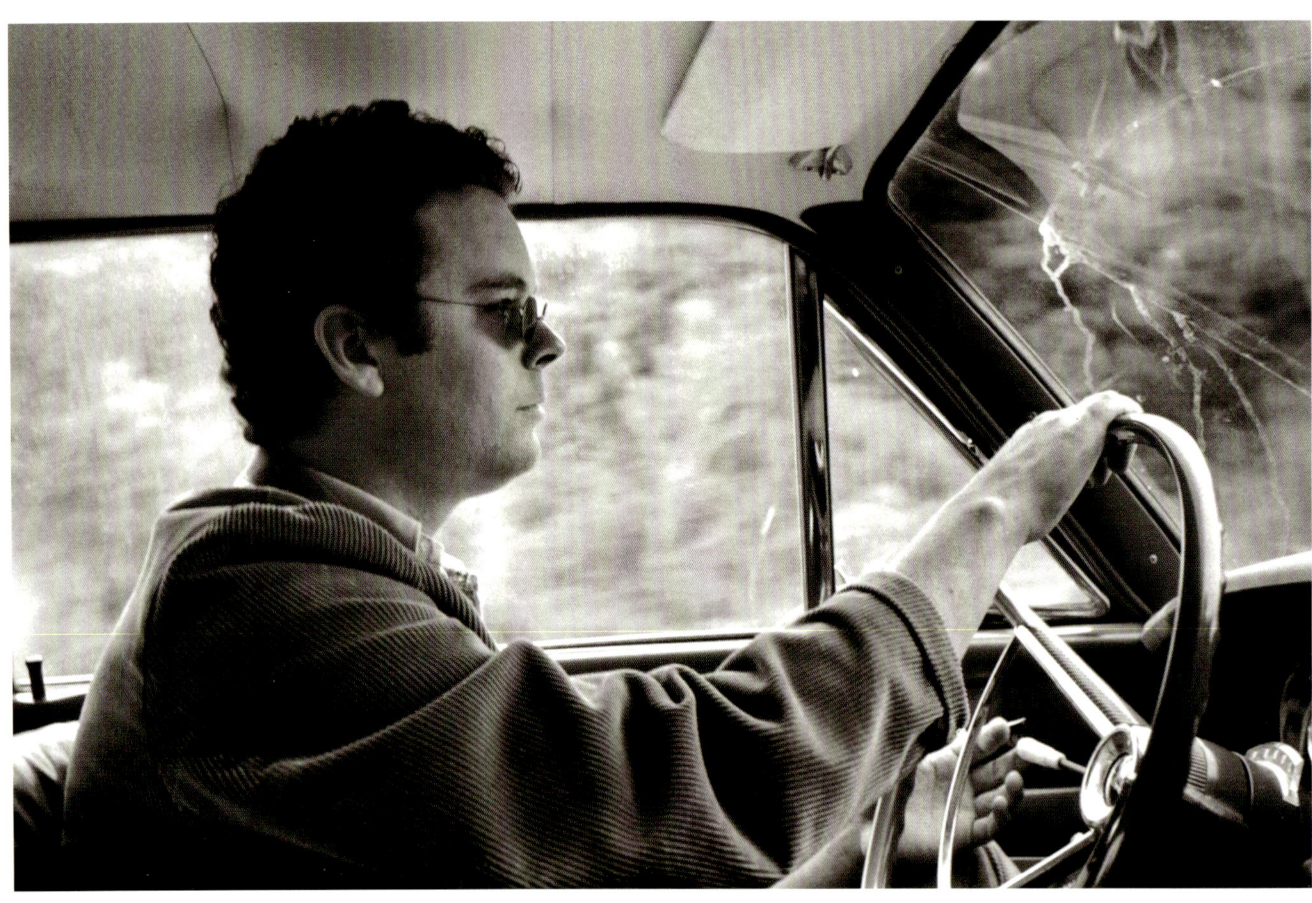

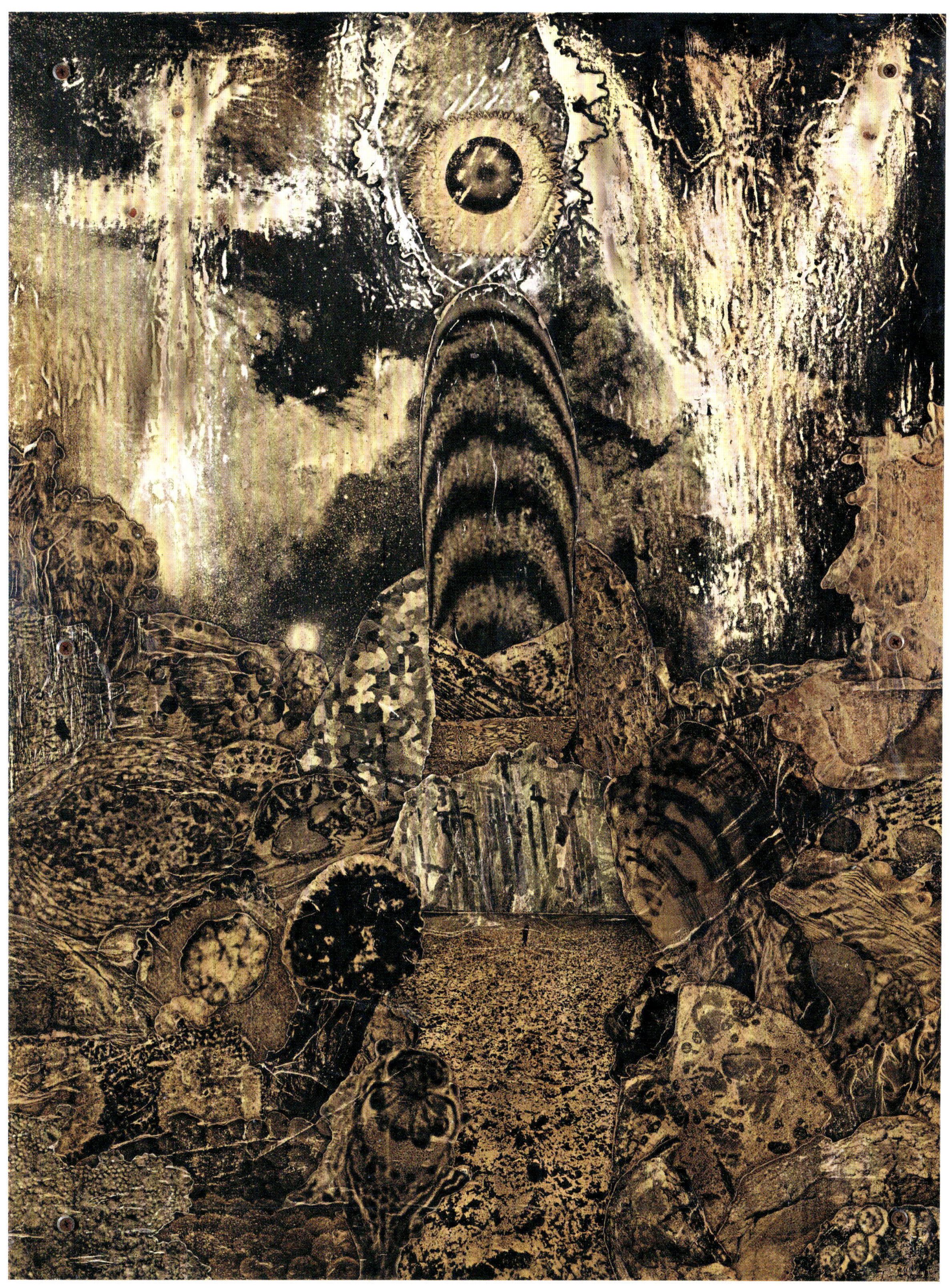

Actor Russel Tamblyn is well-known for his incendiary presence in Robert Wise's musical film of 1961, *West Side Story*. What's less known is that Tamblyn transformed his life completely when he met Wallace Berman.

Born in Los Angeles in 1934, Tamblyn exudes a sunny, boyish charm that made him ideal for the movies of the postwar period, and by the time he was fourteen he was working regularly. Tamblyn made his film debut in *The Boy With Green Hair* in 1948, and eight years later he established himself as a gifted dancer in Stanley Donen's 1954 musical, *Seven Brides for Seven Brothers*. After scoring an Oscar nomination for his work in the 1957 melodrama, *Peyton Place*, Tamblyn was standing on the brink of a major film career; however, his dissatisfaction with the movie world had already taken root. His experience with the 1958 film, *Tom Thumb*, exacerbated his growing sense of alienation.

"I was completely turned off by what happened with *Tom Thumb*," Tamblyn recalls. "The original fairy tale is so good, and it's actually very dark—Tom Thumb ends up being killed by a rat in the story. They eliminated all that from the film and transformed the story into a piece of fluff. I'd just turned twenty one when that film was shot, and they shaved the hair on my chest and my legs, dyed my hair blond, and told me to act like a two-year old."[1]

Tamblyn was drafted in 1958 and spent the next two years in the Army. When he was discharged in 1960, he was looking for something, but he wasn't sure what. In 1960 he married Elizabeth Kempton, whom he met on the set of *Tom Thumb* where she worked as an extra. In 1961 he starred in *West Side Story*, and then he worked with Robert Wise again in 1963, in the classic horror film, *The Haunting*. Tamblyn was making a good deal of money at that point and was living in a sprawling Pacific Palisades mansion with a bowling alley, but he wasn't happy. Then in 1963 he decided to throw a party for his friend Henry Miller.

"The week before the party I ran into Dean Stockwell, whom I hadn't seen in years, and I invited him to the party," Tamblyn has recalled. "Dean came, and he brought Wallace and Shirley, who were absolutely quiet. Wallace didn't like public things and was always like a mouse off in a corner when he was in a group—he preferred one-on-one communication. I hardly spoke to him at the party, but a few days later I received an issue of *Semina* in the mail, with an invitation to visit Wallace in Beverly Glen—and that's when my life began to change. Wallace showed me a film he was working on, which had a tremendous impact on me emotionally. I remember him telling me that the film was in twenty-two parts correlating to the twenty-two letters in the Kabbalah, and that the letters of the Kabbalah are in the shape of God's tongue and are more like a breath."

"Wallace had all the qualities you'd want in a teacher," Tamblyn has said. "When you're in movies you're constantly working to make the viewers head spin, and I was tired of doing things for everybody else. Wallace encouraged me to make art, which is about making your own head spin, and he introduced me to people who lived in

p. 272
Russel Tamblyn, Los Angeles, 1963, Photograph by Wallace Berman.

p. 273
Russel Tamblyn, *Topanga Vision*, 1967–69, Collage on board, with oil paint added in 1969 after the studio fire.

p. 274
Russel Tambyn, Announcement for an exhibition at Mizuno Gallery.

p. 275
Russel Tamblyn, *Open Fist*, 1965, Mixed-media collage and acrylic on wood.

p. 276 left
Russel Tamblyn, *John Dillinger/Self*, 1968, Collaged photographs with oil paint.

p. 276 right
Russel Tamblyn with Jack Hirschman, *HNYC*, Limited edition artist's book published by Russel Tamblyn's Skyline Press.

p. 277 left
Russel Tamblyn, *Book #1*, (Los Angeles: Skyline Press, n.d.).

p. 277 right
Russel Tamblyn, Untitled box collage, 1966, Mixed media, Collection of the Artist.

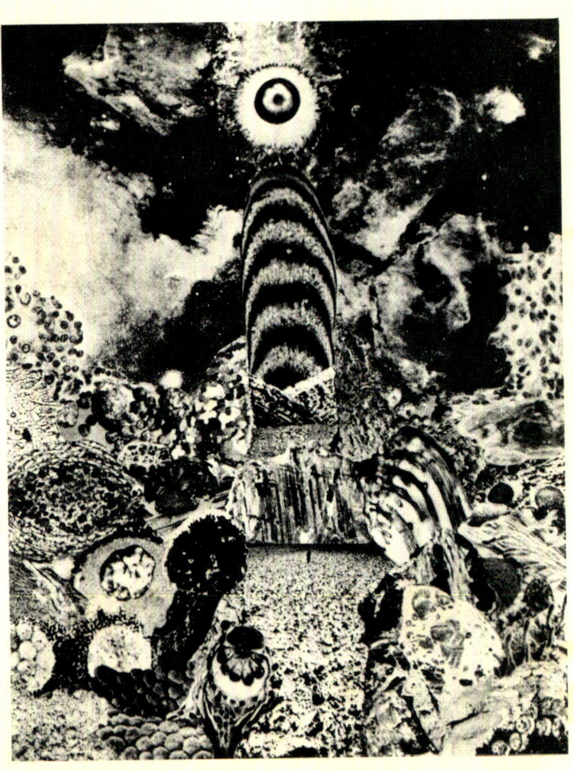

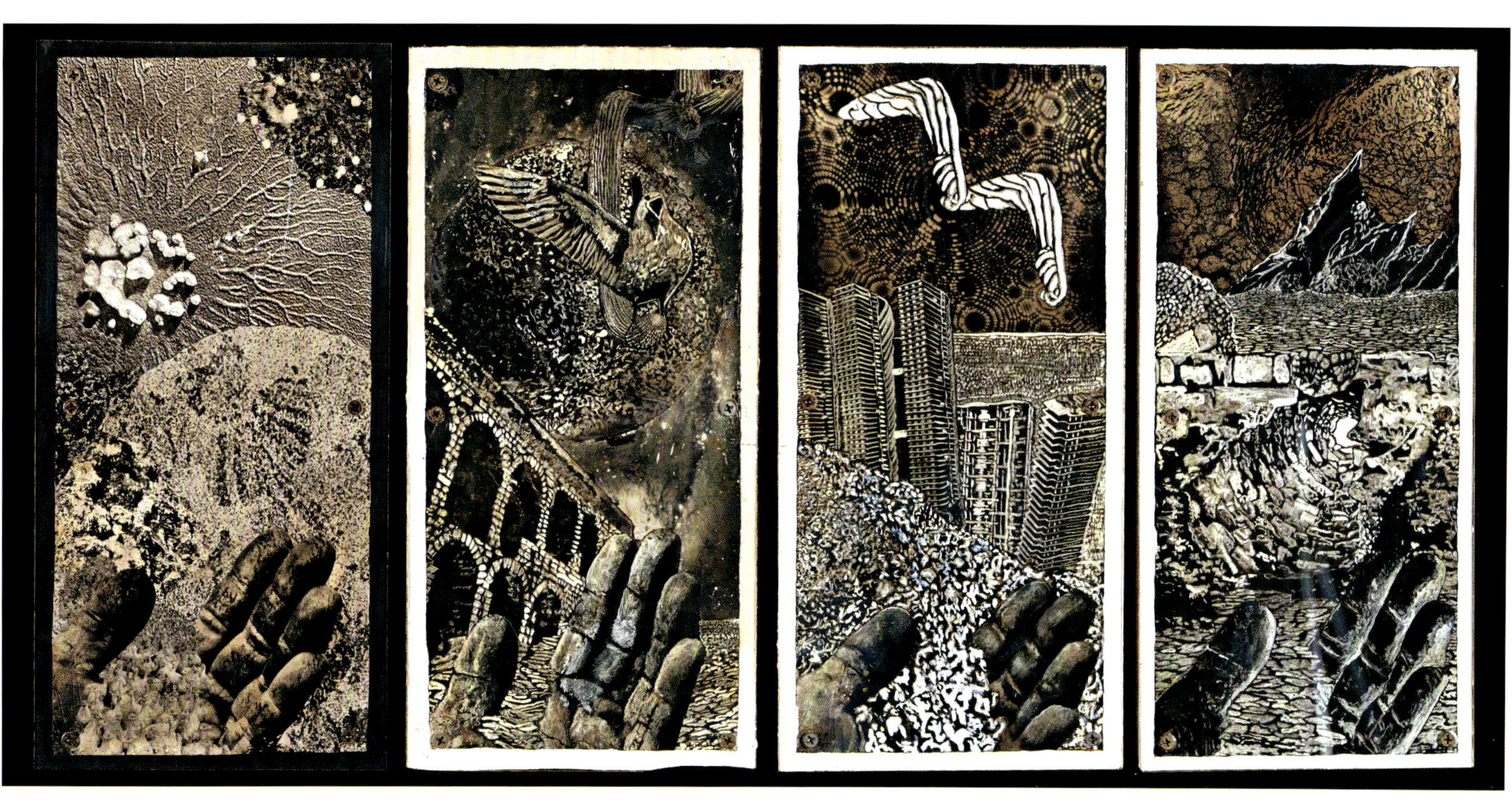

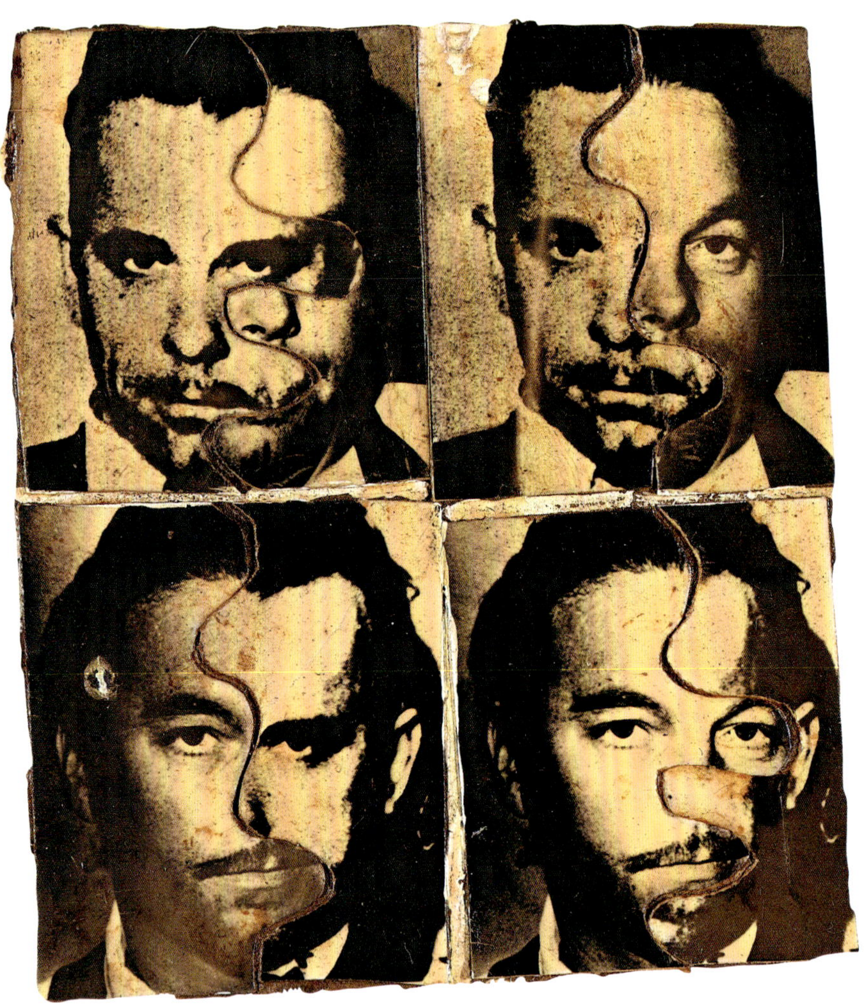

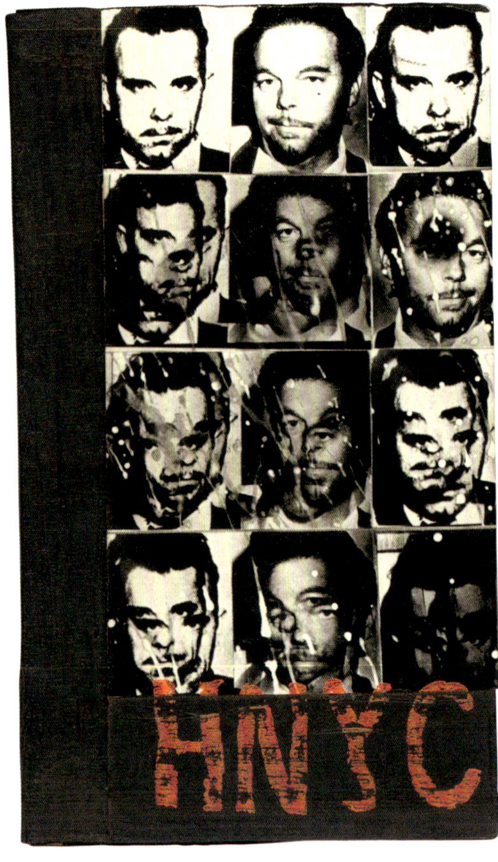
HNYC

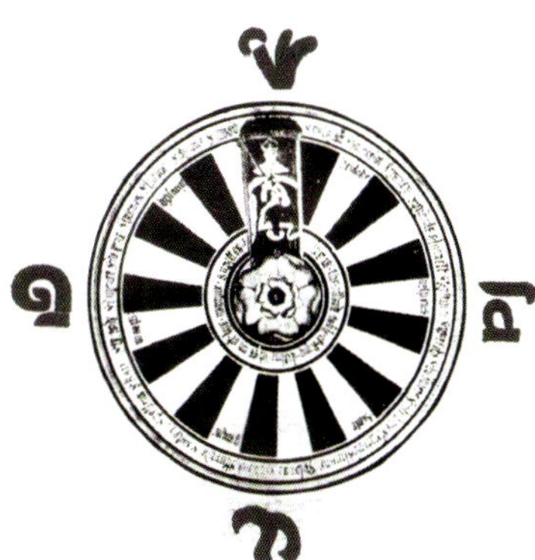

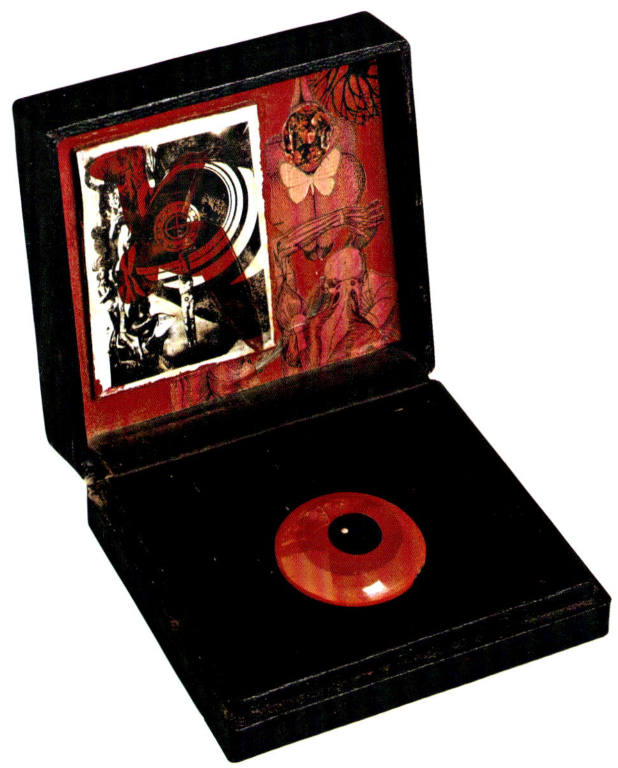

poverty but were incredibly creative. I wasn't working in movies at that point, and I didn't want to work, so I fired the gardeners and let the weeds grow and turned the bowling alley into a theater. Then I sold the house in the Palisades and moved to Topanga in 1964."

At that point Tamblyn threw himself completely into the new creative arena Berman had showed him. He produced collages, paintings, experimental films, assemblages, sculpture, and handmade postcards. Much of Tamblyn's work is infused with a kind of psychedelic pantheism associated with the 1960s, and was particular prominent in the community of Topanga, which then revolved around a back-to-nature vision of utopia. Issues of identity are central to works such as *John Dillinger / Self*, a collaged painting from 1968 that merges Tamblyn's face with Dillinger's. Between 1967 and 1977 Tamblyn's work was exhibited at the Mizuno Gallery, the Los Angeles County Museum of Art, the Topanga Community House, and the Molly Barnes Gallery, among others. His last solo show took place in 1977, in a private exhibition in his Topanga Canyon home.

In 1978 Tamblyn's second marriage ended, and two years later he met musician Bonnie Murray. They moved to Ocean Park together in 1980, married in 1982, and the following year their daughter, Amber, was born. "I took the next two decades off from making art to focus on my greatest work of all," he says of Amber Tamblyn, a poet and actress nominated for several awards in 2003 for her work in the television series, *Joan of Arcadia*.

In 1990 Tamblyn returned to the public eye when David Lynch cast him in a recurring role in the television series *Twin Peaks*. In 2003 two of his experimental films from the 1960s were premiered at the Getty Museum, and from 2003 to 2004 Tamblyn was choreographer, performer, and director of the stage play for Neil Young's multimedia piece, *Greendale*. Young and Tamblyn became friends when they lived next door to one another during the 1960s; thus, the changes in Tamblyn's life wrought by his time in Topanga continue to manifest themselves.

"The death of my own father didn't affect me as intensely as Wallace's death did—everything seemed to go downhill in Topanga after Wallace died," Tamblyn has said. "Things were never the same, and I remember sitting under an oak tree in Topanga and weeping like I'd never wept in my life. I just loved him." *Kristine McKenna*

1 All quotations by the artist from a conversation with Russel Tamblyn, February 10, 1999.

Aya (Tarlow)

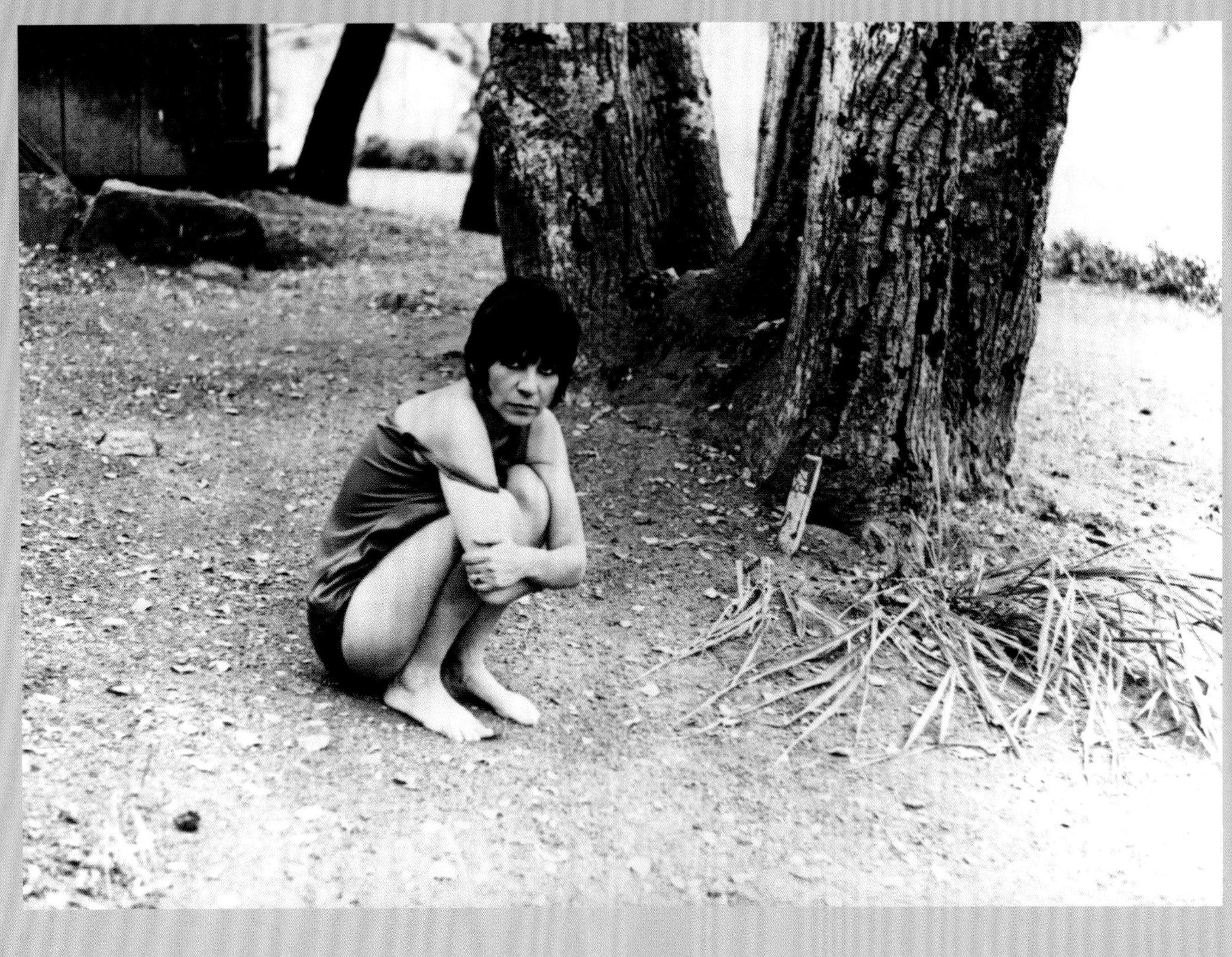

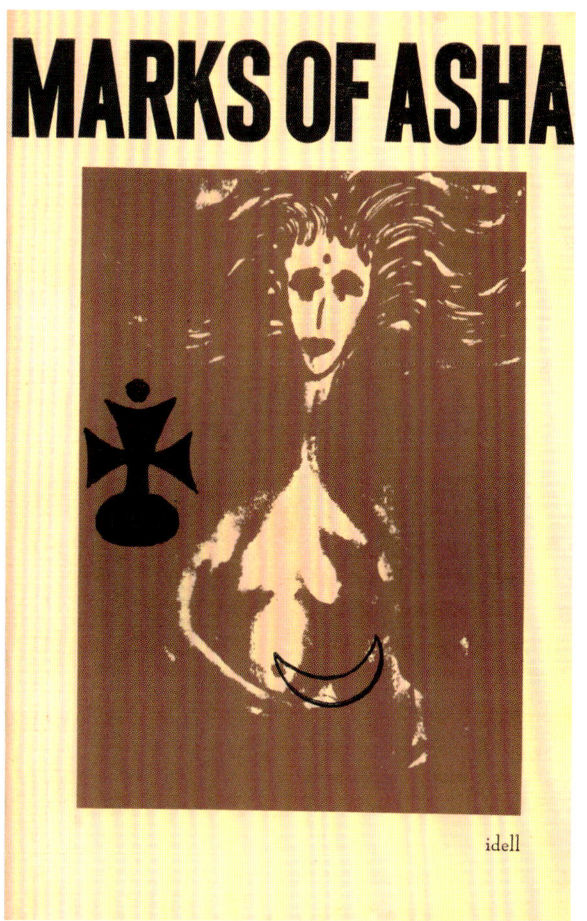
MARKS OF ASHA
idell

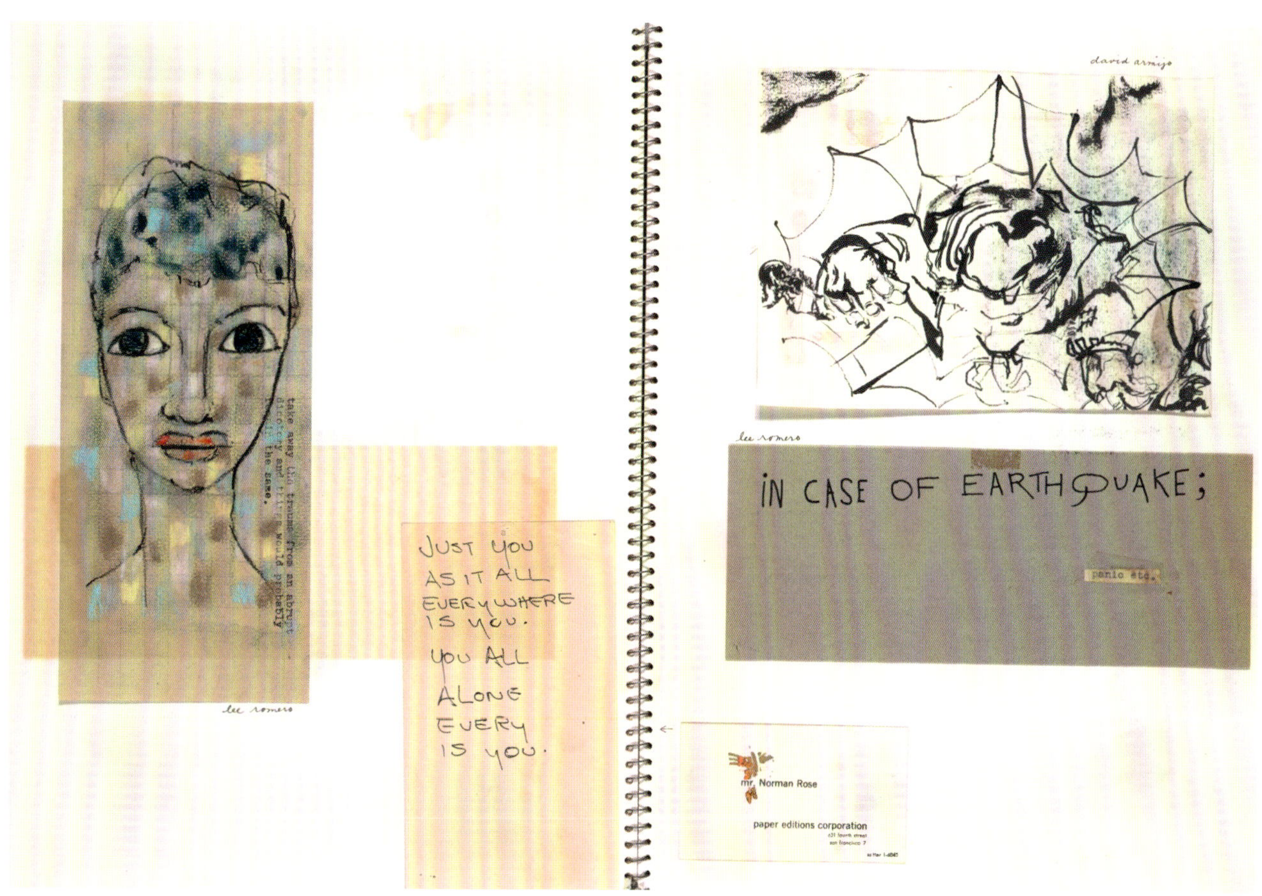
take away the trauma from an abrupt
discovery and things would probably
the same.
lee romero
JUST YOU
AS IT ALL
EVERY WHERE
IS YOU.
YOU ALL
ALONE
EVERY
IS YOU.
david arnigo
lee romero
IN CASE OF EARTHQUAKE;
panic etc.
mr. Norman Rose
paper editions corporation

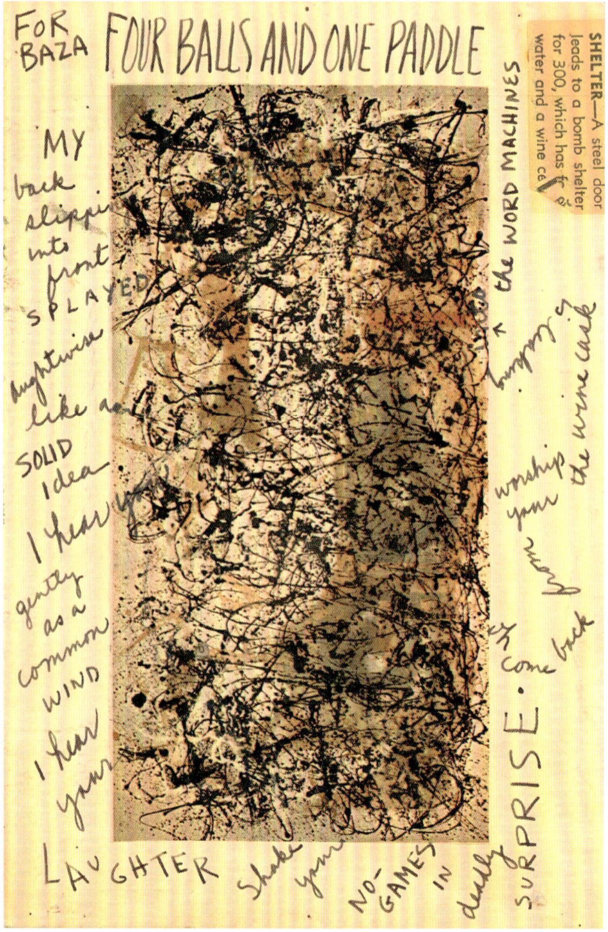

Aya was born Idell Rose Tarlow in Los Angeles in 1932. Her father was a pharmacist who loved the arts, and he encouraged his only daughter to develop a relationship with music, writing, and visual art. As a child she studied ballet and the piano, and by the time she was in high school she was writing poetry and filling sketchbooks with drawings and verse. Aya graduated from John Marshall High School in 1949 and enrolled at Los Angeles City College; however, she quit school after a year to marry artist Fred Glassman. By 1952 she was a young married woman working as a typographer in the art department at the May Company.

In 1954 Aya returned to school where she met Elias Romero in a poetry class. In 1955 she left Glassman to marry him, and she and Romero spent their first few months together living in a farmhouse in Riverside, California. In 1956 they moved to San Francisco, which was in the midst of a cultural renaissance. For the remainder of the decade, Aya read her poetry regularly in the coffeehouses, bars, and bookstores of North Beach, and in 1958 she self-published her first volume of verse, *Poems for Selected People*. During those years Romero was developing light shows, an art form then in its infancy, which went on to become a ubiquitous feature of hippie culture in the 1960s. Throughout the late 1950s Aya and Romero traveled regularly between Northern and Southern California, and established lasting ties with David Meltzer, George Herms, and Berman.

"Wallace was totally laid back and he acted as if artmaking was simply a form of play, but he was an innovator and a creator who just kept working away at things," Aya has recalled. "We used to run into each other at all sorts of events, and I remember him as a low-key person who was actually rather shy and preferred to maintain a low profile. Whether or not it was something he worked at, he had a style I always admired—he was like the Mona Lisa in that he could communicate things of enormous complexity with a smile." [1]

In 1959 Tarlow separated from Romero, whom she divorced in 1962, and moved back to Venice where she reestablished her ties with the Berman circle. In 1962 Paul Beattie published Aya's *Epenome*, and the following year Bob Alexander's Baza Press published her third volume of poetry, *Marks of Asha*. Included in the book is "Note Between Words, for cameron," which opens with the words: "*a witch bewitched / this life stalks itself / watching from the corners / of her own mad eyes*."

In 1965 Aya met Zen master Suzuki Roshi and became a Buddhist practitioner, and two years later George Herms's Love Press published her book, *Zen Love Poems*. It was during this period that she took the name Aya. In 1966 her play, *The Edge*, was staged at the Open Theater in Berkeley, and during the 1960s she continued to develop her involvement with photography. She also deepened her friendships with Cameron—whom she photographed frequently—Rachel Rosenthal, Marsha Getzler, and Anaïs Nin. "That was a highly creative period and it's sadly missed," Aya has said of the 1960s. "It's hard being an artist and working in isolation and we all had each other then."

In 1969 Aya met William Royere, whom she married several months later, and the following year she launched the feminist literary magazine *Matrix: For She of the New Aeon*. During their twenty years together Aya and Royere

p. 278
Aya in Bouquet Canyon, 1969,
Photograph by William Royere III.

p. 279 top
Aya, *Marks of Asha* (Los Angeles: Baza Press, 1963).

p. 279 bottom
Aya, Untitled Beat scrapbook with drawings by Lee Romero, poem by Aya, and Norman Rose business card by Robert Alexander.

p. 280
Aya, *Four Balls and One Paddle (to Robert Alexander)*, 1963,
Collaged mailer.

p. 281 top
Aya, née Idell Tarlow, c. 1958,
Photograph by Warner Jepson.

p. 281 bottom
Aya, Untitled Beat scrapbook, c. 1950s.

p. 282 top
Jack Hirschman and Wallace Berman, 1968, Photograph by Aya.

p. 282 bottom
George Herms, 1970,
Photograph by Aya.

p. 283 top left
Wallace Berman, 1968,
Photograph by Aya.

p. 283 top right
Wallace Berman, 1968,
Photograph by Aya.

p. 283 bottom
Dean Stockwell and Wallace Berman, 1968, Photograph by Aya.

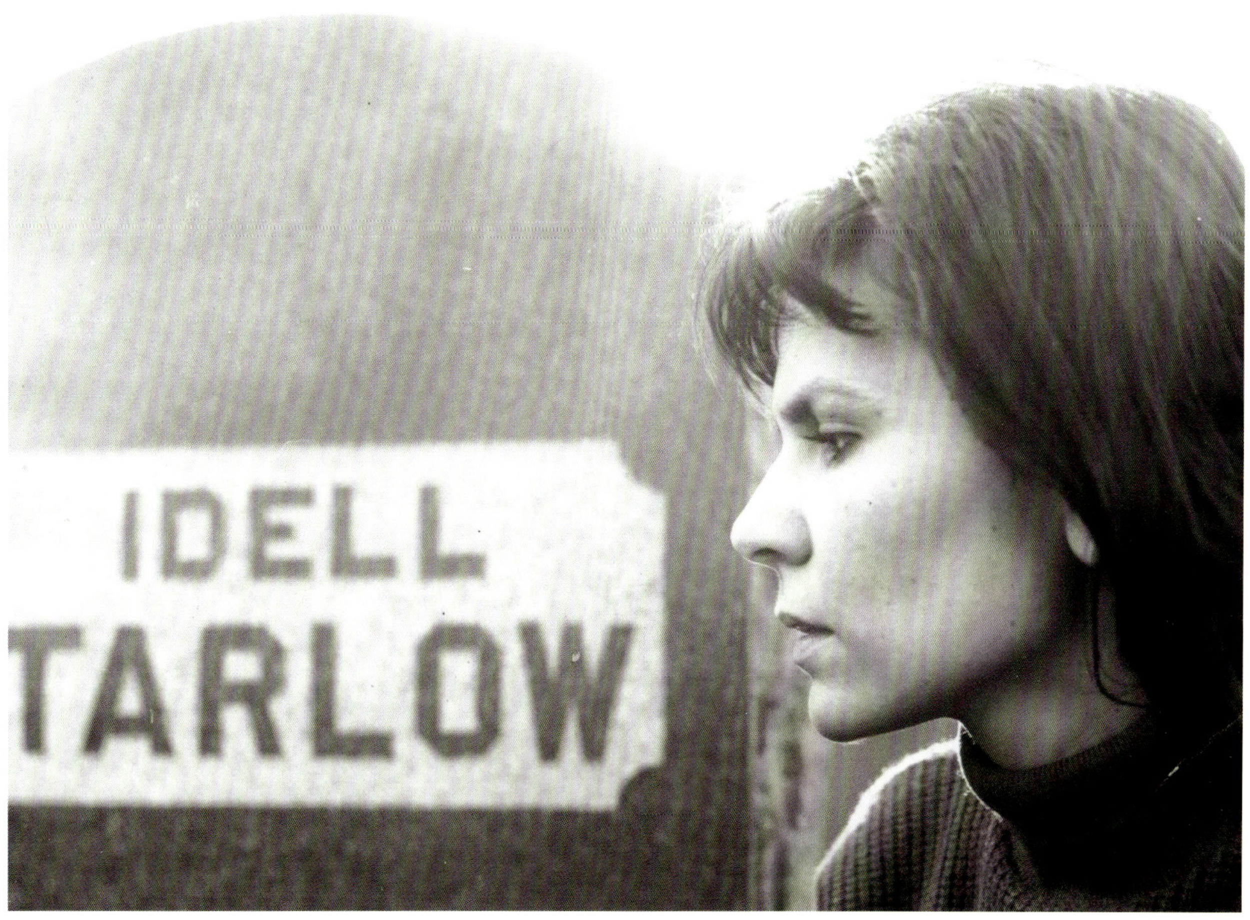

collaborated on several independent films, including shorts with Donovan and Ringo Starr, and a feature-length documentary on the repression of human rights in Vietnam titled *A Religion in Retreat*. During the 1980s she did volunteer work with Tibetan and Vietnamese immigrant communities in Los Angeles.

Following Royere's death in 1989, Aya moved to Sedona, Arizona, where she founded the Wise Woman Lodge, a site for seasonal ceremonies and feminist rituals. In 1990 she took her vows in the Tibetan tradition with Tibetan teacher Erma Pounds, and shortly before returning to Northern California in 2000, she published her first non-fiction book, *Way of the Warrior Priestess*. Aya lives in San Pablo, California, where she continues to write. Since 1992 she has been a certified astrological consultant.

Kristine McKenna

1 All quotations by the artist from a conversation with Aya Tarlow, March 15, 1999.

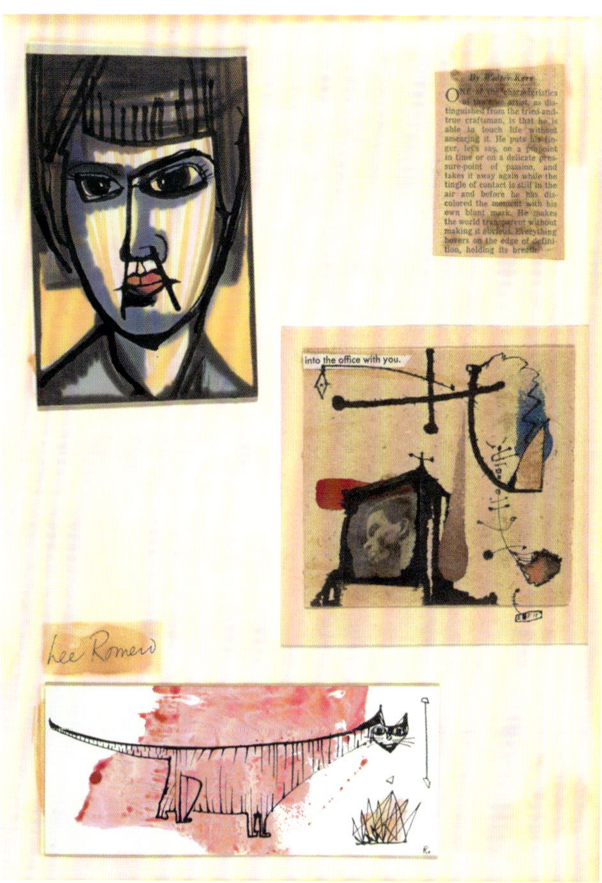

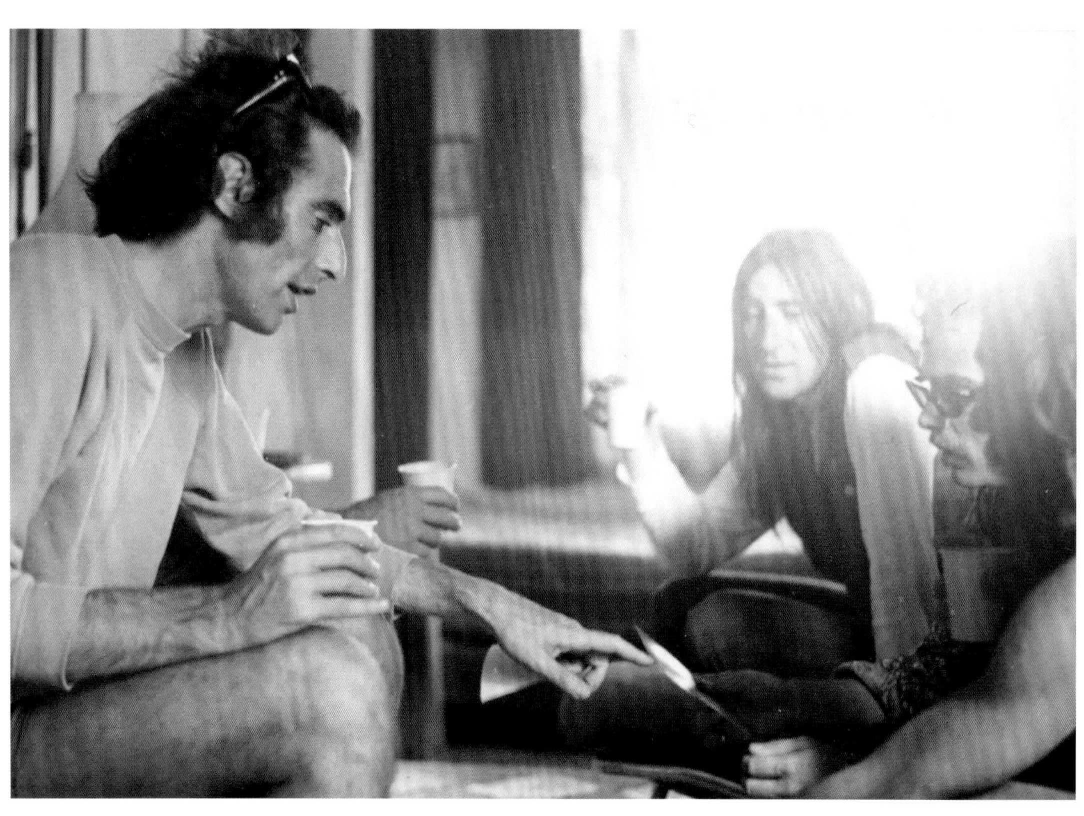

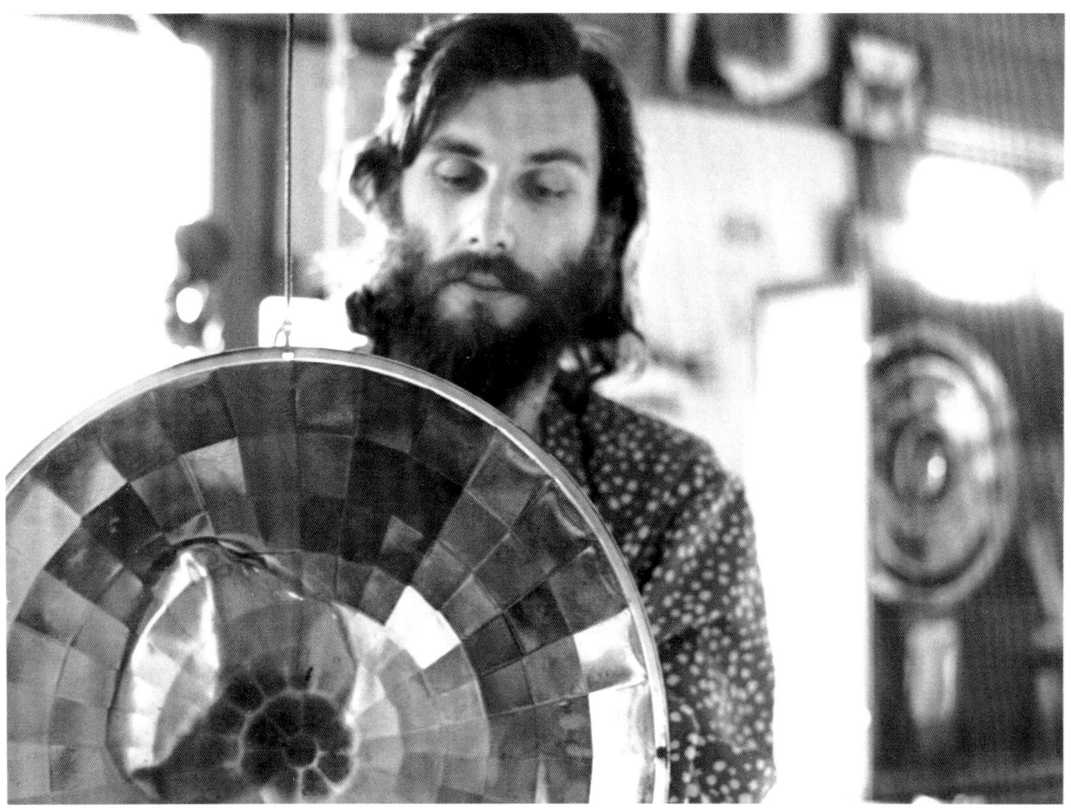

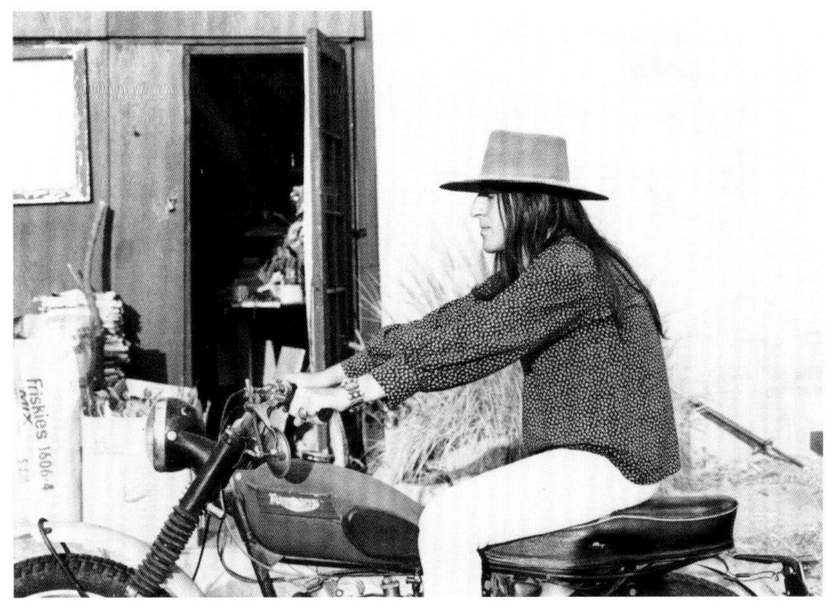

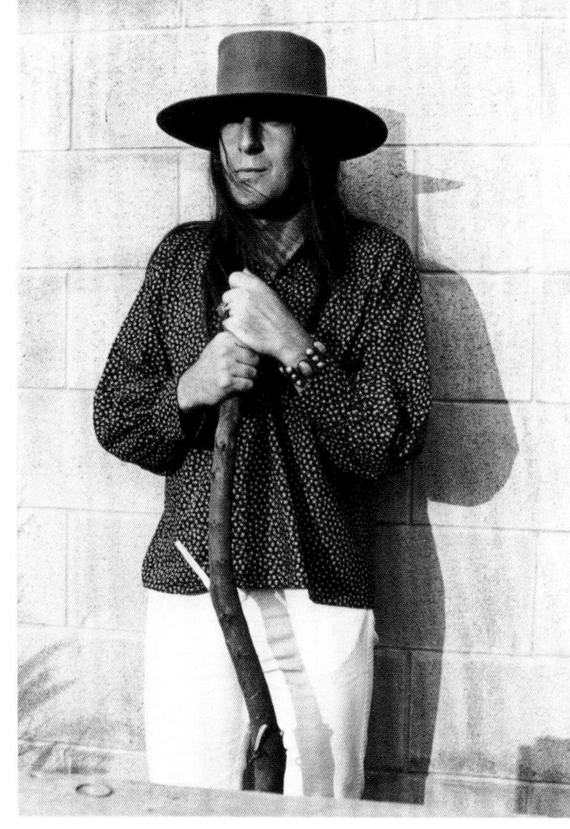

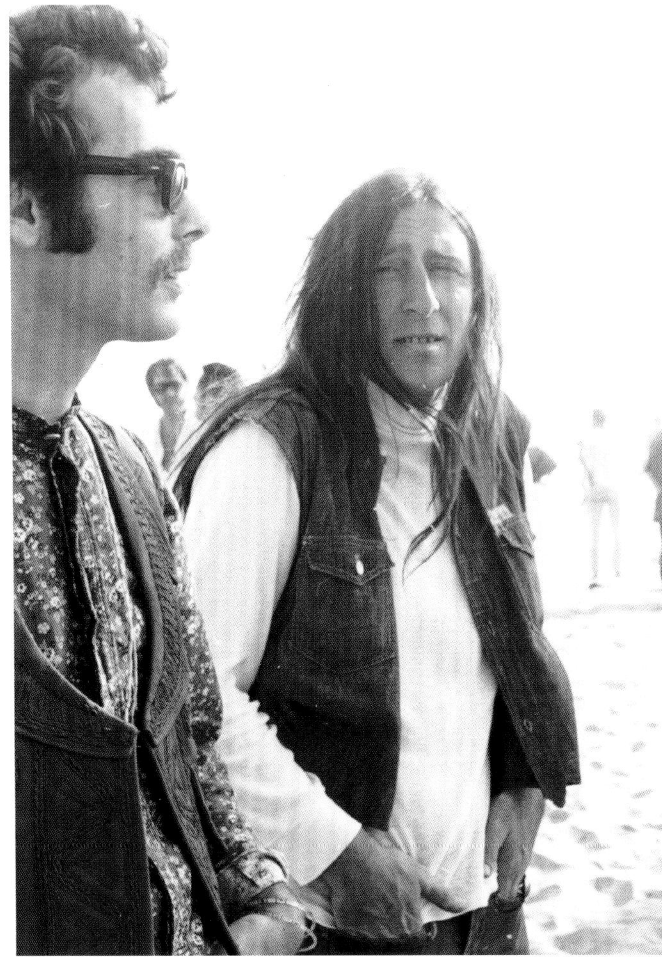

Edmund Teske

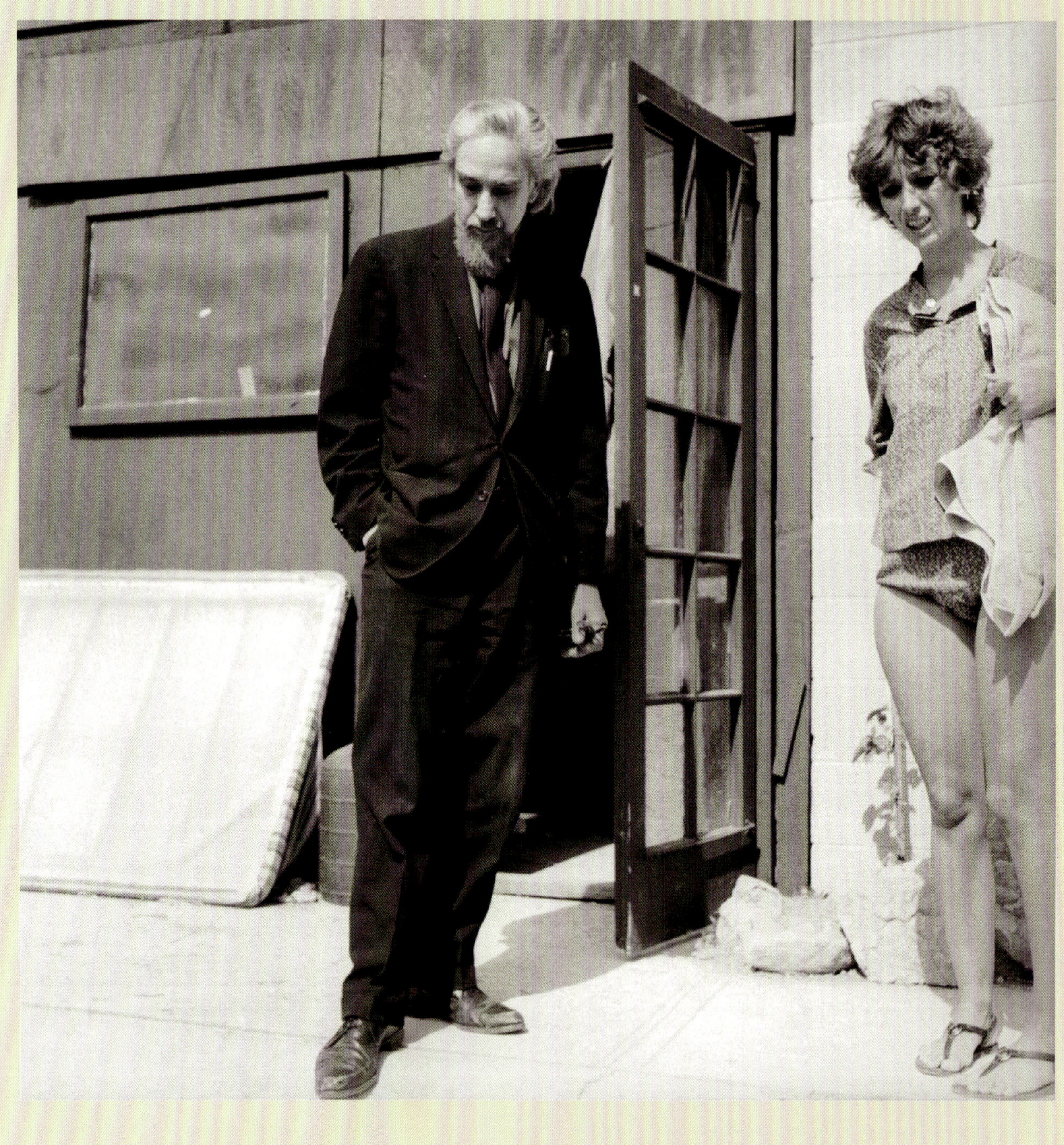

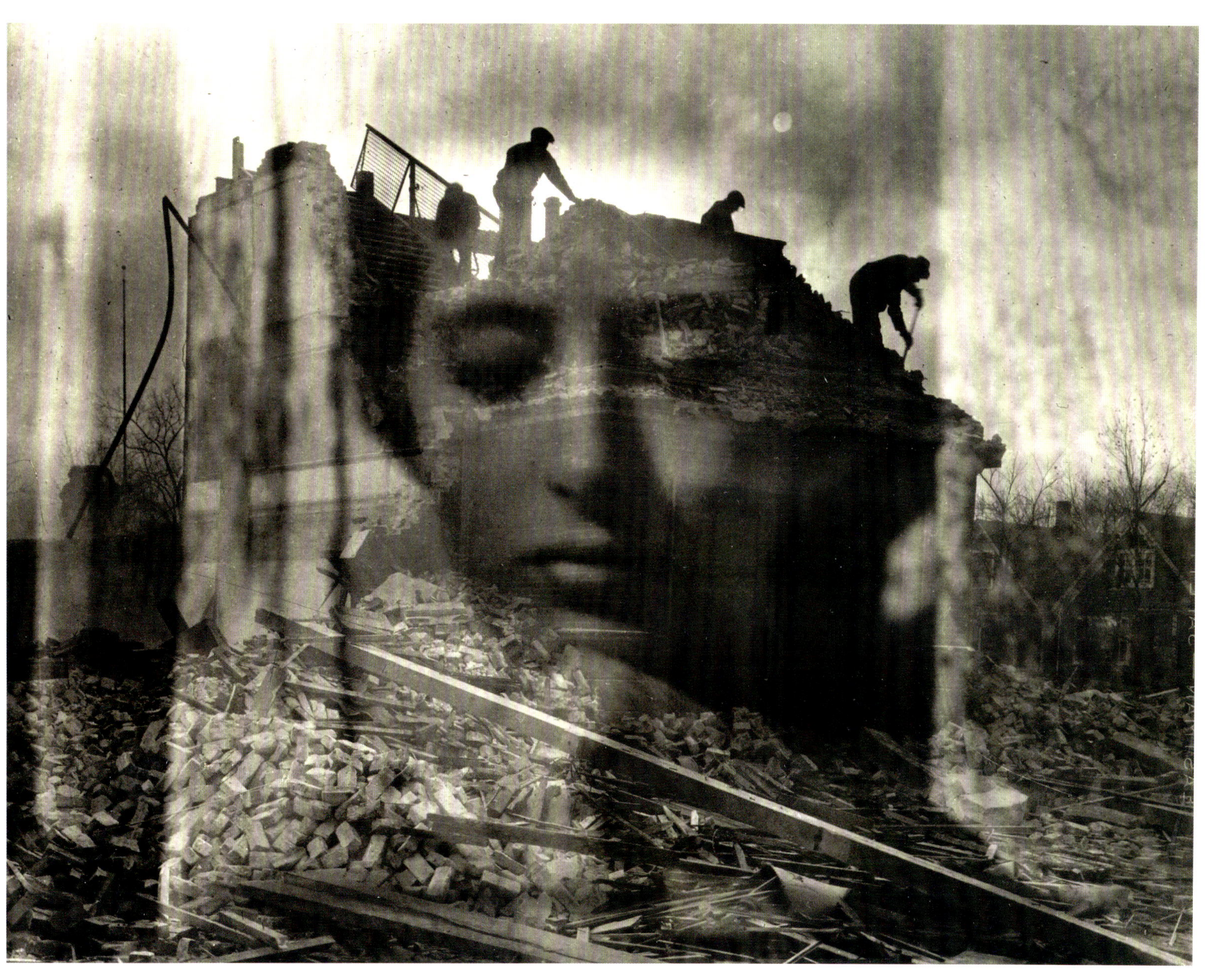

In black-and-white photographs that evoke the sensuous textures of nature and history, Edmund Teske created one of the past century's most lyrical bodies of work. A flamboyant bohemian known for his stentorian pronunciamentos on art and poetry, he suffered neglect during his lifetime from a photography establishment that frowned on his unabashed celebrations of spirituality, nostalgia, and the sensual power of the male nude.

Born in 1911 in Chicago, Teske began taking snapshots with his mother's camera at age seven and began working in a darkroom at age twelve. Employed as a department store clerk after dropping out of high school, he attended art school classes and began to understand the creative potential of photography. An intense reading of Walt Whitman opened him to the expression of his homosexuality and fostered his desire to live as an artist. Soon he was working as an assistant to a variety of commercial photographers, while on his own time making prints of family members and his first male nudes. In 1934, inspired by an exhibition of works by Edward Weston, he purchased a Rolleiflex camera.

Teske's Chicago photographs include images of street detritus, political turmoil, and a remarkable series of straightforward shots taken of streetcar passengers that presage those taken three years later by Walker Evans. He met the artistic elite of Chicago, including gallerist Katherine Kuh, László Moholy-Nagy, and other faculty of the New Bauhaus School of Design. His photographs won the respect of Frank Lloyd Wright who commissioned him—at Teske's expense—to photograph several of Wright's architectural designs in Wisconsin and Illinois. Teske's artistic activities were interrupted in 1942 while he worked for the U.S. Army Corps of Engineers, printing aerial military maps.

p. 284
Edmund Teske and Shirley Berman, Topanga Canyon, 1969,
Photograph by Wallace Berman.

p. 285
Edmund Teske, *Demolition of My Grammar School, Chicago, 1938, Composite with Shirley Berman, Topanga Canyon*, 1956,
Gelatin silver print.

p. 286
Edmund Teske, *Wallace and Shirley Berman #1*, 1955,
Gelatin silver print.

p. 287
Edmund Teske, *George Herms, Topanga Canyon*, 1965,
Gelatin silver print.

His association with Wright led him to photograph Taliesin West in Arizona and Wright's Barnsdall House in Los Angeles. Teske decided to settle in Hollywood and became Alice Barnsdall's assistant, living on her property in Studio Residence B until 1949. In the 1940s Teske became part of the local artistic community, befriending figures such as Man Ray, filmmakers John and James Whitney, Anaïs Nin, Tony Smith and his wife Jane Lawrence, George Cukor, and Christopher Isherwood, who introduced him to Vedantic thought and the ideas of Hindu swami Prabhavananda.

In 1950 Teske began a relationship with actor Will Geer and became a member of his theatrical group in Topanga Canyon. Teske documented a variety of theatrical productions, and used actors such as John Saxon as models for his own work. At about this time, he conceived of arranging his photographs into an epic photo-cycle, *Song of Dust* (finally assembled in 1972–77). Teske accompanied many of his photographs with poems, three of which were published in *Poetry Los Angeles I* (ed. James Boyer May, London: Villiers Publications, 1958).

Always financially strapped, Teske regularly organized "photograbs," at which original prints were auctioned off to friends. Teske was a great admirer of *Semina* and corresponded with Wallace Berman. In 1955 Teske stumbled upon a group of abandoned rusty iceboxes in Cornell, California which he used as a backdrop for a series of hauntingly lyrical photographs featuring Wallace and Shirley Berman and Walter and Shirley Hopps. Shirley Berman and

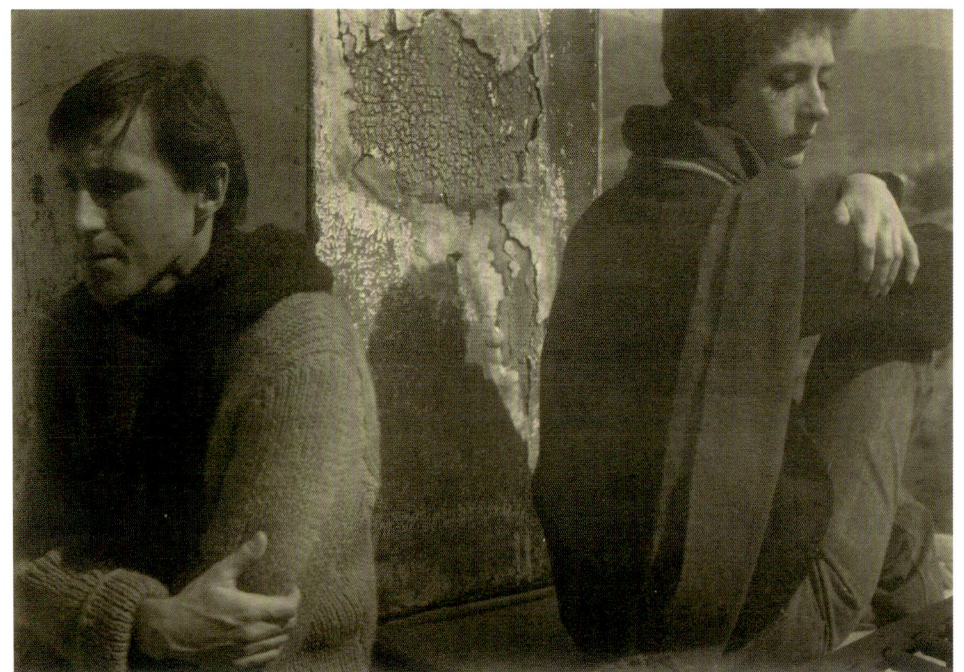

George Herms were frequent subjects of later photographs. Berman featured works by Teske alongside those of George Herms in a 1960 two-man exhibition at Semina Gallery in Larkspur.

In 1958 Teske perfected the technique of duotone solarization, a darkroom process that exposes photographs to quick blasts of light during developing. Teske also experimented with composite printing, combining two or more negatives to create veil-like image overlays. Over the years, Teske met the major photographers of his generation, including Alfred Stieglitz, Paul Strand, Minor White, Frederick Sommer, Imogen Cunningham, and Berenice Abbott. The Museum of Modern Art purchased nine of his photographs in 1959 and two years later retrospectives of his work were held at Pasadena Art Museum and Santa Barbara Museum of Art. In the late 1960s Teske began to teach in local art departments, including a four-year stint at UCLA. In 1970, he photographed the rock group The Doors and made a well-known series of photographs of Jim Morrison.

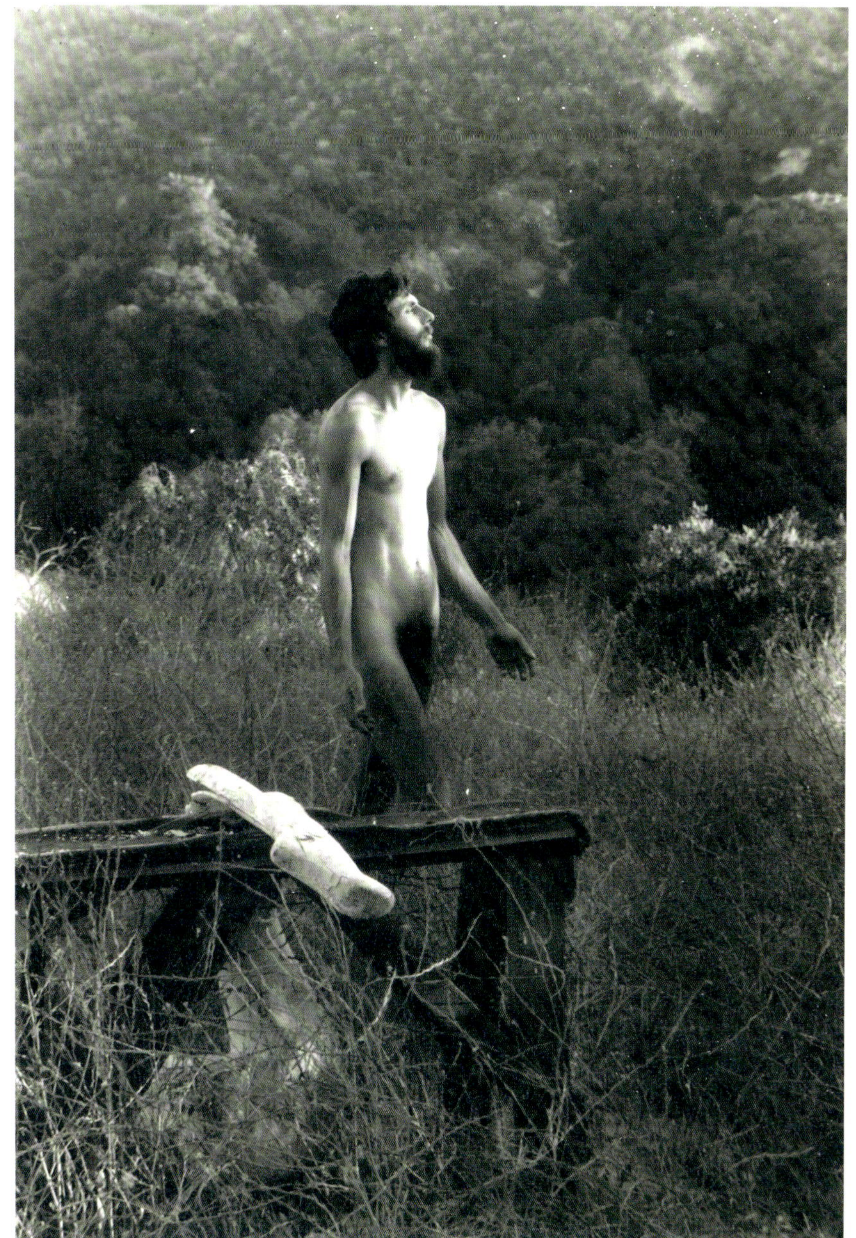

The stains, patinas, and collaged images that result from Teske's experimental processes blur the notion of time, making his photographic images seem like dreams or memories. In Teske's work, the human body is a kind of landscape or natural repository. Photographs of his mother and childhood home were often superimposed on bucolic landscapes, imbuing the settings with a sense of lost time. Other transparent nudes and reclining figures appear over delicately printed fields of grass and ruined buildings.

Teske's unfettered nostalgia seems a philosophical stance, rooted in his commitment to Vedanta, the branch of Hinduism that explores the interconnections of life and nature. The male nude in many of the photographs represents the Hindu principle of Shiva, a passive figure who is close to God. *Shiva Composite with Shirley Berman, Grammar School, Jeff Harris as Shiva* (c. 1970) is an autobiographical reverie featuring the ghostlike image of one of his frequent models, Shirley Berman.

In 1990 Teske was shot by an intruder in his Hollywood studio and four years later his studio was badly damaged in the Northridge earthquake. Undaunted, he worked in his final years on photographs documenting the rock group The Red Hot Chili Peppers. He died at his downtown studio of a heart attack in 1996. The first comprehensive retrospective of Teske's work was held at the J. Paul Getty Museum in 2004. *Michael Duncan*

Alexander Trocchi

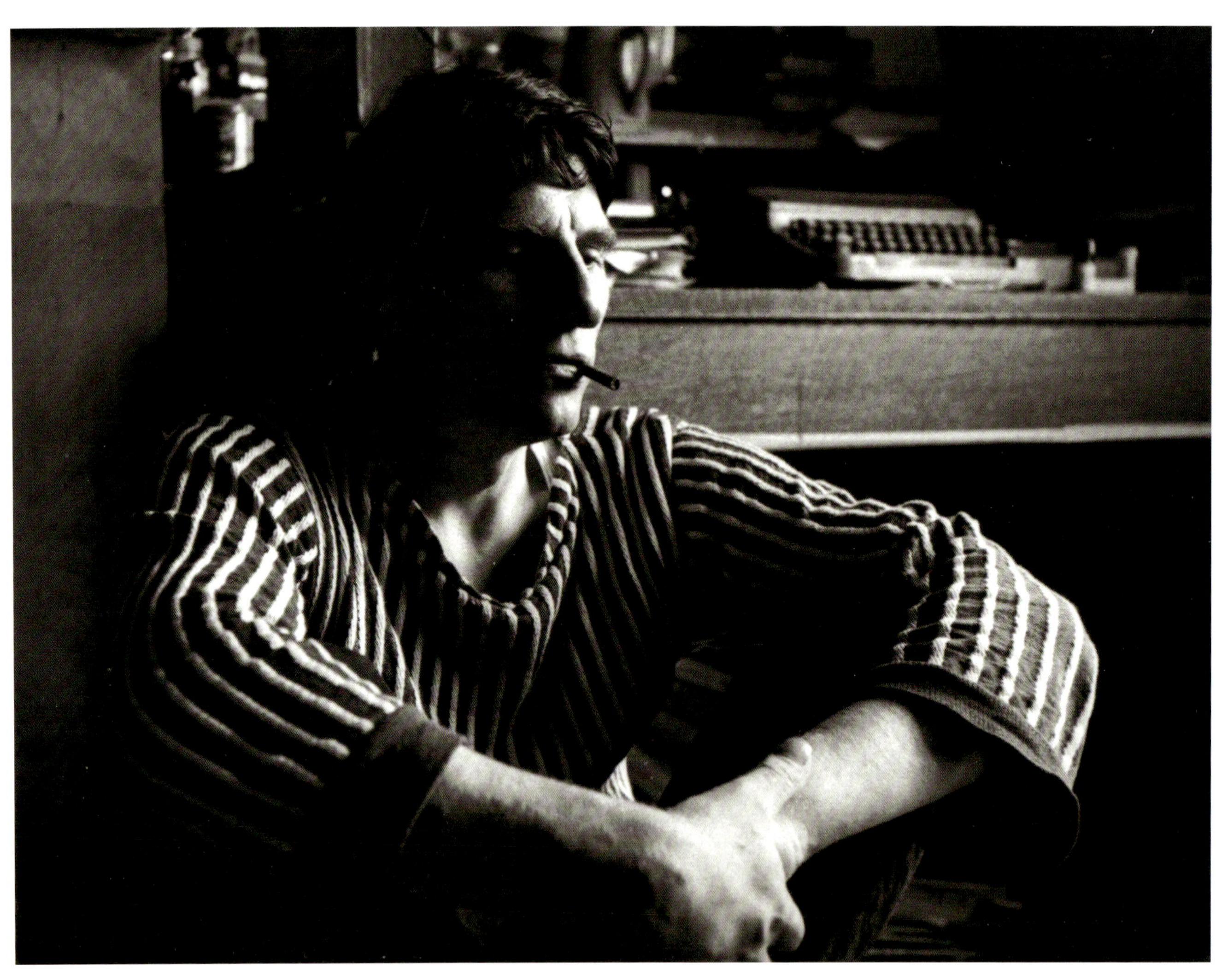

Alexander Trocchi isn't widely known today, but in his time he cut quite a swathe through the counterculture. Born in Glasgow, Scotland in 1925, Trocchi was a brilliant child of great promise, however, his life took a fatal turn when he was sixteen and his mother died. "The last vital link with existence was cut," he said of her death.

When he was twenty-two Trocchi married his first wife, Betty Whyte, who gave birth to a daughter the following year. By 1950 he had completed his degree in English and philosophy at Glasgow University, and in 1951 his second daughter was born. With family in tow, Trocchi moved to Paris in 1952 and the velocity of his life increased dramatically; in the course of a year he left his wife for Jane Lougee and founded the legendary literary magazine, *Merlin*. In 1953 the book-publishing branch of the magazine, Collection Merlin, published Samuel Beckett's novel, *Watt*—Beckett's first English-language translation—and subsequent issues of *Merlin* included contributions from Jean Genet, Eugene Ionesco, Pablo Neruda, and Jean-Paul Sartre. Trocchi's vision as a publisher established him as one of the shining lights of the Parisian postwar demimonde, and his circle included Guy Debord, Terry Southern, and James Baldwin.

In 1954 Maurice Girodias's Olympia Press published Trocchi's first novel, an existential allegory titled *Young Adam*, and in 1956 Trocchi moved to New York City, having "consciously decided to take on the identity of the junkie." Towards that end, he took a job as a scow captain that demanded nothing more of him than that he live on the boat and prevent it from being stolen. He was at the job for a year, which he spent shooting heroin and writing about shooting heroin. The resulting novel, *Cain's Book*, published in 1960 by Grove Press, was hailed as a work of frightening genius. Trocchi was an anarchist intent on discovering "how far a man can go without being obliterated," but in embracing heroin as the central tool for his research, he inadvertently extinguished himself as a writer.

Early in 1957 Trocchi met Lyn Hicks, a twenty-one-year-old New Yorker who had also become a heroin addict by the time the couple married in Mexico in August of that year. Following their wedding, the Trocchis settled in Venice Beach, California, where they lived from August until April of the following year. Trocchi was infamous by that point, and Los Angeles's avant-garde community welcomed him as a visiting dignitary. Word of Trocchi's as yet unpublished novel, *Cain's Book*, preceded him, and Berman had the honor of publishing the first excerpt from it in *Semina Two*.

By the time the Trocchis left Los Angeles to spend five months in Las Vegas, Lyn Trocchi was hooking to support their drug habits. In 1958 they returned to New York where their first son, Mark, was born. Three years later Trocchi was arrested and charged with supplying drugs to a minor; anticipating a prison sentence, he stole two suits from George Plimpton, and with funds supplied by Norman Mailer, fled to Canada where he was met at a Montreal bus station by Leonard Cohen. "He was a very impressive figure, a noble figure," Cohen recalls in *A Life in Pieces*, a portrait of Trocchi published in 1997. "He was very clear about his life. Very unambiguous about what he thought and how he conducted himself. In a certain sense he saw himself as the General Secretary of some new subversive worldwide movement which would overthrow the old sensibility and establish a new one. He had a vision and he had the charisma and the conviction to manifest that vision at any given moment."[1]

Trocchi spent a few days in Canada, then moved to London, where the government then supplied registered heroin addicts with drugs; for that reason, Trocchi remained in the city for the rest of his life. In 1964 he published an essay titled "Invisible Insurrection of a Million Minds" to announce the foundation of Project Sigma, a loose affiliation of anarchists and bohemians bent on creating an international corps of "cosmonauts of inner space." John Lennon, Michael McClure, and R.D. Laing were among those involved, but the organization never amounted to much. "Sigma was simply a way of wasting time and making himself interesting," said British publisher John Calder in *A Life in Pieces*. "Alex loved to be surrounded by admirers."

In 1974 Lyn Trocchi died of chronic active hepatitis at the age of thirty-six, an early end which surprised no one. By the mid 1970s, fans of Trocchi's two novels had stopped waiting for a third, as he was no longer capable of work requiring sustained concentration. "He was terrified of writing," says Sally Childs, his companion at the time of his death of pneumonia in 1984. Trocchi spent his life insisting that "heroin should be placed on the counters of all chemists and sold openly," but in the years prior to his death he advised anyone who asked him against getting started. *Kristine McKenna*

p. 288
Alexander Trocchi in London, 1967,
Photograph by Wallace Berman.

1 Allen Campbell and Tim Niel; *A Life in Pieces: Reflections on Alexander Trocchi* (Edinburgh: Rebel Inc./Canongate Books Ltd., 1997).

Zack Walsh

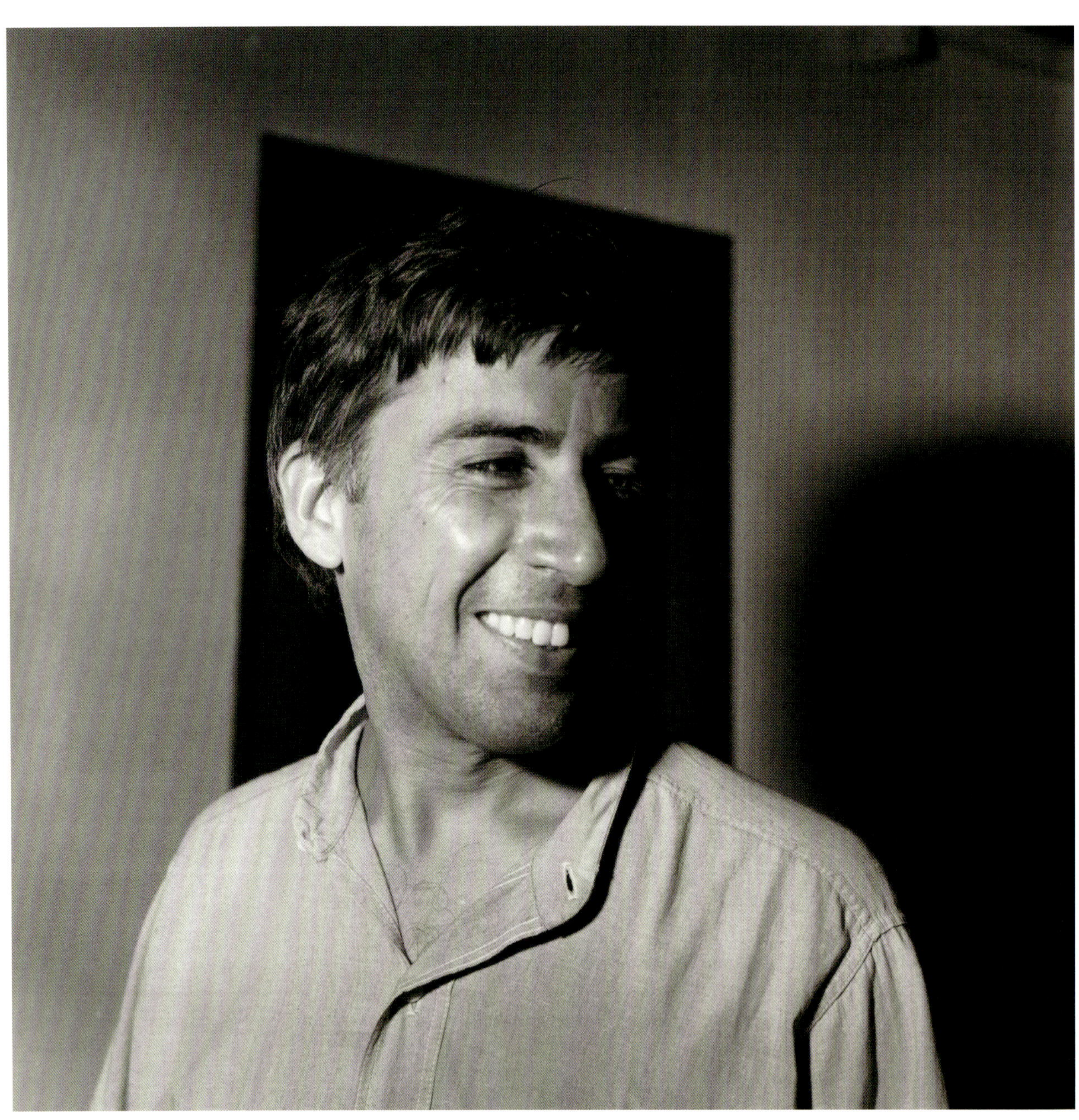

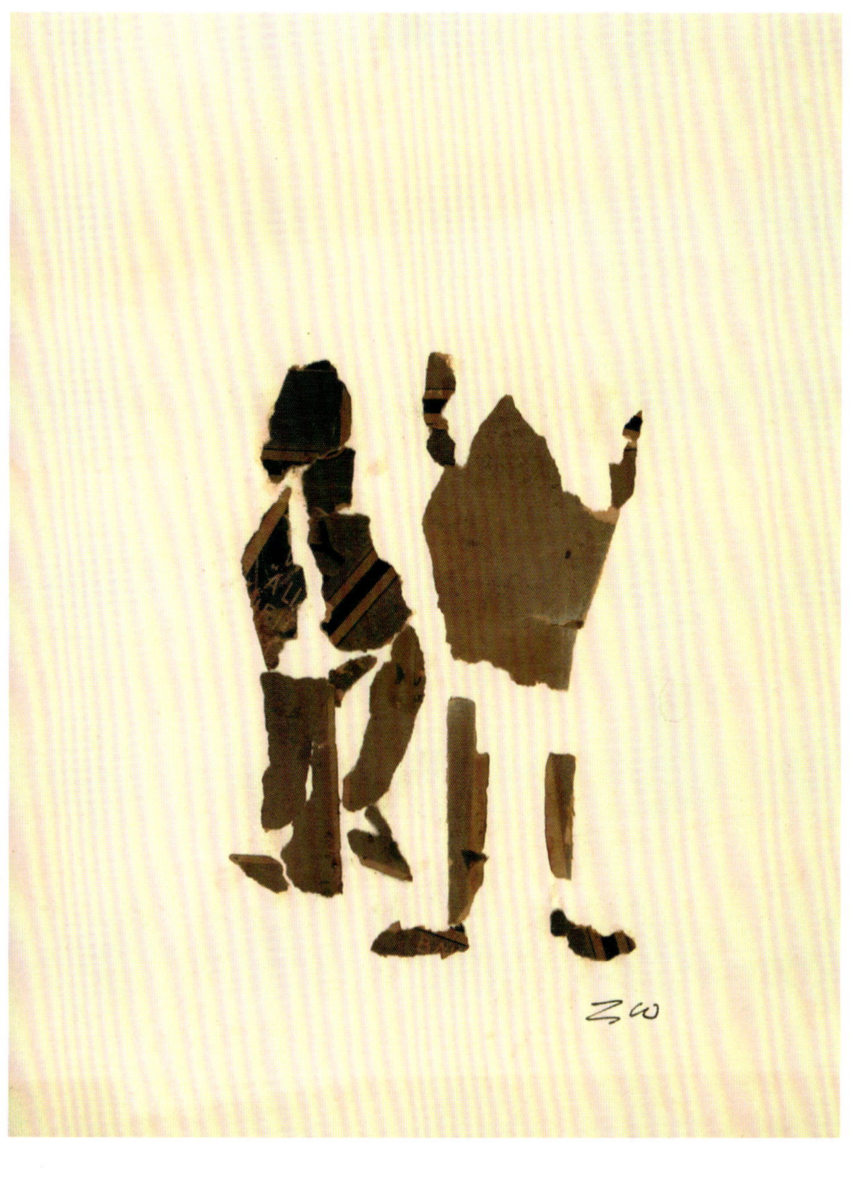
ZW

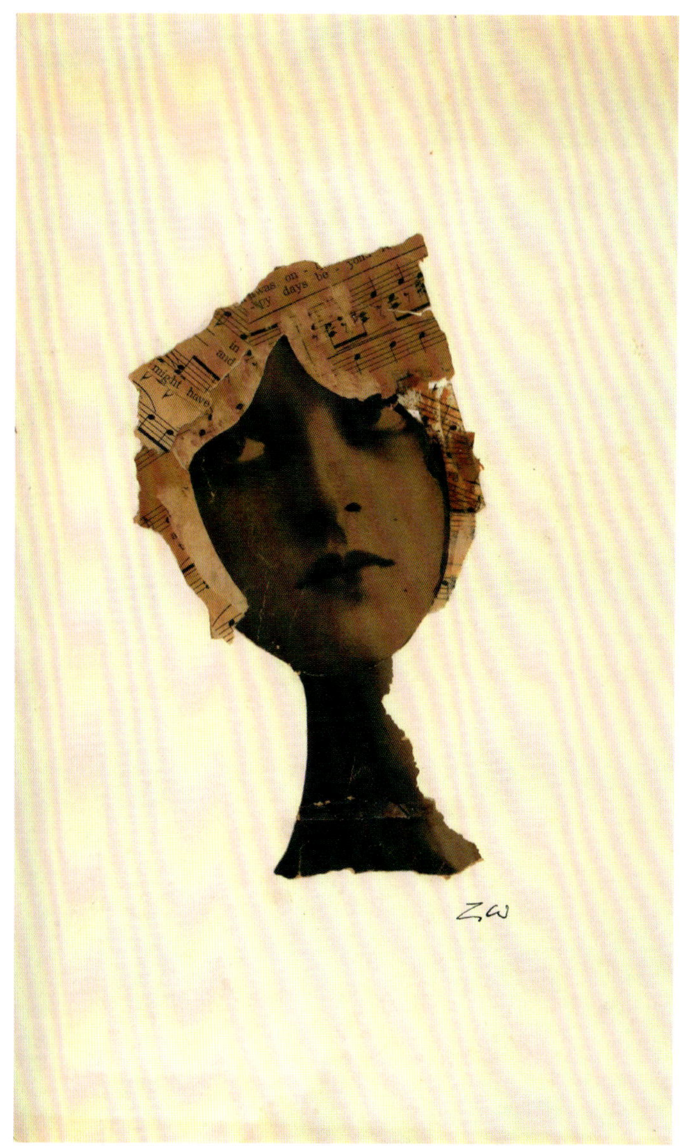
was on - be - yon
days
in
and
might have
ZW

An intriguing poet and artist who warrants further investigation, Zack Walsh was born in Wisconsin in 1924 and grew up in Pasadena. Living off an inheritance, he was a neighbor of Wallace Berman on Crater Lane, and he and his wife Beverly rented the Bermans' house in the late 1950s and early 1960s while they were living in San Francisco and Larkspur. An enthusiastic reader of Krishnamurti, Ouspensky, and Gurdijieff, Walsh wrote spiritually resonant, metaphysical poems with plain-spoken cadences and everyday images. His visual work consisted of lyrical collages, assemblages, and watercolors usually made to accompany his writings.

He published two books of poetry: *Points in Time* (Los Angeles: Baza Press, 1963), featuring a cover photograph by Dean Stockwell and two photographs of Walsh assemblages; and *Sunspots* (Los Angeles: Temple of Man, 1978), illustrated with Walsh's abstract torn-paper collages. Poems by Walsh were included in *Semina Two* and *Semina 8*, as well as in *Poetry Los Angeles I*, edited by James Boyer May (London: Villiers Publications, 1958). In 1977 his drawings and collages were exhibited at Beyond Baroque Gallery, Venice, California.

After his marriage ended in 1965, Walsh fell into problems with drug and alcohol abuse. His son by his second wife, Mary Jo, became his conservator at a young age and took Walsh to live with him in Hawaii where he resided until his death in 2002. *Michael Duncan*

p. 290
Zack Walsh, 1960, Photograph by Charles Brittin.

p. 291
Zack Walsh, Untitled collages, c. 1960.

p. 292 top
Zack Walsh, Untitled poem, 1958 (Published in *Poetry Los Angeles I*, edited by James Boyer May, London: Villiers Publications).

p. 292 bottom left
Robert Alexander and child, c. 1960, Photograph by Zack Walsh.

p. 292 bottom right
Zack Walsh, *Points in Time* (Los Angeles: Baza Press, 1963), Photograph by Dean Stockwell.

p. 293
Zack Walsh, *She*, c. 1960, Lithographic broadside with photograph of Beverly Walsh by Charles Brittin.

**Have you listened
to the first half of the 20th Century
speaking of fabled heroes
from empty head pieces
disguised and covered under
fields of mustard?
Have you watched
fifty beautiful years
glamorizing front page copy
fingerpainting progress
and smiling into history books?
Have you touched the dull fears of your life
into shocks of awareness
that make you wonder how and why
you feel like hiding under flowers?
Or have you seen yourself
in the first half of the 20th Century
pulling a shade to open a music box
that makes it so good
to keep on smiling
you could sleep that lullaby
forever?**

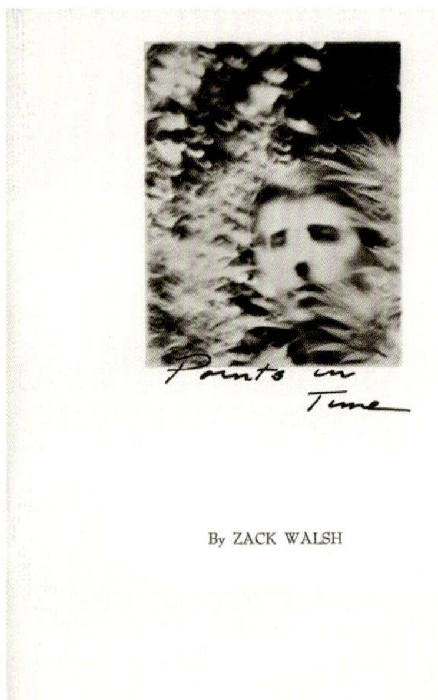

She is the face of the world
hearing misery wail.
The world of the midnight trenchcoat
hangs out the bomb.
The world of the Great Trunk Disappearance
(the heist of the soul)

She is the mask of our ache.
The face of our boxed
screaming flower - -
a cry out of hope
out of need
out of karma
strung in the net
tied in the hoop
the spike that kills
so sad her beauty.

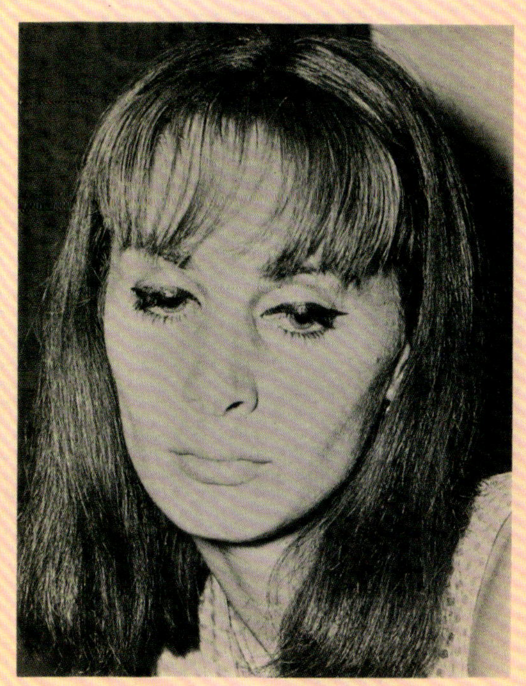

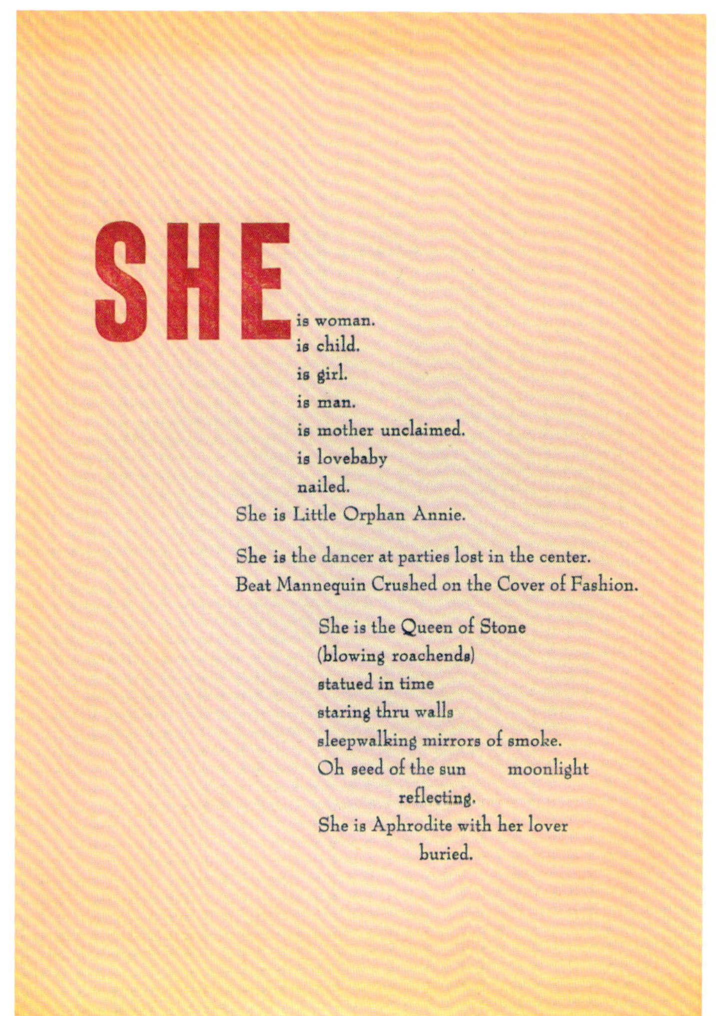

SHE is woman.
is child.
is girl.
is man.
is mother unclaimed.
is lovebaby
nailed.
She is Little Orphan Annie.

She is the dancer at parties lost in the center.
Beat Mannequin Crushed on the Cover of Fashion.

She is the Queen of Stone
(blowing roachends)
statued in time
staring thru walls
sleepwalking mirrors of smoke.
Oh seed of the sun moonlight
reflecting.
She is Aphrodite with her lover
buried.

Lew Welch

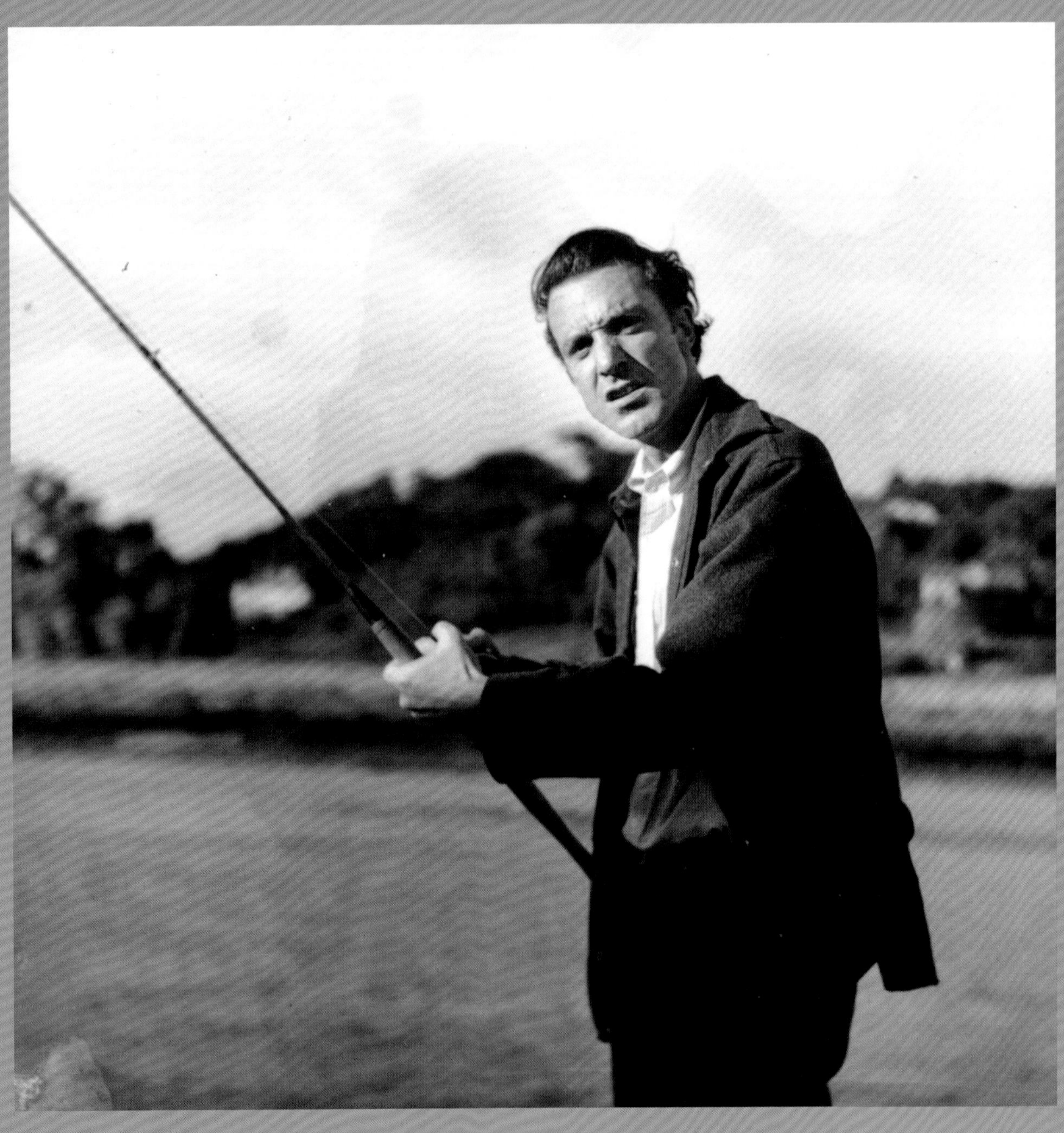

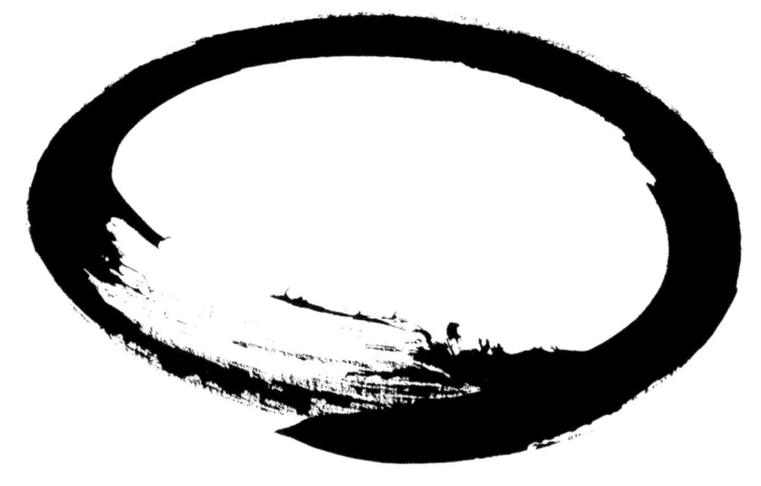

Step out onto the Planet.
Draw a circle 100 feet round.

Inside the circle are 300 things
nobody understands and,
maybe, nobody's ever seen.

How many can you find?

Lew Welch
6/12/64

Lew Welch is one of the lesser-known lights in the Beat pantheon, but those who spent time with him in his actively creative years in the 1950s and 1960s remember him with tremendous affection and admiration.

Born in Phoenix in 1926, Welch was the older of two children in a failed marriage between a spoiled heiress and a ne'er-do-well father who disappeared from Welch's life when he was a child. When Welch was three years old his mother moved to California and the family spent the next fifteen years drifting from one town to another up and down the coast: Because he was perpetually the new boy in class, Welch turned to books and became a serious reader at a young age. Welch had an intensely conflicted relationship with his mother, and he blamed her for many of the problems he struggled with later in life.

p. 294
Lew Welch in Larkspur, California, 1961, Photograph by Wallace Berman.

p. 295
Lew Welch, *Step out onto the planet...*, 1964, Privately published lithographic broadside.

p. 296
Lew Welch, *Sausalito Trash Prayer*, 1969, Illustrated lithographic broadside.

p. 297 top
Lew Welch, *Springtime in the Rockies, Lichen* (San Francisco: Cranium, 1971), Illustrated lithographic broadside.

p. 297 bottom
Lew Welch, *Hermit Poems*, (San Francisco: Writing 8-Four Seasons Foundation, 1965).

After finishing high school, Welch enlisted in the service, but he was in uniform for less than a year. In 1946 he enrolled at Stockton Jr. College where he experienced what he described as "a moment of revelation" when he stumbled across a copy of Gertrude Stein's *Three Lives;* Welch said it was at that instant that he became a writer. In 1948 he transferred to Reed College, and by 1949 he was living with poets Gary Snyder and Philip Whalen. Though he was subject to intense mood swings, Welch produced a voluminous amount of poetry during that period, much of which reflected his admiration for William Carlos Williams. After producing a series of what he referred to as "minimal" poems, Welch wrote "Skunk Cabbage," which he considered his first fully realized work. Speaking in a casual, conversational tone that is alternately humble and indignant, Welch hammered out a style that invariably reveals the perpetual struggle he waged against the darker currents of his mind.

In 1950 William Carlos Williams visited Reed, and Welch established enough of a friendship with him that he was able to visit the poet at his home in New Jersey at the end of the year. Welch was living in Manhattan then and working in a department store, but in April of 1951 he suffered a breakdown that prompted him to join a Dianetics therapy group, and he traveled with the group to Florida, where he spent two months.

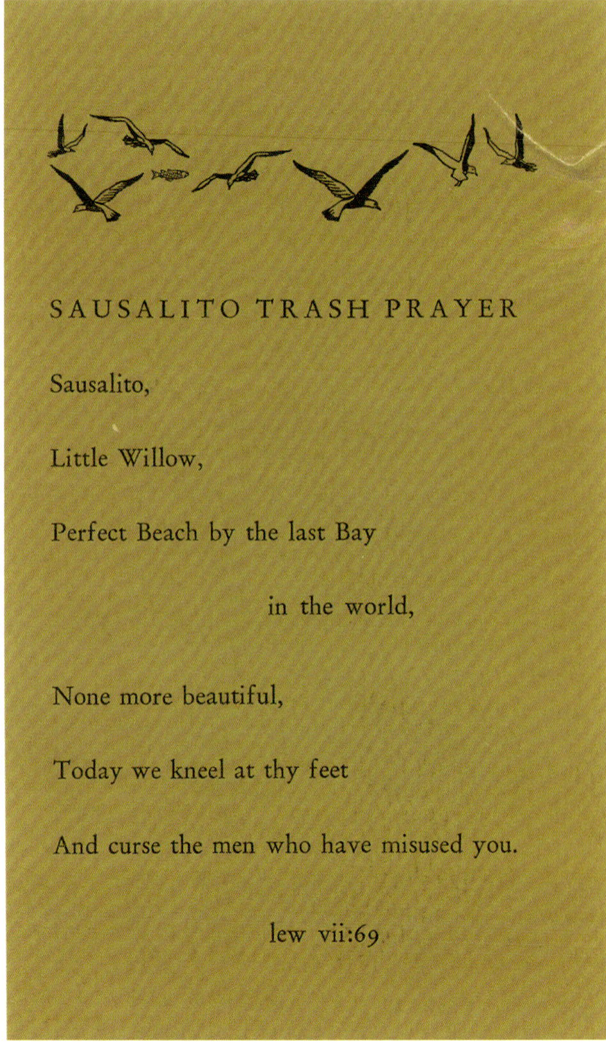

By the fall Welch was back on his feet, and he enrolled at the University of Chicago as a philosophy major. In 1952 he suffered another breakdown and left school to immerse himself in a long program of analysis which stabilized him for the next five years. In 1953 he took a job with Montgomery Ward and married Mary Garber. He continued to write during this period and returned to night school at the University of Chicago. He had begun drinking, though, and as the Beat renaissance gathered steam in San Francisco, he grew increasingly restless. In the fall of 1957 he managed to obtain a transfer to the Oakland office of Montgomery Ward, but was fired shortly after he settled in San Francisco and wound up driving a cab.

"That's how we met Lew—he was a cab driver and he came to pick us up when we were living on Scott Street in 1958," Shirley Berman has recalled. "There were five of us and he said, 'I'm only allowed to take four,' and we said, 'You mean you can't take five starving artists?' He said, 'Only if I can go with you,' and he did."[1]

Welch was drinking heavily by then, and his marriage had completely unraveled. He was hired, then fired, from a job as a rubber cutter at the Bemis Bag Company, so in 1959 he decided to spend some time with his mother, who was living in Reno. When Welch heard that Jack Kerouac was on the scene in San Francisco, he returned to the Bay Area in the new jeep his mother had given him. Kerouac was looking for a lift to his mother's house on Long Island and Welch offered to take him. Poet Albert Saijo decided to go along for the ride, and the three of them collaborated on *Trip Trap*, a book of haiku they compiled as they traveled. Returning to the West Coast, Welch moved in with his mother and devoted himself to writing a novel about his time in college called *I, Leo*. The novel was never finished, but Welch's poetry was beginning to win praise, and in 1960 Auerhahn Press published his *Wobbly Rock*.

In 1960 Welch was living in a communal house in San Francisco when he met poet Lenore Kandel; they fell in love and immediately moved in together. By that point Welch had been diagnosed with cirrhosis of the liver, but he continued to drink heavily, and his episodes of depression became increasingly debilitating. He left Kandel in 1962 and began spending periods of isolation in the countryside of Northern California, occasionally working for the forestry service. During those periods he mostly drank and wrote; *Hermit Poems*, published in 1965, was among the notable works he produced while living alone in the wilds.

In 1964 Welch met Magda Cregg and moved in with her in Marin County. The following year Oyez Press published *On Out*, the first collection of Welch's poetry. From 1965 through 1970, Welch's poetry won an ever larger audience, he worked regularly at odd jobs, gave frequent public readings, and taught several poetry workshops, but he was unable to get a handle on his drinking. He and Cregg broke up, and, in April of 1971, he drove to Gary Snyder's home in Nevada County with plans to build a cabin for himself on adjoining land owned by Allen Ginsberg. On May 23, he took his revolver and disappeared into the woods. His body was never found.

Kristine McKenna

Springtime in the Rockies, Lichen

All these years I overlooked them in the
racket of the rest, this
symbiotic splash of plant and fungus feeding
on rock, on sun, a little moisture, air —
tiny acid-factories dissolving
salt from living rocks and
eating them.

Here they are, blooming!
Tall rock, talus and scree, all dusted with it:
rust, ivory, brilliant yellow-green, and
cliffs like murals!
Huge panels streaked and patched, quietly,
with shooting-stars and lupine at the base.

Closer, with the glass, a city of cups!
Clumps of mushrooms and where do the
plants begin? Why are they doing this?
In this big sky and all around me peaks and
the melting glaciers, why am I made to
kneel and peer at Tiny?

These are the stamps on the final envelope.

How can the poisons reach them?
In such thin air, how can they care for the
loss of a million breaths?
What, possibly, could make their ground more bare?

Let it all die.

The hushed globe will wait and wait for
what is now so small and slow to
open it again.

As now, indeed, it opens it again, this
scentless velvet,
crumbler-of-the-rocks,

this Lichen!

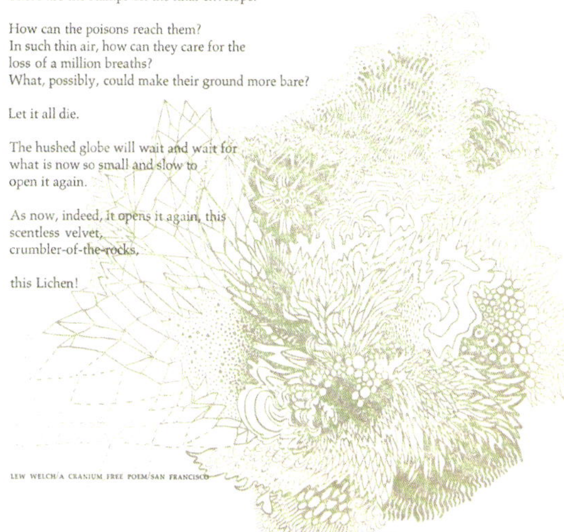

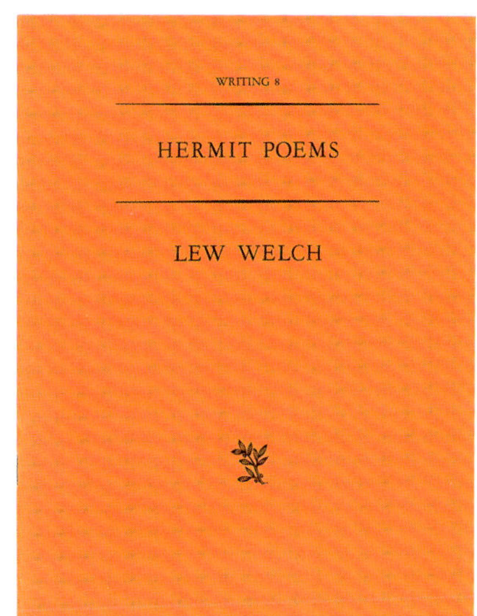

1 Conversation with Shirley Berman, January 9, 1999.

John Wieners

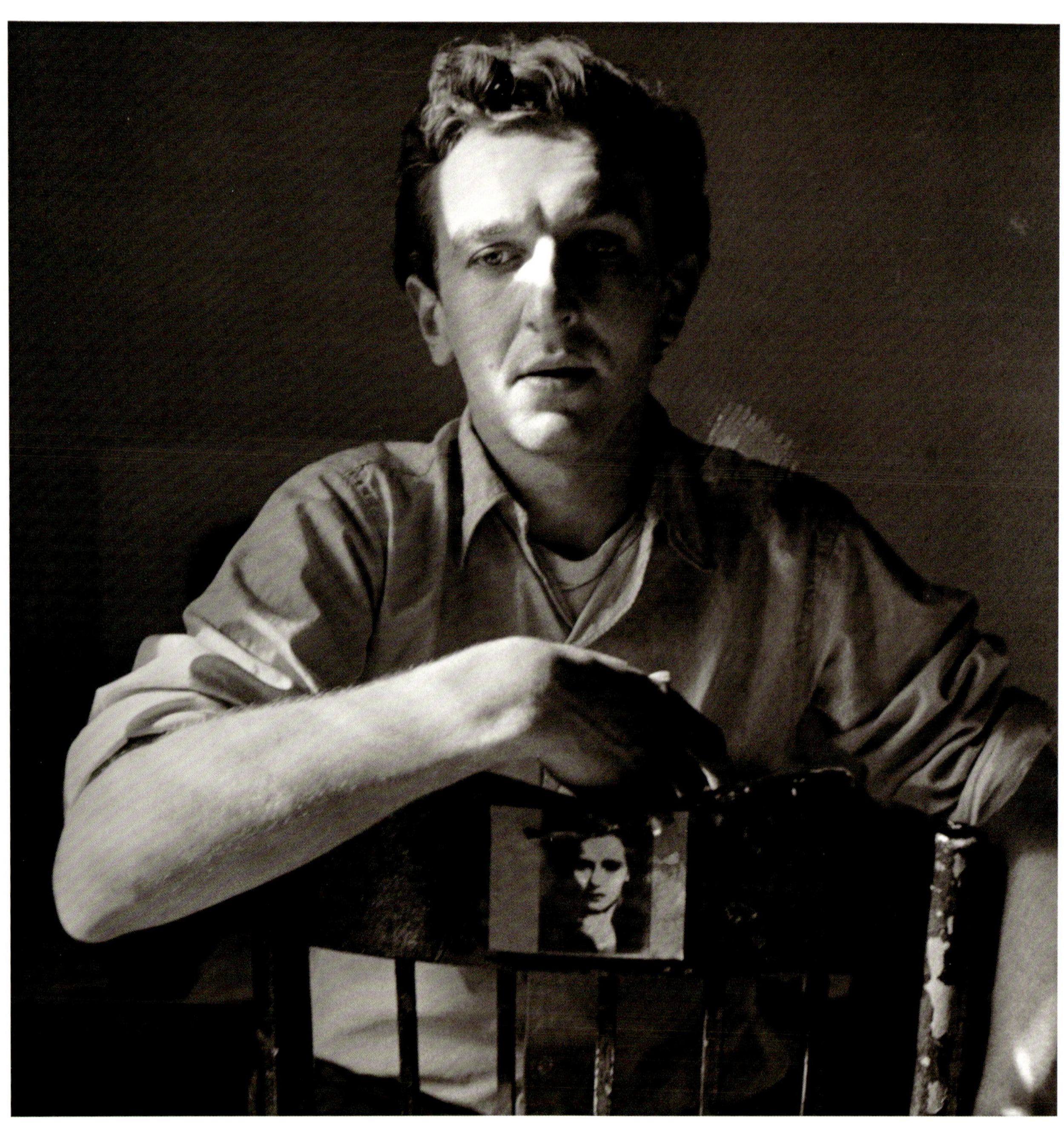

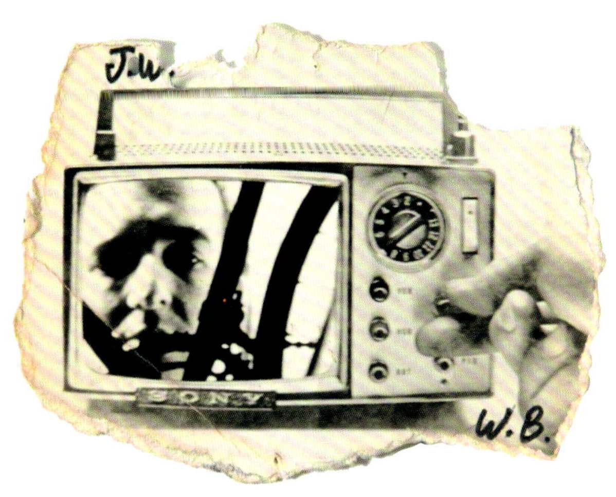

March 13 1960

Dearest Wally:

Sunday evening and I sit in the twilight after supper. Thinking of the big photograph and how much I would like a copy, for the 2nd edition of THE ~~the~~ Wentley Poems, if there is to be one. I'm not sure yet as maybe the first 500 were enough. Anything to displace the drawing by LaVigne.

What are your plans? I am in a state hospital, private room, visitors and family get togethers. Your gift has brought me such balm that it occupies the shadows of ~~the~~ my western window: sill along with ~~the~~ yellow stems, cup and bulb of a dead spring plant.

Lets hope that New England produces a gay May. If you ever want mss for future printing they are in care of Freude 1960 21st Ave. It is hard to write as the TV blares thru out the layers of this ward. And of course most of what we think is channeled to its level. CBPS as my mother wd. say. Corn beef and potato salad. Today her birthday and this fact makes the moon rise fuller.

Until you come through again
measure my spirit by yours JOHN

My love to Shirl and Tosh

A poem for the Definite Article
my grandmother is on the wind this morning
as I sit in a black rocking chair and watch
the sun play on a child playing by the legs
of a woodtable in a whiteroom.

Songs of death
Green peacock eyes wave in the breeze, birds
whistle down the chimmey and the papers
slide to the floor like her tongue
did in the top of her mouth.
The house
is a woman, is Patty Topalian
whosé grandmother slept in a rug,
stealing out of Armenia
to flash her eyes by this chair
and raise the hair under her arms

p. 298
John Wieners at 707 Scott Street, San Francisco, 1959. Photograph by Wallace Berman.

p. 299 top
Wallace Berman, Torn mailer with Berman photograph of John Wieners, undated.

p. 299 bottom
John Wieners, Letter written to Wallace Berman from a Massachusetts psychiatric hospital, 1960. Wallace Berman Archive, Smithsonian Institution.

p. 300
John Wieners, *A Poem for the Definite Article*, With a drawing by Robert Duncan, and an inscription, "To Larry [Jordan] on his birthday, John," 1959. Patricia Jordan Archive, Archives of American Art, Smithsonian Institution.

p. 301
John Wieners, Back cover author photograph for *The Hotel Wentley Poems* by Wallace Berman, 1959.

Poet of poignant and tragic eloquence, born in 1934 of the New England working class in Milton, Massachusetts, John Wieners was educated by the Jesuit brothers of Boston College, for whom inquiring scholarship and Catholic piety were not incompatible. Although Wieners retained a lifelong sense of religious devoutness, it did not deter him from embracing the life of a social reprobate, and the combination of the two is a frequent theme in his poetry, where loftiness and dissoluteness go hand in hand. A self-described "Boston poet," Wieners drew inspiration from the rich literary tradition of his native New England that includes the Transcendentalist poets Emerson and Thoreau, the exquisitely hermetic Emily Dickinson, and the twentieth-century poet Robert Lowell, whose formalism and social refinement often masked a crisis of the mind.

While still in his teenage years, Wieners attended meetings of the genteel Beacon Hill Poetry Society. Wieners's early verse was strongly influenced by Edna St. Vincent Millay, Elinor Wylie, and Sara Teasdale, and later he often spoke of his preference for women poets as less overbearing in temperament, "to their observations of nature, to their love of feeling, and to an abbreviation of expression." Wieners's appreciation and skill for traditional verse forms originates with this period, and would remain an integral part of his work. Wieners's interest in spiritualism and the occult was also awakened in these years, in the likewise genteel settings of Beacon Hill's Theosophical and Vedanta Societies—in keeping with the pioneering studies of the sacred teachings of India and the Far East by nineteenth-century Boston intellectuals.

A turning point in the poet's life came when the twenty-year-old Wieners was passing by the Charles Street Meeting House in Boston, "on the night of Hurricane Hazel, Sept. 11, 1954," as he later recalled. Wieners "accidentally" overheard Charles Olson reading his poetry and stopped in. After the reading Olson handed out copies of the *Black Mountain Review*. The two poets began to correspond, and Olson offered Wieners a scholarship to the experimental Black Mountain College in North Carolina. Poet and teacher Robert Duncan remembered that within a few short weeks of Wieners's arrival, both he and Olson were awed by the "sheer authenticity" of the young poet's talents, and soon regarded him as an equal.

After attending Black Mountain College from 1955–56, Wieners returned to Boston and published the first of three issues of his literary magazine, *Measure*. Shortly thereafter he traveled to San Francisco with his lover Dana, where the San Francisco poetry renaissance was well underway. In 1958 Wieners published his first book, *The Hotel Wentley Poems* (San Francisco: Auerhahn Press), which became an immediate classic of Beat literature. In eight poems written over six days in a hotel room borrowed from the painter Robert LaVigne, Wieners chronicled the lives of his fellow poets, painters, junkies, and homosexuals, in a modern-day *Notes from the Underground*. Amiri Baraka wrote in his autobiography that although Allen Ginsberg's *Howl* was a sensational announcement of a new spirit in poetry, the quiet and understated voice of *The Hotel Wentley Poems* in fact had a more profound effect on many of his contemporaries.

In 1960 Wieners returned to the East Coast, and over the next five years divided his time between New York and Boston. In New York he shared an apartment with Herbert Huncke on the Lower East Side, and oversaw the production of three of his plays at the Judson Poets Theater. He lived largely through the generosity of friends, various small publishers, and the proprietors of small bookstores. In 1965 Wieners enrolled in the Graduate Program at the State University of New York in Buffalo, and served as teaching assistant to Charles Olson. But the poet's excessive drug use, begun in San Francisco, began to take its toll. Wieners was committed to mental hospitals on at least three occasions during the 1960s, and was forced to undergo shock treatment. These experiences are vividly recounted in many of his books, notably *Asylum Poems* (New York: Angel Hair Books, 1969). Despite extreme poverty and personal upheavals, Wieners wrote prolifically throughout the 1960s and early 1970s. *Nerves* (London: Jonathan Cape, 1970) is a stunning summation of Wieners's work from this period, and established him as a poet's poet, placing him foremost in regard amongst his fellow writers.

By the mid 1970s Wieners had settled permanently on Boston's Beacon Hill, at the ironic address of 44 Joy Street. He took an active part in political action committees, educational cooperatives, and the gay liberation movement. In 1975 Wieners published a sprawling masterwork, *Behind the State Capitol, Or Cinncincinnati Pike* (Boston: Good Gay Poets), a book that met with much confusion and even hostility from the poetry community. Although always an experimental poet, Wieners's editors usually favored more technically conservative poems, especially given the poet's skill in handling traditional forms. But in friend and poet Charles Shively, Wieners found an editor and publisher willing to give a free hand to styles both standard and outlandish. Distinctions between poetry and prose are blurred, and schizophrenic shifts of identity vie with stream-of-consciousness narratives. Grammar, syntax, and spelling are broken down and recombined. It is a remarkable picture of "the mind in drag" (Kevin Killian), and a unique poetic document that would prove profoundly inspiring to a younger generation of poets.

Artistically speaking, *Behind the State Capitol* was a rebirth, but sadly it was also a farewell. "Poetry is no longer on my calendar," Wieners curtly told a Boston writer in the late 1970s. Thereafter he seldom committed poem to paper. In later years his rare (and usually brief) poetry readings were often improvised collages of inner voices, old poems, new poems composed that day, interspersed with passages from movie magazines and other popular texts. He remained a reticent but genial figure on the Boston poetry scene, even attending a book party for a friend on the night of his death in 2002.

Raymond Foye

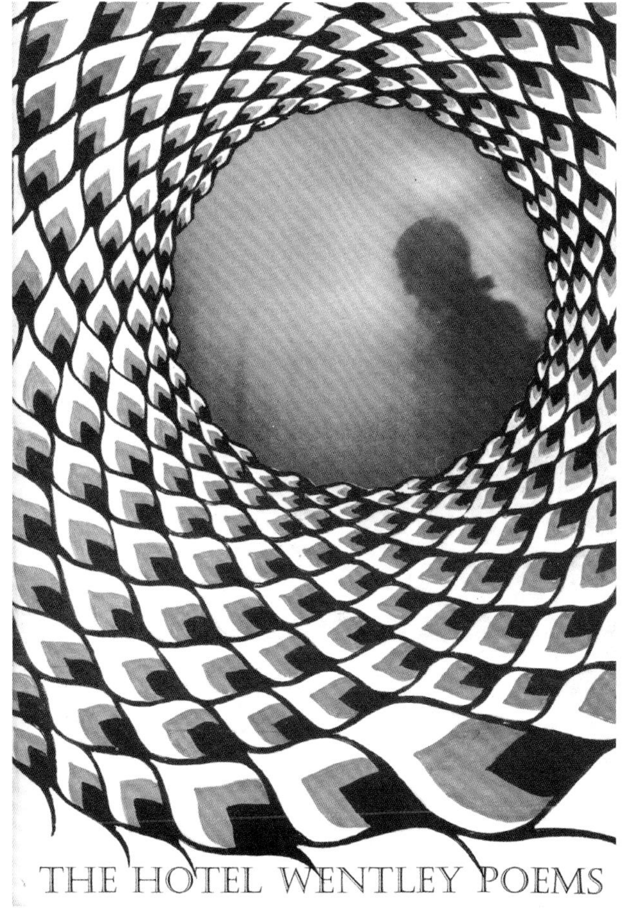

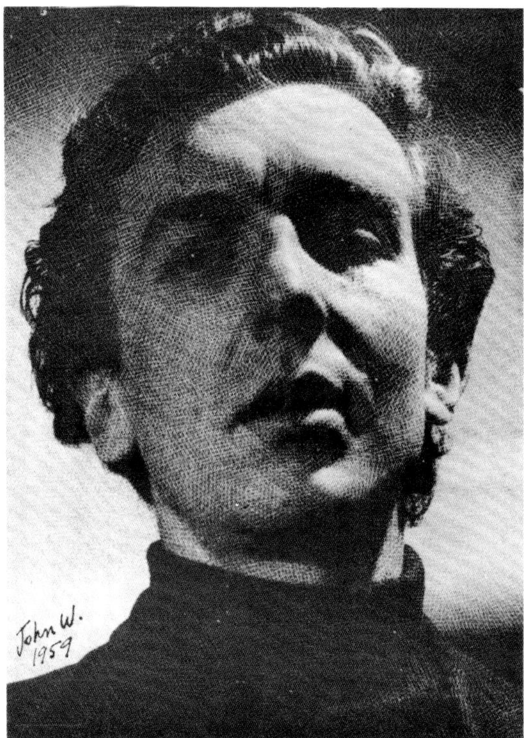

The drawings on the cover and of the poet in *A Poem for Painters* are by Robert LaVigne. The photograph on the front cover was taken in the Hotel Wentley by Jerry Burchard. The photograph of the poet on the back cover was taken by Wallace Berman when the poems were written.

$1.25

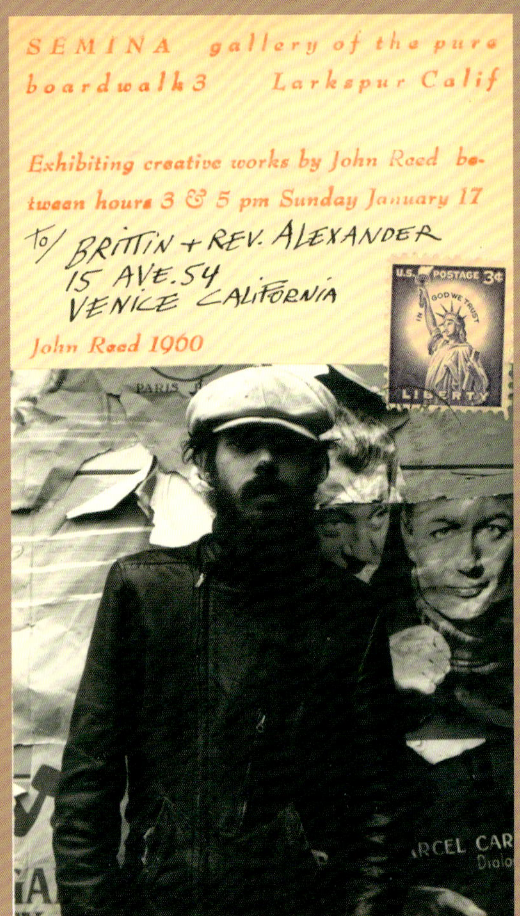

SEMINA art gallery Boardwalk 3
Larkspur Calif 1960

An Exhibition of photographs by Edmund Teske & works by Geo Herms between hours 3&5 pm Sun. May 1

G Herms W.B.

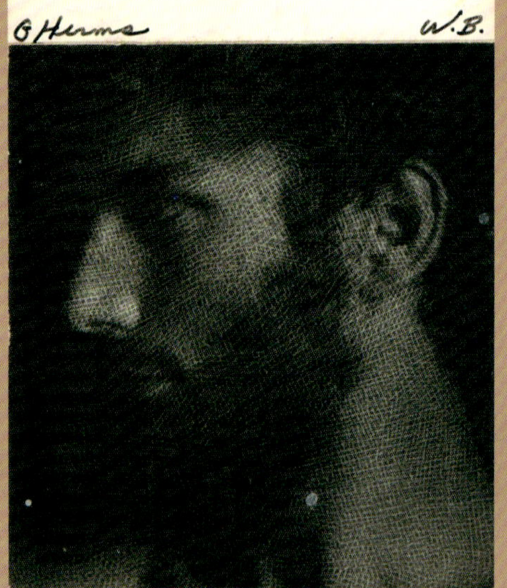

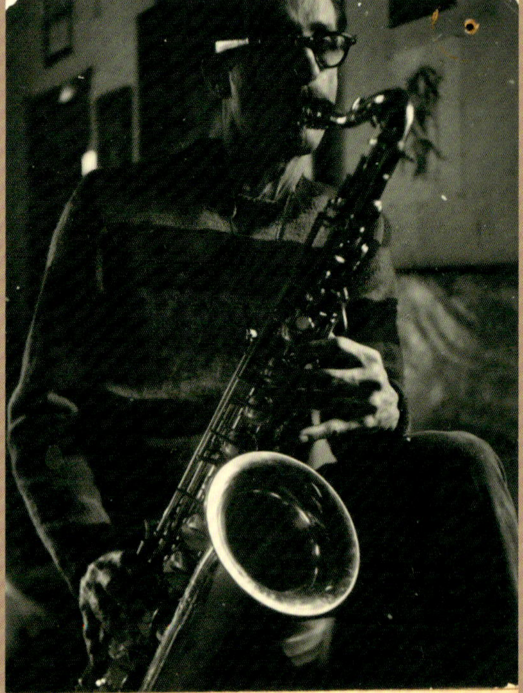

Works by Arthur Richer
Hours 3 to 5 pm Sunday March/5
SEMINA bdwk. 3 Larkspur

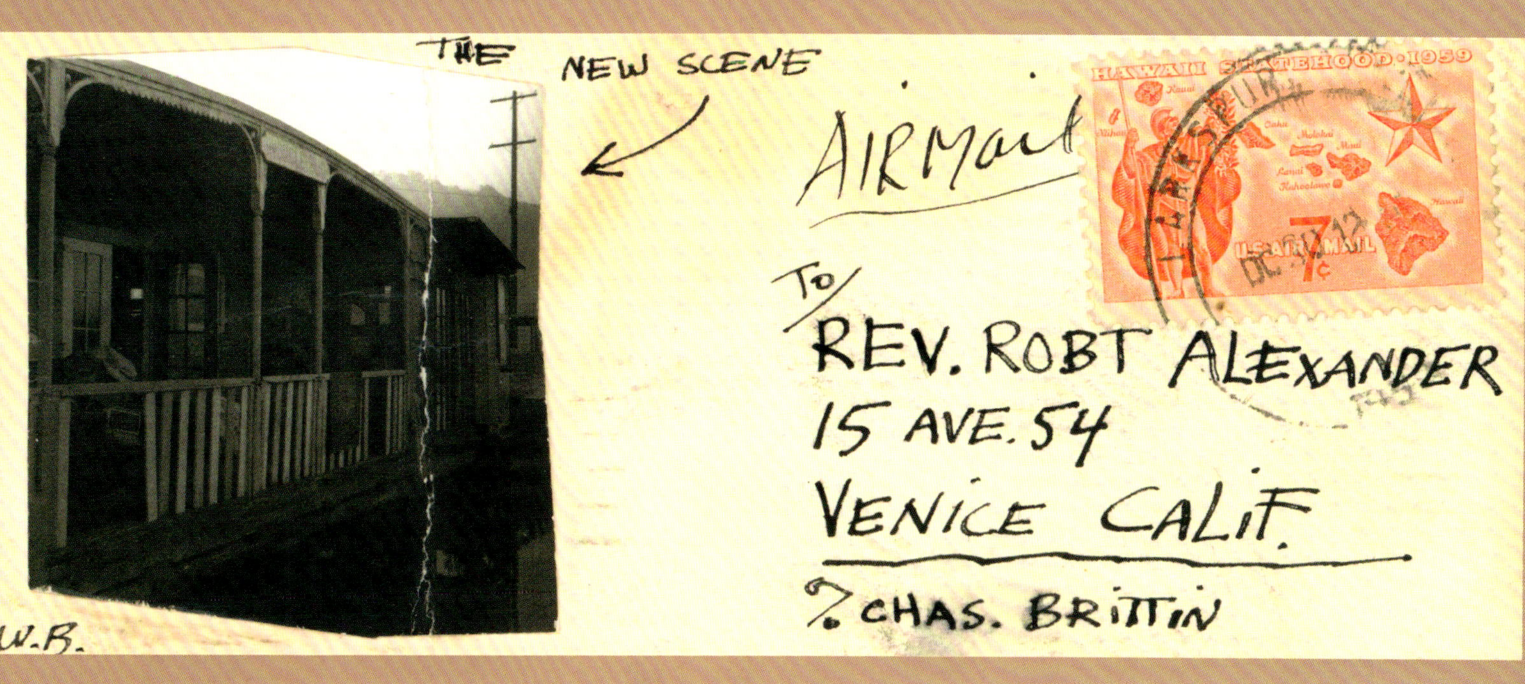

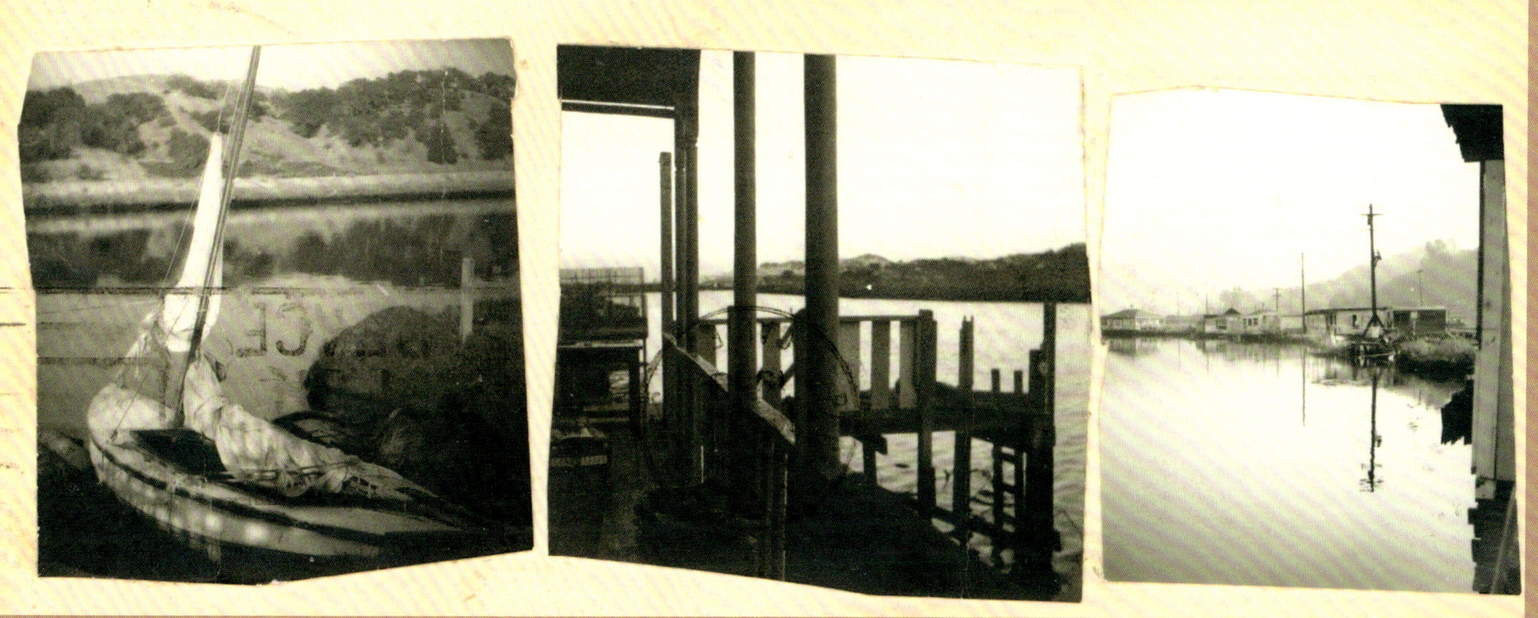

Mailer to Robert Alexander with photographs by Wallace Berman of Larkspur houseboat and piers, 1960. Collection of Charles Britin.

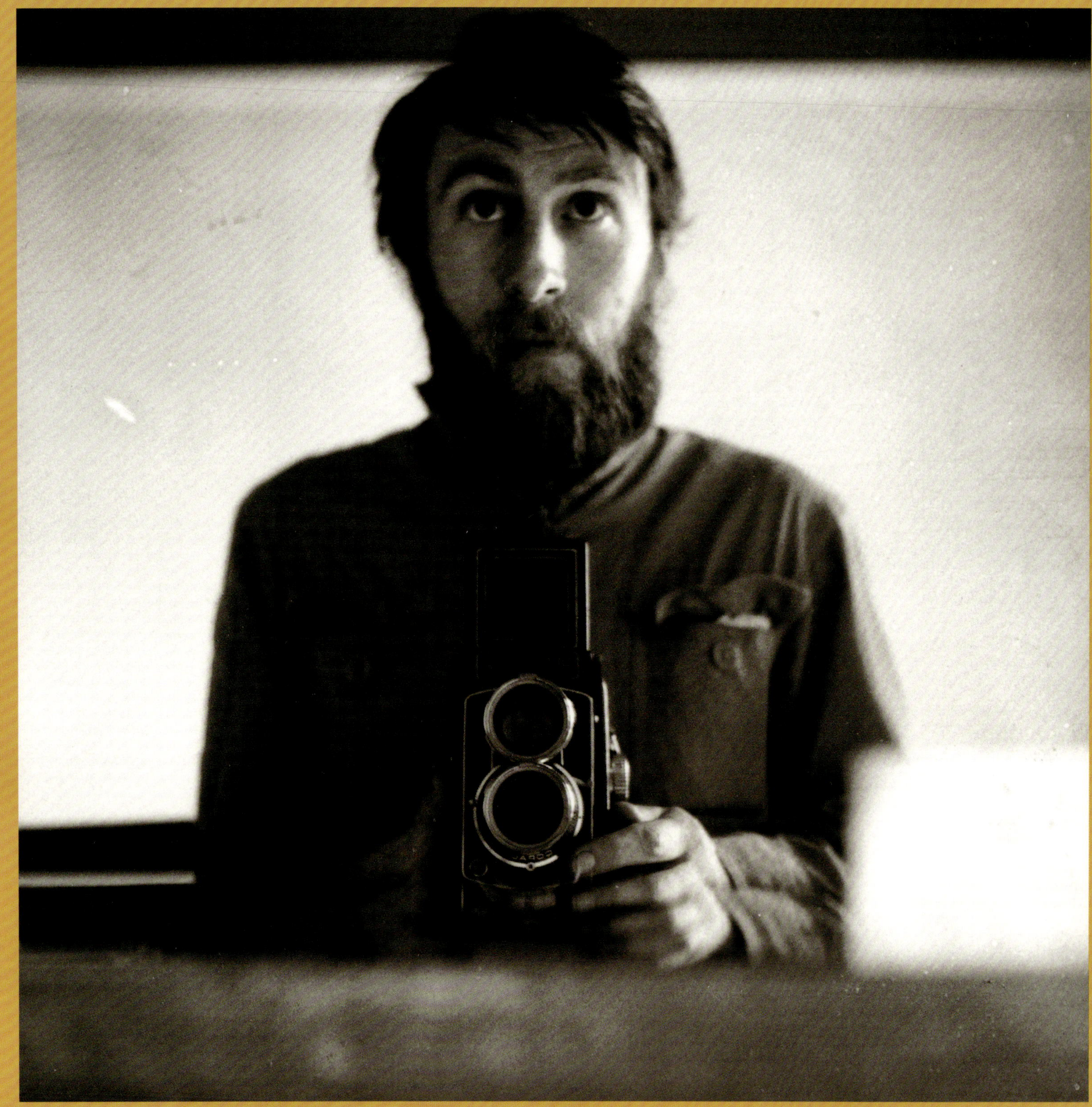

Self-portrait, Larkspur, 1961, Photograph by Wallace Berman, Courtesy Wallace Berman Estate.

Wallace Berman and Photography

Kristine McKenna

Wallace Berman's relationship with photography is as mysterious as everything else about him. People don't think of Berman as a photographer, but in fact, Berman started taking pictures in the early 1950s, and people who knew him back in the day say he always had a camera with him. He took thousands of pictures over the course of his life, but few of his negatives have ever been printed, much less exhibited.

Mechanically reproduced images are, of course, the main ingredient in Berman's Verifax collages, but curiously enough, with one or two exceptions, he never used his own photographs in these works. Nor, with two exceptions, did he ever exhibit his photographs. (In 1959 Berman had a one-day exhibition in his home at 707 Scott Street in San Francisco of a series of photographs he'd taken of Jay DeFeo. After returning to Southern California in 1961, he showed them a second time at his home in Beverly Glen.) So why was he taking pictures? What did he do with them? He did two things that we know of: he displayed them, unframed, around his house; and he cut them up to use on the hundreds of collaged mailers he was forever making and sending to his friends. These activities involved a tiny fraction of the pictures he took, though, so his intentions remain a puzzle.

The approximately twenty-three hundred surviving negatives don't give a complete picture of Berman's photographic practice. The negatives to hundreds of pictures Berman took between the years 1950 and 1965 were lost when the Berman house was destroyed in a mud slide in December of 1965. Thus, it's hard to say if Berman had a clearly identifiable photographic style that evolved, or to compare early pictures with later ones.

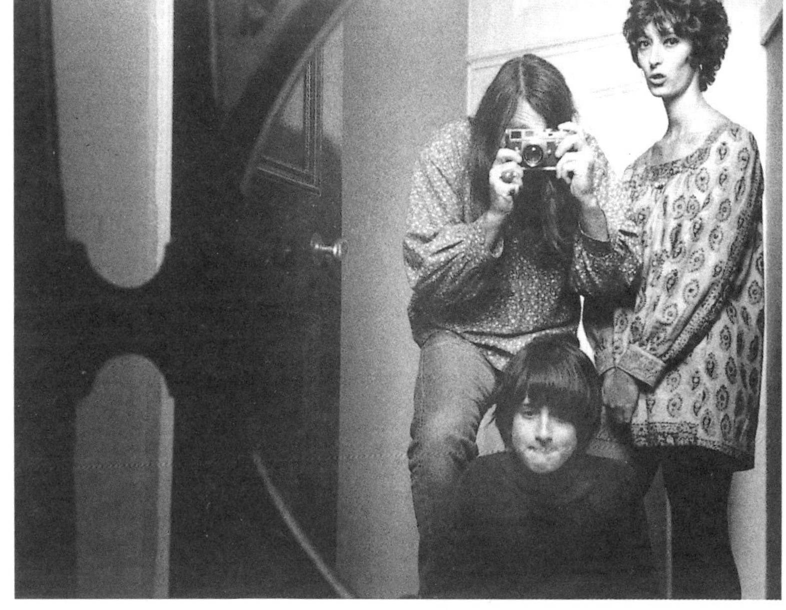

Wallace, Shirley, and Tosh Berman in home of Robert Fraser, London, 1967, Photograph by Wallace Berman, Courtesy Wallace Berman Estate.

The pictures that remain can be loosely broken down into several categories: The first of them is the photographic record Berman created of the art he made. Among the approximately three hundred pictures Berman took of his own artworks, there are images of several destroyed pieces, and documentation of site-specific works comprised of Hebrew letters painted on rocks, most of which were worn away and finally destroyed by the elements.

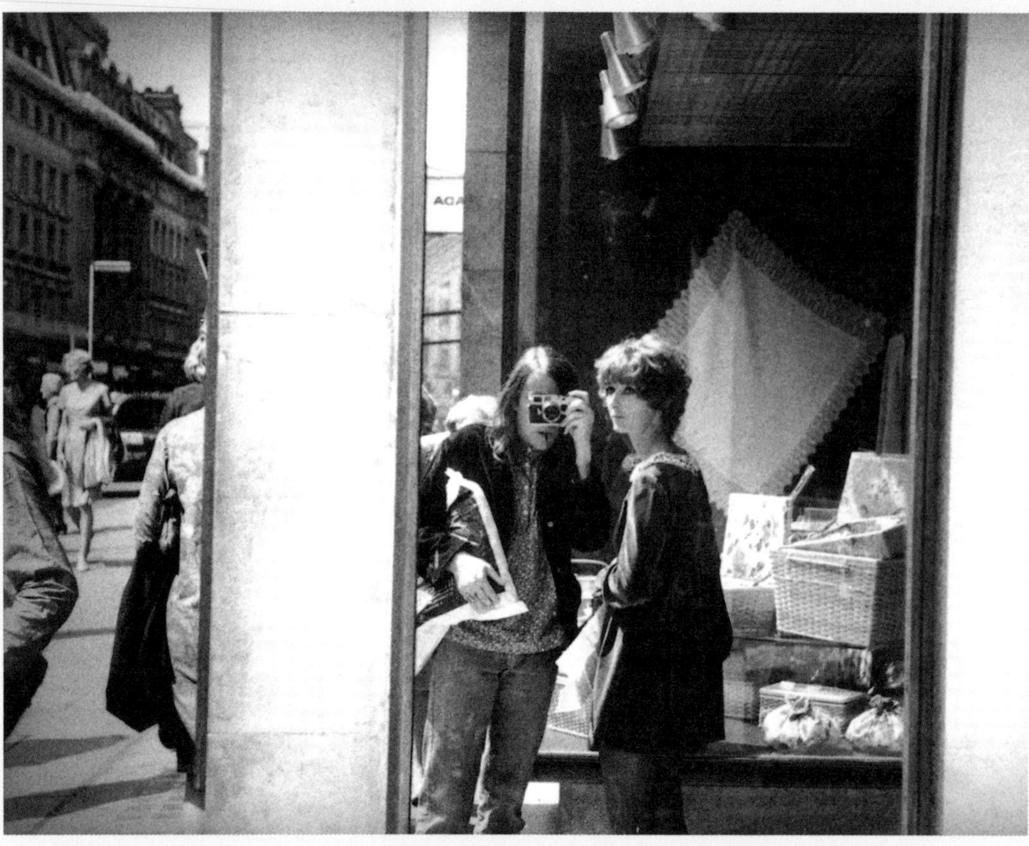

Wallace and Shirley Berman, London, 1967, Photograph by Wallace Berman, Courtesy Wallace Berman Estate.

Berman didn't care much for traveling, and there are very few travel/vacation shots in his archive. There are thirty pictures shot in the early 70s in Taos, New Mexico, taken during a visit to Dennis Hopper at his home there; and one hundred pictures taken in London, where the Bermans spent two weeks during the summer of 1967. "There was something about Hyde Park that fascinated Wallace," says Shirley Berman, "and he shot quite a few pictures there." [1]

The richest vein in the archive comprises Berman's self-portraiture, and the pictures he took of his wife and son. The archive includes a surprising number of self-portraits—approximately 150 in all—most of which appear to have been taken with the use of a timer when he was alone in his studio. More often than not he photographed himself looking straight into the camera lens, with a neutral expression on his face; the resulting pictures are completely inscrutable, yet they have a playful quality.

Berman made forty-one family portraits, eighty pictures of Shirley Berman, and ninety two photographs of Tosh Berman. What emerges from these photographs is the sense of an uncommonly gentle family, a family that lived modestly, but with an acute sensitivity to beauty. Tremendous care was taken with the placement of simple things in the Berman residence, and though their home saw a steady and unending traffic of bohemian types, it bore no resemblance whatsoever to a beatnik crash pad. It looks like a serene and sensible haven, and that's exactly what it was for Berman's friends.

Berman only photographed people that he loved, so the portraits he made of his friends have a palpable sense of intimacy. His archive includes 721 pictures of friends in Northern California, where the Bermans lived from 1958 to 1961, and 840 pictures of the Berman circle in Los Angeles; all of these pictures capture some essential quality of the sitter. "My dad took photographs in a very unself-conscious way, so people were relaxed when he photographed them," Tosh Berman has recalled.[2] It's evident in the pictures that the people close to Berman trusted him completely. His women friends—Jay DeFeo, Patty Jordan, Beverly Walsh—were comfortable having him photograph them in the nude. Philip Lamantia and Robert Alexander allowed Berman to photograph them shooting heroin; Lew Welch, Arthur Richer and Kirby Doyle clowned for his camera; while Bobby Driscoll, Loree Foxx, and Bob Kaufman revealed their despair. "My father was very good at handling extreme personalities," Tosh Berman has observed. As to how he did that, Charles Brittin suggests it was because "there was nothing you could do around Wally that would make you feel foolish. He was enormously tolerant." [3]

Berman apparently had little interest in the nuts and bolts of photographic technique. Tosh Berman has pointed out that "My father didn't know how to load a camera—my mom always did it for him when he wanted to take pictures." Charles Brittin remembers, "Although Wally and I spent a lot of time working on pictures together, I never saw him do a complete darkroom procedure on his own. As far as I know, that wasn't something he knew how to do." Berman commented to Brittin, in a letter written from Larkspur in 1960, "I am no longer completely helpless in darkroom," but Brittin never saw Berman put any newly acquired skills to use. Walter Hopps recalled spending an evening with Berman in 1957, in Hopps's darkroom at his parents's home in Eagle Rock, where they made a series of solarized "darkroom drawings."[4] Berman made no additional work in this mode, however, so it's hard to know how he felt about it.

This isn't to suggest that Berman had a passive relationship with the images he selected to use; in fact, he had an instantly recognizable way of working with photographs that largely revolved around notions of obscuration and erasure. When considering Berman's photographic oeuvre, it's important to remember that he spent two years working in a furniture factory as a distresser, learning how to impart a patina of age and decay to the pieces he worked on. Those skills were key to the body of work he presented in his 1957 exhibition at the Ferus Gallery. The show's twelve parchment wall works, and three free-standing sculptures—*Panel, Temple,* and *Cross*—were all artificially aged, and this aesthetic comes into play with Berman's photographs, too.

One of the most striking things about the library of photographs Berman created is how little he exploited them. However, when he did use one of his own photographs—to include in *Semina,* or collage onto a mailer—he invariably went into the image and somehow altered it. The methodology he devised for working with his photographs boiled down to a few simple techniques. He often tore his pictures into lunette shapes, leaving the edges ragged so as to suggest an effect achieved with a pinhole camera. He did this with pictures of the 1959 Poet's Parade in San Francisco, a portrait of himself with Arthur Richer, the cover art he created for Philip Lamantia's book, *Narcotica*, and the series of portraits of his Larkspur landlady that appear on the cover of *Semina VI*.

Berman often printed his photographs through a patterned transparency that stamped the image with a soft net of cross-hatching, and he also favored a darkroom technique called reticulation, which involves a slight alteration in the process of washing the negative. Because the silver on the negative is still very soft at this point in the developing process, this alteration leaves a pixelated dot pattern on the surface of the picture. Brittin recalls introducing the effect to Berman, who immediately responded to the mysterious, veiled quality it brings to a picture. [5]

The notion of veiling clearly appealed to Berman—it is evident in everything from his labyrinthine Verifax works, which beg to be decoded, to the red filter he overlaid on the image he created for the announcement for Charles Brittin's Semina Gallery exhibition. Doubling is another strategy Berman employed to compound the layers of meaning in his pictures. You can see it operating in a portrait of Tosh Berman taken in 1960, that depicts Tosh standing next to a door collaged with other Berman photographs of Tosh and of his mother. It's there in his picture, included in *Semina 7*, of Jarry Heiserman, standing next to a mirror image of himself, peering from the window of a Mill Valley squat. And it's certainly there in his intervention into the infamous newspaper photo of Lee Harvey Oswald moving into shooting range of Jack Ruby; in Berman's version of the picture, the escorting officer at Oswald's side appears twice.

Berman often entered his photographs by drawing into them. In a self-portrait of Berman reading as he reclines in a Larkspur rowboat, he has drawn the insignia for the Semina Gallery onto the cover of the book he holds. And dozens of pictures were inscribed with a hand-drawn aleph, the monolithic mystery that towers at the center of everything Berman created. Because Berman declined to explain exactly what this symbol meant to him, it's impossible to say how its presence in his photographs—and its absence from others—alters their meaning. Berman was notorious for his refusal to discuss or explain his work, and was comfortable with the fact that the important things in life—the affairs of the human soul—resist articulation. In the end, this is the challenge and the gift his art offers anyone who cares to look.

ENDNOTES

1 Conversation with Shirley Berman, January 9, 1999.

2 All quotations by Tosh Berman from a conversation on January 11, 1999.

3 Conversation with Charles Brittin, December 5, 1999.

4 Conversation with Walter Hopps, August 20, 2004. See Eduardo Lipschutz-Villa, ed., exh. cat., *Support the Revolution: Wallace Berman* (Amsterdam: Institute of Contemporary Art, 1992), p. 89.

5 Conversation with Charles Brittin, September 5, 2004.

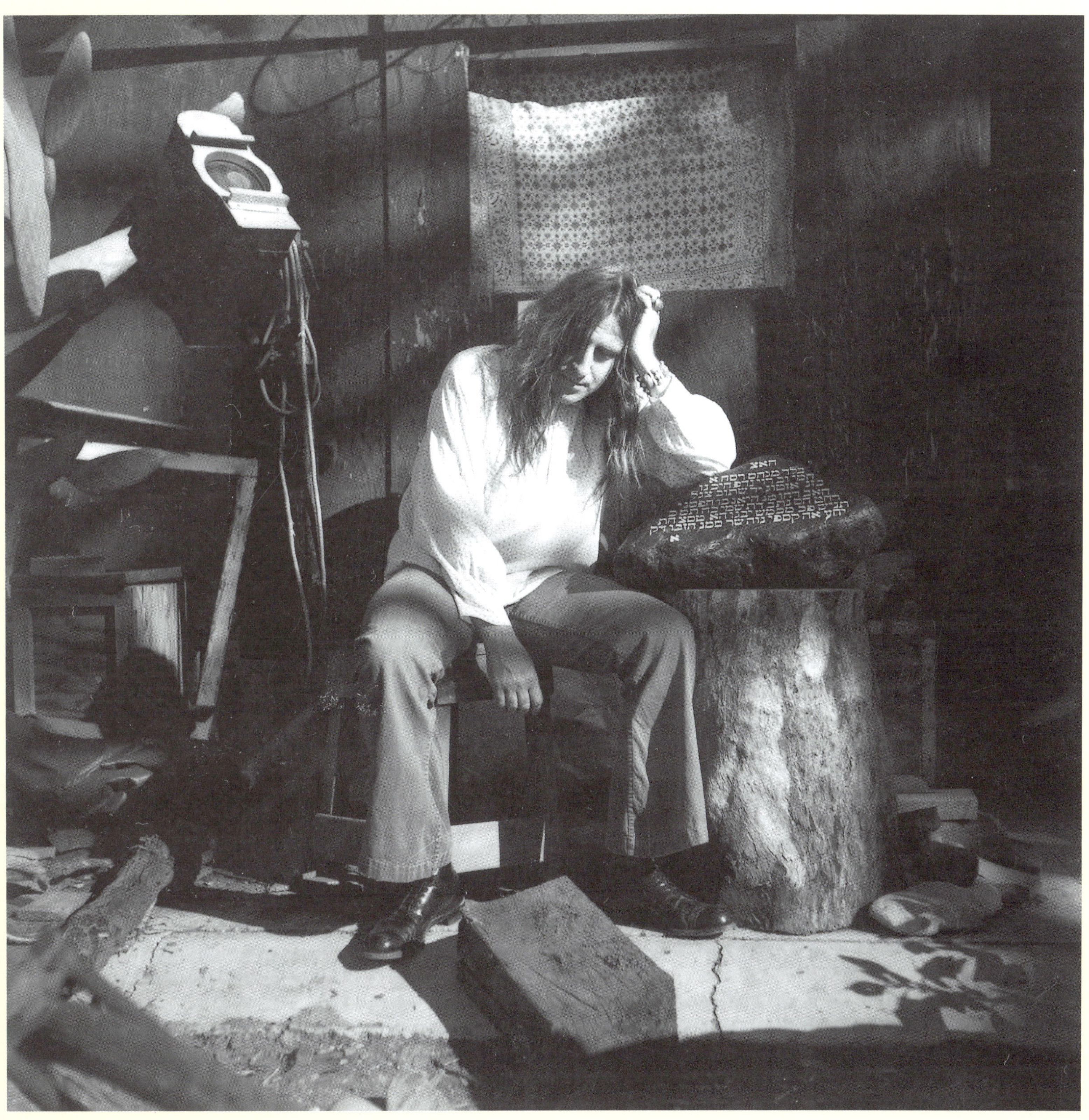

Self-portrait, Topanga Canyon, c. 1973, Photograph by Wallace Berman, Courtesy Wallace Berman Estate.

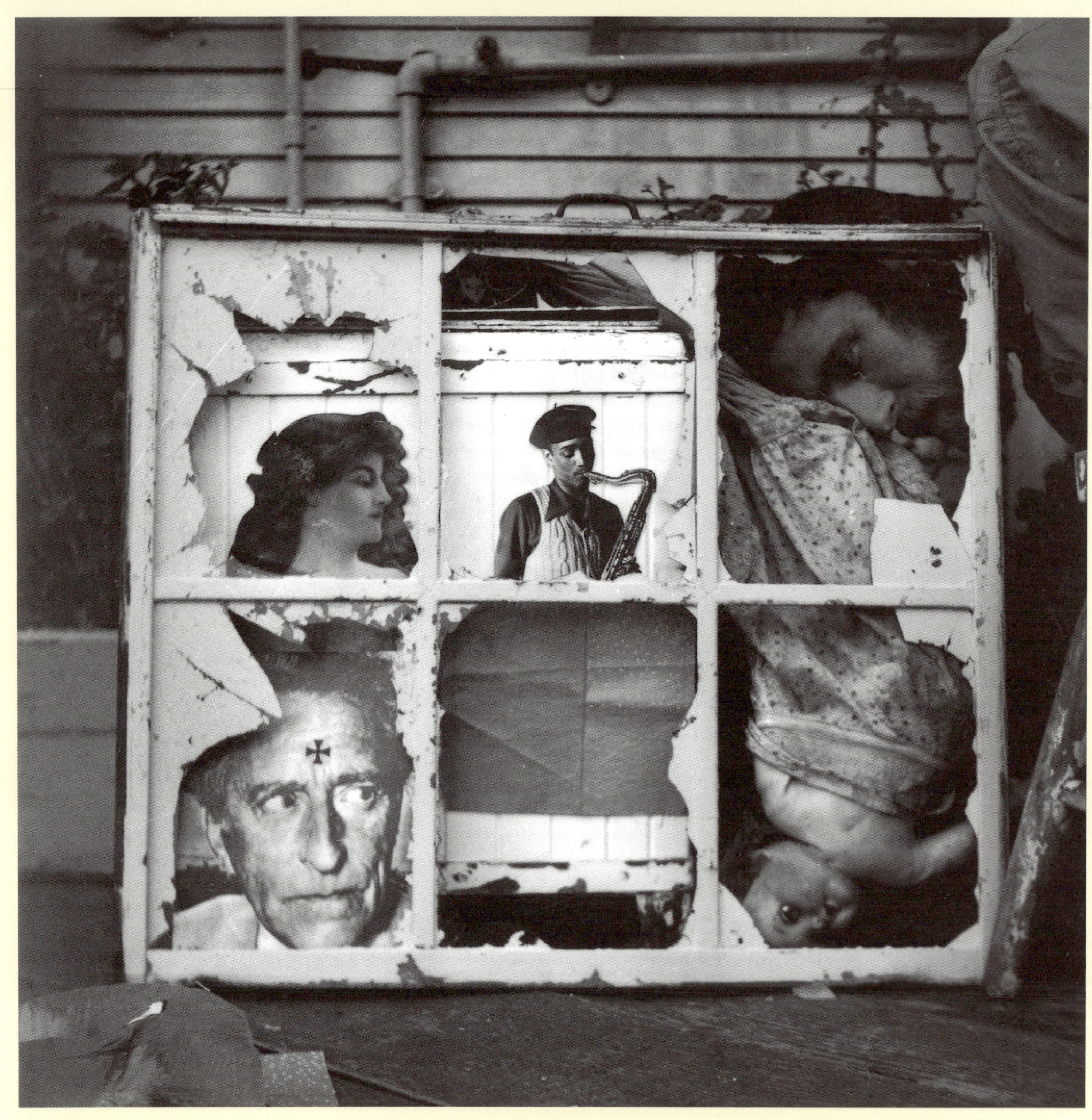

Wallace Berman with an abandoned artwork that includes images of Wardell Gray and Jean Cocteau, Larkspur, 1960, Photograph by Wallace Berman, Courtesy Wallace Berman Estate.

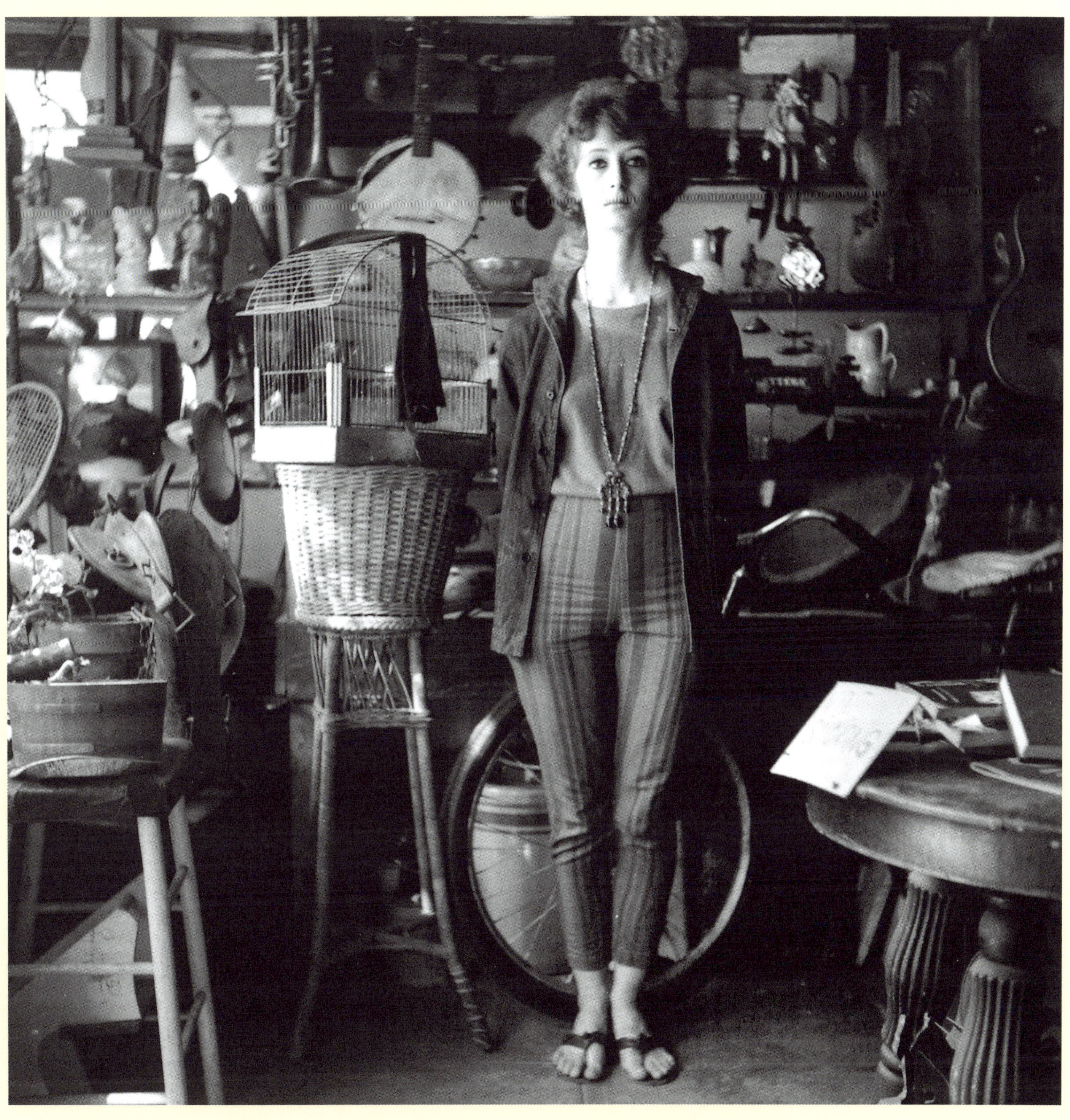

Shirley Berman, McAllister Street junk shop, San Francisco, 1959, Photograph by Wallace Berman, Courtesy Wallace Berman Estate.

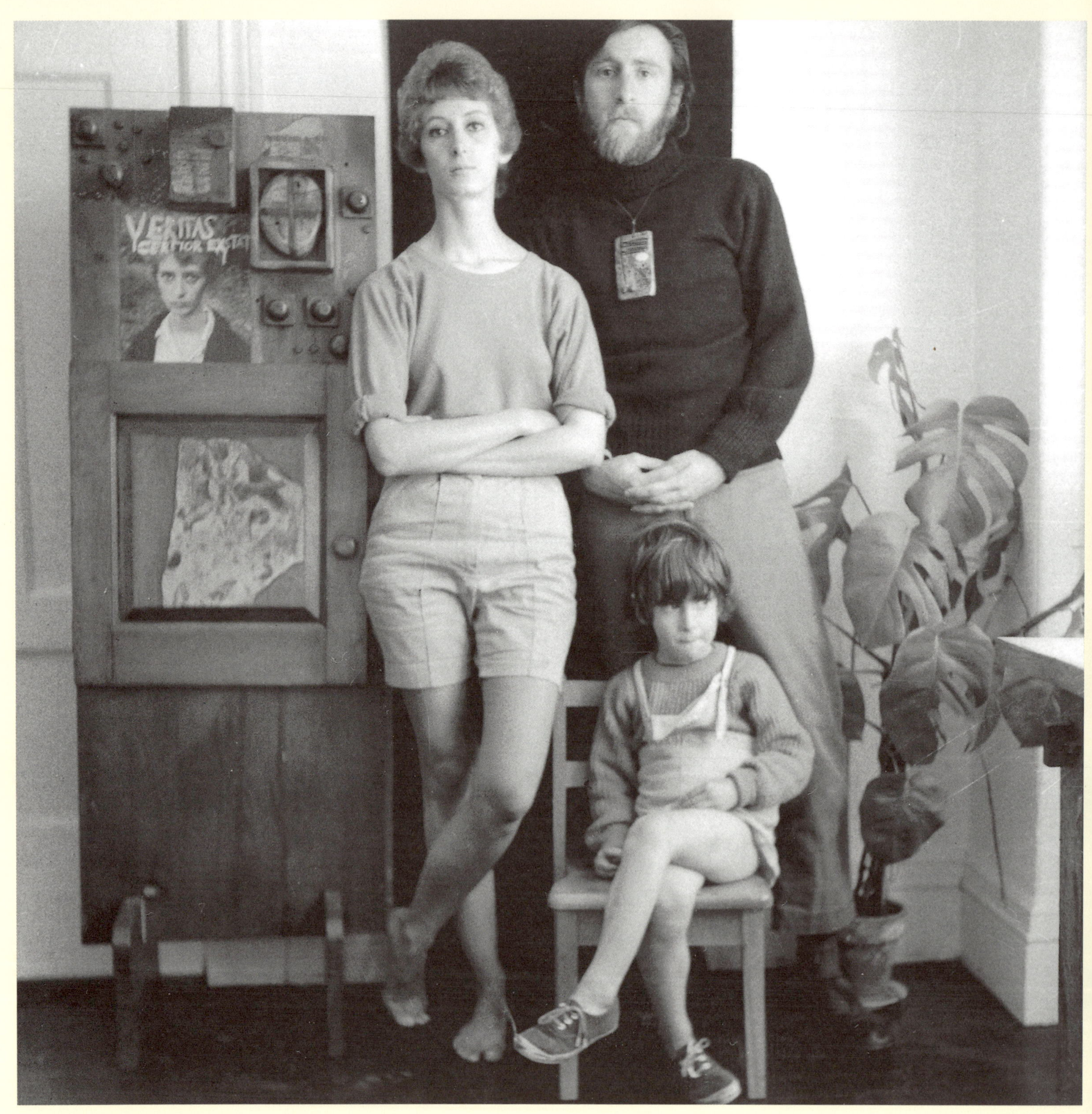

Berman family with *Panel* assemblage, 707 Scott Street, San Francisco, 1959, Photograph by Wallace Berman, Courtesy Wallace Berman Estate.

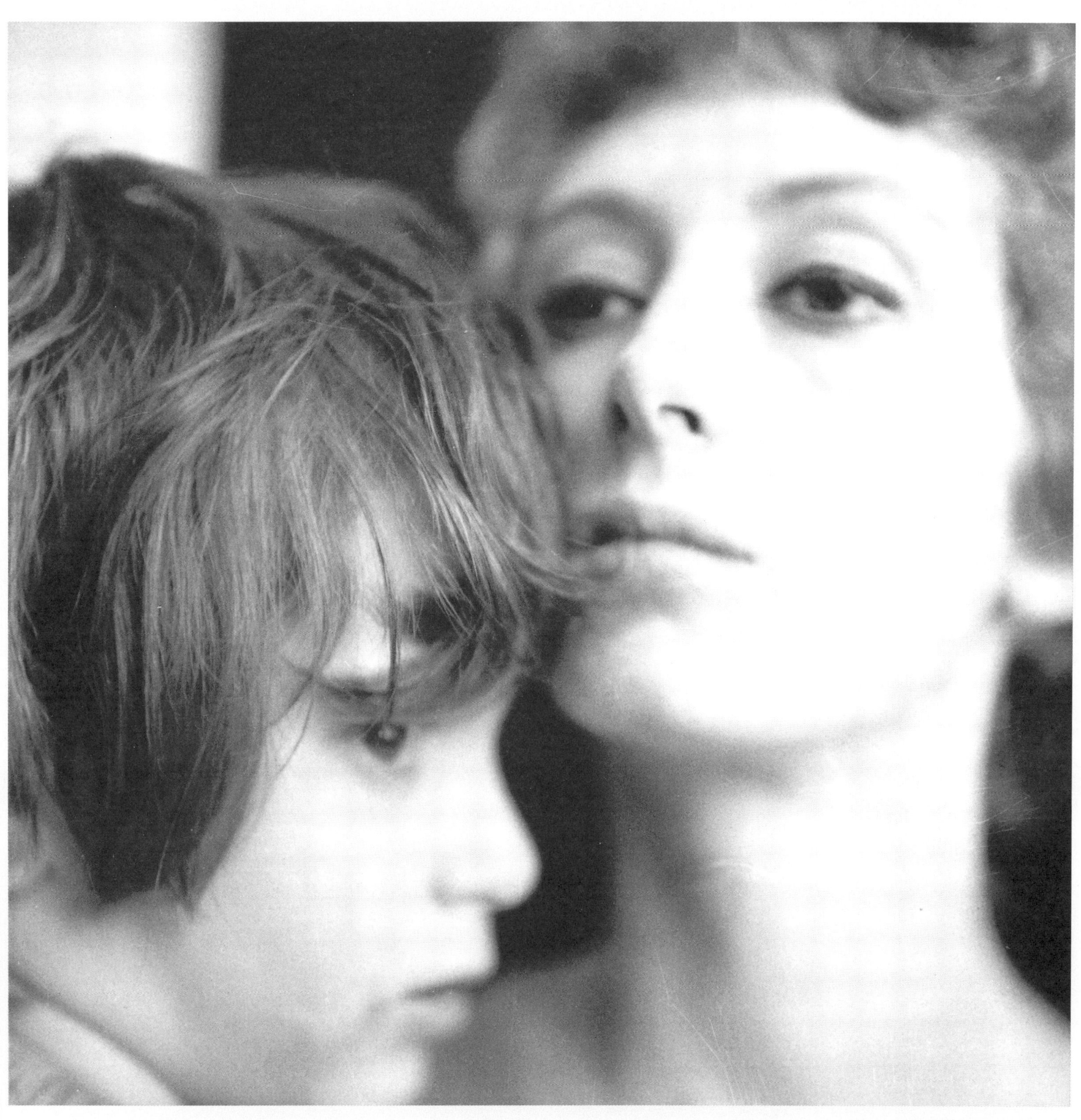

Shirley and Tosh Berman, Beverly Glen, 1956, Photograph by Wallace Berman, Courtesy Wallace Berman Estate.

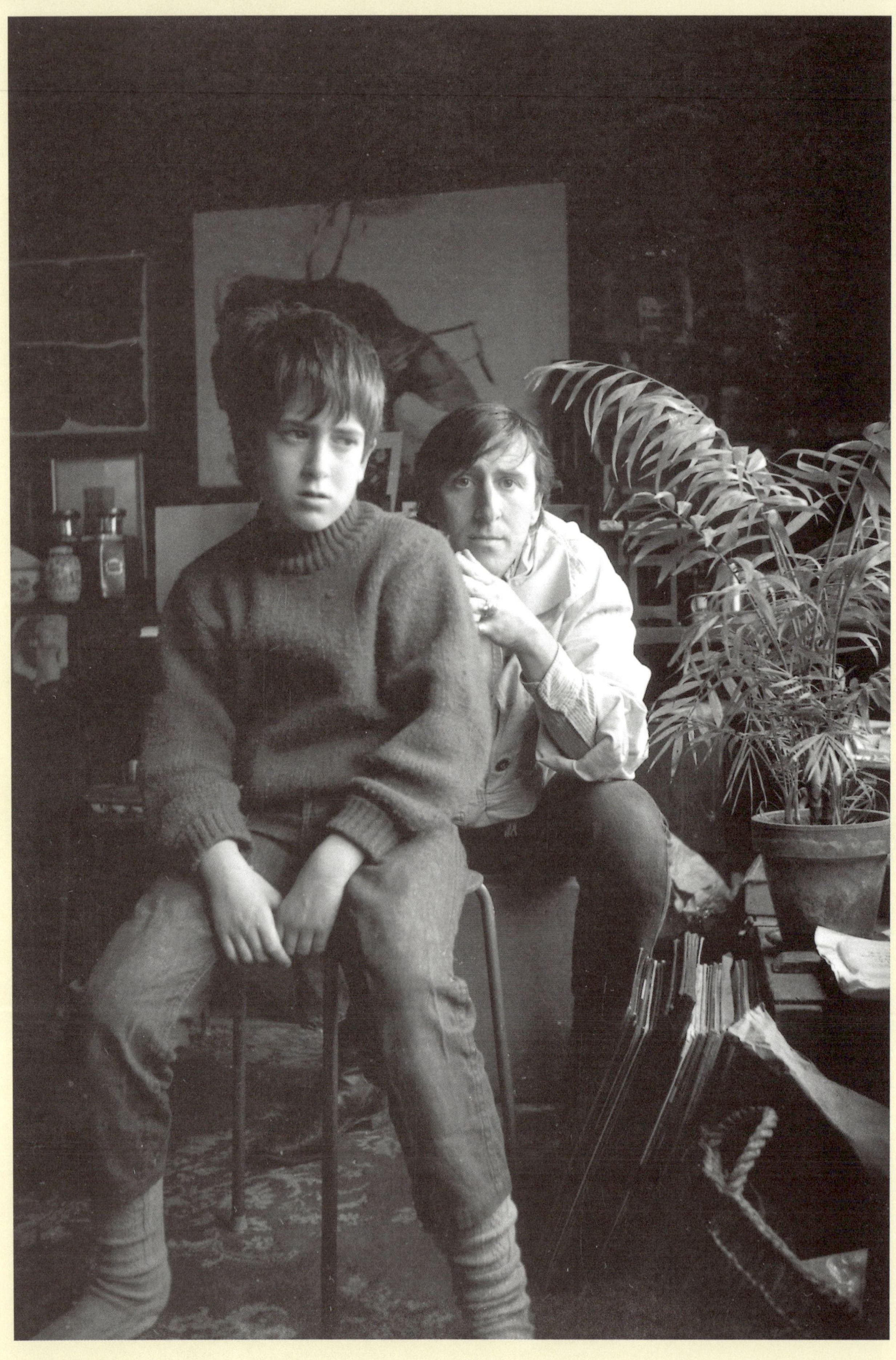

Tosh and Wallace Berman, Beverly Glen, 1963, Photograph by Wallace Berman, Courtesy Wallace Berman Estate.

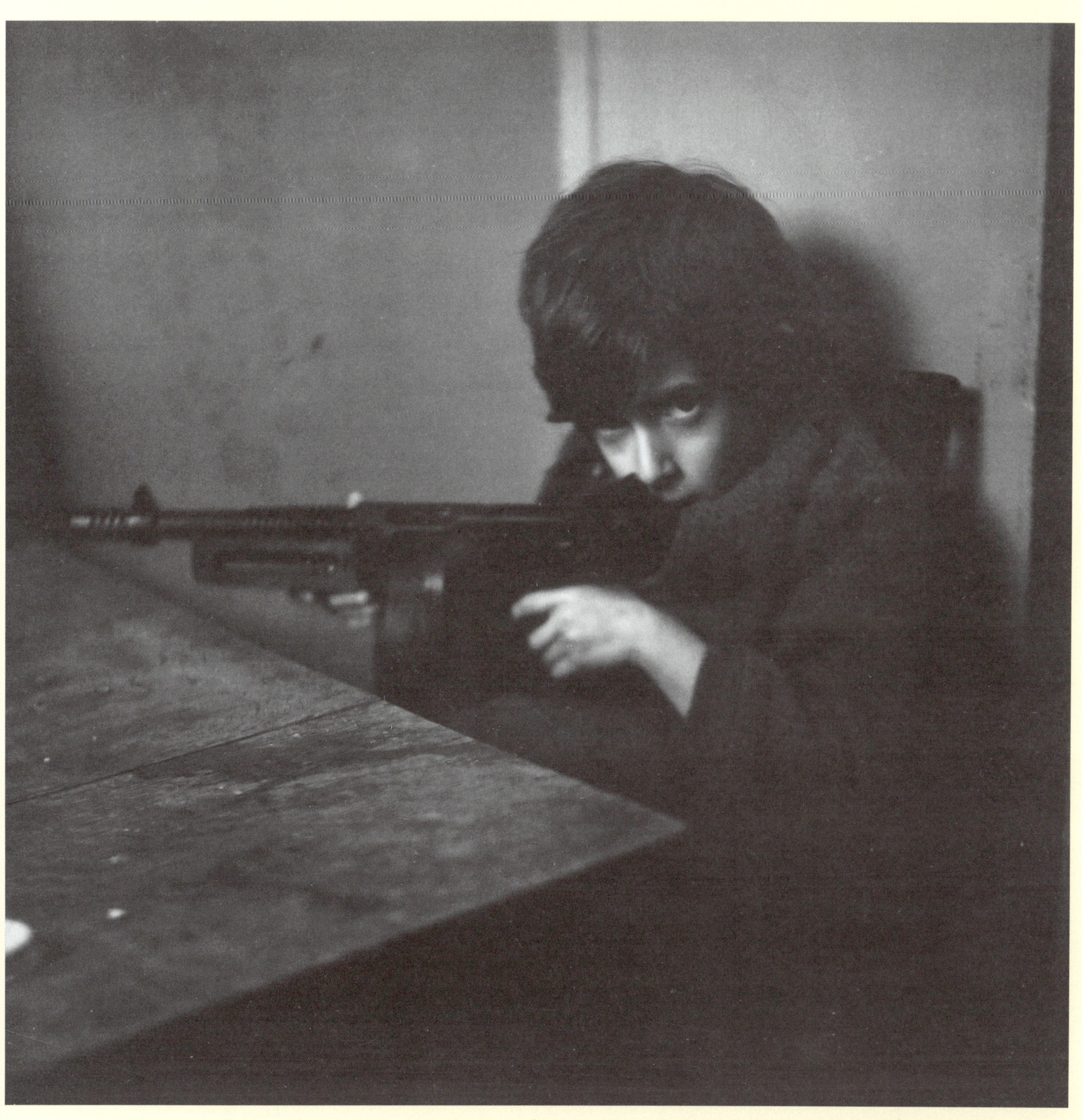

Tosh Berman, Larkspur, 1961, Photograph
by Wallace Berman, Courtesy Wallace Berman Estate.

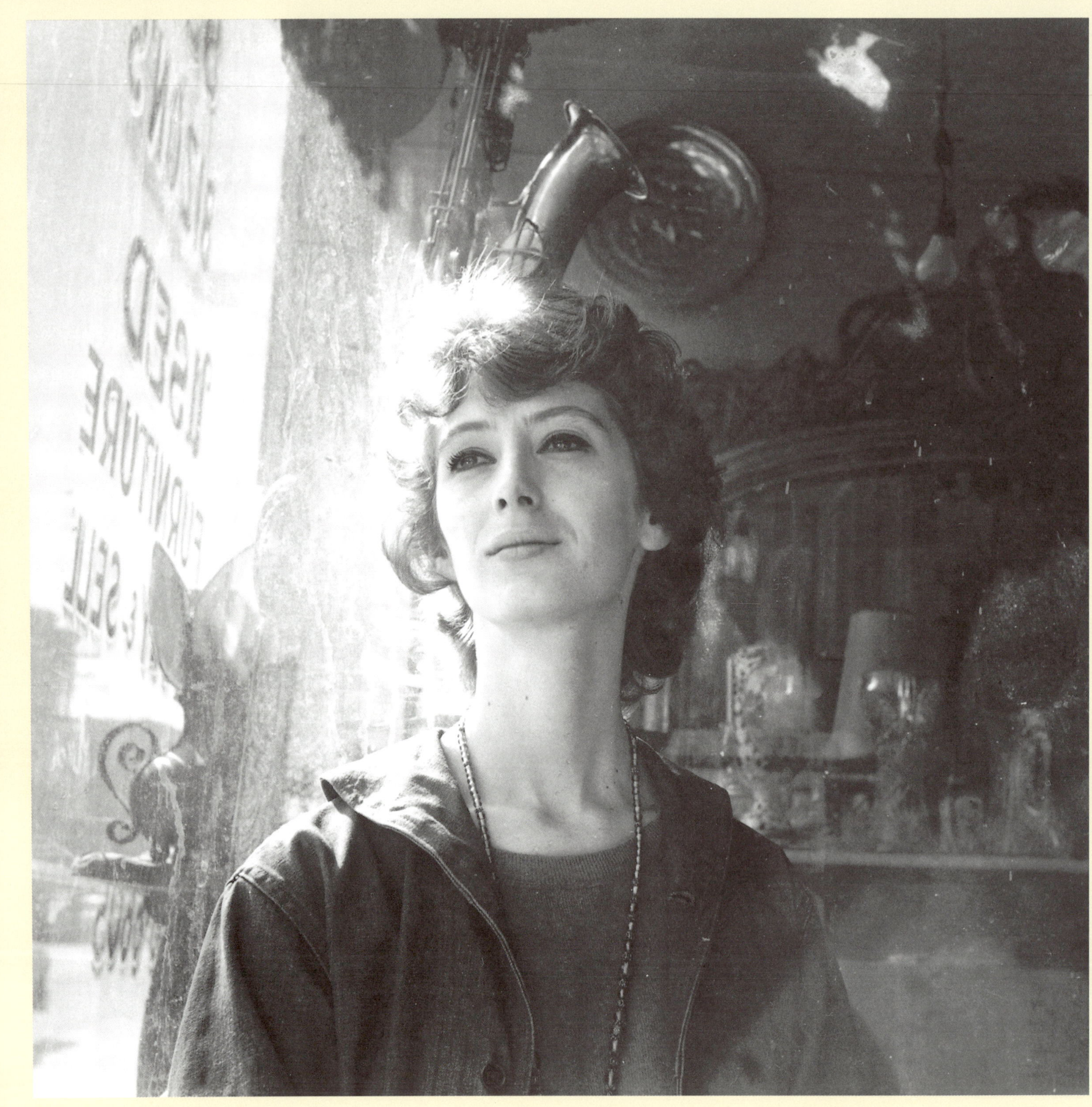

Shirley Berman, McAllister Street junk shop, San Francisco, 1959, Photograph by Wallace Berman, Courtesy Wallace Berman Estate.

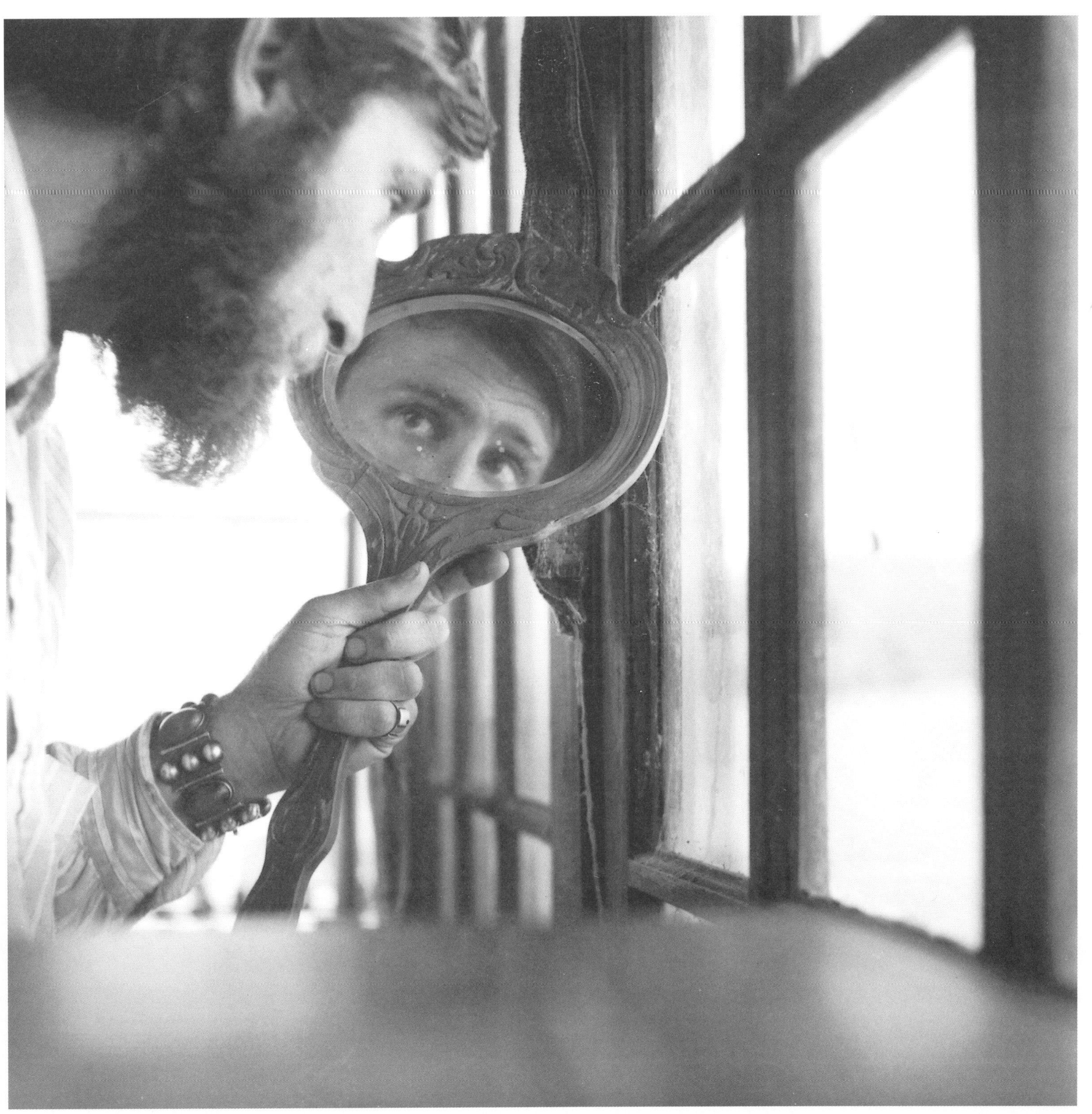

Self-portrait, Larkspur, 1961, Photograph
by Wallace Berman, Courtesy Wallace Berman Estate.

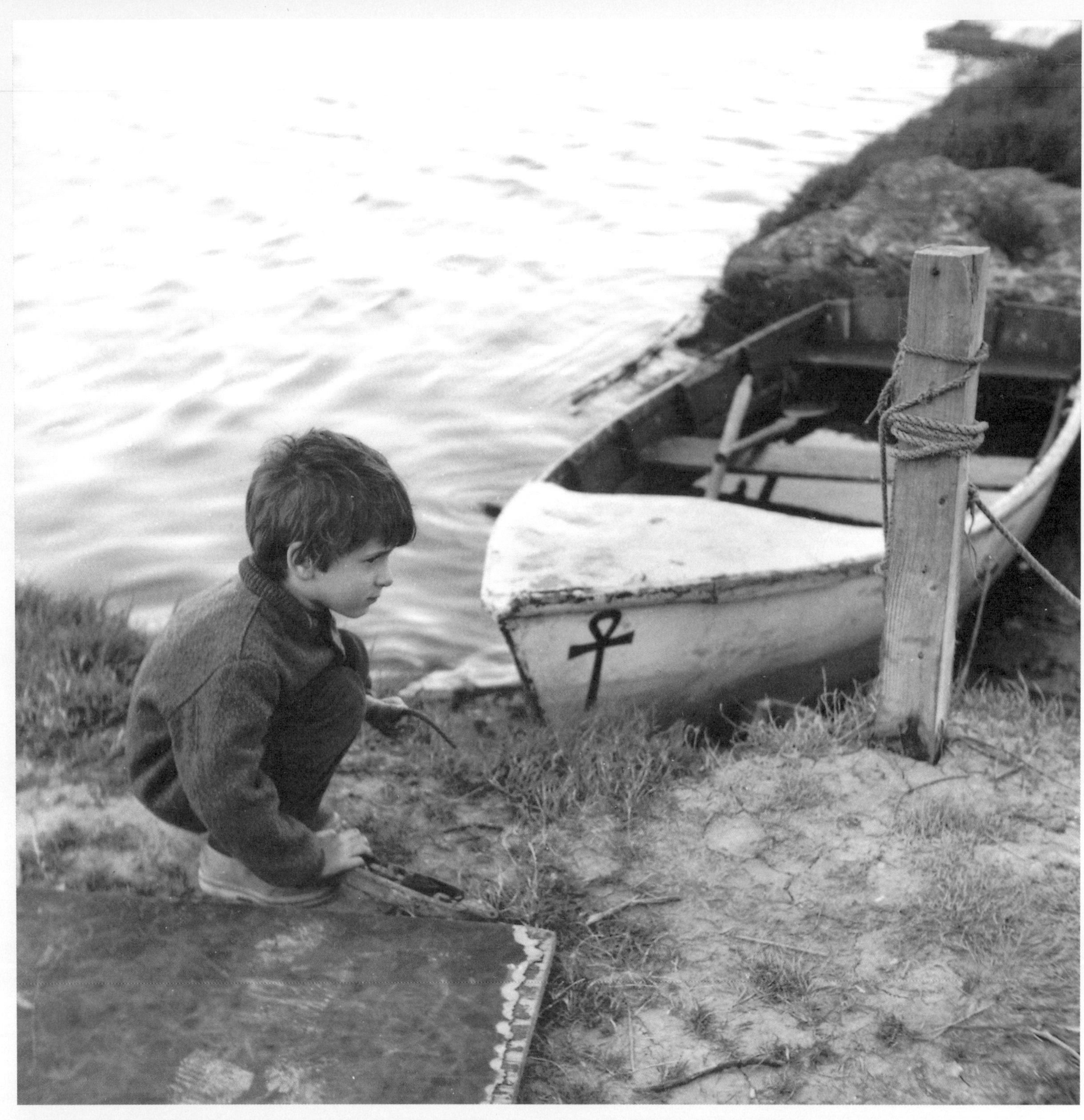

Tosh Berman, Larkspur, 1961, Photograph by Wallace Berman, Courtesy Wallace Berman Estate.

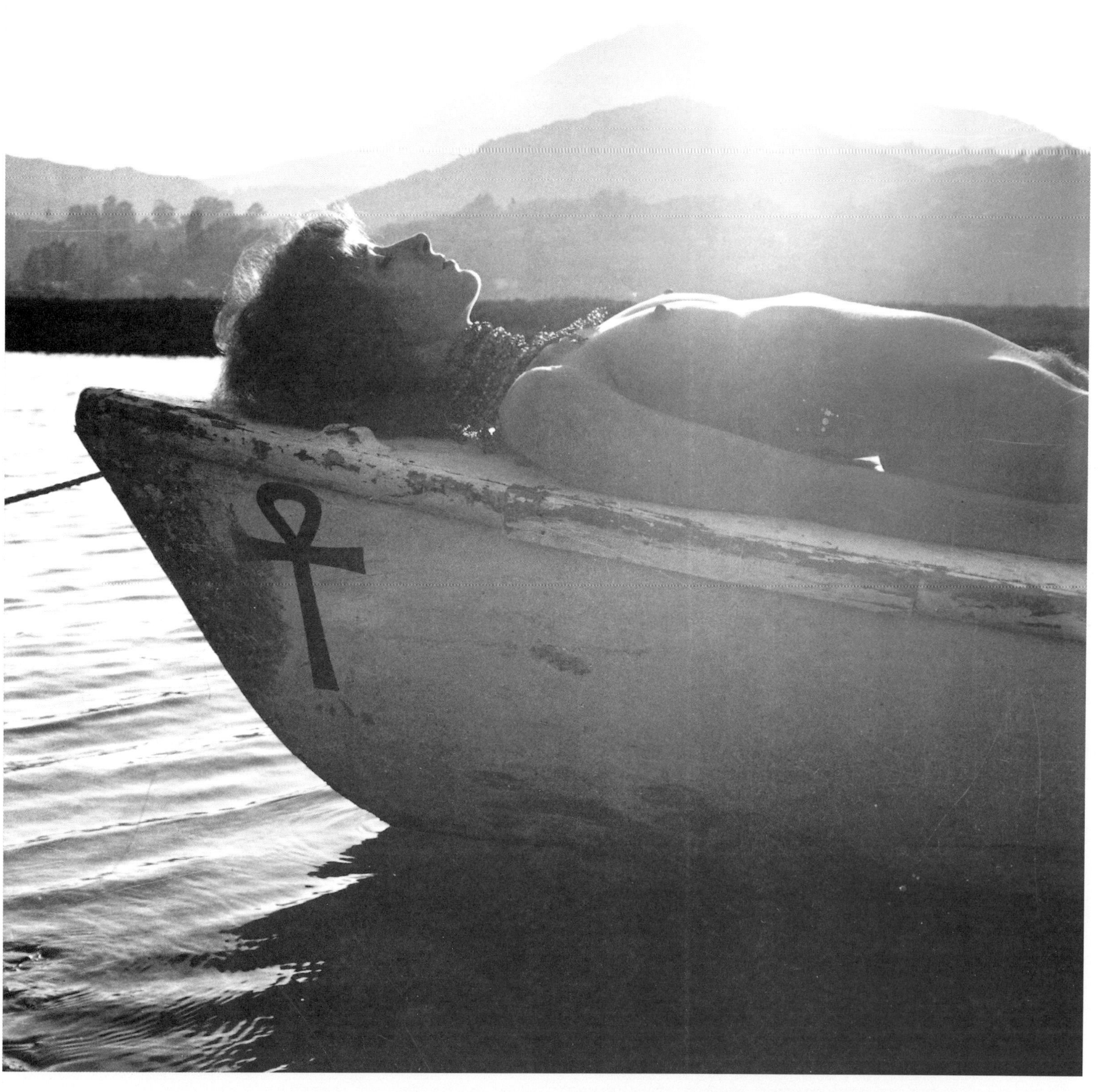

Shirley Berman, Larkspur, 1961, Photograph by Wallace Berman, Courtesy Wallace Berman Estate.

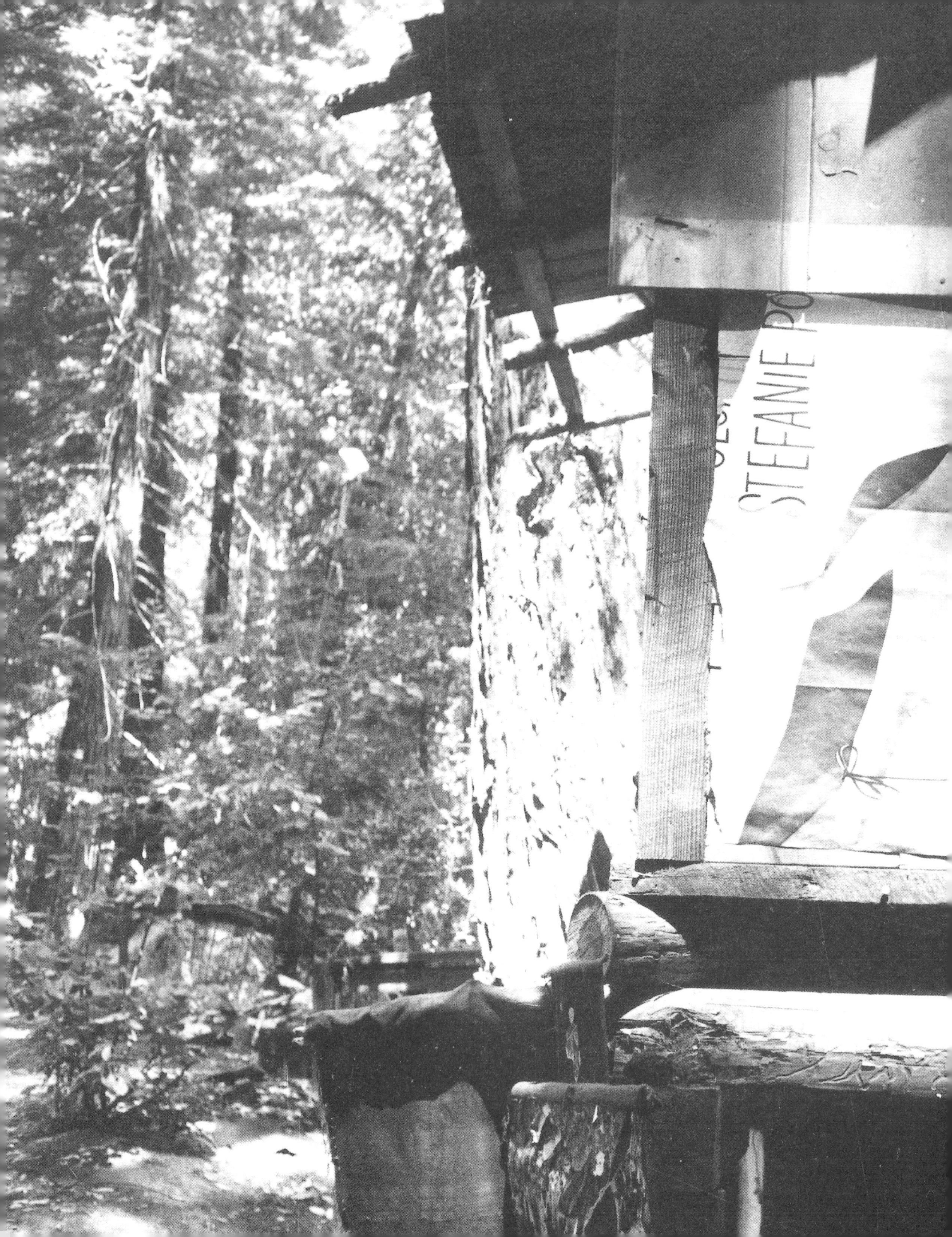
STEFANIE

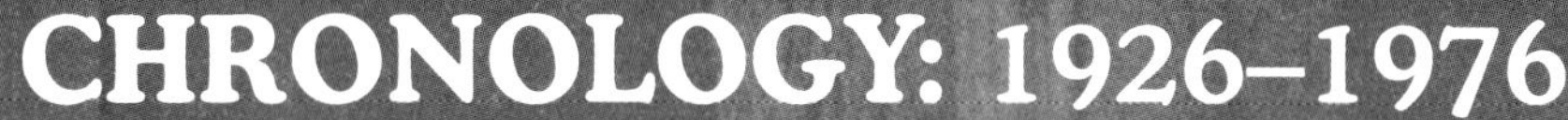CHRONOLOGY: 1926–1976

As is clear in the following chronology, the people in Wallace Berman's community were not without their foibles, and they experienced more than their fair share of drug abuse, emotional illness, wrecked marriages, and prison time. What doesn't come through in the chronology is the way these people functioned together as a community. First, and most importantly, they always made time for one another. Because they rejected mainstream nine-to-five culture, these people lived by a different and dramatically slower clock, one that left plenty of time for long conversations, time to get to the bottom of things, time to wait for new ideas to materialize.

There was a fluidity to the way they lived, perpetually in motion up and down the West Coast, and an open-door policy was the rule of the day. People housed and fed their friends when the need arose, they attended and supported each others' poetry readings, art openings and plays, and they brought their children. Kids were an integrated part of this world, and were rarely left behind with babysitters.

It was a world where art and poetry were created to be given as gifts and as an expression of love, rather than as a means to a career, and there was a respect accorded to poverty that's almost unimaginable today. Berman's community intuitively understood that living gracefully didn't require a fat bank balance; rather, it required an attention to detail, a light touch, a sense of whimsy, and a pagan's appreciation of the sensual.

Berman came of age during the 1940s in Los Angeles' jazz community, and that experience transformed him into a hipster. That hipster aesthetic of tolerance and cool provided the foundation for the beats during the 1950s, and it helped prepare the ground for the social revolution that shook the world in the late 1960s as well. Unfortunately, that revolution turned sour in fairly short order, due to a shortage of viable leaders and an overabundance of bad drugs, and the undertow of the 1960s took its toll on many in the Berman community. Nonetheless, what was beautiful about those people, and the way they chose to live, continues to shine.

Kristine McKenna

Outdoor collage on a tree on the property of the Beattie family, Healdsberg, c. 1960. Photograph by Wallace Berman. Courtesy estate of Wallace Berman.

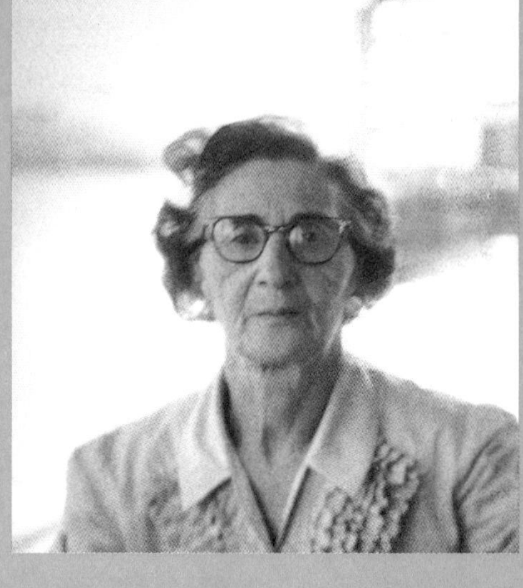

1926

Wallace Berman is born in Staten Island, New York. His mother, Anna Meckler (b. 1891, Russia; d. 1985, Los Angeles), fled the Russian pogroms in 1906, passed through Ellis Island, and found work in New York's garment district. His father, Irving Berman, also fled to New York from Russia and worked in the candy industry. Berman has two older sisters, Marsha (b. 1920, Los Angeles; d.1974, Los Angeles) and Beatrice (b.1923, Los Angeles; d. 1977, Los Angeles).

1936

Berman's father contracts tuberculosis and the family moves to Los Angeles, where they settle in the Jewish community centered in Boyle Heights.

David Rosenfield
(Berman's brother-in-law)
Wallace's father was a simple person and a very ordinary man. He and his brother, Benjamin, ran a small store where they sold penny candies, and by the time I met him he was already very weak—he was consumptive. Wallace's mother, Anna, was the most altruistic person I've ever met and was an easy-going mother—she was never strict with Wallace. Wallace was the funniest one in the family because he was a little devil who was always playing practical jokes. And he was slick. He could take a deck of cards and deal from the bottom of the deck while you were watching him, and he was incredibly good at tennis and ping-pong. Wallace didn't observe Jewish tradition outside the house, but he never went against it when he was home and never brought non-kosher foods into the house.[1]

Edmund Teske (b. 1911, Chicago; d. 1996, Los Angeles) visits Alfred Stieglitz in New York then begins working for Frank Lloyd Wright at Taliesin, in Wisconsin.

1937

Berman's father dies and the family moves to 361 N. Laurel Avenue in Hollywood. Living with the family is Irving Berman's mother, Celia (known as "Bubby"), and Anna Berman's younger brother, Harry Meckler, who becomes a surrogate father figure to Berman. Berman is a slender child with a fragile constitution, and following his father's death he's sent to a camp run by the county in the hills above Monrovia where he spends two years.

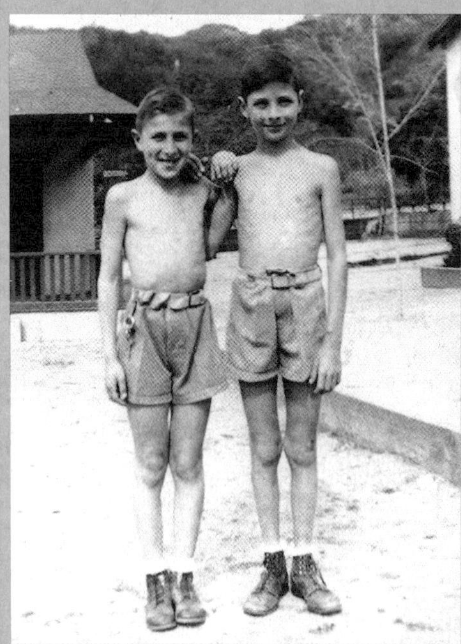

Gary Platt (childhood friend)
It was what was known as a health camp in those days, and Wallace and I were undernourished kids from the city. It was a nice, well-run camp for boys only, and there were around seventy boys there. We all had numbers and lockers, we wore shorts year round, and every other Sunday families were allowed to visit. My family didn't have a car, but Wallace's mother drove and she sometimes brought my mother up. Wallace's mother was very nice, and the fact that she drove a car at that point in time suggested she was an adventuresome type. They used to screen silent movies for us, and when deer came into the camp the cooks used to feed them. Wallace and I were best friends at the camp, and although he was quiet and subdued, he was definitely a free spirit who was always making cartoons. I still have a book he inscribed to me on one of my birthdays.[2]

bottom Berman (L.) and Gary Platt (R.) at an L.A. county health camp in the hills above Monrovia, California, c. 1937, Photographer unknown.

top Wallace Berman's mother, Anna Berman, in Larkspur, Ca., 1961, Photograph by Wallace Berman.

1942

Henry Miller (b., 1891, New York; d. 1980, Pacific Palisades) arrives in Southern California in June and lives at 1212 Beverly Glen until 1943, when he moves to Big Sur. While in Southern California he exhibits his watercolors at the Beverly Glen Green House.

Bobby Driscoll (b. 1937, Cedar Rapids; d. 1968, New York) moves with his family to Altadena, a suburb of Los Angeles. The following year he's cast in the M.G.M. film *Lost Angel* and embarks on a career as a child star that accelerates rapidly.

Bob Alexander (b. 1923, Chicago; d. 1987, Los Angeles) is living in the West Adams district with his father, a pharmacist, and his mother who later operated a small bookstore. During this period he frequents jazz clubs and works as a sideshow barker on the Venice and Santa Monica Beach boardwalk.

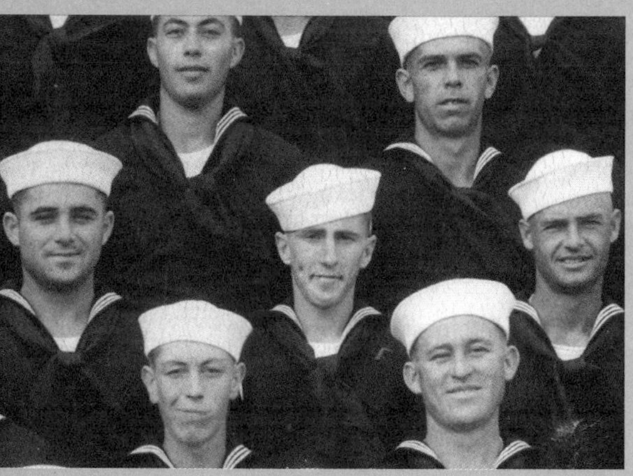

1943

Berman is expelled from Fairfax High School for gambling. He begins a series of pencil sketches of jazz musicians (Slim Gaillard, Nat King Cole, Frank Sinatra) and continues exploring the style until 1947.

Teske moves to Los Angeles; the following year he takes up residence at Hollyhock House, a Frank Lloyd Wright structure owned by Aline Barnsdall.

left Wallace Berman (center figure) during his six-month stint in the Navy in 1944.

center Charles Brittin in 1949, standing outside the apartment on Mariposa Avenue that he shared with his mother while attending UCLA, collection of Charles Brittin.

right Jack Parsons and Cameron shortly after they were married. Photographer unknown, courtesy Cameron Archive/Scott Hobbs.

1944

Berman is arrested for possession of marijuana and the court offers him the choice of jail or the Navy. He enters the Navy; six months later he experiences a psychological breakdown and is given an honorable discharge on December 8.

Circle magazine (1944–1948) begins publication in Berkeley. Edited by George Leite, *Circle* includes contributions from Henry Miller, Robert Duncan, and Philip Lamantia.

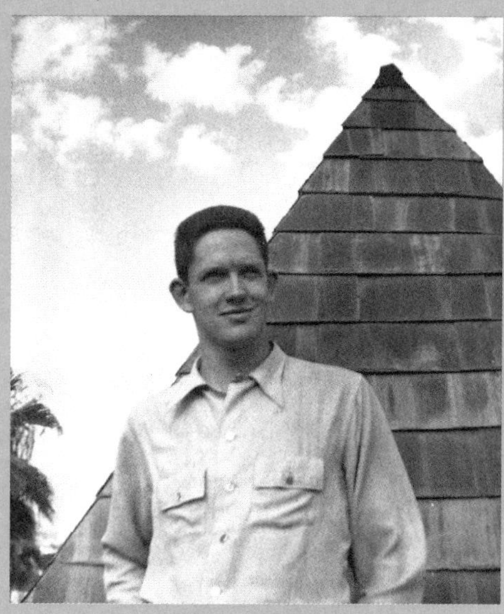

Charles Brittin (b. 1928, Cedar Rapids, Iowa) moves to Pomona, California with his mother.

Alexander's poetry is published in *Sepia*, an African-American magazine specializing in political, antiracist poetry.

1945

Berman meets Bob Alexander through Yvonne "Flip" Dillon.

1946

Cameron (b. 1922, Belle Plain, Iowa; d. 1995, Los Angeles) moves to Pasadena after serving in the Navy in Washington, D.C., during the war. She marries scientist Jack Parsons on October 19, 1946.

Bern Porter publishes *Erotic Poems* by **Philip Lamantia** (b. San Francisco, 1927, d. 2005, San Francisco). A Surrealist poet born to Sicilian immigrants, Lamantia is fifteen years old when taken under the wing of André Breton, who hails Lamantia as "a voice that rises once in a hundred years." Lamantia lives in New York during the 1940s where he works as an assistant editor for legendary Surrealist magazine, *View*.

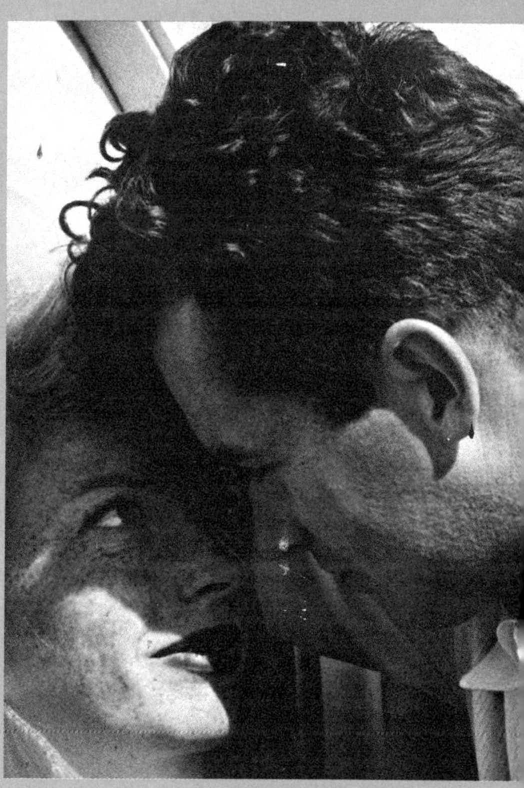

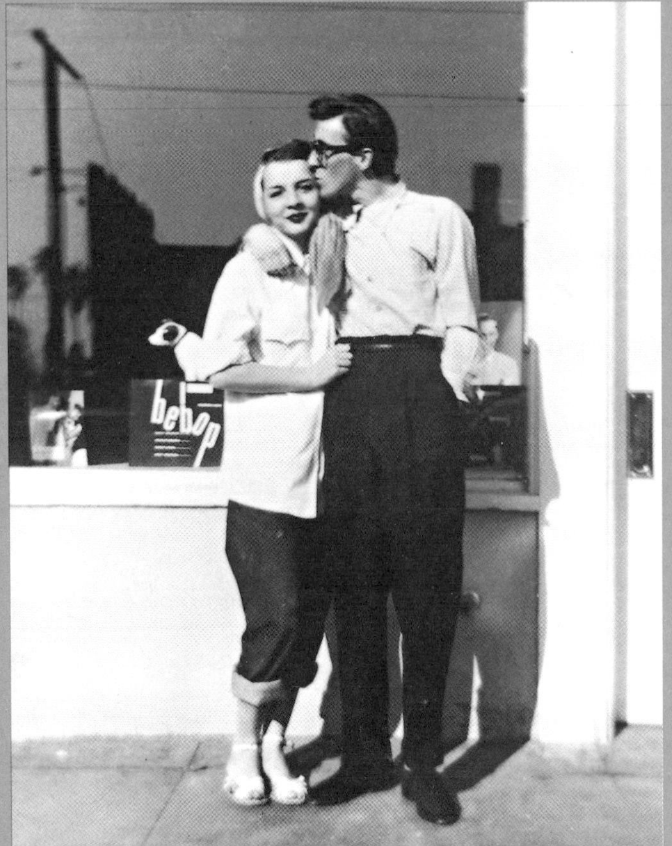

Sid Felsen
(a classmate of Berman's at Fairfax High, who later co-founded lithography workshop Gemini G.E.L.): *During the post-war years Wally spent most of his time in the music world, and he introduced me to a rhythm and blues place at 2133 West Slauson Avenue called The Melody Club, where The Trenier Twins and Jimmy Witherspoon frequently appeared. Wally hung around with Sammy Davis, Jr. quite a bit, and you'd regularly see them at Herbert's Drive-In with a crowd of hot young dancers that included Donald O'Connor.*[5]

1947

Berman meets **Loree Foxx** (b. 1929, Baltimore; d. 1972, Arizona), a former child star whom he dates off and on for the next five years. During this period Foxx makes drawings in a similar style to those by Berman.

Suzi Hicks
(b. 1942, Loree Foxx's niece)
Loree's life was an enigma. She was very independent and sophisticated at a young age, maybe because she'd done a bit of the starlet thing, and she ran with a lot of the dancers on the Hollywood scene. She was a very vain person who never wanted to get old. I was five years old when she started hanging around with Wallace and I always looked forward to seeing him because he was a lot of fun. He used to send me corsages on my birthday.[3]

Berman befriends Ross Russell, founder of Tempo Records, a store on Hollywood Blvd that's a hangout for jazz fans. A tenor-sax player, Russell introduces Berman to Charlie Parker and Dizzy Gillespie. Russell sells the store to Alvin Wilder, whose daughter, Lee Wilder, manages the store and hires Berman to create a mural.

The New Jazz Tempo Newsletter, Spring 1947: *New décor will lift the wigs of all who fall into the wax pad. Jazz murals have been designed by Wally Berman, already the subject of much tongue wagging as a result of his cover design for the 1947 'Be-Bop' album on Dial Records.*[4]

Stuart Perkoff (b. 1930, St. Louis; d. 1974, Los Angeles) moves to Los Angeles and begins publication of the poetry journal, *Ark*. Contributors include Philip Lamantia, Michael McClure and Robert Duncan.

Bern Porter publishes, *Heavenly City, Earthly City*, the first volume of poetry by Robert Duncan (b. 1918, Oakland, California, d., 1988, San Francisco). A key participant in the Black Mountain school of poetry led by Charles Olson, Duncan was one of the first poets to call for a new social consciousness accepting of homosexuality, and was largely responsible for the establishment of San Francisco as the spiritual hub of contemporary American poetry.

Bobby Driscoll moves with his parents to Pacific Palisades and enrolls in The Hollywood Professional School.

Robert Alexander begins using heroin.

1948

Berman begins working at the Salem Furniture Company owned by his friend Lou Wyse; he remains at the job until 1955.

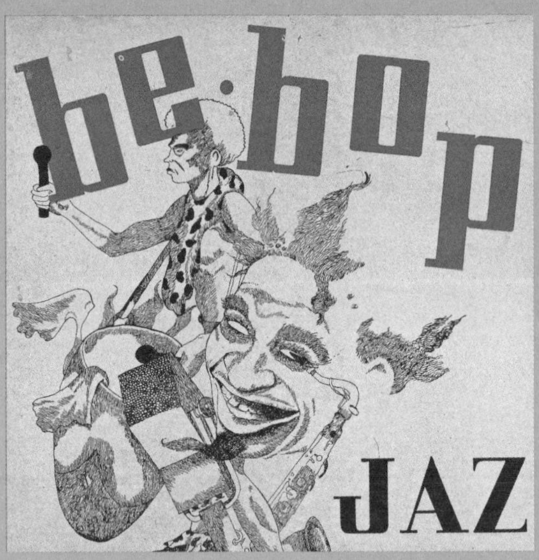

top left Wallace Berman and Loree Foxx in front of Tempo Records, a Hollywood Boulevard hang-out for jazz aficionados, in 1947, Photograph by Lee Wilder, Collection of Charles Brittin.

bottom right *Untitled Be-Bop album cover* by Wallace Berman for Dial Records in 1948.

1949

Jess Collins (b. 1923, Long Beach, California, d. 2004, San Francisco) turns his back on a career in science and moves to San Francisco, where he attends the California School of Fine Art through 1951.

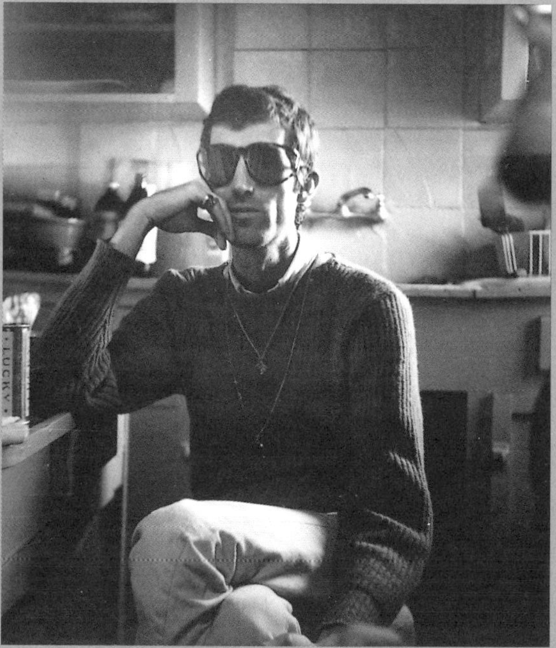

Berman meets Donald Morand.

Donald Morand
(Berman's brother-in-law):
When I was in junior high they had a dance every Friday night at the American Legion on Highland Avenue. Wallace and Loree Foxx were often there and whenever they danced the whole place stopped—they were just amazing. The kind of dancing they were doing verged on gymnastics. Wallace wasn't what you'd call conventionally handsome but he was always surrounded by beautiful women who were completely crazy about him. He drove a blue Buick convertible and wore sunglasses at night, and he was always playing cards. I was finally introduced to Wally, and he told me if I needed to get in touch with him I should call this pool hall where he hung out.[6]

Loree Foxx introduces Berman to Lenny Bruce, a friend and frequent visitor to her apartment.

1950

Loree Foxx marries musician Gil Barrios; the marriage is annulled after five months.

Edmund Teske moves to Topanga Canyon, where he becomes part of Will Geer's theatrical group.

Poet **Bill Margolis** (b. 1927, Chicago; d. 1998, Los Angeles) drops out of Roosevelt College, buys a used 1937 bakery truck, and begins an extended road tour of America.

Arthur Richer (b. 1925, New York; d. 1965, Healdsberg, California) arrives in Los Angeles from New York and attends the Finch-Warshaw Art School while working as a saxophonist.

Poet **Lew Welch** (b. 1926, Phoenix; d. 1971, Grass Valley, California) visits William Carlos Williams in New Jersey, then spends five months in New York.

Bob Alexander and his first wife, dress designer Kathleen Bleiweiss, open Contemporary Bazaar, a store on Ventura Boulevard in Sherman Oaks that carries arts and crafts, clothing, and limited-edition poetry magazines. The store hosts poetry readings and a performance by Lord Buckley.

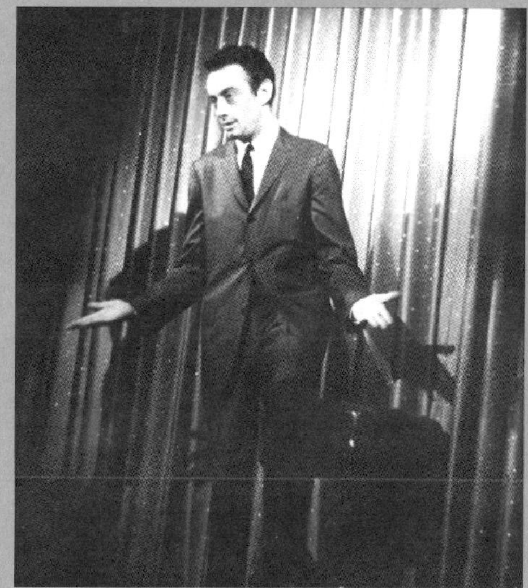

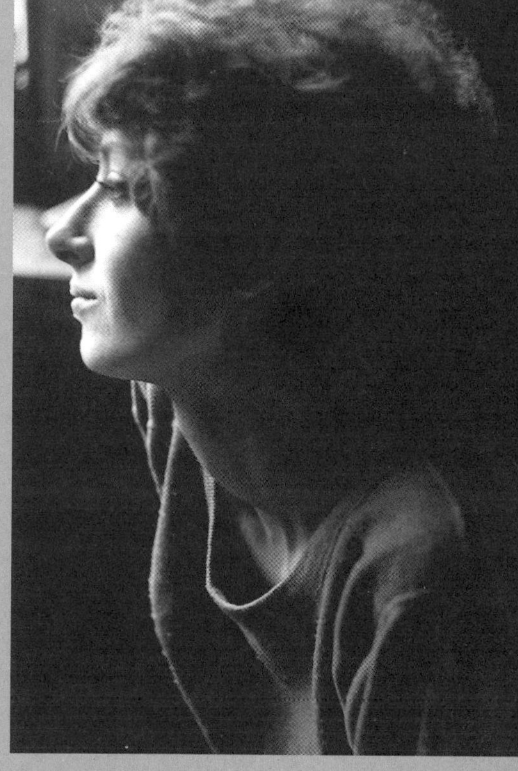

1951

Shirley Morand (b. 1934, Los Angeles) meets Wallace Berman while standing in line to see a Cocteau film at the Coronet Theater. Her brother, Donald Morand, introduces them.

Shirley Berman:
Wallace was a charismatic person with a wonderful sense of humor, and I was immediately drawn to him. He was very involved with Surrealist poetry then and was a self-taught person who spent weekends in the library reading. He also taught himself to draw by making cartoons as a kid, and he could make these really fast drawings that were very funny. Wallace was an extremely private person, and he destroyed a good deal of the poetry and art he created—it was as if he didn't want a record left of what he'd done. He was still painting when we first met, but he destroyed all his paintings. I loved his paintings, and most people who saw them loved his paintings, but he did not love his paintings. [7]

top left Donald Morand in Larkspur, California, 1961, Photograph by Wallace Berman.

bottom center Lenny Bruce performing in a club on Sunset Boulevard in Los Angeles, 1961, Photograph by Charles Brittin.

top right Shirley Berman in Beverly Glen, 1963, Photograph by Wallace Berman.

John Carruthers, a jewelry designer, introduces Wallace and Shirley Berman to Pasadena-based sculptress Julie McDonald, who invites them to a party at Jack Parsons's house in Pasadena, where they meet Cameron.

Loree Foxx, Donald Morand, and Bill Rotsler open an offbeat, short-lived arts-and-crafts shop on La Cienega Blvd.

Lew Welch suffers a nervous breakdown in Chicago, where he had enrolled in the philosophy program at the University of Chicago.

Jess and Robert Duncan meet and become lifelong companions; Jess begins experimenting with collage.

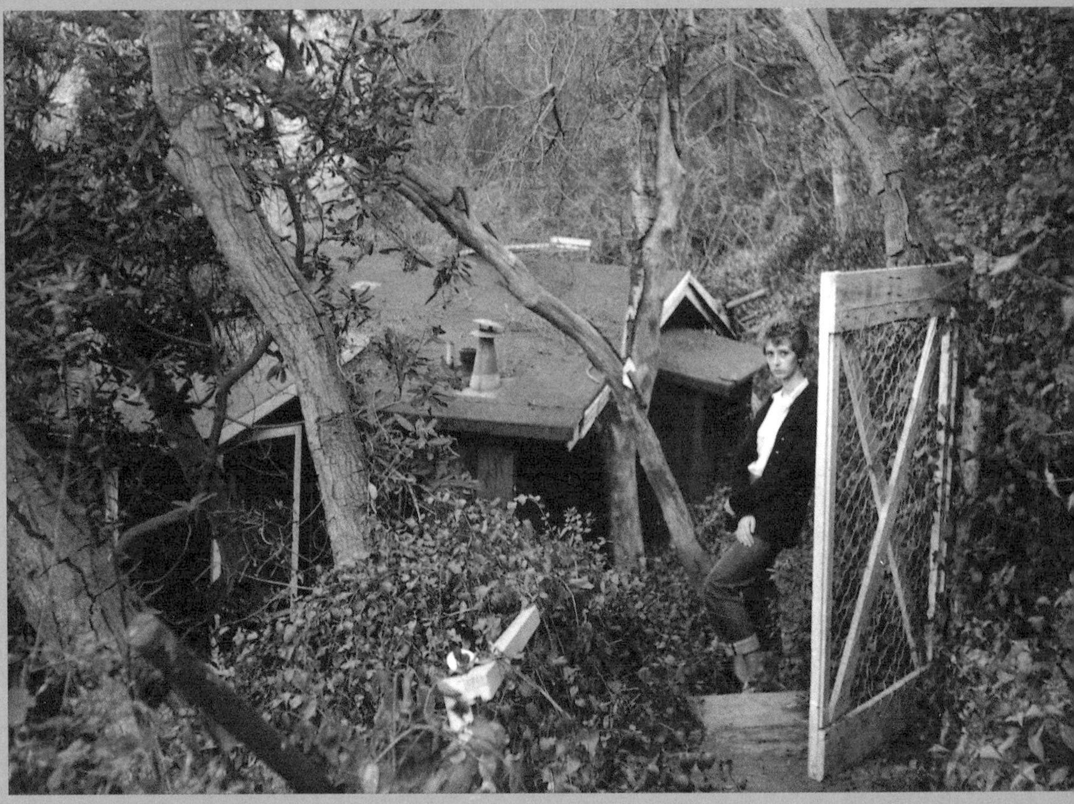

Shirley Berman standing at the gate to the Berman house in Beverly Glen, 1956. Photograph by Wallace Berman.

1952

Poet **Ray Bremser** (b. 1934, Jersey City; d. 1998, New York) is convicted of armed robbery and sent to Bordentown Reformatory, where he remains until 1958. While at Bordentown he begins writing poetry and corresponds with Ezra Pound, Robert Graves, Gregory Corso, and Allen Ginsberg.

Alexander Trocchi (b. 1935, Glasgow, Scotland; d. 1984, London), a Scottish writer based in London who is active in the Situationist International movement, begins working in London as an editor at *Merlin*, *Paris Quarterly* and *Moving Times*. His relationship with all three publications continues to 1955. Throughout the 1950s and 1960s, Trocchi also works as an assistant to Maurice Girodias at Olympia Press.

Donald Morand and Loree Foxx move to New York, where Foxx plans to pursue a career in modeling. They meet Billy Jahrmarkt, a wealthy young artist and drug addict.

Donald Morand:
Loree hated that she was forced to be in movies as a child, and she felt like she had worked her whole life by the time she was eighteen. I guess you could say the experience hardened her because she was manipulative and she was a thief—she wasn't a nice person. I loved her though, and we were always close.[8]

Jack Parsons dies in an explosion on June 17; Cameron leaves Pasadena for Mexico.

Suzi Hicks:
Cameron wasn't a beatnik chick or a starlet type. She was a unique woman and an artist, and she went through an enormous transformation following her husband's death—it was a process of empowerment that involved even a physical change. I think Wallace had tremendous respect for her.[9]

Wallace Berman and Shirley Morand marry on Dec 14, 1952. Shirley wears a pea-green silk afternoon dress, and Wallace wears a gray flannel Brooks Brothers suit.

Shelley Smith
(Berman's niece):
Wallace and Shirley got married at Wallace's mother's house on Laurel Avenue, and I remember thinking how beautiful Shirley was, and overhearing an adult at the wedding say, "They finally got Wallace in a suit!"[10]

1953

Charles Brittin moves to Speedway Avenue in Venice and begins taking photographs of the local community. His friend, Bob Conley, knows Berman from the jazz world and introduces Berman and Brittin.

Charles Brittin:
Wallace and Shirley were an image of something unbelievably good—I'd never seen a couple like that or a world like theirs—and when Wally and Shirley came into my life I began to take myself seriously as a creative person. Many of the people around them were close to having trouble, but Wally and Shirley provided an anchor. Life seemed to be incredibly anxious and frightening yet he remained tranquil.[11]

The Bermans borrow $5,000 from Berman's mother and buy a house at 10426 Crater Lane, in Beverly Glen. Living down the street, on Lisbon Lane, is poet Zack Walsh and his wife Beverly.

Charles Brittin:
Many wonderful things happened at that house in Beverly Glen. If I was too loaded to drive home at the end of the evening, I'd spend the night on the Berman's floor, and my home became that for other people—people would come to the beach and spend the night at my place. John Altoon was teaching at Chouinard then, and he used to take his class down to the water's edge and give them an assignment, then come back to my house and spend the afternoon drinking beer with his girlfriend and me.[12]

George Herms (b. 1935, Woodland, California) visits Los Angeles while on break from his engineering studies at the University of California at Berkeley, and decides to relocate from the Bay Area.

"The Ghost House," the San Francisco residence of many artists and poets—including Jess, Robert Duncan and Philip Lamantia—is demolished.

After providing the voice for the lead character in Disney's animated version of *Peter Pan*, Bobby Driscoll is fired by the studio. His career begins losing steam and later in the year he's arrested for possession of marijuana.

Allen Ginsberg (b. 1926, New Jersey; d. 1997, New York) takes up photography, a practice he continues for the rest of his life.

Jess, Robert Duncan and Harry Jacobus open the King Ubu Gallery at 3119 Fillmore Street.

Idell Rose Tarlow (Aya) (b. 1932, Los Angeles) enrolls at Los Angeles City College and begins having her poetry published in small press magazines.

While living in Chicago, Lew Welch returns to his studies at the University of Chicago, marries Mary Garber, and takes a job with mail-order house Montgomery Ward.

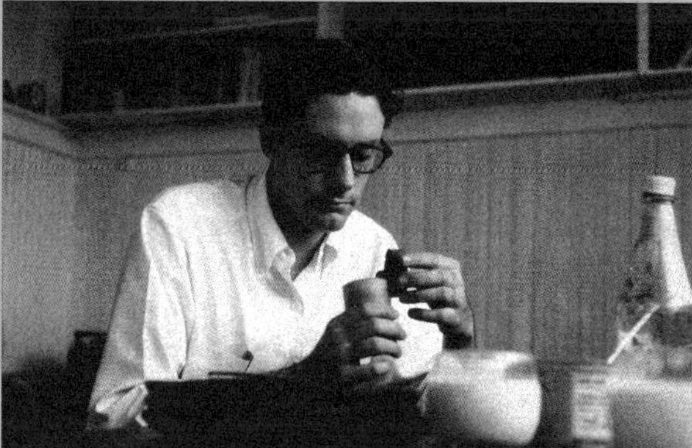

Philip Lamantia attends the peyote rituals of the Washo Indians in Nevada and lives for a period with the Cora Indian tribe in Nayarit, Mexico.

Jay DeFeo marries Wally Hedrick and they move into an apartment at 2322 Fillmore Street.

Michael McClure arrives in San Francisco and moves into the building where DeFeo and Hedrick are living.

Kirby Doyle (b. 1932, San Francisco; d. 2002, San Francisco) marries his first wife, Joanne; within two years the couple have two children.

1954

The Bermans visit San Francisco. Shirley is pregnant at the time, and they stop in Big Sur and visit Henry Miller.

Charles Brittin:
Henry Miller was living up in Big Sur, on Partington Road, and we were all very impressed by him because he represented the American who went to Europe, rejected commerce and lived the life he wrote about. Many of us made the pilgrimage to Partington Road.[13]

While in San Francisco, the Bermans visit Jess and Robert Duncan at their apartment on Baker Street.

Robert Duncan:
There was only the one visit in 1954, but there was in the course of the afternoon an unfolding recognition that we were possibly fellows in our feeling of what art was.[14]

Bob Alexander closes Contemporary Bazaar and commits himself to a heroin detoxification program in Texas.

Shirley Berman:
Bob was a junkie, and although he never stole anything from us, he was extremely negative. Wallace didn't like not seeing Bob but there were periods when it was just impossible to see Bob. He visited us once when Wallace and I were living in San Francisco and he and Wallace actually got into a fist fight, which just broke Wallace's heart. Everyone we knew used drugs for the simple reason that, at that point in time, people were using drugs. But when it came to heroin, Wallace just didn't want that around the house. If someone he adored needed help, though, they could come and stay at our house.[15]

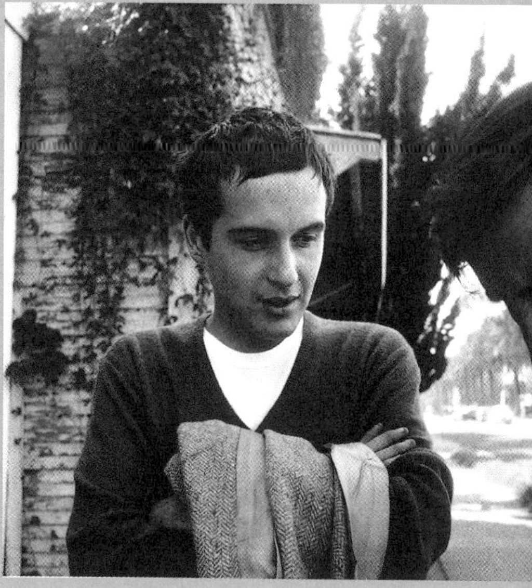

Trocchi publishes his first novel, *Young Adam*.

Bobby Driscoll begins using heroin.

David Meltzer (b. 1937, New York) moves to Los Angeles with his father. Meltzer gets a job in a junk store on Santa Monica Boulevard, where he meets Ed Kienholz whose studio is nearby. Through Kienholz, Meltzer meets the Bermans and becomes involved with the local underground art community.

David Meltzer:
Wallace was a kind of cultural entrepreneur who was very much at the center of an extremely social group that was continually in correspondence—everyone kept in touch by mail, and no matter where you went there was a place for you to crash. There were lots of open doors then, and lots of talented people, many of whom have been forgotten. Artie Richer was immensely talented, but he was self-destructive,as was John Kelly Reed, who was an early casualty of the amphetamine culture that appeared in San Francisco in the late 1950s. John was a highly eccentric person who was in his own world.[16]

top right David Meltzer in Los Angeles, 1957, Photograph by Charles Brittin.

bottom left Walter Hopps in Los Angeles, 1957, Photograph by Charles Brittin.

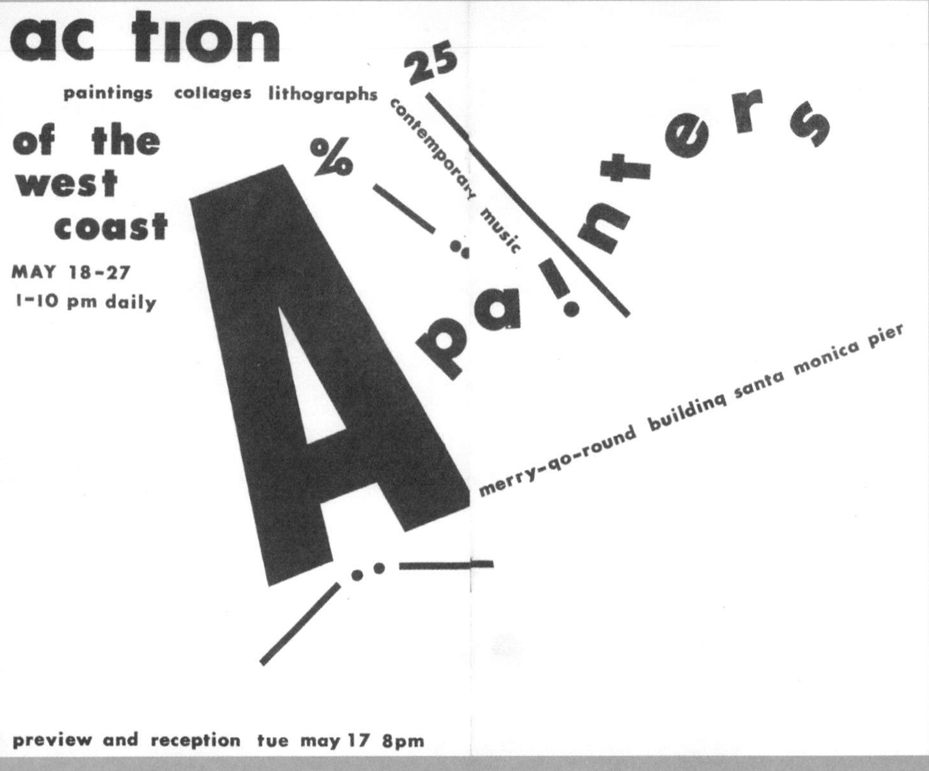

Walter Hopps (b. 1932, Pasadena; d. 2005, Los Angeles) spends time in San Francisco, where he meets Jay DeFeo (b. 1929, New Hampshire; d. 1989, Oakland).

Cameron stars as the whore of Babylon in Kenneth Anger's *Inauguration of the Pleasure Dome.*

Berman acquires an Argus-3 camera and begins spending time with Charles Brittin in the darkroom, learning how to print photographs.

Shirley and Wallace Berman's son, Tosh, is born.

Allen Ginsberg arrives in San Francisco for the summer; he meets Duncan and Jess and renews his friendship with Philip Lamantia.

The King Ubu Gallery closes, and The Six Gallery takes over the space.

Russel Tamblyn (b. 1934, Los Angeles) stars in *Seven Brides for Seven Brothers.*

Artist **Paul Beattie** (b. 1924, Michigan; d. 1987, Healdsburg, California) arrives in San Francisco from Michigan and shows at The Six Gallery.

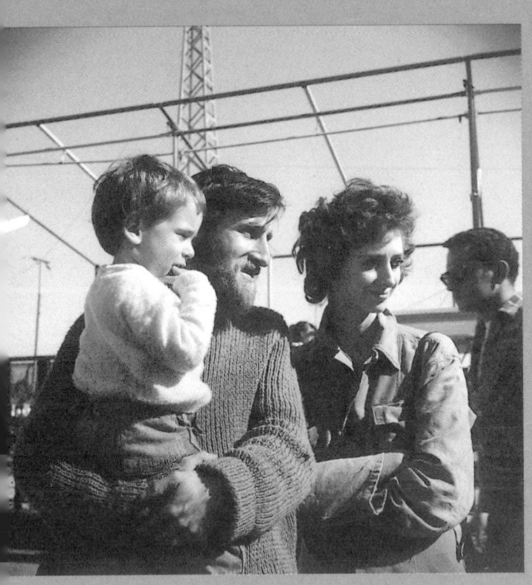

Walter Hopps, Ben and Betty Bartosh, Michael Scoles, and Craig Kauffman open Syndell Studio. Located in Brentwood at 11756 Gorham Ave., Syndell occupies one unit in a three-unit structure built by real estate tycoon W. Brier Schorr out of old telephone poles. The poles are painted white, and black creosote oozes out when their surfaces are pierced with nails. Old doors are used to create bathroom stalls, and beneath the linoleum floor is a layer of felt that provides a soft surface for heavy objects. Hopps and his first wife, Shirley Neilsen, live in the back room of the space.

Lawrence Jordan (b. 1934, Denver) moves to San Francisco after his high-school friend, filmmaker Stan Brakhage, tells him "that's where all the artists are." On arriving, he gets a job as a hospital orderly.

Boston poet **John Wieners** (b. 1934, Boston; d. 2002, Boston) enrolls at Black Mountain College.

Dennis Hopper (b. 1936, Dodge City, Kansas) arrives in Los Angeles to finish high school and pursue an acting career.

1955

Herms spends the first four months of the year in Mexico attempting to live off the land, which he finds he is unable to do. In the summer he moves to Topanga Canyon, where he finds temporary lodgings with sandal-maker Jim Baker. On July 5, Herms' twentieth birthday, Bob Alexander and Wallace Berman drop by and introduce themselves. Herms returns to Berkeley after his parents offer him $100 a month to finish his schooling, and he meets his first wife, Polly Levee, in the theater department.

Joan Brown (b. 1938, San Francisco, d. 1990, Puttaparthi, India) enrolls at the California School of Fine Arts, where she studies with Elmer Bishoff.

Teske discovers a cluster of abandoned iceboxes in Cornell, California, which he uses as a backdrop for portraits of Walter and Shirley Hopps, and Wallace and Shirley Berman.

Donald Morand introduces Billy Jahrmarkt to the Bermans.

Aya Tarlow divorces her first husband and marries Elias Romero; a few months later the couple moves to San Francisco. Tarlow is a regular participant in local poetry readings, while Romero presents light shows with increasing frequency.

top Announcement for Action 1 group show organized by Walter Hopps, Jim Newman and Craig Kauffman and presented on the Santa Monica Pier in 1955, Announcement design by Craig Kauffman, Collection of Hal Glicksman.

left Berman family, Venice Boardwalk, 1957, Photograph by Charles Brittin.

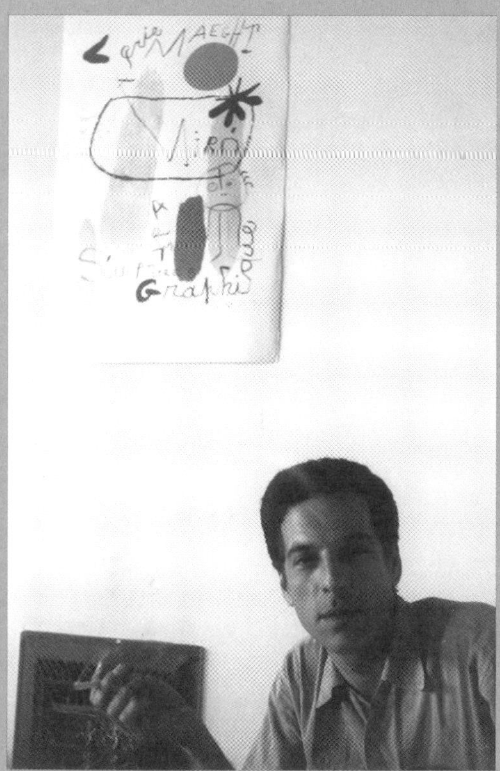

Norman Rose opens Books 55 on La Cienega across the street from the Coronet Louvre Theater. Cameron lives in the back of the store , where Berman first sees her *Peyote Drawing*, the artwork that leads to the closure of his 1957 exhibition at Ferus Gallery.

Lawrence Jordan and Stan Brakhage visit New York where they spend a few weeks with filmmaker Maya Deren. Jordan meets Joseph Cornell when he stops by to visit Deren. After returning to San Francisco, Jordan moves to an apartment at 707 Scott Street managed by poet Bill Margolis and enlists in the Merchant Marines. He periodically ships out to sea over the next four years.

Cameron gives birth to her daughter, Crystal.

Berman purchases a five-by-eight-inch Kelly hand-press through the mail. With assistance from Brittin and Alexander, he begins publishing *Semina*, a limited-edition artists' magazine devoted to poetry, photography, and drawing. The first issue includes contributions from Cameron, David Meltzer, and Bob Alexander.

Charles Brittin:
Semina was a reflection of what Wally was reading, who he was talking to, and what he was excited about. His focus was constantly evolving, the mood of Semina changed enormously from one issue to the next, and they became increasingly simple—in fact, some of the later ones are just single sheets of paper.[17]

Rachel Rosenthal (b. Paris, 1926) arrives in Los Angeles and is hired to teach theater at the Pasadena Playhouse. She is asked to resign a year later when it is decided that she's too avant-garde.

Bob Alexander returns from Texas, separates from his wife, Kathleen, and briefly lives with Norman Rose in Beverly Glen, where they host light shows presented by Elias and Idell Romero. He then moves to a small house at 8205 Santa Monica Blvd. which becomes a hang-out known as the "Baza Shack." (Alexander acquired the nickname "Baza" when, in closing Contemporary Bazaar, he took down the store sign and it broke in half in his hands). Kienholz's Now Gallery gives Alexander his first one-man show.

David Meltzer:
Bob Alexander and Wally were extremely close, but they had conflicting styles; Wally was concealed, cool and cryptic, and Bob was an overt, articulate guy with a booming voice. He had great organizational skills and the charisma of a leader, and people would do anything for Bob until he fell into one of his periodic slumps—at which point he became so whining and wimpy that he became an object of contempt.[18]

Arthur Richer has his first one-man show at Syndell Studio.

Ginsberg reads *Howl* at The Six Gallery; also reading that night are Philip Lamantia and Michael McClure.

Llyn Foulkes (b. 1934, Yakima, Washington) enlists in the Army and is stationed for two years in Germany where he is a clerk typist for the Medical Corps.

Walter Hopps, Jim Newman, and Craig Kauffman organize "Action 1," a group exhibition presented in the merry-go-round building on the Santa Monica Pier from May 18–27.

Robert Duncan gives a reading of his play, *Faust Foutu*, featuring Jess and Lawrence Jordan, at The Six Gallery and disrobes at the conclusion.

Dennis Hopper co-stars in Nicholas Ray's *Rebel Without a Cause*.

David Meltzer enrolls at L.A. City College where he meets Lee and Idell Romero. Meltzer introduces John Reed and **Dean Stockwell** (b. 1936, Los Angeles) to the Bermans.

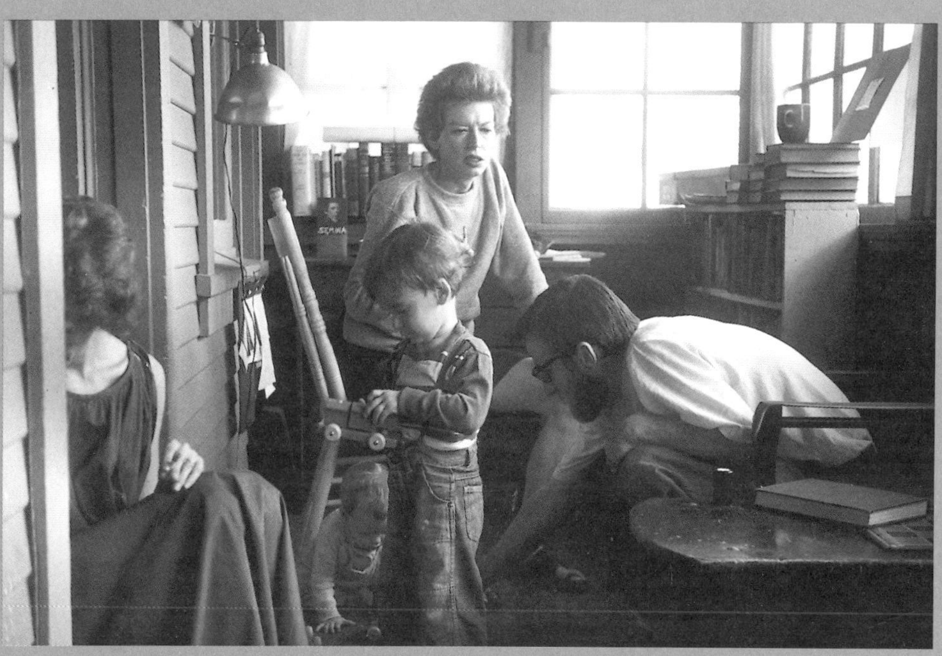

top left Norman Rose at Charles Brittin's apartment in Venice, 1957, Photograph by Charles Brittin.

bottom right Cameron and her daughter Crystal, with the Bermans, at Charles Brittin's Venice apartment, 1957, Photograph by Charles Brittin.

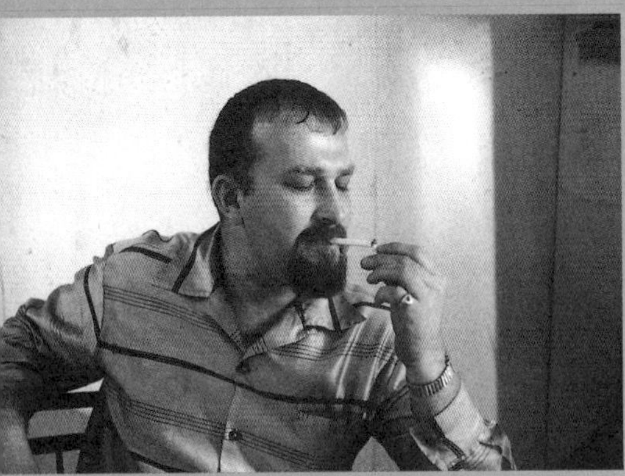

1956

Dean Stockwell introduces the Bermans to Bobby Driscoll and Billy Gray, who starred as Bud Anderson in the television show *Father Knows Best* from 1954 through 1960.

Billy Gray:
The minute I met Wallace I knew he was an extraordinary person. He wasn't classically handsome, but he had a look about him that was profound and moving, and although he was authentic and pure, he also had more guile than anyone I've ever met. I hesitate to use the word mystical, but there was something of that to him. He had a peaceful, unthreatening aura, and a vision that was his own, and he wasn't constrained by conventional boundaries in any area of his life. It was refreshing to see someone who was invulnerable to the slings and arrows that bother most people—Wallace was able to ride on through them and be content with whatever was going on. He didn't try to exploit the things he created beyond making them available to anyone who might be interested, and the way he interacted with people could be described as an attempt to elevate them. He was a very kind person. [19]

Alexander introduces Berman to **Ben Talbert** (b. 1933, Los Angeles; d. 1974, Los Angeles). The son of a truck driver, Talbert was a promising high-school student who had been groomed for a military career, but he turned his back on the military and began studying art at UCLA in 1957.

bottom Suzi Hicks at Charles Brittin's Venice apartment, 1957, Photograph by Charles Brittin.

top left Ed Kienholz Ferus Gallery, 1957, Photograph by Charles Brittin.

top right Joanne Doyle, San Francisco, 1958, Photograph by Wallace Berman, Courtesy Estate of Wallace Berman.

Taylor Mead (b. 1936, Detroit) moves to New York City.

Kirby Doyle's wife, Joanne Doyle, opens a bookstore on Fillmore Street called The Golden Bough; it's here that Doyle meets Lew Welch, Michael McClure, John Wieners, Philip Lamantia, and Wallace Berman.

Bob Alexander introduces Wallace Berman to Arthur Richer and Walter Hopps.

Walter Hopps:
You're in a room where everyone is affecting the posture of being cool, and then Mr. Really Cool walks into the place—that was Wallace. The first time I saw him was at a jazz club on Central Avenue, but we didn't really talk until the first time I visited him in Beverly Glen. I was impressed by Wallace and we hit it off, so I'd often go there for the evening after spending a day at UCLA. It was a simple environment you entered through the kitchen, and the bedroom was basically a kind of nest off to the side of this all-purpose sitting room where people ate, sat around, listened to music, smoked dope or whatever, through the night. An amazing range of people passed through that house. It wasn't as if there was a sign somewhere announcing "come one, come all," but people learned of it by word of mouth. It was similar to the situation with Paul Bowles. Why did people go all the hell over to Tangiers to see Bowles? Because it was an important thing to do, to go see Paul, and in the same way it was important to see Wallace. [20]

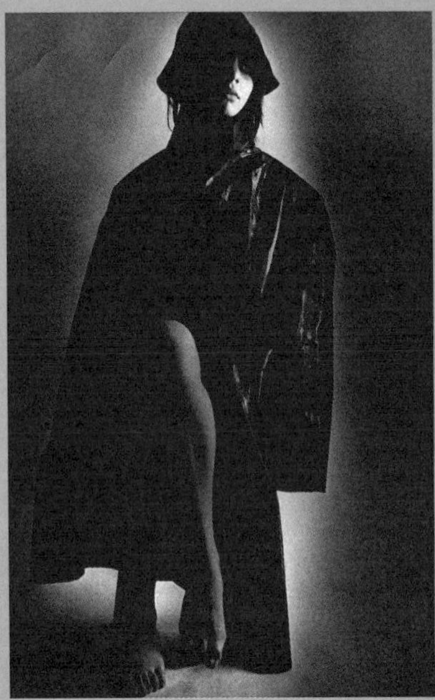

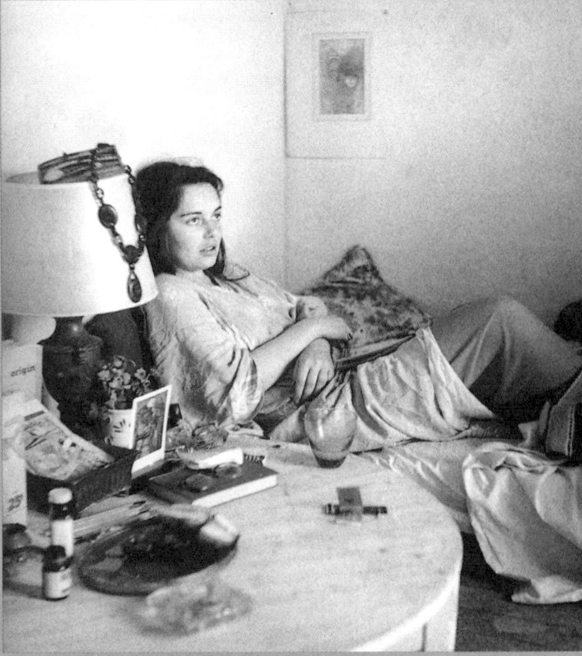

Berman meets Stuart Perkoff whose book, *Suicide Poems* is published this year. In 1960 Perkoff founds Venice West Café, which, along with the Temple of Man, will be one of the few poetry centers in Southern California during the period.

Suzi Hicks:
There were aspects of the poetry scene in Venice that were much more destructive than anything you'd find in Topanga Canyon. I'm not just talking about heroin use—although that was definitely part of it—but the art and the entire sensibility was darker. Stuart had the Venice West Café; so there was Baza at one end of Speedway representing the Wallace faction, and Stuart at the other end. [21]

Bob Alexander introduces Walter Hopps to Ed Kienholz; the three of them collaborate on the Fourth Annual All-City Art Festival at Barnsdall Park. Hopps submits a work of his own, which is removed from the exhibition because it contains a puff of steel wool situated in an explicit location on a loosely rendered female form.

Hopps's Syndell Studio, Alexander, and Kienholz's Now Gallery collaborate on "Action 2," presented from Sept. 5–25 at the Coronet Louvre; Alexander and Hopps install the show.

Ralph Gibson (b. 1939, Los Angeles) enlists in the Navy where he is trained as a photographer.

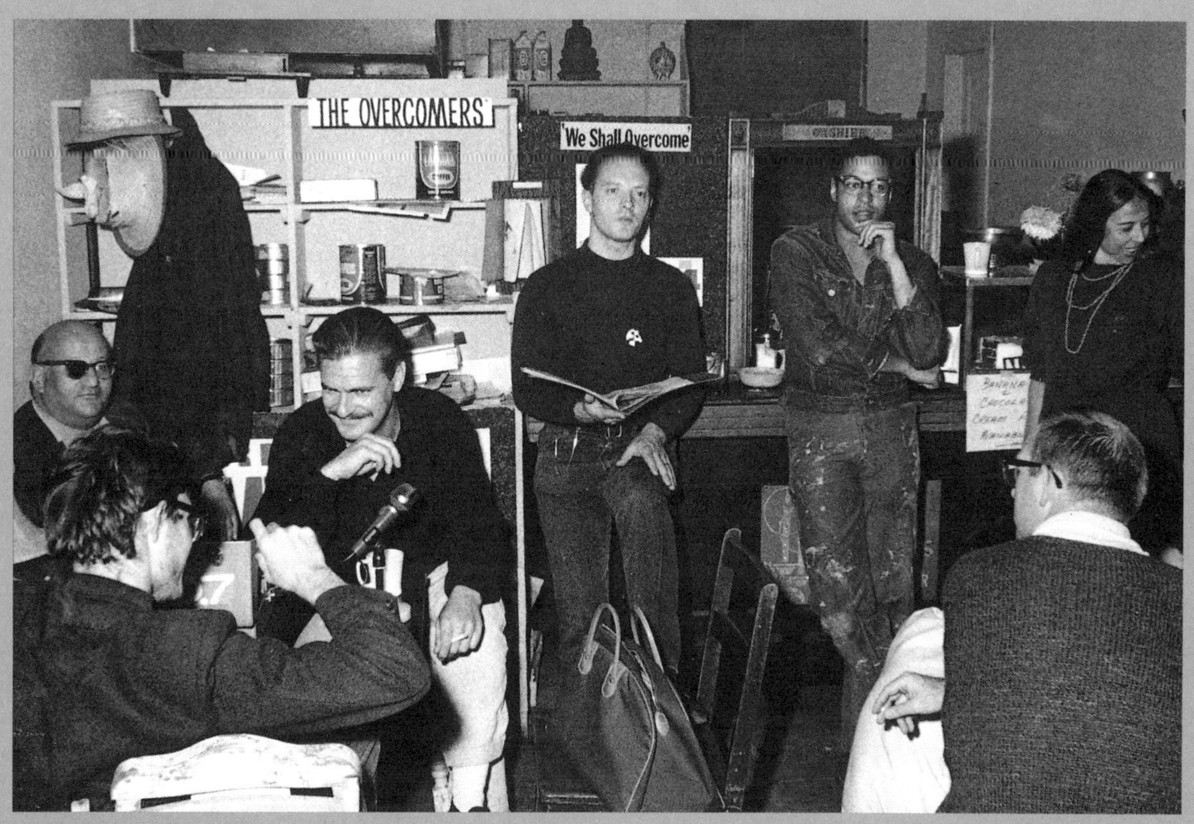

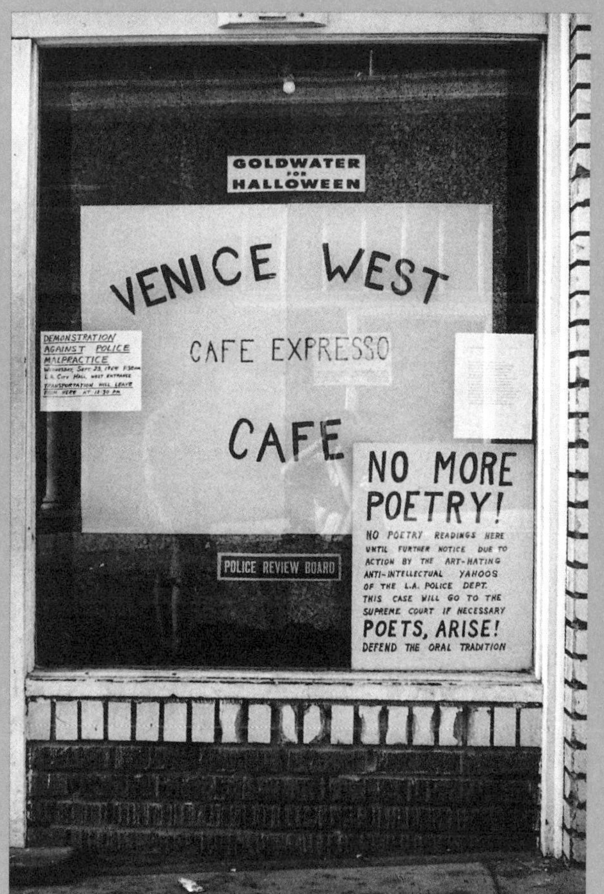

top Venice West Café, the poetry workshop in Venice, California. At the microphone is John Haag, who co-managed Venice West and was later a co-founder of the Peace and Freedom Party. Standing at the far right is Brittin's wife, Barbara Brittin, Photograph by Charles Brittin.

bottom Venice West Café, following the arrest of John Haag in September of 1964, for "providing entertainment without a police permit," Photograph by Charles Brittin.

After completing his studies at Black Mountain College, John Wieners returns to Boston and begins publication of the poetry journal *Measure,* (1957–62). He then relocates to San Francisco, where he contacts Robert Duncan who introduces him to the local community of poets.

Dennis Hopper appears in George Stevens's *Giant*.

In San Francisco, George Herms makes his first assemblage while a student at the University of California at Berkeley—a collaged door valentine for Polly Levee. The couple then move to Hermosa Beach.

In December, Bobby Driscoll and Marilyn Jean Rush get married in Mexico. They have three children before splitting up in 1963.

Michael McClure (b. 1932, Kansas) meets Berman while visiting L.A.

Michael McClure:

I'd been given a copy of the first issue of Semina, and I was deeply moved by the beauty and openness of it. I felt as if it was gleaming in my hand as I looked at it. So I wrote Wallace and told him I'd like to be in his magazine, and later that year I met him when I visited him at Crater Lane. My first impression of him was that he was almost ceremonially "laid back," to use the terminology of the period. Wally had a mystique of being cool, but he was interested in the beautiful, the desperate and the erotic, and there was a dynamism in his eyes that made him a very intriguing person. He spoke slowly and had a soft voice that took on a lilting edge when he said something witty, which was quite often. He and Shirley had beautiful things and a beautiful home, and we all learned to live in a style that essentially started with the Bermans, Robert Duncan and Jess.[22]

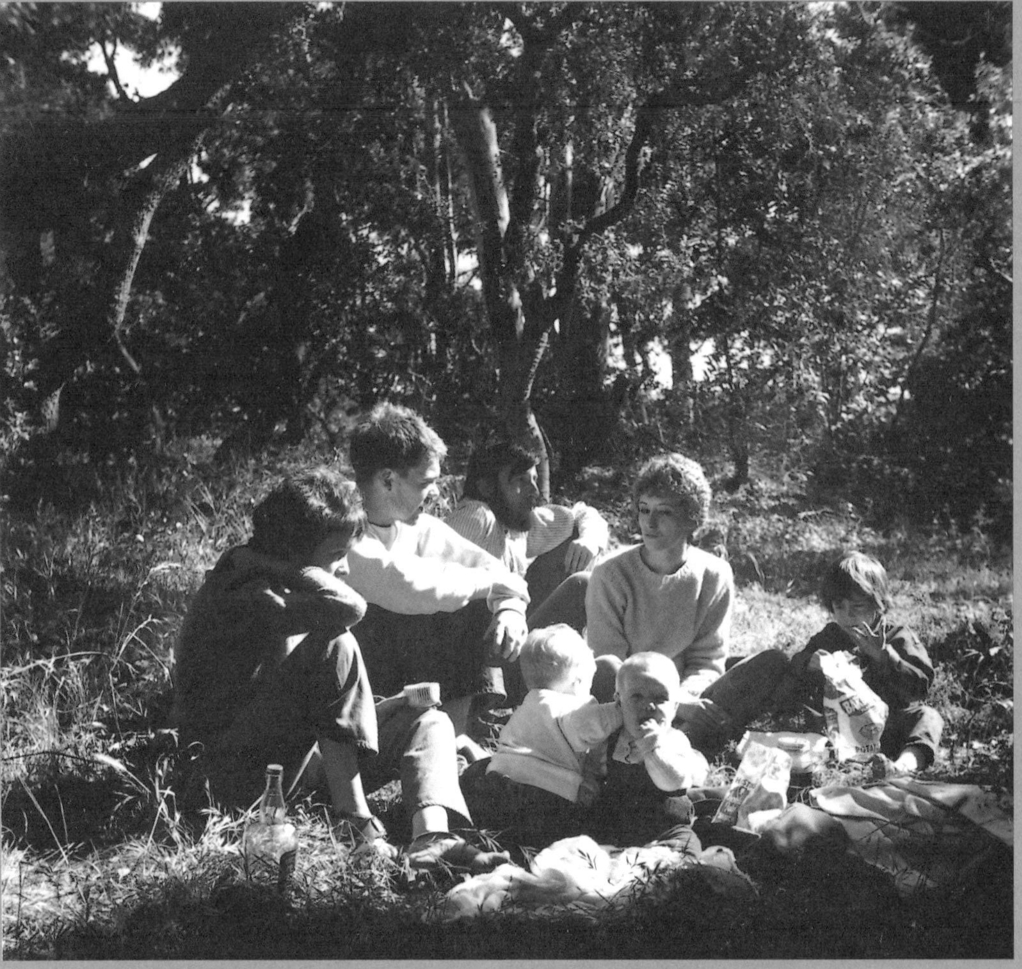

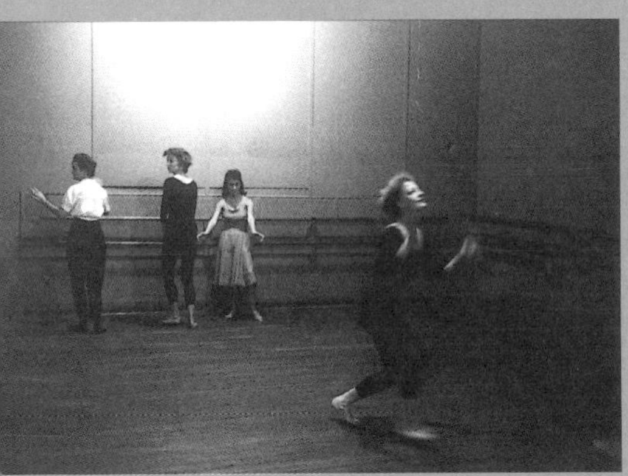

1957

Rachel Rosenthal launches Instant Theater, an experimental performance workshop she operates through 1966. Alexander meets Rosenthal and begins printing announcements for Instant Theater, which the Bermans attend.

Rachel Rosenthal:

Instant Theater was extraordinarily beautiful and wild. It was totally improvised, intensely theatrical, and non-verbal and was largely inspired by Antonin Artaud's Theater and Its Double, *a book I was totally beguiled by. When we went public, our first audience was all the people from the Ferus Gallery—they came every weekend. During those first years Baza created amazing programs and announcements for us that he printed with Popsicle sticks, pages from the phone book, Braille—he was incredibly inventive. I loved Wallace and went to his house several times, but as much as I liked and appreciated them, I couldn't hang out with those people because they were always high and I never took drugs or drank. There was no place there for somebody like me.*[23]

Berman and David Meltzer visit San Francisco; later in the year Meltzer moves there permanently.

David Meltzer:

Wallace and I were picked up at the airport by Lee and Idell Romero. They were already doing what later came to be known as light shows—pouring oil onto a lighted screen and projecting it—and they turned us on in the car on the way home from the airport. Then once we got home they turned us on some more. That was the first time in my life that I really understood what "stoned" meant—I mean, literally, like statuary.[24]

Berman meets Llyn Foulkes, who moves to Los Angeles after being discharged from the Army and enrolls at Chouinard (1957–59).

top right The Driscolls and the Bermans picnicking, Beverly Glen in 1957, Photograph by Wallace Berman.

bottom left Rachel Rosenthal and Instant Theater, Los Angeles, c. 1957, Photograph by Charles Brittin.

Kirby Doyle leaves his wife and family and moves in with **Sharon Morrill**, (b. 1938, San Leandro, CA, d. 1999, Los Angeles), a former airline stewardess known as DiDi.

Lawrence Jordan completes his first film, *Visions of a City.*

Tamblyn is nominated for an Academy Award for his performance in *Peyton Place*.

Ferus Gallery opens at 736A N. La Cienega Blvd. on March 15. Berman's first one-man show opens there on June 7; the L.A. Vice Squad shuts it down two weeks later. Berman is found guilty of exhibiting lewd material and fined $150. During its first year Ferus exhibits work by Jay DeFeo, John Altoon, and Arthur Richer.

Kirby Doyle begins a period of two years of work on the cycle of thirty-six poems which will be published in 1966 as *Sapphobones*.

Herms makes his first full assemblage environment in Hermosa. Titled *The Secret Exhibition*, he shows it to a few friends then destroys it.

PRESS BAZA
8205 santa monica boulevard
OLdfield 4-7070

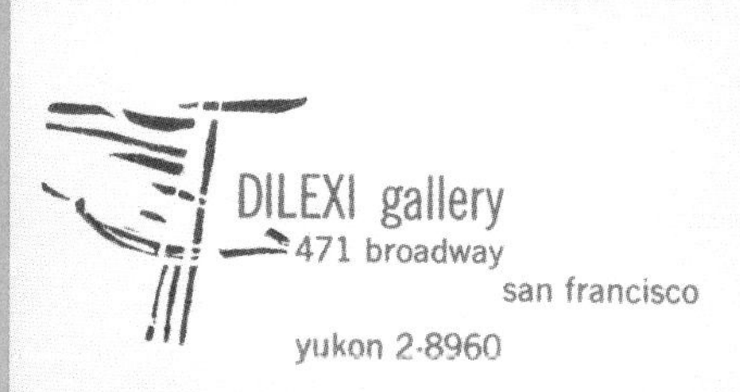

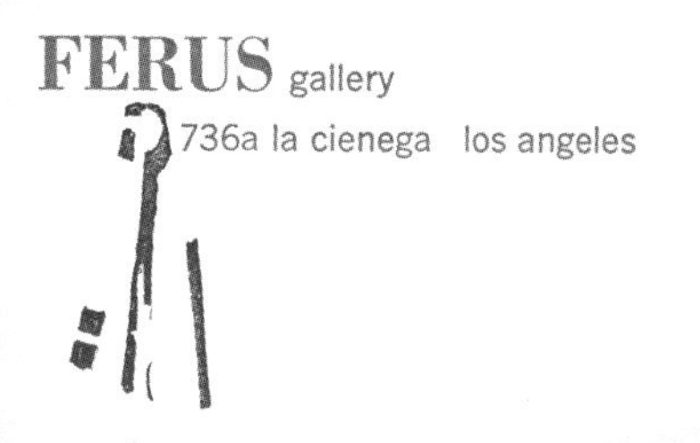

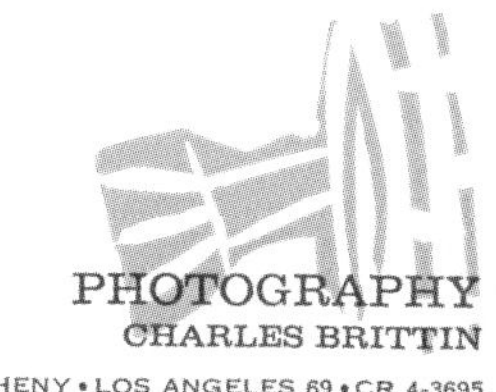

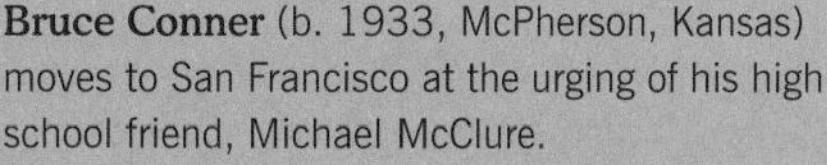

Bruce Conner (b. 1933, McPherson, Kansas) moves to San Francisco at the urging of his high school friend, Michael McClure.

In August Berman and Alexander collaborate on *Collectanea*.

Walter Hopps rents a storefront, on Sawtelle Blvd. in West Los Angeles, for Alexander so he will have a place to print exhibition announcements for Ferus. The place becomes known as Stone Brothers. Stockwell takes Hopper to a poetry reading there and introduces him to Berman.

Dennis Hopper:
Wallace was always a mystery to me, and he was very glamorous. He was a quiet, gentle, humble person, and he had this strange aura about him that was removed, yet not hostile—he was a guy you couldn't really reach. I don't know anybody who didn't respect him, and we all deferred to him because he had a very spiritual quality. He was the guy. Wallace was the guru.[25]

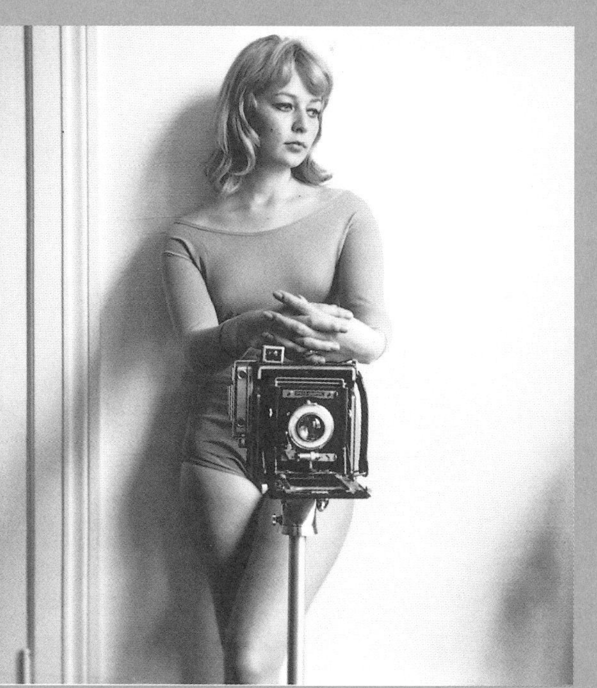

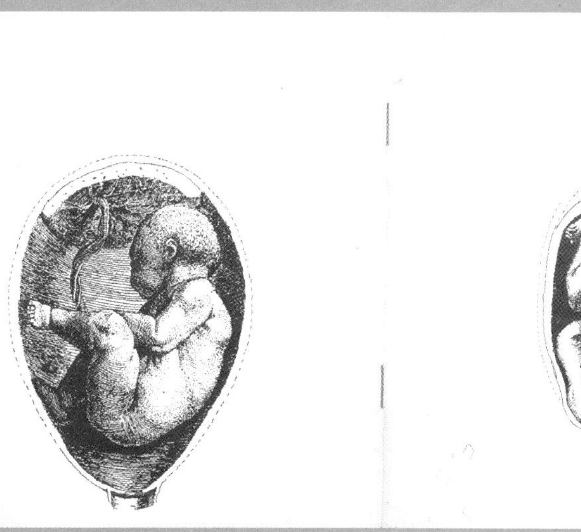

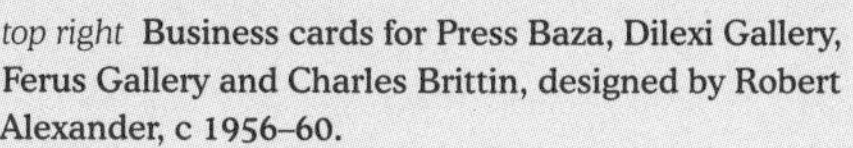

top right Business cards for Press Baza, Dilexi Gallery, Ferus Gallery and Charles Brittin, designed by Robert Alexander, c 1956–60.

bottom left DiDi Morrill, San Francisco, 1958, Photograph by Wallace Berman.

bottom right *Collectanea*, a limited-edition artists book published in 1957 by Robert Alexander, with cover art by Wallace Berman.

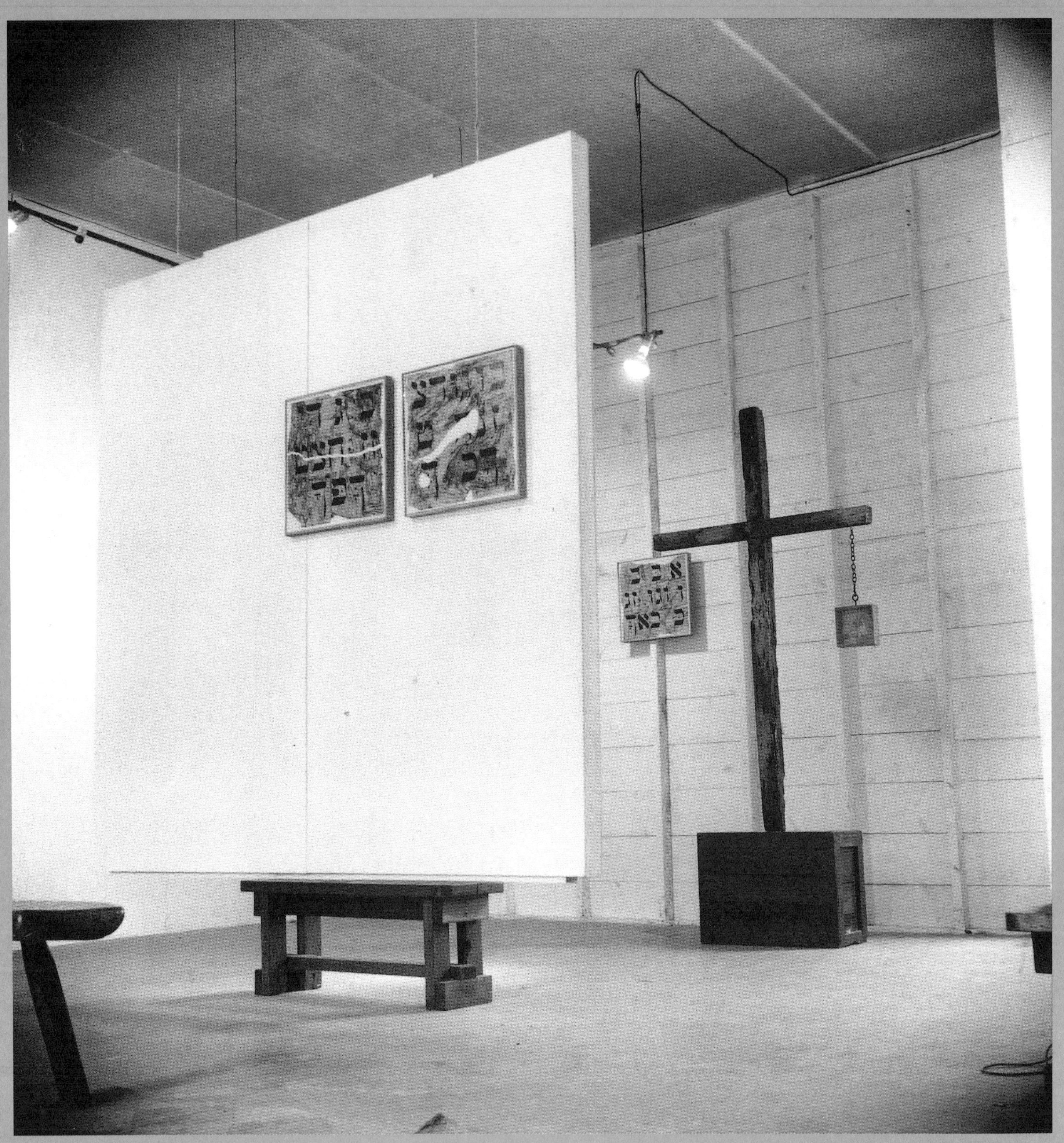

Installation shot, Wallace Berman's exhibition at Ferus Gallery in June, 1957. Visible works include three parchment pieces, and the mixed-media assemblage, *Cross*, Photograph by Charles Brittin.

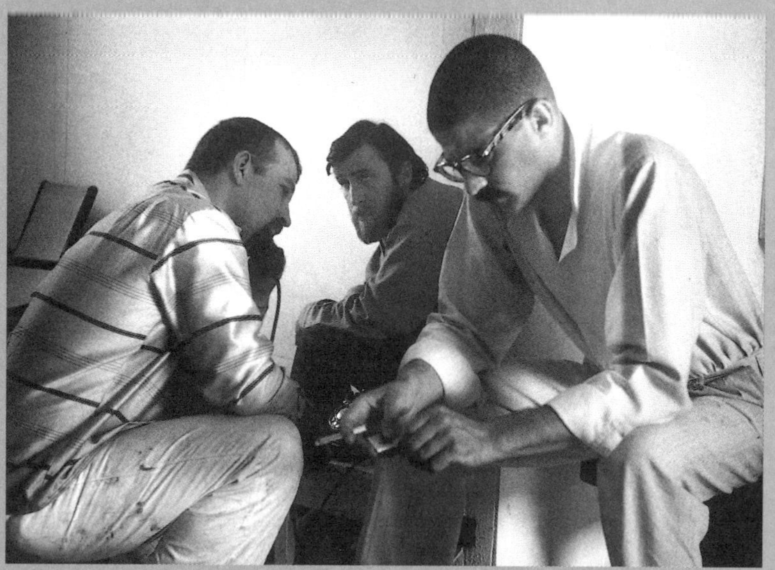

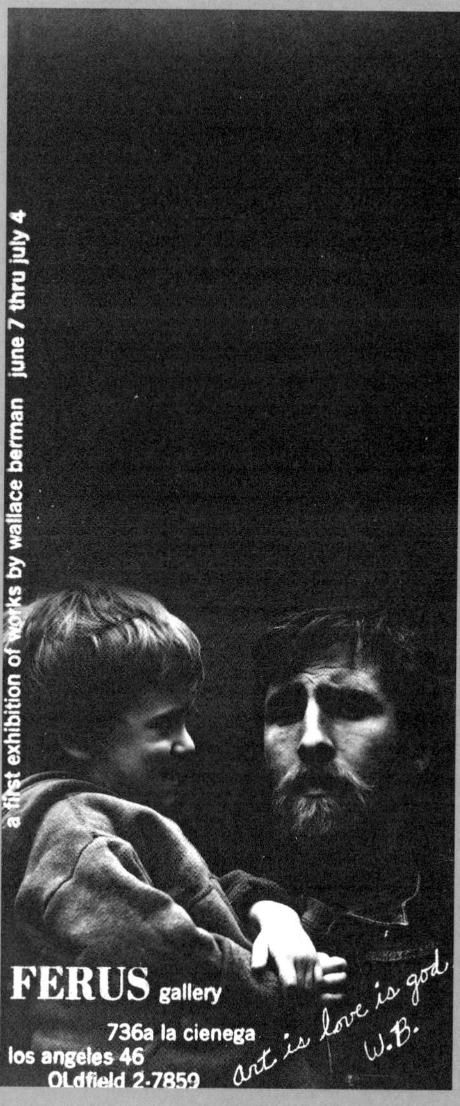

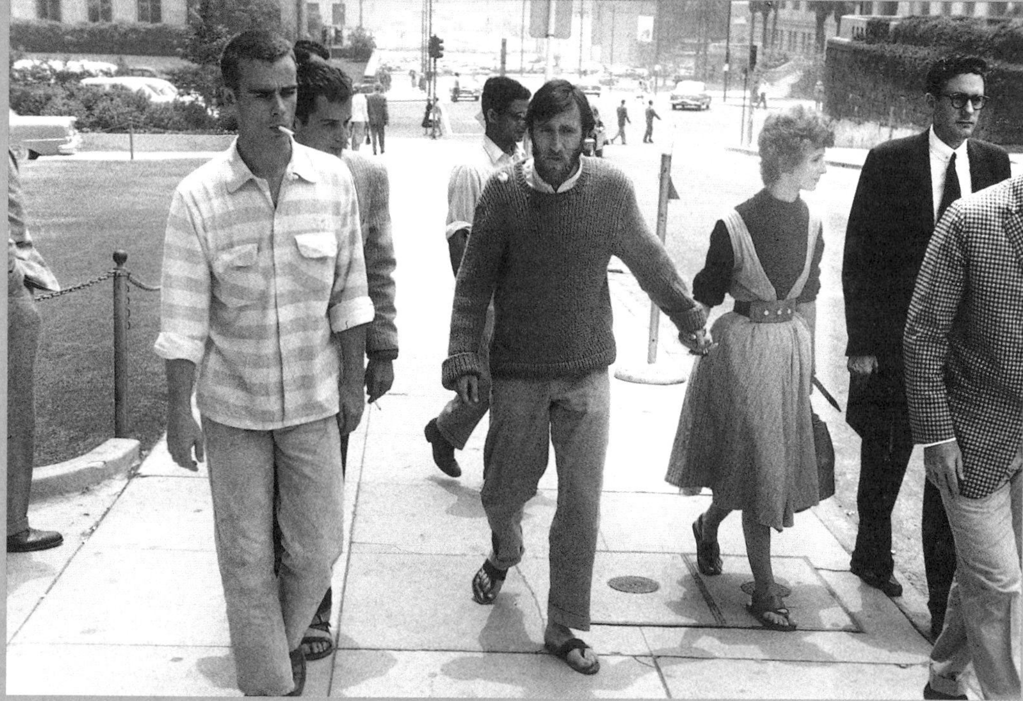

top Ed Kienholz, Wallace Berman, and Robert Alexander at Ferus Gallery, awaiting Berman's arrest on charges of obscenity, 1957, Photograph by Charles Brittin.

right Announcement for Wallace Berman exhibition at Ferus Gallery, 1957, Photograph of Wallace and Tosh Berman by Charles Brittin.

bottom left Dean Stockwell, David Meltzer, Shirley and Wallace Berman, Walter Hopps and Craig Kauffman outside the Los Angeles County Courthouse on the day Berman was tried on charges of obscenity, June 1957, Photograph by Charles Brittin.

Stone Brothers hosts readings by Cameron and Alexander Trocchi, a committed advocate of heroin usage.

Charles Brittin:

Trocchi came to L.A. from London and once he got here he was constantly scuffling for drugs. Trocchi was charming, as destructive people tend to be, but he was a bad influence.[26]

Following the closure of Berman's Ferus exhibition, the Bermans move to San Francisco in December of 1957. Initially they stay in Berkeley with George Herms. During that period Berman completes work on *Semina Two*, which includes contributions from John Altoon, John Reed, David Meltzer, Michael McClure, Zack Walsh, Bob Alexander, Alexander Trocchi, and Walter Hopps. The cover is a photograph of Suzi Hicks taken by Charles Brittin.

The Bermans take an apartment at 2315 Jackson Street in San Francisco where they meet Philip Lamantia who lives a few blocks away.

Philip Lamantia:

I meet this guy and he invites me over, and on the walls are his Hebrew character paintings, so I ask him, "Are these connected to Kabbalah." And he immediately says, "No." He's hip to Kabbalah and has books on the subject, but that isn't what he's doing. He also has books on alchemy and magic, and I recognize that he's interested in the same subjects I am, so we got to know each other pretty well. Wallace was independent and he and Shirley lived in perfect harmony—they had a very cool, interesting relationship. He seemed to have an endless supply of hashish—we never figured out how or where he got it—and we had many up-until-dawn discussions about the oracles, the esoteric—all those matters. Wallace wasn't ambitious, and disinterested people like him were rare in the twentieth century.[27]

While living on Jackson Street, Berman meets Jay DeFeo.

In September, Norman Rose invites Bob Alexander to move to San Francisco and become warehouse foreman for Paper Editions, a paperback book center. Alexander accepts, and Artie Richer and John Reed move north with him.

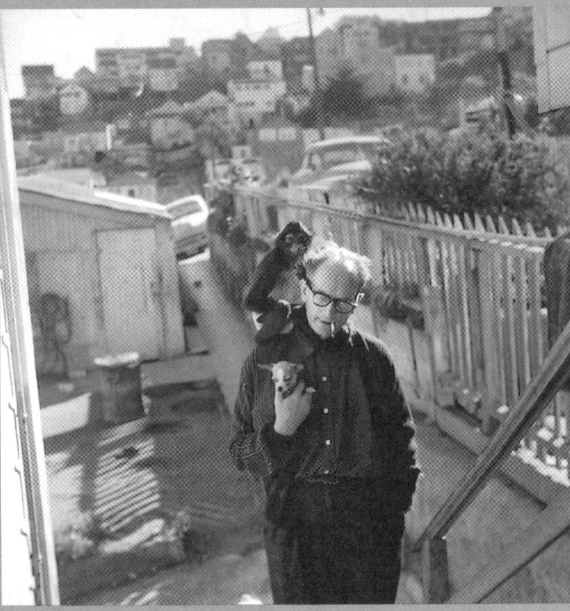

Richer and his family rent a place on Potrero Hill owned by Norwegian physician **Dr. Reidar Wennesland** (b. 1908, Norway; d. 1985, San Francisco), who often rents to artists and builds a substantial collection by accepting artworks in lieu of rent. (Wennesland willed his collection to his alma mater in Norway, the Kristiansand Cathedral School and Adger University College, where it currently resides.)

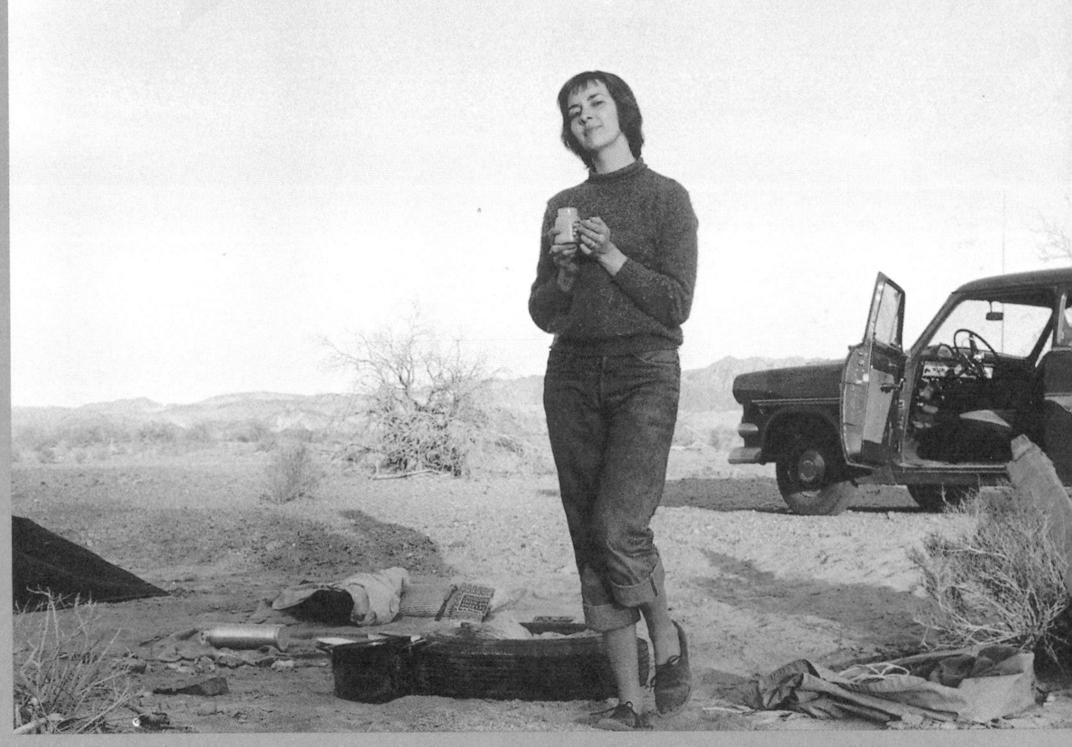

top left John Altoon and Alexander Trocchi, 1957, Photograph by Charles Brittin.

top right Dr. Reidar Wennesland, physician, collector of exotic pets, and landlord of several beat artists in San Francisco during the late 1950s, Photograph by Wallace Berman.

bottom Lyn Trocchi in Los Angeles, 1957, Photograph by Saul White.

Ginsberg's *Howl* is published by Villiers Publications, Ltd. London U.S. customs attempts to ban importation of the book on grounds of obscenity, but the U.S. district attorney refuses to prosecute. Lawrence Ferlinghetti and Shigeyoshi Murao are subsequently arrested for selling obscene material at City Lights Bookstore which stocks *Howl*. The ACLU represents them at trial and Robert Duncan is among those who testify on their behalf.

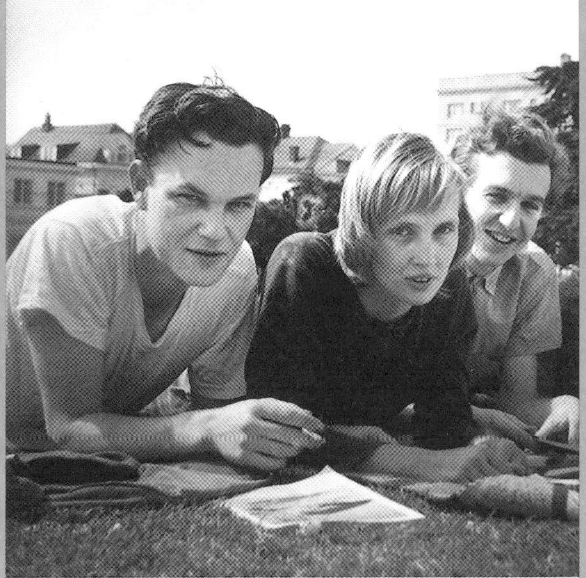

Philip Lamantia:
*Ginsberg was here in the late 1950s, and he wrote a piece about the euphoria of the poets in San Francisco in 1959. There was a whole flurry of us who read together then, and we were euphoric. The closest parallel I can think of for our group was the Surrealists of the 1920s—the theory in both cases being to keep the audience out. Wallace was at the center of the whole thing and was sort of the secret director—in fact, he started a secret magazine—*Semina*—that wasn't offered to the public.*[28]

On September 1 Bruce and Jean Conner marry, then move to an apartment at 2322 Fillmore Street in San Francisco. Conner gets a construction job working with Lawrence Jordan, converting a building in North Beach into a movie theater. In December the Conners meet the Bermans at Michael McClure's apartment at 2322 Fillmore Street.

left Joe Dunn, Jan Balas, and John Wieners in San Francisco, 1958, Photograph by Wallace Berman.

bottom center Announcement for Arthur Richer's exhibition at Ferus Gallery in 1957.

top right Wallace Berman at the front door to 707 Scott Street, 1958, Photograph by Bill Margolis.

Bruce Conner:
By the time Wallace came to San Francisco, he was an underground hero because of the stance he took on sexual censorship. At that point in time just to use certain words could get you thrown in jail, and Wallace was regarded as a kind of martyr because of what happened with his exhibition at Ferus. When I met Wallace he was doing mail art and working on Semina*, and, like many of us, he was working on the outer edges, exploring awareness, consciousness, communication, love and god. He was also involved in the jazz aesthetic, and one-on-one communication is an important part of that. That's reflected in the postcards he sent out—all the postcards were different and were made for specific individuals. Wallace knew who his audience was and how to reach it.*[29]

Lew and Mary Welch move to San Francisco; Welch is hired by the Oakland office of Montgomery Ward and enrolls at San Francisco State.

FERUS GALLERY ANNOUNCES AN EXHIBITION

OF PAINTINGS BY

ARTHUR

RICHER

NOVEMBER 8 – DECEMBER 5, 1957

RECEPTION FRIDAY EVENING, NOV. 8, 8:30 P.M.

736 A N. LA CIENEGA BLVD., LOS ANGELES

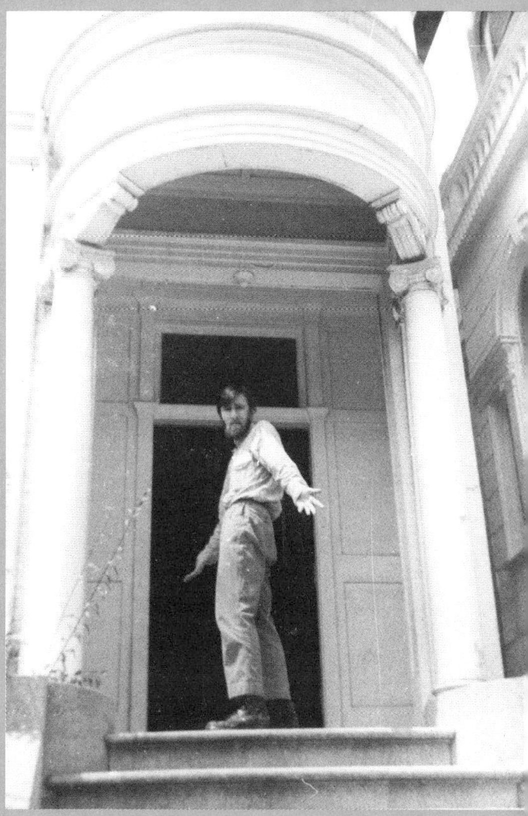

1958

Bruce Conner:
From 1957 through 1965, San Francisco was where it was at. It was a much smaller community and everybody knew everybody. Wallace kept an open door at all times, and there would be food to eat, music people wanted to listen to, which was mostly jazz, and social life.[30]

In June the Bermans move from Jackson Street to the apartment building on 707 Scott Street managed by Bill Margolis. In August, Margolis leaves for New York, and Berman becomes manager of the building. While living on Scott Street, they meet Bob Kaufman (b. 1925, New Orleans; d. 1986, Oakland). The son of a German orthodox Jew and a black woman from Martinique, Kaufman is the third youngest in a family of thirteen children. At the age of thirteen, Kaufman joins the U.S. Merchant Marines and travels around the world nine times. Kaufman arrives in San Francisco a few months prior to meeting the Bermans, having traveled there from Big Sur with his friends Jack Kerouac and Neal Cassady.

Talbert begins making art full-time. He's supported by his wife, Shirley, who works in the art department at UCLA.

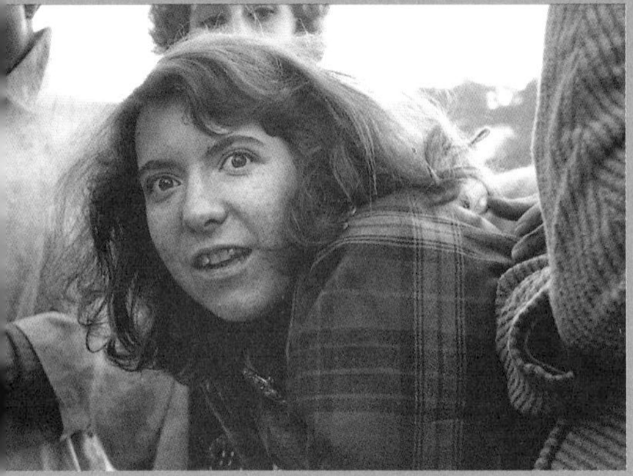

Lew Welch is fired from his job at Montgomery Ward and begins writing poetry full-time.

The Bermans meet Boston poet and publisher Joe Dunn, who works in the San Francisco office of Greyhound Bus Lines. The previous year Dunn launched White Rabbit Press (1957–72) with the publication of Steve Jonas's *Love, the Poem, the Sea & Other Pieces Examined.*

Berman introduces McClure to peyote; McClure writes about the experience in "Peyote Poem," which Berman publishes as *Semina 3*.

Bruce Conner:
Michael was involved with the value of peyote as a spiritual guide, as was I. It had a position in Native American history that resonated for us, and it became important for me to learn about it. When I was at the University of Nebraska, the library had some anthropological papers on peyote cults, which I read. Then I finally took some early in 1958 with a friend named Frank English. All the stuff I'd read didn't mean a thing because there's no way anyone could describe this experience. Everything was bejeweled and sparkling, time and space were all mixed up, and I recognized the realm it took me to as someplace I'd been before. By the mid 1960s everyone I knew smoked marijuana. It was a political drug in that "turning on" made you part of the counterculture, and whenever you visited somebody they'd immediately take out a joint. I discovered I didn't like this at all because it made me paranoid.[31]

David Haselwood launches Auerhahn Press (1958–63) with the publication of John Wieners's *The Hotel Wentley Poems*, which Ginsberg praises as "the work of a naked flower, absolutely REAL." The Bermans meet Wieners, who is living down the street from them above a flower shop at the corner of Washington and Fillmore. Wieners then moves to 707 Scott Street where he lives for eighteen months and writes *The Journal of John Wieners is to be Called 707 Scott Street, for Billie Holiday, 1959,* (published in 1996 by Sun & Moon Press).

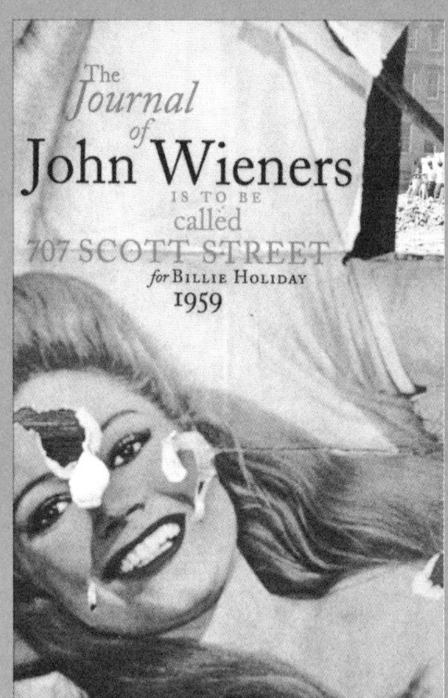

Berman photographs Jay DeFeo standing in front of her painting, *The Eyes*, which was inspired by a Philip Lamantia poem. Later in the year she begins work on her signature painting, *The Rose*, which isn't completed until 1966. Berman photographs her in front of *The Rose* and has a one-day exhibition of the photographs at his Scott Street apartment.

The Bermans meet **Patty Topalian** (b. 1934, Tennessee; d. 1988, San Anselmo).

Herms, Richer, and Meltzer work for Alexander at Paper Editions, and Alexander moonlights at the Jazz Workshop at 721 Broadway. Alexander becomes friends with Jim Newman, who shares his passion for jazz, and they decide to open the Dilexi Gallery above the Jazz Workshop.

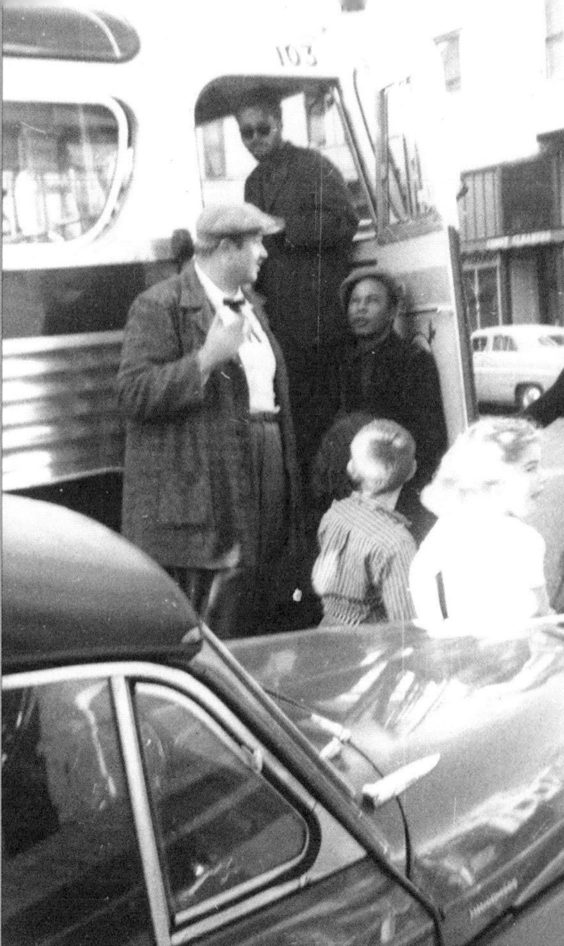

In February Herms and Richer are arrested on drug charges after Herms sells a small amount of marijuana to a colleague at Paper Editions on behalf of Richer. Richer is released, but Herms serves six months at Santa Rita Honor Farm. During that period, his early work is destroyed in a Berkeley fire. Following his release in July, Herms moves to Tuolomne, where his wife has been hired to teach.

The Bermans meet Paul Beattie.

Bruce Conner begins making collages and assemblages and has his first solo show on the West Coast at East West Gallery. During this period Conner also makes his first film, *A Movie*, using found footage.

The Bermans meet Lew Welch.

Bobby Driscoll is arrested on drug charges at his home in Pacific Palisades.

center **The Journal of John Wieners is to be Called 707 Scott Street, for Billie Holiday, 1959. (Los Angeles: Sun & Moon Press, 1996) This journal was written while Wieners lived in the same building as the Bermans. On the cover is an untitled photograph by Louis Faurer, c. 1948.**

top left **Patty Jordan, Semina Gallery, Larkspur, 1961. Standing behind her is Shirley Berman, Photograph by Wallace Berman.**

top right **When San Francisco's hipster community had finally had its fill of being treated as objects of ridicule by the press, they organized a bus "Tour of Squaresville" hosted by Eric Nord. Nord is the heavyset man in the cap, and he's speaking to poet Bob Kaufman, 1958, Photograph by Bill Margolis.**

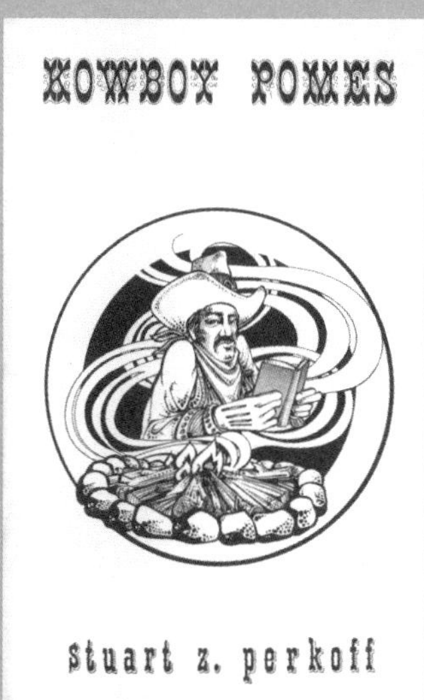

1959

Robert Duncan and Jess launch Enkidu Surrogate, which publishes Duncan's *Faust Foutu: An Entertainment in Four Acts* with cover art and illustrations by the author.

The Ferus Gallery shows work by Arthur Richer, John Altoon, Jay DeFeo, Joan Brown, and Llyn Foulkes.

Irving Blum takes over Ferus and officially drops Berman from the gallery.

Irving Blum:
Wally was an extraordinarily provocative guy who could convince you about anything and somehow I was a bit suspicious of him. Wally's work, somehow, for me, lacked a kind of edge, and it was difficult. Wally stopped working after that one show, didn't do anything for years, so [dropping him from the gallery] wasn't a problem.[33]

Joan Brown moves to 2330 Fillmore Street, where she lives next door to DeFeo and Hedrick, and meets the Bermans, the Conners, the McClures, Duncan, Herms, and Lamantia.

Ray Bremser is released from Bordentown Reformatory after serving six years on an armed robbery charge. He immediately begins participating in poetry readings in New York with Kerouac, Ginsberg and Frank O'Hara.

The Bermans meet Lawrence Jordan at McClure's Fillmore St. apartment.

Lawrence Jordan:
My first impression of Wallace was electric. I'd never had anyone look into my eyes so penetratingly on first introduction, and no one has since. It was powerful. Almost nobody could operate the way Wallace did—he was the ultimate in taste in terms of finding people, bringing out their potential, and choosing poems and photographs for Semina. Wallace had magic, and he made spiritual art that had to do with opening up the soul. The images he used had a heraldic effect, like insignias on medieval banners, and they aroused a shift in gears in your spirit.[32]

Lew Welch takes a job as a rubber cutter for the Bemis Bag Company. His marriage unravels by November, when he collaborates with Jack Kerouac and Albert Saijo on a volume of haiku titled *Trip Trap: Haiku Along the Road from San Francisco to New York, 1959* (Bolinas, Cal.: Grey Fox Press, 1973). Welch moves in with his mother in Reno for six months, then returns to San Francisco and begins living with poet Lenore Kandel.

Bobby Driscoll is arrested for violating his parole.

Joan Brown moves to North Beach with artist Manuel Neri.

Stuart Perkoff begins a two-year period of work on *Kowboy Pomes* (Golden, Colorado: Croupier Press, 1973).

Ray Bremser visits Washington D.C. with members of the Living Theater for a series of readings. He meets Bonnie Frazer (b. 1939, Washington, D.C.) whom he marries three weeks later. Eight months later he is sent to Trenton State Prison for marrying Frazer without permission from the state; He is released after six months when William Carlos Williams intervenes on his behalf.

Jess begins a series of paintings he refers to as *Translations*, which occupy him until 1971.

Berman publishes *Semina 4* which includes contributions from Ginsberg, McClure, Lamantia, Perkoff, Wieners, Reed, and Meltzer. Later in the year he publishes *Semina 5*, with contributions from Lamantia, Jordan, McClure, and Reed. The cover is a photograph taken in Mexico by Brittin.

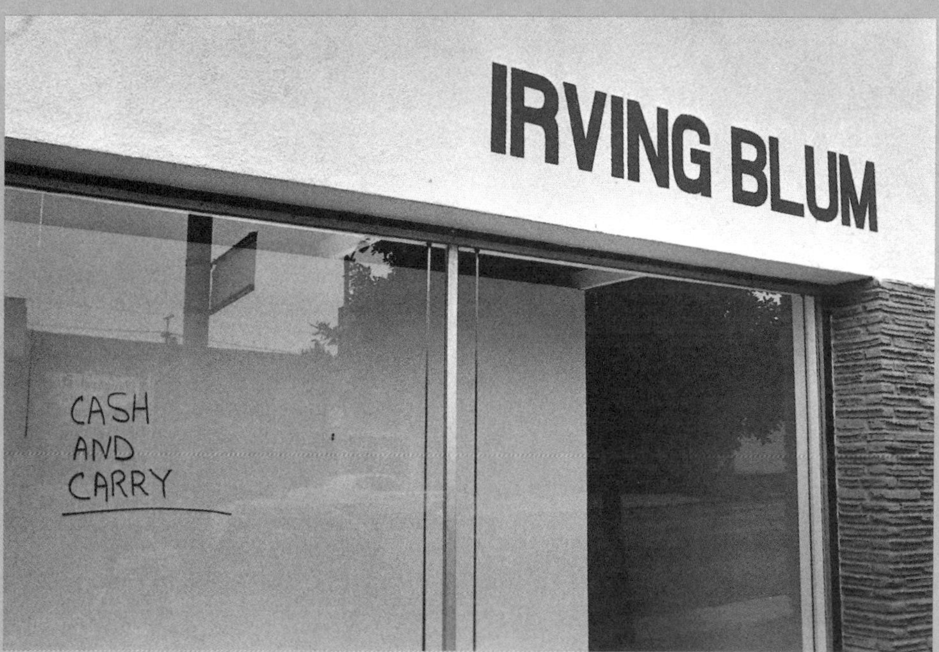

upper left Stuart Perkoff, *Kowboy Pomes* (Golden, Colorado: Croupier Press, 1973).

bottom right Irving Blum gallery, with grafitti, Los Angeles, c. 1968, Photograph by Charles Brittin.

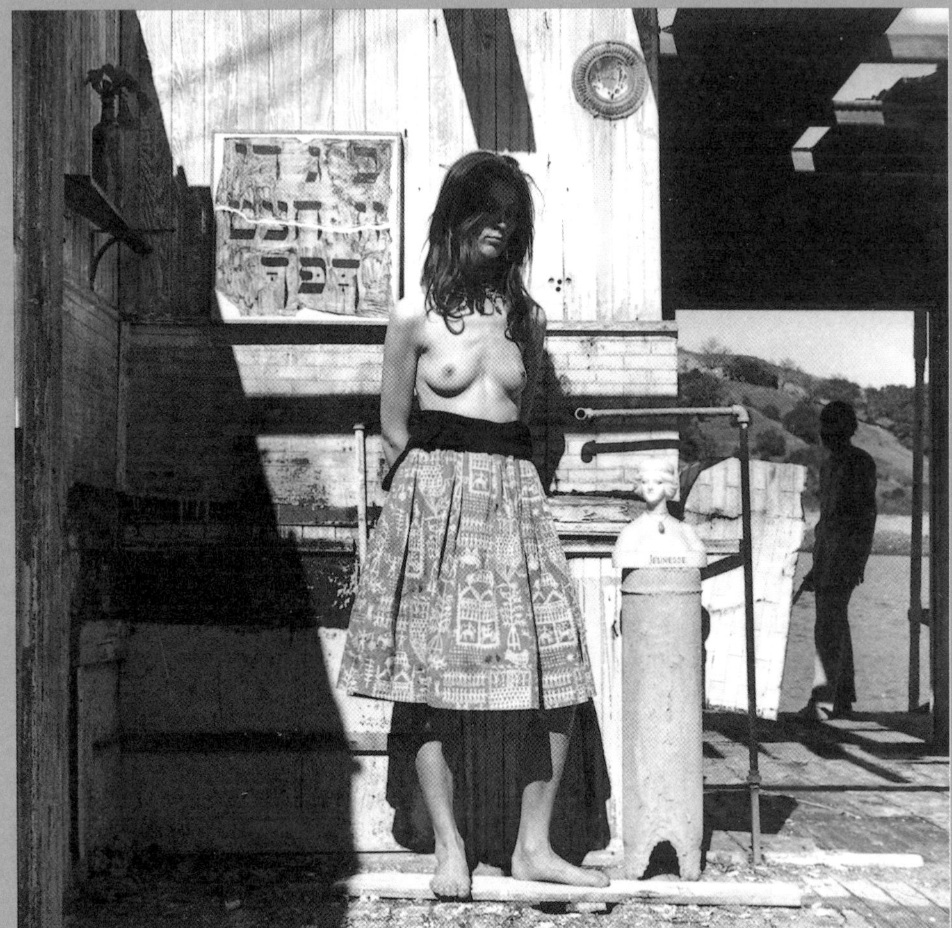

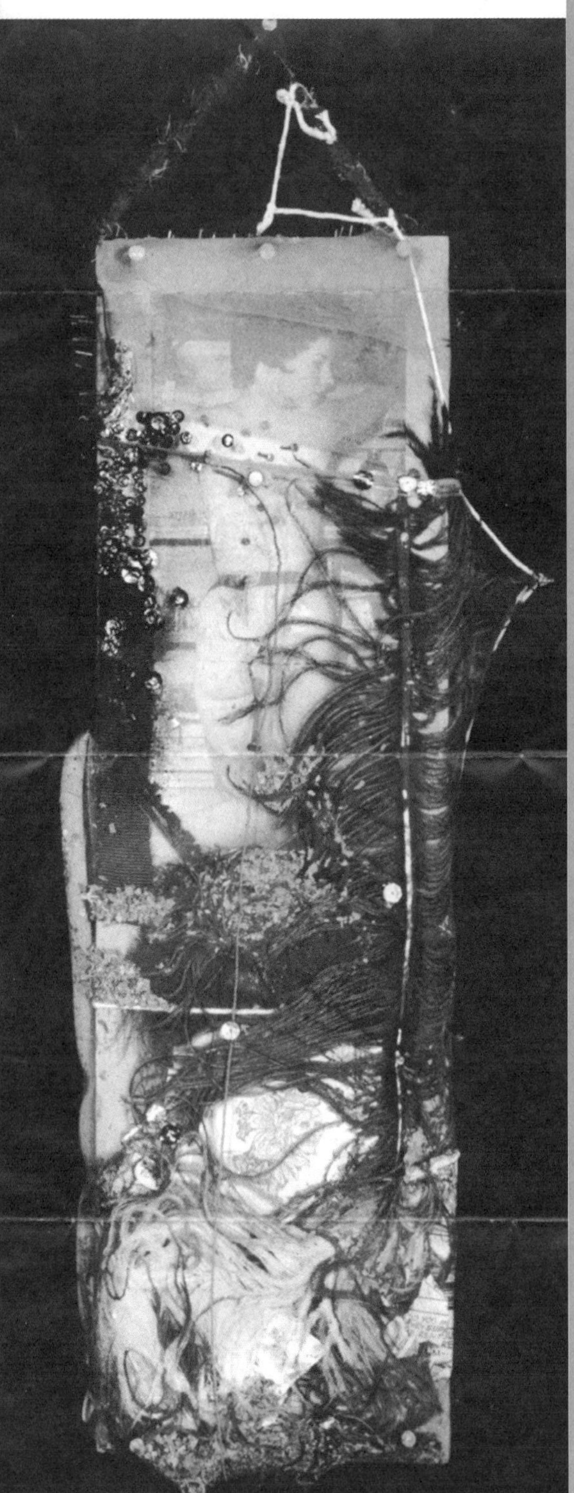

left Louise Herms, Larkspur, California, 1960, Photograph by Wallace Berman.

top Announcement for the opening exhibition of the Batman Gallery, 1960, Collection of Hal Glicksman.

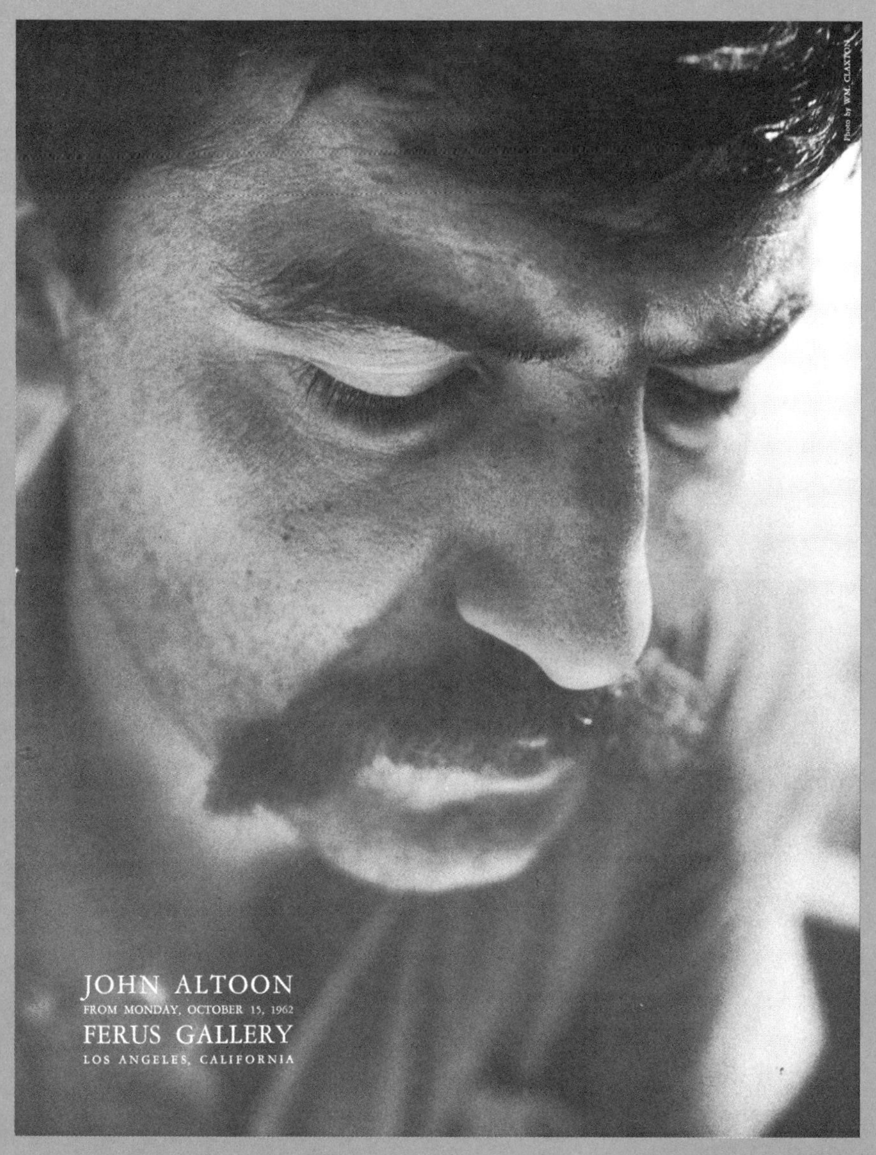

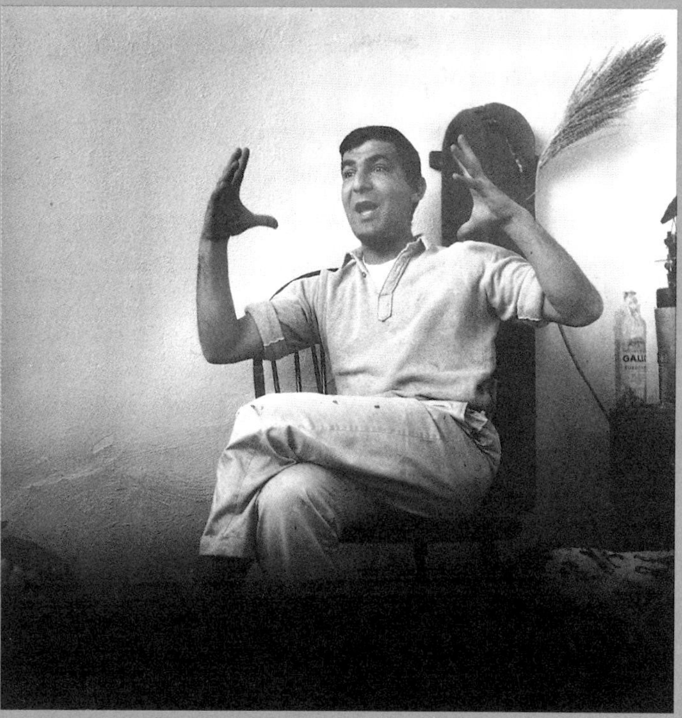

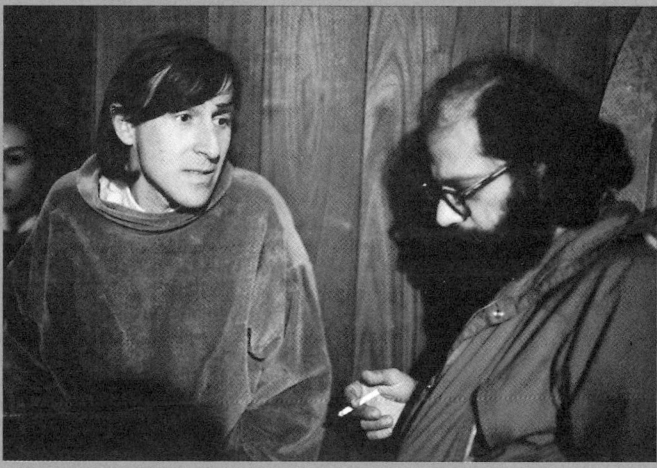

right John Altoon, 1959. Photograph by Charles Brittin.

top left Poster for a John Altoon exhibition at Ferus Gallery, featuring a photograph by William Claxton, 1960.

bottom left Wallace Berman and Allen Ginsberg at the Cinema Theater in Los Angeles, 1957. Photograph by Charles Brittin.

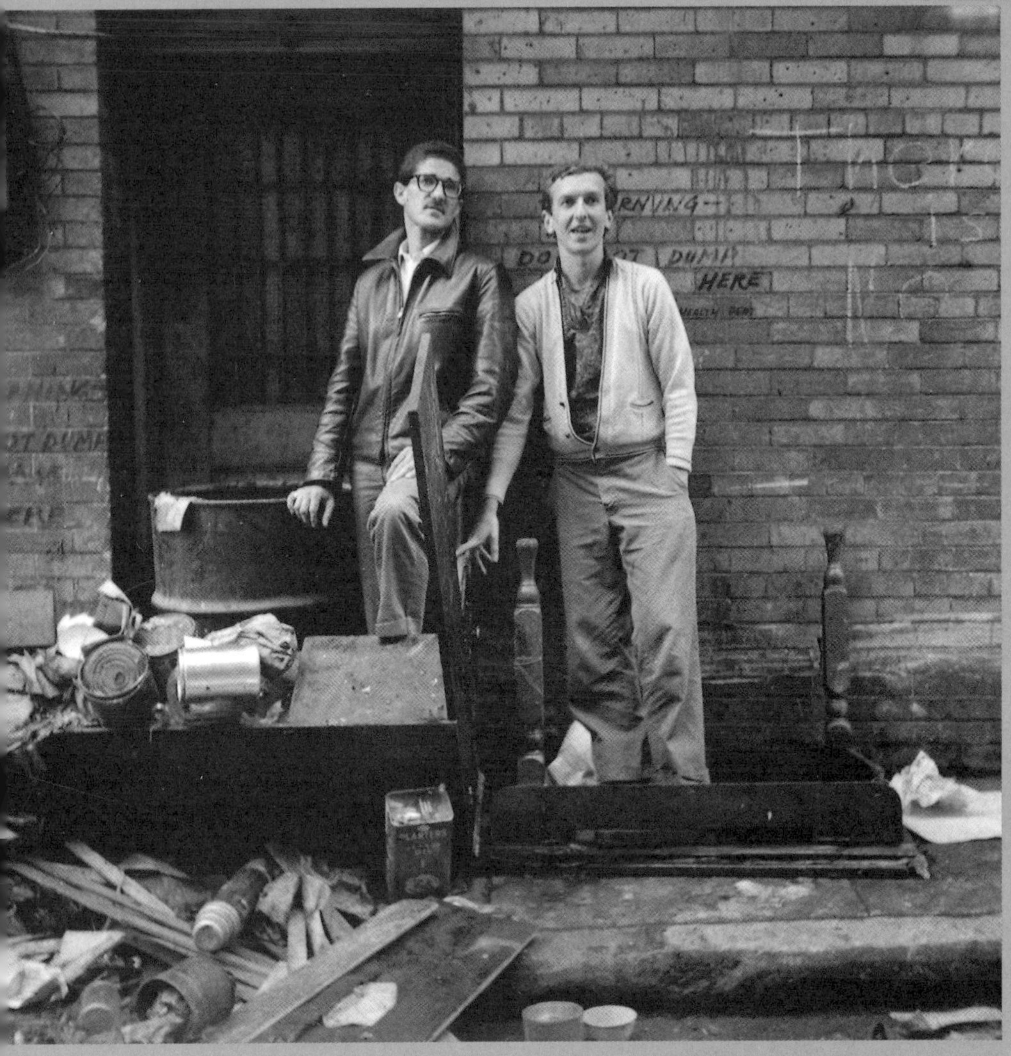

1960

Dean Stockwell stars in Jack Cardiff's film adaptation of the D.H. Lawrence novel, *Sons and Lovers*.

Bobby Driscoll is arrested for assault with a deadly weapon.

Taylor Mead stars in Ron Rice's film, *The Flower Thief.*

Ferus Gallery shows work by Jay DeFeo and John Altoon.

Rachel Rosenthal marries actor King Moody and they move Instant Theater to the Horseshoe Stage Theater (now the Zephyr) on Melrose Avenue.

Bonnie Bremser gives birth to a daughter, Rachel.

Ben Talbert shares a studio with Fred Mason on Brooks Street in Venice. Talbert corresponds with Berman.

Billy and Joan Jahrmarkt move to San Francisco and open the Batman Gallery at 2222 Fillmore Street with a solo show of 99 works by Bruce Conner. The gallery hosts poetry readings—Lew Welch and Kirby Doyle are among those who read there—and Michael McClure presents his play, *The Feast*, which features Doyle in the cast. The gallery closes after presenting 14 shows, including a solo show of Herms with a poster designed by Berman.

Paul Beattie and Warner Jepson experiment with light projections in Ann Halprin's dance studio.

Dean Stockwell stars in *Compulsion*, directed by Orson Welles.

Bob Kaufman, Bill Margolis, Allen Ginsberg, and John Kelly co-found *Beatitude* magazine.

Auerhahn Press publishes two volumes by Philip Lamantia—*Ekstasis* and *Narcotica*—with cover photographs by Berman.

Wieners descends into a depression which prompts him to return to Boston and convalesce in a psychiatric hospital.

David Meltzer marries Christina Meyer and they begin performing bluegrass and folk music together in San Francisco clubs and coffee houses.

George Herms's marriage ends and he leaves Tuolumne and moves to Ed Taylor's Berkeley apartment, a hang-out dubbed "Fort Taylor." He meets his second wife, Louise, at a New Year's Eve party there, and the couple move to an abandoned boathouse in Larkspur a few months later.

Ralph Gibson is discharged from the Navy and settles in San Francisco where he attends the Art Institute for a year.

City Lights Books publishes Bob Kaufman's *The Abomunist Manifesto* and *Second April,* and Kenneth Tynan begins work on *Dissent in the Arts in America*, a film featuring Kaufman. Tynan completes the film the following year and is called to appear before the House Un-American Activities Committee for making it.

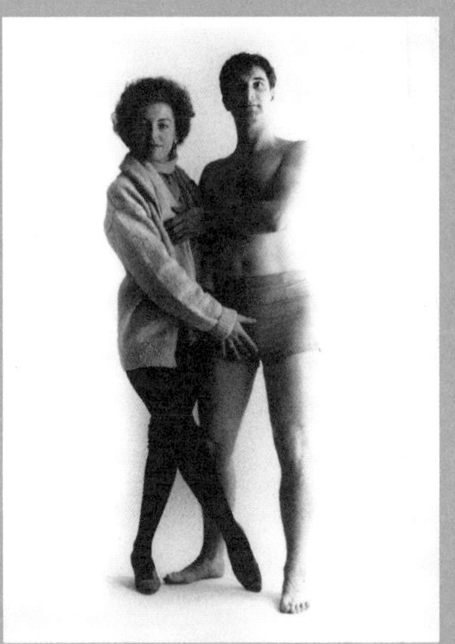

top left Bob Alexander and John Wieners in the alley behind the Jazz Cellar, San Francisco, 1960, Photograph by Wallace Berman.

bottom right Rachel Rosenthal and King Moody in Los Angeles, 1960, Photograph by Charles Brittin.

The Bermans move to Larkspur, where they live in a houseboat moored in the swamps of Corte Madera Creek. Also living there are the Jahrmarkts and the Herms, who live in a boathouse without heat or electricity.

Bruce Conner:
George was living in a little shack out in the middle of the water and you could only get to it during low tide. There was no electricity and no water, and George delivered his first two children there. George was one-thousand percent nature boy, and he could take things from the environment and slap them together into an artwork.[37]

Bruce Conner:
I liked Billy Jahrmarkt, but he was childlike in certain ways. He wanted to open a gallery and said his father in New York would pay for it, so I ran all over town, then I finally found a place. I designed the inside of the place with Ernie Burton, who was an architect, and it was painted black. Michael McClure came up with the name, "Batman," for the gallery, and Dave Haselwood and I did publicity and sent out press releases. The gallery opened and got a fair amount of attention, but after that Billy hardly bothered to keep the place open.[34]

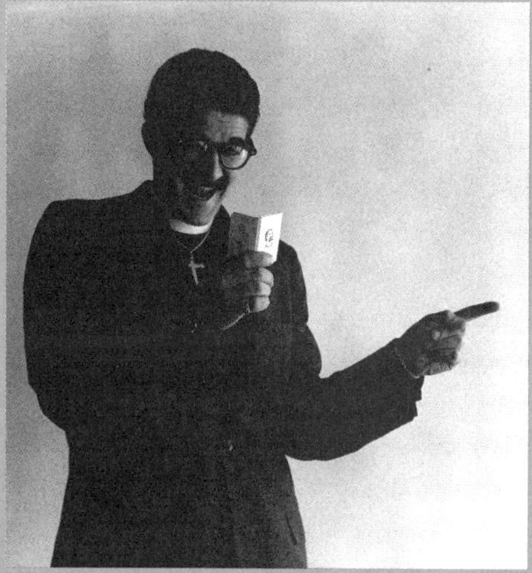

Berman opens the Semina Gallery in a roofless, abandoned houseboat near his home. Over the next year he presents a series of one day shows of work by George Herms, Charles Brittin, Edmund Teske, John Reed, and Artie Richer.

Shirley Berman:
It was a lovely shack on the water and it just looked wonderful with things hanging in it.[38]

Bob Alexander returns to San Francisco to remodel the jazz club, the Cellar, which was damaged in a fire. With assistance from Herms and Richer, Alexander reopens the club, which goes bankrupt after four months.

Suzi Hicks:
Baza was very unpredictable, and you never knew quite what you were getting into with him. The stress of opening the Jazz Cellar put him into a stupor of exhaustion—he was in very bad shape at that point.[35]

Alexander returns to Los Angeles from San Francisco and lives with Charles Brittin in Venice where he founds the Temple of Man, a nonsectarian center for poetry, jazz, and art.

Charles Brittin:
Bob Alexander used heroin off and on for years and he was somewhat sociopathic—he was enormously magnetic and creative and had lots of friends, but everything turned bad at one point and he became increasingly isolated. Bob was always a little menacing, and I never felt at ease with him because you never knew what he was going to do next.[36]

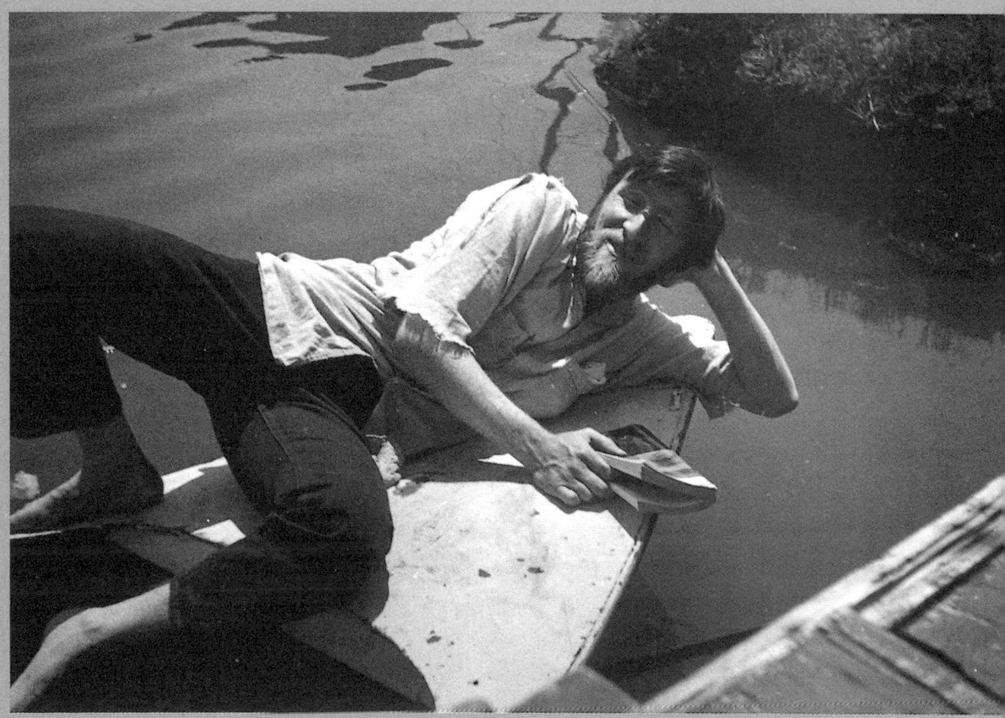

top right Bob Alexander, shortly after the founding of the Temple of Man in 1960, Photograph by Charles Brittin.

bottom right Wallace Berman in Larkspur, 1960, Photograph by Shirley Berman.

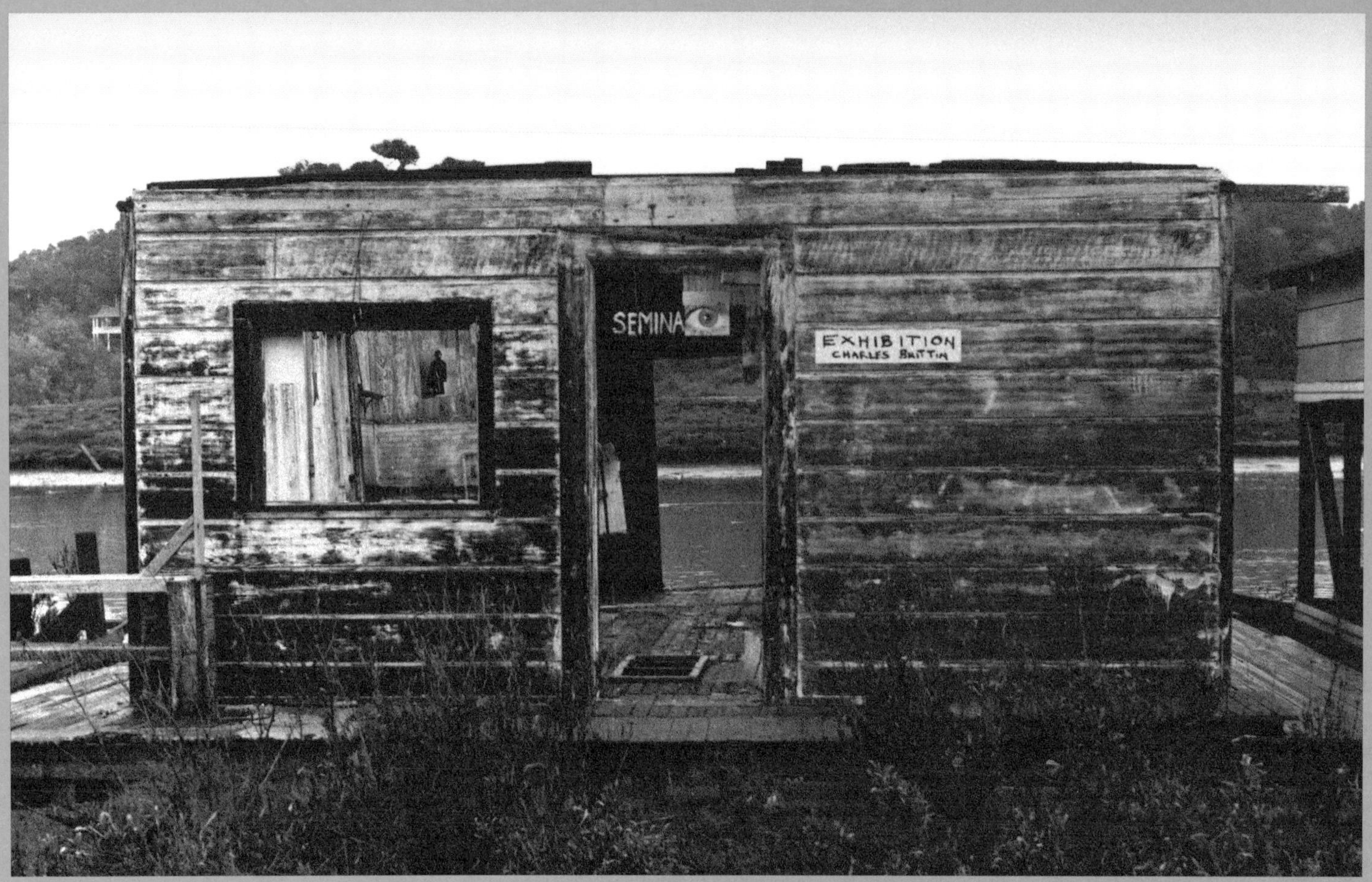

Berman publishes *Semina VI*, which comprises a single poem by Meltzer, entitled "The Clown." Several months later he completes *Semina 7* which features a still from the film *I Want to Live* on the cover. Dedicated to Shirley and Tosh Berman, the issue is devoted entirely to art and writings by Berman.

Tosh Berman:

My father was very much a product of his time. He read everything, and was always intrigued by the criminal element—probably because a life of crime is more interesting than the conventional lives most people lead. He really admired black culture and was fascinated by movements and 'isms' of every type. He wasn't judgmental of any of them, but he had no interest in aligning himself with any specific movement or trend, either. He was just interested. He picked up on everything that was out there and edited what he liked into his artwork.[39]

George Herms meets Edmund Teske in San Francisco and becomes a frequent subject of Teske's photographs.

Ralph Gibson begins working as an assistant to Dorothea Lange; he remains at the job for eighteen months.

Lawrence Jordan and Patty Topalian marry, move to Larkspur, and have a daughter, Lorna. Eighteen months later the family moves to San Anselmo.

Bill Margolis, overwrought from unrequited passion, leaps from a second-story window and is permanently paralyzed.

Kirby Doyle descends into a fog of drug addiction that lasts for five years.

Aya Tarlow divorces Elias Romero and begins taking photographs.

The Bermans meet Ray and Bonnie Bremser. Shortly before Christmas the Bremsers borrow money from Elaine deKooning and flee to Mexico to avoid another imprisonment for Ray. They spend several weeks in Mexico City with Philip Lamantia, who falls into a severe depression and decides to stop writing.

Lew Welch's *Wobbly Rock* is published by Auerhahn Press.

1961

The Bermans return to Crater Lane in June, as do the Jahrmarkts, who live down the hill from the Bermans.

Bobby Driscoll is arrested on a burglary charge and sentenced to six months at the State Narcotics Rehabilitation Center at Chino, California.

Taylor Mead's *Excerpts From the Anonymous Diary of a New York Youth* is published and he begins reading in Manhattan coffeehouses.

Ferus Gallery shows work by Altoon, DeFeo, and Foulkes.

John Wieners moves to New York, where his play, *Still-Life*, is staged at the New York Poets Theatre. He remains in Manhattan through 1963.

Ben Talbert begins his major assemblage, *The Ace*, and has his first solo show, at the Pasadena Art Museum.

Alexander Trocchi publishes a collection of short stories, *The Outsiders*.

Herms returns from San Francisco and lives in Topanga Canyon.

Semina Gallery, Larkspur, 1961, Photograph by Charles Brittin.

Henry Miller's *Tropic of Cancer* is finally published in the United States, after spending twenty-seven years as a banned book. The book is met by an enormous response, both favorable and unfavorable; trials are held across the country and Miller becomes the most litigated author in history.

Bruce Conner comes to Los Angeles to screen six short films at Sandlers, a sandal shop on Santa Monica Boulevard run by Bill House.

Charles Brittin:
Everyone showed up for that and everyone was comfortable with the films. There was a great deal of similarity in people's feelings in the Bay Area and the right circles in Southern California, and if something new happened, people in both places picked up on it quite rapidly and assimilated it without resistance.[40]

Russel Tamblyn stars in *West Side Story*.

While living in New York, poets **Diane DiPrima** (b. 1934, New York) and LeRoi Jones [Imamu Amiri Bararka] launch *The Floating Bear* (1961–71), a poetry newsletter. Subsequent issues are guest edited by Kirby Doyle and John Wieners. DiPrima and Jones, along with others, found the New York Poets Theater.

During a visit to San Francisco, DiPrima meets Robert Duncan at McClure's apartment.

Diane DiPrima:
Robert was clearly not very interested in meeting me. And at one point, I was barely awake, I went over to the window and started brushing my hair, which was very, very long and very, very red. All of a sudden Robert looked up and said "You have the most beautiful hair I've ever seen! Will you come to lunch?"

Robert was probably one of the closest, most intimate lovers I ever had, even though we never had a physical relationship. One thing I learned from him was how precious my life was. How precious the whole ambience of time. A sense of appreciating every minute. Something about this ineffable quality of time and the energy that was there—I can't describe it.[41]

Bruce Conner makes the film, *Cosmic Ray*, using music by Ray Charles. Later in the year the Conners move to Mexico, where Jean gives birth to a son.

David Meltzer, Michael McClure, and Lawrence Ferlinghetti begin publication of *Journal for the Protection of All Beings: A Visionary and Revolutionary Review* (1961–1978).

In the fall Ray Bremser returns to prison (first Trenton State, then Rahway), where he remains for four years. Bremser becomes addicted to heroin while at Rahway.

Llyn Foulkes has his first solo show at Ferus Gallery.

Jack Hirschman (b. New York, 1933) arrives in L.A. to teach at UCLA and meets Berman at a benefit for the magazine, *Coastlines*, at a house in Santa Monica Canyon.

Jack Hirschman:
If you came to Southern California and you were an artist who identified with a certain avant gardism, then you had to see Wallace Berman. Wallace was basically a poet who expressed himself through collage and montage, and he was an outsider—he once told me he regarded himself as a Yiddish Indian. Wally was always right at the center of things, and there was a hipness about him that was always there. He had this really marvelous charisma that was partly attributable to his involvement with the world of jazz, which was the culture of hipsterism, and that's where Wally came from. But he wasn't just some long-haired, fly-by-night hipster—he was a guy who created his own language, and it combined the most ancient languages and the most modern images, images that haunted and upset and involved him. He got a lot of images from television. He'd watch television and then draw images that were counter to television. The word Kabbalah means "reception" and receiving was important to Wallace—he kept the channels open at all times. He loved Cocteau's film, Orpheus, and there's a scene in that film involving a radio that meant a lot to him. The notion of radio reception is a key part of understanding Wallace's work.

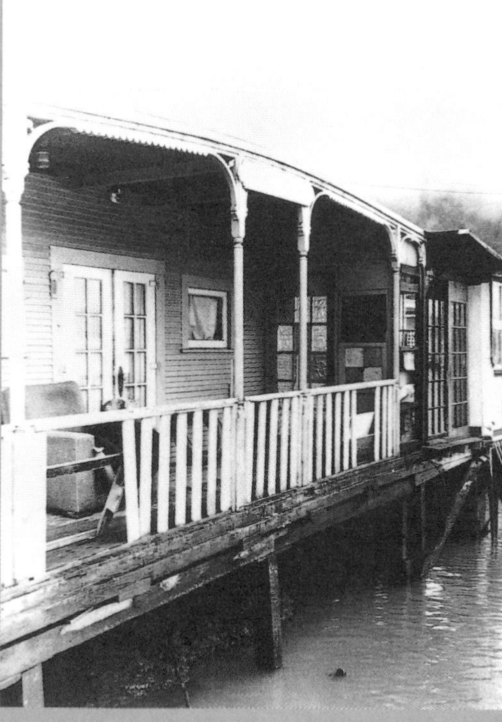

Wallace was conscious of his role as a leader and was aware of the charismatic force he could exert. He always tried to give the impression that he knew less than he actually knew, and he was able to project coolness in a way others could not. I don't mean the coolness of being cold, because he was a very warm and loving guy—he was a real lover. But he could project a certain kind of hip wisdom about virtually anything. He wasn't an intellectual, but he was very quick, and he loved mystery. The notion of the muse was very important to Wally, too, and Shirley was a huge source of inspiration for him.[42]

The Berman family houseboat—called a "wogglebug," Larkspur, 1961, Photograph by Charles Brittin.

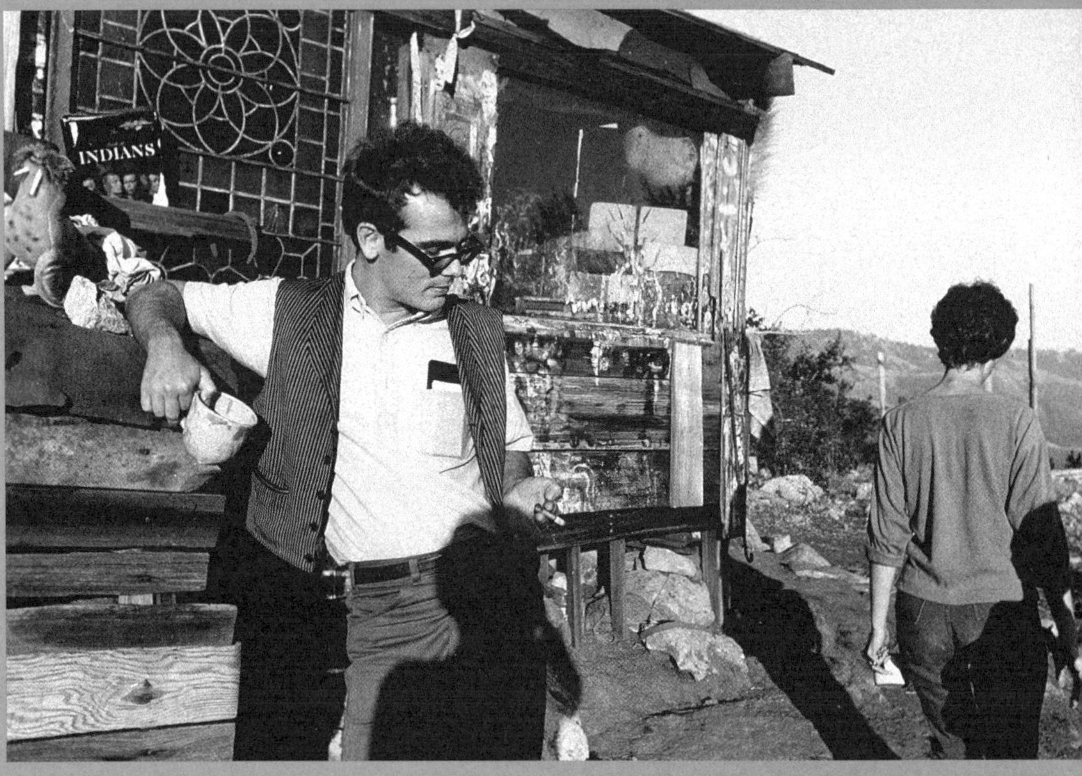

1962

On Sept. 25 Diane DiPrima arrives from New York with her two daughters to stay with the Bermans for a few weeks. Previously acquainted only by mail—DiPrima traded copies of *The Floating Bear* for issues of *Semina*—DiPrima and Berman meet for the first time when he picks her up at the airport.

Diane DiPrima:

Wallace Berman was there to greet us: an apparition like nothing I had ever seen… There was a softness about him— not a gay quality, just a soft female/maleness I couldn't place. I found it disorienting and attractive all at once.[43]

Herms collaborates with Lawrence Jordan on the film *Jewelface*.

Ferus Gallery shows work by Bruce Conner and John Altoon.

Taylor Mead appears in Adolfas Mekas's *Halleluja the Hills*.

Tom Leavitt, Director of the Pasadena Museum of Art, hires Hopps as Curator; following Leavitt's departure a few months later, Hopps becomes Director of the museum.

Stockwell stars in the film version of Eugene O'Neill's *Long Day's Journey into Night*.

Jack Hirschman:

The Dean you see in movies is not the Dean I know. Obviously, he's one of the great actors of his generation, but what you see him do in movies is only a small portion of how talented he is. Dean has one of the best graphic eyes of anyone you'll ever meet—in fact, he did the cover for one of my books—and Russ Tamblyn has a great eye as well. They're known as actors, but in fact, they're visual artists.[44]

Billy Gray is arrested for possession of a few marijuana seeds.

Auerhahn Press publishes Meltzer's tribute to Kenneth Patchen, *We All Have Something to Say to Each Other.*

Charles Brittin and his third wife, Barbara, join CORE; for the remainder of the decade they devote themselves to civil rights, the anti-war movement, and the Black Panthers.

Diane DiPrima marries Alan Marlowe at a Buddhist temple in San Francisco. The McClures, the Jahrmarkts, Kirby Doyle, and DiDi Morrill attend. Three weeks later the newlyweds move to Topanga Canyon.

Bobby Driscoll is arrested on drug charges and sent to jail.

Gibson moves to Beverly Glen and becomes friends with the Bermans.

Joe Dunn's amphetamine use results in his being committed to a hospital for the criminally insane; Graham MacKintosh takes over White Rabbit Press.

Auerhahn Press publishes Philip Lamantia's *Destroyed Works* with a cover collage by Bruce Conner.

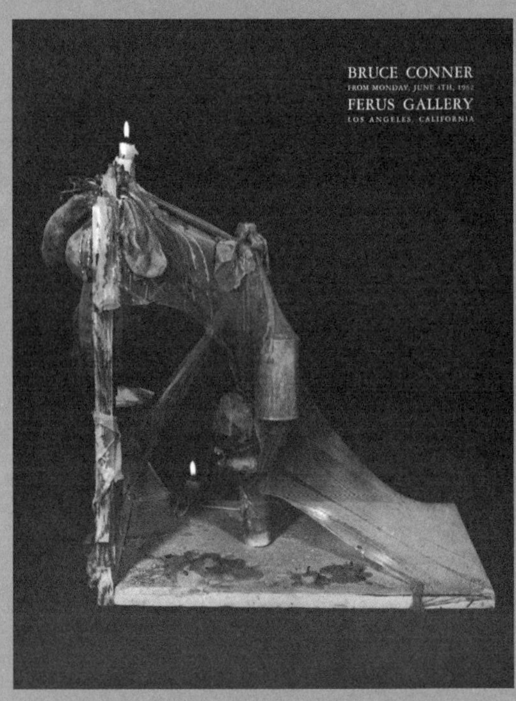

top Dean Stockwell and Shirley Berman in Big Sur, c. 1962, Photograph by Wallace Berman.

bottom Poster for Bruce Conner exhibition at Ferus Gallery, 1961.

opposite page Russel Tamblyn and Dean Stockwell on the set of *Another Day at the Races* (directed by Richard Bailey), 1975.

1963

While visiting Diane DiPrima in Topanga, New York dancer Freddie Herko meets DiDi Morrill. The two fall in love and go to New York together, leaving behind a highly distraught Kirby Doyle. By the end of the year Morrill's relationship with Herko has ended, and she returns to Los Angeles where she begins living with Bobby Driscoll. A few months later Bob Alexander officiates at their wedding at Beverly and Zack Walsh's house on Lisbon Lane.

Bob Kaufman retreats from public life and takes a twelve-year vow of silence after watching John Kennedy's funeral on television. He doesn't speak again until the end of the Vietnam War.

Baza Press publishes Aya Tarlow's *Marks of Asha*.

Jack Smith's film, *Flaming Creatures*, wins the Independent Film Award and becomes a cause celebre in the censorship wars. John Fles arranges a Los Angeles screening of the film at the Cinema Theater. While Smith is in town he screens his first film, a three-minute short titled *Scotch Tape*, at the Berman house in Beverly Glen.

Andy Warhol shoots scenes from *Tarzan and Jane Regained, Sort of…* in the Bermans' yard at Beverly Glen. Wallace and Tosh Berman appear in the film, which stars Taylor Mead.

Gerard Malanga
(artist and Warhol collaborator):
Taylor had this idea for a movie based on Tarzan and when we all came to Los Angeles for Andy's show of the Elvis and Elizabeth Taylor paintings at the Ferus Gallery, we decided to shoot the film in the area where the original Tarzan movies were actually shot. We had a Bolex camera we took with us everywhere we went and everything was done in a very spontaneous spirit. The film was shot in a number of locations and one of them happened to be when we were visiting the Bermans. Wally's profile in New York was very underground at that point—I don't think too many people knew about his work. Artists in New York are so stupid and self-centered that if you mentioned Wally Berman today to any upcoming artists in New York, I guarantee they wouldn't know who he was.[45]

Ferus Gallery shows work by Jay DeFeo.

Toni Basil begins living with Dean Stockwell and becomes friends with the Bermans.

George Herms collaborates with Dean Stockwell on the film *Moonstone*. Herms then moves to Mill Creek in Northern California, where he builds a house with the help of Paul Beattie. Arthur Richer joins them briefly. Herms begins printing books on a hand-press.

Bruce Conner begins work on two films about the Kennedy assassination, one of which is titled *Report*.

Berman publishes *Semina 8* which is dedicated to musician Wardell Gray and includes McClure's poem, "Ghost Tantra."

Walter Hopps organizes a Duchamp retrospective, "By or of Marcel Duchamp or Rrose Selavy," at the Pasadena Museum.

Taylor Mead appears in Ron Rice's *The Queen of Sheba Meets the Atom Man.*

Bob Alexander opens a printing shop at 3303 Sunset Boulevard. He and his second wife, Anita Alexander, live on Hyperion Blvd. in Silverlake, where John Altoon is a neighbor.

Dennis Hopper and Cameron appear in *Night Tide*, directed by Curtis Harrington.

The Beattie family moves to Healdsberg.

Berman meets **Russel Tamblyn** (b. 1934, Los Angeles).

Russel Tamblyn:
I was living this bland, rich life in a big house in Pacific Palisades with a swimming pool and a bowling alley, and Wallace and Shirley came to a party I had for Henry Miller. Wallace and Shirley were extremely quiet at the party—Wallace could be very shy in a crowd—but a few days later I got a copy of Semina *in the mail from him and an invitation to visit him at Crater Lane. I went to see him, and he showed me a film he was working on, and it had such an enormous impact on me that I began to weep. I felt like I'd never seen anything so profound. I'd already begun to turn away from show business because it had come to seem empty to me, but meeting Wallace was the catalyst that made me completely change my life. I was looking for something deeper, and Wallace was a mentor and a father figure to me, and I think he was that for Dean, too. Dean and I had been friends since 1948, when we were both in* The Boy With Green Hair.

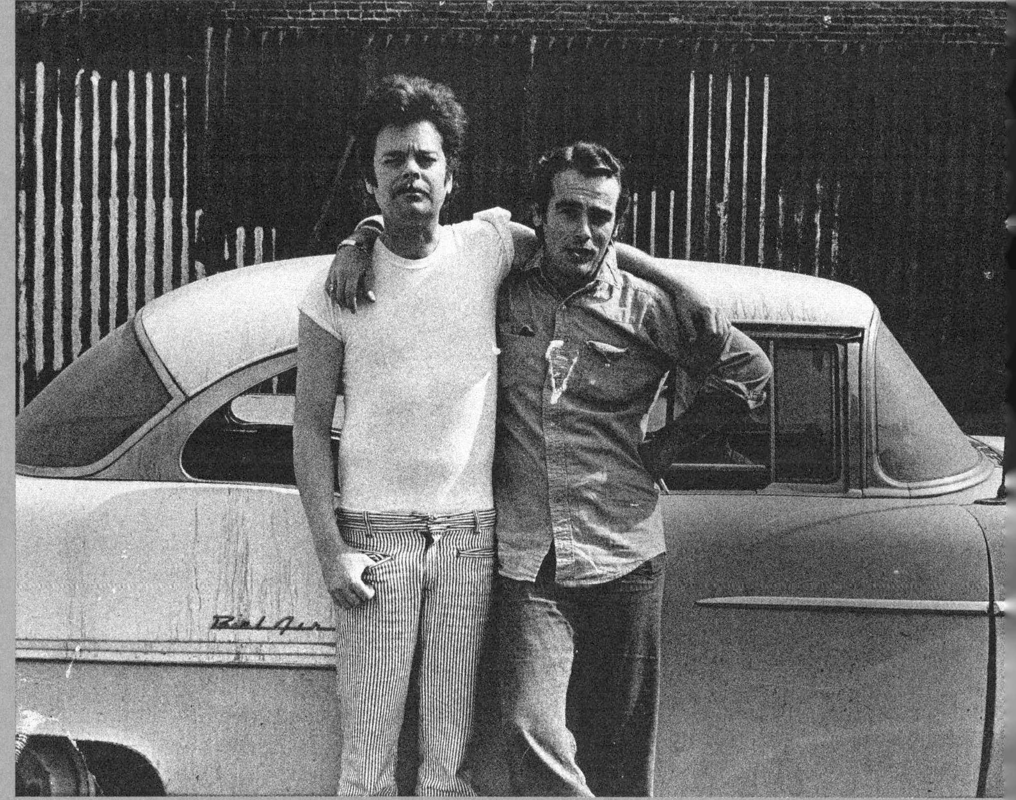

Wallace had this capacity to show you to a door, open it, and let you take it from there, and he had a tremendous aura about him—more than anyone I've ever met. Working in movies I've met a lot of movie stars, and I was friends with lots of them, but I never met anyone with the sort of aura Wallace had. He had a way of inspiring people to channel their energies into something creative without telling them to do this or that. You could see his eyes light up when he saw a spark of creativity in you and it made you want to do more for him. We were once at a party together, and afterwards I said to him, "God, those people were just sitting at your feet," and Wallace replied "Yeah, wait until they find out what I'm really like." The humility reflected in that statement was part of what made him great.[46]

Charles Brittin begins working for Charles and Ray Eames; he remains at the Eames office until 1970.

Lew Welch leaves Lenore Kandel and begins living in isolation in Big Sur where his alcoholism worsens dramatically. A few months later he moves to a cabin in the Trinity Alps.

After returning to New York, Diane DiPrima founds Poet's Press (1963–69). Poet's Press books include seven volumes of DiPrima's poetry, as well as books by Kirby Doyle, Robert Duncan, and Michael McClure.

Philip Lamantia moves to Spain where he studies philosophy and esoterica until 1968.

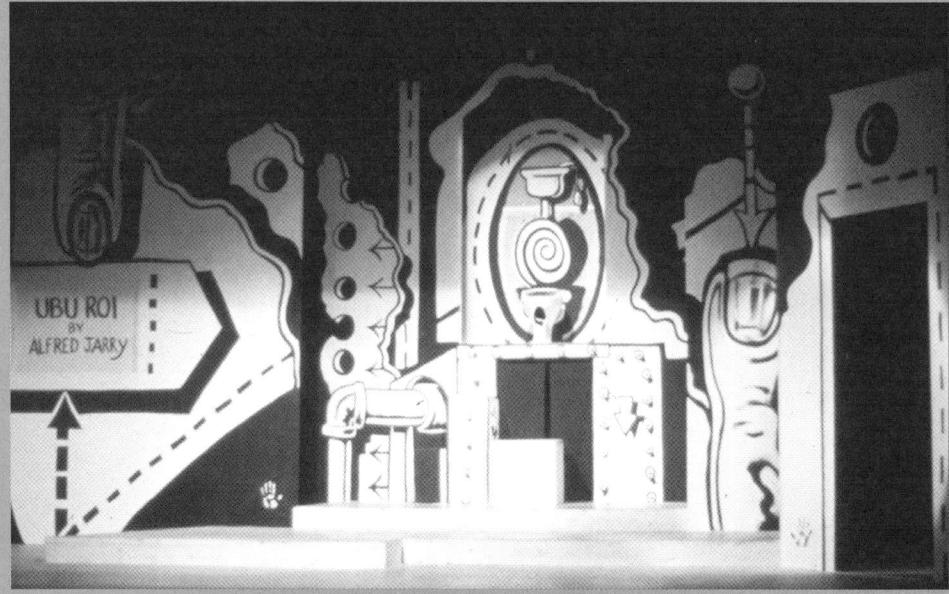

1964

Berman acquires an 8mm Bolex camera and begins work on a film. He also designs the cover for McClure's *Ghost Tantras*, and makes posters for the second and third annual Los Angeles Film-Makers Festivals, organized by John Fles and presented at the Cinema Theater on Western Avenue.

Bobby Driscoll and DiDi Morrill travel to New York for a drug deal that goes bad, forcing them to flee to Montreal. Morrill is on Canada's wanted list for the next fifteen years.

Taylor Mead stars in Robert Downey's *Babo 73*.

Berman publishes *Semina 9* which features a Michael McClure poem and a cover photograph of the shooting of Lee Harvey Oswald.

Lew Welch returns to San Francisco and moves in with Magda Cregg.

Berman begins working in a small studio owned by Billy Jahrmarkt, who gives him a copying machine which he uses to create a series of Verifax collages.

Jack Smith visits Los Angeles to serve as a judge in the Third Los Angeles Film-Makers Festival. While in town he lectures at California State College, Los Angeles, and becomes embroiled in a contretemps with Kenneth Anger, who takes issue with the Festival's screening of his 1954 film, *Inauguration of the Pleasure Dome*.

The Los Angeles Free Press begins publication and features photographs by Charles Brittin on a regular basis.

Ben Talbert designs costumes, posters, and sets for a production of the Alfred Jarry play, *Ubu Roi*, presented at the Coronet Theater and directed by Mark Estrin.

David Meltzer begins study of the Kabbalah and founds Tree Books, which publishes previously unavailable texts on Jewish mysticism.

Toni Basil choreographs *The T.A.M.I. Show*, a pop music variety show staged at the Santa Monica Civic Auditorium, produced by Phil Spector, and recorded in a film given a theatrical release. Basil invites Berman to attend the rehearsal.

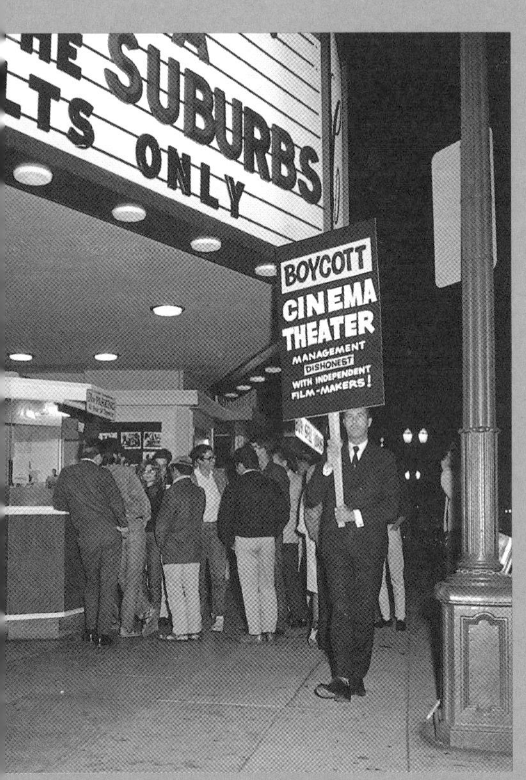

top **Ubu Roi**, a production of the Alfred Jarry play at the Coronet Louvre Theater, with sets by Ben Talbert, 1964.

bottom left Kenneth Anger pickets the Third Los Angeles Film-Makers Festival, 1964. Photograph by Charles Brittin.

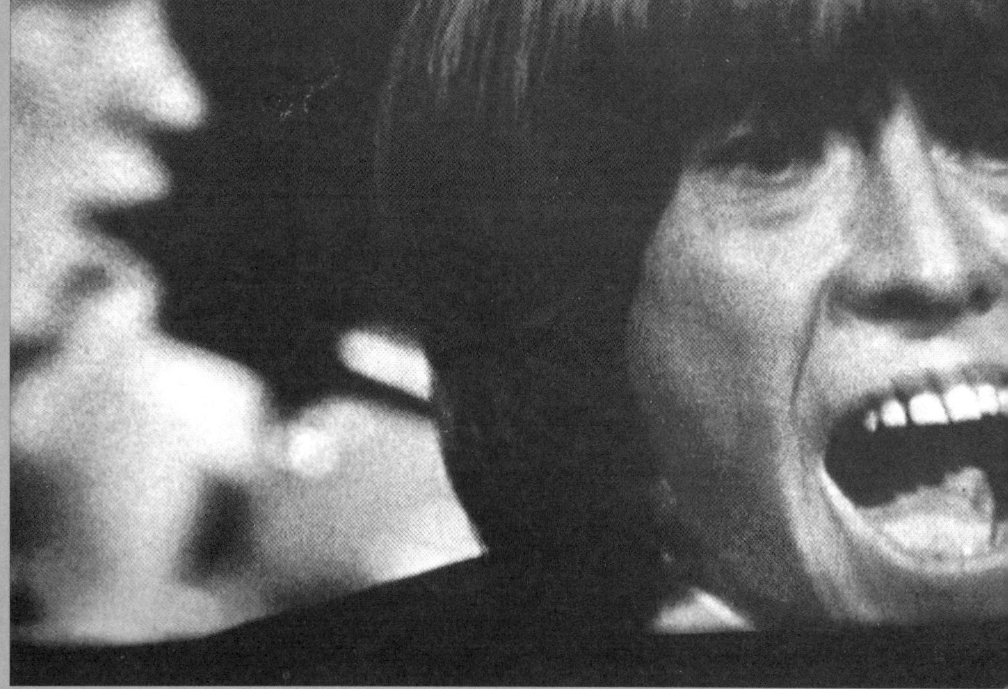

Tosh Berman:
Around that time my dad had an 8mm camera that he carried everywhere he went, and he took the camera and me to the rehearsal. The Supremes were there that day, and we met Mick Jagger and Brian Jones, who struck up a friendship with my father that lasted until Brian died in 1969. We were invited to stay for the show but my father wanted to leave, and although he could've shot film at the rehearsal, he preferred to shoot film of the concert when he saw it a few months later on a movie screen. My dad loved Phil Spector's music and he made a piece for him called You've Lost That Lovin' Feeling. *Phil heard about it and he came to my dad's studio. It was quite dramatic. He arrived at Crater Lane in a limousine with Ronnie Spector and a cane—there he was, a little guy with a cane. My dad liked him a lot.*[47]

George Herms makes films with Paul Beattie, then spends three months in New York working with Freddie Herko and designing sets for McClure's play, *The Blossom or Billy the Kid*, at the American Theater for Poets. He returns to Mill Creek where he makes a film with Jahrmarkt before moving back to Topanga Canyon.

Kirby Doyle goes to New York and begins living with Freddie Herko in an apartment dubbed the Opulent Tower, where they both regularly shoot speed. In October, Herko performs a dance in the living room of his friend, Johnny Dodd, which culminates in his leaping through an open window to his death.

Robert Wilson and James F. Carr publish John Wieners's second book, *Ace of Pentacles*.

Russel Tamblyn moves to Topanga.

1965

Llyn Foulkes begins playing drums in the rock band City Lights, a group he stays with until 1971.

Alexander Trocchi organizes a poetry reading at London's Albert Hall that introduces the work of Ginsberg, Ferlinghetti, and others to a large British audience.

Ben Talbert has a breakdown and moves in with his psychiatrist in a communal home in Topanga. While there he meets Gayle Davis, an exotic dancer who begins supporting him.

Wieners enrolls at the State University of New York at Buffalo for a period of study with Charles Olson that lasts for two years.

Paper Book Gallery publishes Ray Bremser's *Poems of Madness*.

The Conners return to San Francisco from Massachusetts where they'd gone at the invitation of Timothy Leary.

Bruce Conner documents the removal of DeFeo's *The Rose* from her Fillmore Street studio in the film, *The White Rose*.

Arthur Richer dies of a drug overdose at his home in Healdsburg. Later in the year his wife, Betty Richer, also dies. The four Richer children are separated and spend the remainder of their childhoods in different homes.

Dave Haselwood Books publishes *Dream Table, 30 Cards*, and *Unto Caesar* by Michael McClure, and John Wieners' *Chinoiserie*.

Brian Jones and Keith Richards visit Berman in Beverly Glen.

Tosh Berman:
Brian Jones was usually alone when he visited my father, but one time he was with Keith Richards—I remember that night vividly because they looked like perfect pop stars. They were both wearing velvet suits and frilly silk shirts, and they were like walking drugstores—they had compartments in their clothes where various drugs were stashed. Brian really admired my father—not just his artwork, but as a personality—and he was always a perfect gentleman when he visited.[48]

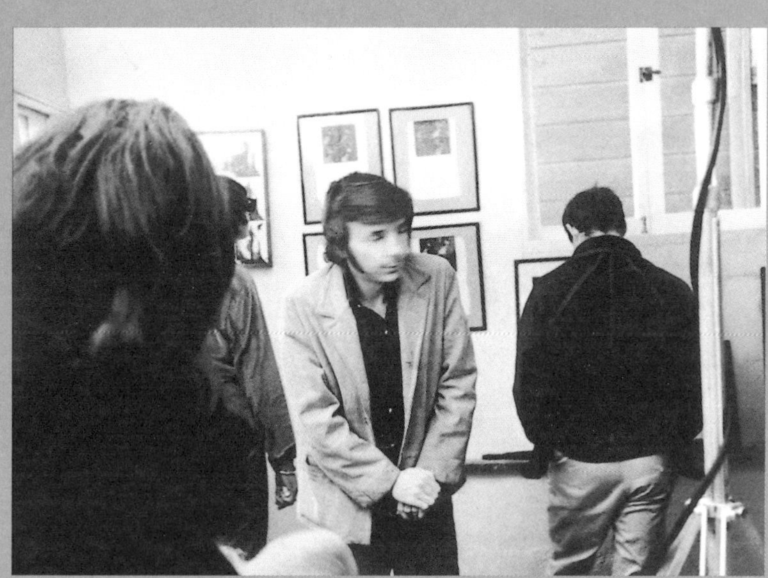

bottom Phil Spector at an exhibition of Wallace Berman's work in his Beverly Glen studio, 1965, Photograph by Wallace Berman.

top Brian Jones in a scene from *The T.A.M.I. Show*, a concert produced by Phil Spector and presented at the Santa Monica Civic Auditorium in 1964, Photograph by Wallace Berman, shot from a movie screen.

Bob Kaufman's *Solitudes Crowded With Loneliness* is published by New Directions.

Berman exhibits his Verifax work from Oct. 10–17 at his Beverly Glen studio.

Dennis Hopper:
I visited Wallace shortly after he started working with the Verifax machine, and I bought the first piece he made with it—a great work called Scope. *Around that time [British dealer] Robert Fraser was visiting Los Angeles and was staying with [Hopper's first wife] Brooke and me, and I took Robert to see Wallace. During that visit Robert bought that great piece,* Papa's Got a Brand New Bag, *and talked about showing Wallace's work in London.*[49]

The Brittins spend three months in the deep south under the auspices of CORE, assisting local black communities in their struggle for civil rights.

Lew Welch's *Hermit Poems* is published by the Four Seasons Foundation. Oyez publishes Welch's *On Out*.

In December, the Berman house is destroyed in a mud slide that results in the loss of hundreds of Berman's photographic negatives, along with artworks by Jess, Joan Brown, Manuel Neri, Ed Moses, and John Altoon. The Bermans temporarily stay with the Jahrmarkts, then move into a Topanga Canyon house that Stockwell buys for them.

Tosh Berman:
It was pouring down rain that day and my dad left to get a passport. My mom and I were in the house when we heard what sounded like huge rocks falling on the house. We went outside to see what was going on, and within seconds the house disappeared down the hill. The house was completely in splinters, and when my father came back and saw it he fainted because he assumed my mother and I were dead.[50]

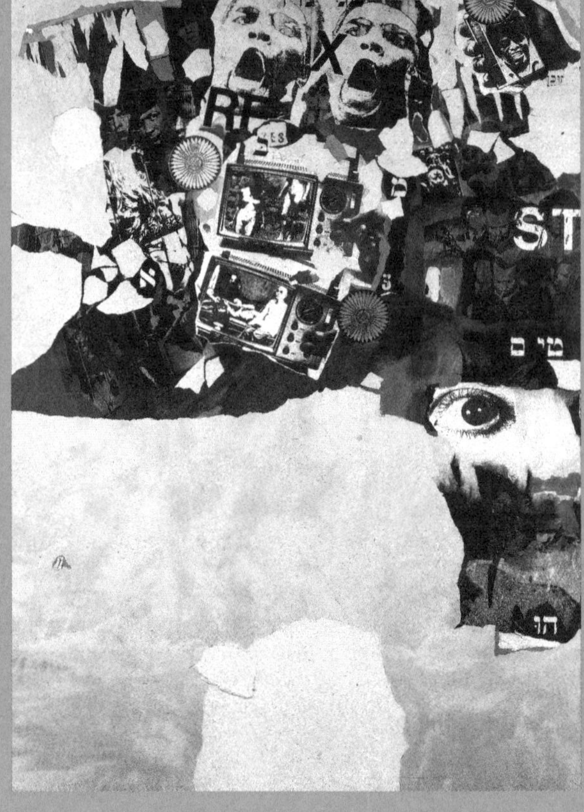

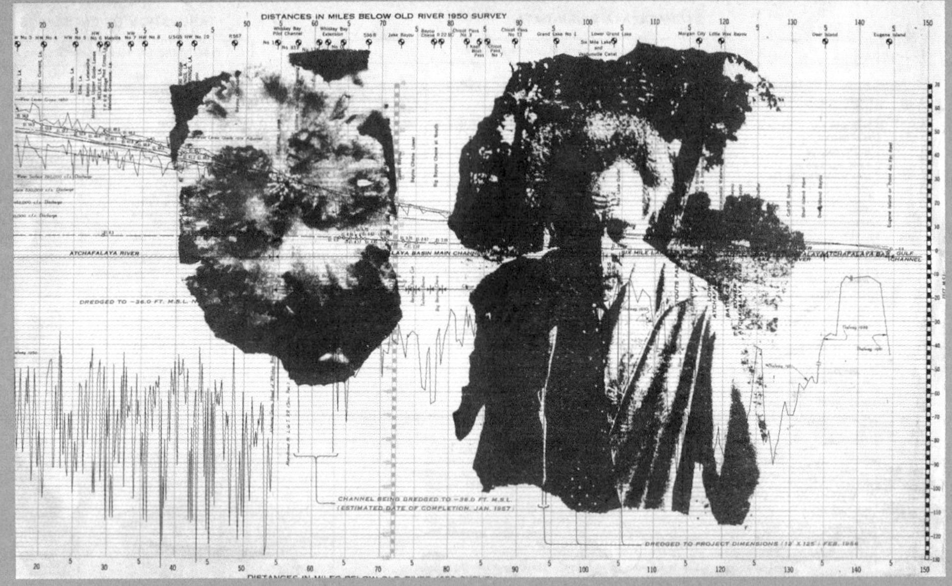

1966

Berman, Jess, Conner and Foulkes are included in "Los Angeles Now," an exhibition that runs from Jan. 31–Feb. 19 at the Robert Fraser Gallery in London.

Aya Tarlow's play, *The Edge*, is staged at the Open Theater in Berkeley.

Ray Bremser is released from prison after serving time on an armed robbery charge. Six months after his release he kicks heroin and begins drinking heavily. The Bremsers move to Central America, where their second daughter, Georgia, is born the following year.

Instant Theater closes.

Walter Hopps has a breakdown and is hospitalized for several weeks to address his amphetamine addiction.

top Wallace Berman, *Papa's Got a Brand New Bag*, 1965, Verifax collage.

bottom Wallace Berman, *Cocteau Verifax Transfer*, 1972.

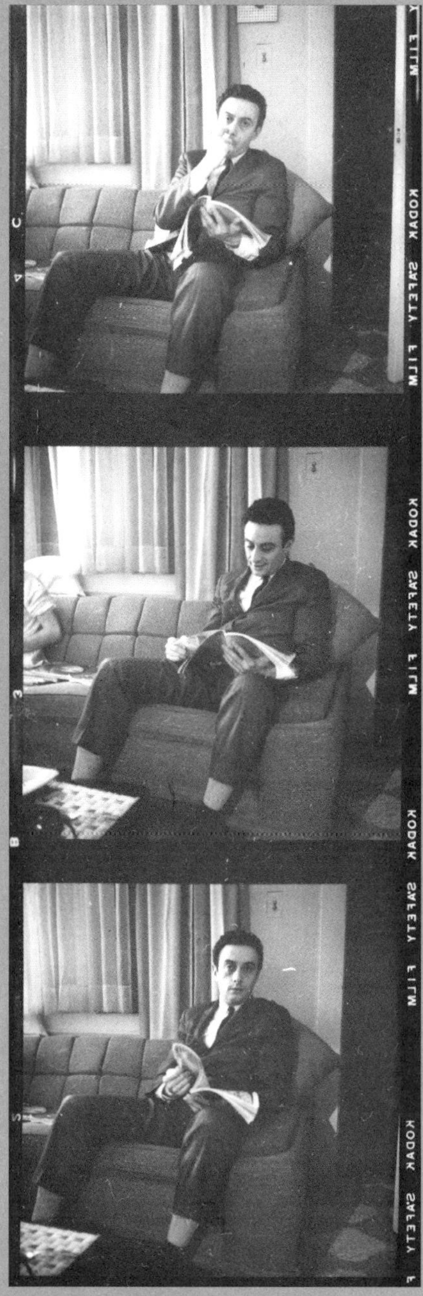

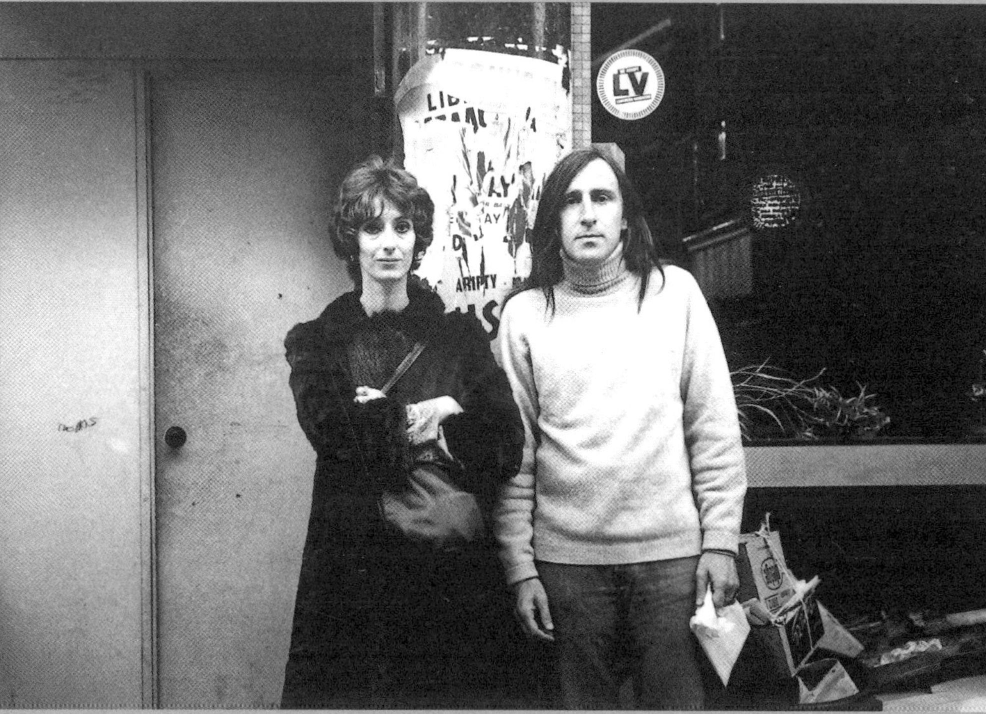

Ralph Gibson moves to New York and works as an assistant to Robert Frank on Frank's films, *Me and My Brother*, and *Conversations in Vermont*.

Lenny Bruce dies of a drug overdose on August 3.

Oyez Press publishes Philip Lamantia's *Touch of the Marvelous*.

Jack Hirschman is fired from UCLA for his involvement in the anti-war movement. He moves to Venice where he lives through 1972.

Artists' Workshop Press publishes John Wieners's *Hart Crane, Harry Crosby, I See You Going Over the Edge*.

Lew Welch
(in a letter to Allen Ginsberg, July 27, 1960): *The saddest thing of all is to see a great temperment (sic), such as Hart Crane's, come to the very lip of this thing—and then do what is so breathtakingly close to the final right action, yet, and because of its closeness, so wrong as to make all the agony go for nothing. Suicide is the last resort of the baby-built accident.... And that is what breaks our heart about Crane and all the many others—to see what was, despite all, so beautiful, become at the last instant so horrible.* [51]

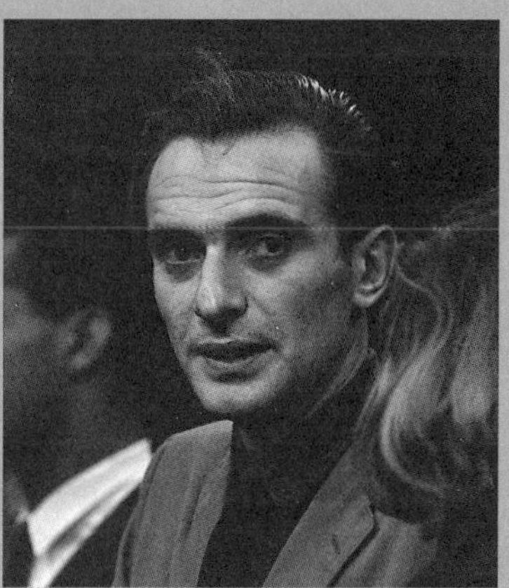

1967

Berman holds a second private exhibition of Verifax collages in Topanga on Feb. 26. During the summer, the Bermans spend three weeks in London where they stay in Robert Fraser's apartment.

Shirley Berman:
Robert was a wonderful person and Wallace really liked him a lot. Robert suggested that Wallace show at his gallery and Wallace was really excited about taking his work to Europe. Robert was supposed to pick us up at the airport but he didn't show up, so we took a taxi to his gallery. We were stopped at a light and we looked over in the car next to us, and there was Robert in a car with the Stones on the way to jail.[52]

Berman is included in the collaged group portrait designed by Peter Blake for the Beatles's album, *Sgt. Pepper's Lonely Hearts Club Band*. While in London, Berman visits Alexander Trocchi.

left Lenny Bruce, Venice, 1957, Photographs by Charles Brittin.

right Wallace and Shirley Berman, London, 1967, Photograph by Tosh Berman.

bottom Jack Hirschman, Los Angeles, 1962, Photograph by Charles Brittin.

1968

Berman has exhibitions at the Los Angeles County Museum of Art and the Jewish Museum in New York.

Taylor Mead appears in Andy Warhol's *Lonesome Cowboys.* His second book, *On Amphetamine and in Europe*, is published by Boss Books.

Walter Hopps is named Director of the Corcoran Gallery in Washington, D.C.

Bobby Driscoll dies of a heroin overdose. His badly decomposed body is found in an abandoned tenement on New York's Lower East Side.

Meltzer begins a series of pornographic novels, published by Essex House, that he refers to as "agit-smut." He completes ten over the next two years. Later in the year, he and Tina Meltzer release their first album, *Serpent Power*, on Vanguard Records.

Kirby Doyle publishes his first novel, *Happiness Bastard*, which was written nearly a decade earlier on long sheets of paper pasted together to form a single roll.

Nova Broadcast Press publishes Ray Bremser's *Drive Suite*.

Stuart Perkoff is arrested on drug charges and incarcerated at Terminal Island Federal Penitentiary until 1971.

Bob Alexander begins working for the Los Angeles Free Press.

Tosh Berman:
I was twelve years old that summer, and when we visited Trocchi in his flat he shot up in front of me. My dad didn't say a word. I'd never seen anything like that before—his arm was totally a mess—but he was very talkative and charismatic.[53]

Bob Alexander and the Temple of Man sponsor a benefit for Idell Romero's Magic Theater at the Topanga Corral. Berman does a poster for the event, Herms designs the announcement, and Elias Romero creates a light show.

Rachel Rosenthal begins a two-year period of studying ceramics with artist John Mason; she exhibits her sculpture frequently for the remainder of the 1960s.

Emmett Grogan's Digger's Communication Company publishes Kirby Doyle's second novel, *Angel Faint*. Doyle stops writing for a period of thirteen years and lives a life of solitude in the California wilderness.

John Wieners's *Pressed Wafer* is published. Devastated by the betrayal of a lover, Wieners begins a downward spiral of depression and substance abuse that continues until 1969 when he enters a mental institution.

Walter Hopps resigns from the Pasadena Museum and accepts a fellowship at the Institute for Policy Studies, a liberal think tank in Washington, D.C.

Tompkins Square Press publishes Ray Bremser's prose poem, *Angel*.

Bruce Conner stops creating assemblages and shifts his focus to film, drawing, and painting.

Berman begins making sculpture from found rocks, and creating site specific paintings on rocks and walls.

Bob Kaufman's second book of poems, *The Golden Sardine*, is published.

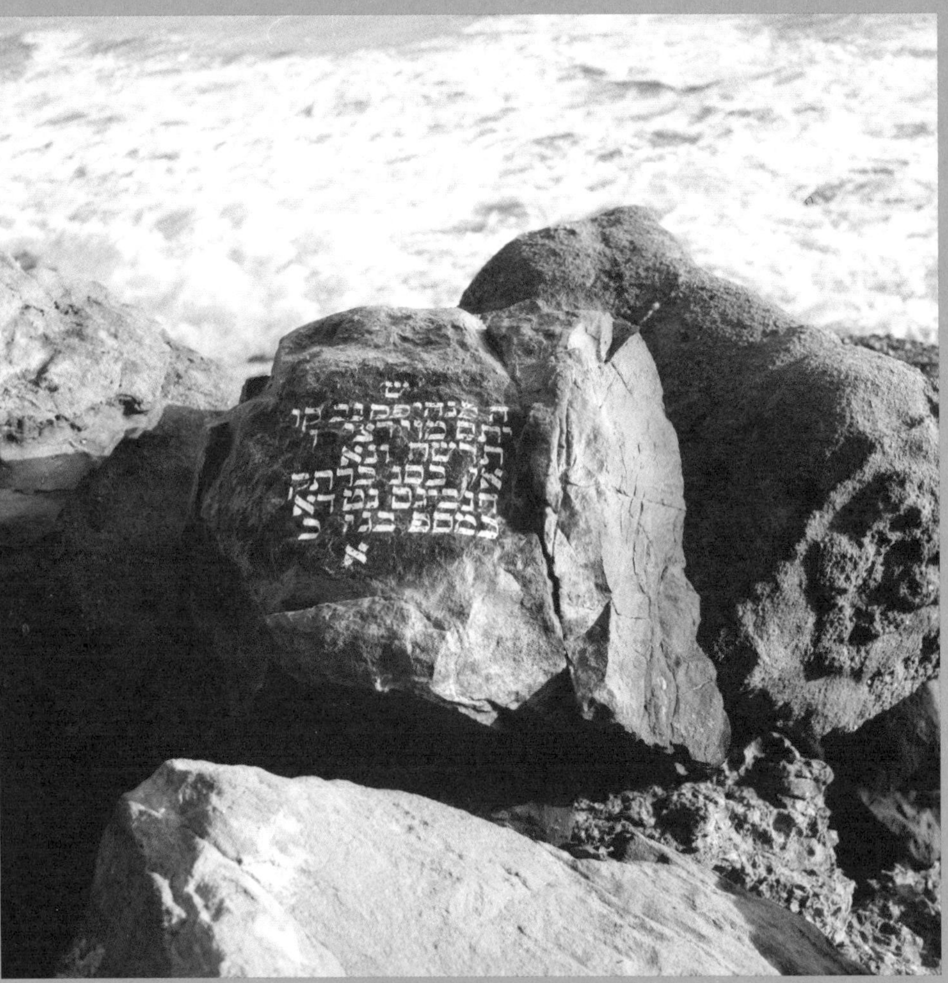

Site specific work combining Hebrew letters and found rocks by Wallace Berman. Early 1970s. Photograph by Wallace Berman.

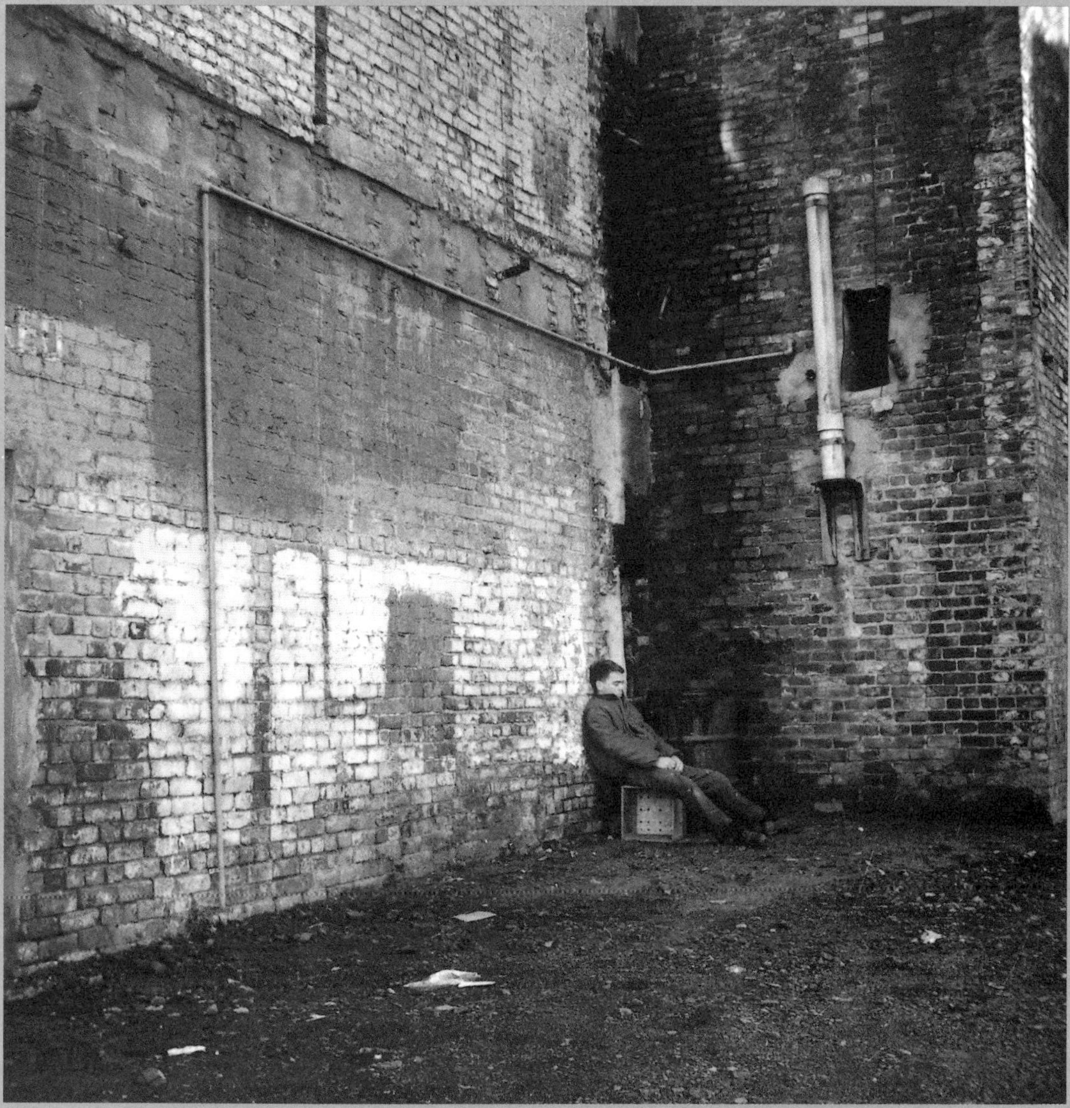

1969

Frontier Press publishes *The Surge*, by Michael McClure.

Herms and Wallace and Shirley Berman appear in *Easy Rider* directed by Dennis Hopper.

Lew Welch's *The Song Mt. Tamalpais Sings* is published.

John Altoon dies of a heart attack.

While the Bremsers are living in Central America, Croton Press publishes Bonnie Bremser's *Troia: Mexican Memoir*, an account of her experiences in Mexico with Ray on the run from the law. She leaves Ray for a ballet dancer and Ray Bremser returns to the U.S. in poor health.

Ray Bremser
(In a letter to Ginsberg, Oct. 29, 1969):
Dear Allen: Bonnie has left me &
the State Department flew me to Miami—
I'm destitute & in a bit of trouble—
my mother is dead. You are my only
friend; so forgive me for imposing again—
I need some money to pay fines for
drunk/disorderly & breaking the peace.
$150 would cover it, and the fare to
New York—I'd never be able to get thru
Georgia & the Carolinas in my shape—
had an accident in Guatemala,
broken shoulder, 4 ribs, elbow, little finger
& sprains. Please help me return to
New York. I'll pay you back
because I'm going to work when I'm back
in the city. Necessary you send money
orders, if possible! Let me know soon—
sorry again, but desperate. Hope you are
well, I'm anxious to see & hear you again.
Best love, Ray[54]

Bremser goes to Ginsberg's farm in upstate New York to recuperate, and Bonnie joins him there in 1970. He continues to live with Ginsberg and Orlovsky until 1974, when he and Bonnie break up for good.

Ralph Gibson founds Lustrum Press. In 1970 he publishes the first book of his own photographs, *The Somnambulist*. In 1971 he publishes Larry Clark's legendary book, *Tulsa*.

Diane DiPrima publishes *Memoirs of a Beatnik*.

Berman creates cover art for issue #37 of *The Floating Bear*, Hirschman's *Black Alephs*, and McClure's *Hymns to St. Geryon & Other Poems*.

Bruce Conner completes the film, *Permian Strata*.

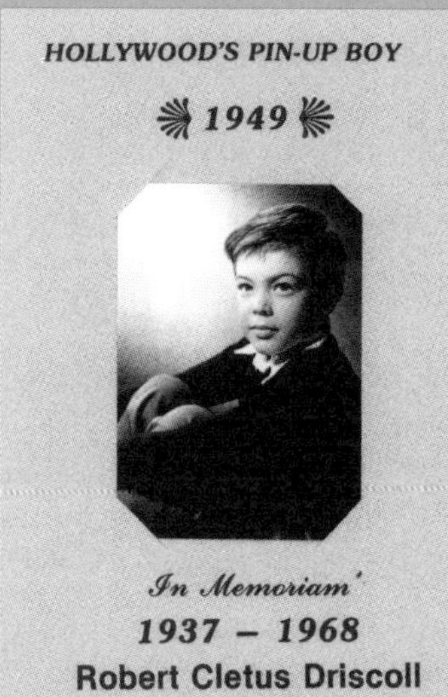

topt Bobby Driscoll in San Francisco, 1959. Photograph by Wallace Berman.

bottom right Memorial card, 1968.

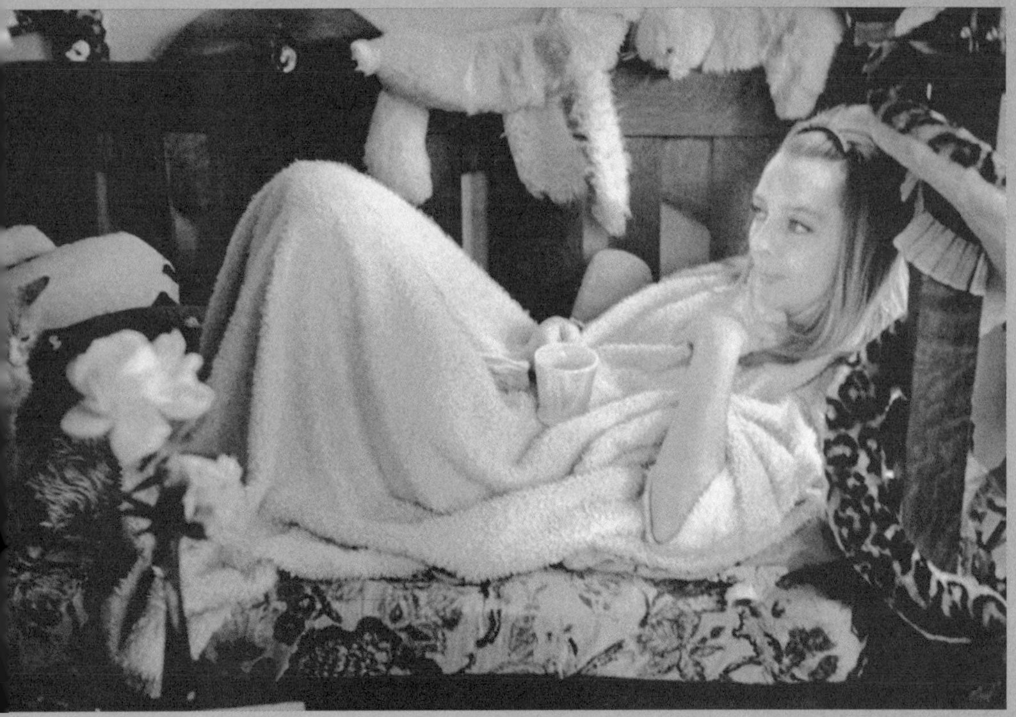

1971

Lew Welch and Magda Cregg separate, and Welch moves to land in the California mountains owned by Gary Snyder and Allen Ginsberg. In May, Welch takes his pistol and disappears into the woods. Snyder goes looking for him and finds a note among the litter of empty beer cans:

I never could make anything work out right
and now I'm betraying my friends.
I can't make anything of it—
never could. I had great visions
but never could bring them together with
reality, I used it all up. It's all gone…
I went Southwest.
Goodbye. Lew Welch[56]

Philip Lamantia visits Walpi, Oraibi and other Hopi villages where he observes the ceremonial practice of the Kachina dancers.

Llyn Foulkes forms a musical group called The Rubber Band.

David Meltzer's Tree Books (1970–78) publishes *Scintilla,* by Jack Hirschman.

Dennis Hopper writes, directs, and stars in *The Last Movie*, an ill-fated western shot in Peru that features Russel Tambyn, Dean Stockwell, and Billy Gray.

1970

The Four Seasons Foundation publishes Lamantia's *The Blood of the Air.*

Tarlow moves back to Los Angeles and begins publishing the feminist literary magazine, *Matrix: For She of the New Aeon.*

Nerves, John Wieners's first international volume, is published to ecstatic reviews. Wieners continues to be periodically institutionalized for the next five years.

Alexander Trocchi publishes his only nonfiction book, *Drugs of the Mind.*

The Meltzers visit the Bermans in Topanga.

David Meltzer:
In the early 1970s my wife and I decided to move our four kids to Europe and on the way out of the country we stopped off to visit the Bermans. That was the last time I ever saw Wally. He'd gotten thicker, heavier, and his hair was long and kind of grayish-white. The T.V. set was on, some sort of sport thing going on, and he took me downstairs to his studio and showed me the work he was making with a Verifax machine—he showed it very casually, as always. He'd recently read a book by Carlos Suarez called The Cipher of Genesis, *involved with retranslating the first chapters of Genesis; upon reading Suarez, Wally began to use not just the Hebrew letters, but their numerical equivalent as well.*[55]

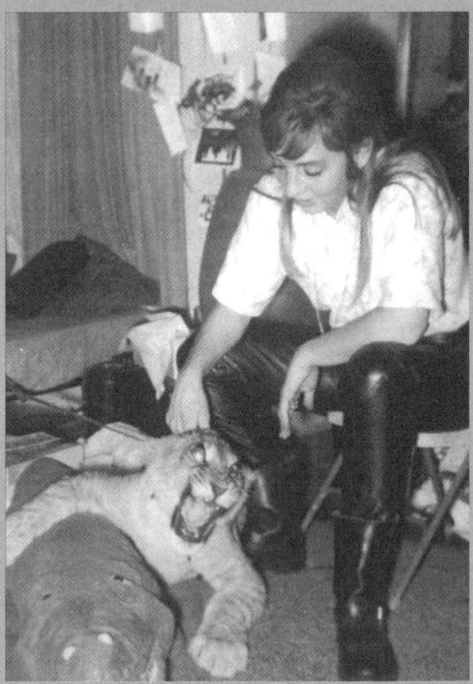

top Loree Foxx, c. 1964, Photograph by Wallace Berman.

bottom Loree Foxx, with one of her pet lion cubs at her home in Joshua Tree, c. 1964, Photographer unknown.

Stuart Perkoff's *Eat the Earth* is published. Later in the year Perkoff moves to San Francisco and attempts to open a bookstore.

Intrepid Books publishes Ray Bremser's *Black is Black Blues*.

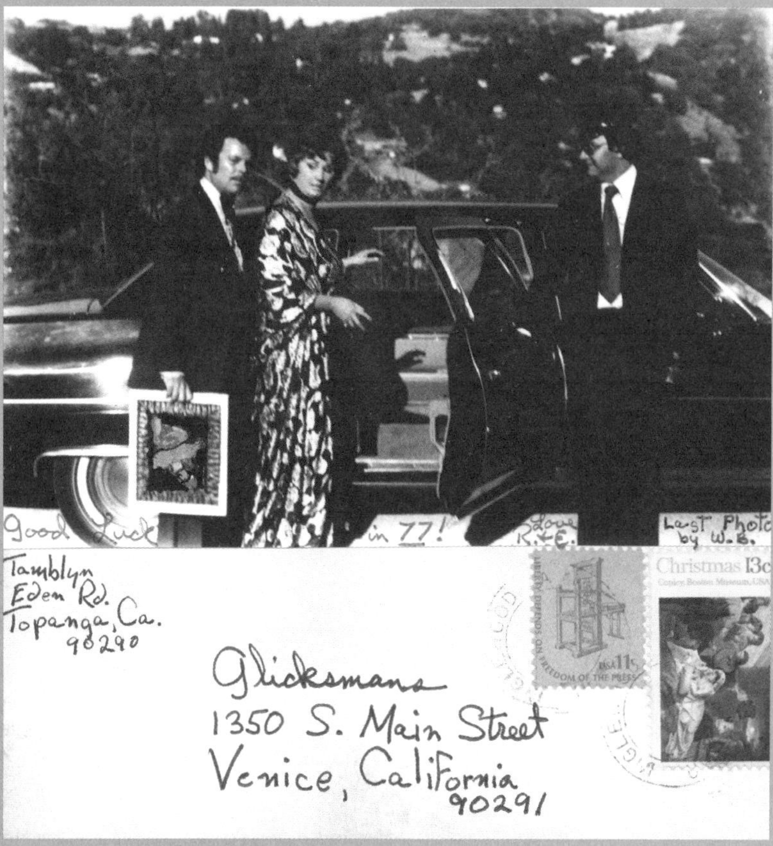

1972

Loree Foxx dies.

Suzi Hicks:
Loree removed herself toward the end of her life. I'd lost touch with her much earlier than that, though. Loree was strange and she'd done Hollywood—although it's more accurate to say that Hollywood had really done her—so she moved out to Joshua Tree with a guy named Dick Constantino. She had a lavender Jaguar she drove around in, and they had lions. I understand that she was in Arizona with a friend of hers named Candy, and they were pulled over and they put her in Arizona State Prison because there were four joints in the car. She had an asthma attack while she was in jail and she died. She was forty-two years old.[57]

Cranium Press publishes *Song for Max Finstein* by Perkoff, *The Mammals* by McClure, and Welch's *Redwood Haiku and Other Poems*.

Alexander Trocchi publishes his first volume of poetry, *Man at Leisure*.

Hopps is fired from the Corcoran and takes a curatorial post at the Smithsonian.

Other Publications publishes Wieners's *The Lanterns Along the Wall.*

1973

Grey Fox Press posthumously publishes Lew Welch's *How I Work as a Poet & Other Essays*, and *Ring of Bone: Collected Poems, 1950–1971*.

Stuart Perkoff returns to Los Angeles and is diagnosed with cancer.

Rachel Rosenthal co-founds Womanspace, a short-lived feminist art collective.

Jahrmarkt dies of an accidental gunshot wound in Afghanistan, where he has moved because of its abundantly available heroin

Meltzer publishes two volumes of poetry: *Bark: A Polemic*, and *Hero/Lil*, which features cover art by Berman, who also does cover art for Perkoff's *Alphabet*. Meltzer also edits *Birth*, an anthology of writings on the subject published by Ballantine Books.

Sand Dollar books publishes McClure's *The Book of Joanna*.

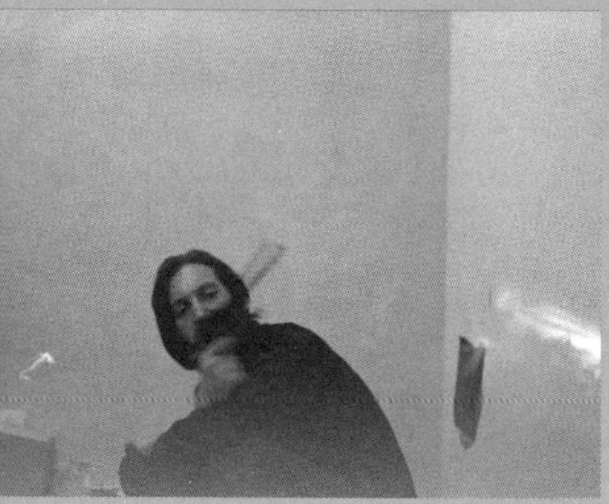

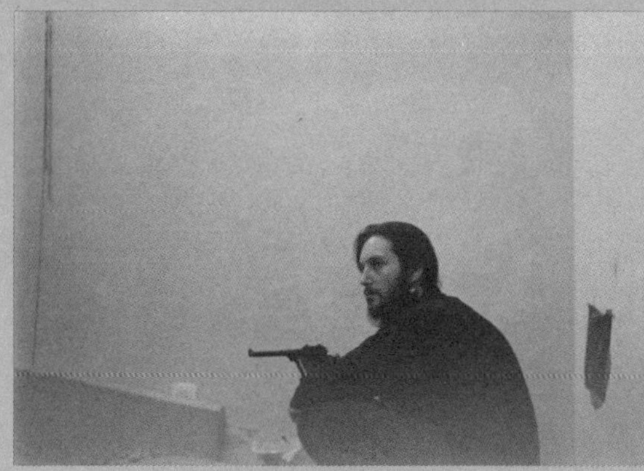

top Russel Tamblyn mailer with photograph of Tamblyn and his first wife Elizabeth, by Wallace Berman, 1976, collection of Hal Glicksman.

bottom Billy Jahrmarkt, c. 1968, Photographs by Wallace Berman.

1974

Angel Hair books publishes John Wieners's *Hotels.*

Ben Talbert dies of an accidental drug overdose.

Foulkes & the Rubber Band perform on Johnny Carson's *Tonight Show*.

Stuart Perkoff dies of cancer.

1975

Rachel Rosenthal presents her first piece as a performance artist, *Replays*, at the Orlando Gallery in Encino. Eleven days later, she performs *Thanks* at Wilshire West Plaza.

Edmund Teske becomes ordained as a minister of Alexander's Temple of Man.

John Wieners's *Behind the State Capitol, Or Cincinnati Pike* is published. Following its publication, Wieners retreats from the literary world and seldom publishes his work. However, he continued to write, as he told an interviewer in 1973, "for the poetical, the people, for the young at heart… Not for myself, merely. Or ever. Only for the better, warm, human loving, kind person."[58]

1976

Meltzer edits *The Secret Garden: An Anthology of Kabbalistic Texts*, published by Continuum Books.

Llyn Foulkes has solo exhibitions in New York and Paris.

Ray Bremser begins a three-year relationship with poet Judy Johnson.

Rachel Rosenthal reopens Instant Theater, which closes after a few months.

Philip Lamantia joins the editorial board of the poetry publication, *Arsenal: Surrealist Subversion.*

Intrepid Books publishes Diane DiPrima's *Brass Furnaces Going Out: Song, After an Abortion.*

Wallace Berman is killed on the eve of his fiftieth birthday by a drunk driver named Ronald "Spike" Miller. A Topanga Canyon drug dealer, Miller attempts to flee the scene of the accident, but is pursued and caught by actor Randy Mantooth, who witnessed the accident. Miller, who'd had seven D.U.I.'s in the year prior to the accident, retains Robert Shapiro to defend him in court. He never serves a day of jail time.

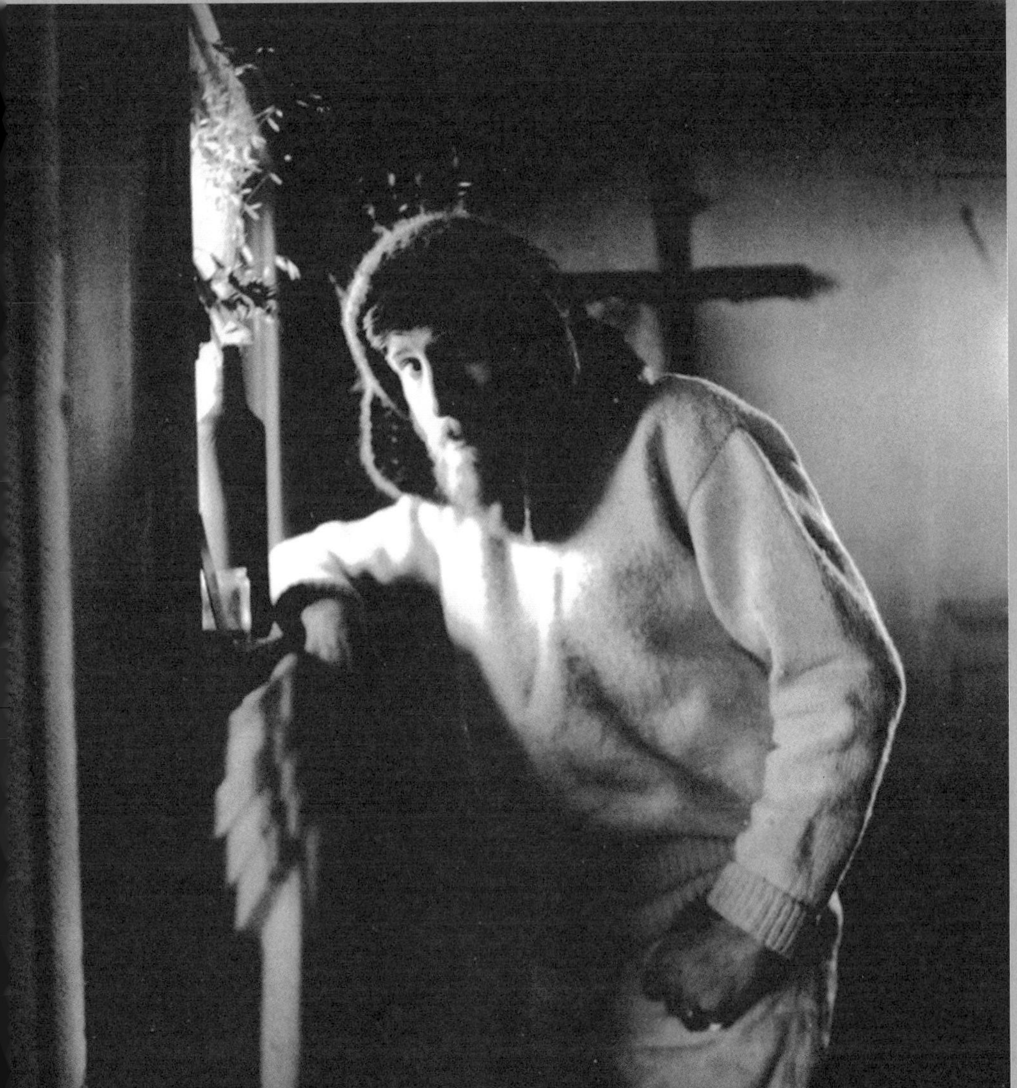

Self-portrait by Wallace Berman, Larkspur, California, 1961.

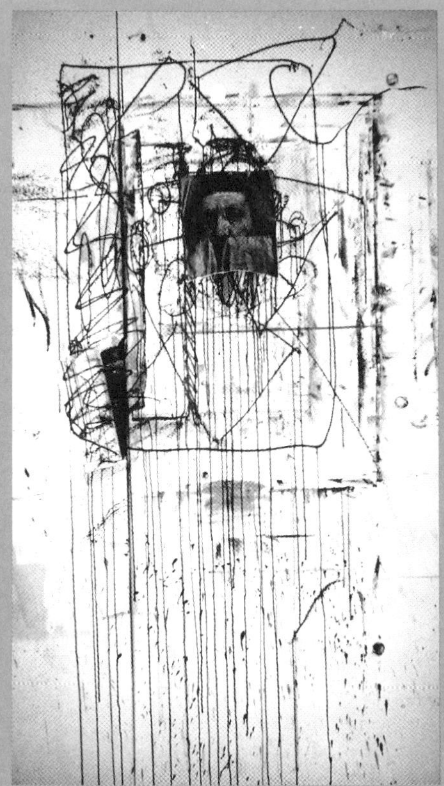

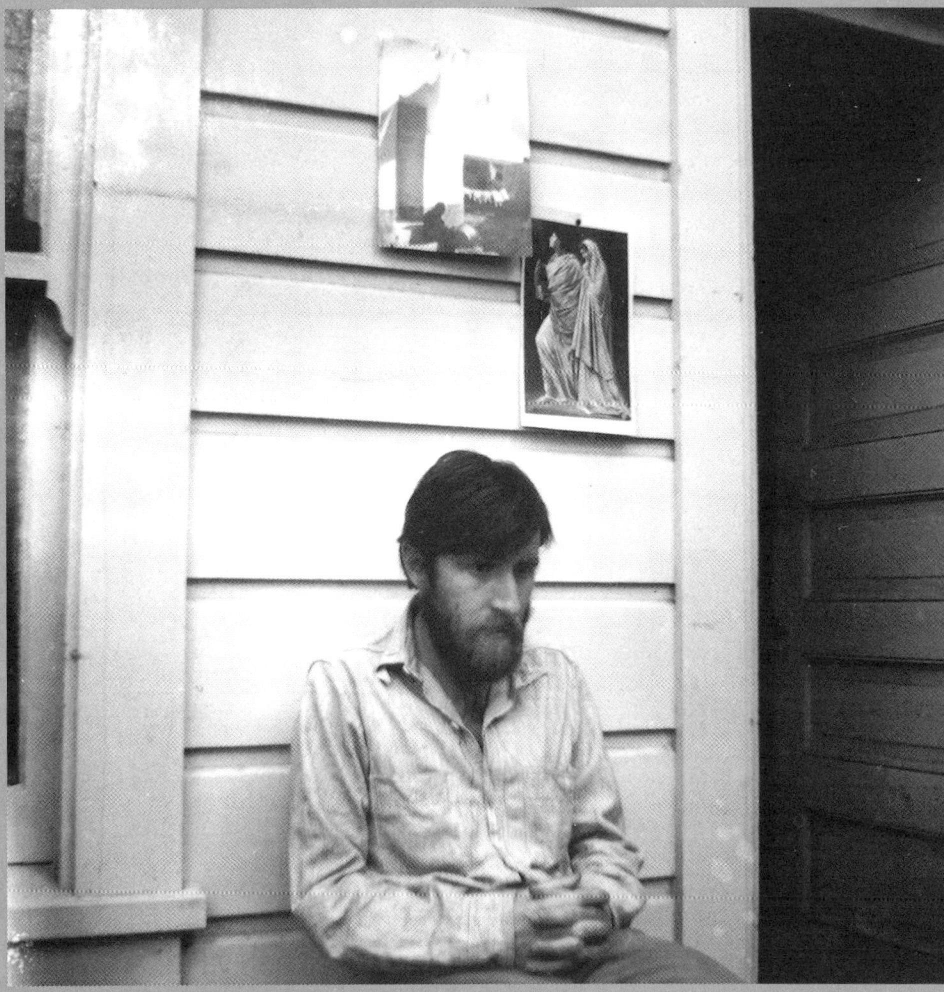

ENDNOTES

1 Conversation with David Rosenfield, June 9, 2000.
2 Conversation with Gary Platt, April 15, 1999.
3 Conversation with Suzi Hicks, December 20, 1999.
4 *The New Jazz Tempo Newsletter*, Spring, 1947, courtesy Kirk Silsbee.
5 Conversation with Sid Felsen, January 18, 2000.
6 Conversation with Donald Morand, January 16, 2000.
7 Conversation with Shirley Berman, January 9, 1999.
8 Conversation with Donald Morand, January 16, 2000.
9 Conversation with Suzi Hicks, December 20, 1999.
10 Conversation with Shelley Smith, December 1, 1999.
11 Conversation with Charles Brittin, December 5, 1999.
12 Ibid.
13 Ibid.
14 Robert Duncan; "Wallace Berman: The Fashioning Spirit," Hal Glicksman, ed. *Wallace Berman Retrospective*, exh. cat. (Los Angeles: Fellows of Contemporary Art, 1978), p. 19
15 Conversation with Shirley Berman, January 9, 1999.
16 Conversation with David Meltzer, January 2, 1999.
17 Conversation with Charles Brittin, December 5, 1999.
18 Conversation with David Meltzer, January 2, 1999.
19 Conversation with Billy Gray, October 13, 1999.
20 Conversation with Walter Hopps, April 15, 1999.
21 Conversation with Suzi Hicks, December 20, 1999.
22 Conversation with Michael McClure, January 29, 2000.
23 Conversation with Rachel Rosenthal, May 24, 2002.
24 Conversation with David Meltzer, January 2, 1999.
25 Conversation with Dennis Hopper, December 30, 1999.
26 Conversation with Charles Brittin, December 5, 1999.
27 Conversation with Philip Lamantia, August 2, 2000.
28 Ibid.
29 Conversation with Bruce Conner, July 9, 2001.
30 Ibid.
31 Ibid.
32 Conversation with Lawrence Jordan, August 21, 2001.
33 *Ferus Gallery oral history transcript/Irving Blum*, interview by Joann Phillips (1976 and 1978), and Lawrence Weschler, (1979). Los Angeles : Oral History Program, University of California, Los Angeles, 1984, p. 57, 71–74.
34 Conversation with Bruce Conner, July 9, 2001.
35 Conversation with Suzi Hicks, December 20, 1999.
36 Conversation with Charles Brittin, December 5, 1999.
37 Conversation with Bruce Conner, July 9, 2001.
38 Conversation with Shirley Berman, January 9, 1999.
39 Conversation with Tosh Berman, January 11, 1999.
40 Conversation with Charles Brittin, December 5, 1999.
41 David Meltzer, ed. *San Francisco Beat: Talking With the Poets*, (San Francisco: City Light Books, 2001). Interview with Diane DiPrima conducted by Meltzer and Marina Lazzara, 1999.
42 Conversation with Jack Hirschman, February 25, 2000.
43 DiPrima, Diane, *Recollections of My Life as a Woman: The New York Years* (New York: Viking, 2001), p. 303.
44 Conversation with Jack Hirschman, February 25, 2000.
45 Conversation with Gerard Malanga, May 15, 2002.
46 Conversation with Russ Tamblyn, February 10, 1999.
47 Conversation with Tosh Berman, January 11, 1999.
48 Ibid.
49 Conversation with Dennis Hopper, December 30, 1999.
50 Conversation with Tosh Berman, January 11, 1999.
51 Letter from Lew Welch to Allen Ginsberg, July 27, 1960, Allen Ginsberg Papers, Box 66, Folder 6, Stanford Library Special Collections, Stanford University.
52 Conversation with Shirley Berman, January 9, 1999.
53 Conversation with Tosh Berman, January 11, 1999.
54 Letter from Ray Bremser to Allen Ginsberg, Oct. 29, 1969, Allen Ginsberg Papers, Box 12, Folder 30, Stanford Library Special Collections, Stanford University.
55 Conversation with David Meltzer, January 2, 1999.
56 Saroyan, Aram, *Genesis Angels, the Saga of Lew Welch & the Beat Generation* (New York: William Morrow, 1979).
57 Conversation with Suzi Hicks, December 20, 1999.
58 Unknown Source cited by Foye, Raymond "John Wieners," in Ann Charters, ed. *Dictionary of Literary Biography 16* (Detroit: Bruccoli Clark/Gale, 1983) p. 583.

left Wallace Berman, Lost work, n.d.
right Self-portrait by Wallace Berman in Larkspur, 1961.

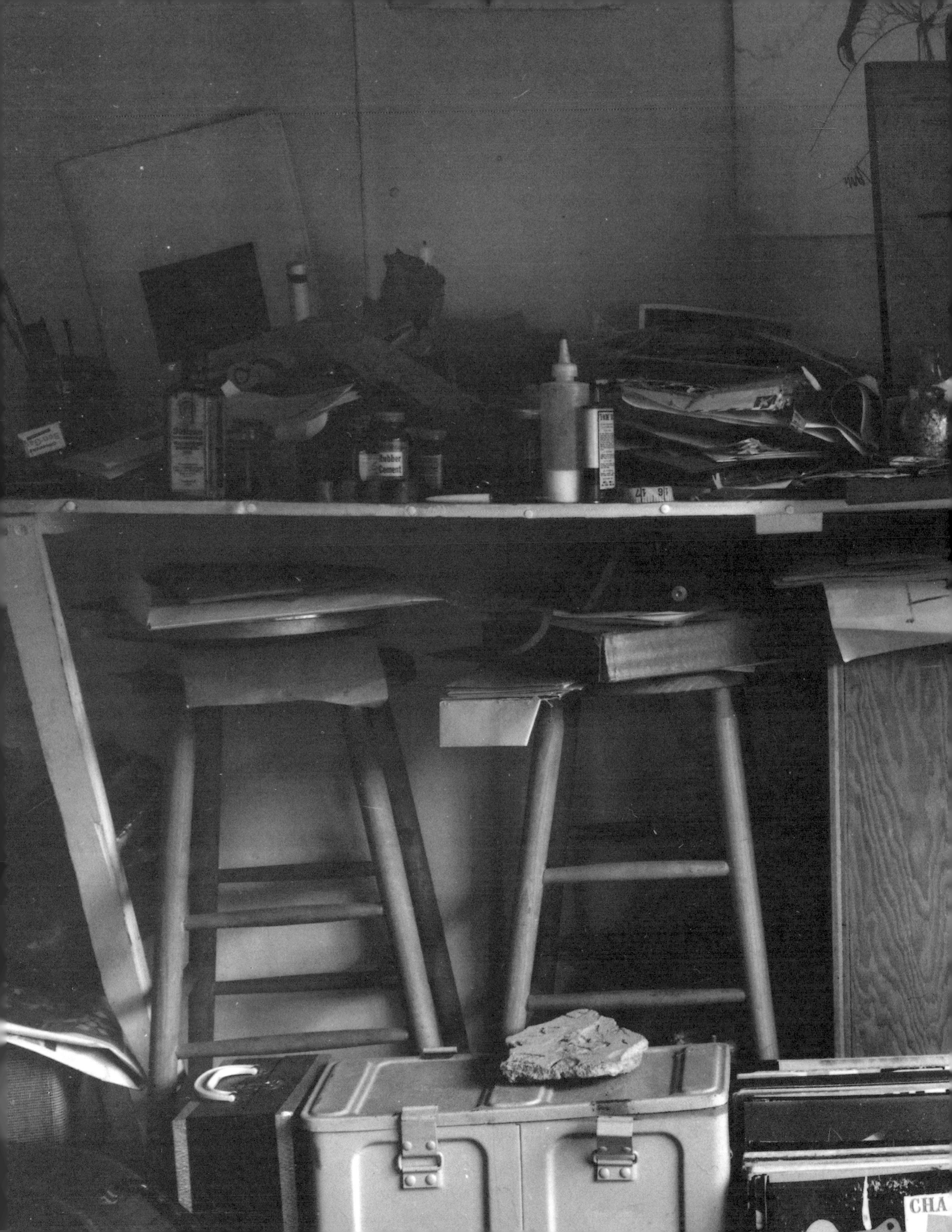
Rubber Cement
CHA

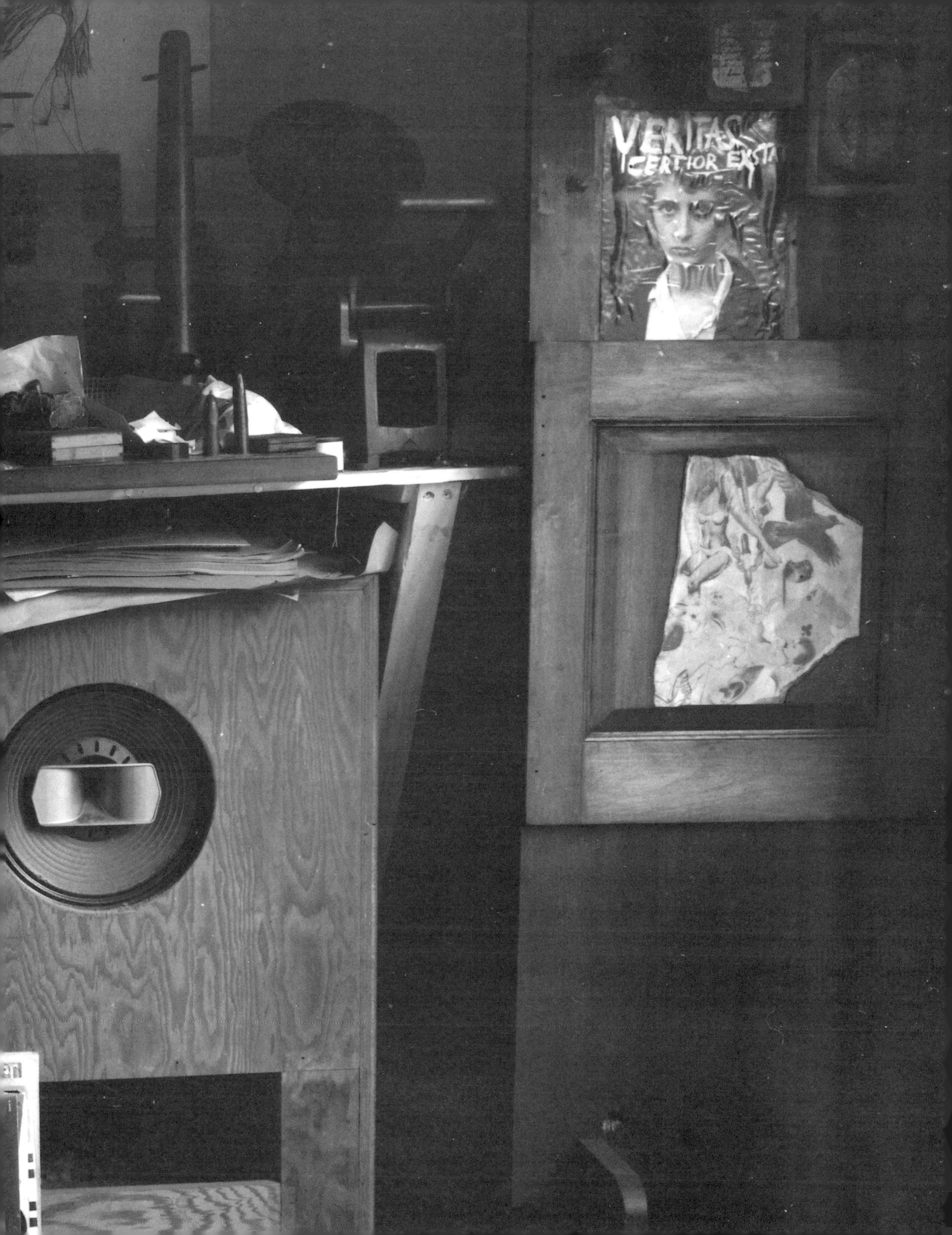
VERITAS
CERTIOR EXSTA

LETTERS

A good deal has been written about Wallace Berman in the twenty-nine years since he died, and there are plenty of photographs of him available to those interested in studying them. Nonetheless, Berman persists in being a man of considerable mystery—which is exactly the way he wanted it. Throughout his life Berman refused to give interviews (the few exceptions to that rule didn't amount to much in terms of what he revealed of himself), and he rarely discussed his work, even with his closest friends. He never taught a class, gave a lecture, or committed his thoughts to paper in the form of a journal or diary. Berman made every effort to tread lightly wherever he went, and leave no evidence that he'd been there once he'd moved on. This makes the handful of surviving letters written by him invaluable and fascinating.

In reading the following letters—most of which were written to poet David Meltzer over a period of years in the early 1960s—it's immediately clear why people were drawn to Berman. He had a fabulous sense of humor and an exquisitely developed sense of the absurd and love of the surreal. He was an unabashed fan and cheerleader for artists he admired in a variety of art forms, ranging from jazz and sports to pop music, film and literature. His command of exotic bits of slang was dazzling and he was a hipster par excellence whose hipness was rooted in his generosity. "Give my love to anyone that would want it," Berman writes at one point. Who could a resist someone capable of a comment like that?

Kristine McKenna

Wallace Berman letters to David Meltzer, 1962–64, collection of Philip Aarons.

David/ midnite here & am smoking
what was in the ancient pillow of
yrs   the one with embroidered d
ragons on it (friend of mine fro
m Turkey);--Jarry arrived few days
ago with bundle on shoulder & man
y stories of many travels thru st
ates & Mexico   Perkoff busted i
n deep Mexico very sick   Charle
s Foster fell off building breaki
ng leg also in Mexico. Bruce Co
nner recently visited & did twist
to 'screamin Jay Hawkins' --rece
ived lenghty letter from John W. &
tells me he swung half thru 15oo.oo
already on framus etc. a grant of
sorts from some group of sorts he
sorts   Measure tho coming any day
from Villiers i think & he awaits
them & then to this coast   visi
ted Geo & Louise today all cool
c'mon down for supper tell Fred
erick i said its cool   yes, the
ref should of stopped it sooner &
i heard that Griffith designs hat
s f.m. is cool & if i had loot i
would buy you one   its not the c
ulture its the lack of advertize
ments Shirley is asleep Tosh is
asleep & Jarry is asleep   i want
to belong so   later

W.B.

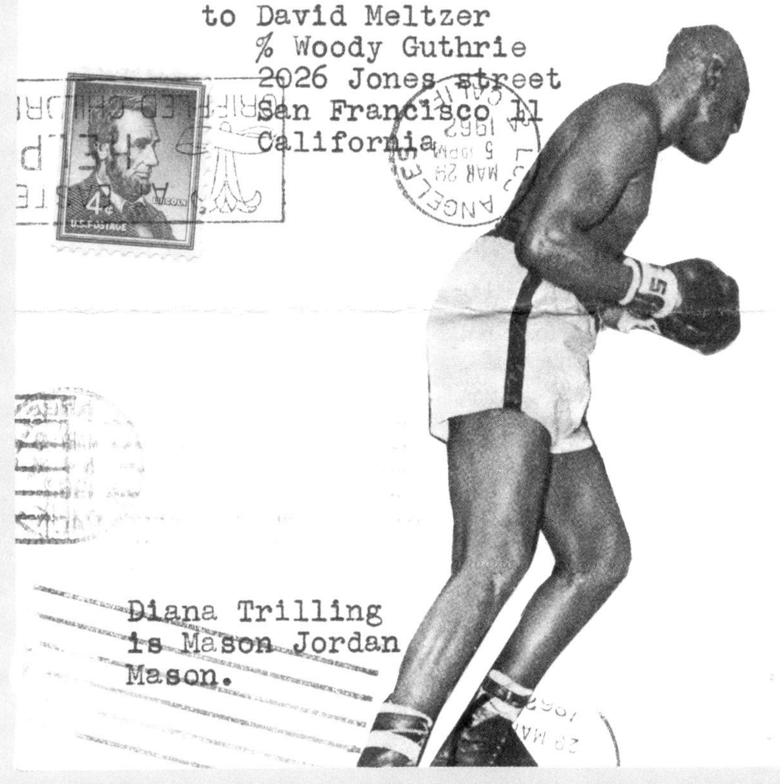

David/ That Dada prizefighter never vanished Motherwell g
oofed & History also like me he dug Romance cuz' withou
t it there is no Mystery & without that there is only --let
me see whats that word ---oh yeh Logic or Death or som
ething or other (fifty or so years for all of us on this
shot) FUCK LOGIC FUCK SCOTT CARPENTER & ALL THE UPMORE CAT
S FUCK yeh that dada cat had cool timing was it Artau
d or Presley who said 'it dont mean a thing if you aint got t
hat swing' Universal Mother David/those cats in the a
lley (are they the realists or is it the chain brass knuckles
shiv club that dominate their brain matter or not) its a nic
e day today & tonite i dig Count Basie Sunday was LSD day &
i fared very cool Sugar Ray pound for pound was the coolest
& he fought Jake many times & when hedid lose it was betting
coup orooney T he Angels here are in fifth place Bo Bel
insky swinging yes yes its points not books while watching
fites some time ago in a bar two spades were about to start t
he first round when the juicer next to me says Wanna bet?? I s
aid yes & he says i'll take the nigger yes its points not b
ooks Mystery is Truth Vision contains Mystery you ask wh
at happened to Kid Gavilan -- hes got a ranch in Cuba & sti
ll wears white shoes Does Bruce Cabot twist?? Dean Stockmo
re does ill wear suit & tie tonite for the count would yo
u believe it hes blowing at the Zenda Ballroom on 7th near
Figeroa yeh history cycle o i go no concert tonite i hat
e concerts its a dance which means you walk around fuck a
round cool around & the band can blow in the correct (traditio
nal manner) no show pieces Kentons nada concerts nada
~~Gunther Shuller nada when he fucks with Jazz~~ i just rememb
ered the many many steps you climb at the Zenda Shirley say
s to buy her shampoo when i go down hill i say what kind she
say Breck i say Dreck

Points & Love
Wallace B.

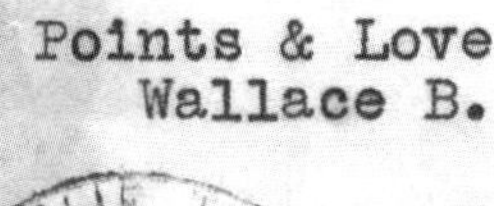

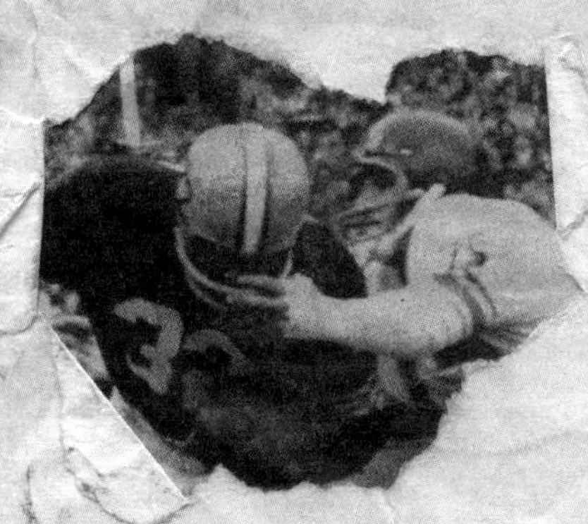

LOS ANGELES, CALIF. TERMINAL ANNEX
MY 29 10 PM
1962

to David Main Event M
2026 Jones st.
San Francisco 11 Cal.

from 1548 Crater lane L.A.24 Calif.

David/ Last week at Pasadena Museum controversy flares supreme as
work by George disturbs ~~suares-a~~ squares in relation to what they
feel is misusing american flag in certain piece show closed tem
porarily opens again with director siding with George etc etc
This morning the discovery that museum has been broken into (sawing
locks-screw rippin' orooney thru barriers etc) & Georges piece rip
ped off wall american flag removed & note left by intruder(co
ntents unknown as police have all frammus) am collecting data via
newspapers & will mail as soon as tomorrows contains todays hanky
panky ok points make it ask the rev Gary Davis am gifted
with 10 gear ultra light aluminum legitimate type racing bike made
in Italy so light like a feather so beautiful in design i stare
towards it continually & dig it so Am producing directing etc
Artauds 'To Have Done With The Judgement Of God' for KPFK have
a complete translation by Wernham can use studios engineer for
what ever too much a producer a director i will try to
find a beret megaphone & wild canvas chair yeh there will be a
week dedicated to Artaud or rather 10 days others involved in
this presentation is the beautiful Anais Nin John Fles who i in
troduced to the Hirschmans head of drama & literature for KPFK
& some UCLA people whom i cannot remember names Tosh received
magazine entitled 'PA'LANTE' from N.Y. excellent pieces by John
Wieners & Mike & Allen G. Johns piece about 707 Scott st. swings
Sport shot continues via Italiano bike & went to first race involv
ing basic looking short called Go Karts of which Dean bought one
& goal to break track record his speed shot is something else
Dean is getting more cool & beautiful had visit from three swing
ers Sandy Wagner from Marin County Sonni from La Pavoni in S.f. &
the most groovy Sharon Kirbys old lady if you have any works of yrs
involving comments thoughts fragments etc of Artaud send down & i
will see that it is included in this week of his work have not ca
sted the voice of Artaud as yet for 'Judgement' tho Dean read it &
flipped to do it (stand back & picture me directing Dean Stockwell)
i think it would be cooler for a non professional to swing behind
it a poet a poet who digs Artaud possibly Lamantia but
Mexico is so far away to try to complete the shot then i keep th
inking of Kirby Doyle whom i remember reading Billy the Kid of Mi
kes to the actors workshop of S.F. & i think he would be comp
atible with this delivery ?? will also do program cover for Ar
tauds week too much Artaud in Los Angeles will try to get Bil
l Spencer to do original music for my shot if not i will swing
myself in this direction coming home from Go Kart races in dism
al Southgate i awoke during Angels baseball game & during lull in
announcing i was fascinated by the crowds sounds would maybe use
this in relation to 'Judgement' am wanting to take a great deal
of liberty with this mother Dean using Patsy Kelly for lead in
his Beckett radio shot remember her a butch comedienne of the
thirtys Goddam the Angels are swinging in second place

love, Wallace B.

to David Meltzer
2026 Jones street
San Francisco Calif.

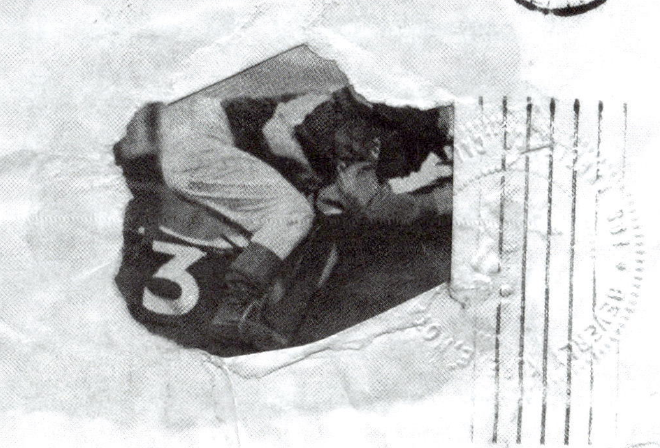

David/ March evening

Just spent a surreal afternoon beginning with Chuck T-
hompson looming up in a Meth fog on Stanley Kramers d-
riveway I veered the caddy towards Sunset off this
scene & am curbed over by a cat in 1963 or 1964 shiny
type of short & its an old friend from pool-room days
-- he reintroduces me to snooker hall under bowling a-
lley in Westwood & i was able to wipe out all our out-
standing bills --tho all i viewed was about three qu-
arters of the table being 'out of my gourd' --snooker
shure cuts pool as it takes a cool frammus with pool
you can bang & bang & the table is fat & ugly & you can
slop them in with power snooker requires sensitivity
--also the table which comes in two sizes is very cool
& the pockets are very small & requires the delicate
air -- o.k. anyway me being in the poolroom set me
wondering about the cycle that some vieneeze degenerate
talked to me for about 4 hours in the Place one nite
--- as its been about a decade & half since i made that
scene--the snooker scene that is & now 'repeat city'
When i asked about Literary scene up thar i was mainly
concerned about the 'Journal'---it was obvious that the
first issue had three editors
Went to wedding that Bob A. officiated & my Shirley was
beautiful maid of honor & all went cool Bob read from the Prophet & this took place in cool pad over rol-
ler-rink near merry-go-round building at Santa Monica
pier much crazy food --japanese shot --as the gr-
oom is jap & his momma cooked up a storm of chicken
Bob looked cool & has a lot of hair on his scull ---
Just received a call from this cat who cut tape for
KPFK here & he said that he & wife just reviewed &
read from 'Auerhahn' 'Hawkswell press' & 'Semina' &
will be on in about two weeks or so --Peyote poem
was read & portion of Clown & separate pieces from
other issues of 'Semina' I dunno what he read from
the other heavyweight presses Big invasion of eastern painters & sculptors here went to Tinguelys
exhibition which had neo-comic movements of mechanical
parts which the viewer participates by stepping on ped-
al which starts movement then his wife had an outside
exhibition in which she blasted with rifle a construction
about 25 feet high of ~~plaster-filled-c~~ paint encased in
plaster & oddsends of cans of paint etc this was all
painted white & as she shot these would explode causing
the colors to stream down construction & in case you
are fashion minded she wore a stretch type outfit -white
with knee-high boots & these had extremely high heels---
some of the shooting she used a pistol handed to her by
Ed Kienholtz Look-Life-Sat.eve.post-Coronet-ReaderDi-
gest-& every fuckin photographer in the whole continent
was shootin away there were more cats with cameras than
there was in Dolcevita then i staggered over to Westwood where Rauschenburg has show & then over to Ferus
where Kienholtz had his go --David/c'mon down
with family & have some supper --
o.k. now we have it --a heavyweight artist in films
'Antonioni' he made L'Avventura which is tremendous f
ilm --an inner involvement slow but with beautiful rythym & now i dug 'La Notte' whew--it contains all
that makes a film a work of Art whereas Dolcevita was
extroverted spectacle Antonioni's shot is inner & not

no.2 page

hung tho --gets over usual humps that hangs others that deal subjectivèly & close La Notte moves slow like La VVentura but this slow & cool rythym makes it under this cats shot cannot remember ever being this impressed with film you should dig it -----have not swung with press since down here except for christmas cards but it rests comfortably & its all ready to go when the Muse insists ------Shirley gigs from 9 to 1 & this makes it cool & we swing the rest of the day Tosh gets picked up by bus at bottom of hill & gets brought back at 2 --so timing seems cool --he is learning to write & read now its a gas he is too much & i love the beatnick ---Kenneth Anger asked for yr address after digging Clown & i gave it to him Cameron living in Venice looking handsome & doing cool things ---received Floating Bear with yr work--- George H. swinging also Nalota & Louise --Bobby D. still in Tehachapi but soon to be released --Been staying close to pad here except for flicks & Friday nite at Barneys beanery as i do the laundry across the street its open all nite then i go across & get juiced on Tap beer & dig fats domino --i always play 13 there and its a cool record cannot remember name of tune but its the only swinger on their jukebox i remember the tune now -its Let the four winds blow Whats happening with yr work//? Are things to be released soon if so send sample-- Give my love to anyone that would want it Tequila gone --still have another 1.90 tho for small bottle --yeh,snooker is cool later

Wallace B.

The cat who called about the KPFK shot just came on station with Mayakowskys poems which he translated sounds cool --- also mentioned on phone his plans to do long tape of Artauds work

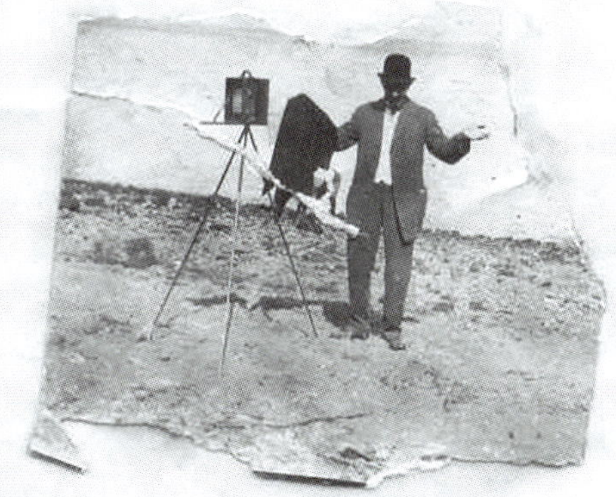

David/ recieved yr book & dug & Dug it or rather re-dug it.
it feels good in the palm have you noticed how when anything is cool it feels right even a completely flat surfa
ce like paper Auerhahn swinging my press is a rusty d
usty mother received a poem from Kirby D. about Fatty Ar
buckle dug it i could even do a shot on Bruce Cab
ot myself & let Michael do up or rather write up Jayne
Mansfield mebbe Geo. on Troy Donahue John Wieners on Ro
chester You on B.Bardot or Agnes Morehead etc etc et
c on the cover Bob Steele balling Lassie No this is n
ot what i want Hollywood is cool what is corny can b
e made beautiful but for real like alchemy & high no
t a shuck solitaire eliminate that cover i shall do
the academy twist who was Rintintin the son of ???
George to swing behind Pasadena museum exhibit Woody Guth
rie is on now & Shirley shoots up the volume full frammus s
ome chick on now singin' Mommy buy be a chinadoll do mommy
do Tosh has fever am anxiously awaiting release here
of 'Last year at Marienbad' the'4 Oaks Cafe up the hiway
here now open til' 2am & faces coming down from hills & i s
ee some fine faces while getting juiced behind Coors Tap bee
r been taking midnite strolls & will have a inn to stop o
ff at before down hiway shot again yes c'mon down & i wi
ll play 'Midnite inMoscow' on the juke there for you Sh
irley beautiful on Mothers day been reading old issues of
'Sports Illustrated' that some cat put out for garbage pick
up & came across cool letter to editor from George Stanley
wait i will get it & copy it & mail you the shot will do
it manana Shirleys Clarks' The Connection the flick wi
ll be here soon & ill dig it been seeing movies & i tell
you 'A walk on the Wild Side' is a lemon fat lemon not b
lind lemon Dean Stockmere doing Beckett for KPFK 8 voic
es Cat said some precious things about me & Semina framm
us etc on kpfk & possibly i will retire now or stay retire
d beautiful sounds here now St James Infirmary too muc
h some chick great brass fat trumpet no cornet
piano brass & zippy drummer yes that large hall sound r
eminds me of my dancehall days Zenda, Park Manor, & the
ones sponsored by some Jewish organizations the ones that
Sammy Davis crooney dug ok the drummer now ommpah
piff piff rrrr ommpahh now 'yer a workin' man when yer
married' same chick yes its true that all the yiddish
known by Jimmie Witherspoon was taught to him by my grandmot
her hes no Muslim his hair has been frammused whew
'Reminicent City' Am i on the way out 'Cycle city'
Repeat City
Hip City
Blind Joe Death City
Blotto City

same chick now 'IM in the Racket' Mommas
in the racket now im in the racket yes
cuz im mitey tired mommas in the racket
'Jack & Jill went up a hill to get some
water & when they got back she had a doll
ar and quarter' yes mommas in the racket
cuz shes tired mommas in the racet now

love
juiced & sad
cuz Tosh has fever/

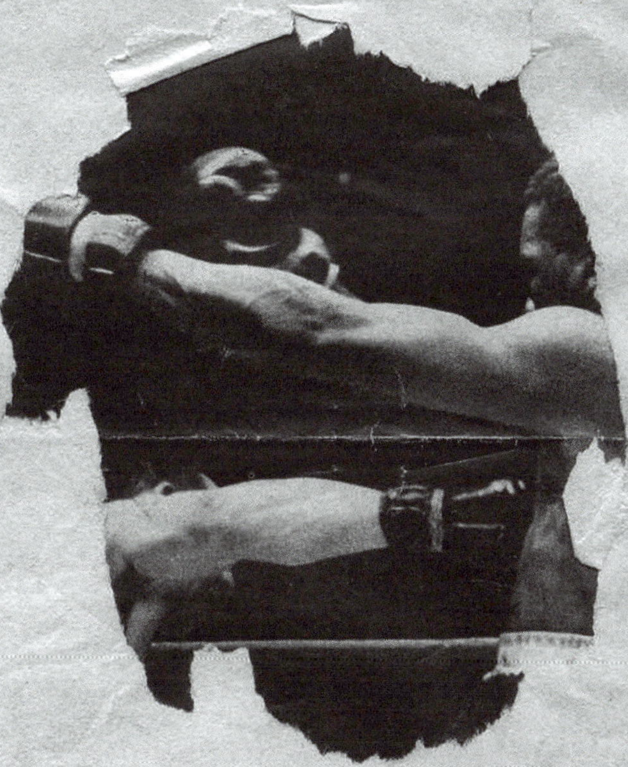

David/ its the Glove & not the book
yes the points involved including
Numerals Judges & claret etc   this
is the fact   if not in there these
cats would be waiting for us in frammus
alley   Griffith should sleep cool
I tell you it was Fullmer who set Paret
up for the Big Natural   not the hat
designer   Fullmer raises Minks therefore
the chopping brutal downwards club
that it takes to wipe out Minks tho
his lumbering rite Jab with bodybulk
behind it is ruff on ribs as you can
observe above as Paret throws arms up
futilely   yes its sports not books
love, Wallace

to David Meltzer
2026 Jones street
San Francisco 11 Calif.

LOS ANGELES, CALIF. TERMINAL ANNEX

from 1548 Crater lane l.a.24 Calif.

David/
would dig getting a book ontitled 'PIN'
by Shwitters & Hausmann   put out by
'Garbocchus' or similar   also wd wa
nt to know prices of'Europa' & Shwitters
in England   if its a hassle to find
out about these   cool it   the same
publishers did all three i believe Tos
h digging 'Treasure Island' now via Wal
t Disney   Tonites T.Monks last nite
locally   will make it   Billy Gray ju
st diggin' Bobby D. & says B.D. playing
a square on abboun account of handing
out a map or somethin'   this happening
on 'Treasure Island'   im facing other
way typing up a Romilar haze   Closeup
now of B.D. & Robt Newton 4 junkeyes
  House investigating Committee in LA
now much picketing pro & con also Rock
well & faggott group re armbands etc
   was peyoted out last week   first ti
me in a year   beautiful   Long John
Silver says to B.D. shipmates   & B.D.
says in answer   shipmates   fadeout &
now some cat swings out with insipid
plea to buy Kodak fuck it   nothing
caps 'Nelson family'   unless its 'Wops
' & Copa'   or similar   digging T.V.
on weekends   o.k.   Giants & midgets
lightweights & heavies in this here to
wn   o.k.   this is'Twist City'
John W. to be here soon than on to S.f.
  --- Paul Beattie down here now   hes
a beautiful cat   healthy vibrations
--- love to Tina & Jennifer & you
W.B.

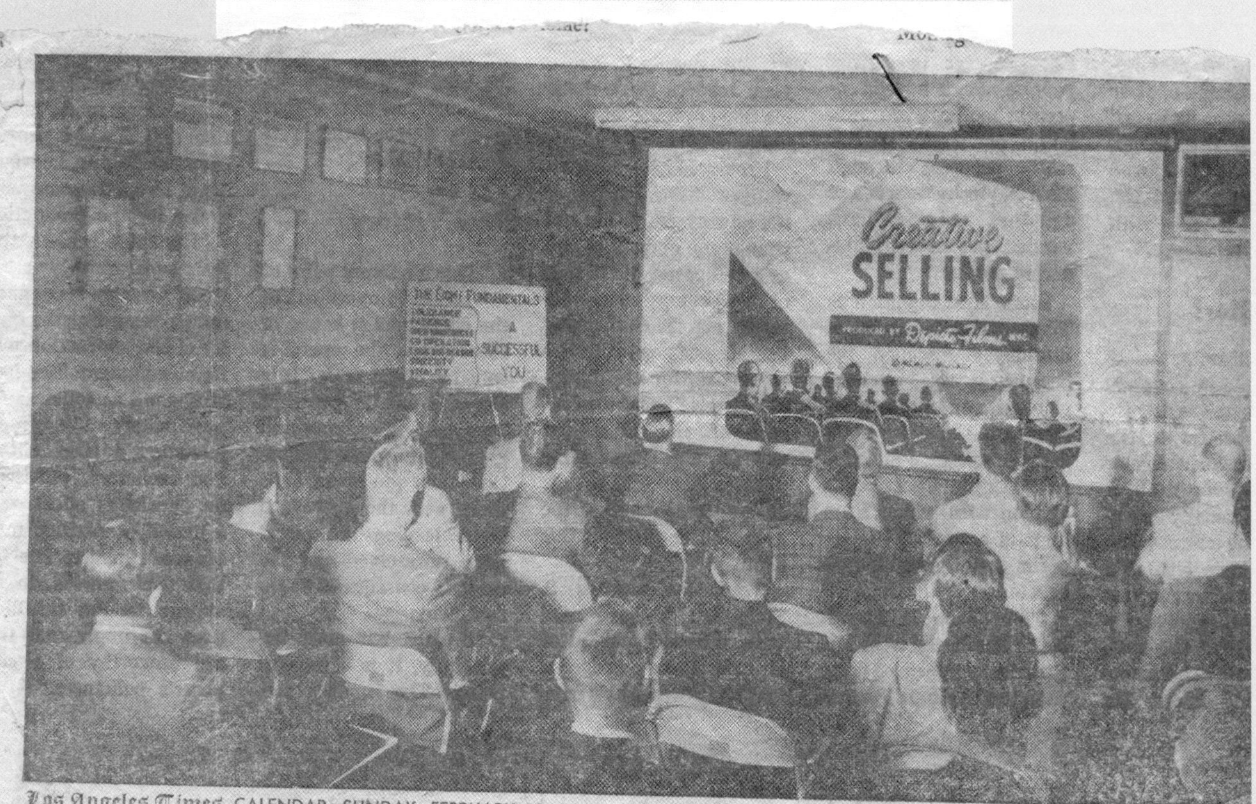

Los Angeles Times CALENDAR, SUNDAY, FEBRUARY 18, 1962

CHECKLIST

Robert Alexander

Untitled ("Art is Love is God"), 1955
Mixed-media assemblage, 6 x 5 x 7 inches
Collection of Charles Brittin, Santa Monica, CA

Baza Press Announcements: Instant Theater: Action 2: four business cards, mid–1950s
Ink on paper, Dimensions variable
Collection of Charles Brittin, Santa Monica, CA

Blood of a Poet, 1956
Mixed-media with artist's blood, 25 7/8 x 17 5/8 inches
Collection of Charles Brittin, Santa Monica, CA

Untitled ("God love masturbating mothers..."), 1956
Mixed-media on paper, 35 1/2 x 24 1/2 inches
Collection of Charles Brittin, Santa Monica, CA

Heartbreak House, 1958
Photographic flipbook, 4 x 8 inches
Collection of Charles Brittin, Santa Monica, CA

Untitled ("Mother"), 1960
Mixed media collage on paper, 11 x 15 inches
Collection of Charles Brittin, Santa Monica, CA

John Altoon

Portrait of a Spanish Poet (Lorca), 1954–59
Oil on canvas, 57 1/2 x 47 inches
Collection of Dr. Leon O. Banks, Courtesy Newspace Gallery, Los Angeles, CA

Untitled (Woman, garden hose, boy), 1966
Ink, gouache on paper, 30 x 40 inches
Private Collection

Lawrence Lipton, *The Holy Barbarians* (London: W.H. Allen, 1960). Cover photograph of John Altoon and friends sitting under Altoon's *Portrait of a Spanish Poet (Lorca)*. Private Collection

Toni Basil

Untitled (Ping Pong Game), 1967–68
8mm film transferred to DVD; TRT: Approx. 3:00
Courtesy the artist

Our Trip, 1967
8mm film transferred to DVD; TRT: approx. 12:00
Courtesy the artist

Our Trip (for Ann), 1967
Film stills, 14 1/2 x 16 inches
Collection of Ann Marshall, Los Angeles, CA

Our Trip (for Teri), 1967
Mixed-media collaged book, 10 x 9 1/4 inches
Collection of Teri Garr, Los Angeles, CA

A Dance Film Inspired by Jim Morrison, 1968
16mm film transferred to DVD; TRT: approx. 1:50
Courtesy the artist

Game of the Week, 1969
8mm film transferred to DVD; TRT: approx. 10:00
Courtesy the artist

Paul Beattie

Vignettes (Wallace & Tosh, Arthur Richer), 1963
16mm film transferred to DVD; TRT: 3:49
Collection of Estate of Paul Beattie, Forestville, CA

Scenes from the Tap City Circus, 1963
16mm film transferred to DVD; TRT 4:29
Collection of Estate of Paul Beattie, Forestville, CA

Game for Angels (collaboration with George Herms), Ed. 50, MC Press, 1963
Ink on 32 cards in cloth bag, Bag: 3 3/4 x 5 1/2 inches; cards: 2 1/4 x 3 1/8 inches each
Collection of Diane DiPrima, San Francisco, CA

George Herms (from footage of *Finger-Water-Light*), 1964
Gouache on board, 9 x 12 inches
Collection of Estate of Paul Beattie, Forestville, CA

Head of Wallace Berman, 1966
Oil on board, 6 3/4 x 4 13/16 inches
Collection of Estate of Paul Beattie, Forestville, CA

Green Disc, 1967
Oil on board, 23 3/4 x 23 3/4 inches
Collection of Estate of Paul Beattie, Forestville, CA

Colliding Galaxies with a Plethora of Globular Clusters, 1976
Pencil on paper, 2 drawings, 3 1/2 x 3 1/2 inches each
Collections of Estate of Paul Beattie, Forestville, CA

Wallace Berman

John Wieners, 707 Scott Street, San Francisco, 1959 (printed in 2004)
Posthumous gelatin silver print, 20 x 16 inches
Private Collection, Courtesy Wallace Berman Estate

Henry and Valentine Miller with Shirley Berman, Big Sur, 1954 (printed in 2004)
Posthumous gelatin silver print, 16 x 20 inches
Private Collection, Courtesy Wallace Berman Estate

Loree Foxx, Los Angeles, 1955 (printed in 2004)
Posthumous gelatin silver print, 14 x 11 inches
Private Collection, Courtesy Wallace Berman Estate

Charles Brittin, Venice Beach, 1956 (printed in 2004)
Posthumous gelatin silver print, 11 x 14 inches
Private Collection, Courtesy Wallace Berman Estate

Rachel Rosenthal, Los Angeles, 1956 (printed in 2004)
Posthumous gelatin silver print, 16 x 20 inches
Private Collection, Courtesy Wallace Berman Estate

Billy Gray, 1957 (printed in 2004)
Posthumous gelatin silver print, 11 x 14 inches
Private Collection, Courtesy Wallace Berman Estate

Robert Alexander, Stone Brothers Printing, 1957 (printed in 2004)
Posthumous gelatin silver print, 11 x 14 inches
Private Collection, Courtesy Wallace Berman Estate

Walter Hopps, Los Angeles, 1957 (printed in 2004)
Posthumous gelatin silver print, 11 x 14 inches
Private Collection, Courtesy Wallace Berman Estate

David and Tina Meltzer and Son, San Francisco, 1958 (printed in 2004)
Posthumous gelatin silver print, 14 x 11 inches
Private Collection, Courtesy Wallace Berman Estate

Joan Brown, Spatsa Gallery, San Francisco, 1958 (printed in 2004)
Posthumous gelatin silver print, 20 x 16 inches
Private Collection, Courtesy Wallace Berman Estate

Bob Kaufman, Co-Existence Bagel Shop, San Francisco, 1958 (printed in 2004)
Posthumous gelatin silver print, 20 x 16 inches
Private Collection, Courtesy Wallace Berman Estate

Philip Lamantia, San Francisco, 1958 (printed in 2004)
Posthumous gelatin silver print, 14 x 11 inches
Private Collection, Courtesy Wallace Berman Estate

William Margolis, Co-Existence Bagel Shop, San Francisco, 1958 (printed in 2004),
Posthumous gelatin silver print, 14 x 11 inches
Private Collection, Courtesy Wallace Berman Estate

Michael McClure, Divisadero Street, San Francisco, 1958 (printed in 2004)
Posthumous gelatin silver print, 14 x 11 inches
Private Collection, Courtesy Wallace Berman Estate

Bonnie and Ray Bremser, 707 Scott Street, San Francisco, 1959 (printed in 2004)
Posthumous gelatin silver print, 11 x 14 inches
Private Collection, Courtesy Wallace Berman Estate

Jay DeFeo, San Francisco, 1959 (printed in 2004)
Posthumous gelatin silver print, 20 x 16 inches
Private Collection, Courtesy Wallace Berman Estate

DiDi Morrill, San Francisco, 1959 (printed in 2004)
Posthumous gelatin silver print, 14 x 11 inches
Private Collection, Courtesy Wallace Berman Estate

Kirby Doyle, Larkspur, 1960 (printed in 2004)
Posthumous gelatin silver print, 14 x 11 inches
Private Collection, Courtesy Wallace Berman Estate

Bobby Driscoll, San Francisco, 1959 (printed in 2004)
Posthumous gelatin silver print, 20 x 16 inches
Private Collection, Courtesy Wallace Berman Estate

Joe Dunn and Tosh Berman, 707 Scott Street, San Francisco, 1959 (printed in 2004)
Posthumous gelatin silver print, 14 x 11 inches
Private Collection, Courtesy Wallace Berman Estate

Paul Beattie, Larkspur, 1960 (printed in 2004)
Posthumous gelatin silver print, 11 x 14 inches
Private Collection, Courtesy Wallace Berman Estate

Arthur Richer, Portrero Street, San Francisco, 1960 (printed in 2004)
Posthumous gelatin silver print, 11 x 14 inches
Private Collection, Courtesy Wallace Berman Estate

Patricia Jordan, Larkspur, 1961 (printed in 2004)
Posthumous gelatin silver print, 14 x 11 inches
Private Collection, Courtesy Wallace Berman Estate

John Reed, Larkspur, 1961 (printed in 2004)
Posthumous gelatin silver print, 14 x 11 inches
Private Collection, Courtesy Wallace Berman Estate

Lew Welch, Larkspur, 1961 (printed in 2004)
Posthumous gelatin silver print, 14 x 11 inches
Private Collection, Courtesy Wallace Berman Estate

Cameron, 1962 (printed in 2004)
Posthumous gelatin silver print, 20 x 16 inches
Private Collection, Courtesy Wallace Berman Estate

Diane DiPrima with Tosh and Shirley Berman, Crater Lane, 1962 (printed in 2004)
Posthumous gelatin silver print, 11 x 14 inches
Private Collection, Courtesy Wallace Berman Estate

Robert Duncan, Crater Lane, 1962 (printed in 2004)
Posthumous gelatin silver print, 11 x 14 inches
Private Collection, Courtesy Wallace Berman Estate

Taylor Mead, Crater Lane, 1963 (printed in 2004)
Posthumous gelatin silver print, 14 x 11 inches
Private Collection, Courtesy Wallace Berman Estate

Jack Smith, Los Angeles, 1963 (printed in 2004)
Posthumous gelatin silver print, 16 x 20 inches
Private Collection, Courtesy Wallace Berman Estate

Dean Stockwell, Crater Lane, 1963 (printed in 2004)
Posthumous gelatin silver print, 16 x 20 inches
Private Collection, Courtesy Wallace Berman Estate

Russel Tamblyn, 1963 (printed in 2004)
Posthumous gelatin silver print, 11 x 14 inches
Private Collection, Courtesy Wallace Berman Estate

Billy Jahrmarkt, Crater Lane, 1964 (printed in 2004)
Posthumous gelatin silver print, 14 x 11 inches
Private Collection, Courtesy Wallace Berman Estate

Toni Basil, Crater Lane, 1964 (printed in 2004)
Posthumous gelatin silver print, 11 x 14 inches
Private Collection, Courtesy Wallace Berman Estate

Ralph Gibson, Crater Lane, 1964 (printed in 2004)
Posthumous gelatin silver print, 14 x 11 inches
Private Collection, Courtesy Wallace Berman Estate

Stuart Perkoff, Venice, 1965 (printed in 2004)
Posthumous gelatin silver print, 20 x 16 inches
Private Collection, Courtesy Wallace Berman Estate

George Herms, Topanga Canyon, 1965 (printed in 2004)
Posthumous gelatin silver print, 14 x 11 inches
Private Collection, Courtesy Wallace Berman Estate

Alexander Trocchi, London, 1967 (printed in 2004)
Posthumous gelatin silver print, 11 x 14 inches
Private Collection, Courtesy Wallace Berman Estate

Jess, Topanga Canyon, 1968 (printed in 2004)
Posthumous gelatin silver print, 20 x 16 inches
Private Collection, Courtesy Wallace Berman Estate

Bruce Conner and friend, Topanga Canyon, 1969 (printed in 2004)
Posthumous gelatin silver print, 20 x 16 inches
Private Collection, Courtesy Wallace Berman Estate

Edmund Teske and Shirley Berman, Topanga Canyon, 1969 (printed in 2004)
Posthumous gelatin silver print, 20 x 16 inches
Private Collection, Courtesy Wallace Berman Estate

Allen Ginsberg, Topanga Canyon, 1971 (printed in 2004)
Posthumous gelatin silver print, 16 x 20 inches
Private Collection, Courtesy Wallace Berman Estate

Wallace Berman, Topanga Canyon (self-portrait), 1975 (printed in 2004)
Posthumous gelatin silver print, 20 x 16 inches
Private Collection, Courtesy Wallace Berman Estate

Untitled (Frank Sinatra), 1943
Graphite on paper, 17 1/4 x 14 1/4 inches
Collection of Dean Stockwell, Rancho de Taos, NM

Homage to Hesse, 1949 (modified 1954)
Wood, 18 x 24 x 24 inches
Collection of Dean Stockwell, Rancho de Taos, NM

Semina (editions 1–9)
Conceived and edited by Wallace Berman with various contributors, 1955–64
Mixed media limited edition artist's publication, dimensions variable
Special Collections and Archives, Utah State University Library, Gift of the Marie Eccles Caine Foundation

Aleph, 1956–66
16 mm film transferred to DVD, TRT: 8:00
Courtesy Wallace Berman Estate

Mock-up for *Semina 2,* 1957
Ink on paper glued to paper, 20 x 24 inches
Collection of Charles Brittin, Santa Monica, CA

Untitled ("Vultus animi"), 1955
Oil on masonite, 5 x 4 inches
Collection of Charles Brittin, Santa Monica, CA

Untitled ("Wardell, Dead"), 1957
Photograph and ink on board, 10 1/2 x 9 1/2 inches
Collection of Tosh Berman, Los Angeles, CA

Untitled (Tondo), 1959
Ink and gouache on paper, 18 3/4 x 18 1/2 inches
Private collection

Mailer to Patricia and Lawrence Jordan ("from Los Angeles (the lowest)"), 1960
Ink, gouache on posterboard, 8 x 8 inches
Patricia Jordan papers, Archives of American Art, Smithsonian Institution, Washington, D.C.

Mailer to Charles Brittin, 1960
Mixed media collage on paper, 2 1/2 x 5 3/4 inches
Collection of Charles Brittin, Santa Monica, CA

Announcement for Charles Brittin exhibition at Semina Gallery, 1961
Photograph mounted on poster board, 7 1/2 x 2 inches
Patricia Jordan papers, Archives of American Art, Smithsonian Institution, Washington, D.C.

Poster for George Herms exhibition at Batman Gallery, 1961
Lithograph on paper, 19 x 13 3/4 inches
Collection of Charles Brittin, Santa Monica, CA

Letter to David Meltzer, 1962
Typed letter with photographic collage, 11 x 8 1/2 inches
Collection of Philip Aarons, New York, NY

Mailer to Robert Duncan and Jess (Marilyn Monroe), 1962
Mixed media on paper, 6 1/2 x 6 inches
Collection of Philip Aarons, New York, NY

Birthday mailer to Shirley Talbert (Charlie Parker), 1962
Mixed media collage on paper, 4 1/4 x 5 3/8 inches
Robert Alexander papers, Archives of American Art, Smithsonian Institution, Washington, D.C.

Mailer to Cameron, 1962
Mixed media collage on cardboard with 1955 photographic portrait of Cameron, 6 1/2 x 6 inches
Collection of Scott Hobbs, Santa Monica, CA

Mailer to Robert Duncan and Jess ("The Contented Little Maiden"), c. 1962
Mixed media collage on paper, 11 x 8 1/2 inches
Collection of Philip Aarons New York, NY

Untitled ("This is the card that reads a 7"), 1961
Mixed media collage on paper, 12 1/2 x 8 1/2 inches
Collection of Dean Stockwell, Rancho de Taos, NM

Untitled (Tuesday 11:30 a.m.), 1963
Typed poetry manuscript, 6 x 4 inches
Collection of Philip Aarons New York, NY

Untitled (Lenny Bruce), 1963
Mixed media collage on paper, 12 x 5 1/2 inches
Collection of Dean Stockwell, Rancho de Taos, NM

Untitled (Jack Ruby), 1964
Verifax collage with manuscript of poem by Michael McClure, 29 1/2 x 29 1/2 inches
Courtesy Wallace Berman Estate

Untitled (Engine, flowers, nuns, pistol), 1964
Verifax collage, 6 x 11 1/2 inches
Courtesy Wallace Berman Estate

Mailer to Matt Beattie (Shells), 1964
Mixed media collage on paper, 6 x 6 1/4 inches
Collection of Paul Beattie Estate, Forestville, CA

Photograph used in poster for Michael McClure's *The Beard,* 1964
Photograph, 9 x 8 inches
Collection of Charles Brittin, Santa Monica, CA

Untitled (A7-Mushroom, D4-Cross), 1966
56-image Verifax collage, 45 1/2 x 48 inches
Collection of Dan Fauci, Los Angeles, CA

Untitled (Cocteau), 1972
Verifax transfer, 8 1/2 x 14 inches
Wallace Berman papers, Archives of American Art, Smithsonian Institution, Washington, D.C.

Untitled (Music), 1974
Ink and letraset on paper, 15 1/4 x 11 3/4 inches
Collection of Dean Stockwell, Rancho de Taos, NM

Untitled (Airborne car and tarot cards), 1976
Verifax collage, 8 1/4 x 10 1/2 inches
Collection of Nicole Klagsbrun, New York, NY

Mailer to Robert Duncan and Jess (Gertrude Stein and Alice B. Toklas), n.d.
Mixed media collage, 9 1/2 x 4 1/8 inches
Collection of Philip Aarons, New York, NY

Mailer to Robert Duncan and Jess (Lust), n.d.
Mixed media collage on paper, 6 x 4 inches
Collection of Philip Aarons New York, NY

Untitled (John Wieners), n.d.
Torn photograph, 2 1/2 x 3 1/4 inches
Patricia Jordan papers, Archives of American Art, Smithsonian Institution, Washington, D.C.

Stephen Mallarmé, *Igitur* (Los Angeles: Press of the Pegacycle Lady, 1974). Translation by Jack Hirschman, cover by Wallace Berman

Ray and Bonnie Bremser

Poems of Madness (New York: Paperbook Gallery, 1965). Private Collection

For Love of Ray (Salisbury, Wiltshire, England: London Magazine Editions 1971). Private Collection

Charles Brittin

John Altoon, Venice Beach, 1955 (printed 2001)
Gelatin silver print, 11 x 14 inches
Courtesy the artist

John Reed, Venice, 1955 (printed 2004)
Gelatin silver print, 14 x 11 inches
Courtesy the artist

Shirley Berman, Ocean Park Pier, 1957 (printed 2004)
Gelatin silver print, 20 x 16 inches
Courtesy the artist

Arthur Richer, Syndell Studios, 1955
Vintage photograph, 8 x 10 inches
Courtesy the artist

Walter Hopps, Ferus Gallery, 1956 (printed 2004)
Gelatin silver print, 20 x 16 inches
Courtesy the artist

Rachel Rosenthal and King Moody, Instant Theater, 1956
Vintage photograph, 10 x 8 inches
Courtesy the artist

Robert Alexander, Ferus Gallery (waiting for police to arrive), 1957 (printed 2004)
Gelatin silver print, 20 x 16 inches
Courtesy the artist

David Meltzer, Ferus Gallery, 1957 (printed 2004)
Gelatin silver print, 14 x 11 inches
Courtesy the artist

The Berman family, Venice, 1957 (printed 2004)
Silver gelatin print, 20 x 16 inches
Courtesy the artist

Lawrence Jordan and George Herms, San Francisco, 1958 (printed 2004)
Gelatin silver print, 14 x 11 inches
Courtesy the artist

Zack Walsh, 1960 (printed 2004)
Gelatin silver print, 14 x 11 inches
Courtesy the artist

Jack Hirschman and Ruth Hirschman-Seymour, outside Cinema Theater on Western Avenue, 1962 (printed 2004)
Gelatin silver print, 11 x 14 inches
Courtesy the artist

Edmund Teske and Bobby Driscoll, Cinema Theater, 1960 (printed 2004)
Gelatin silver print, 11 x 14 inches
Courtesy the artist

Joan Brown

Man on Horseback, 1957
Sculpture
Fabric, burlap, string, wire and wood, 20 x 2 1/2 x 9 1/4 inches
Courtesy the Estate of Joan Brown and Gallery Paule Anglim, San Francisco, CA

Self Portrait, 1958
Oil on canvas, 34 1/4 x 22 inches
Collection of Charles Campbell, San Francisco, CA

Cameron

Untitled ("Heskas Hskin etoz Beahi 1"), 1955
Gouache on paper on cardboard, 21 1/2 x 17 3/4 inches
Collection of Scott Hobbs, Santa Monica, CA

Peyote Drawing, 1957
Ink on paper, 18 1/2 x 24 inches
Collection of Cameron Estate, Los Angeles, CA

Untitled (Winged angel), 1960
Gouache on black paper, 28 1/2 x 21 1/2 inches
Collection of Scott Hobbs, Santa Monica, CA

Untitled (Lady in the lake), 1962
Ink and gouache on paper, 32 x 37 inches
Collection of Scott Hobbs, Santa Monica, CA

Abraxas, n.d.
Mixed media sketchbook, 10 1/2 x 7 inches
Collection of Cameron Estate, Los Angeles, CA

Untitled, n.d.
Mixed media sketchbook, 11 x 9 1/4 inches
Collection of Cameron Estate, Los Angeles, CA

Untitled (Portrait of Crystal), n.d.
Ink and gouache on wood panel, 43 1/2 x 14 3/4 inches
Collection of Scott Hobbs, Santa Monica, CA

Jack Parsons and Cameron (photographer unknown), 1948
Vintage photograph, 26 1/2 x 13 5/8 inches
Collection of Scott Hobbs, Santa Monica, CA

Bruce Conner

September 13, 1959, 1959
Mixed-media assemblage with nylon stockings, black and white photograph, feather, plastic fringe, glass brooch and printed cotton fabric, 22 x 15 1/2 x 1 1/2 inches
Courtesy Michael Kohn Gallery, Los Angeles, CA

Mirror Collage, 1960
Mixed-media assemblage on masonite, 23 x 16 x 2 inches
Collection of Dennis Hopper, Venice, CA

Generic Rat Hand Grenade, 1960
Mixed-media assemblage, 8 x 3 x 2 1/4 inches
Courtesy Michael Kohn Gallery, Los Angeles, CA

Untitled (Music), 1960
Typeface on music paper, 16 x 11 3/4 inches
Collection of Dean Stockwell, Rancho de Taos, NM

Untitled, *9/4/66,* 1966
Pen and ink, 20 x 26 inches
Private Collection

Jean Conner

Floating Head, 1960
Oil on canvas, 24 x 20 inches
Courtesy the artist

Untitled, 1961
Wax, 6 inches diameter x 1/4 inches
Private Collection (originally from collection of Robert Duncan and Jess)

Young Woman with Skull, 1963
Pencil on paper, 23 3/4 x 17 5/8 inches
Courtesy the artist

Mz. Bell, 1969
Paper collage, 11 1/4 x 7 1/2 inches
Courtesy the artist

Jean Conner and Joanna McClure (photographer unknown), c. 1959
Vintage photograph transferred to digital, 14 x 11 inches
Private Collection, Courtesy The Estate of Jay DeFeo, Berkeley, CA

Jean and Bruce Conner in glass case at Batman Gallery exhibition of works by Bruce Conner (photographed by Edmund Shea), 1964 (printed 2004)
Vintage photograph transferred to digital, 8 1/2 x 11 inches
Courtesy of Bruce Conner, San Francisco, CA

Bruce, Robert, and Jean Conner: Untitled family portrait (photographer unknown), 1973
Color photograph and lithograph card, 3 5/16 x 2 3/4 inches
Courtesy Steven Wolf Fine Arts, San Francisco, CA

Jay DeFeo

Footstool (Used during painting of *The Rose,* 1958–1965)
Wood, acrylic, charcoal, graphite, ink and wax pencil, 18 1/2 x 14 1/2 x 14 1/2 inches
Collection of University of California, Berkeley Art Museum, CA. Gift of Bruce and Jean Conner

Untitled *(for B.C.),* 1973
Photocollage, 7 13/16 x 9 13/16 inches
Collection of The Estate of Jay DeFeo, Berkeley, CA

Untitled (Portrait of Wallace Berman), 1974
Synthetic polymer on paper, 17 7/8 x 12 inches
Collection of Whitney Museum of American Art, New York. Gift of the Lannan Foundation

Untitled (Portrait of Wallace Berman), 1974
Synthetic polymer on paper, 23 7/8 x 17 7/8 inches
Collection of Whitney Museum of American Art, New York. Gift of the Lannan Foundation

Temple (for W.B.), 1980
Mixed-media on masonite, 48 x 72 inches
Collection of Mr. and Mrs. Eric Lidow, Los Angeles, CA

The Rose (mounted on paper with note, "one year I sent everyone a slice of *The Rose* for Christmas"), n.d.
Painting fragment, 8 x 10 3/4 inches
Jay DeFeo papers, Archives of American Art, Smithsonian Institution, Washington, D.C.

Announcement for Dilexi Gallery Exhibition (with *The Eyes*), 1959
Ink on paper, 2 x 5 inches
Collection of Charles Brittin, Santa Monica, CA

Diane DiPrima

San Francisco Notebook 5 (Nov. 22–Mar. 31, 1973), 1973
Mixed-media journal bound in hand-decorated, paper covered boards, 8 1/2 x 5 1/2 inches
Diane DiPrima Collection, Rare Book Collection, Wilson Library, University of North Carolina at Chapel Hill

Untitled, 1975
Mixed-media collage on paper, 20 x 16 inches
Courtesy the artist

Flyer for second performance of *Whale Honey* at Point Reyes Theater
Sets by George Herms, flyer designed by Jackson Allen, 1975
Lithograph, 11 x 8 1/2 inches
Collection of Diane DiPrima, San Francisco

West Coast Notebook 13 (Nov. 23, 1975–Mar. 20, 1976), 1975–1976
Mixed-media journal bound in hand-decorated cloth binding, 11 1/4 x 8 1/2 inches
Diane DiPrima Collection, Rare Book Collection, Wilson Library, University of North Carolina at Chapel Hill

West Coast Notebook 14 (Mar. 21–Jan. 9, 1976), 1976
Mixed-media journal bound in hand-decorated cloth binding, 11 1/4 x 8 1/2 inches
Diane DiPrima Collection, Rare Book Collection, Wilson Library, University of North Carolina at Chapel Hill

Darkness Invocation, 1976
Mixed-media collage on paper with poem, 11 x 8 1/2 inches
Courtesy the artist

Diane DiPrima as Mary Shelley and Jackson Allen as Shelley in production of *Whale Honey*, Intersection of the Arts, sets by George Herms (photographer unknown), 1975
2 photographs, 4 x 6 inches each
Collection of Diane DiPrima, San Francisco, CA

Kirby Doyle

Happiness Bastard, 1967
Typed manuscript, 736 x 8 1/2 inches
Collection of Tisa Walden, San Francisco, CA

Sapphobones (Kerhonkson, New York: The Poets Press, 1966). Illustrations by the author. Private Collection

Happiness Bastard (North Hollywood: Essex House, 1968). Private Collection

Bobby Driscoll

Hollywood's Pin-Up-Boy, 1949
Photograph in 1968 memorial card, 7 x 5 inches
Collection of Bonnie and Russel Tamblyn, Santa Monica, CA

Mailer to George Herms, 1958
Mixed-media collage on paper, 3 1/2 x 8 7/8 inches
Collection of Bonnie and Russel Tamblyn, Santa Monica CA

Mailer to the Jahrmarkts, 1964
Mixed-media collage on paper, 5 1/2 x 8 3/8 inches
Collection of Bonnie and Russel Tamblyn, Santa Monica, CA

Untitled (for Wallace Berman), 1964
Mixed-media collage, 5 3/4 x 5 inches
Wallace Berman papers, Archives of American Art, Smithsonian Institution, Washington, D.C.

Untitled, 1965
Mixed-media collage, 5 x 4 1/2 inches
Collection of Bonnie and Russel Tamblyn, Santa Monica, CA

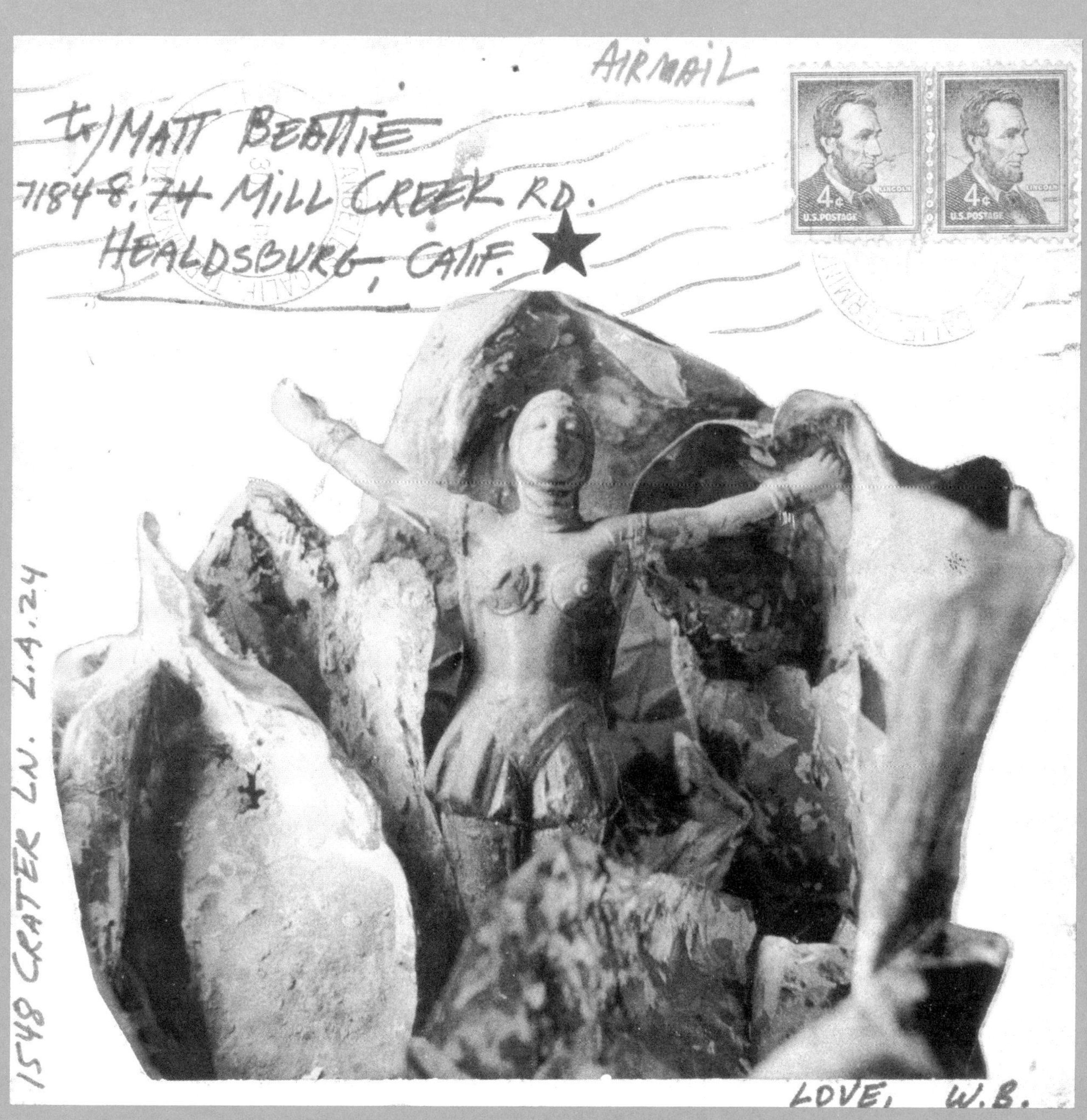

Wallace Berman Mailer to Matt Beattie, 1963,
Courtesy Estate of Paul Beattie.

Robert Duncan

A Winter Sun Yet Dark, 1950
Wax crayon and gold paint on paper, 18 x 14 inches
Collection of Christopher Wagstaff, Berkeley, CA

Fragments of a Disordered Devotion, 1952
Hand-colored artist's book, 8 x 6 inches
Collection of Lorna Jordan, Meridian, ID

Faust Foutu, 1952
Wax crayon with collage on wrapping paper, 40 x 24 inches
Collection of Christopher Wagstaff, Berkeley, CA

A Lisboa, 1954
Wax crayon on paper, 13 x 15 inches
Collection of Nora Eccles Harrison Museum of Art, Utah State University; Marie Eccles Caine Foundation Gift

Joe Dunn

The Better Dreamhouse (San Francisco: White Rabbit Press, 1968). Cover by Jess
Private Collection

Charles Olson, *O'Ryan 1-10* (San Francisco: White Rabbit Press, 1965). Cover by Jess
Private Collection

Robert Duncan, *The Cat and the Blackbird* (San Francisco: White Rabbit Press, 1967). Illustrations by Jess. Private Collection

Llyn Foulkes

Untitled, 1961
Mixed media collage on posterboard, 16 x 16 inches
Collection of Dean Stockwell, Rancho de Taos, NM

Untitled (Cabinet Series), 1961
Mixed-media collage, 12 3/4 x 11 3/4 inches
Collection of Diana Zlotnick, Studio City, CA

Home Studio, 1964
Panoramic photograph, 11 1/8 x 50 1/2 inches
Collection of Diana Zlotnick, Studio City, CA

Loree Foxx

Self-Portrait, 1949
Ink on paper, 14 x 10 inches
Collection of Charles Brittin, Santa Monica, CA

Easter Sunday, 1949
Ink on paper, 10 x 14 inches
Collection of Charles Brittin, Santa Monica, CA

Untitled (Jody and boyfriend, Wallace and girlfriend, and Loree Foxx), 1950
Ink and gouache on paper, 34 x 50 1/2 inches
Collection of Donald Morand, Los Angeles, CA

Ralph Gibson

Whiskey a Go-Go, 1962
Vintage gelatin silver print, 17 x 11 inches
Courtesy the artist

Billy Ferguson in Beverly Glen, 1963
Vintage gelatin silver print, 17 x 11 inches
Courtesy the artist

Wallace Berman, 1974
Vintage gelatin silver print, 17 x 11 inches
Courtesy the artist

Allen Ginsberg

William Burroughs Photographing in NY, 1953
Vintage photograph, 16 x 20 inches
Courtesy Howard Greenberg Gallery, New York, NY

Self Portrait in San Francisco, 1955
Vintage portrait, 20 x 16 inches
Courtesy Howard Greenberg Gallery, New York, NY

Billy Gray

Untitled medallion (Cross), 1962
Leaded stained glass, 9 x 6 inches
Courtesy the artist

Untitled medallion, 1962
Leaded stained glass, 9 x 6 inches
Courtesy the artist

George Herms

Gold Seeds Revolve, 1962
Mixed-media assemblage on wood, 41 x 22 1/2 x 3 inches
Courtesy the artist

Nativity (for exhibition at Rolf Nelson Gallery), 1963
Mixed-media collage on board, 22 x 14 inches
Private Collection

Sets for *The Blossom or Billy the Kid,* 1964
Gelatin silver print, 5 x 7 inches
Collection of Diane DiPrima, San Francisco, CA

Pretender to the Throne, 1965
Ink on paper, 22 5/8 x 17 3/4 inches
Courtesy the artist

Spring Vision, 1965
Oil on canvas, 24 x 30 inches
Collection of Dean Stockwell, Rancho de Taos, NM

Jack Hirschman

Yod (London: Trigram Press, 1966).
Private Collection

Black Alephs: Poems 1960/68 (New York: Phoenix Book Shop in association with Trigram Press, 1969). 3 Verifax illustrations by Wallace Berman.
Private Collection

HNYC (Los Angeles: published by Russel Tamblyn, 1970). Cover illustration by Russel Tamblyn.
Collection of Bonnie and Russel Tamblyn, Santa Monica, CA

Old Timer's Waltz, 1970
Drawing and poem on roll for player piano, 8 1/2 x 31 x 12 inches
Collection of Bonnie and Russel Tamblyn, Santa Monica, CA

Cantillations (Santa Barbara: Capra Press, 1974). Cover by Wallace Berman. Private Collection

Dennis Hopper

George and Nalota Herms, 1962
Gelatin silver print, 16 x 20 inches
Courtesy the artist

Llyn Foulkes, 1964
Gelatin silver print, 16 x 20 inches
Courtesy the artist

Wallace Berman, 1964
Gelatin silver print, 16 x 24 inches
Courtesy the artist

Self-Portrait, 1966
Gelatin silver print, 16 x 20 inches
Courtesy the artist

Billy Jahrmarkt

Homage to McClure, 1960
Mixed-media collage and paint, 12 x 18 inches
Collection of Michael McClure, Oakland, CA

Watch Bat for George Herms, 1961
Clay sculpture on found metal stand, 7 1/2 x 7 1/2 x 4 1/2 inches
Collection of Charles Brittin, Santa Monica, CA

Untitled (Face), 1964
Verifax collage, 11 1/2 x 9 inches
Collection of Dennis Hopper, Venice, CA

Jess

The Door of Many Colord Glass Opend: Imaginary Portrait #1: Robert Duncan, 1952
Oil on canvas, 70 x 33 1/2 inches
The Poetry Collection of the University Libraries, State University of New York at Buffalo

Robert Duncan Reading from "Letters," "The Opening of the Field" (Recordings of radio broadcasts from October 1956, 1958; collaged record jacket by Jess), 1958
Mixed-media on fiberboard, vinyl, 12 x 12 inches
Collection of Nora Eccles Harrison Museum of Art, Utah State University; Marie Eccles Caine Foundation Gift

A Book for Patty (for Patricia Jordan), 1959
Mixed-media hand-made book, 8 1/2 x 6 1/2 inches
Patricia Jordan papers, Archives of American Art, Smithsonian Institution, Washington, D.C.

Armageddon, 1960
Mixed-media collage on paper, 26 3/4 x 26 3/4 inches
Collection of Dean Stockwell, Rancho de Taos, NM

Untitled, 1961–63
Ink on paper, 6 1/4 x 21 inches
Collection of Nora Eccles Harrison Museum of Art, Utah State University; Marie Eccles Caine Foundation Gift

Lawrence Jordan

Portrait of Wallace Berman, 1959
Mixed-media, 9 x 7 5/8 x 2 1/4 inches
Courtesy the artist

Rex in Eternum Vive, 1961
Watercolor on paper, 8 1/2 x 11 inches
Courtesy the artist

Pinkerton Found, 1963
Mixed-media, 17 1/2 x 21 3/4 x 4 1/2 inches
Courtesy the artist

Portrait of John Reed, 1964
Mixed-media, 5 1/2 x 4 1/2 x 2 inches
Courtesy the artist

Patricia Jordan

Kirby Doyle (in the basement of City Lights Books), 1959
Vintage photograph, 10 x 10 inches
Collection of Lorna Jordan, Meridian, ID

Kirby Doyle, Lawrence Jordan, and Wallace Berman, San Francisco, 1959 (printed in 2003)
Posthumous gelatin silver print, 14 x 11 inches
Private collection, Courtesy Patricia Jordan Estate

Wallace Berman ("for Robert and Jess"), 1961
Vintage photograph, 18 x 18 inches
Collection of Christopher Wagstaff, Berkeley, CA

Golden Damsels Descending from the Clouds, 1960–61
Collage, embroidery, feathers, ink, photographs on linen, 67 x 14 1/2 inches
Collection of Lorna Jordan, Meridian, ID

Wallace Berman (in sleeveless vest), c. 1960
Vintage photograph, 10 x 10 inches
Collection of Lorna Jordan, Meridian, ID

Bob Kaufman

Abomunist Manifesto (San Francisco: City Lights Books, 1959). Collection of The Temple of Man Inc., Courtesy Marsha Getzler, Beverly Hills, CA

Second April (San Francisco: City Lights Books, 1959), Collection of The Temple of Man, Inc., Courtesy Marsha Getzler, Beverly Hills, CA

Blues for Hal Waters, 1968
Handwritten manuscript, later published in *Miscellaneous Man,* ed. William Margolis, No. 1, Summer, 1968, 11 x 8 1/2 inches
Collection of The Temple of Man, Inc., Courtesy Marsha Getzler, Beverly Hills, CA

Philip Lamantia

Narcotica (San Francisco: Auerhahn Press, 1959), Cover by Wallace Berman. Collection of Hal Glicksman, Santa Monica, CA

Destroyed Works (San Francisco: Auerhahn Press, 1962), Cover image, *Superhuman Devotion* by Bruce Conner, 1959. Private Collection

The Blood of the Air, (San Francisco: Four Seasons Foundation, 1970), Illustrations by the author. Private Collection

Publication announcement for *Ekstasis* with photograph by Pantale Xantos (Wallace Berman), inscribed to Charles Brittin from Wallace Berman, 1959
Ink on postcard, 3 1/2 x 6 1/8 inches
Collection of Charles Brittin, Santa Monica, CA

William Margolis

Untitled, 1955–1959
Mixed-media journal, 14 x 11 1/2 inches
Collection of The Temple of Man, Inc., Courtesy Marsha Getzler, Beverly Hills, CA

The Anteroom of Hell (San Francisco: Inferno Press, 1957). Collection of The Temple of Man, Inc., Courtesy Marsha Getzler, Beverly Hills, CA

Untitled (Self-portrait), 1959
Pastel on paper, 6 3/4 x 5 inches
Collection of The Temple of Man, Inc., Courtesy Marsha Getzler, Beverly Hills, CA

The Little Love of Our Yearning (San Francisco: Mendicant Editions, 1960), original paste-up. Collection of The Temple of Man, Inc., Courtesy Marsha Getzler, Beverly Hills, CA

(Three Ways) Out, 1962
Handwritten manuscript, 9 x 6 1/4 inches
Collection of The Temple of Man, Inc., Courtesy Marsha Getzler, Beverly Hills, CA

Michael McClure

Love Lion Lioness, 1964
Lithograph on posterboard, 25 1/4 x 32 1/2 inches
Courtesy the artist

Reading at Lion House, San Francisco Zoo (Tape recorded by Bruce "Kansas" Conner), 1964
Collaged box mailer with untitled audio tape and photograph, Ed. 50
4 1/2 x 3 1/4 x 5/8 inches; audio tape TRT: 2:00
Collection of Bonnie and Russel Tamblyn, Santa Monica, CA

Ghost Tantras (San Francisco: City Lights Press, 1964). Cover by Wallace Berman. Private Collection

Poisoned Wheat (San Francisco: Privately published, 1965). Cover by Michael McClure. Collection of Charles Brittin, Santa Monica, CA

Flyer for *The Beard,* 1966
Lithograph on paper, 11 x 8 1/2 inches
Private Collection

Rose Thrust Energy Blessed, 1968
Lithograph on posterboard, 21 1/4 x 28 1/2 inches
Courtesy the artist

Rare Angel (San Francisco: Black Sparrow Press, 1974). Cover from a Verifax print by Billy Jahrmarkt. Private Collection

Taylor Mead

On Amphetamine and in Europe: Excerpts from the Anonymous Diary of a New York Youth, Vol. 3 (New York: Boss Books, 1968). Cover photograph by John Chamberlain. Private Collection

Andy as the Odalisque, n.d.
Oil and acrylic on canvas, 24 x 36 inches
Courtesy the artist

David Meltzer

Amulet (Mandala), 1969
Mixed-media on paper, 10 x 8 1/2 inches
Courtesy the artist

Amulet (Menorah), 1969
Acrylic and ink on canvas, 10 1/2 x 8 1/2inches
Courtesy the artist

Untitled (Bandages), 1969
Mixed-media collage on paper, 9 1/2 x 7 1/4 inches
Courtesy the artist

Untitled (Look Out), 1969
Mixed-media collage on paper, 11 x 12 inches
Courtesy the artist

Luna (Los Angeles: Black Sparrow Press, 1970). Cover by Wallace Berman. Private Collection

Hero/Lil (Los Angeles: Black Sparrow Press, 1973). Cover by Wallace Berman. Private Collection

Henry Miller

Womanish Dreams, 1951
Watercolor on paper, 14 x 20 inches
Collection of Mr. and Mrs. Gary Koeppel, Carmel, CA

Blue Head, 1963
Watercolor on paper, 10 x 11 inches
Collection of Mr.and Mrs. Gary Koeppel, Carmel, CA

Postcard from Henry Miller to Wallace Berman, 1964
Postcard, 3 1/4 x 5 1/2 inches
Wallace Berman papers, Archives of American Art, Smithsonian Institution, Washington, D.C.

Stuart Perkoff

Untitled ("Their skulls are of lead..."), 1959
Mixed-media collage on paper, 11 x 7 7/8 inches
Collection of Hal Glicksman, Santa Monica, CA

Untitled ("Afraid to face the horror..."), 1960
Ink, gouache and collage on paper, 9 3/8 x 6 3/8 inches
Collection of the Temple of Man, Courtesy Marsha Getzler, Beverly Hills, CA

Untitled (Journal), 1960
Mixed-media bound manuscript, 7 7/8 x 5 inches
Stuart Perkoff Papers (Collection #1573), Department of Special Collections, Charles E. Young Research Library, University of California Los Angeles

Untitled (Journal), 1965
Mixed-media bound manuscript, 7 5/8 x 4 1/2 inches
Stuart Perkoff Papers (Collection #1573), Department of Special Collections, Charles E. Young Research Library, University of California Los Angeles

Untitled ("The birds move through the air..."), 1965
Loose page from bound manuscript; ink on paper, 12 1/4 x 7 3/8 inches
Stuart Perkoff Papers (Collection #1573), Department of Special Collections, Charles E. Young Research Library, University of California Los Angeles

Alphabet (Los Angeles & Fairfax: Red Hill Press, 1973). Cover by Wallace Berman. Private Collection

John Reed

Untitled (White), 1955
Oil on canvas, 17 x 36 3/4 inches
Collection of Nancy Reddin Kienholz, Hope, ID

Untitled ("The Unseen Green is Touched and Bounding Back..."), 1955
Gouache on paper, 14 3/4 x 11 3/4 inches
Collection of Charles Brittin, Santa Monica, CA

Poster for Eric Nord Benefit (inscribed to Charles Brittin from Wallace Berman), 1957
Woodcut on paper, 25 x 19 inches
Collection of Charles Brittin, Santa Monica, CA

Announcement for exhibition at Semina Gallery (with photograph by Wallace Berman), 1960
3 x 2 inches
Collection of Charles Brittin, Santa Monica, CA

Untitled, 1960s
Mixed-media hand-made book, 5 x 7 inches
Courtesy Estate of Walter Hopps, Houston, TX

Tongue and Groove, 1970
Wood and metal construction, 10 x 29 inches
Collection of Betty and Monte Factor, Santa Monica, CA

SWOT, n.d.
Collage, mixed media hand-made book, 7 x 5 inches
Courtesy Estate of Walter Hopps, Houston, TX

Arthur Richer

Untitled, 1956
Oil on canvas, 30 1/2 x 20 1/2 inches
Collection of Nancy Reddin Kienholz, Hope, ID

Samurai, 1958
Oil on canvas, 46 x 35 3/4 inches
Collection of Billy Gray, Los Angeles, CA

Announcement for exhibition at Semina Gallery (with photograph by Wallace Berman), 1961
Paper with photograph, 4 3/4 x 2 3/4 inches
Collection of Charles Brittin, Santa Monica, CA

Nuro Muscliar #1, n.d.
Oil on canvas, 16 x 32 3/4 inches
Collection of Nancy Reddin Kienholz, Hope, ID

Rachel Rosenthal

Lee Mullican, Instant Theater, c. 1957
Vintage photograph, 6 3/4 x 9 1/4 inches
Courtesy the artist

Rachel Rosenthal and Lee Mullican, Instant Theater (Photographer unknown), 1956–1957
Vintage photograph, 6 3/4 x 9 1/2 inches
Collection of Rachel Rosenthal, Los Angeles, CA

Rachel Rosenthal, Instant Theater (Photographer unknown), 1956–1957
Vintage photograph, 9 x 6 3/4 inches
Collection of Rachel Rosenthal, Los Angeles, CA

Jack Smith

Vintage composite from *The Beautiful Book,* 1962
Composite silver print, Ed. 200, 4 x 4 inches
Courtesy Steven Wolf Fine Arts, San Francisco, CA

Miracle of Farblonjet, Technicolor Sunset Easter Pageant, 1969
Ink on paper collage, 14 x 11 inches
Collection of Edwin Ruda and Maria Antoinette, Courtesy Mitchell Algus Gallery, New York, NY

Octopus in Skirt, n.d. (c. 1969)
Ink on screenprint on colored paper, 11 x 9 inches
Collection of Edwin Ruda and Maria Antoinette, Courtesy Mitchell Algus Gallery, New York, NY

Untitled ("Your pussy or your life..."), 1969
Ink on paper, 16 x 13 1/2 inches
Collection of Liz Craft and Pentti Monkkonen, Los Angeles, CA

Dean Stockwell

Mailer to Ben Talbert, 1958
Photograph mounted on posterboard, 5 x 4 3/4 inches
Robert Alexander papers, Archives of American Art, Smithsonian Institution, Washington, D.C.

Untitled (from film *For Crazy Horse*), 1958
Letraset collage on 2 found film stills, 9 x 11 inches each
Courtesy the artist

Smith, 1958
Mixed-media collage on posterboard, 9 3/4 x 6 inches
Courtesy the artist

Mailer to Ben and Shirley Talbert (Goodbye party for George Herms), 1963
Mixed-media collage on paper, 3 1/2 x 3 inches
Robert Alexander papers, Archives of American Art, Smithsonian Institution, Washington, D.C.

Untitled (Ram's head), 1965
Mixed-media collage, 17 x 12 1/4 inches
Collection of Helen Winslow, Carmel, CA

Suffragette, 1965
Mixed-media collage on posterboard, 11 3/4 x 10 3/4 inches
Courtesy the artist

Mailer to Jay DeFeo (with photograph of Dean Stockwell and Toni Basil at airport in Cuzco, Peru), 1970
Mixed-media collage on paper, 5 1/2 x 3 1/2 inches
Jay DeFeo papers, Archives of American Art, Smithsonian Institution, Washington, D.C.

Ben Talbert

Shrine of the Great American Weaner, 1962–63
Table, clock case, antlers, baby pacifier, fur, oil, 48 x 24 x 12 inches
Collection of Hal Glicksman, Santa Monica, CA

Ladies' All, 1963
Mixed-media, 16 $1/2$ x 13 $1/2$ inches
Collection of Hal Glicksman, Santa Monica, CA

Stamp Freak, 1963
Mixed-media, 15 $1/2$ x 13 inches
Collection of Hal Glicksman, Santa Monica, CA

Tar Baby, 1963
Mixed-media, 22 x 18 x 2 inches
Collection of Hal Glicksman, Santa Monica, CA

Russel Tamblyn

Open Fist, 1965
Mixed-media collage and acrylic on wood, 4 panels: 18 $3/8$ x 9 inches each
Courtesy the artist

Untitled (animated film), 1965
8mm film transferred to DVD; TRT: 1:20
Courtesy the artist

Topanga Vision, 1967/1969
Mixed-media collage on board, oil paint added after 1969 studio fire, 32 x 25 inches
Courtesy the artist

John Dillinger/Self, 1968
Collaged photographs and acrylic on wood, 7 $7/8$ x 7 $3/8$ inches
Courtesy the artist

Japanese film, 1969
8mm film transferred to DVD; TRT: 7:28
Courtesy the artist

Russel Tamblyn and Dean Stockwell (photographer unknown), 1969
Vintage photograph, 8 $1/2$ x 10 inches
Collection of Bonnie and Russel Tamblyn, Santa Monica, CA

Aya (Tarlow)

"F4-Homo" scrapbook (Including correspondence and artworks by Wallace Berman, George Herms, David Meltzer, John Reed, and others), 1950s
Mixed media hand-made book, 13 $3/8$ x 10 $1/8$ x $1/2$ inches
Aya Tarlow Papers, The Bancroft Library, University of California, Berkeley, BANC MSS 2003/232 c, v.2

Marks of Asha (Los Angeles: Baza Press, 1963).
Collection of Charles Brittin, Santa Monica, CA

Four Balls and One Paddle (to Robert Alexander), 1963
Collage Mailer, 8 x 5 $3/8$ inches
Collection of the Temple of Man, Inc., Courtesy Marsha Getzler, Beverly Hills, CA

Jack Hirschman and Wallace Berman, 1968
Sepia-tone photograph, 3 $1/2$ x 5 inches
Courtesy the artist

Wallace Berman and Dean Stockwell, 1968
Sepia-tone photograph, 3 $1/2$ x 5 inches
Courtesy the artist

Wallace Berman on motorcycle, 1968
Sepia-tone photograph, 3 $1/2$ x 5 inches
Courtesy the artist

Wallace Berman, 1968
Sepia-tone photograph, 3 $1/2$ x 5 inches
Courtesy the artist

George Herms, 1970
Photograph, 7 $1/4$ x 9 $7/8$ inches
Collection of The Temple of Man, Inc., Courtesy Marsha Getzler, Beverly Hills, CA

Aya (Tarlow), San Francisco (photographed by Warner Jepson), c. 1955–59
Vintage photograph, 5 x 7 inches
Collection of Aya (Tarlow), San Pablo, CA, Courtesy Warner Jepson

Aya (Tarlow), Bouquet Canyon (photographed by William Royere III), 1969 (printed in 2004)
Gelatin silver print, 11 x 14 inches
Private Collection

Edmund Teske

Wallace and Shirley Berman #1 & #2, 1955
2 gelatin silver prints, 4 $3/4$ x 6 $5/8$ inches each
Collection of the Nora Eccles Harrison Museum of Art, Utah State University; Marie Eccles Caine Foundation Gift

Demolition of My Grammar School, Chicago, 1938
Composite with Shirley Berman, Topanga Canyon, 1956
Gelatin silver print, 5 $1/4$ x 6 $7/8$ inches
Copyright Edmund Teske Archives, Laurence Bump, Nils Vidstrand
Courtesy Stephen Cohen Gallery, Los Angeles, CA

George Herms, Topanga Canyon, 1965
Gelatin silver print, 8 $1/2$ x 6 inches
Copyright Edmund Teske Archives, Laurence Bump, Nils Vidstrand
Courtesy Stephen Cohen Gallery, Los Angeles, CA

Zack Walsh

She, c. 1960
Lithographic broadside with photograph of Beverly Walsh by Charles Brittin, 8 x 11 $1/2$ inches
Collection of Charles Brittin, Santa Monica, CA

Points in Time (Los Angeles: Baza Press, 1963).
Cover photograph by Dean Stockwell.
Private Collection

Untitled, 1965
Watercolor on card, 4 $1/4$ x 5 $3/4$ inches
Collection of The Temple of Man, Inc., Courtesy Marsha Getzler, Beverly Hills, CA

Untitled (Two standing figures), n.d.
Mixed-media collage, 12 x 9 inches
Robert Alexander papers, Archives of American Art, Smithsonian Institution, Washington, D.C.

Untitled (Flapper), n.d.
Mixed-media collage, 14 x 8 $1/2$ inches
Robert Alexander papers, Archives of American Art, Smithsonian Institution, Washington, D.C.

Lew Welch

Step out onto the Planet..., 1964
Lithographic poetry broadside, 12 $1/2$ x 9 $1/2$ inches
Collection of Magda Cregg, Bolinas, CA

Hermit Poems (San Francisco: Writing 8/Four Seasons Foundation, 1965). Private Collection

Sausalito Trash Prayer, 1969
Illustrated lithographic broadside, 6 x 3 $1/2$ inches
Private Collection

Springtime in the Rockies, Lichen, San Francisco: Cranium, 1971
Illustrated lithographic broadside, 14 x 8 $1/2$ inches
Private Collection

John Wieners

The Hotel Wentley Poems (San Francisco: Dave Haselwood, 1965). Front cover by Robert La Vigne, back cover author's photo by Wallace Berman.
Private collection

L'Abysse
Illustrated by G. Garrick, Ed. of 250, New York: George Robert Minkoff, 1968
Lithographic broadside, 13 x 10 inches
Private Collection

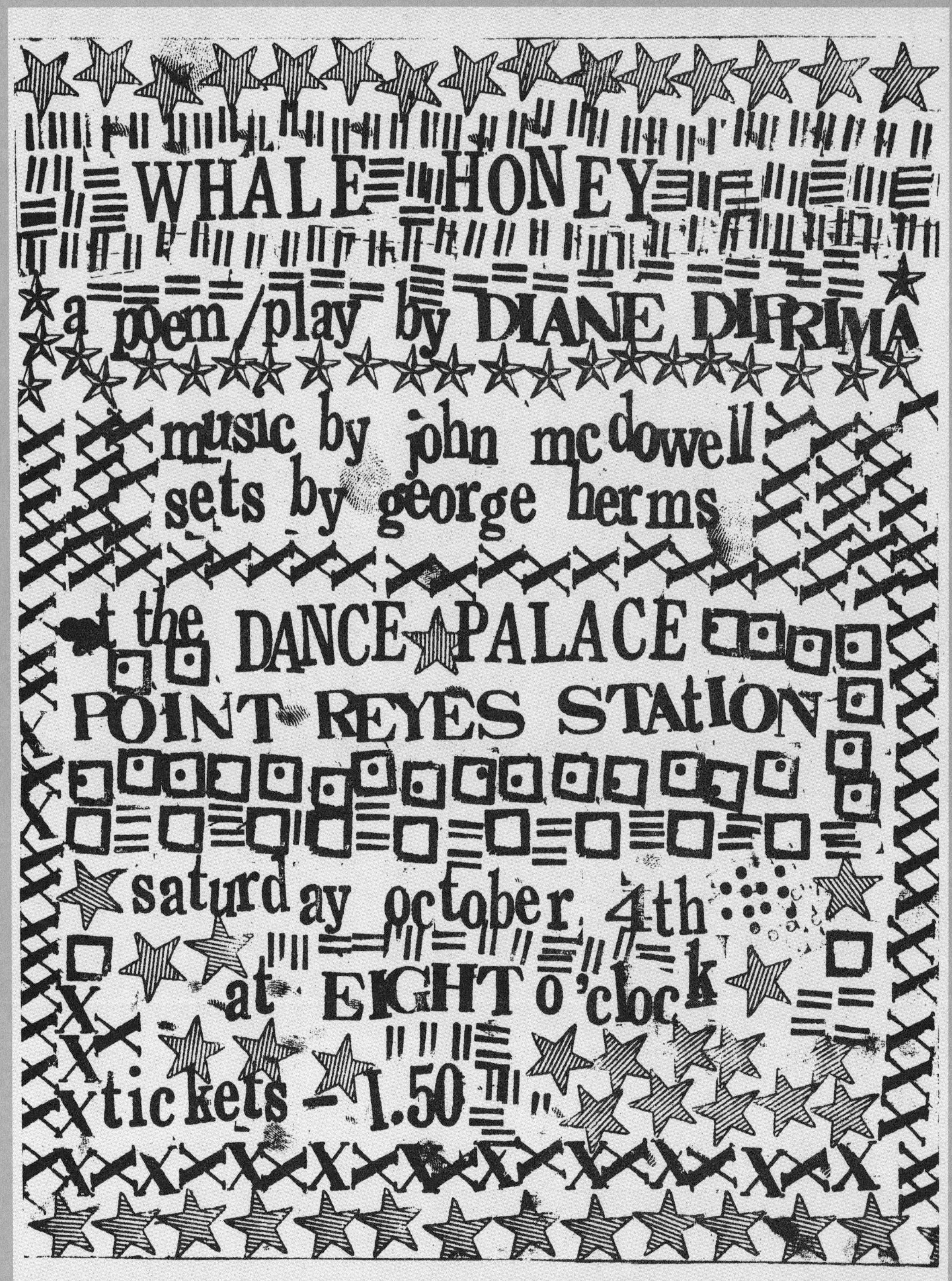

Flyer for second performance of *Whale Honey*, flyer design by Jackson Allen, 1975, Collection of Diane DiPrima.

CURATORS' ACKNOWLEDGEMENTS

Our first thanks go to Shirley and Tosh Berman for their extreme generosity in making accessible Wallace Berman's remarkable photographic archive. Without their blessing and cooperation this project could not have gone forward. Deep appreciation also goes to Elsa Longhauser, Lisa Melandri, and Gretchen Gates at the Santa Monica Museum of Art for their high degree of professionalism and unflagging support for Semina Culture. The brilliant design of Lorraine Wild and Stuart Smith made this book even more beautiful than we dreamed it could be. The faith and support of D.A.P. has also been greatly appreciated.

Special thanks to George Herms, David Meltzer, Dean Stockwell, the late Walter Hopps, Bruce Conner, Russel Tamblyn, and Hal Glicksman who have been invaluable guides through this history. Thanks also to the following individuals who have gone beyond their official capacities in making this exhibition and book possible: Marsha Getzler, Nancy Reddin Kienholz, Richard Jackson, Phil Aarons, Nicole Klagsbrun, Magda Cregg, Diane DiPrima, Karen Marks, Victoria Rowe, Eileen Kaufman, Michael and Amy McClure, Raymond Foye, Rick Pharoah, Donald Morand, Lesley Taplin, Laurie Winer, Clayton Patterson, Mitchell Algus, Jolie Margulies, Noureddine El-Warari, Julian Cox, Bonnie Tamblyn, Lisa Bateman, Tisa Walden, Nils Vidstrand, Paule Anglim, Ed Gilbert, Steven Wolf, Adrienne Fish, Star Jordan, Scott Hobbs, Robyn Beattie, Nick Chase, Leah Levy, Meg Kihn, Leslee Richer Cooke, Christopher Wagstaff, Connie Lewallen, Steven Lieber, Suzi Hicks, Kirk Silsbee, Barry Sloane, Cecilia Dan, Joni Gordon, Sophie Dannenmuller, Taryn Turney, Natasha Selfridge, Diana Zlotnick, and Elizabeth East and Peter Goulds of LA Louver. We offer our gratitude and respect to Merrill Greene, Hal Glicksman, Rebecca Solnit, Anne Ayres, and Sandra Starr Leonard for their pioneering scholarship in this long neglected area of American art history. Finally, we'd like to dedicate this book to Charles Brittin whose generosity and devotion to his artist peers has been an inspiration.

The Santa Monica Museum of Art is grateful to the following foundations and organizations for support of the exhibition Semina Culture: Wallace Berman & His Circle: Philip E. Aarons; LLWW Foundation, the National Endowment for the Arts; and the Pasadena Art Alliance.

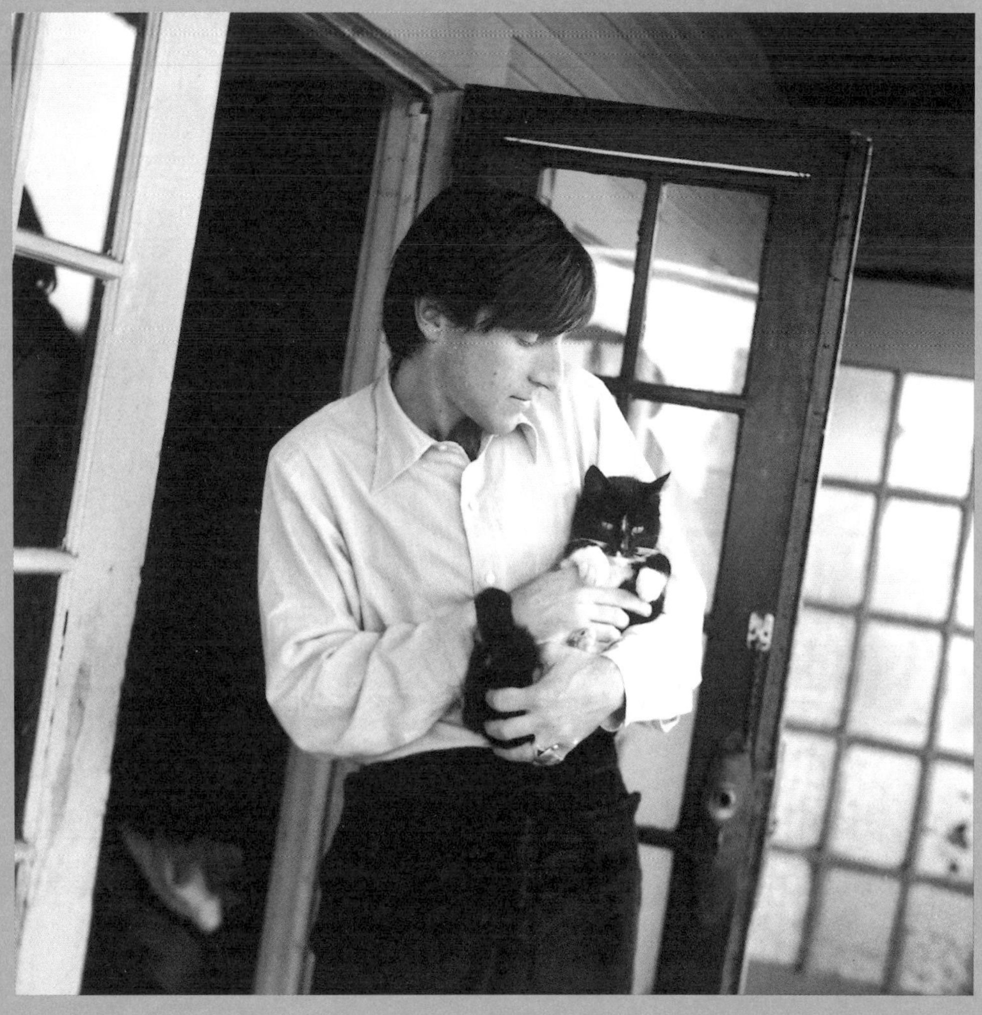

PHOTO CREDITS

Phil Aarons Collection: 29, 361, 362,363, 264, 365, 366, 367, 368; Edwin Ruda and Maria Antoinette Collection, Courtesy Mitchell Algus Gallery, New York, NY: 259; Archives of American Art, Smithsonian Institution, Washington, D.C: Robert Alexander Papers / 265 (upper), 266, 291; Wallace Berman Papers / 2, 125, 133, 350 (left); Jay DeFeo Papers / 121; Patricia Jordan Papers / 186, 302; Dr. Leon O. Banks Collection / Courtesy Newspace Gallery, Los Angeles, Ca: 77 (lower); Collection of the University of California, Berkeley Art Museum: 120; Shirley Berman: 49, 343 (lower); Tosh Berman: 12 (upper), 351 (right); Wallace Berman / Courtesy Estate of Wallace Berman: 6, 8, 12 (lower), 14, 23, 25, 35, 50 (left), 53, 55, 56, 61, 62, 63, 64, 65, 72, 81, 82, 86, 90, 93 (right), 96, 99, 100, 105, 106, 116, 122, 128, 132, 136, 140, 146, 150, 154, 158, 160, 163, 174, 178, 182, 192, 198, 204, 205, 208, 214, 216, 217, 221, 222, 228, 232, 234, 240, 246, 252, 256, 260, 272, 284, 288, 294, 298, 302, 303, 304,305, 306, 309, 310–321, 322 (upper right), 325 (upper left and right), 330 (lower center), 332 (right), 333 (left), 336 (upper right), 337 (left), 338 (left), 340 (left), 342 (left), 346 (upper), 349, 352, 353 (left), 354 (left), 355, 356; Charles Brittin: 2, 3, 10, 20, 51 (lower left), 52 (left), 59 (left), 76, 91, 93, 94, 95, 166, 177, 188, 290, 293 (top), 325 (lower center), 326, 327, 328, 329, 330 (left, center), 331, 332 (left), 334, 335, 336 (left), 339, 341 (lower left, right), 342 (right), 343 (top), 344, 345, 348 (left), 351 (upper left, center), 358–359; The Poetry Collection of the University Libraries, State University of New York at Buffalo: 139; Special Collections and Archives, State University Library, Gift of the Marie Eccles Caine Foundation: 50–69; Charles Campbell Collection, San Francisco, CA: 97; John Chamberlain: 221 (right); Bruce Conner: 81 (upper), 109, 113, 115; Magda Cregg, Bolinas, CA: 295; Jay DeFeo Estate, Berkeley, CA: 112, 118; Diane DiPrima Collection, Rare Book Collection, Wilson Library, University of North Carolina at Chapel Hill: 123; Llyn Foulkes / Courtesy Diana Zlotnick: 144; Ralph Gibson: 151, 152, 153; Allen Ginsberg: 156, 157; Hal Glicksman Collection: 205 (lower), 348 (upper), 355 (right); Nora Eccles Harrison Museum of Art, Utah State University; Marie Eccles Caine Foundation Gift: 137 (lower), 183, 187, 286; Scott Hobbs Collection: 323 (right); Dennis Hopper: 142, 170, 171, 173; Walter Hopps: 175; Walter Hopps Estate: 243; Warner Jepson / Collection of Aya Tarlow: 281; Patricia Jordan / Courtesy Lorna Jordan: 131, 195, 196, 197; Nancy Reddin Kienholz Collection: 250, 251, 244 (upper), 248, 249; Michael Kohn Gallery, Los Angeles, CA: 110, 111; Courtesy L.A. Louver Gallery: 17, 19, 40; Gerard Malanga, Courtesy Sands & Company Fine Art, New York; William Margolis / Courtesy Marsha Getzler & the Temple of Man: 203 (upper, left), 213, 337 (right), 338 (right) 369; Roger Marshutz: 81, 163, 244 (top), 248, 249; Caitlin McCaffrey: 83, 84, 85, 189, 190, 191; King Moody: 254, 255 (right); Stuart Perkoff Papers (Collection #1573), Department of Special Collections, Charles E. Young Research Library, University of California Los Angeles: 235, 237; Rick Pharaoh: 16, 17, 18, 24, 28, 32 (lower), 36, 73, 74, 75, 78, 101, 102, 103, 104, 105, 129, 131, 143, 145, 147, 149, 159, 162, 163 (right), 164, 165, 167, 179, 185, 193, 205, 209, 211, 215, 217 (top), 218, 219, 223, 225, 226, 238, 239, 241, 245 (left), 247, 261, 262, 264, 265 (lower), 267, 268, 269, 270, 271, 273, 275, 276, 277, 293, 347; Gary Platt: 322 (left); Rachel Rosenthal: 253; William Royere III: 278; Edmund Shea / courtesy Bruce Conner: 115; Chas. Stark: 58; Dean Stockwell: 266, 268, 292 (right); Russel Tamblyn: 347, 353 (right); Aya Tarlow: 282, 283; Aya Tarlow Papers, The Bancroft Library, University of California, Berkeley, BANC MSS 2003/232 c, v.2: 279, 281 (lower); ©Edmund Teske Archives, Laurence Bump, Nils Vidstrand, / Courtesy Stephen Cohen Gallery, Los Angeles, CA: 285, 286, 287; Frank Thomas: 23; Zack Walsh: 292 (left); William Warren: 210; Saul White / Courtesy Charles Brittin: 336 (lower); The Whitney Museum of American Art / Gift of the Lannan Foundation: 119 (upper); Lee Wilder: 324 (left); Steven Wolf Fine Arts, San Francisco, CA: 257.

INDEX

Page numbers appearing in *italic* type indicate illustrations.

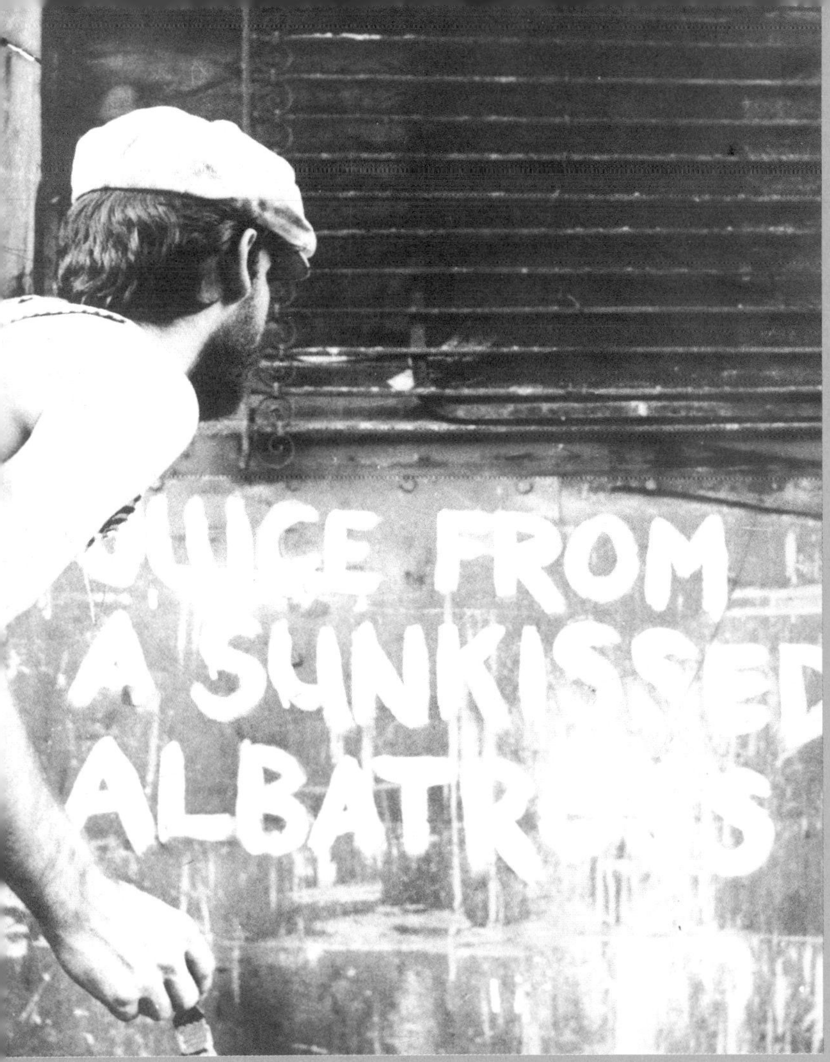

Semina Culture: Wallace Berman & His Circle

Editors: Michael Duncan and Kristine McKenna
Design: Green Dragon Office, Los Angeles,
Lorraine Wild and Stuart Smith
Typeset in: Bodoni, Cheltenham, Cooper, Egyptian,
News Gothic and Monotype Typewriter
Printed by: Oceanic Graphic Printing, China

Published by
D.A.P./Distributed Art Publishers, Inc.
155 Sixth Avenue, 2nd floor
New York, NY 10013
www.artbook.com

A CIP RECORD FOR THE SECOND EDITION IS AVAILABLE FROM THE LIBRARY OF CONGRESS
Second Edition ISBN 978-1-938922-72-5

LIBRARY OF CONGRESS CATALOGING-IN-PUBLICATION DATA FOR FIRST EDITIO

Duncan, Michael, 1953-
Semina culture : Wallace Berman & his circle / Michael Duncan and Kristine McKenna. – 1st ed.
p. cm.
"Catalog of an exhibition at the Santa Monica Museum of Art, Santa Monica, Calif., Sept. 17–Nov. 26, 2005 and 4 other museums" – T.p. verso.
Includes bibliographical references.
ISBN 1-933045-10-8
1. Berman, Wallace, 1926–1976 – Exhibitions. 2. Semina – Exhibitions.
3. Avant-garde (Aesthetics) – California – History – 20th century Exhibitions. I. McKenna, Kristine. II. Berman, Wallace, 1926–19
III. Santa Monica Museum of Art. IV. Title.
N6537.B466A4 2005
700'.9794'07479494--dc22

2005018691

This book was published on the occasion of the exhibition, "*Semina* Culture: Wallace Berman & His Circle," organized by the Santa Monica Museum of Art.

Santa Monica Museum of Art,
Santa Monica, California
September 17–November 26, 2005

Nora Eccles Harrison Museum of Art,
Utah State University,
Logan, Utah
January 10–March 15, 2006

Ulrich Museum of Art, Wichita, Kansas
April 21–July 9, 2006

Berkeley Art Museum and Pacific Film Archive,
Berkeley, California
October 17–December 10, 2006

Grey Art Gallery, New York University,
New York, New York
January 16–March 31, 2007

John Reed at work, c. 1961, Photographer unknown, courtesy of Temple of Man.

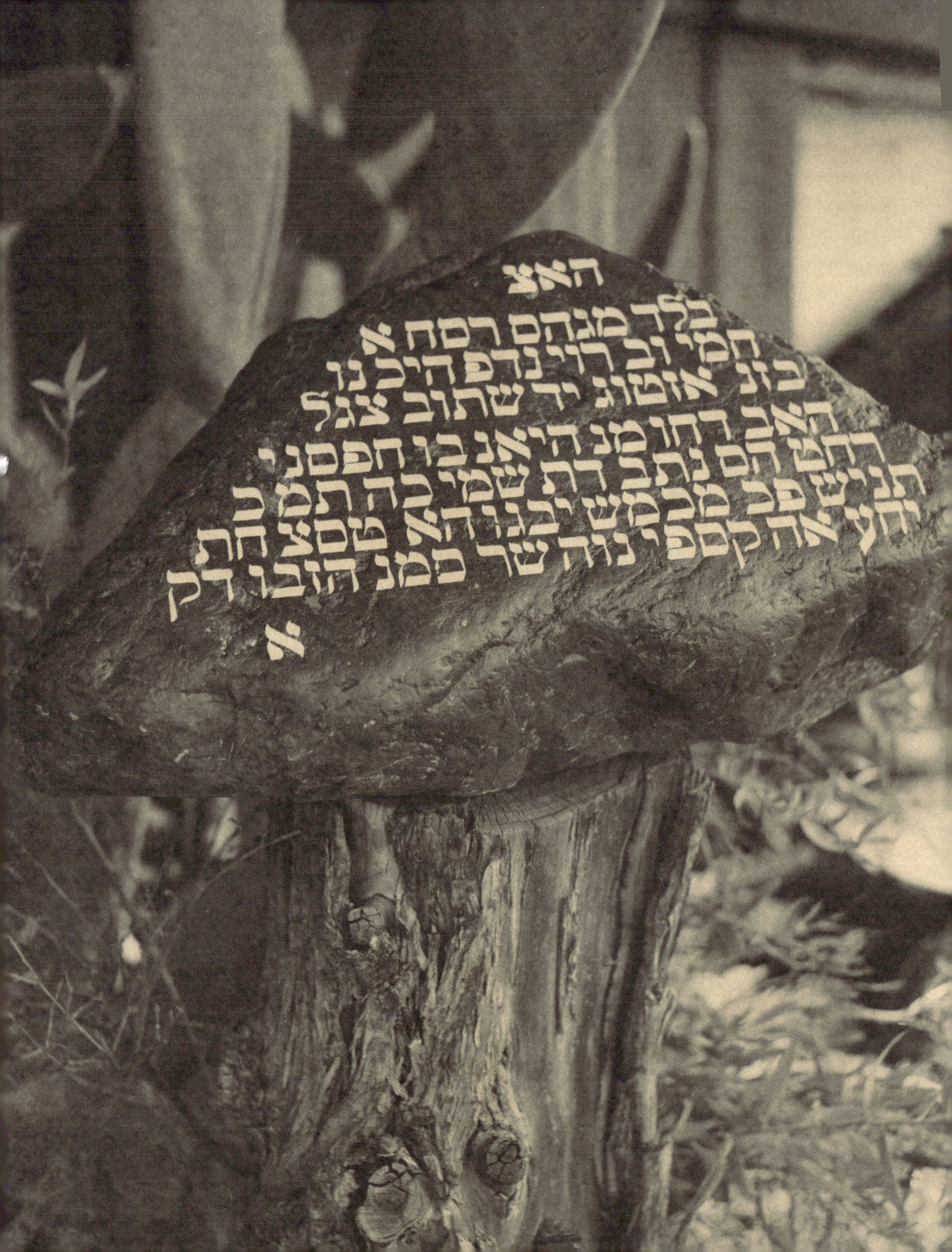